THE MONTH THAT CHANGED
THE WORLD

THE MONTH
THAT CHANGED
THE WORLD

JULY 1914

GORDON MARTEL

OXFORD
UNIVERSITY PRESS

OXFORD

UNIVERSITY PRESS

Great Clarendon Street, Oxford, OX2 6DP,
United Kingdom

Oxford University Press is a department of the University of Oxford.
It furthers the University's objective of excellence in research, scholarship,
and education by publishing worldwide. Oxford is a registered trade mark of
Oxford University Press in the UK and in certain other countries

First Edition published in 2014

Impression: 2

Published in the United States of America by Oxford University Press
198 Madison Avenue, New York, NY 10016, United States of America

British Library Cataloguing in Publication Data
Data available

Library of Congress Control Number: 2013953482

ISBN 978-0-19-966538-9

Printed in Great Britain by
Clays Ltd, St Ives plc

For my darling daughters:
Lisette, Mireille, and Christiane

Contents

PART FOUR: THE AFTERMATH

Preface

This is not another book on the 'origins' of the First World War. The 'origins' of the war lie deeply rooted in the European past—in the concept of the sovereign state, in authoritarianism and militarism, in concepts of masculinity and heroism, of patriotism and honour, in the rise of the nation-state. Historians have traced the roots of the cataclysm back to the unification of Germany by warfare, to the *levée en masse* of the French revolution, to the industrial revolution, to the absolutist monarchies of the seventeenth century, to the wars of religion during the Reformation, to the rise of secular humanism during the Renaissance, to the destruction of European unity with the fall of Rome, to the rise of rationalism and patriarchy in classical Greece. These linkages are all interesting and valid in various ways—but they are not what this book is about.

Nor does this book claim to unravel the mysteries of who or what 'caused' the First World War. The causes—as students are wont to say—are 'many and varied'. Everyone has their favourite, it seems—including professional historians. The usual whipping-boys include: the German emperor, Wilhelm II; the French president, Raymond Poincaré; and the foreign ministers of Russia, Austria-Hungary, and Britain—Sergei Sazonov, Leopold Berchtold, and Sir Edward Grey. Less prominent villains include the chiefs of the German, Austrian, and French general staffs—Helmuth von Moltke, Conrad von Hötzendorf, Joseph Joffre; or ambassadors such as Maurice Paléologue, Prince Lichnowsky, and Aleksandr Izvol'skii. Some are blamed for their villainy; others for their incompetence. Those who prefer a less personalized view of the past can adopt any cause from a long list, or join them together in an almost infinite number of combinations: the quest for empire or national self-determination; finance capitalism or atavistic aristocracies; armaments manufacturers or military strategists.

The aim of this book is more modest. I have attempted to tell the story of how Europe got from A to B: how it moved from the assassination of the heir to the throne of Austria-Hungary on the 28th of June, 1914, to the declarations of war by five of the six Great Powers of Europe at the beginning of August. This is a book about how it happened: how those responsible for making fateful choices—the monarchs and politicians, diplomatists and strategists—grappled with the situation and failed to resolve it without war.

★

My fascination with narrative history can be traced back to my high-school history teacher, Miss MacFarlane. I can see her almost as clearly today as I did fifty years ago, when she would stand at the head of our classroom and instruct us in the complexities of modern history. Even the recent European past was a distant country to us teenagers, growing up in the 1960s on the west coast of North America, with Europe thousands and thousands of miles away, and with the French revolution, the Great Reform Bill and the First World War as remote to us as the Peloponnesian and Punic wars. Miss MacFarlane however, all 90 pounds of her, immaculate in one of her heavy tweed suits, standing there with one hand firmly grasping the wrist of the other, would tell us the story of European history. The fact that she had worked for the United Nations after the war, and travelled throughout the places she described to us, made Europe come alive to students in far-off British Columbia. Her descriptions of the devastation at Monte Cassino, of Franco's soldiers hunting for dissidents in Spanish fields, of conversations with Wehrmacht officers in post-war Paris, merged with her descriptions of Napoleon and Bismarck, the Crimea and the Somme. In her telling of it, European history was made compelling, vivid and exciting.

She also made history challenging and controversial. The narratives were never dead: they opened new doors, new possibilities. There were villains and heroes, tragedies and triumphs, that required identification and explanation. Our questions were routinely answered by questions she threw back to us: whose version of the story did we believe? why did we believe it? We soon discovered that it was not sufficient to recite 'the facts' dished up by the textbook—we needed more than a good memory if we were to impress her. History, it turned out, needed imagination.

That I succeeded in impressing her I attribute to another, earlier teacher. The only classes from 'elementary' school that I now recall were those that took place in the library—where we had, on most days, a 'library' class. Surrounded by books, another Scottish schoolmarm, Miss MacLeod, would sit behind her desk—with the Union Jack proudly displayed on the wall behind her, with portraits of Queen Elizabeth and Prince Philip mounted alongside, and framed photographs of young Prince Charles and young Princess Anne facing us from her desk. And there we would sit, spellbound, while she—with her snow-white hair tied up in a tight bun—read aloud *Treasure Island*, *Bonnie Prince Charlie*, or *The White Company*. Those hours raced by; the next class could not come soon enough. Before long I was getting the books out for myself, reading them by flashlight under the blankets, long after 'bedtime' had passed.

The likes of Miss MacFarlane and Miss MacLeod have now passed into history and are not likely to be seen again. Those of us who had the good fortune to have them as teachers know what we have lost.

★

More direct inspiration for this book came from my work on another project, dating back a quarter-century. Researching the activities of the men employed in the Political Intelligence Department of the British Foreign Office during the First World War, I discovered that most of them had started their careers in intelligence by writing propaganda. One of their works was James Headlam-Morley's *The History of Twelve Days*. Although it was officially sanctioned propaganda, written to justify Britain's entry into the war, the unravelling of the diplomacy that led to the war was compelling nevertheless. With the unprecedented publication of government records, diaries, and memoirs it seemed to me that it would now be possible to construct a more richly detailed and unbiased account of the crisis that led to war.

Although I began assembling materials for this book in the 1990s, its gestation goes back much further. The first history assignment that I undertook as an undergraduate in 1965 was to write a propaganda piece justifying Germany's decision to go to war in 1914. I decided to get a grip on this by going to the public library, where I actually found a wealth of contemporary materials. The 'encirclement' of Germany, the defence of Kultur and other justifications were entirely new to me—neither our texts (nor Miss MacFarlane) had referred to anything of the kind. Clearly, the subject was more complicated than I had imagined. As a senior undergraduate I took a seminar course on the topic—where the final (three-hour) essay-question was 'What caused the First World War?' I tried to utilize the latest theoretical approaches—game theory, etc.—in my answer. It was not a great success. When I proceeded to do my master's degree at the Fletcher School of Law and Diplomacy I took a year-long course on European diplomacy, 1815–1914, with the late Albert Imlah. There was a comprehensive oral examination at the end of the year—at which he asked me to list all of the demands made upon Serbia by Austria-Hungary on 23 July. I think I managed to get seven of the ten (at least I passed).

I still have most of my notes on the 'classic' accounts of the war's origins, written laboriously in longhand on fading sheets of foolscap, from my days as an undergraduate, and then as a graduate student. I have since had the privilege of teaching the subject to my own students for the past forty years—and it was with them in mind that I wrote *The Origins of the First World War* (1987); it appears to have stood the test of time, as it is now in its third (revised) edition (2008). Throughout the years of teaching, however, I had begun to envision what a book aimed at general readers might look like. And it was then that I began to think of combining the approach in *Twelve Days* with Ian Rankin's crime fiction.

How did I imagine that Rankin's approach might be applied to a diplomatic crisis? It seemed to me that the basic narrative structure of the detective gradually discovering the clues through the process of investigation is fundamentally similar to the procedure followed by the historian of diplomacy. Moreover, Rankin's detective, Rebus, is not omniscient: he asks questions, makes mistakes, follows false leads. He must grapple with conflicting evidence and assess the reliability of witnesses and the cleverness—or stupidity—of those he deals with. In Rankin's telling, we move through the story, sifting the evidence as it becomes available—he does not tell us what to look for, what is important and what is irrelevant. He does not talk down to the reader; rather, it is the very complexity of the details that challenges the reader to remain engaged.

I have attempted to adopt this technique in the pages that follow. Practically every word spoken by the characters comes out of contemporary documents—not the rationalizations, justifications, and excuses that they offered after the fact. I attempt to follow the twists and turns of the crisis through the eyes and the ears of the participants. I do not try to point out what to look for or to 'make a case', either for the prosecution or for the defence. I have tried to resist the professorial urge to 'lecture', and have provided only such background information as seemed essential to follow the plot. I believe readers will be able to make their own judgements concerning guilt and responsibility, error and innocence, guile and trustworthiness, as the story unfolds. The July crisis is, and is likely to forever remain, a mystery suffused with tragedy: a complicated plot in which

colourful characters must respond to the challenges that confront them—
and, in so doing, hubris, timing, and happenstance play pivotal roles.

When I decided to try my hand at writing for readers who were not a
captive audience (neither students nor colleagues) I thought it would be
useful to submit Part One (The Killing and The Reaction) and Day One
(Friday, 24 July) to several people whose opinions I could trust. My wife
Valerie and our daughters, Lisette, Mireille, and Christiane, are all avid
readers and astute critics of both fiction and non-fiction—we regularly
exchange books with one another, along with our opinions of them.
I thought if they found the narrative compelling and the tragic tale absorb-
ing that I might be on the right track, and that devoting the next two years
to the writing of this book might be worth the time and effort. They did,
and their positive comments encouraged me to continue. Valerie did more
than give encouragement: she diligently and carefully read each 'Day' of
the crisis as I completed it. Her keen eye, discerning judgement, attention
to detail, and challenging questions were enormously helpful; thank you,
my dear.

I also called upon three former colleagues who have been great friends
and reliable supporters over the past thirty-five years. Although Deryck
Schreuder, Stuart Robson, and Jon Swainger would not claim to be specialists in the world of European diplomacy, I knew I could count on them
to give me incisive criticism and shrewd suggestions based upon their own
work in writing narrative history. They did not let me down. I relied on
their penetrating commentary and helpful suggestions throughout the process. Their support helped to keep me going; thank you, my friends.

I knew I could also count upon several of my academic colleagues who
specialized in the subject of the war's origins to offer the kind of advice and
criticism that only specialists can give. I am deeply indebted to Samuel
Williamson, David Stevenson, Annika Mombauer, and Keith Neilson for
their willingness to assist. They read all (or most) of the manuscript in its
entirety, and their knowledgeable commentary was greatly appreciated.
I would also like to take this opportunity to acknowledge a number of
colleagues in the field whose work, friendship, and support have aided me
and my understanding of this vastly complicated subject over the years:
Richard Bosworth, Volker Berghahn, John Keiger, Holger Herwig, John
Röhl, and the late James Joll. I could sense them peering over my shoulder
daily as I tried to untangle the intricate web of diplomacy and to make it
comprehensible to the general reader. Thank you one and all.

Finally, I am indebted to all of those involved in the publication process at Oxford University Press. Matthew Cotton, Luciana O'Flaherty, Emma Slaughter, Fo Orbell, Anna Silva, and Phil Henderson have been most helpful and professional throughout. Dorothy McCarthy's keen and diligent copy-editing eye was greatly appreciated.

List of Principal Characters

SERBIA

Head of State:
Petar I (1844–1921); king (1903–18)
Aleksandar I (1888–1934); crown prince and regent (1914–21)
Head of Government:
Pašić, Nikola (1845–1926); prime minister (1912–18)

AUSTRIA-HUNGARY

Head of State:
Franz Joseph I (1830–1916); emperor/king (1848–1916)
Heads of Government:
Stürgkh, Count Karl von (1859–1916); minister-president of Cisleithania (Austria) (1911–16)
Tisza, Count István (1861–1918); minister-president of Hungary (1903–5, 1913–17)
Foreign Minister/Secretary of State:
Berchtold, Count Leopold von (1863–1942); common foreign minister (1912–15)
Foreign Office Officials:
Forgách, Count János (1870–1935); section chief, foreign ministry (1912–17)
Hoyos, Count Alexander von (1876–1937); *chef de cabinet* to foreign minister (1912–17)
Ambassadors:
Mensdorff-Pouilly-Dietrichstein, Count Albert von (1861–1945); ambassador at London (1904–14)
Mérey von Kapos-Mérey, Count Kajetan von (1861–1931); ambassador at Rome (1910–15)
Szápáry de Szapár, Count Frigyes (1869–1935); ambassador at St Petersburg (1913–14)
Szécsen von Temerin, Count Nikolaus (1857–1926); ambassador at Paris (1911–14)
Szögyény-Marich, Count László (1841–1916); ambassador at Berlin (1892–1914)
Army and Navy:
Hötzendorf, Count Franz Conrad von (1852–1925); chief of the general staff (1906–11, 1912–17)

GERMANY

Head of State:
Wilhelm II (1859–1941); kaiser (1888–1918)

Head of Government:
Bethmann Hollweg, Theobald von (1856–1921); chancellor (1909–17)

Foreign Minister/Secretary of State:
Jagow, Gottlieb von (1863–1935); secretary of state (1913–16)

Foreign Office Officials:
Stumm, Wilhelm von (1869–1935); director, political department (1911–16)
Zimmermann, Arthur (1864–1940); under-secretary of state (1911–16)

Ambassadors:
Flotow, Count Johannes 'Hans' von (1862–1935); ambassador at Rome (1913–15)
Lichnowsky, Karl Max, Prince von (1860–1928); ambassador at London (1912–14)
Pourtalès, Count Friedrich (1853–1928); ambassador at St Petersburg (1907–14)
Schoen, Baron Wilhelm von (1851–1933); ambassador at Paris (1910–14)
Tschirschky und Bögendorff, Heinrich von (1858–1916); ambassador at Vienna (1907–16)

Army and Navy:
Falkenhayn, Count Erich von (1861–1922); minister of war (1913–14)
Moltke, Helmuth von (1848–1916); chief of the general staff (1906–14)
Tirpitz, Alfred von (1849–1930); state secretary, imperial navy office (1897–1916)

ITALY

Head of State:
Vittorio Emanuele III (1869–1947); king (1900–46)

Head of Government:
Salandra, Antonio (1853–1931); prime minister (1914–16)

Foreign Minister/Secretary of State:
San Giuliano, Antonio, Marchese di (1852–1914); foreign minister (1910–14)

Ambassador:
Avarna, Giuseppe, Duca di Gualtieri (1843–1916); ambassador at Vienna (1904–15)

RUSSIA

Head of State:
Nicholas II (1868–1918); tsar (1894–1917)

Head of Government:
Goremykin, Ivan (1839–1917); chairman, council of ministers (1914–16)

Foreign Minister/Secretary of State:
Sazonov, Sergei Dmitrievich (1860–1927); foreign minister (1910–17)

Ambassadors:
Benckendorff, Count Aleksandr (1849–1917); ambassador at London (1903–17)
Izvol'skii, Aleksandr (1856–1919); ambassador at Paris (1910–17)
Schebeko, Nikolai Nikolaevich (1863–1953); ambassador at Vienna (1913–14)

Army and Navy:
Yanushkevich, Nikolai (1868–1918); chief of staff of the general headquarters (1914–15)

FRANCE

Head of State:
Poincaré, Raymond (1860–1934); president (1913–20)

Head of Government:
Viviani, René (1863–1925); president of the council [prime minister] (1914–15)

Foreign Minister/Secretary of State:
Viviani, René (1863–1925); minister of foreign affairs (1914)

Foreign Office Officials:
Berthelot, Philippe (1866–1934); foreign office (1904–22)

Ambassadors:
Cambon, Jules (1845–1935); ambassador at Berlin (1907–14)
Cambon, Paul (1843–1924); ambassador at London (1898–1920)
Dumaine, Alfred (1852–1930); ambassador at Vienna (1912–14)
Paléologue, Maurice (1859–1944); ambassador at St Petersburg (1914–17)

Army and Navy:
Joffre, Joseph (1852–1931); commander-in-chief of army (1911–16)

BRITAIN

Head of State:
George V (1865–1936); king (1910–36)

Head of Government:
Asquith, Herbert Henry (1852–1928); prime minister (1908–16)

Foreign Minister/Secretary of State:
Grey, Sir Edward (1862–1933); foreign secretary (1905–16)

Foreign Office Officials:
Crowe, Eyre (1864–1925); assistant under-secretary of state for foreign affairs (1912–20)

Nicolson, Sir Arthur (1849–1928); permanent under-secretary of state for foreign affairs (1910–16)

Ambassadors:

Bertie, Sir Francis (1844–1919); ambassador at Paris (1905–18)

Buchanan, Sir George (1854–1924); ambassador at St Petersburg (1910–18)

de Bunsen, Sir Maurice (1852–1932); ambassador at Vienna (1913–14)

Goschen, Sir Edward (1847–1924); ambassador at Berlin (1908–14)

Army and Navy:

Churchill, Winston (1874–1965); first lord of the admiralty (1911–15)

Wilson, Sir Henry (1864–1922); director of military operations (1910–14)

ROMANIA

Head of State:

Karl I (1839–1914); king (1881–1914)

A Diplomatic Lexicon

amour propre self-esteem; used mostly to refer to a situation in which one state cannot permit an action to occur or a state of affairs to arise without losing its self-esteem

casus belli 'cause of war'; used mostly to refer to a specific act that would cause war to be declared

casus foederis 'cause of the treaty'; used mostly to refer to a situation that would cause the terms of an alliance to be applied

chargé d'affaires the person assigned to 'take charge of affairs' in the absence of the person normally responsible for them

démarche 'to march'; used to refer to a wide variety of diplomatic initiatives; most often a diplomatic step to resolve an issue

entente 'understanding'; used to refer to an amicable relationship of an informal kind

fait accompli 'accomplished fact'; used mostly to refer to a situation in which one party has presented others with an irreversible act

minister the head of a legation; i.e. in many 'minor' posts (particularly in the era before 1914) states were not represented by an ambassador heading an embassy, but instead by a legation headed by a minister

modus vivendi 'way of living'; most often used to refer to an accommodation or a working arrangement that enables parties to live with a state of affairs until a permanent arrangement can be agreed to

pourparlers 'conversation'; usually refers to the informal discussions between parties before proceeding to formal negotiations

quid pro quo 'this for that'; in diplomacy, what might be exchanged between two parties in order to arrive at a settlement of differences

rapprochement 'coming together'; used to indicate a reconciliation between parties previously at odds with one another

List of Illustrations

List of Maps

It is half the art of storytelling to keep a story free from explanation as one reproduces it.

Walter Benjamin, *Illuminations: Essays and Reflections*

After the historian has ascertained the facts, there is no further process of inquiring into their causes. When he knows what happened, he already knows why it happened.

R. G. Collingwood, *The Idea of History*

Prologue
The Long European Peace

1914 was the year of Peace in Europe. The last war fought between Great
Powers on European soil had ended forty-three years before, in 1871. That
war, the Franco-Prussian, was now but a distant memory, remembered only
by an elderly few. The conflicts in which Germans, French, Russians,
Italians, Austrians, and British had participated occurred in far-off places:
in Manchuria, South Africa, Indochina, and North Africa. And those who
had fought in them were mainly professional soldiers and volunteers, not
conscripts. The most recent wars had been fought by Turks, Serbs, Bulgars,
Greeks, and Romanians in 1912 and 1913. To western, central, and northern Europeans the Balkans hardly seemed to count as 'Europe', and with
fewer than 100,000 killed, the wars there seemed to amount to little more
than skirmishes. They certainly did not appear to be a warning of things
to come as much as a vestige of a past that civilized Europeans had put
behind them.

No Englishman, Scotsman, Irishman, or Welshman had fought on the
European continent since the Crimean War ended in 1856—some fifty-
eight years ago. The three wars that had created a united Italy had ended in
1866 and cost the lives of fewer than 30,000 soldiers. In the three wars that
united Germany and led to the creation of the German empire in 1860,
1866, and 1870–1, fewer than 25,000 soldiers from Prussia, Bavaria, Baden,
and Württemberg were killed in battle. Wars seemed to be growing fewer,
shorter, less bloody, and farther away from Europe.

What was there to fight over? With the defeat of France and the creation
of a united Germany in 1871, the boundaries of the Great Powers seemed to
be set. Although some in France called for *revanche* against Germany and the
return of the 'lost provinces' of Alsace and Lorraine, their voices became

fewer and less strident over time. By 1914 their recovery had ceased to be a political issue. No one in Austria-Hungary proposed to avenge the lost war to Prussia of 1866, and no one in Denmark dreamed of recovering their lost provinces of Schleswig and Holstein. The re-creation of the Polish state that had disappeared in the late eighteenth century was not on the landscape of practical politics: the governments of Germany, Russia, and Austria-Hungary were working harder than ever to turn their Poles into loyal subjects. A few Italians proclaimed their mission to be the incorporation of *Italia irredenta*—'unredeemed Italy'—into the unified Italian monarchy, but the 'recovery' of the Tyrol and Trentino by war with Austria-Hungary was proposed by no one who mattered in Italy. Officially, Italy was loyal to its alliance with Germany and Austria-Hungary, and if more Italians were to be incorporated into the monarchy this would be achieved only by the peaceful assent of the Austrians.

In all of the feuds, controversies, disputes, quarrels, and squabbles that had arisen over the past forty years, no one in a position of responsibility had raised the possibility of transferring territory from one Great Power to another. No one had raised the prospect of annexing or partitioning the smaller western European states of Denmark, the Netherlands, Belgium, Switzerland, or Luxembourg; no one had proposed to acquire or subjugate the smaller south-east European states of Romania, Bulgaria, Serbia, Montenegro, or Greece. If the frontiers of Europe were fixed, what was there for the Great Powers to fight over?

There was no shortage of quarrels. But these seemed to have less to do with modern Europe and more to do with remnants of the ageing, decaying empires of the past—with the Qing dynasty in China and Ottoman rule in the Middle East; with the remnants of the Spanish, Dutch, and Portuguese empires in the Caribbean, Africa, and the Far East. Europeans generally assumed that Asians and Africans were still far from being able to govern themselves, and that it was therefore inevitable that Europeans would have to govern them for the foreseeable future. But which Europeans, where?

During the long European peace that had endured since 1871, the Great Powers had frequently disputed each other's colonial claims, sometimes coming close to the brink of war: Britain and France over Siam in 1893 and again at Fashoda in 1898; Britain and Russia at Pendjeh in 1885; Germany and France in Morocco in 1905 and again in 1911. Sometimes they went over the brink: the British empire went to war with the Boer republics in South Africa in 1899; the Russian empire went to war with

Japan in 1904; Italy—trying to become an empire—went to war with Turkey in 1911. But the European Powers had avoided war with one another. Peace continued to prevail in Europe. And, while there was peace, Europeans enjoyed unprecedented prosperity—while chaos and conflict prevailed on the perimeter and beyond. No one was surprised. But no one paid much attention. Disputes over barren deserts, fetid jungles, and desolate mountain ranges could not be taken too seriously. No one expected a major war to be fought over the future of the Congo, the Sahara, Afghanistan, or Siam.

It seemed perfectly reasonable to think that, the wars uniting Germany and Italy having finished, there would be peace on the continent for the foreseeable future. The issues that had divided Europeans were now few and far between.

What was there that was worth going to war over? There was no clear ideological divide between east and west, north and south. By 1914 five of the six Great Powers of Europe were constitutional monarchies: how the constitution functioned, and the extent to which it constrained the monarch from acting independently of representative institutions varied from Germany to Britain to Austria-Hungary to Italy to Russia, but the differences did not lead to denunciations of systems deemed to be incompatible. Insofar as there was an ideological divide it was greatest between the French republic and British constitutionalism on the one hand and the tsarist 'autocracy' on the other. Awkwardly, France was allied to Russia, and Britain had grown steadily closer to a *de facto* alliance with Russia since settling most of their colonial differences in the entente of 1907. The German kaiser had for years insisted to the Russian tsar that their monarchical interests bound them closely together in a shared vision of how the political universe ought to function. No European of any standing, representing any political point of view, proposed going to war to eradicate the disease of an alternative political system.

Religion had long ceased to divide Europeans in a way that might lead to war. The Thirty Years War had put that to rest almost 300 years ago. No one suggested that they repeat that horrific experience. Germany—mainly Protestant—was allied with Austria and Italy—mainly Catholic. Catholic France was allied with Orthodox Russia, and both were associated with Protestant Britain. Internal religious differences were far more divisive than external ones: Protestants in northern Ireland were prepared to fight against Catholics in the rest of the island; although Italians were overwhelmingly

Catholic, the papacy regarded the Italian state with disdain verging on disgust; the almost completely Calvinist Hungary regarded Catholic Austria with suspicion; German Catholics, located mainly in Bavaria, had formed their own political party to defend their interests against the majority Protestants. And on it went. No one needed to look beyond their frontiers to find antagonists—they were closer to hand at home. Anyone proposing to fight to alter the religious map of Europe in 1914 would have been laughed at as a lunatic. But no one was proposing any such thing.

If the map of Europe did not need significant revision based on nationality, if Europeans were not divided into hostile camps by political ideology or religious culture, what could be left to fight over? Certainly not wealth. Everyone in Europe had benefited from the long European peace. The economy of the continent had become integrated as never before. Railways, shipping, canals, postal services, telegraphic and wireless communication had led to an unprecedented expansion in trade among nations. The stock exchanges and banking systems had produced an unparalleled interconnectedness: loans, bonds, investments, and ownership no longer knew any nationality. In the decade before 1914 Britain became Germany's best customer. The greatest, and the most popular, economic thinkers of the day argued that peace was essential to prosperity, that internationalism was the way of the future, mercantilism a thing of the past.

Movements to maintain the peace

Among the most popular books in Europe before 1914 was Norman Angell's *The Great Illusion*. He first published his ideas in a 1909 pamphlet entitled 'Europe's Optical Illusion'. He argued that it was a mistake to believe that a victorious war could be made to pay for itself. To the surprise of many, he seemed to prove that the indemnity imposed by Germany on France at the conclusion of the Franco-Prussian war had actually damaged the German economy while stimulating the French. In contrast with the old mercantilist view, wealth could no longer be found in 'gold' but in goods and in the exchange of goods. The futility of indemnities was that the vanquished could pay only if rehabilitated. Wars of conquest no longer served any purpose: they were expensive, wasteful, divisive, and counterproductive. The seizure of Alsace provided no benefit to the German people or state—because Alsace, if it were to function successfully, had to be left in possession of its wealth. All of this demonstrated the interdependence of modern economies and that everyone was hurt by war.[1] The modern capitalist had no country and knew 'that arms and conquests and jugglery with frontiers serve no ends of his, and may very well defeat them'.[2]

Angell's book was immensely popular. It sold over two million copies and was translated into twenty-five languages. In Britain an entire movement, 'Angellism', grew up devoted to his ideas: by 1913 there were more than fifty clubs, as well as study circles and debating unions in at least ten British universities. A £30,000 grant from the Carnegie Endowment for International Peace enabled Angell to establish a journal devoted to his liberal internationalist ideas: *War and Peace*.[3] The idea that war would not, could not, pay was taking root. One Frenchman, Charles Richet, estimated that the cost of a European war would be $50,000,000 per day, per Great Power.

Dire predictions of the economic and human costs of fighting a modern war were everywhere. Almost as popular as Angell was a retired Polish banker and railway magnate, Ivan Bloch, who had made himself rich in Russia's industrial development. In a massive six-volume study that took him eight years to write, Bloch argued in *War of the Future* (1898) that modern technology and techniques had made war suicidal for any state foolish enough to engage in it. He calculated that guns and artillery were now capable of destroying everything within range: in the Franco-Prussian war grenades had burst into about thirty pieces; by 1890 they could burst into 341; the destructive force of artillery had multiplied five times in twenty years and was continuing to grow.

The one-volume edition published the following year—*Is War Now Impossible?*—proved immensely popular. Bloch's enormous compendium of statistics and his detailed analysis of armaments, strategies, and tactics led him to conclude that another war between Great Powers would not be decisive, that it would begin with a slaughter of soldiers unprecedented in history. Soldiers would then entrench themselves and become reluctant to fight. A long, debilitating war of attrition would follow. There would be no decisive battles, only a long, slow bleeding away of precious resources.[4] War could no longer be considered a rational policy: the future of war was 'not fighting, but famine, not the slaying of men, but the bankruptcy of nations and the breakup of the whole social organization'.[5]

Angell and Bloch were not alone in arguing that war was atavistic, an irrational remnant of an unfortunate past. A variety of peace groups had been formed in Europe since the mid-nineteenth century and sporadic meetings had been held. Many of the groups had religious affiliations, and most of them aimed to mitigate the worst effects of warfare, rather than proposing to eliminate it altogether. The first 'Universal Peace Conference' was convened in Paris in 1889, organized by the *Ligue internationale de la paix et de la liberté*. The assembled delegates approved of a proposal to work towards the creation of an international court of arbitration and agreed to reconvene in London the following year. When they met in Rome in 1891 Austro-Hungarian and German delegations were included—a result of the campaign waged by Bertha von Suttner, whose 1889 anti-war novel *Die Waffen nieder* ('*Lay Down your Arms*') was an immediate best-seller and translated into eight languages.[6] Her popularity was instrumental in the formation of the Austrian Peace Society (the *Österreicher Friedensgesellschaft*) in 1890 and the German society in 1892—the *Deutsche Friedensgesellschaft*.

When the Universal Peace Conference met in Berne in 1892 they agreed to establish the International Peace Bureau as a permanent organization that would coordinate the activities of the multifarious groups that were represented and unite in the cause of settling international disputes through the mechanism of a formal arbitration process. Understandably, they were pleased to take credit for the first Hague Conference of 1899 at which the Permanent Court of Arbitration was established.

By 1902 the idea of promoting peace through arbitration was so popular and widespread that Émile Arnaud, president of the *Ligue internationale de la paix et de la liberté*, coined a new term to describe the movement of those who did more than passively support peace, but actively engaged in promoting it—'*pacifisme*'. 'We are pacifists . . . and our ideology is pacifism.'[7]

The movement received a great boost when, in 1896, the Swedish industrialist Alfred Nobel left a vast sum of money in his will to fund an annual prize to be given to the person having done the most or best work to promote fraternity among nations, 'for the abolition or reduction of standing armies and for the holding and promotion of peace congresses'.[8] The first prize was awarded in 1901; in 1910 it was awarded to the International Peace Bureau itself. Andrew Carnegie gave millions to the cause, establishing a trust fund for the Carnegie Endowment for International Peace and building 'temples of peace' around the world—including the Peace Palace at The Hague, which became the location of the Permanent Court of Arbitration in 1913.

By 1914 pacifists were to be found everywhere in Europe. One survey listed 190 peace societies, responsible for publishing twenty-three journals or reviews in ten languages. Over 600 groups representing some one million members supported the work of the International Peace Bureau. When the National Council of French Peace Societies—representing thirty-six separate organizations and several hundred thousand members—met in 1911 they listed seven cabinet ministers on their letterhead. British peace groups came together in 1905 to create a central coordinating committee—the British National Peace Council. The prince of Monaco in 1902 endowed *L'Institut international de la paix* for the purpose of promoting peaceful solutions to international conflicts and encouraging the development of international institutions. In 1904 the headquarters moved from Monaco to Paris. In 1908 an American delegate to the pacifist conference declared: 'If you had been told, ten years ago, that we should have an international tribunal, an international Parliament assured, sixty treaties of arbitration and an international prize court, I say the boldest of dreamers would not have believed it.'[9]

The 'international parliament' was the creation of the Interparliamentary Union, founded on the initiative of a French economist, Frédéric Passy, and a Liberal English parliamentarian, Randal Cremer, in 1889. An advocate of free trade and international arbitration, Passy had earlier been instrumental in establishing the *Ligue internationale et permanente de la paix*, its successor, the *Société française des amis de la paix*, and finally the *Société d'arbitrage entre les nations*. The Interparliamentary Union began by bringing together parliamentarians from Britain and France for the purpose of promoting the cause of arbitration. Conferences were held for eighteen of the twenty-five years between 1889 and 1914. By the time of its meeting at the British House of Lords in 1906, 600 parliamentarians attended—including delegates from the new Russian Duma; in 1908 the delegates met in Berlin—where they were welcomed by the German chancellor. By 1909 almost 3,000 members, drawn from twenty countries, belonged to the Union. Passy was awarded the first Nobel Peace Prize in 1901; Cremer received the award two years later.

By 1914 pacifism had spread far beyond its beginnings as a religious–humanitarian movement. The movement now included legislators, jurists, economists, lawyers, teachers; hundreds of organizations were involved;

annual congresses and conferences were held; trust funds and prizes were established; buildings were built. While 'realist' diplomats and strategists might sneer at the movement no politician dared any longer to denounce the ideas of arbitration and disarmament in public.

Realists might also maintain that it was a dog-eat-dog world in which only the strong would survive, that social life was a struggle that pitted individual against individual, nation against nation, empire against empire. But pacifists were countering these Darwinist notions with ideas of their own. In 1902 the Russian anarchist, Prince Kropotkin, in his hugely influential *Mutual Aid,* cited Darwin's own example of altruistic pelicans who kept alive one of their own who was blind by feeding it fish. They found numerous examples of peaceful coexistence and cooperation in the natural world. The Nobel prize-winning physiologist Charles Richet dismissed the idea that there was such a thing as an 'instinct' for war in his *Peace and War* of 1906. An even greater success was the work of the American scientist, pacifist, and president of Stanford University, David Starr Jordan. He argued in his 1907 *The Human Harvest* that human society had evolved from the fighting of tribal wars to dynastic wars to holy wars. Now that peace had been achieved within the frontiers of the nation-states, the next stage in the evolutionary process would be to achieve peace between nations. A few years later his colleague, the zoologist Vernon Kellogg, dismissed war as a biological stupidity in *Beyond War.* And the Russian-born, French-educated sociologist Jacques Novicow attacked the precepts of social Darwinism head-on in his *La critique du darwinisme social* of 1910. The idea that the 'collective homicide' of warfare could actually promote progress was sheer madness: what war did was to send off the fittest and the bravest to die, leaving behind the cowardly and the sick to propagate the species.[10]

Pacifist ideas and organizations were largely the work of middle-class intellectuals, professionals, and activists. But a strong and determined anti-war movement had also grown within European working-class organizations since the turn of the century. Karl Marx and Friedrich Engels had proclaimed in the *Communist Manifesto* of 1848 that 'the working man has no country'. The socialist movement had formed the First International in 1864 expressly for the purpose of establishing unity among the working classes of the world. But war itself, according to Marx, was not inherently wrong: each was to be judged by whether it hastened or delayed progress in achieving the classless society. And he dismissed pacifists as a bunch of 'hypocritical phrasemongers, [a] squint-eyed set of Manchester humbugs'.[11]

The greatest obstacle to the proletarian revolution was the reactionary regime of tsarist Russia.

By the time that the Second International was founded in 1889 the official position of organized socialism was that war would not be eradicated until socialism triumphed over capitalism. War was inherent in the nature of capitalist society. But it was the working class who paid the price, who were conscripted as soldiers into the mass armies of Europe, and would serve only as cannon-fodder in the wars perpetrated by the bourgeoisie. Socialist leaders hoped that their increasing representation in the parliaments of Europe could be used to starve governments of the funds necessary to fight a modern war: 'Not a man and not a penny to this system' was the slogan of the Social Democratic Party in Germany. And Engels looked forward to the day when most of the conscripted soldiers would themselves be socialists and unwilling to follow the dictates of the bourgeois state.

The syndicalist movement, strong throughout Europe in the years before 1914, and especially popular in France, proposed a different solution to the problem. Fundamentally, syndicalists believed that attempting to influence society through political action, through political parties and representative institutions, was a waste of time. The system was rigged in favour of big business, which had learned to work hand-in-glove with the old aristocracy. The only chance that the working classes had for a better life was to harness the full power of their own labour unions. They proposed to seize control of society through the direct action of a general strike of all organized workers. If the capitalist-controlled government attempted to mobilize the workers to fight their war, that would be the moment to call for the general strike. And if war were to break out, they would call for an armed insurrection against the state. Perhaps this was no idle threat: since 1906 the syndicalists had seized control of the federation of French trade unions, the *Confédération générale du travail*. The threat it posed was sufficiently dire to frighten the government of France, which created a list of dangerous people to be arrested in the event of mobilization—the infamous *Carnet B*.

The section of the Workers' International, the *Section française de l'internationale ouvrière*, differed from the syndicalists in its belief that political action could benefit workers and their cause. In the elections of 1910 the party became the third largest in the Chamber of Deputies; in the spring of 1914 it received 1.5 million votes and became the second largest party. But despite the differences with the syndicalists on political action, it united with them in the *anti-militarisme* campaign. When the government appeared ready to promulgate a law to raise military service from two years to three, the leader of the SFIO, Jean Jaurès, produced a scheme to reform completely the system of national defence. In 1910 he published *L'armée nouvelle*, in which he proposed to make the system more efficient and more democratic by creating a peoples' militia as an alternative to the huge standing army created by conscription. And in 1914 he went further, agreeing with the syndicalists that the most effective way to prevent war was by a general strike—or at least the threat of one.

The Second International was scheduled to meet in Vienna in September. There they planned to discuss the best methods of preventing war and defending workers' interests. But they had no reason to believe that there was any need for hurry—these issues had been percolating and debated for years now. Many socialists believed that strong national defences and large armies were the best guarantee that peace would endure for the foreseeable future, and that peace and security would enable the working-class movement to continue to achieve gains on behalf of those they represented. They were more concerned to ameliorate the hardships of those who were conscripted—and the consequences for their families—than they were with eradicating the armies themselves.

Peace, after all, had endured for decades. And it was arguable that it was the existence of strong armed forces, in which a Europe was divided into two evenly matched sides, that was largely responsible for maintaining the long European peace. Far from armaments and armies making war inevitable, they made it unlikely.

Weathering the storms: the balance of power

The 'system of alliances' had begun decades ago, in 1879, when Bismarck proposed that Germany and Austria-Hungary should recognize that the differences that had led them to war in 1866 were now dead and buried. They shared a mutual interest—and that interest was peace. An alliance between them would enable them to thwart any ambitions France might have to reverse the decision of 1870–1, or any ambitions Russia might have to dominate south-eastern Europe. The terms were purely defensive: 'Should, contrary to their hope, and against the loyal desire of the two High Contracting Parties, one of the two Empires be attacked by Russia, the High Contracting Parties are bound to come to the assistance one of the other with the whole war strength of their Empires'; 'Should one of the High Contracting Parties be attacked by another Power, the other ... binds itself not only not to support the aggressor against its high Ally, but to observe at least a benevolent neutral attitude ...'. In other words, if Russia attacked either of them, they would join together in defending themselves; if France were to attack Germany, Austria-Hungary would keep out of it.[12]

The alliance was expanded three years later to include Italy. Here too the arrangement was purely defensive. 'In case Italy, without direct provocation on her part, should be attacked by France ... the two other Contracting Parties shall be bound to lend help and assistance with all their forces to the Party attacked. This same obligation shall devolve upon Italy in case of any aggression without direct provocation by France against Germany.'[13] And, if one of them should be attacked by two or more Great Powers, the other two would come to its assistance. The agreement also provided for the three Powers to 'take counsel together in ample time as to the military measures to be taken with a view to eventual cooperation'. But the three never came together to coordinate their military plans, and their general staffs were aware of one another's strategy only in broad outline. There were no precise commitments to one another, only vague promises that could not be relied on.

The first treaty of alliance was to last for five years, until 1887. It was renewed then, and repeatedly, in 1891, 1902, 1906, and 1913. Although the terms were revised slightly at each renewal, the fundamental nature of the alliance as defensive, and providing for cooperation in the case of aggression on the part of Russia and/or France, remained unchanged.[14] The most significant development between 1879 and 1913 came in the 1880s when Romania—secretly—joined the alliance.

The Russians learned of the alliance shortly after it was formed, the French a few years later. The Italians gave the French the precise details of the agreement when it was renewed in 1887. When it became clear that Britain was actively cooperating with the Triple Alliance, Russia and France began to discuss the possibility of a counter-alliance. Had they known that Britain had made secret arrangements for cooperation with Italy and Austria-Hungary in the Mediterranean, they might have moved more quickly than they did. After years of fitful negotiations the Russians and the French agreed to counter the Triple Alliance—now, as far as they were concerned, a quintuple alliance—with one of their own.

In 1891 the foreign ministers of Russia and France exchanged letters that led to a formal agreement the following year. As the Russian letter stated, it was the situation in Europe created by 'the open renewal of the Triple Alliance and the more or less probable adhesion of Great Britain to the political aims which that alliance pursues' that led them to their arrangement. They came together because they were united in their desire to maintain the peace, 'which forms the object of their sincerest aspirations'. They agreed to act together on any questions that might 'jeopardize the general peace' and to reach an understanding on what measures they might take if one of them were threatened with aggression.[15]

At first no more than a vague agreement to come to an agreement on measures to adopt in response to a threat of aggression aimed at one of them, by 1893–4 the arrangement had grown teeth. The Franco-Russian alliance became formalized and a military convention established.[16] Like the Triple Alliance, it was purely defensive. The two Powers declared that they were 'animated by an equal desire to preserve peace, and [had] no other object than to meet the necessities of a defensive war, provoked by an attack of the forces of the Triple Alliance'. If Germany were to attack either of them the other promised to attack Germany in support of its ally. If Germany supported an Italian attack on France, Russia promised to employ all available forces to attack Germany; if Germany supported an Austrian attack on Russia, France promised to employ all available forces to fight Germany. If any of the Powers of the Triple Alliance were to mobilize, France and Russia were to mobilize immediately in response 'without the necessity of any previous concert' and were to move the whole of their forces as close as possible to their frontiers. France promised to mobilize 1,300,000 men; Russia 700,000–800,000. Their general staffs were to cooperate in preparing and facilitating the execution of these military commitments.[17]

No time limit was established for the Franco-Russian alliance: it was to last as long as the Triple Alliance endured. Thus, for more than twenty years, Europe was divided into two armed camps, roughly equal in military power, but obliged to act only in the event that the other side committed an act of aggression. Between the Franco-Russian exchange of letters in August 1891 and June 1914 none of the five Great Powers in the alliances fired a shot at another. All military activities were limited to the periphery: south-eastern Europe, north and south Africa, the Far East. The system was stable and peaceful. The leaders of all of the Powers recognized that if they were to undertake an aggressive act their partners could declare their alliance void.

Not only did the alliance system act as a brake on the other side, it restrained the partners within the alliance itself.

Ironically, when tensions arose between the powers in the decade before 1914 (in 1908 and 1911/12 in particular) their peaceful settlement seemed proof that the system worked, that diplomacy could resolve differences without warfare. Only the division of Europe between NATO and the Warsaw Pact established a more stable, predictable, and longer-lasting diplomatic system in the last two hundred years.

During the first decade of the new alliance system the only serious diplomatic quarrels arose not within Europe, but beyond it. And these quarrels were not contests between the Triple Alliance and the Franco-Russian alliance, but between France and Britain, Britain and Russia, Russia and Japan. It was in order to reduce the likelihood that a colonial confrontation might lead to a war between them that the two greatest imperial powers, Britain and France, undertook negotiations to settle their differences. In 1904 they signed a wide-ranging agreement that included provisions that spanned the globe: from Newfoundland to Gambia to Nigeria to Madagascar to Siam and the New Hebrides. Most important, France recognized Britain's dominance in Egypt in exchange for British recognition of French dominance in Morocco.

The Anglo-French agreement, signed in April 1904, which soon became known as the *Entente Cordiale*, was no alliance. There were no provisions for military or naval cooperation, no contingencies anticipated in which one would assist the other in the event of war. No potential enemies were identified. It was, quite simply, a settlement of the differences that had plagued their relationship for the last quarter-century. In a secret protocol to the agreement Britain promised that, if the sultan of Morocco was no longer able to maintain order, France would be given a free hand there.

Although it was no alliance, the entente seemed to signify a shift in the balance of power that had operated in Europe for the last decade. When the French and the Russians had come together to form their alliance, they had assumed that the British were *de facto* members of the Triple Alliance. Despite the fact that the Mediterranean agreements between Britain, Austria-Hungary, and Italy were kept closely guarded secrets, the signs of British cooperation were numerous and public, and contrasted with the friction between themselves, the French, and the Russians. The *Entente Cordiale* threatened to upset this arrangement.

The Germans had been trying for the last twenty years to bring Britain into the fold of the Triple Alliance. But no inducements they could offer had enticed the British to abandon their independence, their so-called 'splendid isolation'. When the Germans undertook to build a high-seas naval fleet in 1898 their hope was that this would induce Britain to join the alliance rather than engage in a costly competition. Surely the British would recognize that their real enemies were the French and the Russians, and that it would be better to join Germany than face a third enemy which—with a fleet—would be in a position to do damage to the British empire? The Anglo-French entente challenged these assumptions.

An opportunity to test the meaning of the new relationship between Britain and France had come early in 1905 when a French military mission was sent to Morocco to 'assist' the Moroccans in reforming their adminis- tration. It would also signify the extent to which the French were now in control of the situation there. The sultan appealed to the Germans for their assistance in resisting the French. And the Germans agreed: on 31 March the kaiser and his entourage disembarked at Tangier, riding through the streets on a magnificent horse, with a military band marching and playing behind him. He announced that Germany would support the independence of the regime in Morocco and that Germany would protect its interests there.

The Germans had decided to test the strength of the new Anglo-French friendship. Would the French be sufficiently emboldened by their arrange- ment with Britain to withstand German pressure in Morocco? If not, if the prospect of a war against Germany on the European continent proved sufficiently daunting to restrain them, the lesson would be clear: that France's imperial future rested not on the entente with Britain, but on the goodwill of Germany. If France, with a much larger fleet than Germany, and with a large army nearby in Algeria, could not act as it saw fit in Morocco because of the German army in Europe, it would demonstrate that it was practically incapable of pursuing an independent foreign policy. The alliance with Russia meant nothing: the Russians were preoccupied with their war against Japan in Manchuria and had just faced the prospect of revolution on 'bloody Sunday' in St Petersburg two months before. The Russians made it clear that they had no intention of fighting a war against Germany for the sake of French ambitions in Morocco. France was on its own.

Or was it? By May the British began to hint that they might be prepared to discuss the possibility of turning the entente into an alliance. And the

French foreign secretary, who had been the architect of the entente, welcomed the prospect. But when the Germans got wind of it they insisted that he be forced out of office—and the French premier, fearing it would end in war, agreed to force his resignation. Germany appeared to have scored a decisive diplomatic victory: the Triple Alliance was supreme in Europe, the Franco-Russian alliance was shown to be hollow, and the Anglo-French entente useless. The Germans confidently called for an international conference to settle the Moroccan dispute.

The balance of power that had been established by the alliance system a decade earlier now appeared to have shattered. When, in the midst of the Russo-Japanese war the kaiser had proposed to the tsar that they might combine in support of one another if attacked by another 'European power', Nicholas II had welcomed the idea. 'Germany, Russia and France should at once unite upon an arrangement to abolish the Anglo-Japanese arrogance and insolence . . . This combination has often come to my mind. It will mean peace and rest for the world.'[18] Things got even worse for Russia when the Baltic fleet finally arrived off the coast of Japan in May— where it was annihilated almost immediately. Two months later when the kaiser met with the tsar in Sweden he persuaded him to sign the defensive alliance that he had proposed the year before.

France's humiliation in Morocco and Russia's humiliation in the Far East prompted Britain to rethink its diplomatic situation. With the Franco-Russian alliance no longer in a position to counter the weight of the Triple Alliance in Europe, combined with the possibility that the new German naval fleet might cooperate with Britain's traditional rivals outside Europe, the future was beginning to look bleak for the British empire. A group of officials at the British Foreign Office argued convincingly that it was only the combined weight of the Franco-Russian alliance that was keeping German ambitions in check. The Moroccan crisis had shown that France could be turned into a pawn of Germany. When a new Liberal government came into power in December the new foreign secretary, Sir Edward Grey, authorized secret discussions between the British and French general staffs to consider joint operations in the event of war. The British were now indicating their willingness to provide military assistance to the French on the European continent in the event of war with Germany.

By the time that the conference was convened at Algeciras in Spain in January 1906 what amounted to a diplomatic revolution had occurred. The sunny prospects for German diplomacy disappeared. France was bolstered by British support. Italy had secretly agreed to recognize the special interests of France in Morocco in exchange for similar recognition of Italy's interests in Libya. Austria-Hungary counselled Germany to act with moderation. The tsar's advisers had persuaded him that a defensive alliance with Germany would mean the abandonment of France, the destruction of the balance of power in Europe, and the encouragement of German expansion into the Middle East. The conference proved to be a humiliation for German diplomacy.

It seemed that Britain had succeeded in restoring the balance of power established in the mid-1890s. To those who managed British policy, the conclusion was clear: the Triple Alliance had grown stronger, and only the prospect of British intervention on the side of France and Russia could maintain the precarious balance between the two alliances. Over the course of the next two years Britain and Russia negotiated an agreement to resolve their differences in Central Asia—in Tibet, Afghanistan, Persia, and the Gulf. Following the Anglo-Russian Convention of August 1907, observers and participants began to refer to the Triple Alliance as facing the 'Triple Entente'. When one member of the British cabinet complained about official usage of the term, Sir Edward Grey replied that it had become 'so exceedingly convenient and common that I can no more keep it out of use than I can exclude split infinitives'.[19] Stability had been restored, the balance recalibrated. The two great alliances again faced one another in Europe, with Britain informally attached to France and Russia.

Although Anglo-French conversations on a combined strategy in Europe continued, there was no alliance, no commitments. To Sir Edward Grey, the arrangement was close to perfect: facing the combined weight of Russia, France, and Britain, the Triple Alliance was unlikely to risk a war; facing the prospect that Britain would only provide assistance if their existence were threatened, neither Russia nor France was likely to undertake the kind of aggressive action that might precipitate a war.

Over the course of the next seven years the newly revitalized balance of power in Europe succeeded in keeping the peace that had endured for the previous thirty-six. The capability of the system to keep the peace was demonstrated repeatedly: in the Balkans in 1908, in Morocco again in 1911, in Libya in 1912, and in the Balkans in 1912 and 1913. Some prophesied that the division of Europe into two armed camps made war inevitable; some strategists argued that this or that moment was opportune for taking military action that would tilt the balance to their advantage in the future. For seven years, what was supposed to be inevitable failed to happen; the advice of those who preached the gospel of war, now, was rejected.

Diplomatists recognized that the harmony of purpose and the coherence of interests that appeared to sustain the unity within each alliance was not as certain as it appeared to be. Within each of the Great Powers there were those who criticized the alliance as inimical to the interests of their nation, state, or empire. In Russia pro-Germans—particularly strong within court circles—argued that the alliance with republican France was unnatural and that Russia's true interests were aligned with the monarchical order of Germany; in France many imperialists—led by the *Comité de l'Afrique française*—argued that the future lay outside of Europe, that the real enemy was the British, and that they ought to abandon the lost provinces to Germany in order to reach an accommodation in Europe; in Germany many criticized the alliance with Austria-Hungary—especially the pan-Germans—for harnessing modern, national Germany to the decadent multicultural empire of the Habsburgs; in Austria-Hungary critics of the alliance argued that Germany would not support them when it counted—in the Balkans and in disputes with Italy; in Italy most nationalists insisted that the real enemy was still Austria-Hungary, which maintained its control of Italians within its boundaries and which showed no sign of agreeing to reconfigure frontiers to reflect national aspirations.

What did these cracks and fissures within the alliances mean? That no one in a position of authority could count automatically on the support of their ally under any given circumstances. Whenever an issue arose a diplomatic initiative would have to be undertaken to determine how far an ally (or allies) might be prepared to go in support. This was at least as important diplomatically as trying to determine how far an adversary might go in opposition. Recognition of this reality contributed to the peaceful, conservative nature of the alliances: allies had to restrain themselves from fomenting a confrontation that might lead to the brink of war only to discover that their ally would abandon them. Without an ally, no single Great Power could stand up to the alliance arrayed against it with any hope of success on the battlefield. If Germany could not fight Russia and France single-handed, Austria-Hungary certainly could not; if Russia could not win a war on its own against Germany and Austria-Hungary, neither could France.

Nor did the revitalized alliance system after 1907 mean the end of negotiations over outstanding issues and potential difficulties. Between 1907 and 1914 France and Germany reached a final settlement of their differences over Morocco; Russia and Germany reached an agreement over Persia and the Baghdad railway; France and Germany reached an accommodation of their differences in the Middle East. The British and the Germans had agreed to wind down their naval race, had arrived at a détente in the Balkans and were negotiating the future disposition of Portuguese colonies in Africa, should Portugal be forced to abandon its position there. Such clouds as there were on the horizon seemed to have disappeared or were in the process of dissipating. One British official—famous for his pessimistic outlook—remarked that since coming to the Foreign Office (some forty-four years ago) he had 'not seen since such calm waters'.[20]

Anyone spoiling to pick a fight had plenty of opportunities to do so in the decade before 1914. Twice, in 1905 and then again in 1911, Germany had challenged France in Morocco. On both occasions the dispute was settled by negotiation. In 1908 Austria-Hungary formally annexed the provinces of Bosnia and Herzegovina, which it had occupied and administered 'on behalf of' the Ottoman Empire since 1878. In Serb eyes, this meant abandoning the dream of uniting all Serbs in a single Serbian state; in Russian eyes, it meant abandoning their Slav brothers to the rule of Germans and Magyars. In the 'annexation crisis' that followed Austria-Hungary refused to reverse its decision and threatened to attack Serbia unless it recognized the legitimacy of the annexation. Neither Russia nor Serbia was prepared to risk war for the sake of the two provinces and they backed down. In 1911 Italy declared war on Turkey and in the 'Guerra di Libia' succeeded in capturing the provinces of Tripolitania, Fezzan, and Cyrenaica as well as the Dodecanese Islands in the Aegean Sea. Although the war lasted for more than a year, and although it could be regarded as an Italian challenge to the Entente in the Mediterranean—and even to Austria-Hungary in the Adriatic—the war did not spread to include any other Great Powers.

In 1912 the Balkan League—consisting of Montenegro, Serbia, Bulgaria, and Greece—attacked Turkey in the first Balkan war. A conference of ambassadors of the Great Powers met in London and eventually succeeded in arranging an end to the war. In 1913 the second Balkan war began when Bulgaria attacked Greece and Serbia; Romania joined in against Bulgaria in a war which lasted less than three months. Although Austria-Hungary and Russia had interests in the Balkans that they regarded as vital, neither intervened directly—partly because it was clear that Germany was not prepared to support Austria-Hungary, and France was not prepared to support Russia, if the war transcended the small Balkan states and involved any of the Great Powers.

Europe had successfully weathered a number of storms by June 1914, and there was no reason to believe that future difficulties might present problems that could not be overcome by negotiation. It was not in spite of the system of alliances that peace was maintained, but because of it. No Great Power on its own felt strong enough to challenge an adversary, given the combined might of the other side. And allies acted as a drag on one another by indicating their unwillingness to risk war over issues in which they had no clear and immediate interest at stake.

The system of alliances was stable, but not set in stone. Negotiations within and across the alliances went on continuously in the decade before 1914. One of the most famous of these was the 'Haldane mission' of 1912, in which the British minister of war was sent to Berlin to negotiate an end to the naval race with Germany that had begun in 1898. The cost of maintaining Britain's naval supremacy frustrated many in the Liberal government who preferred to use the money to fund the new social programmes in pensions and health insurance. But Germany's price was too high: an agreement that Britain would remain neutral in the event of a war in Europe. The negotiations convinced Sir Edward Grey that Germany was attempting to revise the balance of power in favour of the Triple Alliance by removing Britain from the equation. He would continue to encourage France to believe that they might count upon British assistance if attacked by Germany—but that none would be forthcoming if France embarked on adventurous policies that provoked a war.

Although the negotiations came to nothing, they frightened the French into thinking that the British might abandon them. They began to press for a clearer commitment from Britain: if not a partnership in the Franco-Russian alliance, at least a public declaration that Britain and France would cooperate to maintain the balance of power in Europe. Grey was unwilling to go even that far. He would not go beyond cooperation in order 'to maintain European peace'. But the failure of the Haldane mission and the increased German naval building programme that followed convinced the British admiralty that it needed to counter the German threat by moving most of its fleet from the Mediterranean to home waters. France followed suit by moving the fleet stationed in the English Channel at Brest to Toulon in the Mediterranean. The French used these moves to suggest an agreement by which they and the British would discuss how they might act in concert to maintain the peace if either felt threatened by an act of aggression. Britain accepted the basic premise but added that consultation between their experts 'is not and ought not to be regarded as an engagement that commits either Government to action in a contingency that has not arisen and may never arise'. Grey and the French ambassadors exchanged letters to this effect in November 1912. There was still no alliance—only an agreement to consult if either anticipated an unprovoked attack or if something occurred that might threaten the general peace.

The Anglo-French arrangements made war even less likely. They reinforced the basic premise of the balance of power and acted as a brake on any temptation the French may have had to provoke Germany. France might receive the assistance of Britain in the event of war, but could not count on it. Britain immediately undertook fresh negotiations with Germany to resolve issues concerning the Baghdad railway and the future disposition of Portuguese colonies in Africa. The alliance system kept the balance, the concert of Europe settled differences, individual interests encouraged agreements across the alliances.

When the first Balkan war broke out in October 1912 Kaiser Wilhelm declined to hold out to Austria-Hungary any hope that Germany would support them if it chose to intervene. If the Austrians provoked a war because of their determination to prevent Serbia from extending to the shores of the Adriatic 'under no circumstances will I march against Paris and Moscow on account of Albania and Durazzo'.[21] His advisers persuaded him that he was wrong, that if Russia undertook hostile measures against Austria, Germany would have to give its support, even if it meant war with the Entente. Anticipating that a European war was now a possibility, the kaiser asked his ambassadors in Paris and London to report on whether Russia could count on the unconditional support of France, and what side Britain would be on, should it come to war.

Wilhelm did not like what he heard. The ambassador in London reported Lord Haldane as saying that Britain would not tolerate Germany's subjugation of France. And then the chancellor declared in the Reichstag that Germany would stand by Austria-Hungary if it were attacked by a third party and its existence threatened. The prospect of a wider European war led Sir Edward Grey to affirm that Britain would be obliged to come to the assistance of France if it were to face military defeat at the hands of Germany. His statement enraged the kaiser. When he read the ambassador's report he denounced the balance of power as 'idiocy', complained that a 'nation of shopkeepers' was attempting to keep Germany and Austria from defending their interests, and concluded that in the 'final struggle' (*Endkampf*) between Slavs and Teutons, the 'Anglo-Saxons will be on the side of the Slavs and Gauls'.

The kaiser immediately called together his chiefs of the army and navy to discuss how they ought to proceed.[22] He exhorted them to prepare for war. His anger with Britain was palpable: the submarine programme ought to be enhanced in order to torpedo British troop transports and to lay mines in the Thames.

The chief of the general staff argued that war was unavoidable and that the moment was propitious. The Germans enjoyed a military advantage at the moment and they should seize it.

The head of Germany's navy disagreed. He insisted that the navy needed at least a year and a half before it would be ready for war with Britain. The completion of the Kiel Canal, scheduled for the summer of 1914, was essential to the navy's plans.[23]

They did not choose war. The 'unavoidable' was avoided. The discussion that morning has become legendary as the 'War Council of 1912'. But it was nothing of the sort. No minutes were kept, only one military man was present. That three naval men were there signifies the kaiser's wish to lash out at Britain for suggesting that it could not stand by and witness the subjugation of France to Germany. The discussion was only one of dozens, hundreds of such meetings between heads of state or government and their military advisers in the decades before 1914. More often than not the military and naval men present would argue that they needed more men, more guns, more ships before they could embark on war. There was nothing new or surprising in this.

Neither the chancellor nor the secretary of state for foreign affairs attended the meeting that day. The only concrete action agreed upon was that the chancellor should be instructed 'to enlighten' the German people, who needed to know that great national interests would be involved if war were to break out over the Austro-Serbian conflict. The kaiser ordered the staffs of the army and navy 'to prepare plans for a full-scale invasion of England' and for the diplomatic service 'to win allies everywhere'. As usual, his orders produced nothing.[24] War did not break out, the campaign to mobilize opinion fizzled before it began, no new war plans were devised, and the plan to bind Turkey, Albania, Bulgaria, and Romania as a group to the Triple Alliance remained only a dream. As the disappointed Admiral Müller confided to his diary: 'The result was practically zero.'[25]

The German chancellor, Theobald von Bethmann Hollweg, took the kaiser's eruptions in his stride. He had long become accustomed to them. He counselled prudence and caution. The statements of Grey and Haldane had merely reaffirmed what Germany already knew, that Britain was pursuing a balance of power in Europe. This meant that Britain would support France 'if the latter is in danger of being annihilated by us'.[26] And he pointed out that during the crisis in the Balkans Britain had worked closely with Germany and had succeeded in keeping Russia calm. What he hoped for was a long-term solution to the war in the Balkans, which was getting on everyone's nerves and interfering with social, financial, and political progress. He warned the Austrians that they could count on German support only if they were the victims of a Serbian attack. The chancellor was far from advocating an aggressive policy that would lead to war.

Men of peace

But who ruled in Berlin? Kaiser Wilhelm II or his chancellor, Bethmann Hollweg? According to the constitution of the empire created in 1871, the answer was clear: the kaiser did. He alone was given the authority 'to declare war and to conclude peace'.[27] He had the unilateral right to declare that a 'state of war' existed if he deemed the security of the empire to be at risk. He was emperor of Germany, king of Prussia, supreme war lord (*Kommandogewalt*), and commander-in-chief of the navy. He had the authority to appoint and dismiss his chancellor at will, regardless of politics, public opinion, the Reichstag, or the Bundesrat. In fact all of his senior ministers served at his will and were answerable only to him. He, not his chancellor or his ministers, controlled appointments to the army and navy. The chief of *his* general staff and the head of *his* navy reported to him, not to the chancellor. When advice between his civilian and his military advisers conflicted—as it frequently did—he was the final arbiter.

Wilhelm came to the throne somewhat unexpectedly in 1888 at the age of 29. When his grandfather, Wilhelm I, died in March of that year his father had succeeded to the throne. But he ruled for only ninety-nine days, dying of throat cancer in June. His English mother, Victoria, was Princess Royal of England, the daughter of Queen Victoria and Prince Albert, making Wilhelm a cousin of the future King Edward VII and Tsar Nicholas II. A traumatic birth had given him a left arm six inches shorter than the right, an awkward disability for someone who longed to appear as a vigorous man of action, and which he went to great lengths to conceal when on display in public.

By the time Wilhelm acceded to the throne he was well known in court circles for two things: his ambition and his temperament. He made no secret of the fact that he wanted to be known for accomplishing great things, to be a worthy descendant of Otto I and Friedrich der Große (Frederick the Great). In order to realize this dream he believed that he would have to rule 'in person'—unlike his grandfather, who had left most of the real

Wilhelm II (1859–1941); kaiser of Germany (1888–1918)

work of politics, administration, and diplomacy to his chancellor, Otto von
Bismarck. His determination to rule personally led him to clash with the
man who most Germans believed responsible for the victorious wars of
unification and the creation of the German empire. Bismarck realized too
late that he was not indispensable and that he had underestimated the will of
the young kaiser, who dismissed him from office in 1890.

Bismarck's dismissal demonstrated that Wilhelm's talk of personal rule
was more than mere words. It also showed that his anger at slights he
perceived could have dramatic consequences: Bismarck's patronizing manner had wounded and provoked him. Few of his advisers would dare to
disagree with him from that time forward. When they believed him to be
wrong in pursuing his own agenda the best they could do was to try and
manage him—to appease him in some way or to keep him at arm's length,
out of the loop of decisions where he might decide policy based on his
emotional state rather than the needs of the government.

Wilhelm was not a stupid man, although his prejudices and contradictions, his jealousies and his egotism have made it easy to portray him as
foolish and not to be taken seriously. He was extremely adept at languages
and conversed easily in French and English. He had a phenomenal memory
that impressed all those that knew him. He knew a great deal about painting,
sculpture, and tapestry. He was fascinated by science and technology. He
had many admirers. Bernhard von Bülow, on becoming chancellor in 1898,
declared that he was 'by far the most important Hohenzollern ever to have
lived. In a way I have never seen before he combines genius—the most
authentic and original genius—with the clearest *bon sens*. His vivid imagination lifts me like an eagle high above petty detail, yet he can judge soberly
what is or is not possible and attainable. And what vitality! What a memory!'[28]

Wilhelm loved nothing more than dressing up and pretending to be the
conquering hero on horseback—a latter-day Frederick the Great or Napoleon[29]—although he enjoyed commanding his fleet and racing his yacht
almost as much as he did parading through cities in full military attire. But
his attention to military matters was never more than fleeting: he was prone
to issue sweeping orders commanding that this or that be done—and then
disappearing from the scene, forgetting what he had ordered, and frequently
contradicting himself afterwards. He authorized a series of military plans
without paying them much attention. The head of the naval cabinet
described his views on strategy as 'amateurish nonsense'.[30] He was far
more concerned with ceremony than planning, with the design of uniforms

and the awarding of titles than with strategic thought or the careful assessment of personnel.[31] Most often he chose to surround himself with lackeys
and sycophants, with those who enjoyed (or pretended to enjoy) his twisted
sense of humour. Wilhelm craved to be the centre of attention, everywhere,
at all times. The Viennese joked that 'that he insisted on being the stag at
every hunt, the bride at every wedding, and the corpse at every funeral'.[32]

Debate has raged over the thesis that the kaiser's 'personal rule' dominated policies of the empire.[33] It is true that his interventions were spas-
modic, his opinions vacillating, his reactions unpredictable. This meant that
he was never responsible for constructing long-term plans and even less so
for the day-to-day administration of policy. He did succeed in making life
difficult for those who were responsible for planning and administering. 'Far
from being the moving cog at the centre of the German governmental
machine, Wilhelm II was usually a spanner in the works.'[34] But at the same
time, everyone around the kaiser recognized that he would insist on having
the final word on any issue of importance, and that it would be fruitless to
undertake anything of significance without being certain of his support. On
any critical decision—especially one that would determine war or peace—
his would be the opinion that mattered.

The kaiser meddled as much in diplomacy as he did in naval and military
matters. He insisted on having a hand in even the most minor diplomatic
appointments—not just ambassadors, but ministers, envoys, and junior
secretaries. 'The Foreign Office?' Wilhelm once asked; 'Why? I am the
Foreign Office!'[35] He frequently issued personal and private instructions to
Germany's representatives abroad—often unknown to his chancellor and
secretary of state—and instructed them to report directly to him. 'German
diplomats quickly learned that successful careers could best be furthered by
agreeing with the kaiser, and the result was that everything that emerged
from the Wilhelmstrasse was tailored to William II's tastes.'[36]

His emotional eruptions, his repeated threats to do damage to his enemies
have distracted from the fact that he always backed down when the moment
of truth arrived. In the face of clear and determined opposition his confidence would evaporate. This is what happened both at Algeciras in 1906
and at Agadir in 1911. Diplomats and military advisers alike had grown wary
of his dramatic pronouncements on policy because he rarely followed them
up. They had also grown accustomed to his prejudices—against Slavs,
'Orientals' (of all kinds), Gauls, Latins, Jews, and gypsies. And they had
learned to ignore them: they seldom resulted in any kind of coherent policy

or meaningful strategy. His enthusiasms were usually as fleeting as his interventions—he was too lazy and too preoccupied with ceremony and play to conduct the daily business of diplomacy himself. This did not mean he did not interfere, or that he trusted those who did conduct the business: 'You diplomats are full of shit and the whole Wilhelmstrasse stinks.'[37]

The volatile, contradictory, and colourful character of Wilhelm II has distracted attention from the reality that he was essentially a man of peace. Despite the bluster and bravado, he had reigned for more than a quarter-century without engaging Germany in a significant conflict of any kind. During his reign Germany had grown more powerful and much more prosperous. The imperial government had demonstrated that it was capable of maintaining a huge army and constructing a modern navy while providing the benefits of a nascent welfare state to the German people. The alliance system and the balance of power had demonstrably worked to Germany's advantage. No one was threatening to overturn Germany's position in Europe: cries for *revanche* in France had almost disappeared; even the most outspoken francophile in Russia failed to call for war with Germany. The Triple Alliance, which had endured for over thirty years, now included Romania and, it seemed, would likely include Turkey and perhaps Greece and Bulgaria sometime soon.

Outside Europe Germany had established footholds in the few places left in the world that were not already annexed, occupied, or overseen by European colonial powers. And by June 1914 it appeared that Britain was prepared to acknowledge Germany as the successor to Portugal in Africa, while France, Russia, and Britain were willing to watch as the dream of a Berlin to Baghdad railway was realized. On 26 June, in conjunction with the annual sailing regatta, the kaiser presided over the opening of the enlarged Kiel Canal. A contingent of British warships fired a salute in his honour. German dreadnoughts could now bypass the journey around Denmark and sail directly from the Baltic into the North Sea. The recent, peaceful past had been good for Germany—and to the kaiser, the future looked brighter still.

Unlike Kaiser Wilhelm, the emperor of Austria, Franz Joseph, was more inclined to look backward than forward. The greatest days of the Habsburg monarchy appeared to have passed, and the emperor's greatest ambition was to try to keep the empire intact. Also unlike the kaiser, the emperor of Austria and king of Hungary had direct experience of warfare. He had succeeded to the throne in the midst of the revolutions of 1848 when his uncle, the Emperor Ferdinand, had been forced to abdicate in what amounted to a palace *coup d'état*. Franz was only 18—little more than a boy—when he had to deal with the uprising in Hungary that threatened to rip the Habsburg empire in two. Rejecting the advice of his much more experienced ministers, he appealed to the tsar for military assistance against the rebels, and he presided over their defeat in the spring of 1849. He signed off on death sentences for 114 leaders of the rebellion.

He was determined to keep his empire intact, but he wished to be known for something other than repression and bloodletting. His first act when succeeding to the throne was to add 'Joseph' to his name in order to indicate

Franz Joseph I (1830–1916); emperor/king of Austria-Hungary (1848–1916)

his intention of emulating the rule of his enlightened, progressive grandfather, Joseph II. It was his intention to rule as a benevolent autocrat. But it
was questionable whether he would have the opportunity to realize this
ambition. Besides the simmering rebellion in Hungary, Franz Joseph had to
deal with Italian ambitions to unite all Italians within a monarchy under the
rule of the king of Piedmont-Sardinia. In 1859 he met the challenge himself
on the field of battle, commanding his army against the combined forces
of the Italians and the French at Solferino in Lombardy. The Austrians
lost the bloody battle, suffering over 20,000 casualties. He was forced to
cede Lombardy to Napoleon III, who then handed it over to the Italians.
Although he succeeded in retaining control of Venetia, his reputation
suffered a tremendous blow, with crowds demanding that he abdicate in
favour of his brother.

Franz Joseph learned from the defeat the painful lesson that military
adventures could have political consequences. Although he avoided abdication, in the 'October Diploma' of the following year he was forced to
make a number of constitutional concessions, but when these almost immediately proved unacceptable to critics of the regime he was forced to agree
to the creation of a two-chamber imperial *Reichsrat* in the 'February Patent'
of 1861. The lower, elected chamber was given authority over the military
budget. This was not enough to satisfy the Magyars of Hungary, who were
outnumbered by Germans, Czechs, Poles, and others. Hungary refused to
send representatives to sit in Vienna, demanding real autonomy instead.

It took another military defeat for the Magyars to get their wish. In 1866
Franz Joseph decided that he would not permit Prussia to establish its
predominance in the states of the German confederation without a fight.
Although his commander-in-chief advised that defeat was inevitable, the
emperor would not give up without a major battle. When it was fought, at
Königgrätz (Sadova) in Bohemia, it was disastrous for the Austrian armies:
13,000 were killed—compared with Prussia's 1,835—and another 17,000
wounded. The emperor was forced to agree that Schleswig, Holstein,
Hesse-Cassel, Nassau, and the city of Frankfurt would be absorbed by
Prussia, and that Venetia would be ceded to Italy.

And once again there was a price to be paid for undertaking an unsuc-
cessful military adventure. The Habsburg empire was now transformed into
the 'Dual Monarchy' as a result of the *Ausgleich* ('Compromise') of 1867.
The 'lands of St Stephen' (Hungary, Transylvania, and much of Croatia
and Slovenia) were cobbled together as a separate kingdom with almost

complete autonomy. The fact that the crown of St Stephen was placed on Franz Joseph's head at a ceremony on 8 June 1867 did nothing to reduce his sense of personal humiliation.

Twenty years of rebellion, revolution, war, and upheaval had taught Franz Joseph the lessons of a lifetime. Never again would he act recklessly. The next time he made a mistake it would almost certainly destroy the empire and the Habsburg dynasty forever.

After 1867 caution became Franz Joseph's watchword. The 'dual' alliance proposed by Bismarck appealed to him because it seemed to guarantee that Austria-Hungary would be able to live in peace. Promising Germany assistance in the event of a war with France meant little: they shared no common frontier, and there was little that Austria-Hungary could be expected to do to assist Germany. In exchange for this Austria-Hungary received the promise of full military assistance if attacked by Russia. Nothing was more symbolic of Franz Joseph's wish to keep the peace than his willingness to join Austria's recent enemies, Germany and Italy, in the Triple Alliance.

The emperor now settled down to a life of conscientious hard work. He slept on a military field-bed, rose regularly at 4 a.m., put on the uniform of an army lieutenant, and spent several hours reading memoranda, digesting reports, and signing documents. This would be followed by meetings with family and his personal staff, then meetings with ministers, diplomats, and military advisers into the late afternoon. Following dinner he would put in another hour or two of work before retiring for bed at 8 or 9 p.m. His routine became more fixed as the years went by, and he came to resent any alterations to it. He loathed banquets and balls, had no interest in music and the theatre. A daily life more different than that of Wilhelm II would be difficult to imagine.

Those around Franz Joseph regarded him as kind and well-meaning, if rather dull and not particularly bright. He appears never to have read a book. None of his secretaries, advisers, or ministers ever recorded a witty remark or spirited argument. As the years went by, he engendered affection and came to be seen as a father-figure to his people. He became the personal symbol of empire. By 1914 he was the venerable old man, the reliable statesman: statues, photographs, and portraits of him were everywhere. His likeness adorned dinner plates, teacups, coffee mugs, drinking glasses, and beer steins.

His only diversions were shooting birds and animals and liaisons with mistresses. At the age of 23 he had fallen in love at first sight with the 15-year-old sister of a young woman he was supposed to be considering as a possible bride. A year later he married 'Sisi', who became the Empress Elisabeth at the age of 16. At the age of 17 she gave birth to their first daughter, and at 18 to another. When the first daughter died at the age of 2, Elisabeth began to suffer from depression. Although she succeeded in producing a male heir to the throne a few years later, she came to loathe her life at court and began to live a life quite separate from that of the emperor. She loved travel and the theatre; he did not. Their separation, and her depression, was magnified when their son, the Crown Prince Rudolf, shot himself and his mistress at Mayerling in 1889. She went into mourning and wore black for the rest of her life.

After an affair with a Polish countess, and having perhaps fathered a child by his mistress, Franz Joseph formed a lifelong attachment to the actress Katharina Schratt in 1884. He purchased for her a villa overlooking the gardens of his Viennese palace. Intimacy was thus made simple, and he regularly visited her at the villa for breakfast; the empress was only rarely in residence at the palace with him. And then Elisabeth was assassinated by an Italian anarchist while visiting Geneva in 1898.

Unlike Wilhelm II, Franz Joseph was familiar with violence—both personal and on the battlefield. In 1853 he had been stabbed in the neck by a Hungarian tailor. He survived the attack, which elevated his personal popularity. The assassin was executed. His brother Maximilian, the emperor of Mexico, was less fortunate—he was captured by rebels and executed in 1867. And then there was his son and his wife.

By June 1914 the emperor was only rarely seen in public. He seldom left Schönbrunn Palace in Vienna except to make the five-hour train journey to his favourite hunting-lodge at Bad Ischl in the Austrian alps. Since the beginning of 1911 the Austro-Hungarian common council had met thirty-nine times; Franz Joseph had attended none of them. He continued to perform his duties conscientiously, but now 83 years old and having performed these duties for the last sixty-six years, he preferred to do so in quiet, with the assistance of a few trusted advisers. After his early tumultuous years on the throne, he had reigned in peace for the last forty-eight years. He loathed confrontation, avoided excitement, and seldom interfered with the work of his ministers. Nevertheless, he and they knew that he enjoyed more personal popularity than any of them, and that decisions concerning war and peace were still his to make, not theirs.

Despite its provisions for broadly representative assemblies in Austria and Hungary, the constitution left the emperor in a position to determine the country's fate: The 'Fundamental Law Concerning the Exercise of Administrative and Executive Power' of December 1867 was absolutely clear. According to the first article of the constitution, 'The Emperor is sacred, inviolable, and cannot be held accountable.' Article 5 gave him 'supreme command of the armed forces' and the right to 'declare war, and conclude peace'.[38] In spite of receding from public view, and in spite of his increasingly distant relationship with the decision-making process, every important politician, diplomatist, and strategist recognized that Franz Joseph would have the final word.

Above all, the emperor aimed to preserve the 'Habsburg' in the monarchy. Only the dynastic principle was capable of keeping the empire intact—nothing else would suffice. He did not regard *his* empire as ramshackle, incoherent, and doomed to disintegrate. 'The monarchy', he assured a confidant in 1904, 'is not an artificial creation but an organic body. It is a place of refuge, an asylum for all those fragmented nations scattered over central Europe who, if left to their own resources would lead a pitiful existence, becoming the plaything of more powerful neighbours.'[39]

In the years before 1914 his chief of the general staff repeatedly and relentlessly recommended war as the only way to solve Austria-Hungary's problems. The emperor just as relentlessly disagreed: unless waged under the most favourable circumstances, war was likely to end in the disintegration of the empire and the destruction of the dynasty. When it was suggested to him that a favourable moment had arrived to wage a preventive war against Italy in 1911, Franz Joseph declared: 'My policy is a policy of peace . . . It is possible, even probable that . . . [an Austro-Italian] war may come about; but it will not be waged until Italy attacks us.'[40] In 1912 his fellow monarch, Tsar Nicholas II, commented that 'so long as the Emperor Franz Josef lived there was no likelihood of any step being taken by Austria-Hungary that would endanger the maintenance of peace . . .'.[41] In June 1914 the prime ministers of both Austria and Hungary, the foreign minister, and the chief of the general staff knew that they were dealing with an emperor who was now habitually inclined to choose peace over war, caution over risk—and that his word was the final one.

The situation was remarkably similar in Russia. There, the tsar's word was also the final one. There, those around the tsar recognized that he was inherently cautious and averse to running the risks involved in a diplomatic crisis.

Like Wilhelm II and Franz Joseph, Tsar Nicholas II came to the throne unexpectedly. He was only 26 when his father, Alexander III, died suddenly in 1894. As heir to the throne, Nicholas had been groomed to assume the position one day—but that day had arrived much earlier than anticipated. He had had only a minimal introduction to the workings of government. Unlike his fellow monarchs, he had never attended a school; he was educated privately, at home. He proved to be an able student, eventually mastering four languages and developing an impressive grasp of history. He began to receive instruction in government at the age of 17 from some of Russia's leading experts. And at the age of 20 he set out on a grand tour to develop a better grasp of different cultures. He spent almost a year travelling from Greece to Egypt, to India, to Siam, and to China. When he became tsar he was the first to have visited Siberia. On his return to Russia in 1891 he was appointed to serve on the State Council and the Committee of Ministers. But when he acceded to the throne he had not been let in on many secrets; he was not aware of the terms of the Franco-Russian alliance.

Nicholas inherited the Romanov view of the tsarist autocracy. He believed that God had chosen him and his family to rule over their domains, and that he was personally responsible to God for the fate of the empire. This meant that he would make his decisions on the basis of his Christian conscience, informed by the powers of reason that God had granted him. He saw himself as father to his people and believed that they were loyal to him: especially the peasants of the land, who were dedicated monarchists. They distrusted—as he did—the industrial workers of the cities who had lost their connection with the soil, and the bureaucrats who had lost their connection with the soul of Holy Mother Russia.

But this outlook turned the tsar into an increasingly solitary figure as the years went on. He attempted to do all the work of the head of state on his own. Although he was determined to be more than a mere figurehead, he never created a personal secretariat that could have taken on the burden of minor decisions and dealing with paperwork. He frequently neglected major issues in favour of the mass of trivia that confronted him every day. And he did work diligently to deal with the issues. A typical day consisted of rising at 8 a.m., going for a swim, having breakfast, and taking a walk; at 9.30 he would commence his meetings with the grand dukes and court officials,

Nicholas II (1868–1918); tsar of Russia (1894–1917)

and receiving reports from his ministers; lunch would last for forty-five minutes; between 1.45 and 5 p.m. he would receive ambassadors and visiting dignitaries; following a brief afternoon tea he would spend two hours dealing with ministerial reports; dinner was taken at 8, after which he would disappear into his study, alone, often working late into the night.[42]

His conscientious performance of his duties impressed all those around him. No one who knew him criticized his dedication or doubted his sense of duty. His ministers and advisers were less impressed by his other characteristics: he lacked self-confidence; he avoided making difficult decisions; he seemed incapable of acting decisively and quickly. He loathed the petty jealousies that court life, politics, and officialdom seemed to engender—and he did his best to ignore them. He avoided confrontation. He was gentle and courteous to a fault. He much preferred to live life out of the limelight, at home with his wife and children.

His marriage in 1894 to Queen Victoria's granddaughter Alexandra (Princess Alix of Hesse) had reinforced these inclinations. She despised the aristocrats of St Petersburg, with their sense of self-importance, their self-indulgence, their appetite for luxuries, their lusts and their love affairs. Together, she and Nicholas became estranged from Russian high society. As time went on they steadily retreated into the private life of the family, spending most of their time at Tsarskoe Selo (the 'tsar's village') 15 miles south of the capital, and then, characteristically, choosing to live in a villa rather than the palace at their summer retreat at Peterhof, on the shores of the Baltic, 18 miles west of St Petersburg. They were removed not only from high society, but from the new industrial and financial elites that were emerging in Russia, and from the urban working classes, with their long list of grievances, their sense of injustice, and their growing frustration with the political system.

These inclinations of Nicholas and Alexandra to withdraw into their own world were exacerbated by the long-awaited birth of a son and heir to the throne, Alexei, in 1904. When his haemophilia was discovered Alexandra turned to the mystical cleric, Rasputin, as the only one who seemed capable of stopping his bleeding. And she retreated even more into a life of privacy, taking Nicholas with her. Although he continued to carry out his duties conscientiously, and persevered in the performance of his ceremonial roles, he became increasingly isolated from society, politics, and the bureaucracy of the tsarist state.

And then came the disaster of war with Japan and the social upheaval in Russia that resulted in Bloody Sunday in St Petersburg in January 1905, violent uprisings and strikes in most Russian cities, and, in the October Manifesto that followed, a new constitution for Russia. Like Franz Joseph, Nicholas II discovered the terrible price the regime might be forced to pay for foreign adventures. He was required to give up some of his autocratic powers, agree to the creation of a parliament, and grant some civil rights to his subjects. In the years after 1905 the tsar became unremittingly conservative in his approach to foreign policy. As he told his ambassador to Turkey when appointing him to the position in 1911, 'Do not for one instant lose sight of the fact that we cannot go to war. . . . It would be out of the question for us to face a war for five or six years.'[43] His ambitions became entirely defensive. He withdrew even further into the quiet consolations of life with the family. He found the bombastic talk and theatrical manner of Wilhelm II alarming.[44]

Even with the revisions to the 'Fundamental Laws of the Russian Empire' instituted in 1906 Nicholas II—like his fellow monarchs in Germany and Austria-Hungary—retained ultimate control of military affairs and foreign policy. The new constitutional arrangements fell well short of establishing a democratic regime in Russia. The lower house, the Duma, was elected by a complicated system of indirect voting and was far from representative of the Russian people as a whole. And while the Duma was given the right to create legislation and some control over the budget, the tsar could veto anything it did. The tsar himself appointed half the members of the upper house, the State Council. The tsar retained his sovereignty, which was justified as coming from God and history. Nevertheless, the tsar was horrified at having to agree to any reductions to his autocratic powers and was ashamed that he would not be able to pass on what he regarded as his birthright to his son.

The powers that the tsar retained were considerable. He remained commander-in-chief of both army and navy. All of his ministers were appointed by him and answerable to him, not to the prime minister, and certainly not to the Duma. The new constitution enshrined his right to declare a state of emergency and to set aside civil rights. The direction of foreign affairs remained solely his responsibility. The power to make war continued to rest solely in his hands.

In the tsar's hands Russian foreign policy after 1906 was conservative, defensive, and peaceful. Unlike some in Russia, Nicholas II did not believe that Russia had some sort of 'manifest destiny' to rule in the Balkans. He did not even believe that Russia was obligated to support its 'brother Slavs' there on the basis of either race or religion. He welcomed the entente with Britain as reducing the likelihood that their interests would clash in Central Asia or the Middle East. He did worry that Russia's weakness after the war with Japan might encourage a great European power to capture Constantinople—and after the alliance with France and the entente with Britain, this could only mean Germany. He authorized two initiatives to mitigate this fear: diplomatic agreements with Germany to reduce tensions between them in the Middle East, and a massive expansion of the army and a naval building programme to make it clear that Russian power should not be underestimated.

Everything that Nicholas II undertook in the years before 1914 was based on his perception that Russia needed peace and that it was ambition enough for the empire to remain intact and for the tsarist state to endure. By June

1914 Russia had, for the twenty years of his reign, remained at peace in Europe. He intended to continue to live in peace for the foreseeable future.

If the monarchs of central and eastern Europe were, by June 1914, convinced that keeping the peace was in the interests of their regime, this was even truer in the west, in France and Britain. But who mattered there? With no autocratic or authoritarian monarch, in whose hands was the ultimate decision to remain at peace or to go to war?

In June 1914 the French head of state was the most powerful president that France had in the forty-four years since the collapse of the second empire of Napoleon III in 1870. Most Frenchmen believed that some kind of constitutional monarchy would emerge from the ruins of the imperial regime, and a majority of monarchists had been elected to the national assembly in 1871. But it did not. After several failed efforts to turn the presidency into a quasi-monarchy, republicanism succeeded in firmly establishing itself as the legitimate and enduring system of government. The president was given little power beyond that of inviting someone to form a cabinet that would function as the executive branch of government. Although the system endured, it proved to be unstable and chaotic: ministries came and went with dizzying speed. Meanwhile, the president's place in the system became largely ceremonial. This would change when Raymond Poincaré moved from *président de conseil* (usually rendered as 'premier' or 'prime minister' in English) to president of the republic in 1913. He was determined to utilize fully the authority given to the president in the constitution of 1875.

Poincaré brought to the position a dedication, experience, and intellect that provided him with a unique opportunity to transform the presidency. He had witnessed first-hand the tragedy of war, and suffered the consequences of losing a war. He grew up in Lorraine in a thoroughly *bourgeois* family. His ancestors had pursued careers in medicine, science, and public service; his grandfather was a pharmacist, his father an engineer. His cousin, Henri, was one of the twentieth century's greatest mathematicians and theoretical physicists. As a young man, Poincaré was steeped in the traditions of reason, education, and science. Although his mother was a devout Catholic and although young Raymond took communion and did the catechism, he was never an enthusiastic believer—but the influence of his mother set him apart from the vehement anti-clericalism popular with so many middle-class rationalists. As he matured, he appealed for religious toleration and for republicans to recognize that the majority of the French people continued to adhere to their Catholic faith.

Raymond Poincaré (1860–1934); president of France (1913–20)

Poincaré was 9 years old when the Prussians invaded Lorraine in 1870. His family managed to relocate him to Dieppe during the fighting—but when he returned, he discovered that his room in the family home was occupied by a Prussian officer. For the next three years young Raymond lived upstairs in the attic with his family while the Prussian continued to live in their house. The experience left an indelible mark on Poincaré, although not the simple, clear-cut one that might be anticipated. He blamed the government of Napoleon III for having declared war on Prussia, and blamed the government of Bismarck for imposing such harsh terms of peace. He grew into a committed French patriot, and looked forward one day to the restoration of Lorraine to France, but he would never promote war against Germany as the way to achieve this. Having witnessed for

himself the consequences of a failed military campaign, he would never
waver in his belief that France had to be prepared to defend itself militarily
and that it required astute diplomacy to bolster its position.

As Poincaré matured he demonstrated that he was a gifted student. At his
local school he won all of the prizes, and his parents decided to send him to
the most famous *lycée* in France to complete his baccalaureate. He arrived as
a boarder at Louis-le-Grand in Paris at the age of 16. Almost immediately he
established himself as a prodigiously hard worker and a promising intellect.
In the most competitive environment he began once again to win all of the
prizes. He was a brilliant success. Great things were expected of him. His life
there 'was not the clichéd bohemian and licentious student existence of
Paris, but the more sober, ardent life of the future administrative and
political elite'.[45]

Poincaré moved almost naturally into law, easily passing his exams by the
age of 19. But, finding the study of the law rather tedious and uninspiring,
he chose to pursue—simultaneously—an arts degree. The workload was
enormous, but apparently gave him little difficulty. Between the ages of 17
and 21 he managed to publish four novels. And he accomplished this while
doing a year of military service, during which he was promoted to corporal,
then sergeant, and when he completed his service he was made a sub-
lieutenant reserve officer in the *chasseurs à pied* (light infantry). He fulfilled
his year of service while completing his final year in law and, at the age of
20, became the youngest barrister in France.

Although he proved to be an immediate success in the commercial law
firm that he joined, he continued to seek something more. He continued to
write for newspapers and literary journals and became interested in politics.
He stood for election to the Chamber of Deputies in 1887, becoming, at
age 27, the youngest deputy in the chamber. His victory launched a forty-
two-year political career in which he never lost an election.

Given Poincaré's character his long, successful political career seems
surprising. He appeared to lack passion; he was notable for his prudence,
caution, and diligence rather than for his ability to inspire. Two years passed
before he spoke in the Chamber. When he did begin to speak he gave no
sign of ideological enthusiasm, no indication of oratorical skill. He preached
tolerance, patience, and moderation. He established a reputation for prac-
ticality and liberality: 'I am a republican without a label, I am the enemy of
controversy which blocks decisions.'[46] Among his colleagues he became
known for the hard work and thoroughness that he brought to any task, and

for his patriotism and sense of public duty. In 1893, at the age of 33, he was appointed to the cabinet as minister of public instruction—making him the youngest cabinet minister in the history of the republic. This was his first of a long line of appointments in the chaotic ministerial history of *fin-de-siècle* France.

During these early years in office Poincaré became convinced that the political system had become bogged down and unable to modernize and reform France because of the philosophical, religious, and regional divisions that plagued the country. His remedy for this was a revived patriotism, a *patrie* that would bind all Frenchmen together. At the same time he became convinced that, in order to achieve this, the republic required a stronger executive and a more authoritative president. In the mid-1890s there had been four different governments in just over two years.

Poincaré paid little attention to foreign affairs before 1911 when he was appointed *rapporteur* of the Senate commission formed to examine the recent treaty with Germany over Morocco. He had been elected to the senate in 1903. His report defended the treaty against those critics who argued that France had given up too much African territory to appease the Germans. He argued that France had to learn to work with Germany and warned against the 'chronic animosity' that had soured relations for the last forty years. When called upon by the president to form a ministry in January 1912, Poincaré decided to take the position of minister of foreign affairs for himself, in spite of his minimal background in the area.[47] His first significant declaration was a defence of the treaty with Germany, which, he said, 'will allow us to maintain between a great neighbouring nation and France, in a sincerely pacific spirit, courteous and frank relations, inspired by a mutual respect of interests and dignity'.[48]

Officials at the French Foreign Office, the Quai d'Orsay, had grown accustomed to having short-lived, mostly ignorant, ministers in charge of foreign affairs. But Poincaré quickly established that he intended to take charge, to reorganize the office and to take control of policy. He quickly succeeded in reorganizing and centralizing authority at the ministry, placing the direction of power in his hands and a small, loyal, inner circle of permanent officials that he trusted. He appointed an old schoolmate from Louis-le-Grand as political director. He exerted his authority over the ambassadors who had become powerful and virtually independent in the vacuum of power that had existed.

Poincaré aimed to impose a clear direction from the top—and that direction was to preserve the European peace through the maintenance of the balance of power. The alliance with Russia was sacrosanct: it had created a situation in which the two alliance systems had achieved a near-perfect balance. Anything that might upset this could tilt the balance in favour of one side or the other, which was the condition most likely to lead to war. He made it clear that he had no interest in trying to persuade Italy or Austria-Hungary to abandon the Triple Alliance. Such a move would likely make the Germans feel that they were being encircled and might precipitate aggression. When the French ambassador in Vienna attempted to lure Austria-Hungary he had him replaced. Equally, he was not prepared to go too far in moving to a détente with Germany, fearing that it might shake Russia's confidence in the alliance.

As far as Poincaré was concerned the alliance system, which was responsible for maintaining the peace over the last twenty years, was now working almost perfectly. With both sides understanding that war would be disastrous for everyone they were encouraged to coexist in peace, to show restraint in times of crisis, and to resolve difficulties as they arose.

After one year as premier and minister of foreign affairs Poincaré had established control of policy and laid down what this policy was to be. But after that year he also decided to stand for the presidency in the election of January 1913. He defeated Georges Clémenceau to become the youngest president in the history of the republic. His aim now was to restore to the president the authority that he believed was intended for the position, but which had eroded over the past forty-three years. After the usual confusion in establishing a functioning executive in the third republic, René Viviani was installed as premier and minister of foreign affairs. Poincaré was determined that any ministry would support an increase in the size of the army to counter the recent increases in Germany: the term of compulsory service was to be extended from two years to three. Only a strong French army capable of countering Germany could reassure Russia of the vitality of the alliance; only the alliance could assure France of security against Germany and the Triple Alliance. Viviani, profoundly ignorant of foreign affairs, was chosen largely because he was prepared to support the Three Years Bill, but also because he seemed willing to cede the direction of foreign policy to Poincaré.

Unlike the monarchies of Germany, Austria-Hungary, and Russia, the final authority to decide between war and peace in France was not vested in

René Viviani (1863–1925); president of the council [prime minister] of France (1914–15)

a single man. The process provided for in France was linked to responsibility for making foreign and military policy. And here the role of the president was vital: he was responsible for negotiating and ratifying treaties; he was not even obliged to inform parliament except as he deemed it in the national interest; he could sign alliances and give guarantees to foreign powers without legislative approval—or even its knowledge. He was commander-in-chief of the armed forces. While the president had to seek parliamentary approval for a declaration of war, the powers given to him in the constitutional arrangements of 1875 gave him the pivotal role.[49] Insofar as one man above all others was in a position to decide between war and peace that man was Raymond Poincaré. And Poincaré's policy was steadfastly peaceful and conservative, to maintain the balance of power in Europe through the system of alliances.

If the situation was greyer in France than it was in the monarchies of central and eastern Europe, it was muddier still in Britain. There, constitutionally, the decision was still up to the monarch. But in reality the king's power to decide had eroded to the point that his authority was practically non-existent. The decision would be up to parliament. But how would parliament decide? Who held sway? Who had the information upon which to make—if not decisions—recommendations on war and peace that carried conviction?

By June 1914 not power, but influence, was vested largely in the hands of one man: Sir Edward Grey. The 52-year-old foreign secretary was a parliamentarian of considerable experience. He had been elected to the House of Commons in 1885 and retained his seat successfully ever since—just short of thirty years. His election as a Liberal meant that he spent most of his time in opposition until William Gladstone formed his final government in 1892. And his first role in administration was in the field of foreign affairs: he was invited to become the parliamentary under-secretary. As the foreign secretary, Lord Rosebery, sat in the Lords, this meant that much of the responsibility for explaining and defending the government's foreign policy fell to Grey. When the Liberal government was defeated in 1895 Grey held onto his seat, and served as the primary critic of foreign policy while in opposition until the next Liberal government was formed in 1905. He was appointed foreign secretary in December 1905.

Apart from a few radicals in the Liberal and Labour parties, Grey's appointment was widely applauded. He seemed to guarantee that Britain would pursue a responsible and reliable foreign policy. For years he had supported Rosebery's insistence that the conduct of foreign affairs should be above politics, that a foreign secretary should adhere to the principle of continuity, that the interests of the empire were unchanging and must be placed above party politics or special interests. His pedigree seemed a fitting testimonial to these ideals.

Grey had descended from one of the great Whig families in British history. His great-great-grandfather—a distinguished general—had been ennobled as the first Earl Grey; his grandfather's older brother, the second Earl Grey, was famous for the Great Reform Bill of 1832 and has gone down in history as 'Grey of the Reform Act'. His grandfather served several times in Whig–Liberal governments in the mid-Victorian era. His father, a soldier, died young, leaving Grey fatherless at the age of 12. Edward grew up steeped in the traditions of duty, progress, and reform. While most

Sir Edward Grey (1862–1933); foreign secretary of Great Britain (1905–16)

wealthy, landowning Whigs who had supported these principles for the past two centuries had abandoned the Liberal party throughout the second half of the nineteenth century (especially after it adopted the policy of home rule for Ireland), Grey would remain steadfast in his adherence to the principles of progressive reform.

Grey was educated in the manner to be expected of a Victorian Whig–Liberal. After attending preparatory schools he was enrolled at Winchester, one of England's great public schools, where he seemed able to excel without much effort. Following Winchester he went up to Oxford at Balliol College. Although his teachers and classmates regarded him as exceptionally bright, he failed to apply himself and was at one point sent down for his laziness. He showed no apparent aptitude for the classics or history—the path followed by most of those who would form the political and administrative elite of Victorian Britain—eventually graduating with a third-class degree in jurisprudence. He showed much keener interest in cricket, football, tennis, fishing, and hunting than in any academic pursuits.

His failure to obtain any glittering prizes and his apparent absence of application and ambition have rendered him a somewhat mysterious figure. Critics saw (and see) him as someone who combined the absence of any outstanding intellectual ability with a work ethic that was minimal. Admirers point to his steadfast principles, his honesty, and his straightforwardness as the characteristics that account for his political success and his long tenure at the Foreign Office. His friend and fellow liberal imperialist, Richard Haldane, wrote that Grey was 'like steel . . . his display of character is immense . . . it shines out'.[50]

In foreign and imperial policy Grey established himself clearly on the right wing of the Liberal party. Besides following Rosebery's commitment to continuity in foreign policy, he believed in the importance of empire and became one of the leading 'liberal imperialists' who supported Britain's war against the Boers in South Africa—an issue which deeply divided the Liberal party. While his championship of imperialism worried those on the left of the party, it reassured those on the right. His appointment as foreign secretary in December 1905 was received with relief and widespread support: he was a pair of 'safe hands'; his adherence to 'continuity' meant that the Liberal governments faced little criticism from the opposition in the realm of foreign affairs. And it meant that Liberals could get on with their ambitious programmes of social reform without having to pay much attention to foreign policy.

By the summer of 1914 Sir Edward Grey had established himself as a reassuring figure. He had been at the helm of foreign affairs for almost nine years—the longest continuous service in that office since Lord Castlereagh a century before. He had successfully managed a succession of crises, had built upon the entente with France by establishing one with Russia, and his convening and chairmanship of the London conference that resulted in a peaceful conclusion to the first Balkan war—just when it seemed that it might escalate into a general European conflict—cemented his reputation as one of Europe's leading statesmen. And one who was dedicated above all to upholding the long European peace.

Grey too believed in the balance of power. Most of his diplomatic initiatives and interventions since coming into office had been taken for the purpose of upholding it. When it seemed that Germany's great diplomatic triumph during the first Moroccan crisis might reduce France to a second-rate power and disrupt the Franco-Russian alliance, Grey intervened to bolster French will. He then initiated secret Anglo-French staff talks that held out to the French the possibility that Britain would intervene militarily on their side in the event of a continental war. Holding out the possibility of British intervention without promising it was the key to Grey's management of the balance of power. It offered France and Russia the hope of British assistance as long as their policy remained peaceful and defensive: if either appeared inclined to precipitate a war they would not be able to count on Britain's help. Simultaneously, the emergence of something that could be thought of as a 'Triple Entente' served as an almost precise counterweight to the Triple Alliance. And Britain was at the fulcrum of that balance, able to apply its weight when and where it was necessary to keep it working.

The question of who in Britain was in the position to decide between war and peace was not as easily answered as it was in the case of the other European powers. Technically, the decision was still the monarch's to make. But practically, as the 'constitution' (which did not exist) had evolved over the last two centuries, the king could only act upon the advice of his prime minister 'in cabinet'. A declaration of war against the wishes of the government was a practical impossibility—it was never considered. The converse—a refusal to declare war when the government advised it—was equally out of the question. So the real decision between war and peace came down to the cabinet. And here, with the support of the prime minister, Sir Edward Grey dominated the scene. By the summer of 1914 friend and foe alike referred not to the government's foreign policy, but to Grey's. He enjoyed the support of most of the Liberal party, and a good deal of support among the Unionist as well. His advice, while not the law, carried more weight than that of anyone else in Britain. And he was staunchly, determinedly, on the side of peace.

★

In June 1914 the prospects for the European future seemed bright. Diplomatic storms had blown up from time to time over the past decade—but these had always been weathered without war. Quarrels over far-off possessions in Africa, Asia, and the Far East seemed perpetual—but these had become fewer and farther between over the last decade. In the meantime, the voices advocating the peaceful arbitration and conciliation of disputes were growing in number and volume. And those men who counted most when it came to choosing between war and peace seemed, by their own history and sense of national self-interest, to favour clearly the keeping of the long European peace.

PART ONE

The Making of a Crisis

The Killing

As the tragic *Anna Karenina* began with a newspaper report of a suicide, so the tragedy of the First World War began with a newspaper report of a royal visit. Sitting in a Belgrade café on a dreary March day in 1914, Nedeljko Čabrinović studied a newspaper clipping sent to him by his friend in Sarajevo, Mihajlo Pušara. His friend had gone to some trouble in posting it to him, travelling the thirty miles from Sarajevo to Zenica in the hope of eluding the oversight of the Austrian postal officials in Bosnia. Pušara gave the authorities little to go on in the event that they did discover the message: he had simply cut the announcement out of the Zagreb newspaper, the *Srbobran*—'Defender of the Serbs'—written 'greetings' on it, typed Čabrinović's name on the envelope, and mailed it to him at the Golden Sturgeon Café. He trusted that the clipping alone would be sufficient to arouse Čabrinović's interest. The newspaper reported that the *Thronfolger*, the heir-apparent to the imperial throne of Austria-Hungary, the archduke Franz Ferdinand, would attend the army's manoeuvres in Bosnia that summer and that he would be received by the mayor and local dignitaries in Sarajevo on the 28th of June.

The date for the royal visit seemed to have been chosen deliberately to provoke Serbian indignation: 28 June was the anniversary of the battle of Kosovo in 1389 on the 'field of blackbirds' that had extinguished the medieval Serbian kingdom. Bosnia and Herzegovina, provinces of the Ottoman Empire for almost 500 years, had been occupied by Austro-Hungarian forces in 1878, then formally annexed by the Dual Monarchy in 1908. Now, the Serbs of Bosnia were, apparently, to pay homage to the same royal family that blocked their way to creating a Greater Serbia. How were the lost glories of their ancient kingdom to be restored if they were prevented from uniting with their brethren in Serbia?

Pušara's friend Čabrinović had left Bosnia and arrived in Belgrade for the first time as a 19-year-old in 1912. His father removed him from the Merchants' School when he failed his final examination as a 13-year-old in 1908. After trying his hand at various trades, young Nedeljko ('Nedjo') eventually apprenticed as a typesetter and achieved his journeyman status at the age of 15. Although he no longer attended school he continued to read widely amidst the ferment of resentments and revolutionary ideas that permeated Bosnia following the annexation of 1908. He amassed a large collection of anarchist works—until his mother discovered and burned them all.

Before visiting Belgrade in 1912, he had made friends with Gavrilo Princip in Sarajevo. There, the two young men read and discussed books together—including William Morris's *News from Nowhere* (a copy of which survives, signed by them, along with their notations on the need for revolution). But the son's political views clashed with those of his father, who had prospered under the Austrian regime: beginning with only a coffee-grinder, he had set up a social centre in his home, then used the profits to open a *kafana* (café) nearby. In order to obtain the permit necessary for opening the café he had agreed to serve as a police informant. Nedjo decided to leave Sarajevo and to move permanently to Belgrade in March 1913.

The path taken by Čabrinović was one that had become well-worn by young Serbian men coming from Bosnia and Herzegovina. Although life was hard for them in Belgrade, they were welcomed as patriots. Čabrinović, ill, hungry, and unemployed when he arrived there, was helped by the Serbian nationalist organization, the *Narodna Odbrana* ('National Defence'), which provided him with sufficient funds to survive his first months there on his own. By October 1913, the organization had assisted him in finding a job as a typesetter in the state printing office. He was employed there when he received the newspaper clipping that announced the archducal visit.

By 1914 Čabrinović had accumulated a little money, a few friends, and many resentments. He was ashamed of his father for taking Austrian money to serve as an informant, a shame that he perhaps confided to veterans of the recent Balkan wars and other émigrés at one of their favourite, rather shabby, cafés situated in the *Zeleni Venac* marketplace: the *Zlatna Ribica* or the *Žirovni Venac*.[1] It was probably at the *Žirovni Venac* where Čabrinović showed the newspaper clipping to Princip over lunch. It did not take them long to come up with a scheme. At dinner later that day Princip proposed

Nedeljko Čabrinović (1895–1916)

that they kill the archduke and suggested that they include in their plans a third young friend, Trifko Grabež.

Like his friend Nedjo, Gavrilo was little more than a boy when he first made his way from Sarajevo to Belgrade in 1912 at the age of 17. Also, like his friend, he had had his troubles in school, where the authorities had tried to put a stop to his political activities against the Austrian regime. He blamed the Austrians for all of the ills that beset his fellow Serbs in Bosnia: 'I have seen our people being steadily ruined. I am a peasant's son and know what goes on in the villages.'[2] He told the truth: he came from a *kmet* (serf) family who had lived for centuries in a remote part of western Bosnia. And he was a witness to the growing colonization of Bosnia and Herzegovina by Austrians and Hungarians: in the 1880s there had been only 16,000 Austro-Hungarian subjects in these provinces; by 1910 the number had grown to 108,000. The dominant ethnic group in Hungary, the Magyars, had used

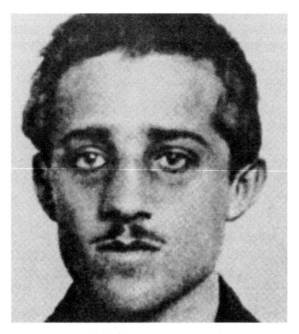

Gavrilo Princip (1894–1918)

the autonomy they gained at the creation of the Dual Monarchy in 1867 to promote their national identity. A Budapest bank encouraged Magyarization by purchasing the lands of impoverished Bosnian peasants and offering them for lease or sale to Magyars.

Determined to turn the tide against the new Austrian and Magyar oppressors, Princip was befriended soon after his arrival in Belgrade by the secretary of the *Narodna Odbrana*, Major Milan Vasić. When Serbia joined Greece and Bulgaria in attacking Turkey in October 1912, Vasić encouraged young Princip to sign up as a fighter in a *komitadji* (guerrilla) unit. Although he did try to enlist, Gavrilo was rejected for service as too weak, with indications that he may have been suffering from incipient tuberculosis. Dismayed by his failure, he returned to Bosnia for the winter of 1912–13, but by March had decided to return to Belgrade to resume his studies.

Princip found schooling in Belgrade much more congenial than that offered by the Austrian-run *gymnasium* that he had attended in Sarajevo. The *Narodna Odbrana* assisted him—along with many other young Bosnians—with the funds necessary for him to survive while he pursued

Trifko Grabež (1895–1918)

his diploma. And the curriculum, with its emphasis on Serbian language, literature, and history, was more attractive than the classical focus on Latin and Greek back in Bosnia. Although life was hard, with barely enough money to survive on bad food and in dismal lodgings, 'Gavro' (as he now preferred to be called, after Victor Hugo's heroic boy in *Les Misérables*) and his friends thrived in the atmosphere provided by their new schools. Most of them passed their examinations easily, with Princip completing three years of schooling in one—after the minister of education personally permitted him to take privately the examinations for the fifth and sixth class.

While studying for his final examinations he shared a room with Trifko Grabež—and the two young men were living together when Čabrinović approached them with the announcement of the upcoming visit of the archduke. In the emotionally charged atmosphere of Belgrade in the spring of 1914 it was not quite so surprising that Čabrinović, Princip, and Grabež discussed the idea of murdering the imperial archduke in Sarajevo.

★

This was to be a special 'moment' for Serbia. The nation and the national idea seemed to be riding the wave of history. In the two Balkan wars of 1912 and 1913 Serbia had succeeded in defeating first Turkey and then Bulgaria.

Map 1. The Adriatic

In the process, it had doubled its territory and increased its population by 50 per cent (from 3 to 4.5 million). The dream of a Greater Serbia, of a restored Serbian empire that would unite all Serbs, suddenly seemed now to be within reach—were it not for Austria-Hungary's opposition to it. Not only had the Austrians occupied and then annexed Bosnia and Herzegovina—containing over 2 million Serbs—but they had denied Serbia its goal of acquiring an outlet on the Adriatic Sea.

When Serbia joined Montenegro, Bulgaria, and Greece in attacking and defeating Turkey in the first Balkan war, one of the fruits of victory was then to set it free of its landlocked condition. Access to the sea would mean greater freedom for its commerce, which remained largely dependent on Austro-Hungarian railways. At the conference of ambassadors which met in London to bring about an end to the war, Austria had succeeded in getting sufficient diplomatic support from the other great European powers to create an independent Albanian state that it hoped would block forever Serbia's path to the Adriatic. Fused with these nationalist aspirations and hatreds were the ideas of Kropotkin, Bakunin, Herzen, and other anarchist and revolutionary ideologues that were imbibed by the young émigrés who arrived in Serbia between 1908 and 1914.

One such émigré was Vladimir Gaćinović, the son of an Orthodox priest from Herzegovina. Gaćinović fled his village in 1908 at the age of 17, at the time of the Austrian annexation. Although he had been designated to follow in his father's footsteps and enter the priesthood, he decided instead to flee to Belgrade and volunteer as a *komitadji* fighter in the war that he expected would soon erupt between Serbia and Austria. When that war failed to materialize he returned to his studies, enrolling at the University of Belgrade—but without abandoning his hopes of a revolution against the Austrian occupation. He travelled to Switzerland in 1911, where he was inspired by expatriate Russian revolutionaries such as Leon Trotsky. A year later he received a Serbian scholarship that enabled him to enrol at the University of Vienna. Gaćinović was one of an elite: in 1902 there were only thirty inhabitants of Bosnia and Herzegovina with a university education. Wealthy Serbs and Croats alone could afford to send their sons to the universities in Vienna, Prague, or Zagreb.

While studying in Vienna, Gaćinović adopted Prince Peter Kropotkin as his guiding light. Gaćinović was less interested in the core anarchist philosophy of 'mutual aid' based on cooperation among small groups and the dismantling of the centralized state, than he was in Kropotkin's defence of violence as a legitimate means to a noble end. The end that Gaćinović had in mind was the creation of a Greater Serbia—and Kropotkin had outlined the means by which this might be attained. 'Propaganda by deed' could be a powerful weapon: Kropotkin argued that a dramatic act of violence or martyrdom could succeed in arousing ordinary people from their lethargy and awaken their natural, but latent, rebellious instincts. Gaćinović, attuned to this argument, discovered just such a martyr in the shape of Bogdan Žerajić, a fellow Serb from Herzegovina.

★

The government of Austria–Hungary had raised the volatile temperature of Serbian politics by deciding (in 1910) to formalize the annexation of the occupied provinces through the proclamation of a constitution.

His Royal and Apostolic Majesty, the emperor Franz Joseph, was to attend in person the opening of the new *Sabor* (parliament) in Sarajevo. This was meant to be a grand gesture of paternal good will: granting limited representative government to his new subjects. But the gesture quickly backfired: although political parties were now permitted, strict limitations were imposed on what could be printed and what could be said; the franchise was restricted, electoral districts were based on religion, and ethnographical quotas were built in.

The announcement of the imperial visit unsurprisingly outraged young Serbs, a number of whom were determined to disrupt the celebration. Žerajić, a 22-year-old medical student, was inspired to go much further: he would do no less than assassinate the emperor. And, in spite of extensive security measures taken by the Austrian authorities, he nearly succeeded. At the last moment however, he appears to have had second thoughts. Instead of attempting to kill the aged emperor, he aimed his weapon at the Austrian governor of the province, General Varešanin. Although he managed to fire five shots from close range at the general, he missed with all five. Rather than allowing himself to be captured, Žerajić then used his last bullet to shoot himself dead.

The authorities quickly arranged to have Žerajić buried secretly in the section of the Sarajevo cemetery reserved for suicides and vagrants. Yet in spite of their precautions he was transformed almost overnight into a martyr for the Serbian cause. Žerajić's fame—and the legend of his martyrdom— blossomed when Gaćinović immortalized him in an anonymous pamphlet, *The Death of a Hero*. Kropotkin's principles seemed to be working precisely as the anarchist philosopher had envisioned: spontaneously, a wide array of informal groups, organizations, and societies sprang up around the memory of the young martyr—which came to be referred to collectively as *Mlada Bosna* ('Young Bosnia'). Never a formal organization, young Bosnians located Žerajić's grave, decorated it, and transformed the site into a nationalist shrine. The martyr's dying words were, according to Gaćinović, 'I leave it to Serbdom to avenge me.'

Gavrilo Princip, for one, was deeply moved when he read the pamphlet. He vowed on Žerajić's grave to avenge his death. Gaćinović's call for action reverberated with Čabrinović, Grabež, and many others as well: 'The Serb revolutionary, if he wants to win, must be an artist and a conspirator, must have talent for strength and suffering, must be a martyr and a plotter, a man of Western manners and a *hajduk*, who will shout and wage war for the unfortunate and downtrodden. Revolution never comes from despair, as is mistakenly thought, but out of revolutionary thought, which grows in national enthusiasm.'[3] Gaćinović appealed simultaneously to modernity and tradition, to anarchist ideas and to Slavic heritage: a *hajduk* was popularized in Serbian folklore as a heroic fighter against the Turkish overlords.

★

Organized terror now surfaced. The epicentre of *Mlada Bosna* activism and violence was the high school in Mostar (the capital of Herzegovina) founded in 1893—where the Habsburg authorities had refused to permit the formation of student groups of any kind and threatened students with expulsion if they were discovered to have joined one. The result was to encourage the creation of numerous secret societies, most of which were small and disorganized but were grounded in the intense populist emotions that erupted spontaneously among the youth of the occupied provinces. They were inspired by the life and the rhetoric of the Italian nationalist hero, Giuseppe Mazzini, and they modelled themselves on his '*Giovane Italia*'—the idea that the youth of a nation should be in the vanguard of those struggling for liberation. 'There is no more sacred thing in the world than the duty of a conspirator, who becomes an avenger of humanity and the apostle of permanent natural laws.'[4]

Young Bosnians worked to organize resistance. An umbrella organization, *Narodno Jedinstvo* ('National Unity', also referred to as *Narodno Uje-dinjenje*—'National Unification') undertook the task of coordinating their activities, and struck a committee to resolve differences among the various groups. And some of them began publishing a newspaper in Hungary in 1912, the *Novi Srbin* ('The New Serb') which declared as its goal that 'The new Serbs must elevate the belief in the freeing and uniting of the South Slavs to the level of religion.... If a higher authority commands that we either abandon our desire for freedom or give up our life, we as new Serbs will die, in death still victorious over the enemy, since we cannot be empowered in our lives and will glorify our brief lives with the beautiful gesture of a hero's death.'[5]

While the groups in *Mlada Bosna* may have been inchoate and disorganized, its progenitors in Serbia itself, the *Narodna Odbrana* ('National Defence') and the *Ujedinjenje Ili Smrt* (henceforth 'Union or Death'), were not. Both became highly disciplined and well organized. Gaćinović (whose pamphlet had turned Žerajić into a martyr) joined both groups.

The *Narodna Odbrana* was formed in Belgrade on 8 October 1908, the day after Austria-Hungary proclaimed its annexation of Bosnia and Herzegovina. Immediately after the proclamation the Serbian foreign minister, Milovan Milovanović, invited twenty civic leaders to meet at the city hall. Here they were persuaded by a leading dramatist, Branislav Nušić, to form a society dedicated to defending the Serbian 'idea'. The fledgling group immediately succeeded in procuring funds, producing propaganda, and attracting members. It soon established a national organization. An officer of the Serbian army, General Bozho Janković, chaired a central committee in Belgrade which took responsibility for coordinating the activities of district committees, which in turn directed the activities of local committees. By 1914 over 400 local committees had been established, and where no committee had been formed 'confidential men' were identified to act in their place. Under the guise of cultural, gymnastic, shooting, and sporting societies, the *Narodna Odbrana* aimed to undermine the loyalty of Serbs to the Austrian regime in the occupied provinces. Its members undertook to spy on Austrian officials and train to engage in guerrilla action against the authorities. It encouraged young Bosnians to come to Belgrade, where it assisted them in finding jobs or with the funds necessary to enable them to continue their education—as it had done with Princip, Čabrinović, and Grabež.

The *Narodna Odbrana* succeeded in establishing a highly visible presence in Serbia before 1914, engaging in public activities and attracting leading politicians, officials, and military men to serve openly on its committees. Two of the more prominent figures in the organization, Colonel Dragutin Dimitrijević and Major Voiya Tankosić, were instrumental in the formation

Dragutin Dimitrijević, 'Apis' (1876–1917); chief of military intelligence, Serbian general staff (1913–16)

of another, secret, society that grew out of the *Narodna* and from which it actively recruited its members. 'Union or Death' was formed on 29 May 1911, on the eighth anniversary of the assassination of the Serbian king and queen, Aleksandar and Draga, by the officers who had participated in the murders: 'the Men of 29 May'. Dimitrijević and Tankosić were two of the leading regicides. The new organization was created 'with the object of realizing the national ideal: the union of all Serbs', which was to be accomplished through the instrument of the Kingdom of Serbia, and through 'terrorist action', which it preferred to 'intellectual propaganda'. Theirs was to be a clear departure from the tactics of the *Narodna Odbrana*. Union or Death aimed to 'organize revolutionary action in all the territories inhabited by Serbs' and was prepared to use 'every means available to combat the adversaries of the national idea'.[6]

★

Although the name 'Union or Death' succinctly summarized the nature of the organization, it has come to be more dramatically known as the 'Black Hand' (*Tsrna Ruka*) because of the symbol they adopted, which featured a death's head, a dagger, a bomb, and poison, all symbolizing the ethos of the organization.

Membership was restricted only to the most dedicated zealots: members were expected to 'forfeit their personality', in return for which they would receive 'neither glory nor personal profit'. Members were bound in 'absolute obedience' to the committees that directed their activities, and membership was permanent: once someone joined there was no going back, no way of withdrawing or resigning. Members were required to convey to the central committee anything of interest that they learned, either as a private individual or in their capacity as a state official. A member who injured the organization in any way was to be punished with death.

Joining the Black Hand was no small undertaking, and a ceremony was developed to highlight the extent of the commitment to which members were pledged. New recruits were ushered into a darkened room, lit only by a small wax candle. On a table covered in black cloth in the middle of the room lay a cross, a dagger, and a revolver. The regulations of the organization and the responsibilities of membership were solemnly explained before the recruits were asked whether they were prepared to join. When they gave their assent, a delegate of the central committee, masked and silent, would enter the room to listen to the recruits recite the oath of allegiance:

> 'I, . . . on becoming a member of the organization Union or Death, swear, by the Sun that warms me, by the Earth that nourishes me, before God, by the blood of my ancestors, on my honour, and on my life, that I will from this moment till my death be faithful to the laws of this organization, that I will always be ready to make any sacrifice for it. I swear before God, on my honour and on my life, that I will take all the secrets of this organization with me to my grave. May God confound me and may my comrades in this organization judge me if I trespass against or either consciously or unconsciously fail to keep my oath.'

At this point the delegate would shake the hands of the new recruits and, still hooded, withdraw in silence. A network of implacable and toxic cells was soon in creation.

★

Vladimir Gaćinović, the devotee of Kropotkin, acquaintance of Trotsky, and biographer of the martyred Žerajić, joined Union or Death in 1912. He immediately set about facilitating the creation of a network of revolutionary cells—*kružok*—in Bosnia. He was engaged in this work when, in the autumn of 1913, he received instructions from Tankosić on behalf of the central committee, that he should meet in Toulouse, France, with others who were prepared to participate in an imperial assassination attempt.

In mid-January 1914 Gaćinović accordingly met with two other members of the Black Hand at the Hôtel St Jérome in Toulouse. The plan called for the participation of five conspirators, but the two coming from Paris could not afford the train fare and failed to arrive. Summoned to the meeting were two young Muslims who had grown up together in the same village in Herzegovina: Mustafa Golubić and Mehmed Mehmedbašić. Many Bosnian Muslims had also been outraged by the annexation of 1908, and a Muslim People's Organization (*Muslimanska Narodna Organizacija*) had formed to denounce the negation of the Ottoman sultan's sovereignty. They had appealed to the signatories of the Treaty of Berlin to reverse the annexation, but their appeals went nowhere.

Neither Golubić, attending the University of Lausanne, nor Gaćinović could afford the train fare to Toulouse, but Mehmedbašić, the son of an impoverished feudal lord, granted freedom to his two remaining *kmet* (serfs) for cash in order to finance the journey for all three of them.

At their meeting in Toulouse, Gaćinović preached the ideals of terrorism. He proposed that they undertake a dramatic act calculated to inspire the peoples of Bosnia and Herzegovina to rise in revolt against Austria-Hungary. They agreed to choose a relatively 'soft' target: the governor of Bosnia, General Oskar Potiorek. Gaćinović provided the Muslim boys with the guns, and the cyanide capsules with which they were to poison themselves in the event that they were captured.

It was a bold plan but their nerves failed them. When their train crossed the frontier into Austria from Ragusa the would-be assassins feared that their guns would be discovered by customs officials; panicking, they threw the weapons out of the window and the conspiracy disintegrated.

★

Secret talks about some kind of terrorist attack on the Austrian administration still continued, however, with the upcoming visit of the archduke to Sarajevo later that summer now offering an even more dramatic opportunity.

The leadership of the Black Hand had learned of the visit well in advance of anything that appeared in the newspapers. Indeed, Dimitrijević had his own sources of information. By 1913 he had risen to the position of head of the intelligence service of the Serbian general staff. Rumours of the visit had begun circulating in Vienna in the autumn of 1913 and were reported to Belgrade.

Plans to murder the archduke were being hatched, almost simultaneously, both from above and from below. Another secret society, the *Smrt Ili Život* ('Death or Life'), appears to have been formed in April 1914. It too was guided by a central committee of seven members who called one another *duhovi*: (spirits) of the Avengers of Kosovo. Members took an oath of allegiance, were sworn to secrecy and obedience to the committee, and promised to commit suicide on behalf of the cause if necessary. The committee in the spring of 1914 drew up a list of nineteen young men who were qualified to act as assassins of the archduke. Included on the list were Gavrilo Princip, Nedjo Čabrinović, and Trifko Grabež.

Princip returned to Bosnia from Belgrade during the winter of 1913–14, having contacted Gaćinović while they were both in Sarajevo. In March, Princip moved back to Belgrade to complete his studies, where he learned of the archduke's visit and began discussing the assassination with Čabrinović and Grabež. The would-be killers quickly identified the things they would need if they were to succeed in their mission: weapons; means by which to get into Bosnia with their weapons; and additional accomplices— because the archduke was certain to be well guarded.

Around Easter Princip approached his closest friend in Bosnia, Danilo Ilić, a member of the Black Hand *kružok* in Sarajevo. Ilić's father, a cobbler, had died when Danilo was only 5 years old, forcing his mother first to take in laundry in order to support them, and then later to accept paying lodgers. Her support enabled Danilo to attend the Merchants School in Sarajevo, from which he graduated in 1905. After several years of wandering around Bosnia, picking up odd jobs, he won a scholarship to attend teachers' college. Although he obtained his teaching certificate in 1912, he worked only briefly as a teacher before falling ill. Encouraged by his friend Gaćinović, Ilić travelled to Switzerland to meet with Russian revolutionaries there—but then Bulgaria attacked Serbia in June 1913. The second Balkan war had begun. He returned to Serbia to volunteer, spending the war working as a male nurse, caring for those stricken by cholera. During this time his friends, who gave him the nickname 'Hadžija', listened to his tales of meetings with revolutionaries 'as Moslems listen to their pilgrims returned from Mecca'.[7]

One of the schoolboys who lodged with Danilo's mother was the 13-year-old Gavrilo Princip. Jovo Princip, his older brother, had taken him to Sarajevo in August 1907 with the intention of enrolling him in military school—because the Austrians were offering free tuition, board, and uniforms for those who enrolled. But Jovo was persuaded in a chance meeting with a merchant friend that the boy's prospects for a prosperous future would be enhanced if he joined the Merchants School instead. After enrolling, Princip began to share a room with Ilić, four years his senior, and continued to do so—off and on—until 1910. Gavro gradually grew unhappy with the curriculum at the Merchants School, and decided that he would prefer to transfer to the high school with its classical curriculum, and in August 1910 he succeeded in passing the entrance examination in Latin and Greek. Although he did well at the school, he was expelled in February 1912 for participating in demonstrations against the Austrian authorities in Sarajevo. He chose to leave Bosnia altogether and moved to Belgrade in the spring. But he remained in touch with his former room-mate, and it was to Ilić that Princip turned when he, Čabrinović, and Grabež decided that they would need additional recruits in the conspiracy to kill the archduke. Ilić, who had earlier recruited Mehmedbašić to join Union or Death, now approached him and Golubić, successfully persuading them to join in the terrorist conspiracy.

Another of Princip's café confidants agreed to assist in procuring the weapons for the assassination. As they had no money, this was not going to be easy. It took days for them to make the necessary arrangements. A friendly waiter at the Oak Garland had introduced Milan Ciganović, a fellow Bosnian émigré—and member of the Black Hand—to Princip not long after his arrival in Belgrade. Ciganović had left Bosnia following the annexation in 1908 and fought as a *komitadji* in the Balkan wars, for which he was honoured with a medal for bravery. Like many such fighters, he had returned to Belgrade after the war with a small supply of hand grenades—which Princip knew about, having lived briefly with him. Before agreeing to provide the grenades however, Ciganović said that he would have to discuss the idea with a 'certain gentleman'—who turned out to be Tankosić, his *komita* battalion commander, who had recruited him as member No. 412 in Union or Death. Tankosić, now a major in the regular Serbian army, after consulting Dimitrijević, gave Ciganović the go-ahead, promising to provide the revolvers and instructing him to give Grabež shooting lessons—in order to avoid another fiasco such as Žerajić's having fired five shots at Varešanin from close range and missing with all five. Princip and Čabrinović practised their shooting in Košutnjak Park on the outskirts of Belgrade, where Princip quickly proved himself to be adept. Before they set out for Sarajevo, Ciganović gave Princip, Čabrinović, and Grabež six hand grenades, four revolvers, some money, a map of Bosnia, cyanide, and a note to an official instructing him to assist in their crossing at the frontier between Serbia and Bosnia on their assassination mission.

★

By the end of May the three young assassins were now ready to set out on their killing. The funding provided by the Black Hand was far from lavish: Princip was forced to pawn his winter coat for 8 dinars. Crossing the frontier into Bosnia a month before the archduke arrived was likely to be easier than it would be later when security was certain to be enhanced. Even so, eluding frontier guards and customs officials was going to be no easy task—especially when their possession of revolvers and grenades gave such compelling evidence of their intentions.

On the 28th of May the three boarded a steamer in Belgrade to carry them up the Drina River to the frontier at Šabac where they were to utilize one of the tunnels (*kanal*) of Union or Death to cross into Bosnia. A series of these tunnels (modelled on the underground railroads that provided an escape route for fugitive slaves in the USA) had been set up to smuggle people, propaganda, and weapons from Serbia into the occupied provinces.

When they arrived in Šabac a Serbian official provided them with false documents indicating that they were Serbian revenue officers. They then travelled by rail to Loznica, where they split up: Čabrinović walked to Zvornik, with a teacher helping him cross the river and get to Tuzla; Princip and Grabež, with the six grenades strapped around their waist and with revolvers in their pockets—a cumbersome arrangement which made walking very difficult—crossed near Lyeshnitsa on 29 May, where they were assisted by several 'confidential men' of the *Narodna Odbrana*.

The mission almost failed before it began. The Serbian government, which employed numerous spies and informants of its own within Serbia, learned of the plot and attempted to quash it. The leadership of Union or Death, supported by some high-ranking army officers, was aiming to bring down the socialist government of Nikola Pašić's ruling Radical Party. As far as they were concerned, Pašić was too liberal and too reluctant to challenge Austria-Hungary. The chief of the Serbian general staff, General Radomir Putnik, tried to convince the king to dismiss him when Pašić made it clear that he wanted to bring the 'new Serbian' territories acquired through the Balkan wars into the constitutional system enjoyed by the rest of the country; the military, ruling these territories under military occupation,

Map 2. Assassination routes

objected. King Petar, himself a moderate constitutionalist, refused to dismiss the prime minister, but Pašić, hoping to solidify his rule, called for an election to be held on 1 August. As an assassination attempt on the heir to the throne of the Dual Monarchy was bound to lead to a crisis with Austria and play into the hands of his political opponents, Pašić sent a directive to Serbian frontier officials at Loznica, instructing them to intercept the three would-be assassins. But the officials, who turned out to be members of Union or Death, claimed that the message had arrived too late for them to act, and that the conspirators had already crossed the frontier.

Eventually, Princip and Grabež arrived in Tuzla, after implicating a number of Bosnians in the plot—mainly peasants who would pay with their lives for the assistance they had provided. Čabrinović, who made it to Tuzla before the others, was lounging in a café when he met a police agent who knew his father and who had, in fact, seen him just the day before. But, in spite of Čabrinović's well-known propensity for indiscretion and braggadocio, he did not arouse suspicion. When the three of them departed from Tuzla for Sarajevo by train, the police agent, who joined them on the train, again spotted Čabrinović. For the remainder of the journey the two of them chatted about the situation in Serbia and the upcoming visit of the archduke. When the agent asked him who his long-haired, dark-eyed friend was, Čabrinović told him: 'Princip'. The agent again failed to regard them as suspicious, and the three arrived unimpeded in Sarajevo, where they reported to Danilo Ilić. In fact, Princip moved in with Ilić's mother at 3 Oprkanj Street—and, as required by the Austrian authorities, dutifully proceeded to the police station to register his place of residence.

★

Imperial power began to lose local authority. If Serbian authorities had now failed in their efforts to stop the conspirators at the frontier, the Austrian authorities had lamentably failed to detect them carrying their weapons across the countryside, and the police had failed to notice anything suspicious about them and their behaviour. Yet another initiative might have prevented the assassins from carrying out their mission. The Serbian minister in Vienna, Jovan Jovanović, contacted Count Berchtold, the Austrian foreign minister, to warn him that there might be trouble connected with the archduke's visit. However, Jovanović, who had made no effort to hide his fervent pan-Serb views, was disliked and distrusted by Berchtold, who refused to meet with him. Instead, he directed him to deal with Ritter von Biliński, the Polish minister responsible for the administration of the imperial provinces of Bosnia and Herzegovina. Pašić would later claim to have issued the instructions to his minister to take this initiative, but Jovanović countered that he had acted on his own when he became concerned by reports of the mounting resentment in Bosnia arising from the archduke's visit. Whoever was responsible, it is clear that Jovanović met with Biliński on or about 5 June—one week after the assassins had crossed the frontier, and with plenty of time left to arrest the conspiracy and apprehend the assassins.

When they finally met in Vienna, Jovanović outlined his concerns to Biliński. He pleaded his case with the minister: that the scheduled visit to Sarajevo on Vidovdan (St Vitus' Day)—the anniversary of the Serb defeat at Kosovo—would provoke the Serbs. 'Among the Serb youths,' Jovanović argued, 'there may be one who will put a live cartridge in his rifle or revolver instead of a blank one. He may fire it, and this bullet may strike the commander.'[8] So Jovanović sketched a scenario in which one of the Serb recruits might shoot the archduke during the manoeuvres. He therefore urged that the manoeuvres not be held in Bosnia or, at the very least, not on Vidovdan.

Biliński still did not take the warning seriously. Jovanović neither offered anything specific nor suggested that there was a conspiracy unfolding,

Leon Ritter von Biliński (1846–1923); common finance minister of Austria-Hungary and minister responsible for Bosnia-Herzegovina (1912–15)

giving Biliński little evidence with which he might try to persuade the military authorities to call off the long-planned manoeuvres. Besides, he told Jovanović, Bosnia appeared to him to be fairly quiet at the moment. Biliński decided not to pass on the warning to either the emperor or the archduke. The minister was well aware that the archduke disliked the moderate policies of reform that he was attempting to initiate in Bosnia—policies that Biliński believed most likely to ameliorate Serb antagonism and gradually to win them over to Austrian rule. The archduke preferred the

Oskar Potiorek (1853–1933); Austro-Hungarian military governor of Bosnia-Herzegovina (1912–1914)

hard-line policies championed by the military governor of Bosnia and Herzegovina, General Oskar Potiorek.

Biliński was not on good terms with Potiorek, whom he regarded as a pig-headed reactionary who was doing his best to block the economic and social reforms necessary to accommodate Serbs to Austrian rule. When young Serbs in Bosnia were radicalized by Serb victories in the Balkan wars, and then outraged by the Albanian settlement, the civilian head of government had been replaced by a military officer. General Potiorek, the *Pogladvar* ('the chief'), believed that the 'south Slav question' could not be solved by reform, but only by war with Serbia. Without compelling evidence of a conspiracy, Biliński was unlikely to be able to convince either the general or the archduke to alter plans for the visit. If his warnings came to nothing it would only further discredit him in the eyes of the future sovereign. In spite of his responsibilities for the provinces, Biliński had not even been consulted about the manoeuvres or the visit. So, instead of dealing directly with the archduke, he chose to consult the civilian authorities who worked under him in Sarajevo.

After the warning from Jovanović, Biliński asked his officials for an assessment of the risks involved in the visit. Their forecast was bleak. The chief of the political department at Sarajevo reported that the police force was insufficient to guarantee the safety of the archduke, particularly given the lengthy route that he was scheduled to follow from the railway station along the Miljačka River to the Vijećnica, the city hall. Potiorek dismissed these concerns: 'The archduke comes here as a general and you have nothing to do with the matter.'[9]

The archduke himself made it clear that he wished his visit to be a strictly military affair. He chose to ignore the concerns of the civilian authorities and they were left out of the planning and security arrangements. As conscientious bureaucrats, they consequently declined to take any responsibility for the visit—and they communicated their position to the court. The archduke dismissed their worries. He had his own very personal reasons for wishing to keep the visit 'strictly military': namely, his wife.

★

Franz Ferdinand had married the Countess Sophie Chotek against the wishes of his uncle the emperor. Rather than a traditional arranged marriage between members of related noble households, that between Franz Ferdinand and Sophie was a love match. The archduke, who was expected to marry the daughter of the Archduchess Isabella, instead fell in love with one of her ladies-in-waiting. Although she was not regarded as a great beauty, she was a handsome and dignified woman of 27 when Franz Ferdinand was introduced to her. She came from an old, aristocratic Bohemian family, but it was neither of noble standing nor rich. In fact, by this time the family was relatively impoverished. She was one of eight children, and one of five girls. Her father, who kept the family on his salary, and then on a pension, made it clear that the girls would have to find employment if they did not marry, and thus at the age of 20 she had taken up a position as lady-in-waiting to the Archduchess Isabella.

The emperor determined to put a stop to what he and the court regarded as an entirely unsuitable union—one that demeaned the Habsburg name. According to Habsburg 'house rules' a Habsburg could marry only eligible

Franz Ferdinand (1863–1914); archduke and inspector-general of armed forces of Austria-Hungary (1913–14); Sophie, duchess of Hohenberg (1868–1914)

partners, which meant either someone of Habsburg descent, or one of those stipulated in a list of families of the ruling dynasties in Europe, supplemented by a few princely ones. To marry a mere lady-in-waiting showed a shocking disregard for Habsburg tradition. Consequently, the emperor threatened to expel Franz Ferdinand from the family—but this would have left his sickly brother Otto as heir (wracked by disease, he would die, probably of syphilis, six years later).

In the face of these threats the archduke proved implacable and immovable. Franz Joseph was eventually forced to agree to the marriage, but only on the condition that it be morganatic—a concept that stretched back to the Roman *Matrimonium ad Morganiticam*, which dealt with marriages between free and unfree persons, but which had evolved over the centuries to deal with unions between unequal couples in general. In this case, the arrangement made was that neither Sophie nor her offspring would possess the titles and rights that would normally have come with marriage. Neither she nor the children could succeed to the throne.

The terms of the marriage were imposed in an 'oath of renunciation' on 28 June 1900. Held in the Secret Council Chamber in an apartment of the Hofburg Palace in Vienna, the emperor stood on a platform to address those assembled before him. Gathered there were all fifteen adult archdukes, government ministers, and senior officials of the court. To them Franz Joseph read the full text of the oath. Franz Ferdinand then swore the oath on a bible and signed the declaration. The ceremony, which lasted less than half an hour, embittered the archduke against the emperor forever.

Two days later, on 30 June, Franz Ferdinand and Sophie were married at a castle owned by one of her family in Reichstadt in northern Bohemia. None of the archdukes attended—only two archduchesses, Franz Ferdinand's own half-sisters, were willing to participate. The ceremony was performed by the village priest. That morning the archduke received a telegram from the emperor announcing that Sophie would be raised from 'Countess' Chotek von Chotkova und Wognin to Princess 'Hohenberg'—a title associated with the Habsburgs, arising from their medieval possessions in southern Germany, which brought her, symbolically at least, closer to the family. Henceforth she could be addressed as 'Princely Grace'. But members of the royal House of Habsburg were archdukes and archduchesses—not princes and princesses—and dukes and duchesses, counts and countesses were mere aristocracy. Eventually, after giving birth to her third, and last, child, the emperor promoted her again to 'Duchess Hohenberg', which meant she was now to be addressed as 'Your Most Serene Highness'.

But Sophie was still not a member of the royal family, and she never would be. She was routinely humiliated in court circles. In order of precedence, she came after the youngest of the archduchesses. In royal processions, the archduke would walk at the head; the archduchess would come last, walking alone, without an escort. She could not sit at the head table during state dinners; she could not share the royal box when attending the theatre or the opera. Instead of submitting to such humiliation, she preferred to avoid most official functions. When the archduke represented the emperor at foreign courts the morganatic arrangements meant that she could not even attend.

These arrangements were more than a mere annoyance to Franz Ferdinand. By 1914 his bad temper had become legendary in Austrian court and military circles. He frequently flew into a rage over the smallest matter, with one of his close friends describing him as 'unbalanced in everything: he did nothing like other people'.[10] Once, when travelling on the imperial train on his way to meet the German kaiser, something in his carriage proved to be unsatisfactory—whereupon he drew his sword and hacked the upholstery to pieces. Although close friends and family found him to be genial, kind, and loyal, he was abrasive and cold to outsiders. He seemed unwilling to make any effort to cultivate popular affection among those he was to rule over. The contrast with his uncle was striking: although austere and remote, by 1914, having ruled for sixty-six years, the emperor Franz Joseph was now regarded with affection as the 'father' of the Dual Monarchy. His portraits and statues were to be found everywhere.

Franz Ferdinand was incensed at having to deal with the humiliations endured by his wife. But when the emperor appointed him to the position of inspector-general of the imperial army he saw the possibility that Sophie might at last be accorded the treatment befitting an empress. The visit to Sarajevo offered just such an opportunity. Rather than—literally—taking a back seat to her husband the archduke, as wife of the inspector-general of the *k.u.k.* (*kaiserlich und königlich*, 'imperial and royal') army she would sit at his side in an open carriage during the procession, and take a place of honour next to him when he spoke at the city hall. Thus the archduke was determined that the entire affair of his visit should be kept as 'military' as possible—and if this meant ignoring and offending the civilian authorities, so be it. He had little use for the 'politicians' in any case.

★

The preparations for the archduke's visit in 1914 were very different from those made for the emperor in 1912. For the emperor's visit to Sarajevo, which became the occasion of Žerajić's martyrdom, a double cordon of troops, numbering many hundreds, had lined the route of Franz Joseph's procession. But for Franz Ferdinand's visit two years later there were to be slightly more than 100 police available to protect him and his wife. One week before the visit the police did issue an order that all students residing temporarily in Sarajevo must return to their villages. But that order, which would have emptied the city of almost all of the conspirators, was not enforced. The Sarajevo police had advised against the choice of Vidovdan for the visit, but their warnings were ignored. In 1912 'strangers' had been forbidden to view the procession of the emperor unless they first submitted to an interview with the police, while hundreds of residents deemed to be dangerous were confined to their homes for the duration of the visit. No such precautions were taken in 1914: the archduke got his wish that the visit should be a strictly military affair. General Potiorek, who took control of the proceedings, did little to safeguard the heir to the throne, in spite of having under his command some 70,000 troops from the manoeuvres.

The lack of precautions and the failure of authorities to take seriously warnings and signs of danger led some to believe that a second conspiracy may have been operating on the 28 June: one that involved Austrians who wished to see the *Thronfolger* dead—especially if this were to happen at the hands of Serbs. The archduke had made no secret of the fact that he regarded the emperor—'the old boy'—as a procrastinating compromiser who was endangering the future of the monarchy. Franz Joseph regarded the *Ausgleich* (compromise) of 1867 as having salvaged the rule of the Habsburg dynasty after the empire suffered a crushing defeat at the hands of the Prussian army. But Franz Ferdinand regarded its principal arrangement, the creation of an autonomous and co-equal Hungary, as a disaster that was leading the monarchy down the road to ruin.

The archduke offered an alternative vision of the monarchy's future: the political structure should be reformed in order to accommodate and encourage 'the nationalities' of the empire. The presence of Czechs, Slovaks, Poles, Romanians, Italians, Slovenes, Serbs, Croats, and Ukrainians made the 'dual' monarchy a truly multinational empire. But Franz Ferdinand believed that the Magyars of Hungary had been given too much power in 1867, which they were now using to abuse the minorities under their control, alienating them from the Habsburg dynasty. When meeting with a delegation of Slovaks, the archduke blamed the Magyars for their difficulties: 'It was bad taste' on their part 'ever to come to Europe'.[11]

★

While the emperor persisted in his belief that the arrangements of 1867 were reasonable and workable and that it would be dangerous to reopen the constitutional discussion, the archduke argued that fundamental reforms were necessary. What he believed to be needed was a new federalism that would recognize, in particular, the rights and responsibilities of Czechs, Romanians, and Slavs, who, under the arrangements of 1867, were relatively disenfranchised. In the Hungarian parliament of 1914, for example, eight million non-Magyars were represented by forty-two deputies; eight and one-half million Magyars by 392. One antidote to this, which was contemplated by the archduke, was to introduce universal suffrage; another was to divide the monarchy into fifteen autonomous states based on nationality, but with German as the common language and with the emperor heading a central government, with a small federal parliament elected on the basis of population. This proposal was bound to alienate the Magyars, who currently enjoyed equal status with the Germans in the monarchy and predominant status over the minorities within Hungary.

Franz Ferdinand did not care: he despised the Magyars. When attending a regimental dinner in Hungary where the hussars performed their traditional *csardas* he declared 'Just look at that animal dance! That's one of the first things I shall do away with!'[12] And look forward to inheriting the throne, he did: he secretly had a full-sized portrait painted of himself—in full regalia as emperor.

Between his politics and his personality by 1914 Franz Ferdinand had accumulated numerous enemies who hoped that rumours that he was fatally ill would turn out to be true. Those who disliked and distrusted him looked forward to the possibility that his more reasonable and less ambitious brother, Karl, would take his place as heir. It was widely assumed that if Franz Ferdinand were to ascend to the throne, he would issue a manifesto announcing his plans for reform of the constitutional arrangements. This would initiate an immediate political crisis. It was also widely believed that he would ask the Pope to annul the morganatic oath upon the death of Franz Joseph, and that his good friend, Wilhelm II of Germany—who shared his antipathy to the Magyars—had already agreed to recognize Sophie as empress.

One final scheme for reform supported by the archduke was particularly relevant to the conspiracy to kill him in 1914. Although Franz Ferdinand preferred the 'federalist' solution to the monarchy's woes, he was also prepared to countenance a 'trialist' experiment. This idea involved the creation of a new entity that would transform the 'dual' monarchy into a triad: a third state consisting of Serbs, Croats, and Slovenes. The great attraction of this scheme was that it would reduce Magyar influence within the monarchy. But this scheme also worried Serb nationalists—especially those of Union or Death and the *Narodna Odbrana*—because it might, by unifying south Slavs within the monarchy and elevating their status to that of co-equals of the Germans and Magyars, subvert the movement to unite all Serbs under the Serbian umbrella, or all south Slav peoples within an independent 'Yugoslavia'. Dimitrijević and Tankosić regarded the trialist scheme as the greatest threat to their plans; the archduke as their greatest enemy.

So Franz Ferdinand's decision in the autumn of 1913 to attend the military manoeuvres in Bosnia the following June had a political purpose as well as a personal one. It was intended to encourage elements loyal to the monarchy there and to assure them that they would not be abandoned to the aspirations of the Greater Serbia movement. In spite of the warnings and threats received in the meantime, on the evening of 23 June the archduke and his suite met at the South Station in Vienna to set out on their journey to Bosnia. On the morning of the 24th they boarded the battleship *Viribus Unitis* at Trieste; on the 25th they boarded a smaller vessel to make the journey up the River Narenta to Metkovitch in Dalmatia. Crowds gathered on the river banks, waving, and calling out to the archduke as the steam launch made its way up river. In Metkovitch the party boarded a train to take them to Mostar, the capital of Herzegovina, where, after a drive around the town, they proceeded to Ilidže, a small Bosnian spa town outside of Sarajevo, where Sophie was waiting for them. The town was decorated in Austrian and Hungarian flags; they did not see the Serbian and Croatian flags that residents had also displayed, because General Potiorek had ordered them to be removed.

The circuitous route by sea was chosen as a deliberate affront to the Hungarians. To reach Sarajevo by railway meant going via Budapest— which Franz Ferdinand refused. But neither would he subject Sophie to the extra forty hours of travel that his route entailed, so she went by rail and reached Ilidže before him.

Later that evening a state ball was held at Ilidže. None of the officials from the ministry of finance, who were responsible for the administration of the province, was invited to attend. The archduke had issued explicit instructions that they were not to receive invitations. The official reason for their exclusion was that this occasion was strictly military—but the officials regarded their exclusion as an insult directed at them because of their advice to cancel the visit. For the next two days the archduke, in his role as inspector-general of the armed forces of the empire, viewed the army manoeuvres in the mountains just south of Sarajevo. The weather was unpleasant and unseasonal, with snow on the ground in June. When the manoeuvres ended, late in the afternoon of Saturday the 27th, Franz Ferdinand and Sophie took a leisurely drive through Sarajevo in an open carriage, where they appeared to be warmly welcomed by those who saw them. At dinner that evening the duchess told a leading Bosnian politician who had warned General Potiorek that the visit ought to be cancelled, that the people of Sarajevo had proven him wrong, that everyone had treated her and her husband with friendliness and true warmth. But others continued to worry. The chamberlain of the archduke's household tried to persuade the archduke to cancel the official visit to the city on the next day, but Potiorek's aide-de-camp, Lieutenant-Colonel Merizzi, argued against the cancellation and persuaded the archduke to proceed with the itinerary as planned.

★

Wandering through the bazaars of the town on that Saturday afternoon, Gavrilo Princip almost came face-to-face with the man he intended to kill. Later that evening Danilo Ilić handed out the weapons to the conspirators and directed them to the locations that they were to stake out the next day. He also introduced one of the new recruits, Mehmedbašić, to Princip, who had not yet met him. At a Sarajevo café on that Saturday evening Ilić warned the conspirators that he had reason to believe the police had discovered the plot. On Friday a police detective had telephoned headquarters from Ilidže to tell them that Čabrinović, who had been expelled from Bosnia two years ago, had been spotted in the street.

But when the message made its way up to the chief of police, he gave instructions that Čabrinović was to be left alone. Why? Čabrinović's father, in order to get permission to open his Sarajevo café, had to agree to perform services for the police—and the son admitted to one of his fellow-conspirators that his primary motive for participating in the assassination was to atone for the sins of his father in collaborating with the Austrians.

Meanwhile, after attending mass in Ilidže on the morning of Sunday the 28th, the archduke and the duchess set out by train for Sarajevo. The weather had propitiously changed: it was now a brilliant and warm summer day. Their appearance in the city was to be splendid and precedent-setting: the Duchess of Hohenberg was, for the first time on Habsburg territory, to receive the honours consistent with royal status. She was resplendent in her full-length white dress with red sash tied at the waist; she held a parasol to shelter from the sun, along with a fan to cool her; gloves, furs, and a splendid hat finished off the outfit.

The day was a very special one for Serbs. For years it had been an occasion for national mourning, in memory of the defeat suffered at the hands of the Ottoman Turks at the battle of Kosovo in 1389 which had extinguished the medieval Serbian kingdom. After 523 years the decision had been reversed when the Serbs triumphed over the Turks at the battle of Kumanovo in the first Balkan war of 1912. Celebrations had been planned for 28 June 1913, but these were cancelled when war with Bulgaria appeared imminent: Bulgaria attacked Serbia on the 29th. In 1914 Serbs everywhere, including those in Sarajevo, were planning to celebrate the defeat of the Turks and the reversal of history after half a millennium. As the laws of coincidence would have it, the 28th of June was also the fourteenth anniversary of the act of renunciation that Franz Ferdinand had been compelled to agree to—and the royal treatment that Sophie was to receive was partly intended to serve as a kind of apology for the humiliations that she had endured ever since. Thus, there was another, more personal, reason for neglecting the warnings of scheduling the visit on Vidovdan.

★

The route that the royal party was to follow after they arrived at the railway station had them driving along the Appel Quay, a broad street running alongside the Miljačka River. The details of the route had been published in the local *Bosnische Post*, in order that spectators would know where they could view the royal procession. After all, the political point of the visit was to demonstrate the support of the people for the Austrian regime in general, and for the heir to the throne in particular: the mayor had issued on 23 June a proclamation calling on the people of the city to welcome the archduke and to demonstrate their feelings towards him. They were directed to decorate their homes appropriately.

Ilić placed the assassins, who now numbered seven, at each of the three bridges spanning the river. Besides Princip, Čabrinović, and Grabež, Ilić had recruited Mehmedbašić once again. When the young Muslim received Ilić's telegram in Stolac on the 26th, he immediately applied to the police for a pass to travel to Mostar to visit a dentist. When he reached Mostar he simply failed to alight and continued on to Sarajevo, where he booked a room at the main hotel. Joining these five were two new additions: Vaso Čubrilović and Cvetko Popović. Čubrilović had come to Ilić's attention as a Serb patriot when he had been expelled from the high school in Tuzla for walking out of a ceremony when the Habsburg anthem had been played to begin celebrations of Saint Sava, the patron saint of Serbians. In June 1914 he was 17 years old and enrolled in the high school in Sarajevo. Vaso introduced Ilić to his even younger friend, Cvetko, a 16-year-old who was attending teacher's college in Sarajevo. On the evening of Saturday the 27th Ilić gave Čubrilović and Popović one grenade and one revolver each; Mehmedbašić was given a grenade. Before going to bed that night, Čabrinović and Princip each paid a visit to Žerajić's shrine at the cemetery.

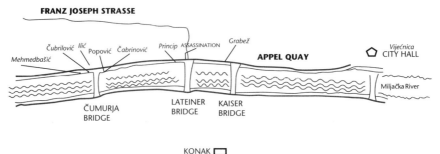

Map 3. The Sarajevo assassination

The next morning Ilić met with Princip, Grabež, and Čabrinović at a cake shop. Princip gave Čabrinović a grenade and a cyanide capsule. Čabrinović had arrived having just had a fight with his father, who wanted to hang the Habsburg flag in honour of the archduke. After leaving the cake shop Čabrinović met up with an old school friend and the two of them went to have their photographs taken to immortalize the assassination. The photographer took and developed the pictures within an hour; Čabrinović had six copies made and arranged for his friend to send these to his grandmother, sister, and friends. He was quite certain that he was about to be martyred for the cause. Before taking his place on the route, he gave away all of his money and his belongings.

The seven assassins mingled with the gathering crowds for over an hour before the motorcade arrived. Ilić had assigned Čabrinović a place across the street from Mehmedbašić and Čubrilović, who were in front of the garden at the Mostar Café, situated across from the first bridge on the route, the Čumurja, with Popović and himself on the other side of the street. Princip was placed 200 yards further along the route, at the second bridge, the Lateiner. Grabež was placed at the third bridge, the Kaiser. All were in their places by the time that the royal party arrived at the station at 10 in the morning.

★

The royal procession consisted of six automobiles. The first was supposed to be manned by four special security detectives assigned to guard the archduke, but something soon went awry. Only one of the detectives actually managed to take his place; local policemen substituted for the others. The next car was to carry the mayor, Fehim Effendi Čurčić, wearing his red fez, and the chief of police, Dr Edmund Gerde—who had warned the military authorities about the dangerous atmosphere in Sarajevo and had advised against the visit on this day.

The archduke and the duchess were to be seated next to one another in the third car, facing General Potiorek and the owner of the limousine, Count Harrach. Thus arranged, the archduke and duchess conducted a brief inspection of the Philippović military barracks before setting out on the journey to the city hall. Once they arrived there, they were to be greeted with a formal welcome and reception, after which they were to open the new state museum and then proceed to the military governor's residence. Lunch was to be hosted by General Potiorek there, at the *konak*—formerly the administrative headquarters under the Ottoman regime.

Ten minutes before the motorcade reached the Čumurja bridge, Čabrinović was approached by a policeman and asked to identify himself. He was left alone when he produced a permit that purported to have been issued by the Viennese police, but not before asking the policeman which car was carrying the archduke. 'The third', he was told.

Minutes later he took out his grenade, knocked off the detonator cap, and threw it at the limousine carrying the archduke and the duchess. Although Čabrinović and the others knew that there was a twelve-second delay between knocking off the cap and the explosion, he was unable to wait that long. He hit the limousine with it, but it bounced off before exploding under the next car, immobilizing it and wounding Colonel Merizzi, General Potiorek's aide-de-camp, and injuring a number of spectators. The only damage that had been done to the royal couple was a slight wound inflicted on the duchess's cheek, where she had been grazed by the grenade's detonator. Čabrinović fell to the ground, swallowed the cyanide, then jumped over the embankment into the river. The cyanide failed and the river had been reduced to a mere trickle in midsummer. Čabrinović was captured immediately by a policeman who asked him if he was a Serb. 'Yes, I am a Serb hero', he replied.[13]

The procession continued on its way to the splendid new city hall, the Vijećnica. The building had been designed in a neo-Moorish style meant to evoke the Alhambra. This was part of the 'neo-Orientalist' policy of the Austrian administration meant to cultivate the support of Bosnian Muslims, and the Vijećnica was decked out in Bosnia's 'national' colours. Once the royal party arrived, the mayor began to read his effusive speech in their honour—apparently unaware of the near calamity that had just occurred behind him.

The archduke interrupted the speech, angrily demanding to know what the mayor meant by speaking of 'loyalty' to the crown when a bomb had just been launched at the heir to the throne. But the duchess, playing her accustomed role, managed to calm him down and the mayor continued with his elaborate, prepared remarks. When it was the archduke's turn to reply he had to wait for the staff officer to arrive with the copy of his speech, which was splattered in blood. After the speeches, the duchess was received by a delegation of women, with the formal welcome to her given by the head of the Muslim school.

Subsequent to the speeches and the reception, the party discussed how they ought to proceed. Potiorek proposed that they could either return immediately to Ilidže, driving at full speed along the Appel Quay, or they could go straight to his residence, which was only a few hundred metres away. The archduke insisted that he wished to visit the military hospital to see Colonel Merizzi, and then to proceed to open the museum, as planned. The duchess changed her itinerary: she was to have gone to the governor's residence following the ceremony at the city hall, but now decided to accompany her husband: 'It is in time of danger that you need me.'[14]

The royal couple, along with Potiorek, climbed into a new car, with Count Harrach standing on the footboard to shield the archduke from any other would-be assassins. Upon being informed that Čabrinović had been arrested, Franz Ferdinand is reputed to have said, 'Hang him as soon as you can, or else Vienna will send him a decoration.'[15]

In order to reach the hospital, the motorcade was forced to retrace its route along the Appel Quay. Princip, who had almost abandoned hope of getting a shot at the archduke after the arrest of Čabrinović, was still near the Lateiner bridge, but when the police began clearing the crowd he had crossed the street in order to have a better position if the procession turned to go to the museum. When the driver of the first car turned right, in accordance with the original plan, the driver of the second car—a soldier with no familiarity with the city—followed him, along the route which would have taken them to the museum.

Potiorek immediately recognized the mistake and ordered his driver to stop. The car then began to reverse slowly in order to get back onto the Appel Quay—with Count Harrach now on the opposite side of the car to Princip, who was standing at the corner of Appel Quay and Franz Joseph

Street, in front of Schiller's delicatessen. Seizing the unexpected opportunity, Princip stepped out of the crowd.

His moment had arrived. Instead of throwing a grenade—because it was too difficult to take it out of his coat and knock off the detonator cap—he fired with his revolver from 30–40 feet. A policeman, seeing him raise the gun, tried to stop him, but Mihajlo Pušara, a friend who had accompanied Princip, kicked the policeman in the knee and knocked him off balance. The first shot hit the archduke near the jugular vein; the second hit the duchess in the stomach. 'Soferl, Soferl!' Franz Ferdinand cried, 'Don't die. Live for our children.'[16]

But the duchess was already dead by the time they reached the governor's residence. The archduke, unconscious when he was carried inside, was also dead within minutes—before either a doctor or a priest could be summoned. Later that night a sculptress and a painter were brought to the *konak* to make death masks of the royal couple.

The crowd was attempting to lynch Princip when the police managed to rescue him. He tried to swallow the cyanide capsule, but vomited it up. An Austrian judge interviewed him almost immediately afterwards: 'The young assassin, exhausted by his beating, was unable to utter a word. He was undersized, emaciated, sallow, sharp featured. It was difficult to imagine that so frail looking an individual could have committed so serious a deed.'[17]

The Reaction

Week One: 28 June–5 July

On the morning of 28 June Judge Leo Pfeffer took his daughter to the Appel Quay to view the royal procession. They were nearby when the grenade thrown by Čabrinović exploded. The judge sent his daughter home and walked to the city hall. He was called to the first-aid room, where he met the bleeding Čabrinović. By the time the bloodied and bruised Princip arrived, the judge had been assigned to interview the assassins and report to Vienna. By evening Princip had been charged with the assassination. Along with Čabrinović, he was taken to the military prison and put in chains. Neither expressed remorse for their actions, although Princip did say he was sorry about the duchess, whom he had not intended to kill.[1]

Ilić was arrested that afternoon. All of Čabrinović's family was rounded up and taken to jail—along with all of the employees who worked in their café. Mehmedbašić, Čubrilović, Popović, and Grabež managed to flee Sarajevo. Grabež was arrested when he arrived at the Serbian frontier because he lacked the special permit required for travelling. It took several days, until 3 July, before the police were able to track down and arrest Čubrilović and Popović. Mehmedbašić managed to elude them, escaping to Montenegro.

On the evening of the assassination, crowds of young Croatian and Muslim men began to gather and march through Sarajevo, singing the Bosnian anthem and shouting 'Down with the Serbs'. Around 10 p.m. about one hundred of them began stoning the Hotel Europa, owned by a prominent Serb and frequented by Serbian intellectuals.

The next morning Croat and Muslim leaders held a rally to demonstrate their support for Austrian rule. They sang the national anthem of the monarchy, displayed black flags, and carried portraits of the emperor. Sporadic demonstrations now escalated into full-scale rioting. Crowds gathered in front of Serb societies and businesses. They began smashing windows, ransacking the Serbian school, the *Narod* and *Srbska Riječ* newspapers, and the Hotel Europa, stoning the residence of the head of the Serbian Orthodox Church in Sarajevo, and besieging the homes of prominent Serbs. Čabrinović's home and his father's café were attacked. The rioting continued for hours before martial law was proclaimed.

No effort was made to arrest the rioters. Since the annexation of 1908 officials had favoured the Croats and Muslims as useful allies in building a model province; in return they received enhanced status and greater opportunities. And Franz Ferdinand's 'trialist' project seemed to offer more hope for the future. Instead of acting against the rioters, the police in Bosnia rounded up and arrested hundreds of Serb businessmen, journalists, writers, and priests.[2]

★

News of the assassination arrived in Belgrade around 5 p.m., in the midst of celebrations of the anniversary of the battle of Kosovo in 1389. At 10 p.m. officials ordered people to return to their homes. Nevertheless, celebrations continued well into the night. The secretary of the Austrian legation reported that the people of the city were delighted with the news of the murders; some had declared that 'It serves them right, we have been expecting this for a long time', or 'This is revenge for the annexation.'[3]

A few Serbian newspapers denounced the killings the next day while criticizing the Austrian military manoeuvres in Bosnia as a deliberate provocation. The scenario played out during the manoeuvres had envisioned an invasion of Serbia. One newspaper praised Princip as a martyr.[4] On the other hand an editorial in the newspaper of the governing Radical Party, the *Samouprava*, anticipated what would become the official government response: it denounced the killings and expressed sympathy for the Habsburg family and the people of the Dual Monarchy. The editorial blamed the murders on 'mentally unbalanced youths'.[5]

Prime Minister Pašić was on board a train bound for Kosovo to celebrate the anniversary of the battle on the evening of the 28th when news of the killings reached him. Although shocked, he continued his journey and attended the celebration. He was in the midst of an election campaign in which he and his party were challenged by opponents demanding a more aggressive foreign policy. Pašić could not afford to be seen as less patriotic than the opposition. But he had been working to improve relations with Austria-Hungary, believing that Serbia needed a long period of peace to consolidate the gains made in the Balkan wars. Those wars had cost 370 million dinars: three times the entire budget for 1912. The army was in a desperate state, and the minister of war estimated that it would take ten years to rebuild it. Pašić wanted to avoid a confrontation with Austria.

★

In Vienna, all public performances were cancelled immediately. The people of the city remained calm through the evening of the 28th, but by the next day some Viennese newspapers were blaming Serbia for the killings. Although they might not yet have the details of the conspiracy, they had no doubt who to blame: 'Ten years ago they butchered their own King and Queen by night; they have now murdered the Austro-Hungarian heir in open daylight on the street.'[6]

On Monday afternoon a mob gathered in front of the Serbian legation and the police had to be brought in. The next day an article appeared in the *Militärische Rundschau* headed 'To Belgrade!'. The chief of the general staff insisted that Austria 'must draw the sword' against Serbia.[7]

Many of the leading Viennese newspapers, however, including the *Fremdenblatt*, the *Neue Freie Presse*, and *Pester Lloyd*, argued against a campaign of revenge. In the immediate aftermath of the assassination it was far from clear how the government of Austria-Hungary would respond.

The emperor's reaction may have shocked the people of Vienna. He was blaming himself for the killing: permitting the archduke's marriage had been an affront to God, for which he was now being punished. He told his closest confidants that the assassination was unlikely to have any political consequences. And why should it? 'This is just another of those tragic occurrences which have been so frequent in the Emperor's life. I don't think he regards it in any other light.'[8]

Decisions had to be made concerning a memorial service. The emperor had only recently recovered from a prolonged illness. He had now recovered sufficiently to return to Vienna from his beloved hunting lodge at Bad Ischl (about 300 kilometres from Vienna) the morning after the assassination. He quickly made it clear that any service would be minimal. The reason given was that Franz Joseph must be spared the fatigue of an elaborate ceremony. The real reason was the continuing animosity towards the duchess.

As far as the court was concerned, Sophie did not meet the criteria for a formal state ceremony. The official in charge proposed a full ceremony for the archduke, with the body of the duchess to be left at the train station until it was shipped to the crypt that the archduke had built for them at his castle in Artstetten. When friends of the royal couple objected, the ceremony was downgraded. Heads of state were not to be invited, only ambassadors already available in Vienna.

On Monday the 29th the bodies of Franz Ferdinand and Sophie left Sarajevo by train for Trieste. On the same day Count Conrad von Hötzendorff, the chief of the general staff, proposed to Count Berchtold that they attack Serbia immediately, without warning. His advice came as no surprise to the Austrian foreign minister. The general had been preaching war for years.

★

Conrad was born in 1852 only half a mile from the emperor's residence at Schönbrunn palace in Vienna. He came from the 'service nobility': his great-grandfather had been ennobled in 1815 after fifty years as a finance official. Conrad entered the Theresian Military Academy in 1867, graduated tenth in a class of eighty-eight, and was commissioned as a lieutenant in 1871. While he was a student, the Franco-Prussian war of 1870–1 was being waged: Conrad developed a lifelong obsession with the lessons to be learned from it and became the army's leading expert on it. In 1874 he was admitted to the rigorous two-year programme offered at the War School. He graduated at the top of his class and was immediately appointed to the General Staff.

Conrad was no ordinary soldier. While at the academy, he mastered Russian and Czech while developing an interest in philosophy. Throughout his life he continued to read Kant, Darwin, and his favourite philosopher, Schopenhauer. But he was also a young man of action: when the Muslims of Bosnia revolted against the Austrian occupation in 1878 he pleaded to be sent there. He found an unconventional, dirty war fought in rugged terrain, and in 1882 he published an article proposing a new strategy for wars fought in the mountains. Instead of marching in file in long columns along mountain paths, where the men could be picked off by snipers, he proposed advancing on a broad front, confronting the difficulties posed by the difficult terrain. While in Bosnia he taught himself Serbo-Croat, which he mastered sufficiently to be sent into Serbia as a spy in 1881.

Count Franz Conrad von Hötzendorf (1852–1925); chief of the general staff of Austria-Hungary (1906–11, 1912–17)

His linguistic skills, philosophical interests, and military experience led to Conrad's appointment as instructor of tactics at the War School in 1888. Three years later he would publish a book of 815 pages: *Zum Studium der Taktic* ('Toward the Study of Tactics') in which he argued that the morale of the men was the crucial factor in determining victory or defeat. To win meant crushing the enemy's morale—which could not be accomplished by standing on the defensive.

A decade later, in the third edition of *Taktic*, he attacked pacifist 'dreamers'. War was inevitable. The state had to maintain a strong army and cultivate a warlike spirit (*kriegerischer Geist*) in order to survive. Recognizing that all life was a struggle for existence constituted the only 'real and rational basis for policy making. . . . Whoever remains blind to the mounting danger, or whoever recognizes it but remains too indolent to arm himself, and is too undecided to deliver the blow at the proper moment, deserves his fate.'[9]

Conrad was a bold, unconventional figure. He found in Darwin's laws a message more powerful than that offered by Christianity. Soldiers must be trained to kill their neighbours, not to 'love them as thyself'. Thou shalt not kill? 'A hypocrisy'. He was no courtier: when he became chief of staff he met weekly with the emperor, but they never became friendly. Conrad was brusque and opinionated. He had few friends. The emperor and the arch-duke, deeply devout Catholics, were disturbed by Conrad's absence of Christian feeling. He did not share their love of hunting and he dismissed the pomp and circumstance of court ceremonies and military parades as a waste of time and energy.

When Conrad's wife died of stomach cancer in 1905 at the age of 44 he was heartbroken. He had suffered occasional bouts of depression through-out his life, but these now threatened to become debilitating. And then, attending a dinner party in 1907, he met a beautiful, elegant, and rich young woman. By March he was declaring his love and announcing his intention to marry her. But there was a problem: she was already married, with six children. Eventually, she confessed that her marriage was loveless, and they became lovers. Between 1907 and 1915 he wrote more than 3,000 letters to her—some of them sixty pages long.[10]

The liaison did not satisfy Conrad. Although Gina's husband agreed to the arrangement because it enabled him to take a mistress, Conrad was determined that they should marry. He dreamed that a great success in war would elevate his status at court and in society to a level that would enable them to overcome the difficulties of divorce and remarriage. As he had climbed the chain of command from general to *Feldmarschalleutnant* to chief of the general staff in 1906, he began to preach the advantages of striking first. He insisted that an aggressive foreign policy, made possible by a strong and unified army, was the key to revitalizing the Habsburg empire and overcoming domestic difficulties. During the Bosnian crisis of 1908–9 he itched for the opportunity to attack the Serbs when they objected to the annexation. He was deeply disappointed when they backed down. After-wards, he complained incessantly that Austria-Hungary had missed a golden opportunity to solve the Serbian problem.

Conrad also wanted war with Italy. When the Italians invaded Tripoli and launched their war against Turkey in 1911, he proposed to attack them.

Italian forces that guarded the frontier with Austria were depleted: Austria could crush them quickly and easily. His advice cost him his job as chief of staff in November 1911. The foreign minister complained to the emperor about his interfering in foreign policy and his sneering contempt for anyone who dared disagree with him. Franz Joseph agreed that the idea of an aggressive war against an ally contradicted his policy of peace.

When the first Balkan war broke out Conrad hoped that it would give Austria the opportunity to intervene. After Turkey was defeated, Serbia and Montenegro could be incorporated into the Habsburg empire 'somewhat like Bavaria or Saxony in the German empire'.[11] But the opportunity was missed. Returning as chief of staff in December 1912, Conrad again urged the necessity of war with Serbia.

A successful war was Austria-Hungary's only opportunity for salvation. Even if defeated, war was worth the gamble. In December 1913 Conrad wrote to Gina that 'more and more' he believed 'that our purpose ultimately will be only to go under honorably . . . like a sinking ship'.[12] When news of the assassination at Sarajevo reached him he wrote that he foresaw nothing good for the future of the monarchy, that Serbia and Romania would become 'the nails in its coffin', that Russia would give them its strong support, and that the struggle would be hopeless. Nevertheless, 'it must be pursued, because so old a Monarchy and so glorious an army cannot go down ingloriously'.[13]

★

Franz Ferdinand and Sophie were murdered on Sunday. The next day Conrad was pleading with Berchtold to attack Serbia. The foreign minister seemed disinclined to take such a drastic step. By Tuesday, however, Berchtold had been persuaded that the conspiracy had been designed in Belgrade. He believed the young men had been carefully selected to do the killing because, by Austrian law, the death penalty could not be applied to anyone under the age of 18.[14]

In Vienna, the Serbian minister tried to meet with Berchtold, but was passed along to an under-secretary. Jovan Jovanović wanted to assure the Austrians that his government condemned the outrage and would not tolerate any illegal proceedings within its territory that might disturb relations with Austria. But he could not restrain himself from airing accumulated Serbian grievances against Austria, such as its championing of an independent Albania, the creation of which prevented Serbia from gaining access to the Adriatic.

In Belgrade, the secretary of the Austrian legation asked what steps the Serbian police had taken to follow up clues to the crime that were to be found there. 'The answer was that the matter has not yet engaged the attention of the Serbian police.'[15] Later that day, however, the minister of the interior ordered the chief of police in Belgrade to investigate any links between the assassins and government officials.

Within forty-eight hours of the assassination the spectre of a crisis between Austria and Serbia began to emerge. The Austrians would point to the responsibility of the Serbian government for the killings; the Serbs would proclaim their innocence. The Austrians would point to Serbian sponsorship of a 'Greater Serbia' as the root cause of the unrest in Bosnia; the Serbs would claim that Austria's opposition to the legitimate aspirations of the Serbian people was the cause of the problem.

Where these accusations and disputes might lead was still far from clear. Would Austria follow the advice of Conrad and seize the opportunity to attack Serbia? Would Serbia attempt to placate the Austrians by taking vigorous action against those elements in Serbia responsible for the Greater Serbia movement? If a real crisis emerged, could it be limited to Austria and Serbia, or would the great powers of Europe become involved?

Serbia had no ally, but Austria had two, perhaps three. In fact Serbia, created as a principality following the Napoleonic wars, had enjoyed friendly relations with Austria throughout most of the nineteenth century. Austria promoted Serbia as a buffer between itself and Russia; later, between itself and Russia's client state, Bulgaria. For several decades following the Crimean War, Austria acted as Serbia's patron, Russia as Bulgaria's. In 1881 Austria and Serbia had signed a secret alliance and Serbia played the part of loyal client until the 1890s. The Russians, who had never shown any particular affection for the Serbs, had placed their Balkan hopes on Bulgaria until it turned to Austria for support. Bulgaria appeared a more useful buffer against Russian expansion into the Balkans; the Austrians were happy to support it. In July 1914 it was unclear whether Serbia could hope for more than sympathy from Russia in any contest with Austria.

Austria, by contrast, enjoyed the longest-standing alliance in Europe through its agreement with Germany. The 'Dual Alliance' would celebrate its thirty-fifth anniversary in October 1914. The Italians had made it a Triple Alliance by joining the combination in 1882 and the Romanians had secretly signed on the following year. The Triple Alliance had been renewed five times since, giving the Austrians every reason to believe that in any diplomatic crisis arising from the assassination they would enjoy political support that the Serbs could not hope to match.

Appearances were deceiving. Italy had outstanding claims against Austria: the 'unredeemed' Italian-speaking peoples of the Trentino who remained outside of Italy—*Italia irredenta*—as well as the multi-ethnic city of Trieste on the Adriatic, whose governing language was Italian. Once united, Italy had developed expansionist aspirations along the Adriatic—where it could claim to be the heir to the Venetian empire. Many Italians regarded Austria as an enemy. And the secret adherence of Romania to the Triple Alliance was politically complicated: the large Romanian population in Hungary was restive under the Magyar domination—to the point that the Romanian government dare not make public its alliance with Austria.

So support for Austria in the Balkans boiled down to Germany, and the signs were not encouraging. When Berchtold met with the German ambassador in Vienna on 30 June, Heinrich Leopold von Tschirschky und Bögendorff preached caution. Many Austrians wished for a final reckoning with the Serbs, but he advised them not to act in haste. They should first decide clearly what they wanted to achieve and weigh their options carefully. Neither Italy nor Romania was likely to offer support for an energetic response.[16]

Tschirschky's caution would have surprised his colleagues in the diplomatic corps. He was widely believed to have urged Austria to take aggressive steps on numerous occasions during his seven years as ambassador in Vienna. A member of the Saxon nobility, Tschirschky began his career as personal secretary to Otto von Bismarck's son, Herbert, in 1885. He served in Vienna, Constantinople, and St Petersburg before returning to the Wilhelmstrasse and his appointment as secretary of state for foreign affairs in 1906. Although he became an intimate friend of Kaiser Wilhelm II, frequently accompanying him on his foreign travels, he did not enjoy his position and the chancellor found him disappointing. Married to the daughter of a Hungarian-Jewish sugar baron, he was comfortable in Vienna where he established close working relationships with successive Austrian foreign ministers. His words carried weight in Vienna, and he was relied upon in Berlin as a trustworthy representative.[17]

While Tschirschky was advising caution in Vienna, Germany's acting secretary of state for foreign affairs was assuring the Serbian minister in Berlin that he did not believe his government to be responsible for the assassination. He encouraged the Serbian government to cooperate with the

Heinrich von Tschirschky und Bögendorff (1858–1916); German ambassador at Vienna (1907–16)

Austrian authorities in Bosnia in their investigation of the plot, and thus to dissociate themselves from the crime.[18] He confided to the Italian ambassador his fear that the Austrians might adopt measures 'too severe and provocative'—and that Germany would have to undertake the 'continuous and laborious task' of restraining Austria.[19]

His officials did not yet know how the kaiser would respond. He was known to be friendly with the archduke and had greatly enjoyed his visit with Franz Ferdinand and Sophie at their Bohemian castle at Konopiště in early June. On the weekend of the 27th–28th Wilhelm was at Kiel, taking the helm of his racing yacht, the *Meteor*, at the annual regatta there. News of the assassination reached him at 2.30 p.m. on Sunday. He decided immediately to return to Berlin so that he could personally take charge of affairs in order to 'preserve the peace of Europe'.[20] He arrived at Potsdam on Monday afternoon.

★

Could the situation be defused? Would the Serbian government cooperate with an Austrian investigation into the roots of the conspiracy? The Serbian prime minister, Nikola Pašić, who was no friend of the 'Men of 19 May' and its connection with the Black Hand, knew that the most zealous nationalists were plotting to overthrow him. He had been trying to improve relations with Austria-Hungary. On Wednesday he instructed Serbian representatives to explain that his government had taken steps to suppress anarchic elements within Serbia, and that it would now redouble its vigilance and take the severest measures against them. 'Moreover, Serbia will do everything in her power and use all the means at her disposal in order to restrain the feelings of ill-balanced people within her frontiers.'[21]

Would Pašić's assurances satisfy the Austrians? The Serbian minister in Vienna reported three days after the assassination that Viennese mobs were demonstrating in front of the legation and that hatred was being spread by 'lower Catholic circles', the press, and the military. He predicted that Austria would not decide what steps to take until after the funeral for the archduke and duchess, whose bodies were not scheduled to arrive in Vienna until Thursday. The German ambassador concurred: what Austria would demand of the Serbs would depend on whether their inquiry in Bosnia found any 'highly suspicious facts against Belgrade'.[22] Tschirschky could not envision anything more than a demand that Serbia cooperate with their investigation into the killings.

The German government seemed to agree with the ambassador's warnings that Austria should proceed carefully. The chancellor, Theobald von Bethmann Hollweg, persuaded the kaiser to abandon his intention of attending the funeral ceremony—even if only as a 'personal friend' of the murdered archduke rather than as emperor of Germany. The public explanation for his absence was to be his physical indisposition; the explanation given to Franz Joseph was fear for the kaiser's personal safety. Berlin had received warnings that other assassins might now be gunning for him. A third, political, reason was Bethmann Hollweg's wish to avoid further inflaming the situation.

The kaiser was flammable material. Since the beginning of his reign he had established a pattern of erupting angrily whenever he perceived an insult—either to himself personally, or to the German Reich. The assassination of a friend and future monarch enraged him now. So who knew what might be said and agreed upon in the heat of the moment in Vienna were he to attend the funeral, where he would be surrounded by Austrian military men, led by Conrad, itching for a fight with Serbia? Bethmann Hollweg had good reason to fear the consequences should the kaiser intervene personally, but if he could restrain the kaiser perhaps a crisis could be averted. The Austrians would not move without German support.

★

By Wednesday, 1 July, things seemed to be moving slowly and judiciously. Since martial law had been declared in Bosnia, calm had been restored. Attacks on Serb businesses and institutions had ceased. Serbia had promised to restrain its hotheads. The memorial for the archduke and duchess in Vienna was to be a low-key affair. Only a couple of extremist right-wing newspapers in Austria and Hungary were calling for revenge on Serbia; most preached caution. The minister-president (prime minister) of Hungary, Count István Tisza de Borosjenő et Szeged, wrote directly to the emperor to urge that the assassination not be used as an excuse for a 'reckoning' with Serbia. It would be a fatal mistake to proceed unless they could prove the complicity of the Serbian government in the plot. He warned that the strategic outlook was bleak: Romania was virtually lost to the Triple Alliance and Bulgaria was still too exhausted from its war with Serbia to be counted on.[23]

Few expected the conscientious and cautious foreign minister of Austria-Hungary to disagree with the Hungarian premier's advice. By the summer of 1914 Leopold Anton Johann Sigismund Joseph Korsinus Ferdinand, Count von Berchtold, was widely regarded as intelligent but weak, hard-working but unambitious, charming but effete. He was one of the richest men in Austria-Hungary: a nobleman who had inherited vast estates in Moravia, at the intersection between Germans, Hungarians, Czechs, and Slovaks—and then married the daughter of a rich Magyar aristocrat. He had been educated privately, at home, until reaching the age of 20. Besides classical Latin and Greek, he became fluent in Czech, Slovak, Hungarian, and French. He entered the diplomatic service at the age of 30 in 1893, serving in Paris and London before being appointed ambassador to St Petersburg in 1906. He chose to retire from the service in 1911, preferring to tend to his estates, collect art and other treasures, and to establish a first-class stable of

racing horses rather than continuing to deal with the tiresome work of
diplomacy. He was reluctantly persuaded to come out of retirement and
serve as foreign minister when Count Aehrenthal died in February 1912.

After more than two years in office, Berchtold's reputation for prudence
had been confirmed. He had demonstrated his commitment to upholding
the status quo. In the succession of Balkan crises that arose after he assumed
office, he had moved closer to Britain, accepting the vision of Sir Edward
Grey's 'concert of Europe' to resolve diplomatic difficulties. He had become
frustrated with the lack of support offered by Germany—with its support for
Italy during the war with Turkey and with its opposition to his initiatives to

Count Leopold von Berchtold (1863–1942); common foreign minister of Austria-
Hungary (1912–15)

draw Bulgaria into the Triple Alliance. Berchtold was especially annoyed when, in the spring of 1914, he had suggested the possibility of using force to prevent the unification of Serbia with Montenegro. The idea left the kaiser 'completely cold'; Vienna was 'crazy' to consider it.[24]

Sitting on Berchtold's desk was a memorandum that he had asked a senior official at the foreign office to draft in early June. It had nothing to do with the assassination per se: Baron Franz von Matscheko had completed his assignment by 24 June, four days before the killings.

As instructed, Matscheko assessed the situation as it had evolved in the Balkans after the upheavals of the last two years. A few changes worked to the benefit of the Triple Alliance: the creation of an independent Albania now acted as a barrier to the expansion of Serbia; Greece, although allied to Serbia, might not necessarily be counted as an enemy of Austria–Hungary and Germany; and, most promising, Bulgaria had been awakened 'from the hypnosis of Russia' and was now seeking to establish closer relations with the Triple Alliance.[25]

In spite of these positive signs the situation had not worked out to the advantage of Austria–Hungary. Turkey, with which they had shared a 'natural community of interests' and which had served as a counterweight to Russia and the independent Balkan states, had been pushed out of Europe almost entirely. Serbia, which had been hostile to Austria–Hungary for years, was 'entirely under Russian influence', had enormously increased its territory and population and might be further enlarged if united with Montenegro. Perhaps worst of all, Romania, which had allied with Serbia in the Balkan wars, was still acting in solidarity with Serbia. Moreover, public opinion in Romania had shifted in favour of Russia; it might be lost to the Triple Alliance.

Matscheko warned that Russia and France had developed a coherent plan to take advantage of these changes. Austria–Hungary, Germany, and even Italy were conservative and aimed to preserve the peace, but Russia and France aimed to overturn the status quo. The Franco-Russian alliance was an offensive arrangement that was forestalled only by the military superiority of the Triple Alliance. Russia's 'intense diplomatic activity' aimed to unite the Balkan states in a Balkan league in order to overcome the military superiority of Austria and Germany. It was holding out the prospect of territorial expansion to adherents of such a league—which could only be accomplished at the expense of the Dual Monarchy.

Matscheko concluded that it would be 'irresponsibly negligent' and put the defence of the monarchy at risk, to remain 'more or less passive' in the face of developments in Romania. He did not propose, promote, or predict war. Rather, he outlined a long-term diplomatic strategy to be pursued jointly by Austria-Hungary and Germany in order to counter the growing influence of Russia in the Balkans. When news of the assassination arrived in Vienna on the evening of the 28th, he and his colleague, Count Forgách, sat down to revise the memorandum. By 1 July Berchtold himself had redrafted their revision, turning it into a plea for German support and a manifesto for the coercion of Serbia.

Berchtold's revised memorandum argued that Russia was aiming to encircle (*Einkreisungstendenzen*) the monarchy—a design ultimately aimed not at Austria-Hungary, but at Germany. If Russia succeeded in encircling Austria-Hungary it would be impossible for Germany to resist, and Russia would achieve political and commercial supremacy. It was short-sighted to argue, as some German critics did, that in the Balkans Germany was standing up only for Austro-Hungarian interests.[26]

Three days after the assassination Berchtold decided that opportunity had now knocked, that this was the moment to bring Germany back onto the side of Austria-Hungary in vigorous support of its interests in the Balkans. The question was, how to do it?

★

The tactic adopted by Berchtold was determined, in part, at Berlin. When Bethmann Hollweg convinced the kaiser that it was best not to come to Vienna for the archduke's funeral, it meant that Berchtold and Franz Joseph would be deprived of the opportunity to deal with him directly. They could, however, be quite certain how Wilhelm would respond to the murder of his friend and fellow royal. In the absence of a meeting, Berchtold had a letter drafted for the emperor to send to the kaiser—a 'personal' letter, to be written in Franz Joseph's own hand.

On Thursday, the 2nd of July, the emperor wrote the letter, expressing his regret that he would be deprived of the opportunity to speak directly with the kaiser about the political situation. In place of a conversation, he was enclosing a memorandum—the Matscheko memorandum—drafted, he said, before the catastrophe of Sarajevo. The crime committed against his nephew (no mention of the duchess) had resulted directly from the agitation conducted by 'Russian and Serbian Panslavists' who were determined to weaken the Triple Alliance and 'shatter my empire'. It might prove impossible to prove the complicity of the Serbian government in the conspiracy but it was clear that the plot had been well organized and could be traced back to Belgrade. There was no doubt that the aim of the Serbian government was to unite all south-Slavs under the Serbian flag, encouraging crimes such as the one perpetrated at Sarajevo and posing a lasting danger 'to my house and to my countries'.[27]

An international crisis was now on the agenda. How was it proposed that the dangers posed by Panslavism be avoided? Serbia must be isolated and reduced in size. Only a few days after the killing Austria had delineated its aim and explained it to Germany.

The emperor also outlined the methods by which Austria's objective could be achieved. Romania, although a secret partner in the Triple Alliance since 1883, could no longer be relied upon as an ally. King Karl of Romania had informed Austria twice in recent months that—in spite of his personal wishes—he would find it impossible to do his duty as an ally in view of 'the excited and hostile sentiments of his people'. Franz Joseph complained that Romania was establishing 'bonds of friendship' with Serbia, while tolerating within its realm the same kind of hateful agitation against Austria as was found in Serbia. The Romanians were aiming to create a Balkan league directed against the Dual Monarchy. This was not unprecedented. Early in King Karl's reign Romania had been about to launch a similarly adventurous policy when, Franz Joseph told Wilhelm, 'your late grandfather interfered in an energetic manner' and Romania became a reliable supporter of 'order'.

Austria's message was clear. Giving advice to Romania would no longer suffice. The only way to prevent the formation of a new Balkan league 'under the patronage of Russia' would be to secure the adherence of Bulgaria to the Triple Alliance. Bulgaria should be persuaded that its real interests 'tally with ours' and be prevented from turning 'to its old love for Russia'. Once this was achieved, a new friendship between Romania and Bulgaria could be encouraged; Romania might then abandon its dangerous policy of seeking the friendship of Russia and Serbia. If this strategy succeeded the Triple Alliance could then attempt to reconcile Greece with Bulgaria and Turkey. 'A new Balkan league could then be formed under the patronage of the Triple Alliance'—the aim of which would be to stop the 'Panslavist flood'.

The plan was ambitious. Success could be achieved only by 'pushing aside' Serbia and preventing it from 'becoming a factor of power in the Balkans'.[28] Unspoken (or unwritten) was the implication that only if Germany took an active role against Serbia could the threat of Russian domination be stopped.

The long, 4,000-word Matscheko memorandum that supplemented the emperor's letter outlined the perilous future that awaited the Germans unless they adopted Austria's strategy. The original draft had been altered to emphasize the aggressiveness of the Franco-Russian combination and to highlight the unreliability of Romania as an ally. Russia's policy was 'immanently aggressive'; its aims were 'constant and far-seeking'. In spite of Russia's unprecedented expansion over the past two centuries, it still lacked access to the sea—which explained why it aimed to unite the Balkan states against Austria. Germany must see that if Russia succeeded in isolating Austria and detaching it from the Triple Alliance it would be impossible for Germany to resist Russia's ultimate political and economic supremacy. The extraordinary growth in Russian armaments, its extensive preparations for war, and the building of strategic railways were all aimed at Germany, not Austria. And Russia could continue to count on French support, given their desire to avenge the lost war of 1870–1 and recover the lost provinces of Alsace and Lorraine.

Austria could proceed vigorously against Serbia only with the support of Germany. But securing this support was not the only challenge confronting Berchtold: he could not act against Serbia without Tisza's support.

★

The peculiar constitutional arrangements of the Dual Monarchy had made Hungary an equal partner in the empire since 1867. Without its approval, Austrian military action was impossible. At the same time that Berchtold was revising the Matscheko memorandum and drafting Franz Joseph's letter to Wilhelm, Tisza was warning against any peremptory step.[29] Austria-Hungary should not run the risk of being considered by the entire world as 'the disturbers of peace' and he would refuse to take any responsibility for such a policy.

Tisza was no soft-minded peace-loving pacifist. He was a smart, stern, tough-minded Calvinist who had no fear of pursuing controversial or unpopular policies. After studying at universities in Berlin, Heidelberg, and Budapest he was elected deputy to the Hungarian chamber of deputies

Count István Tisza (1861–1918); minister-president of Hungary (1903–5, 1913–17)

in 1886, at the age of 25. By 1903 he was leader of the Liberal Party and minister-president. He left politics briefly when his party was defeated by a coalition of opposition parties, but returned in 1910 after reconstituting the Liberal Party as the 'Party of Work' and by 1912 was again minister-president. Between 1912 and 1914 he fought several duels, wounding a number of opponents severely with his sabre. He had established an iron grip in Hungarian politics, and it would be impossible for Berchtold to take any initiative without his support.

In Vienna they were aware that Tisza was opposed to acquiring any Serbian territory. The Serbs were already too numerous and to add to their number would energize the demands for a 'trialist' federation in the monarchy—which would reduce Hungary's role. But Tisza also feared the growing strength of Russia in the Balkans—particularly its appeal to the sizeable Romanian minority within Hungary. He had laid out his concerns and his suggestions for Franz Joseph in a memorandum in March 1914.[30] He warned that a Balkan league under Russian leadership might act as the catalyst for a world war—and losing such a war would spell the end of the Dual Monarchy. So Austria-Hungary must convince Germany that the two empires shared identical interests in the Balkans. Together they should support Bulgaria, which would check Romania, lead to a reconciliation with Turkey and Greece, and isolate Serbia. Russia's plan to encircle Austria-Hungary would fail. Matscheko's June memorandum built on the foundation laid down by Tisza in March.

The Hungarian minister-president made it clear that he was not opposed to war, but to the risks involved in going to war in unfavourable circumstances. They could easily find a pretext for declaring war whenever they wanted, once they had succeeded in creating a 'diplomatic constellation' that would alter the military balance in their favour. Any energetic Austrian policy in the Balkans required German assistance, and this could not be assured until the kaiser's well-known inclinations to prefer Serbia over Bulgaria were overcome. Only when Bulgaria became an ally and Romania made public its membership in the Triple Alliance could Austria-Hungary risk war.

Tisza shared the popular social-Darwinist views of relations among states. He wrote in an essay 'From Sadowa to Sedan' that there are some territories that are within the sphere of interest of several states. 'For such territories, world history knows only one solution, force, until this solution leads to a final result that forces the weaker adversary to reconciliation and to the appropriate modification of its aspirations.'[31] He was prepared to fight—if the conditions were right.

★

Days after the assassination the question remained: would the most powerful men in Austria-Hungary seize the opportunity to 'solve' the Serbian problem once and for all? How far would Franz Joseph, Berchtold, and Tisza go? Berchtold told Conrad that he had drafted a memorandum for the emperor to send to the kaiser dealing with the 'whole array' of Balkan questions. He asked the chief of the general staff to provide him with a note illustrating the military consequences that would arise from Romanian neutrality—and possible hostility—in a European war.[32]

Conrad's reply was discouraging. Romania's neutrality would be equivalent to the loss of twenty divisions—about 400,000 men. If Romania joined
their enemies the cost would double to forty divisions and 800,000 men. He
explained that the Austro-Hungarian army was to bear most of the burden
in fighting Russia, to enable Germany to win a swift and decisive victory
against France. But Austria-Hungary's only hope of success depended on
the assistance of Romania. If they could no longer count on Romania it
would be necessary to erect permanent fortifications in order to prevent an
unhindered invasion of Transylvania. What they needed was an 'open treaty
of alliance' binding Romania to the Triple Alliance.[33]

Conrad's concerns affirmed Tisza's reservations. Unless Germany could
find a way to compel Romania to come out publicly as a member of the
Triple Alliance, Austria-Hungary would have no choice but to embark on a
long-term programme of fortifying the frontier between Hungary and
Romania. There seemed to be no prospect of defeating Russia without the
cooperation of Romania.

★

Romania was one issue flagged by Tisza. Proving the complicity of the
Serbian government and officials in the assassination was the other.

By Thursday, the 2nd of July, a preliminary police investigation into
the assassination had identified the seven principal conspirators. Six of them
had been taken into custody (Mehmedbašić having managed to escape).
Interrogations of the prisoners already indicated that they could be linked to
highly placed men in Belgrade. And from Belgrade the Austrian military
attaché was sending reports linking the conspiracy to Tankosić and Dimitrijević (Apis) and to the *Narodna Odbrana*. The pieces of the puzzle seemed
to be fitting into place.

Any decisive action against Serbia still depended on the support of
Germany. And both the German ambassador in Vienna and the acting
secretary of state in Berlin had advised caution in the immediate aftermath
of the assassination. When Berchtold met with Tschirschky again on
Thursday he argued that Austrian and German interests alike demanded
action against Serbia's systematic intrigues against the monarchy. Tschirschky
tried to assure him that Germany would stand by Austria, but Berchtold
complained that in spite of such assurances Berlin had not always supported
him in the past. The ambassador, speaking privately, told him that this was
because Vienna was 'always expounding ideas, but had never formed a

definite plan of action'. If Austria were to do so now, Berlin would make
Vienna's cause 'its own'. But Austria first had to be clear how far it intended
to go and what it proposed to do with Serbia afterwards. And before
proceeding they had to be certain of Romanian and Italian support.

Berchtold dismissed the notion that much could be done to guarantee the
support of the Romanians: they had, after all, attacked 'defenceless Bulgaria'
against the interests of Austria, and Germany had given him to understand
that he must keep quiet about it. He asked Germany to use its influence over
Romania 'when we, to save the integrity of the monarchy, strike a blow
against Serbia'.[34]

Tschirschky agreed with Berchtold about Romania but insisted that Italy
be consulted before any action was taken that might lead to war. Berchtold
replied bluntly and clearly: if they were to consult Rome the Italians would
certainly ask for compensation—probably Valona (Vlore), the Albanian
port city opposite Brindisi (and once part of the Venetian empire). He
expected the Germans to explain to the Italians that Austria would be
fighting for its very existence and that the terms of the Triple Alliance did
not justify any demands for compensation.

The emperor himself intervened. In a long conversation with Tschirschky,
Franz Joseph expressed his fears of Russian-supported Serbian expansionism,
his belief that Romania could no longer be counted upon as an ally, and his
fears that Austria faced 'a very dark future'. It seemed that he was to be
granted no peace during the last days of his life.[35] He trusted that the kaiser
would understand the dangers that Austria was now facing. The only
glimmer of hope that he perceived was the improved relations between
Britain and Germany—and consequently between Britain and Austria.

Tschirschky quashed even this optimistic supposition. It was most
unlikely that the British could be parted from their French and Russian
friends any time soon. Probably the best they could hope for was a gradual
improvement in relations.[36] Tschirschky continued to throw cold water on
the idea of Austria undertaking bold action against Serbia. Romania must be
handled; Italy must be compensated; Britain was unlikely to separate from
France and Russia.

The kaiser was incensed when he learned that his ambassador was
counselling caution and restraint. When he received a copy of Tschirschky's
report of his 30 June conversation with Berchtold he demanded to know
who had authorized him to make such remarks. 'It is none of his business.'[37]
How the Austrians responded to the outrage of Sarajevo was entirely their

own affair. The ambassador was to drop such nonsense: the Serbs must be dealt with decisively and immediately.

Tschirschky did not yet know of the kaiser's reaction when he sat down between midnight and 1 a.m. on 2–3 July to compose a report on his conversation with Franz Joseph. As he did so, he could hear a great crowd demonstrating in front of the Russian embassy. Eventually dispersed by the Viennese police, the mob marched off, singing the Austrian national anthem and the '*Wacht am Rhein*'.

★

The bodies of the archduke and duchess arrived in Vienna on the evening of 2 July. They were to lie in state in the Hofburg Palace until a requiem mass was conducted on the 4th. They would then be transported to their final resting-place in the chapel at the archduke's castle at Artstetten. In the meantime, marauding bands of Croats and Muslims continued to attack Serb properties in Bosnia—the mobs sometimes waving Austrian banners and portraits of the emperor. Martial law was declared throughout the entire province.

These developments barely seemed to register with the so-called 'Triple Entente'. When the French cabinet met for the first time following the assassination on Tuesday, the 30th of June, the situation arising from Sarajevo was barely mentioned. Raymond Poincaré did not alter his plans to attend a number of public functions in which he was expected to participate in his ceremonial role as president of the French republic. After offering expressions of regret and condolence for the outrage and the deaths, Britain, France, and Russia appeared content to sit back and wait for events to unfold.

It was not that they expected nothing to happen. The British ambassador in Vienna, Sir Maurice de Bunsen, reported that it was 'not unlikely' that 'great tension' would arise between the Dual Monarchy and Serbia.[38] 'Moritz' de Bunsen, the grandson of a Prussian minister to Britain, was a veteran diplomat, having entered the service in 1877 following his time at Rugby and Christ Church, Oxford. It had taken him almost thirty years to rise to the rank of ambassador (to Spain) at the age of 54 in 1906, and he had been in his post at Vienna for less than a year. He reported privately that he had heard the army was straining at the leash to go against Serbia, but he could not believe they would be 'let slip'.[39] Newspapers in Vienna and Berlin assumed that the conspiracy had been planned in Belgrade and they blamed the Serbian government for creating the atmosphere of political extremism that led to the crime.

In London, Paris, and St Petersburg the Serbian government was advised to proceed cautiously. The French government suggested that it should maintain an attitude 'of the greatest possible calm and composure'.[40] The Serbian government ought to restrain their press from treating the assassins as martyrs and inflaming opinion further against them in Austria and Germany. If everyone remained calm, a crisis could be averted.

Entente diplomats in Vienna discussed the possibility of war erupting. The Russian ambassador, Nikolai Schebeko, did not believe that the Austrian government would allow itself to be rushed into a war. He assured the British ambassador that Austria knew an attack on Serbia would compel Russia to intervene. A 'Serbian war meant a general European war'—a war for which Austria was not prepared. While the press might blame Serbia for the murders, the government could hardly be held responsible simply because the plot had been prepared on its soil, and 'he did not think the Austrian Government would be induced by a few violent articles in the press to act upon it'.[41]

De Bunsen was not so certain. Everything he heard suggested that the middle classes, the army, and even officials at the Ballhausplatz—the eighteenth-century building in which the Austrian foreign ministry was situated—were incensed against the Serbs. People of moderate and sensible views on foreign affairs were expressing the opinion that Austria had to show its strength by settling accounts once and for all with Serbia and 'by striking such a blow as will reduce that country to impotence for the future'. The French ambassador, Alfred Dumaine, while sharing these apprehensions, believed that the emperor would restrain those seeking revenge; Austria would probably not go beyond making threats.[42]

The apprehensions of the ambassadors did not seem to be shared outside of Vienna. In London, the permanent under-secretary of state for foreign affairs, Arthur Nicolson, doubted that Austria would undertake any 'serious' action. He expected the storm to blow over. In Berlin, the French ambassador, Jules Cambon, announced that it was his intention to take his vacation as planned for the last two weeks of July.[43] One week after the killings, by Sunday, 5 July, it was far from clear how the situation would unfold. Perhaps it would not become a crisis, perhaps it would just fade away.

Entente representatives were cautiously optimistic. It seemed likely that the Serbs could be persuaded to cooperate with the Austrian authorities in their investigation of the crime. The Serbian government was indicating that it was prepared to move against individuals or groups that had aided or encouraged the assassins. Germany appeared to be counselling caution and warning of the diplomatic complications that might arise with their allies if Austria acted without consulting them in advance of any bold step. It seemed likely that calmer heads would prevail in Vienna.

At the Wilhelmstrasse in Berlin, they seemed to share the opinion that the crisis would blow over, that 'it will not come to a war between Austria and Serbia'. Neither Russia nor France had any desire to start a war: they were both suffering from financial difficulties and were preoccupied with domestic issues. Britain also wished to avert a war: the times are past 'when she could leave the peoples on the continent to slaughter each other'.[44]

Any possibility that Austria could use the assassination to 'solve' its Serbian problem 'once and for all' depended on the support of Germany. Count Tisza had made it clear that he would not consent to any dramatic steps being taken against Serbia without a promise of such support. It was to determine the extent of German support that Berchtold, on 4 July, despatched his *chef de cabinet* at the foreign ministry, Count Alexander Hoyos, to Berlin on a special mission. He was to take with him the emperor's personal letter to the kaiser, along with the revised Matscheko memorandum.

The choice of Hoyos was indicative of where Berchtold now stood. Hoyos, 36 years old, and a diplomat since 1900, led a group at the Ballhausplatz widely referred to as the 'Young Rebels' for their promotion of an aggressive foreign policy as an antidote to the monarchy's apparent decline. That he came from a family of Magyar magnates would add to his credibility with Tisza.

Hoyos had been given some confidential advice from a German journalist several days earlier—just as Berchtold was revising the Matscheko memorandum and drafting the emperor's letter to the kaiser. Victor Naumann, an influential publicist, told Hoyos that in Germany's army and navy circles— and even in the foreign office—they regarded the possibility of a preventive war against Russia with 'less disfavour' than they had a year ago. And Wilhelm von Stumm, an important official at the Wilhelmstrasse, had told him when they met recently that Germany could have a war with Russia when it wanted to, and that the foreign office did not consider this to be impossible.[45] Hoyos found this encouraging.

Count Alexander von Hoyos (1876–1937); *chef de cabinet* to foreign minister of Austria-Hungary (1912–17)

Naumann urged the Austrians to seize the opportunity: the Monarchy was facing a question of 'life or death'. The crime of Sarajevo must not go unpunished. Serbia must be annihilated. Germany would then see whether Russia was willing to go to war over it. In Berlin they no longer counted on Romania as an ally and they were now prepared to bring Bulgaria and Turkey into the Triple Alliance. He assured Hoyos that the kaiser was horrified by the Sarajevo murder and would back Austria against Russia if he was approached in the right way. The kaiser believed that the monarchical principle was in danger, and his officials at the foreign office would not attempt to change his opinion because they regarded it as a favourable moment 'to bring about the great decision'. Naumann predicted that if Austria did not act decisively now it would be finished as a monarchy and as a Great Power.

Hoyos assured the German journalist that he shared his views. Austria must seize the opportunity to solve the Serbian question. It would be most valuable if they could be certain that Germany would 'cover our rear'. After reporting the conversation to the foreign minister, Berchtold decided to send Hoyos to Berlin on a special mission to hand over the emperor's letter to the kaiser and the revised Matscheko memorandum. He was not willing to entrust the delicate mission to the Austrian ambassador.

Berchtold did not trust Count László Szögyény-Marich, in spite of the fact that he knew Germany intimately, having served as ambassador there for over twenty years. Berchtold believed he was past it: Szögyény was

Count László Szögyény-Marich (1841–1916); Austro-Hungarian ambassador at Berlin (1892–1914)

72 years old, almost deaf, and had been scheduled to retire almost a year ago. The 'mental decline of this Nestor among our ambassadors', the foreign minister had told Franz Ferdinand, was bound to worsen over time.[46] But Szögyény was an affable, cultivated companion who enjoyed the patronage of Franz Joseph and had established himself as one of the few foreigners in Wilhelm II's inner circle. Even after all these years he still spoke German with a Hungarian accent, leading the kaiser to label him as 'the wrinkled gypsy'.[47] Perhaps his affability, as much as his age, made him suspect in Berchtold's eyes.

Hoyos arrived in Berlin on the morning of the 5th. After discussing with Szögyény the documents that he had brought with him, he met over lunch with the under-secretary of state, Arthur Zimmermann, acting in place of Gottlieb von Jagow—who was away in Switzerland on his honeymoon. While Hoyos and Zimmermann were meeting, ambassador Szögyény was meeting separately with the kaiser in Potsdam over lunch, where he presented Franz Joseph's letter.

Kaiser Wilhelm expressed some apprehensions. If Austria were to undertake severe measures against Serbia—which he expected them to do—it could lead to serious complications. Nevertheless, he authorized Szögyény to convey to the emperor that Austria could rely on the full support of Germany. Russia was bound to be hostile, but he had been preparing against this 'for years'. He did not believe that Russia was ready for war at the moment but would attempt to incite France and Britain against Austria and fan the flames in the Balkans. Even if it came to war with Russia, Germany would, the ambassador wrote, 'stand at our side'. He would regret it if Austria failed to seize the moment 'which is so favourable to us'.[48]

The kaiser's words would afterwards become legendary as the 'blank cheque'—even though there was no mention of a cheque, blank or otherwise. What he meant by standing at Austria's side and giving his 'full support' remained to be seen. The kaiser told the ambassador that he would have to discuss the situation with his chancellor before his assurances could be considered official.

Bethmann Hollweg was summoned from his estate at Hohenfinow to Potsdam where he and Zimmermann met with the kaiser that evening. They were joined by Falkenhayn, the Prussian minister of war and chief of the kaiser's military cabinet.[49] They discussed the possibility that the Russians might intervene, but concluded that this was unlikely: 'though friends of Serbia' the Russians 'will not participate'.[50] The sooner the Austrians moved against Serbia the better. The minister of war was not alarmed. Neither he nor the chancellor believed that the Austrians were 'really in earnest', even though the language they used sounded more resolute than in the past.[51] Falkenhayn wrote to the chief of the general staff—who was enjoying a spa vacation—that war was unlikely to arise. He departed for his annual vacation a few days later.

Bethmann Hollweg and Zimmermann were designated to continue the discussion with the Austrians the next day. In the meantime, the chancellor advised the kaiser to proceed as if the affair would remain a purely localized one, not requiring his personal attention. He encouraged him to depart for his annual North Sea cruise the next day.

Week Two: 6–12 July

A week after the assassination, by Monday, 6 July, it remained unclear whether there would be a crisis, uncertain what the next steps would be. Publicly, Germany attempted to create the impression that the world was unchanged: the kaiser departed on the *Hohenzollern* for his cruise. Behind the scenes, the ground was being cleared for more dramatic steps. When Bethmann Hollweg met with Szögyény and Hoyos on Monday he confirmed what the kaiser had indicated the day before: Germany would stand shoulder-to-shoulder with its Austrian ally.

Bethmann Hollweg usually managed to get along reasonably well with the kaiser—in spite of their starkly contrasting personalities. Where Wilhelm was bombastic, Bethmann Hollweg was reserved; where Wilhelm loved jokes and horseplay, Bethmann Hollweg was serious, solemn, and lacking any apparent sense of humour; Wilhelm loved the pomp and circumstance of ceremony and military display, while Bethmann Hollweg avoided the public eye as much as he could. But the kaiser recognized in Bethmann Hollweg a highly capable administrator who shared his distrust of democratic institutions, his dislike of Poles, and his disgust with socialists and socialism.[52] On the other hand, Bethmann Hollweg's professorial demeanour frequently annoyed the kaiser, who felt he was being lectured to—while his chancellor found distressing the kaiser's absence of tact, his frivolousness, and his tendency to make hasty decisions without careful consideration of the consequences. When his wife Martha died in May 1914 Bethmann Hollweg became even more serious, further withdrawing

Theobald von Bethmann Hollweg (1856–1921); chancellor of Germany (1909–17)

from the society life that the kaiser loved, and more inclined to adopt a fatalistic view of life. Although they continued to work closely together, the chancellor never established a warm personal relationship with the kaiser.

The Bethmann Hollwegs had risen from fairly humble beginnings. Theobald's great-grandfather Johann Jacob Hollweg—a baker—married Susanna Elisabeth Bethmann—the daughter of a Frankfurt banker—in 1780, and adopted the double-barrelled name at the same time that he assumed the directorship of her father's bank. In mid-century his grandfather had served as minister of culture during the reign of Friedrich Wilhelm IV. His father and uncle used the considerable wealth accumulated by the family to purchase a large estate of 3,000 hectares at Hohenfinow, 30 miles from Berlin, and ascended to the Prussian nobility.

Theobald, born in 1856, was educated privately by a tutor until the age of 12, when he was sent to an elite private school that offered the most rigorous classical education in Germany. Proving himself to be an exceptionally able student, he graduated from the University of Berlin with a doctorate in law at the age of 24 in 1880. He decided against a career in law, accepted an administrative appointment, and by 1899 had risen to the position of *Oberpräsident* of the Mark Brandenburg, the highest administrative office in Prussia. A year later his father died and Theobald inherited the estate.

In 1905 the chancellor, Bernhard von Bülow, appointed Bethmann Hollweg to serve as Prussian minister of the interior. His primary goals in the post were to counter the rise of socialist 'subversion' and to continue the 'Germanization' of Poland. Two years later he was promoted to vice-chancellor. When Bülow was forced to resign the next year he recommended that Bethmann Hollweg succeed him: 'neither as a thoroughbred nor as a jumper, but as a good plow-horse, plodding along slowly and steadily'.[53] The kaiser, somewhat reluctantly, agreed.

In office, Bethmann Hollweg's two greatest challenges were the kaiser and the Reichstag—the national parliament created by the constitution of imperial Germany in 1871. He bridled at Wilhelm's personal interventions into administrative and policy matters that the kaiser knew little about, and he found uncongenial the political manoeuvring required to manage the Reichstag. Elected by universal manhood suffrage and the secret ballot, the Reichstag was becoming increasingly difficult to deal with. A born administrator, Bethmann Hollweg attempted to govern from the centre, but depended on the Right for support. He found it increasingly difficult to pursue the kind of moderate, modernizing, reformist policies that he preferred.

Bethmann Hollweg also found it difficult to deal with Wilhelm II's dream of building a great navy. He regarded it as far more important that Germany, surrounded by potential enemies in Europe, should have a strong army. The price of building a great high-seas fleet was starving the army of the funds it needed, while challenging the British empire and pushing it closer to France and Russia. Until now Bethmann Hollweg pursued two goals in defence and foreign policy: building a stronger army and reaching an accommodation with Britain by offering an arrangement in which Germany recognized British naval superiority in exchange for a promise of neutrality in the event of a European war. At the time of the assassination Bethmann Hollweg was actively engaged in promoting agreements with Britain concerning the future disposition of the Portuguese colonies in Africa and over the future of the 'Berlin to Baghdad' railway in the Middle East.

Everyone expected the German chancellor to proceed carefully. For seven years he had attempted to restrain the kaiser's inclinations to react suddenly and emotionally to international events. Although Bethmann Hollweg believed that Germany needed its 'place in the sun' and shared the Darwinist belief that growing organisms must expand or die, he preached caution at every turn. As he told the kaiser's son, the crown prince, 'In any war which is unleashed without compelling reason, not only the Hohenzollern crown but the future of Germany is at stake. . . . to rattle the sabre at any diplomatic entanglement without having honor, security, or the future of Germany endangered is not only bold beyond reason, but criminal.'[54] How then, would this circumspect, cautious, and careful man react to the proposals brought by Hoyos from Vienna to Berlin?

★

Acting upon the kaiser's instructions, the chancellor told the Austrians that Germany agreed with their argument that Russia's plan for a 'Balkan league' threatened the Triple Alliance and that they should attempt to induce Bulgaria to join them. He would therefore authorize the German minister in Sofia to open negotiations with the Bulgarians in coordination with the Austrians. He would also instruct the German minister in Bucharest to inform King Karl of the negotiations and to advise him to stop the 'Romanian agitation' against Austria. He would leave Austria to decide how to proceed with Serbia, but the Austrians 'may always be certain that Germany will remain at our side as a faithful friend and ally'.[55]

Bethmann Hollweg pressed Austria to act quickly. The moment was favourable for solving their Balkan problems. How long this might last was uncertain. Questions remained: how far might Russia go in defending Serbia? would the French encourage the Russians to support the Serbs? where would the British stand? Without any tangible interests of their own in the Balkans, would the British restrain the Panslavist sentiments of the Russians?

★

The German ambassador in London, Prince Lichnowsky, had been brought out of retirement specifically for the purpose of improving relations with Britain. The German decision to build a high-seas fleet; the kaiser's inflammatory telegram to President Kruger of the Transvaal encouraging Afrikaners to stand up to British imperialism; German sabre-rattling at the time of the first Moroccan crisis; the competition with British commercial interests in building a 'Berlin to Baghdad' railway—all these things had gradually embittered Anglo-German relations.

When in 1912 Bethmann Hollweg had proposed to appoint an official at the Wilhelmstrasse, Wilhelm von Stumm, as ambassador in London the kaiser had refused. 'No! He is far too *afraid* of the English! And hates my Fleet!' He would only appoint someone 'who has *My* trust, obeys *My* will, carries out *My* orders'.[56] The kaiser believed he knew someone he could trust.

Prince Karl Max Lichnowsky was born in 1860, the son of the fifth Prince Lichnowsky. The family estates in Silesia and Austria had made them rich: their holdings were fertile and contained rich deposits of coal. The young

Karl Max, Prince von Lichnowsky (1860–1928); German ambassador at London (1912–14)

prince entered military service in the exclusively aristocratic *Leibgardehusar-enregiment* at the age of 22, but within a year he moved to the foreign ministry. A succession of minor diplomatic postings soon followed, during which time he came to be patronized by Prince Bülow while serving under him at Bucharest—when it was widely believed that he had become Princess Bülow's lover.

Although the family possessed considerable holdings in Austria (over 4,000 hectares around Grätz) Lichnowsky had little respect for the Austrian system. It was too feudal and too clerical for his tastes. He complained that Austria was ruled by 'a pitiable old man and his unruly nephew and a Roman-Slavic priesthood'.[57] Although the Austrians neither loved nor understood the new German empire, he believed that they were essential to Germany's political and strategic position in Europe. Fortunately, as Lichnowsky saw it, the Austrians had little choice but to continue to rely upon their alliance with Germany, giving the Germans a relatively free diplomatic hand.

Lichnowsky returned to Berlin and by 1900 was a councillor in the political division—one of six or seven working directly under the secretary of state. His most important role was as head of the appointments board, where he was responsible for testing candidates for admission to the service and for advising the chancellor on appointments to legations and embassies. When he failed to be appointed to an ambassadorship of his own after several years at the Wilhelmstrasse, he took indefinite leave from the service. He had come into his inheritance in 1901 and became a very wealthy man. A few years later, at the age of 44, he married Mechtilde, the Countess of Arco-Zinnebe—a direct descendant of the Habsburg empress, Maria Theresa. When she gave birth to a son the following year, the kaiser insisted on being made his godfather, and the son was named Wilhelm.

For years they led lives of cultured aristocrats, dividing their time between Berlin and their estates. Mechtilde established herself as a distinguished writer of novels, plays, and assorted works. He devoted himself to his books (his library at Grätz contained over 15,000 volumes). They were connoisseurs of good food and conversation, holding lavish dinner parties where writers, artists, scholars, and businessmen mingled with nobles and aristocrats. Still, Lichnowsky hoped that he would return to the diplomatic service and an appointment as ambassador one day. When the Paris embassy was vacated in 1910 he expected to receive the appointment. When it failed to come he petitioned to be granted formal release from the service.

Then, in 1912, Lichnowsky published an article on Anglo-German relations. He was responding to a former British prime minister and foreign secretary, Arthur Balfour, who had written that a large fleet was not necessary for Germany, whereas for Britain it was a matter of life and death. Lichnowsky replied that Germany could not leave itself defenceless against the British navy and that the existence of the German fleet was a fact of life that the British would have to learn to accept. It was this article that convinced the kaiser that he had found his man for the embassy in London. But Bethmann Hollweg, as staid and conservative as always, argued that Princess Lichnowsky was unsuitable for an ambassador's wife: 'she is consumed by her interests (almost exclusively art, music, and more especially the theatre), has little understanding of her husband's social position, gives him no support in this direction and therefore has not known how to establish herself in either the Berlin or the Silesian society'.[58] The kaiser, as usual, prevailed and after some delay Lichnowsky was appointed ambassador in October 1912.

Lichnowsky immediately set out to establish friendly relations with the leading statesmen of Britain. He and Mechtilde were soon on good terms with the prime minister and his wife—Herbert and Margot Asquith—and were frequent weekend guests at the Asquith country house on the Thames. He quickly formed a warm and respectful relationship with the foreign secretary, Sir Edward Grey. And Lichnowsky went to great efforts to be accepted into court circles and the society of English businessmen.

Within two years of his appointment to London, Lichnowsky believed that he had accomplished much that he had aimed for. By midsummer 1914 Anglo-German relations seemed to be much better than they had been for years. The two states had cooperated in the Balkans during the wars of the previous year, had come to an arrangement over the future disposition of Portuguese colonies in Africa, and settled their differences over the 'Berlin to Baghdad' railway. He was feeling pleased and optimistic about their relations in the future.

Lichnowsky returned to London from a brief vacation in Germany on Monday, 6 July and proceeded immediately to the foreign office. Acting on instructions from Bethmann Hollweg, he arranged to meet with Sir Edward Grey that afternoon in order to persuade him that Britain and Germany should agree to 'localize' any dispute between Austria and Serbia.

Lichnowsky told Grey that Austria would be justified in demanding satisfaction from the Serbian government as it had already been shown that Belgrade had provided support to the conspirators. Although he did not yet know what form this satisfaction would take, it was likely to result in 'strained relations' between Vienna and Belgrade. He hoped that Grey would use his influence at St Petersburg to induce the Russians to persuade the Serbs to acquiesce to the Austrian demands. He told Bethmann Hollweg that Grey appeared to understand that Austria would have to adopt severe measures and had promised to 'keep in touch' with Germany on this question.[59]

Lichnowsky had also attempted to paint a picture of the 'uneasiness' that had arisen in Berlin as a result of Russia's enormous armaments programme and the construction of strategic railways. Grey replied that he did not believe that Russia had any warlike intentions. On the 'delicate subject' of Anglo-Russian relations the ambassador assured the foreign secretary that he did not doubt his word that no secret political agreement existed between Britain and Russia. But he was concerned by rumours of an Anglo-Russian naval understanding for mutual cooperation against Germany in the event of war. Perhaps, Lichnowsky suggested, although there may be no political agreements or binding compacts, 'certain discussions' might be going on between their naval authorities?

In fact, Lichnowsky knew that these were more than rumours: a German spy working in the Russian embassy in London had transmitted to Berlin the correspondence of the Russian ambassador. They knew that Anglo-Russian naval conversations had begun. Lichnowsky warned that a naval agreement would strengthen the tide of nationalistic feeling in Russia and the clamour in Germany for increased armaments. It would also make it difficult for the German government to oppose demands for exceeding the limits on naval expenditure that were currently fixed by law. In other words, the Anglo-German naval race, currently quiet, and apparently won by Britain by the summer of 1914, might begin anew if an Anglo-Russian naval partnership were to be formed.

Grey gave a rather different account of the same conversation. The ambassador had told him—privately—of the anxiety and pessimism that he had found in Berlin. Lichnowsky believed the Austrians intended to do 'something' and that it was not impossible that they might undertake military action against Serbia. Surely, Grey replied, the Austrians were not thinking of taking Serbian territory? No, Lichnowsky said, they would not know what to do with it if they did. But they did believe that they must have some compensation, and that Serbia must be humiliated. This put the

Germans in an exceedingly difficult situation: if they advised the Austrians to do nothing they would be accused of always holding them back and failing to support them; but if they let events take their course there was the possibility of very serious trouble.

According to Grey, Lichnowsky recounted Berlin's fears of the expanding Russian army and the possibility of an Anglo-Russian naval agreement. The ambassador worried that the feeling was growing in Germany that it was better not to restrain Austria and 'let the trouble come now, rather than later'.[60] Although Lichnowsky did not share the belief that Russia was ill-disposed towards Germany, he had found Bethmann Hollweg pessimistic and he wanted to raise these delicate matters privately with Grey at the first possible opportunity.

Grey was now forewarned that Germany was inclined to support the humiliation of Serbia by Austria. But just how far were the Austrians prepared to go? Lichnowsky warned that they might take military action, but he did not believe they would attempt to partition Serbia. While he suggested to Grey that Germany would support Austria, he gave no hint what form this might take.

Lichnowsky had returned to London full of anxieties. He tried to get an old friend, the Romanian ambassador, to convince the Romanian government to convince the Serbs to accept without quibbling any demands made by Austria. Once the crisis had passed and the danger of war had disappeared, the terms could then be quietly revised in Serbia's favour.[61]

Bethmann Hollweg did not trust his ambassador. 'Lichnowsky', he told his closest confidant, 'is much too gullible. He allows himself to be taken in by the English.'[62] Bethmann Hollweg outlined his many worries to Kurt Riezler, his favourite *Legationsrat* (counsellor) in the imperial chancellery (the bureau that the chancellor used to coordinate the various administrative branches of government). The Anglo-Russian naval talks, and the possibility that this could lead to a landing in Pomerania, frightened Bethmann Hollweg. Russia's military power was growing rapidly; its construction of railways could make Germany's strategic situation untenable. In the meantime, Austria was becoming weaker and could not be counted upon to go to war for the sake of a German problem. If Germany let Austria down over Serbia it could go over to the western powers, 'whose arms are open'. Germany would then lose its last dependable ally.

★

What would the Austrians make of Germany's assurances of support? In Vienna on 7 July Berchtold invited the German ambassador to meet with him, Tisza, Count Karl Stürgkh (the Austrian prime minister), and Hoyos, just returned from his mission to Berlin. Hoyos read a memorandum that he had drawn up following his meeting with Zimmermann, along with one from Szögyény. Berchtold asked Tschirschky to convey to both the kaiser and the chancellor his sincere gratitude and that of the Austrian and Hungarian premiers for the position Germany had adopted, 'so clearly in accord with the bonds of alliance and the dictates of friendship'.[63]

But Berchtold and Tisza also stressed that what Hoyos had said to Zimmermann should be regarded only as his personal opinion—particularly his comment that Vienna was considering a partition of Serbia. The ultimate aim of Austria's intentions in Serbia remained unknown. Tschirschky complained that a ministerial conference to be held later that day would be devoted to a discussion of measures to be taken within Bosnia and Herzegovina.

Tschirschky was being misled. Afterwards, Berchtold reported to Franz Joseph that the ministerial conference had discussed 'the question of an eventual warlike action against Serbia'.[64] In fact, in the 4,000-word memorandum on the meeting, almost no consideration was given to the question of internal measures to be taken in Bosnia and Herzegovina.

In theory the emperor should have presided over meetings of the Austro-Hungarian common ministerial council, which brought together the two prime ministers and the three 'common' ministers shared by Austria and Hungary who were responsible for foreign policy, war, and finance. In practice, Franz Joseph normally delegated the responsibility of chairing these meetings to his foreign minister. On the morning that the council was due to meet the emperor left Vienna for his retreat at Bad Ischl—which was five hours by train from Vienna—where he would remain for the next three weeks. From now on, Berchtold would have to make the journey by train to have Franz Joseph ratify any decisions made by the council.

The primary concern at the meeting of 7 July was the issue of war with Serbia. The earlier rift between Berchtold and Tisza now turned into one between Tisza and the common ministerial council as a whole. As Berchtold tactfully expressed it, a 'perfect identity of opinion' between the emperor's ministers could not be reached.

Berchtold chaired the meeting. The premiers of Austria and Hungary were present, along with Biliński (minister of finance and responsible for the administration of Bosnia–Herzegovina) and Krobatin (minister of war). Hoyos, back from his mission to Berlin only that morning, took the minutes. Berchtold proposed that they ought to decide whether the moment had come to render Serbia's intrigues harmless forever (*für immer unschädlich zu machen*). As such a decisive step could not be taken without diplomatic preparation, he had consulted the German government. The result had been highly satisfactory: both the kaiser and the chancellor had promised Germany's support in the event of 'warlike complications' with Serbia. Berchtold did not believe that this would necessarily involve them in a war with Russia. If the monarchy failed to act decisively now, the Romanians and their own south Slavs would interpret this as a sign of weakness. Austria-Hungary must act now to prevent the further decline of its prestige as a great power.

Tisza agreed that the result of the judicial inquiry and the attitude of the Serbian press had increased the possibility of war with Serbia. But he would never consent to the kind of surprise attack suggested by Hoyos during his visit to Berlin. This would discredit them in the eyes of Europe and among all the Balkan states except Bulgaria, which—still reeling from its losses in the second Balkan war of the previous year, was too weak to offer effective help. He insisted that a diplomatic initiative must come before military action, that they must address demands to the Serbs—and only if these were rejected, then present them with an ultimatum. If their demands were accepted the monarchy would score a splendid diplomatic success and enjoy an immense increase in its prestige. If Serbia refused their demands, he would vote for war.

While Tisza was willing to reduce the size of Serbia, he was not prepared to annihilate it. Russia would fight to the death to save Serbia. Nor would he agree to annex any part of Serbia. In spite of Germany's encouragement, he did not believe war to be necessary at the moment—a war in which they would have to protect themselves against an attack from Romania. Better to seize this opportunity of securing Bulgaria and Turkey for the Triple Alliance as a counter to Serbia and Romania.

Berchtold disagreed. He complained that Austria's diplomatic victories in the Balkans—in the annexation crisis and in the creation of Albania—had not improved its position. Only by the exertion of force could Austria solve the fundamental problem: the propaganda for a Greater Serbia which was initiated from Belgrade and whose corrupting effects were felt in Austria 'from Agram to Zara'.

Stürgkh, the Austrian prime minister, agreed with Berchtold. General Potiorek had declared that internal measures in Bosnia and Herzegovina would have no effect unless they first dealt a forcible stroke against Serbia. It might prove impossible to hold the provinces unless they dealt promptly with Serbia. The events of the last few days suggested a solution 'at the point of the sword'. While he agreed with Tisza that the decision for or against war was not for the German government alone to decide, Austria should be strongly influenced by their promise of unreserved loyalty and their advice to act without delay. Tisza ought to consider this and recognize that a weak and hesitating policy now might jeopardize German support in the future. If a surprise attack was not feasible they would have to find some other way. He urged the council to decide whether or not it was absolutely necessary to have a war. The details of how to proceed could be worked out later, but if it were agreed that it was necessary to undertake a diplomatic initiative for international reasons, this should be taken with the understanding that it could only end in war.

Three options were on the table: an immediate surprise attack on Serbia; a diplomatic initiative designed to produce war with Serbia; or a diplomatic initiative in which Austria might be satisfied with the humiliation of Serbia.

Biliński, the minister responsible for Bosnia-Herzegovina, agreed with Stürgkh and Berchtold. In spite of his earlier differences with Potiorek, he argued that the general was in the best position to judge the situation. He agreed that a decisive conflict was unavoidable and that Germany could be counted on to stand on Austria's side. Unlike Tisza, he would not be satisfied with a mere diplomatic success: the Serbs were not amenable 'to anything but force'.

Krobatin, the minister of war, concurred: a mere diplomatic success would be interpreted as weakness. Better to go to war immediately because the balance of forces over time would change to Austria's disadvantage. Perhaps they need not even declare war: there had been none in either the Russo-Japanese or the Balkan wars. Austria should begin by mobilizing against Serbia as secretly as possible, then present an ultimatum while postponing a general mobilization until it became clear that Russia would act. Many reservists were engaged in bringing in the harvest, so delaying a general mobilization would be advantageous.

Tisza tried to convince the others that internal reform in Bosnia was both possible and necessary. The Bosnian police must be in an 'indescribable state' if they had permitted six or seven assassins—who were known to them—to place themselves along the route of the royal party, armed with guns and grenades. Perhaps Austria's position could be improved by adding Bulgaria to the Triple Alliance. In the 'present circumstances' a war would be a terrible calamity, whereas Russia might, in the future, be absorbed by difficulties in Asia.

Berchtold dismissed these arguments: Austria's enemies were preparing for a decisive conflict. Romania was assisting Russian and French diplomacy and could not be won back for the Triple Alliance as long as the Serbian agitation continued. The agitation for a Greater Romania followed the Serbian one for a Greater Serbia and would end only when Romania was isolated following the annihilation of Serbia.

Every minister except Tisza was convinced that a mere diplomatic victory was unacceptable. Even a glaring humiliation of Serbia would be worthless. Nevertheless, the strength of Tisza's political position and the absolute necessity of Hungarian support for any measure to be adopted convinced the ministers that they had to agree to his insistence that there be no mobilization until concrete demands had first been presented to Serbia. Once these were refused, an ultimatum could then be presented. Everyone but Tisza believed that such stringent demands should be made as to make refusal 'almost certain' and thus open the door to a military solution.

Tisza pleaded that while the demands should be stringent, they ought not to appear to have been designed to be impossible to accept. They must be framed in order to provide 'a lawful basis for our declaration of war'. He insisted that he be given the text of the note to be presented to Serbia— which must be composed with utmost care—before it was sent. If the council disregarded his point of view he would be forced to draw 'the obvious conclusion'.

★

The council adjourned for lunch. When they reconvened that afternoon they were joined by Conrad as chief of the general staff and by Admiral Kailer, representing the head of the navy. The council wanted to know from Conrad whether it was possible to mobilize only against Serbia at first, whether it was possible to retain sufficient troops in Transylvania to intimidate Romania, and where they would take up the fight with Russia. Conrad responded to these questions privately and asked that his answers not be recorded in the minutes.[65] The council discussed the disposition of forces, 'the probable course of a European war', and the demands to be made in the note to Serbia. Tisza stuck to his guns, insisting that the council consider carefully the points that he had raised. Although the council did not formulate precisely the conditions of the ultimatum to Serbia, it established a 'clear idea' of what was to be asked.

Berchtold summed up the situation: despite differences of opinion between members of the council and Tisza, agreement had been reached 'as the proposals of the Hungarian Premier would probably lead to war with Serbia'. Tisza and all members of the council recognized this. Berchtold would travel to Ischl tomorrow (the 8th) to report their discussions directly to the emperor. Tisza asked him to give a memorandum explaining his views to the emperor; Berchtold agreed to do so.

After the meeting concluded Berchtold wrote to Franz Joseph to ask that he be permitted to delay their meeting for a day to allow Tisza to compose his memorandum. He forewarned the emperor that the council had been unable to reach 'a perfect identity of opinion' because of Tisza's reservations. The rest of the council was unanimous in believing that they should utilize this opportunity 'for warlike action against Serbia'.

★

By the morning of Wednesday, the 8th of July, the government of Austria-Hungary—with the possible exception of Tisza—seemed prepared for war. At the Ballhausplatz, officials began to draft an ultimatum to Serbia. But a new impediment to quick action then surfaced. Conrad had discovered two days earlier that key military units at Agram, Graz, Pressburg, Cracow, Temesvár, Innsbruck, and Budapest were on leave and were not scheduled to return to barracks until 25 July. They had been released when landowners complained that they could not bring in the annual harvest without their help. To recall them publicly at this moment would be regarded as preparatory to war—when it was too early for such a signal to be sent.

The Austrian timetable was now altered to meet the demands of military logistics: 22–23 July was established as the earliest date by which an ultimatum could be presented to Serbia, because mobilization could not begin until the 25th. This was hardly the speedy response to the assassination that the kaiser had insisted was crucial when he had met with the Austrian ambassador in Berlin three days earlier. Berchtold suggested that the chief of the general staff and the war minister should take their vacations.

Other difficulties and uncertainties remained. Would the emperor agree with his ministers? Could Tisza persuade him to change course? Was Tisza willing to divide the monarchy when it stood on the brink of war? Would

Germany stand with Austria when the moment came? Could Serbia be isolated and the war localized?

Tschirschky offered an answer to one of these questions on the morning of 8 July. Having just received a telegram from Berlin, he met with Berchtold to report that the kaiser had instructed him to declare 'emphatically' (*mit allem Nachdruck*) that he expected Austria to act against Serbia. Germany, he said, would not understand if Austria neglected this opportunity.[66] In fact, negotiating with Serbia would be a confession of weakness which would damage Austria's position in the Triple Alliance and might influence German policy in the future. Berchtold explained the concerns raised by Tisza. If Franz Joseph agreed with the Hungarian prime minister, the foreign minister would propose that they present concrete demands to Serbia—and that these demands be of such a nature 'as to preclude the possibility of their being accepted'.[67]

At the Ballhausplatz they believed that Germany could be counted on. Count Johan Forgách was confident that they were 'completely at one with Berlin'.[68] The kaiser and the chancellor were determined as never before and were willing to back Austria against Russia, even at the risk of a world war. Forgách was elated. This was the opportunity to recover his reputation following an earlier debacle.

Forgách, as Austrian minister at Belgrade, had played a vital role in the Bosnian annexation crisis of 1908. He was one of the 'Young Rebels' who believed that establishing Habsburg dominance in the Balkans could cure Austria-Hungary's internal stagnation and provide a unifying force throughout the empire. But he had discredited himself the year after the crisis when, at what would become an infamous treason trial at Agram, it was discovered that he had supplied the court with forged documents. He had been sent into professional exile afterwards, occupying a minor post at Dresden, until he was given a chance to redeem himself when appointed chief of the political section at the Ballhausplatz in late 1913. After the assassination of Franz Ferdinand he had joined Matscheko in revising his memorandum of 24 June.[69] He combined with Hoyos and Baron Alexander Musulin (the Croatian head of the chancery) in arguing that Austria must launch a pre-emptive strike against Serbia. A *Flucht nach Vorne*—'flying into the eye of the storm'—was needed to prove that Austria was no longer weak and vacillating.[70] They preached this sermon in their evening meetings with Berchtold.

Berchtold used Germany's promises of support in trying to persuade Tisza to agree to act against Serbia. If they vacillated, Berlin would regard it 'as a sign of weakness' and Austria's position within the Triple Alliance would be damaged.[71]

Berchtold succeeded. Tisza was persuaded that they must act.[72] After recounting all of the reasons why he had opposed an immediate attack on Serbia in the council meeting, he assured the emperor that he would support an attack on Serbia if it rejected the 'just demands' made on it by Austria. He outlined briefly what he believed these should consist of. If war came, they should conquer Serbia and award parts of it to Bulgaria, Greece, and Albania. Austria itself should not participate in the partition except for some minor rectifications along the Serbian frontier. Nevertheless, if Serbia did yield to pressure and agreed to the Austrian demands, Tisza believed they would have to accept the diplomatic victory and the blow to Serbia's pride that this entailed.[73]

★

In Berlin Bethmann Hollweg worried that Austria would fail to act. He thought that 'the old emperor' in Vienna might decide against it and that an opportunity would be lost. He believed that they could win a war if Germany assisted Austria. And if a general war did not break out because the tsar decided against it or because France counselled peace, this might break the Entente apart.[74] In Berlin by Thursday they envisioned the crisis ending in either a successful war fought by the Triple Alliance against France and Russia or in a diplomatic triumph that could disrupt the Triple Entente. Both outcomes required a determined and energetic policy on the part of Austria.

Tisza, however, continued to oppose any attack on Serbia that had not been properly prepared by diplomacy beforehand. The suggestion made by Hoyos that Austria might attack Serbia immediately was 'unauthorized sabre-rattling'.[75] But Franz Joseph saw things Berchtold's way: he agreed that they should act against Serbia because failing to do so would 'discredit' Austria in German eyes.[76] Tisza's was now the only significant voice of caution in Austria-Hungary. In Germany no one of importance, not the kaiser, not the chancellor, not the war minister, not the chief of staff, made any effort to restrain Austria. Instead, they were all calling for an energetic and determined initiative.

When Gottlieb von Jagow, the German secretary of state, finally returned to Berlin from his honeymoon, he took up Bethmann Hollweg's line. It would have been difficult to differ, even had he been so inclined. The role of secretary of state was far more limited than that of foreign ministers in Austria-Hungary and Italy, Britain, and France. In Germany, he was an administrative appointment made by the chancellor, and answerable to him. He was not a member of the imperial council and ranked well below the chief of the general staff and the chief of the naval staff. German diplomats regarded ambassadorial appointments as more important and prestigious. But Jagow, although he came from a long line of Prussian nobles, was landless and with no prospects of an inheritance—which meant he was dependent on his official position for his income. Although ambassadors received a considerable stipend, no one could afford the expenses involved without a substantial private income. Thus, when Jagow, serving as ambassador at Rome, was offered the position as secretary of state in 1913, it meant a considerable improvement in his personal finances. And things got even

Gottlieb von Jagow (1863–1935); secretary of state of Germany (1913–16)

better in July 1914 when—at the age of 51—he married a woman with a considerable fortune of her own.

When Jagow met with the Italian ambassador on the 9th of July, he explained to him that Germany would indeed counsel moderation to Austria, but that Austria could not be too submissive when confronted by a Serbia 'sustained or driven on by the provocative support of Russia'. Neither did he believe that 'a really energetic and coherent action' on the part of Austria would lead to a conflict. He envisioned a diplomatic victory for the Triple Alliance.[77]

★

In London, the German ambassador was sketching a rather different picture of Germany's attitude. Lichnowsky confided to Sir Edward Grey that he had some hope that his government had succeeded in 'smoothing' Austrian intentions with regard to Serbia.[78] The ambassador failed to mention this in his report to Berlin. Instead, he detailed the reassurances that Grey had given to him concerning Britain's position: there were no secret agreements with France and Russia that entailed obligations on Britain in the case of a European war. Britain wished to preserve the 'absolutely free hand' that would enable it to act according to its own judgement and the government had assured parliament that it would not commit itself to secret liabilities.[79]

Lichnowsky, trying to maintain Anglo-German harmony, gave Grey the impression that Germany would exercise a moderating influence on Austria while conveying to Berlin the impression that Britain might restrain Russia.

Grey did not wish his position to be misconstrued. He told Lichnowsky that British relations with France and Russia remained intimate. Although there were no commitments that imposed obligations on Britain, he would not deny that conversations had taken place between the naval and military authorities on both sides—stretching as far back as the first Moroccan crisis of 1905—but these had absolutely no aggressive intent. As he anticipated that Austria might feel compelled to adopt a stern attitude toward Serbia, he was endeavouring to persuade Russia to adopt a peaceful view and assume a conciliatory attitude. Much would depend on whether Austria's measures would arouse 'Slavic sentiment' sufficiently to make it impossible for Russia to 'remain passive'. Lichnowsky concluded that Grey was confident, cheerful, and 'not pessimistic' about the situation.[80]

When Grey met with the Russian ambassador the day before, he had expressed his fears that the strength of public opinion might force the

Austrians to act against Serbia. Berchtold's position was weak and the Austrian government 'might be swept off their feet'. He had received reports from Vienna and Budapest detailing the feeling and the demonstrations against Serbia. He supposed that some discovery during the trial of the assassins might give Austria grounds for a charge of negligence against Serbia.[81] Count Benckendorff was more hopeful. He thought that the Germans could be counted upon to restrain Austria, and he did not believe they wished to precipitate a quarrel.

Grey worried that fear of Russia might influence Germany. He had information that the Germans were 'uncomfortable and apprehensive' regarding Russia, because they had learned of the Anglo-Russian naval conversations. He believed they imagined that there was more to these talks than was the case, that they might fear some coup was being prepared against them. He urged Russia to reassure Germany that this was not so. Benckendorff agreed: he was quite conscious of the apprehension felt in Berlin, and of the danger that this represented. Neither he nor Grey was aware that the Germans were encouraging the Austrians to respond quickly and vigorously to 'solve' the Serbian issue forever.

★

On Friday the 10th, Berchtold briefed Tschirschky on his meeting with Franz Joseph at Ischl on Thursday. The emperor wished to express his gratitude to the kaiser for his support and he shared Germany's opinion that they must put an end to the 'intolerable conditions' that existed with Serbia. The emperor favoured putting concrete demands to the Serbian government, and Berchtold now agreed that this would be preferable to the odium that Austria would incur if it were to attack without warning. Putting demands forward would place Serbia in the wrong and make it easier for the British and the Romanians to remain neutral.[82]

But what demands? Berchtold had a few suggestions: they might demand that an agency of the Austro-Hungarian government be established at Belgrade to monitor the Greater Serbia machinations; they might insist that some organizations be dissolved and some army officers dismissed. They might allow Serbia only forty-eight hours to agree. As it would be very disagreeable if the Serbs were to give in, Berchtold was considering what demands might be made that would be impossible for them to accept. What did they think in Berlin?

Berlin chose not to think anything. Jagow instructed Tschirschky to tell Berchtold that Germany could not take part in formulating the demands to be made on Serbia. Germany's guiding principle was established: a diplomatic distance would be maintained; nothing was to be done that might suggest Germany was behind Austrian policy. Jagow advised Vienna to collect material to demonstrate that agitation in Serbia threatened Austria's existence and that the whole of this should be published before submitting the ultimatum to Serbia.

At the same time, the kaiser was becoming irritated and agitated. He complained that it was taking the Austrians too long to act. Almost two weeks had passed since the assassination and nothing had been done. The Austrians had had 'time enough' (dazu haben sie Zeit genug gehabt) to formulate their demands—although he agreed that making demands was preferable to an immediate attack. But the Austrians should demand 'all' the items proposed by Berchtold—and these should be unambiguous.[83]

In fact, the kaiser suggested they go further: they should demand that the strategically valuable Sanjak of Novibazar, currently occupied by the Montenegrins, be handed over to them. This would begin 'the row' immediately: it would prevent the union of Serbia and Montenegro and stop Serbia getting to the coast.[84] There was no doubt where the kaiser stood: for immediate, vigorous action that would extinguish the Serbian threat to the Dual Monarchy and 'stop Panslav agitation for all time'.[85]

★

The Austrian chief of the general staff entirely agreed with the kaiser. Since the annexation of Bosnia and Herzegovina in 1908, when the Austrians had withdrawn their forces from Novibazar, Conrad had regretted the decision. He now looked forward to recovering the territory and wanted Berchtold to tell him whether war was a certainty or merely a possibility. He argued against protracted diplomatic negotiations: Austria's antagonists would gain valuable time for military preparations. 'Peaceful intentions should be feigned' only in order not to alarm their enemies. Austria should present an ultimatum with a short deadline; if Serbia's response was negative, Austria should mobilize immediately.[86]

Signs of an impending war were hard to hide. The French consul-general in Budapest reported that artillery and ammunition were being sent to the frontier.[87] Stocks on the Viennese exchange were falling precipitously. Tisza attempted to allay growing fears in Hungary that war was around the corner. He declared in the Chamber of Deputies on the 9th that no steps would be taken until the judicial inquiry had completed its investigations.

The British ambassador did not know what to make of all this. Nothing was really known about the government's intentions 'and it may well be that they will hesitate to take a step which might lead to a position of great international tension'. The Serbian minister assured him that he had no reason to expect a threatening communication would be addressed to his government.[88] Meanwhile, officials at the Ballhausplatz were preparing the list of demands designed to be unacceptable.

But the Austrians did face diplomatic difficulties. Germany seemed reliable, but how far could they go without the support of Romania and Italy? Conrad had made it clear that he regarded Romanian support—or at least neutrality—as vital to his war plans: a hostile Romania posed a strategic threat to Austria, which had no plans to defend itself against a Romanian attack in Transylvania.

Reports from Bucharest were not encouraging. The German minister reported on 10 July that King Karl, a Hohenzollern prince installed on the Romanian throne in 1866, had told him that he had twice recently indicated to the Austrians that he would be unable to carry out his alliance obligations to them in the event of war because of the hostile feeling in Romania against Austria. Hungary's treatment of its Romanian population had exacerbated the demands in Romania to unite all Romanians under one flag; the Romanian people, and most of their politicians, now regarded Austria, rather than Russia, as their primary enemy. King Karl refused to believe that the Serbian government was connected with the assassination.

In fact, the king complained that they seemed to have lost their heads in Vienna. Berlin should exert its influence at the Ballhausplatz to extinguish the 'pusillanimous spirit' (*kleinmütigen Stimmung*) in the ascendance there. He disparaged the political abilities of Berchtold and blamed the administrative mismanagement of the Austrians for their difficulties in Bosnia. While the Russian foreign minister recently assured him that the Russians had no intention of going to war, he also made it clear that they could not tolerate an Austrian attack on Serbia. In such an event, the king said, 'Romania would be under no further obligations.' Far from reaffirming the Romanian commitment to the Triple Alliance, practically every issue raised by King Karl pointed in precisely the opposite direction.

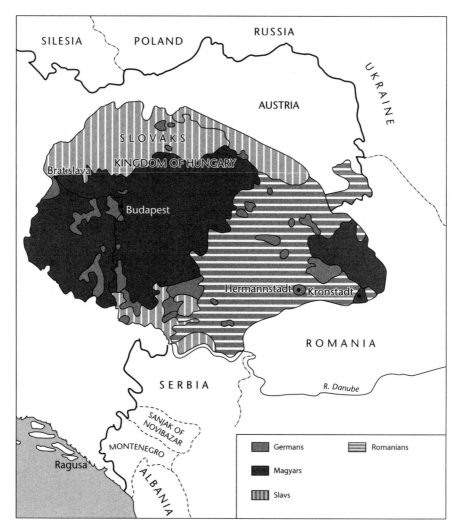

Map 4. Ethnic composition of Hungary

The only positive note struck in this conversation was the king's belief that St Petersburg might induce Belgrade to restrain the anti-Austrian movement in Serbia, because what had happened at Sarajevo 'might just as well happen at Petersburg tomorrow'. The king was prepared to exercise his influence at Belgrade in the same direction. The unscrupulous and disorderly nagging of

the press in Serbia kept public feeling constantly aroused, and it ought to be
stopped. But the press in Austria ought to be restrained as well.

Would the attitude of Romania give the Austrians pause? Their grand
design for a new Balkan League of Romania, Bulgaria, Turkey, and Greece
surrounding Serbia seemed to have little to sustain it. How far could they go
without Romanian support?

★

Even more problematic in Austro-German strategy was the role to be
played by Italy. Berchtold had been aware from the outset that any move
against Serbia was likely to produce an Italian demand for compensation in
the Balkans. Any such demand he was determined to resist. As early as 3 July
he insisted that Berlin must explain to Rome that Austria was fighting for its
existence. The stipulations of the Triple Alliance providing for compensation to be given to Italy if Austria expanded in the Balkans did not come
into effect because no Turkish territory was in question.

Berlin was reluctant to do as Vienna asked. Jagow explained to the
German ambassador in Rome that Germany had promised to support
Austria in taking whatever steps against Serbia that it deemed appropriate,
and to assist the Austrian alliance initiatives at Bucharest and Sofia. But, as he
expected that the Italian foreign minister, San Giuliano, would be predisposed to favour Serbia, the ambassador ought not to notify him of the steps
Germany was taking in support of Austria.

Italy's response was not encouraging. San Giuliano said that he was
advising Belgrade to be moderate and he expected his advice would be
followed. But governments of democratic countries 'could not be held
accountable for the transgressions of the press', and Austria should not be
unfair.[89] In other words, he rejected the Austrian argument that the Serbian
government was responsible for the assassination because of what had been
said in Serbian newspapers.

Could Italy be counted on? The answer depended almost entirely on San
Giuliano. The prime minister, Salandra, had little or no interest in foreign
affairs and was content to leave matters in the hands of his foreign minister.
The king of Italy, according to the Italian constitution of 1861, 'alone has
the executive power. He is the supreme head of the state, commands all the
armed forces by sea and land, declares war, makes treaties of peace, of
alliance.'[90] But in practice, the tiny, cynical, malicious, and sarcastic Vittorio
Emanuele III took little interest in politics and was usually content to leave

Vittorio Emanuele III (1869–1947); king of Italy (1900–46)

matters to his ministers. It would prove difficult to persuade the king to leave his home in Piedmont to come to Rome and its stifling summer heat, even at the height of the crisis.

The direction of Italian policy was left almost entirely in the hands of Antonino Paternò-Castello, the sixth Marchese di San Giuliano, a rich and distinguished Sicilian aristocrat. He was born in the baroque Palazzo San Giuliano in the town square of Catania in 1852, where his family—the most famous and powerful in the city—had lived since the early eighteenth century. A brilliant and hard-working student, he was elected to the Chamber of Deputies in 1882 at the age of 29—making him the youngest deputy elected. By the 1890s he had become a proponent of Italian colonial expansion, arguing that Eritrea could become Italy's Canada, Australia, or

Antonio, Marquis di San Giuliano (1852–1914); foreign minister of Italy (1910–14)

even the United States. If Italy failed to exert itself in the Mediterranean it might lose its position 'in the vast and world theatre of the great struggle for hegemony between the Slav race and the Anglo-Saxon race'.[91] San Giuliano, an anti-clerical Freemason, combined a progressive, rationalist outlook with a belief in the social Darwinist struggle among nations.

After the turn of the century San Giuliano developed an additional expansionist goal. After visiting Albania in 1901 he proposed a series of initiatives to compete with Austria in the Balkans: Italy should invest in banks, schools, and railways and should be prepared to spend money to promote Italian culture. Elected president of the Italian Geographical Society in 1906, he declared: 'In the grandiose struggle of the nations for prosperity and power Italy must not be the last...'.[92] That same year he was appointed ambassador to Britain.

His time in London convinced San Giuliano that Italy shared Britain's interest in maintaining an equilibrium in the Mediterranean. He founded an Anglo-Italian association. He saw no conflict between good relations with Britain and belonging to the Triple Alliance. After almost three years in London he served briefly as ambassador in Paris before being appointed foreign minister in 1910. Once in office, he continued to express Italy's loyalty to the Triple Alliance while warning that Italy could not risk war with Britain. He was determined to keep sentiment and nationalist aspirations outside of decision-making. Italy's choices should be made purely on the basis of rational self-interest.

By July 1914, however, San Giuliano was ill and in constant pain; he had suffered from gout for the last thirty years, and was now plagued by arthritis and troubled by a bad heart. He had to take sedatives to help him sleep, which he would then counteract with stimulant injections to keep him going during the day. Nevertheless, he continued to direct Italian foreign policy throughout the crisis and was practically free of restraint in pursuing the policy he believed to be correct. Berchtold was uncertain how to handle him. He expected to have the demands during the week of 12 July. But the German government, 'with whom we are acting in perfect harmony', agreed with him that the Italian government should not be informed.[93] Berchtold wondered whether it might be advisable to inform San Giuliano before the demands were presented—by a day or at least a few hours—to avoid giving offence.

Week Three: 13–19 July

Two weeks after the assassination, by 13 July, it was still far from clear how events would unfold. One of Austria's hopes was dashed. The special emissary sent from Vienna to Sarajevo to investigate the assassination reported that he had been unable to find any proof that the Serbian government was implicated in the crime.[94] The Austrians responsible for putting together the case against Serbia now had to refocus their efforts: instead of accusing it of complicity in the crime itself, they would have to demonstrate that Serbia had failed to live up to its promise of 1909 that it would live on good terms with the Dual Monarchy. This was going to make the public-relations battle in Europe much more difficult.

On the other hand, the one significant voice of restraint in Austria-Hungary had now changed its tune: Tisza had abandoned his initial opposition. He had begun to fear the consequences of appearing weak in German eyes by failing to act decisively and forcefully even when their support was promised. Franz Joseph had now made the decision to act and was attempting to pressure the Hungarian prime minister to join in a united front. On the 12th he urged Tisza to settle his differences with the other ministers as soon as possible. The emperor urged that the demands made on Serbia should be formulated 'so that no loophole would be possible'. A 'showdown' was necessary: there would be difficulties ahead, but things would never become easier.[95]

Franz Joseph, Berchtold, and Tisza had good reason to believe that the moment was opportune. The political situation and social unrest within the powers of the Entente made it seem unlikely that Austria would face a determined and united response. In Russia, most attention was focused on the strikes of working men that were gathering momentum in the major cities. Since the beginning of the year, sixteen new strikes had broken out every day, totalling 3,534. The police deemed 2,565 of these to be 'political'. Out of 242,000 industrial workers in St Petersburg, 180,000 were now on strike. In France the sensational trial of Madame Caillaux—the wife of an important cabinet minister accused of killing a journalist—was set to begin on 20 July and promised to absorb the attention of the press and the French people when it did. In Britain the politicians were most concerned that a civil war might break out in Ulster over the Home Rule Bill. The chancellor of the exchequer, David Lloyd George, declared in a speech that the situation in Ireland, combined with an impending strike by railwaymen, transport workers, and miners, presented the gravest situation that any British government had dealt with 'for centuries'.

Apart from a few murmurs of disquiet in London and St Petersburg there was nothing to suggest that the Entente intended to stand up for Serbia. British, French, and Russian diplomats counselled moderation on the part of Belgrade and advised the government to restrain its press. In the meantime, the Entente continued to wait for the Austrian response, hoping that it might be reasonable and measured. No one predicted that the Austrians were devising demands that no sovereign state could be expected to swallow.

The British ambassador in Vienna reported rumours that officials at the Ballhausplatz were proposing military action to uphold Austria's standing as a great power. He discounted them. Sir Maurice de Bunsen believed that Berchtold was 'peacefully inclined' and that it would be difficult for anyone to persuade the emperor to sanction 'an aggressive course of action'. Tisza's cautious pronouncements in response to questions in the Hungarian parliament suggested that moderate counsels were likely to prevail.[96] If Franz Joseph, Berchtold, and Tisza were all inclined in the direction of peace, the virulent opinions expressed in the right-wing press in Vienna would count for little.

In London on 17 July J. A. Spender, editor of the influential *Westminster Gazette*, published a long article advising Serbia to recognize that Austria-Hungary's anxieties were reasonable. Serbia would be well advised to do whatever it could to allay these anxieties without waiting for pressure that might lead to 'warlike complications'.[97] Officials at the German Foreign Office had the article circulated amongst the German press as a 'semi-official pronouncement' by one 'close to Sir Edward Grey'. There is every reason to believe that Grey agreed with Spender. He may have inspired the article.

★

In St Petersburg, however, the Russian foreign minister was taking a very different line. Although Sergei Dmitrievich Sazonov condemned the assassination, he also criticized the Austrian administration in Bosnia for permitting attacks on Serbians in its aftermath. He dismissed those loyal to the Austrian regime there as amounting to little more than a few 'Mohammedans and Catholics'. And he denied that the assassination was part of a plot to create a Greater Serbia for which the Serbian government could be held responsible. The assassination was perpetrated by immature young men acting on their own. The German ambassador believed that Sazonov's attitude could only be explained by his 'implacable [*unversöhnlichen*] hatred' of Austria-Hungary, 'a hatred which is absolutely clouding more and more all clear and calm judgement here'.[98]

Sazonov, who came from an aristocratic family of large landowners, was a cautious and careful career diplomat. He had entered the foreign ministry in 1883 at the age of 23 and served in a variety of posts before being appointed foreign minister in 1910. Since then he had established a reputation as being intelligent but unreliable. It usually took him some time to make up his mind on an issue—and then he was prone to change it. Sir Arthur Nicolson complained that 'one never knows precisely how far he is prepared to go' and he had warned in an earlier crisis that Britain would look foolish if

Sergei Dmitrievich Sazonov (1860–1927); foreign minister of Russia (1910–17)

it backed Russia 'and then found that Sazonov more or less deserted us'.[99] But to the Austrian ambassador on the 13th of July the foreign minister appeared adamant, angry and determined to reject Austria's argument that responsibility for the assassination could be traced to the government in Belgrade. Would his anger dissipate? Would he waver, change course, or back down?

★

On the same day that Berchtold received the report that the assassination could not be traced back to the Serbian government he broke the bad news to Tschirschky. Austria could not release the results of the inquiry; it could do no more than publicize the general trend of Serbian policy and the results it produced. Nevertheless, Berchtold resolved to act: he would try to reach agreement with Tisza the next day, and ask for Franz Joseph's authorization of the ultimatum to Serbia on the following day. They would then present it immediately to Belgrade—ideally, just hours before the French president and premier were scheduled to board the *France* for their visit to St Petersburg.[100]

Tisza disrupted Berchtold's plan. Although he agreed on the fundamentals of the ultimatum—including a forty-eight-hour limit for a response—he insisted that the final draft be submitted to the two governments before it was presented to Serbia. This could not happen before the 19th.

The alteration in the timetable meant that the ultimatum could not be presented before Poincaré and Viviani left France for St Petersburg. The Austrians now believed that it would be preferable to delay its presentation until after their visit had been completed: if they presented it while the French statesmen were in Russia this might be interpreted as intended to provoke them. And if Poincaré was able to discuss their response directly with the tsar, Russia might assume a more determined opposition.

In order to get Tisza's approval of the ultimatum, Berchtold had been forced to make more concessions. The Hungarian minister-president would not agree to present the ultimatum unless the council of ministers first approved a resolution that the monarchy was not striving to acquire territory; at most, there might be slight rectifications of the Austro-Serbian frontier. Moreover, although it could be taken as given that the note made war probable, Berchtold was forced to concede it was possible that a peaceful arrangement might be made if Serbia gave way in time. If Serbia were to agree to Austria's demands it would be a 'profound humiliation' (*tiefe Demütigung*) and a blow to Russian prestige in the Balkans.[101]

These changes altered the course of the crisis. Tisza now seemed convinced that abandoning any territorial gains, in addition to alleviating Hungarian opposition to the acquisition of more Slavs in the monarchy, might also mitigate hostile international reaction to the Austrian demands. Nor was it any longer taken as a given that the demands must result in war. Although this still seemed probable, the governments of Austria and Hungary now agreed that a humiliation of Serbia might be adequate. New uncertainties arose: would the promise of 'no territorial acquisitions' alleviate international opposition to Austria's demands? Would Serbia go so far in accepting the demands that Austria might be contented with its humiliation?

Berchtold, now envisioning a diplomatic resolution to the crisis, added a new issue: if Serbia accepted the demands, Austria would demand that it pay for the costs of their mobilization.

Tisza and Berchtold reported these changes directly to the German ambassador. Tisza went to see Tschirschky at the embassy; Berchtold asked him to come to the Ballhausplatz. Both were anxious to explain the delay in presenting the ultimatum; they wanted to assure Germany that they were now resolute and united. Tisza explained that he was now 'firmly convinced' that war was necessary: the monarchy must demonstrate its vitality and end the intolerable conditions it faced in the south-east. Tisza pressed Tschirschky's hand warmly and said 'Together we shall now look the future calmly and firmly in the face.'[102]

Berchtold guaranteed that the emperor would approve the ultimatum. Although it had been decided to delay its presentation, 'they could feel absolutely assured in Berlin that there was *not a thought of hesitation or uncertainty*' in Vienna.[103] In the meantime they would try to maintain the appearance of calm: Conrad went on vacation on the 13th, followed by Krobatin, the minister of war, on the 15th. In Berlin that evening Bethmann Hollweg confided that Germany would continue to support Austria even if it meant taking 'a leap into the dark'.[104]

On the same day, an enormous celebration was held in Belgrade to celebrate the life of the Russian minster, Nicolas Hartwig, who had died suddenly and unexpectedly a few days before. Known as an ardent Panslavist and advocate of Russian support for a Greater Serbia, rumours swirled around Belgrade that he had been murdered in an Austrian plot: he had suffered a fatal heart attack while visiting the Austrian legation. Prime Minister Pašić decided to give him a state funeral, and requested that he be buried in Belgrade. The Russian government agreed, but advised Serbia to prevent demonstrations against Austria. In his funeral oration Pašić praised Hartwig's commitment to Panslavism while praising the tsar as the 'mighty protector of all Slavs'.[105] Would he protect them? Where did Tsar Nicholas stand?

★

According to Berchtold, the tsar was the reason for delaying presentation of the ultimatum. It would be unwise to take this 'energetic step' at a moment when the 'peace-loving, reserved' Tsar Nicholas might be under the influence of those 'who are always for war': namely, Poincaré and Izvol'skii, the Russian ambassador at Paris.[106] The influence of Izvol'skii was especially worrying. He had been forced out of his position as Russian foreign minister because of his disastrous diplomatic failure during the Bosnian annexation crisis of 1908. Everyone who knew him—friends and foes alike—believed he was determined to avenge the humiliation he had endured. He regarded loyalty to the French alliance as essential to Russian foreign policy, and his appointment to Paris as ambassador in 1910 signalled the government's determination to strengthen the alliance.

In Berlin they were dismayed by the Austrian decision to delay, no matter what reasons were given for it. Although the secretary of state appreciated the reasons for it, he feared that public support for Austria would diminish in Germany and within Austria-Hungary itself as time went on, as they became further removed from the horror of the assassination. Still, Jagow did not propose to reconsider Austro-German strategy. Far from it. He decided that the moment had arrived to bind Italy fast to the Triple Alliance.

Jagow insisted that Vienna must reach an understanding with Rome. Italy had a right to claim compensation for any change in the Balkans that worked to the advantage of Austria. Minor concessions—such as ceding the port city of Valona in Albania—would not suffice. In strict confidence, he told Tschirschky in Vienna that only the acquisition of the Trentino was

Aleksandr Izvol'skii (1856–1919); Russian ambassador at Paris (1910–17)

likely to be adequate: 'This morsel would be delicious enough' to shut up Austrophobic public opinion in Italy. He recognized that surrendering the Trentino would be difficult for the Austrians, but they must ask themselves what value they placed on Italy's attitude, and how the price compared with gains to be won elsewhere. Italy's attitude would have considerable influence on Russia and, should 'a general conflagration' arise, Italy 'would be of great military importance for us'. He instructed Tschirschky to discuss this thoroughly and confidentially with Berchtold.[107]

Jagow knew he could count on Tschirschky to follow instructions; he was much less certain of Lichnowsky in London. The ambassador's reports were pessimistic, pointing out that British opinion had long favoured the principle of nationality, and that 'sympathies here will turn instantly and impulsively to the Serbs' if Austria resorted to violence. Approval for punishing the killers would not be translated into support for Austrian military action: this would be antithetical to the sensibilities of the nation 'and to the tastes of the (Liberal) Party'.[108]

Jagow was not pleased. He instructed Lichnowsky to use the assassination of King Aleksandar and Queen Draga by the 'Men of May' to show that the system of illegality and violence continued to rule in Serbia. The ambassador also seemed to be missing the point: they were concerned with 'a preeminent political question'. This occasion might be the 'last opportunity' for Austria to deal a death-blow to the menace of a Greater Serbia. If they failed to seize it Austria's prestige 'will be finished'—and Austria's 'status in the world' was of vital interest to Germany.[109]

Jagow, beginning to despair of Lichnowsky, attempted an end-run around the ambassador. On the same day that he tried to bring him to heel, he wrote to a Hamburg businessman, Albert Ballin, the director-general of the Hamburg-America (Hapag) steamship line, and a well-known, long-time proponent of good relations with Britain. Jagow told him that the rumours of Russia seeking a naval agreement with Britain were true. Although 'the good Lichnowsky' did not seem willing to believe it, Russia was seeking very broad military and naval cooperation with Britain. Whatever the details of such an arrangement—and even if the English 'with their unique casuistry' built in reservations—it was bound to encourage Russia's aggressive tendencies.

Jagow proposed to Ballin a tactic that might cause the Anglo-Russian negotiations to fail. Perhaps Grey could be scared off if the Liberal Party could be alarmed, or if some cabinet member were to object. Could Ballin use one of his many intimate connections 'with Englishmen in positions of authority' to this effect? Perhaps Ballin could write a letter warning of a new, inevitable, and intense naval scare arising from an Anglo-Russian convention. Ballin might also suggest that at the Wilhelmstrasse they were beginning to question whether the work of establishing a rapprochement with Britain might be ruined. The impression that this would create in Germany of an 'iron ring closing around us' might lead to serious consequences when added to the increasing strength of Russia and the aggressive tendencies inherent in Panslavism.[110]

Ballin proposed to go to London. Without informing Lichnowsky, he arrived on 20 July and immediately began discussions with his English friends.

Jagow was trying to buy off Italy and frighten off Britain. Bethmann Hollweg addressed France. He explained to the secretary of state for Alsace-Lorraine that Germany aimed to 'localize' any conflict between Austria and Serbia. He believed that the French, burdened by 'all sorts of troubles', could be expected to do everything possible to prevent Russia from interfering. Their task would be made easier if French nationalists were deprived of any cause for agitation in the next few weeks. Bethmann Hollweg, who had arranged that there would be no polemics in the German press against France, instructed the secretary of state to do the same at Strasbourg and to postpone any measures which could be used to stir up agitation in France. Keeping the French quiet would have 'a most favourable effect on the Franco-Russian alliance'.

By mid-July Germany's diplomatic goal seemed clear: it was, as Bethmann Hollweg put it, of 'the utmost importance' to localize the dispute.[111] Britain and France could be used to restrain Russia's inclination to intervene on Serbia's behalf. At the same time, they aimed to solidify the Triple Alliance by promising territorial compensation to Italy and keeping Romania in the fold. This may have seemed simple when viewed from Berlin, but the German diplomats responsible for carrying out this strategy in London, Rome and Bucharest saw things rather differently.

★

In London, Lichnowsky could barely conceal his contempt for Berlin's manoeuvres. Writing directly to Bethmann Hollweg, he dismissed the essence of the entire strategy. The assumption that the Serbo-Croat peoples could continue to be divided into a series of different entities—some of them under the rule of Austria, others under Hungary—was false.

Attempting to maintain the status quo was likely to lead to 'the total collapse of the political house of cards' on which it was erected. He doubted that there existed any plan in Vienna capable of solving the south Slav problem: this would require a political transformation for which they lacked the will and the leadership. The Austrians preferred to satisfy the needs of the moment and to postpone political difficulties in order to go along in 'the old groove'. A mere military 'correction' of Serbia could not solve the south Slav problem.[112]

Would Russia and Romania stand by and leave Austria a free hand to deal with Serbia? Lichnowsky believed Count Benckendorff, the Russian ambassador in London (who happened to be his cousin), when he gave his assurances that Russia had no desire to go to war with Germany. Whether this could be translated into Russian passivity in the case of an Austro-Serbian conflict was uncertain. But it was clear to Lichnowsky that Germany, which faced no imminent danger from Russia, and which could not hope to detach Britain from the Entente, was risking everything for the sake of what he regarded as 'mere adventure'. War with Serbia would neither solve the south Slav problem nor annihilate the Greater Serbia movement. So what was the advantage to Germany in acting as the guarantor of Austrian policy? Could they count on Austrian gratitude for their assistance? He very much doubted it.

The German ambassador in Rome, Hans von Flotow, was equally discouraging. San Giuliano had made it clear to him that neither he nor the Italian government would regard as legitimate any attempt to make the Serbian government responsible for people who were not its subjects. If Austria believed it could suppress the Serbian national struggle by adopting violent methods 'it would be quite impossible for any Italian Government to accompany her along this path'. The idea of nationalism and the principles of liberalism would deter Italy from supporting Austria against Serbia.

When Flotow attempted to challenge San Giuliano in order to get some hint on whether he might assist his ally in a crisis, the foreign minister refused to commit himself. The ambassador concluded that it would be extremely difficult, perhaps impossible, to persuade Italy to follow Germany's lead in supporting Austria.[113] San Giuliano, a champion of the Triple Alliance, predicted that if Austria succeeded in dissolving the Greater Serbia organizations they would simply go underground and transform themselves into secret societies. Not even the occupation of Belgrade could extinguish national aspirations of such strength. Austria was making its old mistake of believing in the supreme power of police measures.[114] Flotow advised Berlin that the only hope of getting Italy to support Austria–Hungary was by offering significant compensation. He suggested that Germany take the lead and put pressure on Vienna to reach a deal with Rome.

Flotow's attitude further complicated Austro-Italian relations: the Austrian ambassador in Rome, Kajetan Mérey von Kapos-Mére, suspected that his German counterpart might have revealed Austria's intentions to San Giuliano. 'This would not be the first instance that in delicate questions between us and Italy, Germany tries to render service to the latter at our expense.'[115] San Giuliano, suffering from a weak heart and a debilitating attack of gout, had decamped from the stifling heat of Rome to the coolness of the medieval hill town of Fiuggi, 50 miles to the south. A modern spa had recently been opened at the foot of the old town, based on the miraculous properties of the healing waters of the spring there—the *acqua di Fiuggi*. Flotow was staying at the same hotel, giving him direct access to San Giuliano.

It seems that Flotow, when Jagow had informed him of the general direction in which Austria intended to move against Serbia, had sketched the plan to the Italian foreign minister. San Giuliano had then informed his ambassadors that Austria intended to present unacceptable conditions to Serbia and would then use this as a pretext for an attack. Germany would support them. He encouraged Russia and Romania to express their opposition to this plan in Berlin and Vienna. Austrian code-breakers in Vienna had intercepted the message, and thus the Ballhausplatz knew that the information had gone to their enemies in Serbia and Russia.

Keeping secret the demands that Austria intended to make on Serbia was becoming increasingly difficult. The Russian ambassador in Vienna reported that when the judicial inquiry was concluded Austria would make 'certain demands on Belgrade'. The Austrians, he suggested, were counting on Russia not to intervene. He urged Sazonov to make it clear to the Austrians how Russia would react if they made demands on Serbia 'unacceptable to the dignity of that state'. When Sazonov forwarded this message to the tsar, Nicholas commented that in his opinion 'a state should not present any sort of demands to another, unless, of course, it is bent on war'.[116]

While this leak was happening in Rome, another occurred in Vienna. The British ambassador there was let into the secret by a retired Austrian diplomat, Count Lützow, formerly ambassador at Rome. Lützow had a

place in the country near de Bunsen's and a day after meeting with
Berchtold at the Ballhausplatz, he invited de Bunsen to come over for
lunch. Lützow asked him if he realized how grave the situation was: Austria
would not stand for Serbia's insolence any longer. A note was being drawn
up that would demand effective measures to prevent the manufacture and
export of bombs and to put down insidious and murderous propaganda
against the Dual Monarchy. Austria would not tolerate futile discussions. 'If
Servia did not at once cave in, force would be used to compel her.'[117]
Berchtold was certain of German support and he did not believe that Russia
would intervene. When de Bunsen suggested that he could not believe
Russia would stand by and allow Austria and Serbia 'to have it out in a
cockpit' Lützow insisted that Austria was determined to have its way this
time and would refuse to be deterred by anybody.

Sir Maurice de Bunsen (1852–1932); British ambassador at Vienna (1913–14)

De Bunsen concluded that this point of view coincided with what was being said in the Austrian press and by most of the people he met. He predicted that they would have an anxious time of it. Still, he could not bring himself to believe that Austria would resort 'to extreme measures'.[118]

★

On Saturday the 18th Jagow requested the exact particulars of the route to be taken by the kaiser, cruising on board the *Hohenzollern*, from the 23rd on. That was the date now set for presentation of the Austrian note at Belgrade. As Germany aimed to localize the conflict between Austria and Serbia 'we cannot afford to alarm the world by the premature return of His Majesty'. But after the 23rd the kaiser had to be within reach in case of unforeseen circumstances which might make important decisions—such as mobilization— necessary.

Jagow was not alone in his alarm. The Serbian prime minister had been warned by his minister in London on the 16th not to believe the 'calcu-lated peace-loving statements from Austro-Hungarian circles'.[119] A well-informed source told him that they were preparing to put enormous pressure on Serbia, which might result in an armed attack. On the 18th Pašić, who had received similar information from several other sources, sent urgent telegrams to Serbian diplomats at midnight, instructing them to request the assistance of foreign governments in restraining Austria. Serbia would not accede to demands it deemed to be unacceptable 'to any state which guards its independence and dignity'.[120] Reports from St Petersburg were not encouraging. The Serbian minister reported that Sazonov still did not believe that Austria would do anything. Serbia began to call up its reservists. The Austrian navy began to mobilize for a Balkan war.[121]

Although it was becoming more difficult to maintain the appearance of calm, Germany tried to do what it could. Jagow arranged to have a newspaper article on the Austro-Serbian situation published in the *Nord-deutsche Allgemeine Zeitung* on Sunday the 19th. This was meant to be reassuring, to suggest that the dispute would be resolved peacefully. Every-one knew that the newspaper was 'officially inspired' and would interpret it as representing the views of the German government. So Jagow instructed Tschirschky to explain to the Austrians that the article had been written for the sake of European diplomacy—to avoid giving alarm prematurely. 'Please take care that this is not wrongly interpreted': it was not meant to restrain them in Vienna.[122]

Jagow was attempting to deal simultaneously with Flotow's indiscretions at Rome, Berchtold's intransigence on Italian compensation at Vienna, and Lichnowsky's opposition to Austro-German policy at London. In a desperate attempt to persuade his ambassador to uphold the government line, Jagow wrote personally to Lichnowsky. He accepted the ambassador's reservations about 'that ever-increasing, disintegrating composition of nations beside the Danube'. Austria's lack of vigour meant that it barely counted as a great power any longer—and this had weakened the Triple Alliance. But the assassination offered the Austrians the opportunity to demonstrate that they were still capable of action. If Germany tried to hold them back it would deprive them of their last chance of 'political rehabilitation', accelerate the process of internal decay, and Austria's standing in the Balkans 'would disappear forever'. The alternative was a Russian hegemony, and this Germany could not permit.[123]

Jagow explained that the success of Germany's strategy of localizing the conflict depended on Russia's reaction. The greater the determination with which Austria behaved, the quieter Russia was likely to remain. Russia was not ready to strike at the moment. Neither France nor Britain wanted a war. But Russia would be prepared to fight in a few years, and then 'she will crush us by the number of her soldiers'. Russia wanted to keep the peace for a few more years while building up a fleet in the Baltic and developing its strategic railways. That portion of Russian opinion that was favourably disposed to Germany was growing weaker while the Slavic element was becoming increasingly hostile. If Germany failed to localize the Austro-Serbian dispute and Russia were to attack Austria, a *casus foederis* would arise—that is, the terms of the Austro-German alliance would be activated. 'We could not then abandon Austria.'[124]

Jagow admitted that Lichnowsky was correct concerning British opinion. Britain's lack of sympathy for Austria was to be expected, but this was far from a willingness to participate in a European war. Sir Edward Grey ought to understand that the balance of power that he wished to maintain in Europe would be destroyed if Germany deserted Austria, which would then be demolished by Russia. It was in Britain's interest to assist Germany in attempting to localize the conflict.

Jagow, finishing his letter at 1 a.m. in the morning of 19 July, ended with a plea: if Lichnowsky failed to find his arguments convincing, he trusted him to 'stand behind them' nevertheless. The secretary of state was becoming more apprehensive and nervous. On the 20th the deputy chief of the admiralty staff found him 'unsure of himself, fidgety and timid'. Jagow gloomily sketched the political situation and said that a general European war was no longer out of the question.[125]

★

In Vienna the Ballhausplatz had finally finished putting together the list of demands. The common council would convene at Berchtold's private residence on the morning of Sunday the 19th to consider them.

Hoyos confided that the demands were such 'that no nation that still possessed self-respect and dignity could possibly accept them'.[126] Members of the council arrived quietly, in unmarked cars. They quickly agreed to the terms proposed. This time there was little discussion and no controversy.

The meeting was devoted mainly to the logistics of the delivery of the note and the mobilization that they anticipated would follow. Berchtold proposed that the note be handed over to the Serbian government at 5 p.m. on Thursday the 25th—to coincide with the departure of the French president and premier from Kronstadt. They would demand a reply within forty-eight hours. When the deadline expired on Saturday evening they would publish the orders to begin mobilization. Berchtold advised against any further delay in presenting the demands because 'Berlin was beginning to get nervous' and news of Austria's intentions had already reached Rome. The council agreed.

The only contentious issue was once again raised by Tisza. Hungary would agree to proceed only if the council agreed—unanimously—that the monarchy had no plans to annex Serbian territory, apart from some small frontier rectifications. Berchtold, although willing to forgo the annexation of Serbian territory by Austria 'in the present political situation', proposed that large portions of Serbia be surrendered to Bulgaria, Greece, Albania, and Romania. This would so reduce Serbia in size that it would cease to be dangerous. He could also envision circumstances in which Austria might have to annex some territory: Russia might intervene at Sofia and install a government hostile to Austria; Albania was unreliable and it could be a mistake to enable it to expand.

Tisza continued to insist that the council agree—unanimously—to his point of view. Rejecting the annexation of territory was necessary for domestic political reasons and because Russia would resist 'to the limit' (à outrance) if Austria were to insist upon the complete annihilation of Serbia.

The best diplomatic card that Austria could play was a declaration to the powers disavowing the intention of annexing Serbian territory.

Neither the minister of war (Krobatin) nor the Austrian premier (Stürgkh) was prepared to forgo territorial acquisition altogether. Krobatin wanted to establish a bridgehead on the other side of the Sava River; Stürgkh wanted to see Serbia reduced to dependence on the monarchy by deposing the dynasty, imposing a military convention, and other measures. The council unanimously agreed that as soon as the war began the monarchy would declare to the powers that they did not intend a war of conquest nor the annexation of Serbia. This was not to preclude frontier rectifications or the reduction of Serbian territory to the advantage of other states. And the temporary occupation of Serbian territory might be unavoidable. Berchtold declared that on all points 'the council is perfectly agreed' and closed the meeting.

Five awkward days were to elapse before the ultimatum would be presented to Serbia. Austria's alliance partners were becoming restive. The Germans were impatient; they wanted to know the terms of the note immediately they were agreed upon. Jagow insisted that he needed this information in order to prepare *démarches* toward the other powers.[127] Kaiser Wilhelm, still sailing on the *Hohenzollern*, had ceased to pay much attention to the situation until the 19th, when he received word that Austria had now prepared the demands against Serbia. He now entered into a state of 'high anxiety'.[128]

The Italian ambassador at Vienna, the Duke d'Avarna, tried to get what he could out of Berchtold, but the little that he got was misleading. When asked if it was true that a stiff note was to be presented at Belgrade, Berchtold replied that the investigation was ongoing. Although it was probable that 'a communication would have to be made eventually' to the Serbian government it was too early to say what the contents of the note would be. At the Consulta, the eighteenth-century baroque palazzo that housed the Italian foreign ministry, they anticipated that Austria would put itself in the wrong by making its demands too far-reaching.[129]

The diplomats of the Entente remained in the dark. From Vienna, on the day that the common council agreed on the ultimatum, de Bunsen reported that the Russian ambassador, who had been due to take his annual leave but had postponed it, now felt it was safe to go away for two or three weeks. The French ambassador believed that—in the end—the Austrian government would see the wisdom of avoiding armed conflict with Serbia.

The British ambassador himself, in spite of his recent conversation with Lützow, trusted that his colleagues were correct in their belief that 'warlike complications' would be avoided.[130]

Week Four: 20–23 July

The waiting continued. In London, Sir Edward Grey assured Lichnowsky that he remained optimistic and believed that a peaceful solution would be reached. He might have been less optimistic had he known how far the Austrian demands would go. Lichnowsky warned him that Berchtold would demand satisfaction from Serbia and guarantees for the future. Grey replied that everything would depend on the form of the satisfaction to be demanded, whether moderation would be exercised, and especially on whether the accusations against Serbian complicity were convincing.[131] And he thought they might: it was possible that the Serbian government had been negligent and that it could be shown that the murder of the archduke was planned on Serbian territory. If Austria's demands were kept within 'reasonable limits' and, if the necessary justification were provided, he hoped that 'every attempt' would be made to prevent a breach of the peace.[132]

Grey seemed prepared to fall in line with Germany's position: he hoped the quarrel might be settled and localized. He hated the idea of war between any of the great powers: 'that any of them should be dragged into a war by Servia would be detestable'.[133]

The waiting would not continue much longer. On Monday the 20th of July, Berchtold met with the emperor and received his approval of the ultimatum. The details were sent immediately to the Austrian minister in Belgrade, who was instructed to present them on Thursday afternoon, the 23rd, between 4 and 5 p.m. Instructions were sent to Austria's ambassadors in Berlin, Rome, Paris, London, St Petersburg, and Constantinople and to ministers in Bucharest, Sofia, Athens, Cetinje, and Durazzo to present to the respective governments to which they were accredited the details of the note on the following day, Friday the 24th.

Not even Germany was let in on the secret of the demands to be presented. Jagow again asked to be 'exactly informed' of the note's contents in order to facilitate the handling of publicity in Germany.[134] But ambassador Szögyény had been told to inform the government in Berlin of the details on the 24th, at the same time as all the others.

As for Austria's other partner in the Triple Alliance, Berchtold was willing to inform Italy that Austria intended to present a note to Serbia only one day beforehand—'this seemed sufficient courtesy towards so unreliable an ally as Italy'.[135] Jagow was distressed that Berchtold was not prepared to do more to secure Italy's support. He continued to urge the Austrians to offer compensation to the Italians: perhaps they could encourage the Italians to seize Valona?

Berchtold now realized that he could use Tisza's insistence that Austria renounce any annexation of Serbian territory to his advantage. The renunciation meant there could be no justification for Italy's demand for compensation. And, as for an Italian move into Valona, Austrian opinion was so strongly against this that he could not possibly consent to it. Berchtold suggested that instead of pressing Austria to come to an agreement with Italy, Berlin should point out to San Giuliano the contradictions in his policy: claiming on the one hand that Italy required a strong Austria-Hungary as a wall of defence against Slavism, while at critical moments following a policy that brought him 'into contact with the chief power of Slavism'—Russia—preventing Austria-Hungary from keeping its possessions intact.

According to Berchtold, while Italy might express its indignation in words, it would 'scarcely follow them up with deeds'. As a result of their war with Turkey, the Italians were not eager for battle. Austria did not need their cooperation or support; neutrality would suffice. He would go no farther than to consider something that might pacify Italian subjects within the monarchy itself.[136]

With only two days left before the Austrian demands were to be presented to Serbia, the Triple Alliance remained in disarray. The Austrian ambassador in Berlin pleaded with Vienna to coordinate action with the Germans. Szögyény objected to the instructions he had received not to communicate the details of the Austrian demands until the 24th: in his 'humble opinion' the details ought to be communicated to Germany immediately.[137] Jagow believed that Germany ought to be informed of the details of the ultimatum before other governments. Szögyény explained to Berchtold in a personal letter that the kaiser 'and all the others in high offices' had loyally promised to support Austrian action from the very first. To fail to inform Germany of the details of the demands until all the other powers were informed as well 'might give offence'. Jagow had again promised that Germany would stand by Austria 'with all its forces' but he wanted to know whether Austria planned only a temporary occupation of Serbian territory or whether—as Hoyos had hinted earlier to Bethmann Hollweg—Austria was considering the partition (*Auftheilung*) of Serbia.[138]

Berchtold relented. He agreed to put Germany in the picture. Claiming that it had never been his intention to treat the Germans on the same footing as the other powers, he instructed that Tschirschky should be given a copy of the ultimatum on the evening of the 21st.[139] The Wilhelmstrasse received the details of the note by the next day, Wednesday the 22nd—the day before the ultimatum was to be handed to the Serbian government in Belgrade.

★

While Austria and Germany were sorting out their differences, the French delegation had arrived in Russia. On the evening of the 15th of July Poincaré, accompanied by René Viviani (who combined the functions of *président du conseil*—equivalent to 'premier'—and foreign minister) and Pierre de Margerie (the political director at the Quai d'Orsay), had departed, with great fanfare, from the Gare du Nord on the presidential train. At Dunkirk, they had embarked on the battleship *France* for their tour of Scandinavia, scheduled to last until 31 July. They arrived in Russia on the 20th, where they were greeted by cheering crews, the firing of ships' guns and shore batteries. A Russian band played the *Marseillaise* while the president and the premier boarded the imperial yacht, the *Alexandria*, where the tsar and the foreign minister were waiting for them, along with ambassadors Paléologue and Izvol'skii. They then travelled to Peterhof where a spectacular banquet awaited them.

The next day they arrived in St Petersburg, where the mayor offered the president bread and salt—according to an old Slavic custom—and Poincaré laid a wreath on the tomb of Alexander III, 'the father' of the Franco-Russian alliance. In the afternoon they travelled to the Winter Palace for a diplomatic levee. Along the route they were greeted by enthusiastic crowds: 'The police had arranged it all. At every street corner a group of poor wretches cheered loudly under the eye of a policeman.'[140] Another spectacular banquet was held that evening, with ninety-six guests at the French embassy.

Not unexpectedly, the Russian tsar and the French president proclaimed their devotion to the alliance. More surprisingly, they spent little time talking about the Austro-Serbian situation. When, at the French reception for the diplomatic corps on the 21st, the British ambassador expressed his fear that Austria was about to present a stiff series of demands to Serbia, Poincaré took the opportunity to question the Austrian ambassador about it.

Count Frigyes Szápáry de Szápár dissimulated: the inquiry was ongoing, he said, and he claimed not to have been informed of the results. He lied. He had, in fact, received the terms of the note already. Nevertheless, he took offence at Poincaré's attitude: the French president delivered a kind of lecture, arguing that a government could not be held responsible for anything for which there was no concrete proof. Poincaré warned Austria not to forget that Serbia had friends. His tactless behaviour 'was almost threatening'.

'Fritz' Szápáry had been ambassador in St Petersburg for only a few months. For the previous six years he had served in Vienna as chief of the political department at the Ballhausplatz; and before that he had served in a variety of diplomatic posts in Rome, Berlin, and Munich. He was a Magyar aristocrat, a hereditary member of the Hungarian upper house, and chamberlain of the emperor's court in Budapest. Vastly wealthy, a graduate of the most famous school in Austria, the Theresianum, always impeccably dressed, he was the archetypal diplomat.

Berchtold had appointed Szápáry to St Petersburg largely because he believed that he would be less accommodating to Russia than his predecessors had been. During the Balkan wars Szápáry had argued that Austria-Hungary should take an aggressive stand against Serbian expansionism. Although he had been appointed to his new post in the autumn of 1913 he did not take it up until February, and then, in late May, he had returned home to be with his wife and young son, who were both ill. Only on 20 July, after his son died, did he return to St Petersburg. The day after his return he met with Poincaré. He concluded that the French president would not have a 'calming influence' on Sazonov.[141]

French and Russian politicians and diplomats spent little time discussing the Serbian situation. Instead, they considered the tensions between Russia and Britain over railways in Anatolia, the prospects of the Anglo-Russian naval conversations, and the future of the Three Years' Law in France.[142] On the 22nd, the day before the Austrian ultimatum was to be presented, Poincaré casually assured the Serbian minister in St Petersburg that France

Count Frigyes Szápáry de Szápár (1869–1935); Austro-Hungarian ambassador at
St Petersburg (1913–14)

would 'help you to make it better'.[143] At the same time he confided to his
diary that he was not convinced Russia would support Serbia.[144]

Sazonov appeared to be speaking clearly and forcefully. He warned the
German ambassador of 'powerful and dangerous influences' that might
plunge Austria into a war—even at the risk of starting a world-wide
conflagration. He acknowledged that Franz Joseph and Berchtold were
'friends of peace', but an aged monarch and a weak foreign minister
might not be able to overcome the warlike inclinations of those around
them. The influence of men such as Count Forgách—'an intriguer of the
basest sort'—and Count Tisza—'half a fool'—was increasing.[145]

Count Friedrich Pourtalès argued that the Serbian government had
permitted the Greater Serbia agitation to go on and that the assassination
itself had been planned in Belgrade. Sazonov retorted that a whole country
could not be held responsible for the acts of individuals. Besides, the

murderer of the archduke was not even a Serbian subject. He blamed bad government on the part of Austria for the agitation that went on within its own borders. There were those in Austria who wished to take advantage of this opportunity to annihilate Serbia—but Russia could not look on indifferently while Serbia was humiliated. And Russia was not alone: the situation was now being taken very seriously in Paris and London.

But was it? Notwithstanding Poincaré's tough talk in St Petersburg, French diplomats were giving—and sending—mixed messages. In Vienna, when the French ambassador, Alfred Dumaine, met with Berchtold he seemed to reinforce the president's warnings: a war between Austria and Serbia might turn into a war of the 'Slav races' against the monarchy. But Dumaine immediately watered this down by reporting to the Austrian foreign minister his conversation with the Russian ambassador—from which he had concluded that Russia did not intend to stand up much for Serbia in the dispute and might give no more than 'moral' support. In the event of war between Austria and Serbia, Dumaine believed that Russia would not take an active part and would do what it could to 'localize' it.[146]

A career diplomat, the 62-year-old Dumaine had served either at the Quai d'Orsay or in the diplomatic service for thirty-seven years. He was profoundly anti-British, knew no English, and was disgusted by British customs and public life. He consistently discounted warnings that Germany was prepared to provoke a war.[147] While he was watering down warnings of any vigorous reaction against Austria on the part of the Entente, the Russian ambassador had departed on his vacation from Vienna, satisfied with the assurances that had been given to him at the Ballhausplatz.

Things were no clearer in London than they were in Vienna or St Petersburg. The British ambassador at Berlin had been on leave from his post since the assassination, and the foreign secretary was not sufficiently concerned about the situation to order him to return. Grey was fully aware of the mounting apprehensions that Austrian demands might be made on Serbia that could precipitate an international crisis, but he continued to believe that Berlin would have a moderating effect on Vienna.[148]

Grey's main concern was what would happen if Russia stood by Serbia in resisting any Austrian demands. He suggested to the Russian ambassador the kinds of things that he would consider doing, were he in Sazonov's place: he might send for the Austrian ambassador, refer to press reports that Austria was going to make demands on Serbia, emphasize the strength of pro-Serb feeling in Russia, ask the Austrian government to take Russia into their confidence by telling them exactly the extent and nature of their grievance against Serbia, and what they felt it necessary to ask of the Serbian government. It might then be possible for the Russian government to get the Austrian demands kept within reasonable limits.[149]

The British foreign secretary was obviously working in the dark: he offered these hypothetical suggestions days after the Austrian demands had been finalized and the day before they were to be presented at Belgrade.

On the eve of the crisis the Entente and the Triple Alliance were both in disarray. Dire warnings of a world conflagration, predictions of war between the Slav races and the multinational monarchy were counterbalanced by talk of moderation, assurances of peaceful intentions, and suggestions of quiet diplomatic discussions resolving the dispute. Entente diplomats were aware that demands were about to be made on Serbia, but exactly when they would be presented and how far they would go remained uncertain. The French ambassador in Berlin, Jules Cambon, was convinced that Germany had no intention 'of playing the role of mediator' and intended to support Austria with all of its authority.[150] But the ambassador in London, his older brother Paul—who always referred to Jules as '*mon cher enfant*'—continued to believe that Germany would restrain Austria because no German interests were involved. For his part, Sir Edward Grey was prepared to urge Serbia to give Austria assurances that it would prevent future plots from forming if Austria could prove that the assassination had been prepared and organized on Serbian territory.

The Italian foreign minister saw things more clearly than most. San Giuliano warned the British ambassador that Austria's demands had been carefully drafted in order to be unacceptable to Serbia. He had now abandoned any hope that the emperor might act as a moderating influence: Austria was determined to take this opportunity to crush Serbia. He assured the French ambassador that Germany 'would make no effort to restrain Austria'. Vienna seemed to believe that Russia would stand by and let Serbia 'be violated'. Once the Austrian ultimatum was presented, he predicted that Austria 'will make it a duty to obtain what she has demanded'.[151] Everyone would find out the next day, on Thursday, 23 July, which was more accurate—San Giuliano's gloomy prediction or Grey's hope for moderation.[152]

★

By 23 July twenty-five days had passed since the assassination. Twenty-five days of rumours, speculations, discussions, half-truths, and hypothetical scenarios. Would the Austrian investigation into the crime prove that the instigators were directed from or supported by the government in Belgrade? Would the Serbian government assist in rooting out any individuals or organizations that might have provided assistance to the conspirators? Would Austria's demands be limited to steps to ensure that the perpetrators would be brought to justice and such outrages be prevented from recurring in the future? Or would the assassination be utilized as a pretext for dismembering, crushing, or abolishing the independence of Serbia as a state? Was Germany restraining Austria or goading it to act? Would Russia stand with Serbia in resisting Austrian demands? Would France encourage Russia to respond with restraint or push it forward? Would Italy stick with her alliance partners, stand aside, or join the other side? Could Britain promote a peaceful resolution by refusing to commit to either side in the dispute, or could it hope to counterbalance the Triple Alliance only by acting in partnership with its friends in the entente?

On Monday, 20 July, Berchtold had instructed the Austrian minister in Belgrade to present the note containing the Austrian demands to the Serbian government between 4 and 5 p.m. (local time) on the 23rd.[153] Baron Wladimir Giesl von Gieslingen, formerly a major-general in the Austrian army, had arranged accordingly to deliver the note at 4.30 p.m. On Tuesday Berlin received information that Poincaré would not depart on the *France* from the harbour at Kronstadt until 11 p.m., meaning that if the note were delivered in Belgrade as scheduled the French president would not yet have left.[154] On Wednesday Tschirschky was instructed to bring this to Berchtold's attention. On Thursday, the day the note was to be delivered, Berchtold instructed Giesl to delay its presentation until 6 p.m.[155] The Germans and the Austrians regarded it as vital that Poincaré should have departed from Russia before the details of the note became known.

The delivery of the note was further complicated because of the absence of the Serbian prime minister from Belgrade. Berchtold had assumed that the note would be delivered to Pašić but, in the midst of the Serbian election campaign, the prime minister was not scheduled to be in the capital on the 23rd, or for several days after. Berchtold instructed Giesl on the 21st to inform the Serbian foreign office in advance that he would be presenting an important communication on the 23rd, and that this made it desirable that the prime minister should return to Belgrade. But Giesl was also to make it clear that the prime minister's absence would not delay the presentation of the note—it would simply be handed to the prime minister's representative or the official next in rank at the Serbian foreign office. In spite of this, Pašić chose not to return to Belgrade earlier than scheduled.

This was not the only unexpected complication faced by Austria and Germany in the days leading up to delivery of the ultimatum. Bethmann Hollweg found himself forced to complain to the kaiser that the activities of his son, the crown prince, threatened to disrupt German diplomacy. Prince Wilhelm had begun flirting with the pan-Germans years earlier. Led by a former inspector of cavalry in the Bavarian army, the pan-Germans advocated a *Staatsstreich*—a counter-revolutionary strike by the crown itself against socialism and liberalism. They proposed to abolish universal suffrage, dismantle parliamentarism, and bring in anti-Jewish legislation. They also viewed the Habsburg monarchy, with its polyglot, multinational character, as the greatest impediment to the creation of a unitary 'German' state. The kaiser had warned his son against associating with them: they were 'dangerous people' led by a 'fanatical odd-ball' and were more dangerous to the stability of the monarchy 'than the wildest Social Democrat'.[156]

In spite of the prince's promises to the contrary, he had gone public with his support for pan-German publicists and their attacks on 'the men whom Your Majesty has placed in responsible offices'. In November 1913 he had tried to convince his father to dismiss Bethmann Hollweg. The chancellor had begged the prince to desist from supporting the pan-Germans, especially as this had attracted the attention of Entente journalists, who were reporting that the prince was urging war. Bethmann Hollweg now feared that when the Austrian ultimatum to Serbia was made public, the prince's position would be regarded as 'warmongering' whereas it was the chancellor's task—according to the kaiser's admonitions—to localize the dispute. He therefore requested 'most humbly' that the kaiser forbid the crown prince by 'immediate telegraphic order' to refrain from interfering in politics.[157]

'Papa Wilhelm' immediately telegraphed to his son to explain how painful and grievous it was to have had the chancellor point out to him that the prince had broken his promises. He appealed to his son's 'duty and honour as a Prussian officer' to keep his promise to refrain from any sort of political comment 'which can only serve to disturb My policies and those of My responsible advisers'.[158] The chastened crown prince apologized and promised to behave henceforth. Bethmann Hollweg might be spared at least one complication in the days that followed.

But the chancellor worried even more about the kaiser's own activities. Wilhelm had ordered the German fleet to be kept together following its annual manoeuvres, which led Bethmann Hollweg to worry that 'as soon as the ultimatum is refused' the kaiser might order 'conspicuous fleet movements'.[159] When the chancellor asked for the admiralty's opinion he was told that if there was a possibility of Britain declaring war on Germany they must prepare for the possibility of a sudden attack on the fleet. Given Germany's numerical inferiority, this meant not allowing the fleet to be exposed. The fleet should be recalled six days prior to war breaking out.[160] On the 23rd, with the Austrian ultimatum to be presented at 6 p.m., the chancellor advised the admiralty to prepare for the possibility of 'a sudden attack on our fleet' by the British.[161]

Bethmann Hollweg anticipated that the Serbs would reject the Austrian demands. Kaiser Wilhelm dismissed British hopes that he would use his influence to restrain Austria. 'Why should I do any such thing?' Austria was perfectly within its rights: 'The rascals have added murder to agitation and must be humbled.' Lichnowsky ought to tell Grey 'plainly and seriously' that the Austrian demands were Austria's affair and Germany would not attempt to influence them. 'Serbia is nothing but a band of robbers.' He refused to interfere. Emperor Franz Joseph alone was competent to judge the situation. And the kaiser resented Britain's condescending way of giving orders.[162]

From the perspective of Berlin and Vienna, things now looked promising. Bethmann Hollweg looked forward to a diplomatic victory: if things went well, if Russia did not mobilize and a war was avoided, a Russo–German understanding should be possible because of Russia's disappointment with its Entente partners.[163] In Germany and Austria-Hungary there appeared to be widespread support for a vigorous diplomatic initiative. In Russia, France, Britain, and even in Serbia itself, there seemed to be chaos, division, and uncertainty. The chief of the kaiser's military cabinet assured his wife that although there were thunderclouds on the horizon, crises like this one had been averted in the past and it was difficult to imagine a world war being unleashed by a Serbian 'gang of murderers'.[164]

On the final day of the visit of the French president and premier, thousands of striking workers chopped down telegraph poles, then combined them with paving stones to erect barricades, stretching wires across the streets to prevent Cossacks from charging them on their horses. Strikers cut the telephone cable between St Petersburg and Finland and then wrecked the power station, which meant that trams had stopped running by evening. At the Nikolaieff shipyard another 8,000 workers joined the strike, along with thousands more from the government Obukhoff gun factory. Strikers marched through the streets singing revolutionary songs and waving red flags. Thousands assembled in front of the imperial porcelain factory, throwing stones through the windows and calling for the workers inside to join them. By now over 100,000 workers in St Petersburg were on strike— many of whom were leaving the city to return to their villages. Employers had decided to lock their workers out for two weeks and the council of ministers was scheduled to meet the next day to consider a declaration of martial law—once the French visitors had departed.

Although things were quieter in Paris, attention was focused not on the Austro-Serbian situation, but on the sensational trial of Madame Caillaux. On the 23rd Caillaux's first wife, Madame Gueydan, took the stand and testified to how she had discovered the liaison between her husband and a woman she had believed to be her friend. Her husband had lied to her and deceived her, but she had obtained proof in the form of love letters she discovered from his mistress. When he had promised to end the affair she had given the letters back to him—after which he announced his intention to divorce her. But he was unaware that Mme Gueydan's sister had taken photos of the letters before handing them back. Mme Caillaux's lawyer defended her killing of the newspaper editor on the premise that she was trying to retrieve copies of the letters that had been given to him. But Mme Gueydan refused to hand over the letters to the judge. The courtroom was packed to overflowing. Readers of newspapers could not get enough about the trial. Balkan matters faded into the background.

The affair threatened to topple the government. In St Petersburg, Viviani was much more concerned with the trial than he was with Franco-Russian diplomacy. He regretted having left Paris: 'What are we bloody well doing here anyway?'[165]

In London, things were not much better. The king had caused a sensation when he had declared that 'the cry of civil war is on the lips of the most responsible and sober-minded of my people'. A conference had been called to bring representatives of the government, Unionists, and Irish Nationalists together at Buckingham Palace in the hope of finding some way of resolving the crisis that had arisen because of the Home Rule Bill. But the conference seemed to be getting nowhere, with Unionists and Nationalists unable to agree on a formula to apply to the four northern counties of

Ulster. The collapse of the government or even civil war seemed entirely possible.

And then, 'at the striking of the clock' at 6 p.m. on Thursday, the 23rd of July, the Austrian note was presented in Belgrade to Pašić's deputy, the chain-smoking Lazar Paču.[166] Paču immediately arranged to see the Russian minister to beg for Russian help.[167] Even a quick glance at the demands made in the note convinced the Serbian regent, Prince Aleksandar, that he could not possibly accept them. The chief of the general staff and his deputy were recalled from their vacations; all divisional commanders were summoned to their posts; railway authorities were alerted that mobilization might be declared; regiments on the northern frontier were instructed to prepare assembly points for an impending mobilization. The crisis had finally begun.

PART
TWO

The July Crisis

Day One
Friday, 24 July

On the morning of 24 July all European governments received copies of the Austrian ultimatum to Serbia. Four days earlier, Austria's ambassadors and ministers had received their copies of the note, along with an explanation of the Austrian position, and instructions on how they were to proceed. The only change made between Monday and Thursday was the delay in the presentation to Serbia of one hour in order to be certain that Poincaré and Viviani had left St Petersburg. Nothing that anyone said or did during that week altered the course that had been agreed upon in Vienna by the common ministerial council on Sunday the 19th.

A preamble to the list of demands asserted that a subversive movement that aimed to 'disjoin' portions of Austria-Hungary had grown 'under the eyes' of the Serbian government. This had resulted in acts of terrorism, attempts at murder, and actual murders beyond the frontiers of the Serbian kingdom. The Serbian government had done nothing to suppress this movement: it had tolerated the criminal activities of societies and organizations; it had tolerated outrageous language in its press and the glorification of instigators of plots against Austria; it had allowed its officers and officials to participate in subversive plans and had tolerated an 'unhealthy propaganda' in its public instruction. This had caused the people of Serbia 'to hate the monarchy and despise its organization'.

Austria's investigation had confirmed that the murder in Sarajevo had been prepared in Belgrade, that the murderers had received their weapons and bombs from Serbian military officers and government officials who belonged to the *Narodna Odbrana*, and that the murderers and their weapons had been conveyed to Bosnia with the assistance of Serbian officials at the border. The Austrian government could no longer maintain its attitude of patient observation now that the peace of the monarchy was threatened and it must put an end to such doings. They therefore demanded that the

Serbian government condemn the propaganda aimed at Austria–Hungary and pledge itself to suppress 'with all the means in its power' this criminal and terrorist propaganda. In order to give its solemn pledge to this effect, the Serbian government was required to declare on Sunday, the 26th of July that:[1]

> The Royal Servian government condemns the propaganda directed against Austria–Hungary, that is the entirety of the ambitions, whose ultimate aim it is to disjoin parts of the territory belonging to the Austrian-Hungarian monarchy and regrets sincerely the horrible consequences of these criminal ambitions.
>
> The Royal Servian government regrets that Servian officers and officials have taken part in the propaganda above-mentioned and thereby imperilled the friendly and neighbourly relations, which the Royal government had solemnly promised to cultivate in its declaration of the 31st March 1909.
>
> The Royal government, which condemns and rejects every thought and every attempt to interfere on behalf of the inhabitants of any part of Austria–Hungary, considers it a duty to warn officers, officials and indeed all the inhabitants of the kingdom, that it will in future use great severity against such persons, as will be found guilty of similar doings, which the government will make every effort to suppress.
>
> The Royal Servian government will overmore pledge itself to the following:
>
> 1. To suppress every publication likely to inspire hatred and contempt against the monarchy or whose general tendencies are directed against the integrity of the latter;
> 2. to begin immediately dissolving the society called: *Narodna odbrana*, to seize all its means of propaganda and to act in the same way against all the societies and associations in Servia, which are busy with the propaganda against Austria–Hungary; the Royal government will take the necessary measures to prevent these societies continuing their efforts under another name or in another form;
> 3. to eliminate without delay from public instruction everything that serves or might serve the propaganda against Austria–Hungary, both where teachers or books are concerned;
> 4. to remove from military service and from the administration all officers and officials who are guilty of having taken part in the propaganda against Austria–Hungary, whose names and the proofs of whose guilt the Imp. and Roy. government will communicate to the Royal government;

5. to consent that Imp. and Roy. officials assist in Servia in the suppressing of the subversive movement directed against the territorial integrity of the monarchy;

6. to have a judicial inquiry instituted against all those who took part in the plot of the 28th June, if they are to be found on Servian territory; the Imp. and Roy. government will delegate organs who will take an active part in these inquiries;

7. to arrest without delay major Volja Tankosić and a certain Milan Ciganović, a Servian government official, both compromised by the results of the inquiry;

8. to take effective measures so as to prevent the Servian authorities from taking part in the smuggling of weapons and explosives across the frontier; to dismiss from service and severely punish those organs of the frontier service at Schabatz and Loznica, who helped the perpetrators of the crime of Sarajevo to reach Bosnia in safety;

9. to give the Imp. and Roy. government an explanation of the unjustified remarks of high Servian functionaries in Servia as well as in foreign countries, who, notwithstanding their official positions, did not hesitate to speak in hostile terms of Austria-Hungary in interviews given just after the event of the 28th June;

10. to inform the Imp. and Roy. government without delay that the measures summed up in the above points have been carried out.

After weeks of anticipation the Austrian response to the assassination was official and clear. The rumours and speculations ceased. The time for action had arrived.

★

A copy of the note was read aloud by the Austrian ambassador to the Russian foreign minister in St Petersburg at 10 a.m. on the 24th. Sazonov, Szápáry reported, listened in comparative quiet. He declined to indicate how Russia might respond to the *démarche*. But it was obvious to him that Austria wanted war with Serbia: 'You are setting fire to Europe!'[2] He predicted that in London, Paris, and other European capitals Austria's conduct would be regarded as an unjustified act of aggression. Austria's demands were unacceptable: Serbia was not responsible for the assassination and would not agree to disband the *Narodna Odbrana*. He objected to the demand that Austrian officials should actively participate in the suppression of subversive movements: Serbia would no longer be master in its own house! He blamed

Count Forgách, implying that Forgách, who had attempted to use forged documents at the Agram treason trial five years earlier, might be up to his old tricks. He asked what proof Austria actually had that the series of attempted murders referred to had originated in Belgrade. But Austria hardly need bother furnishing a dossier with the proof: the very fact of presenting an ultimatum demonstrated that it was not interested in an impartial judgment on the case. 'What you want is war, and you have burnt your bridges behind you.'

Szápáry came away from their meeting with the impression that Sazonov was more saddened and depressed than excited. He seemed deaf to the argument that all monarchies had a common interest in acting against political assassination: 'the monarchical idea has nothing to do with this affair at all', he said.[3] He never once mentioned Russia, Slavdom, or the Orthodox Church; instead, he repeatedly referred to Britain and France and to the impression that Austria's action would make on Europe and the rest of the world. Although Sazonov remained calm throughout the hour-and-a-half discussion, his attitude was, from first to last, 'disagreeable and hostile'.[4]

Following their meeting, Sazonov immediately placed a telephone call to the tsar—an unprecedented step. The Austrians, he told Nicholas, had to know that Serbia could not possibly comply with their demands, and that they must therefore intend to attack Serbia. Nor would they have presented such an ultimatum without the backing of Germany. The tsar directed that the council of ministers, which was scheduled to meet at 3 p.m. in order to discuss the strikes plaguing Russia, instead focus their discussion on Russia's response to the ultimatum.

Before the council met, Sazonov arranged to meet with the British and French ambassadors at the French embassy. When they convened over lunch at 12.30, Sazonov explained that he believed it urgent for the three of them to discuss the situation because the ultimatum meant that war was imminent. Austria's conduct was provocative and immoral. Some of the demands were impossible for Serbia to accept. As Germany must have been consulted by Austria beforehand and must be cooperating with it, he hoped that Britain would likewise proclaim its solidarity with Russia and France.[5]

The French ambassador, Maurice Paléologue, made it clear that France would support Russia diplomatically and fulfil its obligations under the terms of the alliance if the necessity arose. He advised Paris that only the 'solidarity of the Triple Entente' could deter the provocation of the 'Germanic Powers'.[6] His opinion would come as no surprise to officials at the Quai d'Orsay.

★

Paléologue was another career diplomat, but one with an unusual background. His father, a Romanian of Greek extraction, had gone into exile for political reasons; his mother was a Belgian musician. The young Paléologue, baptized in the Greek Orthodox Church, became a naturalized French citizen. His family's wealth and his intellectual gifts enabled him to shine academically, first at the Lycée Henri IV, then at the Lycée Louis-le-Grand, where he became acquainted with Raymond Poincaré, Paul and Jules Cambon, and other pillars of the French republican elite. He entered the

Maurice Paléologue (1859–1944); French ambassador at St Petersburg (1914–17)

French diplomatic service in 1880 at the age of 21, but was called to serve at the Quai d'Orsay in 1887, where he worked for the next twenty years.[7]

Everyone was impressed with Paléologue's intelligence and his erudition. He attained a degree in law, was fluent in English, German, and Italian, and began to demonstrate an impressive literary flair as a young man. His critics regarded him as 'too imaginative' to be suited to diplomacy; he was too vain, too inclined to self-promotion, and too excitable to be relied upon. Nevertheless, he participated in the negotiations that resulted in the alliance with Russia, which he regarded as essential to France. Appointed to St Petersburg as ambassador in January 1914, he believed Germany was aiming to divide France and Russia. He preached the need for Franco-Russian solidarity and the inclusion of Britain in the alliance—a position he reiterated throughout the visit of Poincaré and Viviani.

The British ambassador, Sir George Buchanan, was more guarded than his French colleague. While he promised to report to Sir Edward Grey the arguments made by Sazonov and Paléologue, he did not believe that Britain would give an unconditional engagement to Russia and France to support them by force of arms. He pointed out that Britain had no direct interests in Serbia and that British public opinion would never sanction a war on Serbia's behalf.

Sazonov countered by asserting that Serbia was only part of the general European question. He seemed to suggest that Britain should join Russia and France in communicating to Austria that they would not tolerate its interference in the internal affairs of Serbia. Buchanan asked: did this mean that Russia would declare war on Austria if it proceeded to embark on military measures? Sazonov replied that he was not yet able to answer this. He believed Russia would have to mobilize in any case, but as the council of ministers was meeting to discuss the situation that afternoon, no decision was likely to be taken before tomorrow, when the tsar would preside over a further meeting.[8]

Buchanan argued that their most immediate objective should be to induce Austria to extend the forty-eight-hour time limit. Paléologue disagreed: Austria had either made up its mind to go to war or it was bluffing. In either case, the only chance to avert war was for the Entente to adopt a firm and united attitude. Buchanan avoided any promises; they first needed to know how far Serbia might go in meeting the Austrian demands. Sazonov reiterated that some of the demands were simply unacceptable. He and Paléologue continued to press Buchanan for a declaration of British solidarity, but he would go no farther than to suggest the possibility that

Sir George Buchanan (1854–1924); British ambassador at St Petersburg (1910–18)

Grey might be willing to make 'strong representations' to the German and Austrian governments that an attack on Serbia would endanger the peace of Europe. Grey might add that such an attack would probably mean Russian intervention, which would then involve France and Germany, in which case it would be difficult for Britain to keep out.[9]

Buchanan did not hold out any false hopes. Since arriving in his post at St Petersburg in 1910 at the age of 55, he had warned London that there was a distinct possibility of a Russo-German rapprochement. A determined advocate of the entente with Russia, he had occasionally suggested to Grey that Britain ought to consider the possibility of an alliance to keep the Russians onside. He was, however, an experienced diplomat—having served abroad for almost all of his thirty-eight years in the diplomatic service—and was careful not to encourage the Russians to believe that they could rely on British support under any circumstances.

He did not go far enough to satisfy Sazonov. If war were to break out, the foreign minister warned, Britain would be dragged in sooner or later. War would be more likely if the British did not make common cause with the Russians and the French from the outset. Buchanan concluded from the discussion that even if Britain declined to join them, France and Russia 'are determined to make a strong stand'.

★

When the Russian council convened at the neoclassical palace on Yelagin Island in the Neva River delta in St Petersburg at 3 p.m. that afternoon Sazonov began by suggesting that Serbia would probably turn to them for advice and assistance. The Russian government ought to prepare its answer in advance. He focused the attention of the council not on Austria, but on Germany. Russia, he argued, had made numerous concessions to Germany whenever their interests had come into conflict over the last decade, but the Germans had taken this only as proof that Russia was too weak to stand up to them. Russia had thus unwittingly encouraged Germany's aggressive methods—and the time had now come to make a stand. The Austrian ultimatum had obviously been drawn up with Germany's connivance. If Serbia complied with its demands, it would be turned into a *de facto* protectorate of the central powers. If Russia failed to stand up on behalf of the Slav peoples its prestige would collapse utterly: it would be regarded as decadent and treated as a second-rate power. But standing up on behalf of Serbia would mean running the risk of war. Were they prepared run this risk?[10]

Others at the meeting argued there would be difficulties in rising to the challenge of fighting a major war, but Russia was prepared for them. The meeting was chaired by the weak and ineffectual premier, Ivan Goremykin. Critically important were the views of the most powerful figure in the government, Aleksandr Krivoshein, the minister of agriculture. He had established himself as someone able to make connections and build coalitions within the fractious Duma, and impressed the tsar in doing so. Since 1912 he had also come to be regarded, along with the minister of war, as leading a war party in the council. He advised his fellow ministers to 'believe more in the Russian people and their age-old love for the homeland, which was greater than any accidental preparedness or unpreparedness for war'.[11]

Krivoshein believed that the government must act boldly in standing up to Germany and Austria: firmness, not conciliation, was most likely to prevent war. If the government failed to act boldly when Russia's vital interests were at stake, he warned, 'public and parliamentary opinion would fail to understand why'.[12] The heads of the army and the navy explained that while the reforms instituted following the Russo-Japanese war had yet to be completed, and although the Russian army had yet to achieve numerical superiority over the central powers, there was no military reason why Russia could not stand firm. The council agreed to back Serbia in spite of the risks.

The ministers agreed that Sazonov should approach the other Great Powers and suggest that they induce Austria to extend the deadline for the Serbian reply. This would enable them to acquaint themselves with the documents that the Austrian government had put together in its investigation of the crime at Sarajevo.

Sazonov proposed they advise Serbia not to offer any resistance if it was unable to protect itself against an armed invasion by Austria-Hungary. Instead, Serbia ought to announce that it was yielding to force and entrusting its fate to the judgment of the Great Powers. The ministers agreed.

The defence ministers were to request the tsar's permission to mobilize the military districts of Odessa, Kiev, Kazan, and Moscow and the Black Sea fleet—when circumstances warranted it.[13] They were also to request authorization for the minister of war to begin gathering stores of war material and for the minister of finance to 'diminish the funds' of the ministry 'which may be at present in Germany or Austria'.[14]

The council meeting lasted four hours. When it finished at 7 p.m. Sazonov immediately met with the German ambassador. He disputed Count Pourtalès' assertion that the situation between Austria and Serbia could be 'localized' because it concerned only the two of them. The affair, he insisted, was a European one. Serbia's promises of good behaviour had been made to Europe, not to Austria, and it was for Europe to examine the dossier of charges against it. Austria could not act as both accuser and judge. He was not prepared to accept as proven the facts alleged by Austria. In fact, he was deeply suspicious of Austria and was not prepared to stand by: 'If Austria-Hungary devours Serbia, we will go to war with her.'[15]

Less than twenty-four hours after the presentation of Austria's demands on Serbia, the Russian council threatened to turn the situation into a

European crisis. War seemed to be a real possibility. But the tsar had not yet authorized the actions proposed by his ministers.

Sazonov believed that he had stated the Russian position clearly and forcefully to the German ambassador. Pourtalès reported that the foreign minister was 'very much excited' and refused to be persuaded by the ambassador's arguments. When Pourtalès tried to argue that Russia could not possibly act as 'the advocate of *regicides*', Sazonov replied that the situation had nothing whatever to do with the monarchical principle. Now, almost a month since the assassination, the horror of the deed had receded. The atmosphere had changed.

Given the forcefulness with which he expressed his views, Sazonov might have been surprised had he seen the ambassador's report of their conversation. Pourtalès, instead of focusing on the apparent willingness of Russia to resort to war, advised that the reference to Austria 'devouring' Serbia meant that Russia

Count Friedrich Pourtalès (1853–1928); German ambassador at St Petersburg (1907–14)

would take up arms only if Austria attempted to acquire Serbian territory. He concluded that Sazonov's desire to 'Europeanize' the dispute meant that the 'immediate intervention' of Russia was not to be anticipated.[16]

Count Friedrich von Pourtalès, an aristocratic cousin of Bethmann Hollweg, conducted diplomacy in the style of the grand *seigneur*. When he arrived in St Petersburg in 1907 he brought with him seventeen vanloads of furniture. He had risen to ambassadorial rank largely because of his success in colouring reports to fit what he believed Berlin wished to hear. In his diary, he drew a rather different conclusion from the meeting: his impression was that the council of ministers had considered the possibility of a breach with Austria-Hungary and Germany and were resolved 'not to hang back from an armed conflict'.[17]

Bethmann Hollweg believed what Pourtalès told him. The effect of the ultimatum had not been unfavourable: it was crucial that Sazonov, although angry, had not committed himself. The chancellor was not worried about the prospect of an Austro-Serbian conflict: Paris was 'aghast' at the cold shoulder they had received from London; everything now depended on whether Russia mobilized immediately.[18]

★

The Austrian tactic of waiting for the departure of Poincaré and Viviani from St Petersburg seemed to have achieved the desired effect. Sazonov was reduced to discussing the situation with the French ambassador rather than coordinating Russo-French policy directly with the French president and premier. On the 24th Poincaré and Viviani were both at sea on board the *France*, having departed only minutes before the note was received in St Petersburg. A copy of the Austrian note was given to the acting minister for foreign affairs, Jean-Baptiste Bienvenu–Martin, in Paris the next morning. He then attempted to provide Poincaré and Viviani with a summary via wireless message to the *France*. Communications, however, were difficult: not only was radio telegraphy in its infancy, but the Germans were attempting to jam messages from their telegraphy centre at Metz.

Bienvenu-Martin, the minister of justice in Viviani's cabinet, had no experience in foreign affairs. But he suddenly found himself at the centre of a political storm. Although he could depend upon a permanent official at the Quai d'Orsay, Philippe Berthelot (the political director), for direction and advice, he had little choice but to meet directly with foreign diplomats in Paris.

Late in the afternoon of the 24th the German ambassador read aloud to him a formal statement outlining his government's position. Not surprisingly, Germany supported the Austrian demands and warned that, if Serbia failed to comply, the Austrian government would have no choice but to adopt strong measures including—if necessary—military means. As far as Germany was concerned the most important point was that the dispute should be settled exclusively between Austria-Hungary and Serbia and that the great powers should endeavour to localize it. Because of the system of alliances, the interference of other Powers would have 'incalculable consequences'.[19]

The views expressed by the interim foreign minister in Paris contrasted starkly with those of Sazonov in St Petersburg. Bienvenu-Martin agreed with the German ambassador that Austria's demand to punish all those implicated in the crime of Sarajevo was legitimate. On the other hand, he believed that Serbia could not be expected to comply with demands that impinged upon its dignity and sovereignty; to do so would be to run the risk of revolution. He suggested that a third option ought to be considered: neither outright acceptance nor refusal, but an agreement that Serbia would punish all those involved in the crime and suppress anti-Austrian propaganda. Was the Austrian note to be regarded as a simple '*mise en demeure*' (a summons to appear in court), he asked? Or was it to be considered an ultimatum? Ambassador Schoen could not answer him.

Like Pourtalès reporting from St Petersburg, Schoen's record of the meeting was optimistic. Bienvenu-Martin, he said, was 'visibly relieved' by Germany's position that the conflict between Austria and Serbia should be settled by the two participants alone. The French government 'sincerely shares the wish' to localize the dispute and would work for this in the interest of maintaining peace in Europe. Bienvenu-Martin did warn him however that Russia had to reckon with Panslavism at home and as a result might find it difficult to take a disinterested attitude. Russia's position would be made more difficult if Austria insisted upon the immediate fulfilment of all its demands, including those that were incompatible with Serbian sovereignty or were impracticable to carry out at once. The French government had already advised Serbia to make all concessions possible and hoped that Austria would agree to discuss individual points at issue with Serbia.

Baron Wilhelm Edler von Schoen was also accustomed to reporting what he believed Berlin wished to hear. A representative of the 'new Germany', he was the son of a wealthy south German industrialist who had been ennobled in 1885—when Wilhelm was 34. One of his aristocratic colleagues complained that he 'smelled of leather'. He had served in the Franco-Prussian war before joining the diplomatic service in 1877. He became a member of the kaiser's entourage, frequently joining him on cruises and learning to ingratiate himself by never disagreeing with his master. A courtier and a society man, the kaiser chose to appoint him as ambassador to St Petersburg in 1905, writing to the tsar that Schoen 'is married to an elegant and most charming wife . . . and is a loyal, quiet discreet man, a personal friend of mine . . . and a good lawn tennis player, in case you should need one'.[20] The kaiser's patronage led to his appointment as secretary of state for foreign affairs in 1907. Although competent, Schoen was too compliant and weak for Bethmann Hollweg, who wanted someone stronger in the position. He was moved from Berlin to become ambassador in Paris in 1910.

From Schoen, the German government might reasonably conclude that if Russia agreed to localize the dispute, the French would be relieved and happy. From their ambassador in St Petersburg, they might reasonably believe that Austria's renunciation of territorial acquisitions in Serbia would be sufficient for Russia to treat the dispute as a 'localized' Austro-Serbian one.

★

Would these optimistic impressions be countered in Berlin? Both the Russian and the British ambassadors were absent on leave. Only the French ambassador, Jules Cambon, was present—having just returned from vacation the day before. Although he had received no instructions on how his government proposed to respond to the Austrian note, he met with Jagow on the afternoon of the 24th and offered the foreign minister his personal views of the situation.

Cambon was blunt. He made it clear to Jagow that he distrusted the claim that Germany was ignorant of the scope of the Austrian note; he complained about the shortness of the time-limit; he expressed his dismay that 'all means of retreat have been cut off'. But his views failed to make much of an impression on the secretary of state.

Jagow dismissed the ambassador's concerns. He expected no more than 'a little excitement' on the part of 'Serbia's friends'. Cambon concluded from his reaction that Germany was prepared to support Austria with 'unusual energy'—which he attributed to the assumption in Berlin that the monarchies would stand together.[21]

Jules Cambon (1845–1935); French ambassador at Berlin (1907–14)

The French ambassadors in Berlin and St Petersburg arrived at fundamentally the same conclusion on the first day of the crisis. Cambon and
Paléologue both reported that Germany seemed determined to support
Austria and must have known the terms of the ultimatum and approved
of it in advance. Only 'the solidarity of the Triple Entente' could prevent
the Germanic powers from pursuing their provocative attitude.[22] From
London, Paul Cambon added his voice to the chorus: he and the Russian
ambassador there agreed that Austria would not have despatched the ultimatum without the agreement of Berlin beforehand. If Germany had
wished to stop Austria it could have done so. The situation was as grave
as could be imagined 'and we see no way of arresting the course of events'.[23]
Paul Cambon predicted that in two days Austria would march into Serbia
because the Serbians could not possibly accept the Austrian demands; Russia
would then be compelled to react.

Paul Cambon (1843–1924); French ambassador at London (1898–1920)

That the three ambassadors shared the same perspective was not surprising. They, along with the ambassador at Rome, Camille Barrère, had formed a kind of diplomatic cabinet over the last decade. With a series of ever-changing, weak, and usually uninstructed foreign ministers, they had filled the gap. By July 1914 they were more accustomed to telling the Quai d'Orsay what policy should be than they were to follow directions they received from Paris. The Cambons and Paléologue had all studied together at the famous Lycée Louis-le-Grand (whose graduates included Voltaire, Robespierre, and Victor Hugo, as well as Raymond Poincaré and Jean Jaurès). Jules Cambon had married Paléologue's sister. Though they varied on the extent to which a rapprochement with Germany was possible, they were all committed to the view that the alliance with Russia was essential for

France's position in Europe, and that the entente with Britain was essential for France's future overseas.

Sir Edward Grey agreed with the assessments of the Entente ambassadors in London. When he met with the Austrian ambassador that morning he told him that he was shocked by the extent of the Austrian demands. The foreign secretary had never before seen 'one State address to another independent State a document of so formidable a character'.[24] The demand that Austria-Hungary might be given the right to appoint officials who would have authority within the frontiers of Serbia could not be consistent with Serbia's sovereignty. Nevertheless, as far as the British government was concerned, it had no interest in the merits of the dispute between Austria and Serbia; its only concern was the peace of Europe. Grey was greatly apprehensive and promised to 'exchange views' with other powers in order to determine what might be done to mitigate the situation.

Grey did have a suggestion for the French ambassador. He saw an opportunity to exercise a mediating or moderating influence: Germany, Italy, France, and Britain—the great powers who had no direct interests in Serbia—could 'act together for the sake of peace' simultaneously in Vienna and St Petersburg. He was going to see the German ambassador following a cabinet meeting that afternoon and he would put the suggestion to him then. Paul Cambon agreed that the idea was worth pursuing, but warned that once Austria attacked Serbia it would be too late for any mediation. Time was quickly running out.[25]

★

The council of ministers in St Petersburg had been scheduled to meet not to discuss the European crisis but to deal with striking workers. The British cabinet was scheduled to meet at 3.15 that afternoon in order to discuss the crisis in Ireland. The conference of the four party leaders meeting at Buckingham Palace had failed to come to an agreement, and now an armed revolt in Ulster seemed a distinct possibility. But Grey took the opportunity of the meeting to present an alarming summary of the situation in Europe: the prime minister believed that a 'real Armageddon' was within sight. Nevertheless, Asquith reassured his beautiful young mistress that 'there seems . . . no reason why we should be more than spectators'.[26]

When he met with the German ambassador that afternoon Grey reiterated his position that he had no concern with the ultimatum to Serbia as long as it did not lead to trouble between Austria and Russia. But given the 'extraordinarily stiff character of the Austrian note', the shortness of the time-limit, and the wide scope of the demands on Serbia, he was very apprehensive of the view that Russia would take.[27] He confessed that he felt quite helpless to influence Russia on his own. The only possibility of exercising a moderating influence was for the four disinterested powers to work together at Vienna and St Petersburg. The immediate danger was that Austria might, a few hours after the deadline, march into Serbia. This would arouse demands in Russia to step in to help the Serbs. The only chance of persuading Austria to delay military action was if Germany joined Britain in a diplomatic initiative at Vienna.

When Lichnowsky reported the conversation to Berlin he emphasized Grey's anxieties. The Austrian note, the foreign secretary had told him, 'exceeded anything he had ever seen of this sort'.[28] If Serbia accepted the terms unconditionally it would cease to count as an independent nation. If Austria invaded Serbia there would be an immediate danger of war—a war that would exhaust and impoverish Europe. Industry and trade would be ruined, the power of capital destroyed; revolutionary movements like those of 1848 would result.

In spite of these grim predictions, Lichnowsky also gave Berlin reason for optimism. Grey, he said, had emphasized that the European war that he foresaw would be fought between Russia, Austria-Hungary, Germany, and France. He had given no hint that Britain might become involved.

Lichnowsky, distrustful of the Austrians in general and of Berchtold in particular, suggested privately to Grey that the Serbs should not reply negatively to the ultimatum, that they must respond favourably to some points at once. This would give Austria an excuse for not taking immediate action. He did not report this suggestion to Berlin.

Grey was persuaded. Immediately after meeting with Lichnowsky he telegraphed to Belgrade that the only possibility of averting Austrian military action was for Serbia to avoid giving an absolute refusal to the demands and to reply favourably to as many points as the time-limit allowed. Serbia ought to express its regret and promise Austria the 'fullest satisfaction' in dealing with any Serbian officials who were proved to have been accomplices in the murder of the archduke.[29]

★

The Serbs were becoming desperate. Prime Minister Pašić returned to Belgrade at 5 a.m., dejected and anxious. He convened a meeting of the cabinet at 10 a.m., which then met most of the day with the regent, Crown Prince Aleksandar, in the chair. Rumours were circulating throughout the city: that the government would relocate to Nish; that a telegram had been received from St Petersburg promising Russian support; that Montenegro had promised to march with Serbia if Austria attacked; that the military were insisting on war; that full mobilization had begun; that the crown prince had appealed to both the tsar and to the queen of Italy for support.

The last two rumours were true. Following the meeting of the cabinet, Aleksandar sent a telegram to the tsar appealing for his support. He assured him that the Serbian government condemned the outrage at Sarajevo and that it would open an inquiry into it if the complicity of Serbian subjects were proved at the trial in Austria–Hungary. The demands contained in the Austrian note, however, were unnecessarily humiliating and incompatible with Serbia's dignity as an independent state. Nevertheless, Serbia was prepared to accept those conditions compatible with Serbian independence 'as well as those to which your Majesty may advise us to agree'. But some of the demands required changes in legislation which could not be carried out within the time-limit. The Austrian army was concentrating on the frontier. Serbia was unable to defend itself. Prince Aleksandar begged the tsar to come to Serbia's aid as soon as possible. 'The much appreciated goodwill which your Majesty has so often shown towards us inspires us with the firm belief that once again our appeal to your noble Slav heart will not pass unheeded.'[30]

The news from St Petersburg was not encouraging. The Serbian minister, who had been on vacation at his summer villa in Finland until he got word of the ultimatum, managed to see Sazonov that evening, after the Russian council of ministers had met. After they discussed the situation for an hour Spalajković was able to report that Sazonov condemned the ultimatum: no sovereign state could accept such demands. Russia was prepared to help, but it was not clear how: there was no promise of military support. In fact, Sazonov suggested that Serbia should not resist an Austrian invasion. Instead, the government should withdraw to the south and appeal to the Powers for their assistance. Russia might mobilize and might issue a communiqué promising to protect Serbia.[31]

Meanwhile, the Serbian minister of war ordered that the bridges over the Sava River connecting Austria and Serbia be mined, and that the railways prepare to be taken over by the military authorities. The cabinet as a whole believed on the 24th that Austria was likely to attack as soon as the ultimatum expired on the evening of the 25th.

Time was now of the essence—or so it seemed. By Friday evening fewer than twenty-four hours remained before the Austrian deadline was set to expire. While the Serbian cabinet was still trying to decide how to respond, the Austrian minister in Belgrade received detailed instructions on how to proceed the next day. Serbia must accept the demands unconditionally; anything less would be taken as a refusal. Assuming that the Serbs would refuse, Giesl and the legation staff were to leave Belgrade on the 6.30 p.m. train for Semlin. Once across the Austrian border, he was to use the official railway telephone at the station to call Tisza in Budapest. Tisza would then convey the message to Berchtold, who would expect to receive it as early as 7 p.m. on Saturday. If Serbia surprised them and accepted the demands, Giesl could send one of his staff to do the telephoning from Semlin to Budapest.

Everything appeared to be moving as the Austrians had anticipated. The Serbs seemed certain to refuse at least some of the demands; the French and the British appeared reluctant to become involved and would perhaps restrain the Russians; the Russians might complain and bluster, but a determined Austro-German combination should be enough to deter them. War, when it came, would be localized. Serbia could not possibly withstand the armed might of the Austrian armies.

★

The reports they were receiving in Vienna did nothing to weaken or deflect Austria's determination. From Berlin, the ambassador reported that the newspapers there were full of praise for the Austrian note. From Rome the ambassador reported that the secretary-general (equivalent to the permanent under-secretary at the British Foreign Office)—representing San Giuliano—agreed that Austria's action was 'purely defensive'.[32] From Paris, the ambassador reported that Bienvenu-Martin—representing the minister of foreign affairs—expressed the hope that the dispute would end peaceably 'in a manner to satisfy our wishes'.[33] From London, the ambassador reported that Sir Edward Grey, while regretting the form of the note and the brevity of the time-limit, 'is at one with us in wishing to localize the conflict'.[34]

Equally encouraging, the Germans appeared to be supporting the Austrians as promised. The German ambassador in Paris assured his Austrian colleague that he had informed the French government that Germany regarded the

Austro-Serbian controversy as one that should be resolved exclusively by the two governments involved. More pointedly, if a third state were to interfere in the dispute Germany would be faithful to its duties as an ally and 'place itself on our side'.[35] The Austrian ambassador, Count Nikolaus Szécsen, reported to Vienna that the German ambassador's manner of speaking to Bienvenu-Martin 'appears to have been very energetic'.[36]

The diplomacy of the day emboldened Austria. Tisza's earlier hesitations and reservations disappeared: an unsatisfactory Serbian reply ought to be followed by an immediate Austrian mobilization, he now told Berchtold. At the Ballhausplatz they were preparing for war. The Hague conventions stipulated that Serbia must be served with a formal declaration of war. This ought to be presented after Austria had completed its mobilization but before military operations were launched. But the procedure already laid down had provided for the Austrian minister and his staff at the legation to depart from Belgrade immediately upon receiving an unsatisfactory reply to the Austrian demands. Thus, there would be no Austrian official available to present the declaration in the prescribed manner: telegraphic communication would likely have been severed and the mails would be unsafe. Serbia was unlikely to permit a specially selected person to cross the frontier to deliver the declaration to them. The Austrian government therefore asked the German chancellor whether Germany would undertake to transmit the declaration of war through its minister at Belgrade.[37]

Germany declined the request. As its position was that the quarrel with Serbia was an internal Austro-Hungarian affair, Germany must not appear to be mixed up in it in any way. Only if Russia were to intervene would Germany be drawn into the conflict. A declaration of war coming from the German legation would, especially to that portion of the public unacquainted with diplomatic custom, make it 'appear as though we had incited [gehetzt] Austria-Hungary to go to war'.[38]

Berlin was determined to adhere steadfastly to the line that it had played no part in the formulation of the Austrian demands. Although Germany's ambassadors were instructed to reinforce this at every opportunity, their explanations were beginning to ring hollow. Late on Friday evening the Wilhelmstrasse notified Germany's ambassadors in Paris, London, and St Petersburg that the opinion prevailing in those capitals seemed to be that Germany had incited Austria to direct a 'sharp note' to Serbia and had 'participated in its composition'. The ambassadors were to refute this. They should reaffirm that Germany had exercised no influence of any kind regarding the contents of the note. Nor could Germany advise Vienna to retract: the Austrian government had determined to take a strong stand on its own initiative, and its prestige—both internal and external—'would be completely lost' if it were to back down from its stand.

While Germany was disavowing responsibility and refusing to put any pressure on Vienna, it continued to worry about Italy's reaction. The ambassador in Rome reported that the Austrian ultimatum distressed San Giuliano. Expecting a backlash among Italians, he instructed prefects to suppress any anti-Austrian demonstrations and to prevent volunteers from enlisting to fight on the side of Serbia. He feared that the short time-limit would create an unfavourable impression and he complained that Austria, in proceeding without first advising its allies, had acted against 'the spirit of the Triple Alliance'.[39] Did this mean that Italy would break from its partners?

Jagow could not hide his frustration when he received word of San Giuliano's displeasure. He complained that the Austrians seemed not to have kept their promise to inform the Italians beforehand. He suggested they tell San Giuliano that Germany found itself in the same boat: it had not been informed 'in detail' about the Austrian note—nor did it wish to be informed, as the matter belonged to Austria-Hungary's internal affairs.[40] He suggested they remind San Giuliano that Italy had failed to inform its allies at the beginning of the Libyan war, that it had presented them with a fait accompli.

A conversation between Jagow and the Italian ambassador in Berlin clarified the problem confronting the alliance. Riccardo Bollati had previously occupied the important post of secretary-general at the Italian Foreign Office, so he was well acquainted with San Giuliano's attitude to the Triple Alliance. He assured Jagow that Italy would maintain a friendly and benevolent attitude towards Austria. He promised that Italy would cooperate with its allies in all Balkan questions—but only after receiving assurances concerning compensation. If such assurances were not forthcoming, Italy would aim to prevent the 'territorial aggrandizement' of Austria-Hungary.[41] Bollati confided to Jagow—in the strictest confidence—that Italy would demand the Trentino as compensation for any extension of Austrian territory; if Austria took any part of Albania, Italy would expect to receive Valona.

Jagow agreed with the Italians. He instructed Tschirschky to point out to Berchtold that Article VII of the alliance spoke of the *régions des Balkans*— therefore the Austrian interpretation that the compensation clause referred only to *Turkish* territory was erroneous. More to the point, it seemed to Jagow that a 'theoretical' discussion concerning the interpretation of the article was misplaced under the circumstances. 'Politically useful decisions are needed.'

San Giuliano was adamant. In spite of his illness, he returned to Rome later in the day to meet with the prime minister and the German ambassador. In an excited discussion lasting several hours, he argued that the spirit of the alliance demanded that Austria should have come to an understanding with its allies before embarking on such an aggressive move. If a general European war broke out it would be the result of 'an act of provocation and aggression' on the part of Austria.[42] He insisted that Article VII meant that they should come to an agreement prior to any alteration of the status quo in the Balkans and that there should be compensation for any territorial changes. Ambassador Flotow found the situation awkward and frustrating: Mérey, the Austrian ambassador, was sick in bed; the counsellor of the Austrian embassy, who was filling in for him, was 'incompetent'. He did not hold out much hope of shifting Austria's position at Rome.[43]

After almost a month of encouraging, prodding, and cajoling, the Germans had failed to move the Austrians any closer to the Italians. Their warnings that something must be done in order to bind Italy closer to the alliance had been ignored. The Austrians had offered nothing. In fact, they had made it quite clear that they did not intend to offer any compensation to the Italians both because they did not believe that the terms of the alliance warranted it and because they themselves had disavowed any intention of acquiring Serbian territory.

The first day of the crisis found the Triple Alliance in disarray. But it was still far from clear what form Italy's complaints would take and how far its reservations might influence the policies of Germany and Austria. In recognition of the political difficulties faced by the Italian government in opposing any movement for national unification, the German and Austrian ambassadors had been authorized to bribe journalists. This was referred to euphemistically as 'financially influencing the local press'. By 24 July this initiative had accomplished little, if anything.

The other initiative, to shore up the partnership with Romania by bringing Bulgaria into the Triple Alliance, was stalled. King Karl, although sympathetic, faced insurmountable political opposition to publicizing Romania's membership in the alliance. And although the kaiser had swallowed his contempt for King Ferdinand of Bulgaria and authorized discussions of an alliance in Sofia, these had gotten nowhere by 24 July. The kaiser now gave his permission for a new initiative: to take advantage of Turkey's apparent desire to join the alliance.[44]

In spite of these complications, one day into the crisis neither Austria nor Germany showed any sign of wavering in their determination. Berchtold made his position clear to the Russian chargé d'affaires in Vienna that afternoon: 'the very existence of Austria-Hungary as a Great Power' was at stake; Austria-Hungary must give proof of its stature as a Great Power 'by an outright *coup de force*'.[45] Nothing that the Austrians or the Germans heard after the presentation of the ultimatum disabused them of the belief that the dispute could be contained, that it could be 'localized' between Austria and Serbia. From everything that they heard, neither the French nor the British wished to be involved and their reluctance might be sufficient to restrain the Russians from offering support to Serbia.

The biggest question remained unanswered: how would the Russians respond? Early indications were not encouraging. In St Petersburg Sazonov defended the Serbs and argued that they would under no circumstances agree to disband the *Narodna Odbrana*. He was unmoved by arguments of monarchical solidarity. In London the Russian ambassador declared that it would be impossible for Russia to advise Serbia to accept the conditions of the Austrian note: if Serbia complied it would 'sink to the level of an Austrian vassal'.[46] Public opinion in Russia would not tolerate this.

In Vienna the Russian chargé d'affaires, Prince Kudashev, asked how Austria would respond if the time-limit were to expire without a satisfactory answer from Serbia. Berchtold told him that Giesl and his staff had been instructed in such circumstances to leave Belgrade and return to Austria. The prince, after reflecting on this, exclaimed, '*Alors c'est la guerre!*'

Day Two
Saturday, 25 July

Would there be war by the end of the day? It seemed so: the Serbs had only until 6 p.m. to accept the Austrian demands. Berchtold had instructed the Austrian representative in Belgrade that nothing less than full acceptance of all ten points contained in the ultimatum would be regarded as satisfactory. If the Serbs failed to comply with the demands, the Austrian minister and the entire legation were to leave the country immediately.

The Austrian position was clear. It had not moved since the ultimatum was presented on Thursday evening. The only uncertainty seemed to be how and when a formal declaration of war would be made. No one expected the Serbs to agree to the demands in their entirety—certainly not the Austrians.

Nothing had happened on Friday the 24th to persuade Austria to alter its course. That the Russians complained about the note was no surprise. The reports received in Vienna from St Petersburg were actually quite encouraging: the Russians, although angry and bitter, seemed likely to respond slowly and carefully. According to the Austrian ambassador, Sazonov appeared saddened and depressed, complaining that the Austrians seemed to want war, that they were burning their bridges behind them and setting fire to Europe. But instead of threatening the Austrians with war, Sazonov only warned them that Russia would not permit them to 'devour' Serbia— from which the German ambassador concluded that this, along with the proposal to bring the dispute before a European 'court', indicated that Russia was not likely to undertake a 'warlike response'.[1] Sazonov did little more than warn that Austria would encounter the combined displeasure of the Entente.

Was the threat of a combined opposition to Austria real or imaginary? Early indications suggested that the Russian threat lacked substance: with the French president and premier literally 'at sea' on board the *France*, the

French did not seem likely to undertake any forceful policy. And the caretaker back in Paris, Bienvenu-Martin, actually appeared to accept the logic of Austria's legal arguments in its complaints against Serbia: he agreed with the Austro-German position that the dispute was one that concerned Serbia and Austria alone. In London, Sir Edward Grey was on the spot and in charge but gave no indication that Britain would stand shoulder-to-shoulder with the Russians in a conflict over Serbia. Like Bienvenu-Martin, Grey's only concern seemed to be that the crisis should be contained, that it be limited to a dispute between Austria and Serbia. 'I do not consider that public opinion here would or ought to sanction our going to war over a Servian quarrel.'[2] But if a war between Austria and Serbia were to occur, 'other issues' might draw Britain in. This he was anxious to prevent. Instead of warning Austria that Britain might support Russia if it came to a conflict, however, Grey proposed that the four 'disinterested' Powers—Britain, France, Germany, and Italy—might attempt to mediate the dispute.

Without a guarantee of French and British support would the Russians be prepared to run the risk of war with Austria and Germany? On the first day of the crisis the French and the British had both indicated that they would encourage the Serbs to respond as positively as possible to the Austrian demands and that they should declare their willingness to submit the dispute to arbitration or mediation.[3] Neither Britain nor France was prepared to go as far as Sazonov in declaring the demands of Austria to be 'unacceptable'. In St Petersburg Sazonov was unable to get any clear indication of what the Entente would do: the French ambassador promised that France would live up to its alliance commitments, but the British ambassador warned the Russians not to expect Britain's unconditional support. In Paris, the British ambassador assured his Austrian counterpart that Russia would not fight.[4] And Paléologue's promise of French support was of questionable value: the terms of the alliance provided only for French assistance in the event of an attack on Russia. Nothing in those terms envisioned France taking up arms in support of a Russian attack on Austria in defence of Serbia. So what was the promise to live up to the commitments of the alliance actually worth?

For close to a month since the assassination the diplomats of the Entente had stood on the sidelines, waiting for the Austrians to act. Everyone anticipated that when they finally did so it would be dramatic and determined—but no one had guessed that their demands would be deliberately designed to make them impossible for Serbia to accept. When the Austrian ultimatum was finally presented, the scene suddenly shifted from

Vienna and Berlin to St Petersburg and London. Everything, it seemed, would now depend upon how the Entente responded: were they prepared to stand by and see Serbia attacked or reduced to a vassal of Austria-Hungary? Entering the second day of the crisis it was far from clear what their response would be.

★

By midday Saturday the Russians seemed to have reached a decision. They prepared to take dramatic military steps. In the morning at Krasnoe Selo, Tsar Nicholas presided over a meeting of the Russian Grand Council—which included those who had met as the Council of Ministers on Friday, but added members of the royal family and high-ranking officials. The council agreed to mobilize the thirteen army corps designated to take action against Austria-Hungary. And by the afternoon the preparations to mobilize in the military districts of Kiev, Odessa, Moscow, and Kazan had begun.[5] The German military attaché reported that the regiments had been recalled to their garrisons, that summer manoeuvres had been cancelled, and that military cadets were to be commissioned immediately rather than later in the autumn. He anticipated that all necessary preparations were being made for mobilization against Austria.[6]

What the council had agreed upon, and the tsar had approved, was to declare 'the period preparatory to war'. This had been defined on 2 March 1913 as 'a period of diplomatic tension which precedes the beginning of war operations'. The council was acting on information that preparatory measures for mobilization were already under way in Austria-Hungary and Italy. The Serbian minister in St Petersburg reported to Belgrade that Russia was preparing to launch an offensive against Austria-Hungary if it attacked Serbia. The tsar believed that Russia and France could defeat the Triple Alliance, and that the war might end in the partition of Austria-Hungary. Spalajković suggested that the moment had arrived to 'achieve the full unification of the Serbs' and that it would be desirable if Austria attacked Serbia.[7]

At 8 p.m. the chief of the general staff met with his department heads and announced that the decision had been made to reply to the Austrian ultimatum 'in a manner worthy of Russia'.[8] Shortly after midnight the fortresses of Warsaw, Ossovyets, Novgorod, Brest-Litovsk, Ivangorod, Vilna, and Grodno were placed on a war footing; bridges over rivers near the frontier were to be placed under guard; St Petersburg and Warsaw were declared to be in a 'state of extraordinary protective activity'. Censorship and security were tightened; horses and wagons assembled for transporting men and munitions, harbours were to be mined.

Did these steps mean 'war'? Apparently not. Russia would not begin military operations until Austrian troops crossed the Serbian frontier. 'In order to avoid major diplomatic complications' operations were to be confined solely to action against Austria, and the remaining military districts would be mobilized only in the event that Germany joined Austria.[9]

Having decided on their first military steps, the Russians tried to seize the diplomatic initiative. After the meeting of the council on the previous day Sazonov had instructed Prince Kudashev (still acting in place of the absent ambassador in Vienna) to propose an extension of the time-limit on the ultimatum in order to provide sufficient time for the Powers 'to acquaint themselves' with the findings of the Austrian inquiry into the circumstances of the crime of Sarajevo.[10] Russian representatives in Berlin, London, Paris, and Rome were to remind the other Powers that they had not been informed of the Austrian demands on Serbia until twelve hours following the delivery of the note, making it impossible for them to resolve the dispute peacefully. As Austria had indicated its willingness to provide the Powers with the results of their inquiry into the assassination plot, surely sufficient time ought to be given for them to form an opinion on the matter? To fail to do so would be at variance with 'international ethics'.[11]

But Kudashev was unable to meet directly with Berchtold. When he appeared at the Ballhausplatz first thing Saturday morning, he discovered that the foreign minister had left Vienna to be with the emperor at Bad Ischl when the ultimatum expired that evening. The best the Russian chargé d'affaires could do was to present the arguments for an extension of the time-limit to Berchtold's *chef de cabinet*. But Baron Macchio was not encouraging; in fact he behaved with an 'icy coldness': there was 'no chance' that Austria would agree to extend the time-limit. He dismissed as a misapprehension the Russian argument that time was needed to consider the Austrian position and to examine the dossier: Austria had not informed the Powers of the demands they had made upon Serbia in order to learn their opinion. On the contrary, Macchio insisted that the affair concerned Austria and Serbia alone. Austria had provided the Powers with the dossier only in order to comply with international 'etiquette'.[12]

Macchio promised to communicate Sazonov's request to Berchtold, but this was not enough for Kudashev. He desperately despatched telegrams directly to the foreign minister, both to Ischl and to the train: 'I am urgently instructed to ask the Imperial and Royal government for a prolongation of the term fixed in the ultimatum to Serbia.' The telegram reached Berchtold on board the train somewhere between Linz and Ischl. Kudashev admitted to the French ambassador that he did not expect a positive result.

Sazonov did not believe that his arguments alone would persuade Austria to extend the deadline. His hopes rested with Germany. When he met with the German ambassador in St Petersburg on Friday evening, he had urged Pourtalès to present his argument for an extension to Berlin on the premise that Europe required more time to form an opinion on the issues raised by the ultimatum. After all, he argued, the promises made by Serbia in 1909 to behave as a good neighbour to Austria, and which Austria was now using as justification for the extraordinary demands it was making on Serbia, had been made not to Austria alone, but to Europe as a whole. And 'Europe', he insisted, could not permit Serbia to be sacrificed to the threat of violence from her more powerful neighbour.

Pourtalès had not been encouraging. During their conversation on Friday he stuck to Germany's position that the question was one to be settled between Austria and Serbia alone, that it was in the interest of Europe that the dispute should be 'localized'. He had gone even further, arguing that Sazonov's proposal would amount to summoning Austria to appear before a 'European tribunal': the judicial inquiry it had conducted into the assassination would be subjected to the supervision of the Powers. This would be humiliating, and Austria could not agree to it without abandoning its status as a Great Power.[13] Moreover, the procedure suggested by Sazonov was impracticable: what would be the point if Austria's friends lined up on one side and its opponents on the other? The effect would be to turn a local dispute into a European crisis. Was that really what the Russians wanted? It could mean a European war. Were the Russians prepared to run this risk for the sake of Serbia?

The ambassador's arguments failed to convince Sazonov. He insisted that his suggestion be transmitted to Berlin for consideration. But he was under no illusion: he recognized that Germany was 'prejudiced' (*voreingenommen*) in Austria's favour and had predetermined its position. Becoming increasingly irritated as he reviewed the situation, he implied that there would be dire consequences if Europe did not intervene to prevent Serbia from being 'devoured' by Austria. If this happened Russia was prepared to go to war with Austria.

Sazonov's immediate aim was to extend the deadline. Recognizing that the Austrians would not agree to this on their own, he attempted to get Germany to put pressure on them. And to persuade Germany he was prepared to threaten war.

Pourtalès dismissed this as a hollow threat. The fact that only once during their long interview did Sazonov allude to the possibility of an armed intervention by Russia led him to conclude that no 'precipitate steps' in the direction of war were likely at present. The ambassador did not know that the Russian Council of Ministers had already decided to advise the tsar to authorize a partial mobilization directed against Austria. Instead of taking the threat seriously, and in spite of Sazonov's 'excited mood', Pourtalès concluded that the foreign minister's real aim was to temporize—and thus his proposal to involve Europe. He anticipated no immediate intervention on Russia's part; it was likely to take up arms only if Austria attempted to acquire Serbian territory.[14]

When Sazonov warned against Austria 'devouring' Serbia, he had an unintended effect. He seemed to confirm Tisza's argument that if Austria-Hungary promised not to take any Serbian territory, Russia might refrain from military intervention. Angry, apprehensive, and fearful, Sazonov hoped that a firm and united front on the part of the Entente might convince Germany to put pressure on Austria. He knew that his legalistic arguments concerning the agreement of 1909 would have little effect unless backed by real political authority and the possibility of military consequences. Although the French government was practically absent, and although Bienvenu-Martin had seemed to swallow the Austro-German line, the French ambassador in St Petersburg continued to give his personal assurances that France would live up to its alliance commitments. But for the moment these assurances meant little, if anything. Sazonov saw only two choices for Russia: either deter Austria by mobilizing in preparation to defend Serbian sovereignty, or trust that French and British pressure in Berlin might result in a mediated settlement.

Why would Sazonov not allow Austria to deal with the Serbs as they wished? Because, he told the British ambassador, 'Austria's action was in reality directed against Russia.' The real goal was to overthrow the status quo in the Balkans and to establish an Austrian hegemony there.[15] Sazonov had sketched his nightmare scenario to the German ambassador on Friday evening: the Austrians would devour Serbia, then Bulgaria, and then 'we shall have them on the Black Sea'.[16] Russia could not contemplate such an outcome.

By Saturday afternoon three options seemed open to the Russians: to allow Austria to 'devour' Serbia and establish its hegemony in the Balkans; to prepare for war with Austria on behalf of Serbia; to bring sufficient pressure to bear to persuade Germany to restrain Austria and submit the dispute to mediation. No one in the Russian government seriously considered abandoning Serbia to the Austrians. The second and third options seemed to merge together: Russia might begin taking the military steps necessary for fighting a war with Austria, but such steps might also have the effect of bringing Austria and Germany to the negotiating table.

Sazonov assured the British ambassador that in taking the first steps to mobilization Russia had no aggressive intentions and would undertake no military action until forced to do so by Austria. He maintained that, as Serbia was prepared to punish those guilty of perpetrating or assisting in the crime at Sarajevo, it could not be expected to submit to Austria's political demands. If Austria attacked when the deadline expired he suggested that the Serbian government abandon Belgrade, withdraw their forces into the interior, and appeal for the assistance of the Powers. 'Leaving the enemy to occupy the land without fighting and making a solemn appeal to the Powers' might succeed in internationalizing the question.[17] Thus, by Saturday afternoon, with the deadline looming in only a few hours, it seemed possible that a general European war could still be delayed or averted. If Europe were to become involved in an attempt to settle the crisis diplomatically, even an Austrian invasion might not lead immediately to war. Russia—according to the foreign minister—was prepared to countenance an Austrian invasion and occupation of Serbia. Sazonov had still not suggested to anyone—not to the Austrians or the Germans; not to the British or the French—that Russia would immediately go to war if Austria attacked Serbia.

★

The question now was whether the dispute would be 'localized' as Austria and Germany wished, or 'internationalized' as Russia wished.

Where the British and the French stood remained uncertain until Saturday. On Friday the acting French foreign minister had indicated that he agreed with the Austro-German position on 'localization'. The British foreign secretary had refused to commit himself: on the merits of the dispute between Austria and Serbia Britain had no opinion or interest. As long as the dispute did not lead to an Austro-Russian confrontation, Britain would not concern itself in the matter.[18] No one knew what would happen when the Austrian deadline expired at 6 p.m.

By Saturday afternoon hope was vanishing that Austria might extend its deadline. But what would this mean? The Austrians assured the British that it need not necessarily mean war. In London, the Austrian ambassador promised Grey that if Serbia failed to comply with the demands Austria would only break off diplomatic relations and begin military preparations— 'not operations'. This, Grey told his ambassadors in St Petersburg and Paris, 'makes the immediate situation rather less acute'.[19] Sometime on Saturday afternoon the looming deadline of 6 p.m. began to appear less cataclysmic than might have been anticipated.

Nevertheless, military preparations, and still less military mobilizations, were not to be undertaken lightly. Quite apart from the tensions they created and the increased likelihood of an armed confrontation of some kind, they were hugely difficult and expensive. So efforts to convince the Austrians to extend the deadline continued until the last moment. In Berlin the Russian chargé d'affaires, still acting in place of the absent ambassador, attempted to meet with the German secretary of state to present Sazonov's proposal to extend the deadline and to involve the European Powers in a settlement of the crisis. Jagow agreed to meet with him—but not until 4.50 in the afternoon—barely an hour before the deadline was to expire. So the chargé submitted a written note outlining the Russian proposal, pleading with the secretary of state to instruct the German ambassador in Vienna to assist in bringing about an extension.[20] He reported to St Petersburg that he was not hopeful.

Everyone now regarded Germany as the key. Without German pressure on the Austrians to submit the dispute to mediation there seemed no possibility that they would alter their course. Sazonov tried to convince the British that the only thing that would induce the Germans to pressure Austria was Britain standing firmly by the side of Russia and France. He did not believe that the Germans really wanted a war. But their attitude would be determined by Britain's: if the British failed to take a firm stand now, 'rivers of blood would flow' and, in the end, they would be dragged in anyway.[21] If Britain wished to maintain the balance of power in Europe, Austria must not be permitted to triumph.[22]

★

Two very different strategies emerged over the course of the day Saturday in St Petersburg. Sazonov insisted that the only way the Austrians could be stopped from crushing Serbia was if the Germans were to restrain them—and the only way that the Germans would exercise such restraint was if they believed that they would run up against the combined forces of the Entente if they failed to do so. Sir George Buchanan offered Grey's alternative to this scenario: that Britain should offer its diplomatic services as a 'friend' at Berlin and Vienna—a friend who, if its councils of moderation were disregarded, might then be converted into an ally of Russia. Sazonov countered that Germany seemed to be convinced that it could rely upon the British remaining neutral in any conflict. Buchanan warned that, if the Russians mobilized, Germany would not allow them the time to carry this out and 'would probably declare war at once'.[23]

Buchanan's gloomy forecast failed to deter Sazonov. Russia, he insisted, could not allow Austria to crush Serbia and become the predominant power in the Balkans. Even without Britain—with only the support of France—Russia was willing to run the risk of a European war over Serbia. With the French ambassador continuing to assure him of French support, Sazonov told Buchanan that Grey needed to decide: he could choose now to stand with Russia and perhaps succeed in averting a cataclysmic war by frightening Germany into pressuring Austria, or he could stand on the sidelines and be forced into the war once it broke out.

Grey refused to choose. He was unwilling to give the kind of unconditional promise of support that Russia was seeking. But neither did he propose to stand on the sidelines. The 'sudden, brusque and peremptory character' of the Austrian demands on Serbia made it 'almost inevitable' that Russia and Austria would shortly mobilize their forces against one another.[24] This scenario suggested to him that there was still an opportunity to avert war: Britain and France, Germany and Italy could, he suggested, 'hold the hand' of their partners in attempting to mediate the dispute.

The Russian ambassador in London, Count Aleksandr Benckendorff, disliked Grey's suggestion. A career diplomat, Benckendorff had followed his father's footsteps when he joined the diplomatic service in 1868 at the age of 19. Appointed ambassador to London in 1903 he had worked hard to promote the idea of an entente with Britain. He was one of those moderate progressives who believed that a closer relationship with Britain would promote constitutionalism in Russia and stimulate political reform and economic development. A rapprochement with Britain was worth the

Count Aleksandr Benckendorff (1849–1917); Russian ambassador at London (1903–17)

price of abandoning some of Russia's ambitions in Central Asia, and combined with the French alliance it would strengthen Russia's ability to withstand Austro-German expansionism in the Balkans and the Middle East.[25]

By 1914 Benckendorff believed that he had accomplished most of his goals. He had established himself in British society: he was a frequent weekend guest of King George V and enjoyed close friendships with leaders of the Liberal government—the prime minister, Herbert Asquith, and the first lord of the admiralty, Winston Churchill, as well as important figures within the Unionist opposition. But he now feared that his work might be undone. He feared that Grey's proposed four-Power mediation would give Germany the impression that Britain and France had become detached from Russia. He pleaded with Grey to give some indication to Germany that Britain would not stand aside if there was a war.

Grey maintained that he had not done this, that he had given no indication that Britain would stand aside in the event of war. Paradoxically, he now suggested that the likelihood of Austro-Russian mobilizations might actually make war less likely: their mobilizations would have the effect of turning the 'localized' Austro-Serbian dispute into a wider one that necessitated the intervention of Europe in order to preserve the peace. In effect, Grey was suggesting that the German government should now ask Austria 'to consider some modification of her demands, under the threat of Russian mobilisation'.[26]

Grey admitted that it would not be easy to persuade the Germans. He feared they would interpret it as throwing away their military advantage because, with them, mobilization was a matter of hours, whereas with Russia it was a matter of days. And he understood he was asking the Germans that, if Russia mobilized against Austria, they should suspend their own mobilization and join with Britain in a diplomatic initiative instead. Surely the Russians ought to see that his proposal would be advantageous to them, as they would gain time for their mobilization?

Sazonov's pleas in St Petersburg, along with Benckendorff's in London, fell on deaf ears. Grey reiterated that he had said nothing to indicate whether Britain would or would not take part in a war: he simply 'could not say'. He would not warn Germany of an armed intervention by Britain, but neither would he promise to remain neutral. Instead, he maintained that his proposed four-Power mediation—now referred to as the mediation *à quatre*—'was the best proposal to make in the interests of peace'.[27]

Grey believed that he had little choice. He saw no indication in Britain of a willingness to fight a European war for the sake of Serbia. There was no appetite in government to join the Entente in a war for the sake of Russian interests in the Balkans. The British public was not interested in the issues at stake and there was considerable political opposition to any continental commitment—especially within the Liberal party. Things might be different if France was threatened with German aggression, but this did not appear to be the case on Saturday, 25 July.

Although Grey told the Russians that Germany was the only impediment to his mediation strategy, he was in fact equally concerned that Russian intransigence could wreck it. Buchanan was reporting from St Petersburg that Paléologue was promising French support to the Russians and that this was emboldening them: 'it almost looked as if France and Russia were determined to make a strong stand even if we declined to join them'.[28]

Grey somehow had to convince Germany to persuade Austria to come to the negotiating table while at the same time restraining Russia from going too far too fast—and yet it was only the threat of a vigorous Russian response that might induce Germany to insist on a negotiated settlement. If Russia failed to make a determined stand, Germany would have no incentive to risk offending the Austrians by holding them back.

Grey was attempting to perform a complicated diplomatic juggling act: trying to restrain Russia from going too far while using its military preparations as bargaining tool; failing to threaten Germany with British intervention while refusing to promise that Britain would remain neutral if war broke out.

Grey regarded France as essential to the success of his juggling act. Acting on his instructions, the British ambassador in Paris, Sir Francis Bertie, met with Bienvenu-Martin—still acting as foreign minister on behalf of the absent Viviani—and pointed out to him on Saturday afternoon that in 'democratic countries such as England and France' war could not be undertaken without the support of public opinion. And Bertie declared himself to be quite certain that British public opinion would not sanction a war in support of a Russia which 'as protector of Slavs' had picked a quarrel with Austria over the 'Austro-Serbian' difficulty.[29]

Francis Bertie, the second son of an earl, had entered the Foreign Office directly from Eton at the age of 19 in 1863. There he had remained for the next forty years, rising to the position of assistant under-secretary of state before moving to the diplomatic service in 1903. By 1914 he had served as the ambassador in Paris for nine years, where he performed in style, driving to the Elysée Palace in a splendid coach with his coat-of-arms emblazoned on the side. His staff nicknamed him 'the bull' for his obstinate manner and outspoken opinions. He had been a leading proponent of the Anglo-French entente even before coming to Paris, as he had gradually become convinced that France was the only counterweight to Germany's ambition to dominate Europe. He promoted a closer relationship than the entente, pressing Sir Edward Grey to consider an alliance, and encouraging the French to believe it might be a possibility. He feared that the alternative to a clearer commitment might be a Franco-German détente.

Bertie took a decidedly less favourable view of the entente with Russia. He consistently argued against drawing any closer to the Russians and complained of the difficulties they presented to Britain in central Asia. Now, he privately assured Grey that French public opinion would not

Sir Francis Bertie (1844–1919); British ambassador at Paris (1905–18)

back up the Russians 'in so bad a cause'. And he trusted that the French government would advise Russia against 'excessive zeal' in protecting 'their Servian client'.[30]

If Bertie was right, even lukewarm French support ought to be sufficient to restrain Russia from behaving too aggressively. From Grey's perspective, while military preparations—or even mobilization—might bring war closer, they might also encourage negotiations. If France could act as a drag on Russia's willingness to go to war over Serbia, perhaps Germany could be induced to do the same with Austria.

★

When Grey met with the German ambassador in London on Saturday morning, he was encouraged to believe that his proposed mediation *à quatre* might succeed. Prince Lichnowsky told Grey that he had received a telegram from Berlin affirming that Germany had not known the terms of the Austrian demands beforehand and had no more responsibility than any of the other Powers for the 'stiff terms' of the note. On the other hand, those demands now having been presented made it difficult for Austria to retreat from them. Still, Lichnowsky believed Austria might accept 'with dignity' the mediation *à quatre* contemplated by Grey.[31] If Germany agreed to mediation, Grey believed that France would as well.

Lichnowsky could nevertheless feel the opportunity to avert disaster beginning to slip away. The opinion had already taken hold in Britain that Germany was at the very least 'morally responsible' for the Austrian demands. It was unthinkable that such demands would have been made without Germany's encouragement. He warned Berlin that if Germany were now to refuse to participate in Grey's proposed mediation *à quatre* the effect would be ruinous: 'confidence in us and in our peaceful intentions will be ruined once and for all.'

The ambassador assured Grey that he regarded his proposal favourably. He told the truth. On Saturday afternoon he wired Jagow privately to urge him to accept Grey's suggestion and to announce this in both Vienna and St Petersburg. 'I see in it the only possibility of avoiding a world war.' Germany had everything to gain in adopting the mediation proposal and nothing to lose. Mediation was still possible as long as Germany was not mobilized—but, after that, who knew? The ambassador warned that if Germany refused the proposal, Grey would not bestir himself again. Refusal would have a very disagreeable effect in Britain, and if France were drawn into the dispute he did not believe that Britain would dare to remain disinterested.[32]

In the meantime, Grey had already acted on Sazonov's request that he support his proposal for an extension of the time-limit imposed in the Austrian ultimatum. Although he had little hope that this might succeed, he had instructed the British chargé in Berlin, Horace Rumbold, to support the proposal there.

Simultaneously, Lichnowsky was exhorting his government to pressure Austria into extending its deadline. After meeting with Grey in the morning he had immediately wired Berlin to 'urgently advise' agreement with Grey's request that the deadline be extended. If Germany were to refuse to do so it would create the impression in Britain that it had not tried to do everything possible to maintain peace. This might influence the position Britain would take in the future. And he tried to disabuse them in Berlin of any notion that Britain's current domestic difficulties would influence the government's foreign policy: the nation would stand firmly behind it 'no matter what it may be'.[33]

In Berlin, Jagow appeared to support the idea of extending the deadline. In practice, he did little more than 'communicate' the proposal to Vienna. He told the British chargé that he had instructed the German ambassador in Vienna to speak with Berchtold about it. He reiterated to Rumbold what he had already told Lichnowsky: that given the timing involved, and with the Austrian foreign minister at Ischl awaiting the Serbian reply, such a proposal was unlikely to succeed at this late stage. In spite of Jagow's assurances, however, there is no evidence that Tschirschky was instructed to discuss the idea with Berchtold, and none that he proposed the extension to the Austrians.[34]

The Austrian ambassador in Berlin gave a very different picture of opinion at the Wilhelmstrasse. Officials there, Szögyény reported, believed that a negative reply by Serbia to the Austrian demands ought to be followed immediately by an Austrian declaration of war and the beginning of military operations against Serbia. Any delay would be dangerous because it would create an opportunity for other Powers to interfere. The Wilhelmstrasse was urgently advising Austria to proceed quickly and thus present the world 'with a fait accompli'.[35] The ambassador concurred.

Paradoxically, the proposal of the Entente powers that the deadline be extended may actually have prompted Germany and Austria to act even more quickly. And Grey's hint that France might be counted upon to restrain Russia if Germany did the same with Austria may also have had the opposite effect to the one he intended: the Wilhelmstrasse concluded that France would attempt to avoid a general conflict.[36] The German ambassador was reporting from Paris that although the press there condemned the Austrian ultimatum, Germany's statement advocating 'localization' had made a great impression.[37] The Austrian ambassador was equally optimistic: the attitude of the French press was not as hostile as might have been expected, and there was a 'certain understanding of our demands'.[38] All the more reason, then, for Austria to act quickly and decisively—because without the promise of support from France or Britain, how likely was it that Russia would risk war?

Lichnowsky was trying to persuade Berlin that it would be a mistake not to support Grey's proposal for a mediation à quatre, even if it was now too late to extend the Austrian deadline. When he again saw the foreign secretary that afternoon, he found him more hopeful than he had been on

Friday. Grey gave no sign 'of irritation or ill-feeling'. He anticipated that mobilization by Austria would be countered immediately with mobilization by Russia—at which point the moment would have arrived for the four Powers to begin mediating between them. Grey reiterated his position that as long as the dispute involved only Austria and Serbia he did not wish to become involved; but the escalation of the crisis into a dispute that led to conflict between Austria and Russia would mean 'a world war'.

Grey argued that the situation now was similar to the crisis of the previous year, when war had been averted by means of the conference of ambassadors in London. Although Britain was not committed by any binding agreements, it could not regard European complications as 'a matter of indifference'. He therefore wished to cooperate with Germany in the interest of European peace. He hoped that an Anglo-German mediation (which both France and Italy were likely to join) would once again succeed in preventing a European war. Finally, Lichnowsky pointed out that Grey was fully prepared to recognize the justice of Austria's demand for satisfaction and the punishment of all those connected with the murder; a mediation might also succeed in reaching agreement on this aspect of the dispute.[39]

Lichnowsky tried to present Grey's attitude in the most favourable light. The foreign secretary, who was calm and judicious, seemed anxious to walk 'hand-in-hand' with Germany. Grey had implied that the mediators would satisfy Austria's demands for the punishment of the perpetrators of the crime at Sarajevo. From this, the ambassador concluded that the British government was striving to maintain a friendly attitude in its relations with Germany and would adopt a non-partisan position in the Balkan dispute. He warned however that this attitude would last only as long as the British were convinced that Germany honestly desired peace and was willing to cooperate with them in averting 'the European thunderstorm'. If Germany refused Grey's proposal for a mediation à quatre, or if it displayed an attitude that suggested it wished to bring about a war with Russia, this would 'probably have the result of driving England unconditionally over to the side of France and Russia'.[40]

Lichnowsky was well aware that a friendly relationship with Britain was the key element in the foreign policy of the German chancellor. Although Bethmann Hollweg had failed to achieve the political understanding with Britain that he had sought at the time of the Haldane mission of 1912, he had succeeded in resolving the Baghdad railway dispute, arranging for the future disposition of Portuguese colonial possessions in Africa, and achieving a détente with Britain in the Balkans. Both the chancellor and the ambassador knew that the head of the German navy, Admiral Tirpitz, believed Germany would not be ready for a naval conflict with Britain for some years yet. Bethmann Hollweg was determined to secure British neutrality in the event of war.

The immediate supervision of German foreign policy rested in the hands of the secretary of state, not those of the chancellor. Bethmann Hollweg remained on his estate at Hohenfinow, rather than taking charge of the situation himself—although he did have a special telegraph line put in to improve his communications. Jagow knew where the chancellor stood on the issue of British neutrality and he assured Lichnowsky that he agreed with his suggestions. Germany, he said, was prepared to join the other great Powers in initiating a mediation 'subject to our well-known alliance obligations' should a conflict develop between Austria and Russia.[41]

Was Jagow backing away from full German support of Austria-Hungary? At a meeting with an influential Berlin journalist, Theodor Wolff, that morning he agreed with him that the Austrian note was not good and assured him that he had no knowledge of it beforehand. It would, he said, have been better to concentrate on two or three crucial points instead of listing everything that could be thought of. Meeting with Horace Rumbold later that afternoon, he complained that the Austrian note left 'much to be desired as a diplomatic document' and reiterated that he had no knowledge of it beforehand.[42]

In responding to Grey's proposal, Jagow made his acceptance of it conditional on it taking effect only if 'localization' failed. Only in the event of an Austro-Russian conflict would Germany agree to participate in a mediation. He was pleased that Grey agreed with the German position that the dispute between Austria and Serbia concerned no one but themselves. He told Wolff that the surest way to avoid a European war and to prevent Russia from intervening was for Austria to stick to its terms.[43]

★

There was reason to be hopeful that a settlement of the dispute could be negotiated. In Belgrade, Pašić had convened another meeting of the Serbian cabinet in the morning in order to agree on their response to the Austrian demands. By the time they met the Serbs had received clear advice from Russia, France, and Britain urging them to be as accommodating as possible.

No one promised military assistance. Serbia's Balkan allies, Greece and Romania, had both advised against war with Austria. On Friday, the Serbian cabinet had seemed prepared to be defiant; by Saturday afternoon news began to filter out that it was now willing to go a considerable distance in order to placate the Austrians. The British chargé d'affaires in Belgrade reported to London that the Serbs were drafting a 'most conciliatory' reply and that they were willing to meet most of the Austrian demands. The French minister in Belgrade had fallen ill on 14 July and Paris had received no despatch or communication of any kind from the Serbian capital until this day, when the new minister wired that Serbia was prepared to comply with almost all of the Austrian demands.[44] The British and French representatives alike believed that Russia had been instrumental in convincing the Serbs to reply in such a conciliatory manner—another hopeful sign.

While attempting to follow the advice of the Russians, the French, and the British in going as far as possible in complying with the Austrian demands, the Serbs also began to prepare for the worst. The cabinet was still determined to resist points 5 and 6 in the Austrian ultimatum, as these were deemed to go too far in impinging upon the principle of national sovereignty. Anticipating that this might prove unsatisfactory to Austria, arrangements were made to evacuate the royal family from Belgrade. The national bank, the railways, and the foreign ministry were preparing to have gold, currency, and documents shipped to the interior. The garrison in Belgrade left the city to relocate at Kragujevac, a fortified town 60 miles to the south. The ammunition depots of the fortress were evacuated and ambulance units left for the south. Prince Aleksandar signed the order for general mobilization and drums were beaten outside of Belgrade cafés, calling up conscripts. This led the Austrian minister to report that mobilization began at 3 p.m.—three hours in advance of the ultimatum deadline. Mobilization did not, in fact, begin until midnight.

Two minutes before the 6 p.m. deadline, the formal French text of the Serbian reply was handed over to Baron Giesl in Belgrade.[45] The reply began with an expression of hope that their answer would 'remove every misunderstanding' that jeopardized the 'friendly and neighbourly' relations between themselves and Austria. Since 1909 Serbia had given numerous indications of its 'pacific and moderate' policy and it was now prepared to place before a court of law any Serbian subject 'regardless of position or rank' for which there was evidence of participation in the 'crime of Sarajevo'. The government was prepared to publish tomorrow—Sunday—in the official gazette a declaration that 'The Royal government of Serbia condemns all propaganda directed against Austria-Hungary, that is, it condemns all efforts leading to the ultimate result of disjoining parts of the territory of the Austro-Hungarian monarchy, and it deeply regrets the sad consequences of such criminal dealings.' There then followed a point-by-point response to the ten demands contained in the Austrian note:

1. When the Skuptschina meets next time in the ordinary way, a paragraph will be inserted in the Press-law, threatening severe punishment to whoever incites to hatred or contempt against the monarchy, and to all publications whose general tendency is directed against the territorial integrity of Austria-Hungary.

When the forthcoming revision of the constitution takes place, an addition will be made to Article XXII of the constitutional law, by which it will be possible to confiscate such publications, a thing that cannot be done according to the present determinations of the Article.

2. The government has no proofs, nor does the Note of the Imp. and Roy. government give any such proofs, according to which the 'Narodna odbrana' and similar societies have up to this time committed criminal actions, such as are here in question, through any of their members. Still the Royal government will comply with the demand of the Imp. and Roy. government and dissolve the 'Narodna odbrana' and every other society, which shows itself hostile to Austria-Hungary.

3. The Royal Servian government promises to remove without delay from public instruction in Servia, all propaganda, that might be considered as directed against Austria-Hungary, if the Imp. and Roy. government will demonstrate such propaganda.

4. The Royal government is also prepared to dismiss from military and civil service all officers and officials of whom judicial inquiry will affirm that they have been guilty of actions against the territorial integrity of the monarchy; the government expects that to make inquiry possible the Imp. and Roy. government will without delay communicate the names of these officers and officials and the deeds they are accused of.

5. The Royal government confesses that it does not quite understand the sense and the extent of the Imp. and Roy. government's demand, according to which the Royal Servian government is to approve on its own territory the collaboration of organs of the Imp. and Roy. government, but it declares that it would consent to such collaboration, inasmuch as it was based upon the principle of nations rights and penal procedure and would not violate friendly and neighbourly relations.

6. The Royal government considers it a duty to order judicial proceedings against all those persons, who were or were supposed to be implicated in the crime of the 15/28[46] June and who would be found on Servian territory. But the government cannot consent to the collaboration of organs of the Imp. and Roy. government, delegated for this express purpose, as this would be a violation of the constitution and of the law of penal procedure.

But the Austro-Hungarian organs might in some cases be informed of the results of the inquiry.

7. The Royal government ordered the arrest of Major Voislav Tankosić on the very evening, when it received the Note.

As to Milan Ciganovič, who is a subject of the Austro-Hungarian monarchy, and who up to the 15th June was employed in the Railways Direction (as aspirant), the authorities have not been able to find him and a warrant was issued against him.

The Imp. and Roy. government is requested to communicate the grounds, on which these persons are suspected and the results of the inquiry of Sarajevo that regard them, with as little delay as possible, so that an inquiry can be instituted.

8. The Royal government will extend the measures, which already exist against the smuggling of weapons and explosives across the frontier.

It need not be said that the Royal government will immediately institute an inquiry and will use the severity of the law against those officials of the frontier service on the line Sabac Loznica who have neglected their duty and have allowed the criminals to cross the frontier.

9. The Royal government will very willingly give explanations on the enunciations of its officials in Servia and in foreign countries, made in interviews after the crime of Sarajevo, which the Imp. and Roy. government declares to be hostile, if the Imp. and Roy. government will show up these speeches and give us the proofs that they were really held by the functionaries in question.

The Royal government will cause the material for this research to be collected.

10. The Royal government will inform the Imp. and Roy. government of the execution of the measures promised in this Note, and will communicate the ordering and carrying out of every point, except where this Note already brings things to a close.[47]

What did the reply amount to? The Serbs were willing to swallow every demand that had been made upon them with the exception of points 5 and 6 in the Austrian ultimatum. In response to the demand that Serbia agree to allow Austrian officials to assist 'in the suppressing of the subversive movement directed against the territorial integrity of the monarchy' the Serbs expressed some uncertainty concerning the role of Austrian officials in conducting investigations on Serbian territory. But even here they expressed their willingness to collaborate with Austrian officials as long as this was based upon the principle of national rights and penal procedure. On point 6, where the Austrians had demanded not only that a judicial inquiry be instituted against all those who had participated in the plot of 28th June but that Austria would 'delegate representatives who will take an active part in these enquiries' on Serbian soil, the Serbs agreed to institute judicial proceedings against those accused of participating, but would not consent to direct Austrian participation as this would violate the Serbian constitution and 'the law of penal procedure'.

How would Austria respond? Even before he received a copy of the Serbian reply, Sir Edward Grey had become more optimistic. Based on reports that the Serb reply would go far to accommodate the Austrian demands, he conveyed to Lichnowsky his hope that Germany would influence Austria to take a favourable view of it.[48] He expressed this opinion in a letter to the German ambassador, written in his own hand: 'It seems to me that it ought to produce a favourable impression at Vienna.'[49]

But the signs were confusing. From Vienna, one hour before the deadline expired, the French ambassador concluded that the Austrian government 'is determined to inflict humiliation on Serbia: it will accept no intervention from any Power until the blow has been delivered and received full in the face by Serbia'.[50] Nevertheless, given the extraordinary extent of the Serb concessions contained in their formal reply, surely there was ground for negotiation?

Berchtold's instructions to Giesl in Belgrade had been crystal-clear: nothing other than complete acceptance of each of the demands in their entirety would suffice. When the Austrian minister received the Serb reply at 5.58 on Saturday afternoon, he could see instantly that their submission was not complete. He announced that Austria was breaking off diplomatic relations with Serbia and immediately ordered the staff of the legation to leave for the railway station. By 6.30 the Austrians were on a train bound for the border. As arranged beforehand, when Giesl reached Semlin, the first train-stop in Austrian territory, he telephoned Budapest to inform the government that the Serb reply was unsatisfactory.[51] His message was then forwarded to Vienna and Ischl.

Was war now imminent? Giesl reported that the Serb government and diplomatic corps had already left Belgrade and that a general mobilization of Serb forces had been proclaimed at 3 p.m. Excitement gripped Vienna as soon as the news became known. Tisza, who had earlier had his reservations about taking dramatic and drastic action against Serbia, was now fully committed to the cause. He had urged Franz Joseph the day before to order mobilization at once if the Serb answer was deemed unsatisfactory. 'The slightest delay or hesitation', he warned the emperor, 'would gravely injure the reputation of the Monarchy for boldness and initiative.'[52] That evening, in the Kaiservilla at Bad Ischl, Franz Joseph signed the orders for mobilization of thirteen army corps.

When the news reached Vienna the people greeted it with the 'wildest enthusiasm'.[53] Huge crowds began to form, gathering at the Ringstrasse and bursting into patriotic songs. The crowds marched around the city shouting 'Down with Serbia! Down with Russia!' In front of the German embassy they sang '*Die Wacht am Rhein*'; police had to protect the Russian embassy against the demonstrators. In Budapest, demonstrators braved a rainstorm to parade and sing.

In Berlin, a crowd numbering in the tens of thousands had begun to gather in the late afternoon, waiting for news outside of the newspaper offices. This had become common practice, as newspapers would print special edition broadsheets throughout the day when there was important news to report. Special editions began to appear between 7 and 8 p.m., at first reporting that Serbia had agreed to the demands, and then, some time between 9 and 10 p.m., that they had rejected them. Most people went home. But those who did not began to stage spectacular demonstrations of support for Austria. They marched down Unter den Linden and gathered in front of the Austrian embassy where they sang '*Gott erhalte Franz den Kaiser*'. Some gathered around the Siegessaül—the victory column commemorating Prussia's victory over Denmark in 1864. Other groups formed around the statue of Bismarck in front of the Reichstag, in front of the kaiser's palace and the chancellor's residence—but the kaiser was still at sea on the Baltic and the chancellor on his estate at Hohenfinow. At the chancellor's residence the crowd heard one speaker declare that there 'lived the man who was the blacksmith of the German Empire and the Triple Alliance. Today the Triple Alliance faces its greatest test. [I] hope that Bethmann Hollweg will show himself worthy of Bismarck.'[54]

Berlin cafés filled to overflowing, with patrons calling on the orchestras they employed to play patriotic tunes, particularly '*Deutschland, Deutschland, über alles*'. Around midnight a crowd gathered in front of the Russian embassy, calling out 'Down with Russia!' By then the crowds consisted mainly of young people—university students especially—who continued to parade and sing, in spite of pouring rain—until 3 or 4 in the morning.

Apart from Berlin and Vienna, Budapest and Munich, and a few other large cities in Austria-Hungary and Germany, there was little enthusiasm. The excited response to the news of the evening was limited mainly to the cities—and even here those on the Left were inclined to denounce the Austrian ultimatum and the decision to sever diplomatic relations with Serbia. On Friday the socialist *Vorwärts* had described Austria's demands as 'more brutal than any ever made upon a civilized state in the history of the world'.[55] On Saturday it insisted that 'Not one drop of German blood should be sacrificed for the power-hungry Austrian rulers and the imperialistic profit interests.'[56] The executive committee of the Social Democratic Party (SPD) issued a proclamation to workers: 'The ruling classes, who in peacetime oppress you, despise you, exploit you, want to use you as cannon-fodder. Everywhere the cry must ring in the despots' ears: "We want no war! Down with war! Long live international brotherhood!"'[57]

In London and Paris on Saturday people continued to be more concerned with domestic affairs than with anything that was happening in the Balkans. The political crisis over Ulster continued to dominate the attention of the British, although King George did finally mention the Austro-Serbian crisis in his diary that day for the first time since the assassination. Within an hour of Giesl's departure from Belgrade Sir Edward Grey left London for the country, where he intended to spend Sunday fishing. His chargé d'affaires in Berlin was not so calm: in the afternoon he wrote to his wife that 'the Austrians will probably be in Belgrade by Monday. The Lord only knows what will happen then'; in the evening he witnessed a crowd gathered around Bismarck's statue in front of the Reichstag, laying a wreath and singing patriotic songs.[58]

In Paris, people still paid little attention to anything other than the Caillaux trial, which seemed to be reaching new heights of sensationalism. It seemed briefly that the presiding judge might challenge another of the judges to a duel for publicly insulting him. When the love letters from Mme Caillaux to M. Caillaux were finally read out in court she began to cry and then fainted; M. Caillaux rushed to the dock and carried his wife out of the courtroom. The trial had to be adjourned for three-quarters of an hour.

Behind the scenes, the French government were active, both in Paris and in Stockholm. The acting premier, Bienvenu-Martin, fearful of the approaching Austrian deadline, requested that Paul Cambon come home for consultations. The ambassador left London that afternoon, with the explanation that he was going to attend the birth of his first grandchild. Two hours after Austria severed diplomatic relations with Serbia, the French minister of war ordered generals and commanders on leave to return to their garrisons. When the chief of the general staff received this instruction he requested permission to execute the '*Instruction sur la préparation à la mobilisation*' and proposed to cancel troop movements and to recall all those on leave or furlough.

By this time Poincaré and Viviani had reached Stockholm, where the president considered whether they should now return to Paris. He decided against it: returning to France was likely to excite the French public and give the impression that France was directly involved in the crisis. Privately, he confided to his diary that he regarded Sazonov's advice to Serbia that it should appeal to Europe and withdraw its forces to the south as giving in to Austria-Hungary. He could not see how he could influence the outcome: France could not 'be more Slav than the Russians'.[59] He anticipated that Austria would succeed in humiliating Serbia. He had not yet learned of the military measures approved by the tsar at the meeting of the Grand Council earlier that day.

★

What would Austria do now? The German ambassador was assured that a declaration of war on Serbia was imminent. Franz Joseph, however, after endorsing mobilization, was reported to have commented that 'the breaking off of diplomatic relations does not necessarily mean war'. He may have gotten this line from Berchtold, who, while on board the train headed for Bad Ischl, had received the telegram sent by Kudashev requesting that the deadline be extended. Before reaching his destination the foreign minister had telegraphed from Lambach to Vienna that he would not agree to prolong the deadline. But, he added, 'even after the breaking off of diplomatic relations' the Serbs could bring about a peaceful solution—if they were subsequently to accept, unconditionally, the Austrian demands.[60] In such an eventuality, however, Austria would demand repayment of the costs involved in mobilization.

In other words, both the emperor and the foreign minister did not rule out a peaceful solution of the crisis, even after diplomatic relations were severed, and even after the army was ordered to begin mobilizing.

Even if war were to come, what sort of 'war' would it be? In Berlin the chancellor reassured the kaiser that Paris and London were working 'zealously' to localize the conflict.[61] When the day began Paléologue had appeared to confirm this impression from St Petersburg: Sazonov was acting with moderation and proposing that even if Austria invaded, Serbia should refrain from combat and instead denounce the infamy of Austria to the civilized world.[62] The French ambassador told both the head of the chancellery at the Russian Foreign Office and the Italian ambassador that although the situation was critical it was by no means hopeless. Now that the crisis was evolving into one between Germany and Russia, he could not believe that Germany would continue to support Austria in the face of the combined opposition of France and Russia, and with Britain and Italy using their influence at Berlin to persuade the Germans to agree to mediation.[63]

★

By the end of the day on Saturday, 25 July, there remained at least four possible scenarios: Serbia could still comply with the Austrian demands to an extent that might satisfy Austria, even though the deadline had passed; Austria and Russia could agree to the mediation *à quatre* proposed by Grey; Austria could invade Serbia, but the Serbs could refuse to fight them and trust Europe to intervene on their behalf; or an Austrian attack on Serbia would precipitate an armed intervention by Russia and thus a wider European conflict. Even after the Austrian legation had departed from Belgrade and diplomatic relations had been severed, even after the Serbian government had ordered mobilization and departed Belgrade for the south, the outcome of the crisis was still far from clear.

Meanwhile, those on the periphery were becoming increasingly concerned. The Belgian minister in Berlin expressed his anxiety about how events were unfolding, believing that Austria and Germany saw an opportunity to take advantage of a situation in which Russia, Britain, and France were distracted by domestic difficulties.[64] In Brussels the foreign minister drafted a note to be used if the situation between Germany and France became dangerous. Belgian representatives to the states that had guaranteed the independence and neutrality of Belgium—Germany, France, and Britain—were, if so instructed, to present the note informing them 'of our fixed determination to fulfil those international obligations that are imposed upon us by the treaties of 1839'.[65] The note, however, was undated and was to be kept strictly confidential until the foreign minister issued fresh instructions.

Day Three
Sunday, 26 July

The deadline for the Serbs to comply with the Austrian demands made in their ultimatum of Thursday, 23 July had come and gone. The Austrians had departed from Belgrade and were back on Austrian soil by Saturday evening; the Serbian government, the Belgrade garrison, and the legations of Russia, France, Britain, and Italy had abandoned the city for the safety of the south. And yet the sky did not fall. Shells did not rain down on Belgrade. There was no declaration of war. The morning of Sunday, the 26th of July, remained peaceful, if not calm. Throughout Europe most people attended their churches and prepared to enjoy their day of rest. Few said prayers for peace; few believed divine intervention was necessary. Europe had weathered many storms over the last decade. Only pessimists doubted that this one could be weathered as well.

Contrary to the rose-coloured memories of those recollecting July 1914 years afterwards, the summer was not brilliant. Snows had plagued the Austrian military manoeuvres in the mountains near Sarajevo during the archduke's visit at the end of June. On 23 July, the day the Austro-Hungarian ultimatum was presented in Belgrade, a hurricane hit Budapest. The 24th of July marked the third day in a row that France was deluged with torrential rains—especially in the normally arid south. Between the 23rd and the 26th the warmest day in London reached 66° Fahrenheit. On the 25th and 26th demonstrators in Berlin and Vienna, Munich and Budapest, had to face chilling rain and wind when they went out into the streets.

By midday Sunday almost everyone in Europe had heard or read the news that the Austro-Hungarian government had deemed the Serbian reply to their ultimatum to be unacceptable, had broken off diplomatic relations, and was beginning to mobilize. And they knew that the Serbian government and court had departed from Belgrade to seek safety in the south and that the Serbian mobilization had begun. The demonstrations that had begun on Saturday evening continued into Sunday—particularly in Berlin and Vienna, but now in some other cities as well.

In Austria-Hungary the right of assembly, the secrecy of the mail, of telegrams and telephone conversations, and the freedom of the press were all suspended. Pro-war demonstrations were not only permitted but encouraged. Giesl, alighting from his carriage at the railway station in Vienna that morning, was greeted by cheering crowds. Demonstrators filled the Ringstrasse, marched on the Ballhausplatz, gathered around statues of national heroes and sang patriotic songs. That evening the Bürgermeister of Vienna told a cheering crowd that the fate of Europe for centuries to come was about to be decided, praising them as worthy descendants of the men who had fought Napoleon. Newspapers supporting the government continued to publish without restriction: the *Alkotmány*, published by the Catholic People's Party, declared on Sunday that 'History has put the master's cane in the Monarchy's hands. We must teach Serbia, we must make justice, we must punish her for her crimes.'[1]

In London it was announced that all Austro-Hungarian subjects liable for military service were being summoned to join their regiments. Any men who had deserted or avoided doing their military service were promised an amnesty if they returned home at once and presented themselves for service.

In New York a gathering of over 10,000 was sponsored by the Allied Germanic Societies of Brooklyn. After singing '*Die Wacht am Rhein*', '*Deutschland über Alles*', and the Austrian national anthem, a cable was sent to the German kaiser to congratulate him for his stand in supporting Austria-Hungary: 'We desire that this great, important hour shall find a happy solution, and that by the course of events the supremacy of the German race in Europe shall be established for the future in the interest of civilization and humanity.'

In Paris, in spite of the pouring rain, a crowd of Serb demonstrators gathered in front of the Austrian embassy, shouting 'Down with Austria!' and 'Long live Russia!' while burning and then trampling an Austrian flag in the mud. When police intervened they marched to the Russian embassy where they sang the Serbian national anthem. By evening crowds were parading the boulevards, singing the *Marseillaise* and shouting 'Long live the army!'

How urgent was the situation? In London, Sir Edward Grey had left town to go to his cottage at Itchen Abbas to spend Sunday fly-fishing. The Russian ambassadors to Germany, Austria, and France had yet to return to their posts. The British ambassador to Germany was still on vacation. Kaiser Wilhelm was on his annual yachting cruise of the Baltic. Emperor Franz Joseph was at his hunting lodge at Bad Ischl. The French premier and president were visiting Stockholm. The Italian foreign minister was still taking his cure at Fiuggi; the Austrian minister of war was on vacation. The chiefs of the German and Austrian general staffs remained on leave; the chief of the Serbian general staff was relaxing at an Austrian spa.

★

Sir Edward Grey had already proposed that Britain, France, Germany, and Italy ought to mediate between Austria and Russia—the mediation *à quatre*. As long as Austria and Germany maintained that the dispute was a 'local' one concerning Austria and Serbia alone, his proposal got nowhere. Grey had admitted that as long as the dispute could be contained Britain had no concern with it. Austria's refusal to accept the Serbian reply as a basis for negotiation was almost certain to trigger military preparations in Russia, which threatened to transform the crisis into a European one.

   Late Saturday evening the Foreign Office in London had received a long telegram from Sir George Buchanan, the ambassador in St Petersburg, recounting his meeting with Sazonov that afternoon. The foreign minister had informed him that the meeting of the Russian council—presided over by the tsar that morning—had sanctioned the drafting of an Imperial *ukase* that would authorize the mobilization of 1,100,000 men.[2] But this was not to be published, and would not take effect, until Sazonov judged that the moment had come to issue it. In the meantime it would be necessary to take preliminary steps to prepare for the mobilization, and these were to be initiated immediately. Buchanan had warned him that if Russia were to mobilize, Germany, in order to prevent Russia from mobilizing fully beforehand, would probably declare war on Russia at once.

   Grey was already at his cottage by the time the telegram was received and it was left to the permanent under-secretary of state, Sir Arthur Nicolson, to decide how to respond to Buchanan's warning. Nicolson, who as ambassador to Russia had been instrumental in promulgating the Anglo-Russian entente, had thus far taken a cautious position on the crisis, advising against anything that might propel Russia forward against Austria and Germany. But he did fear the consequences if Britain let Russia down. In April he had told Buchanan that he favoured the negotiations for a naval agreement with

Russia because he believed a more definite arrangement might be necessary
to keep Russia onside: 'I do not know how much longer we shall be able to
follow our present policy of dancing on a tight rope, and not be compelled
to take up some definite line or other. I am also haunted by the same fear
as you—lest Russia should become tired of us and strike a bargain with
Germany.'[3]

Nicolson now thought he could see a general European war looming if
they did not act immediately. He suggested to Grey that they take up
Sazonov's apparent willingness to participate in a conference to deal with
the crisis. He proposed that Berlin, Paris, and Rome ought to be asked to
authorize their ambassadors in London to meet in a conference chaired by

Sir Arthur Nicolson (1849–1928); permanent under-secretary of state for foreign
affairs of Great Britain (1910–16)

Grey. Pending this, Vienna, Belgrade, and St Petersburg should be asked to abstain from active military operations. He explained that he believed this was the only hope left of avoiding a general conflict.[4]

Nicolson drafted the instructions to Britain's ambassadors and by mid-afternoon Grey had taken time off from his fishing to wire his approval. Half an hour later the instructions were sent out. The under-secretary admitted that he was not optimistic: 'but in any case we shall have done our utmost'. He pointed his finger at the Germans. Jagow, instead of supporting the earlier proposal for a mediation *à quatre*, had only 'passed on' the suggestion in Vienna. 'Berlin', he told Grey, 'is playing with us.'[5]

Playing how? What did Nicolson think the Germans were up to? They were, he believed, trying to persuade them in London that the Russians would not act, while spreading the word that the British would remain quiescent. He pointed out that they were using the younger brother of the

George V (1865–1936); king of Great Britain (1910–36)

kaiser, Prince Heinrich—formerly commander of the German high-seas fleet, and now a Grand Admiral—to draw his cousin, King George V, into this game. On Sunday morning the prince had breakfast with the king. Heinrich warned him that if Russia took action there would be a revolution and the dynasty would be overthrown. Nicolson dismissed this as nonsense, but suggested that it showed what the Germans were up to.

Other Germans further complicated things by attempting to use Prince Heinrich's initiative for their own purposes. The German ambassador, Prince Lichnowsky, reported to Berlin on the breakfast meeting before the morning was out. His version of the discussion emphasized that King George had conveyed to Heinrich his 'intense desire' (lebhaften Wunsch) that Britain and Germany, assisted by France and Italy, would cooperate in the proposal for a joint initiative to maintain the peace.[6] This was Lichnowsky's desire, too—to convince Berlin to go along with Grey's suggestion. The German naval attaché in London, Captain von Bülow, contradicted the ambassador. In an 'absolutely confidential' telegram sent on the same day to the Imperial Naval Office he reported that the king had told Prince Heinrich that Britain would remain neutral in the event of war on the continent. The British fleet had discharged the reservists called up for annual manoeuvres and given leave to naval crews as scheduled.

Prince Heinrich had seen Lichnowsky after the breakfast meeting and asked him to convey the gist of their conversation to the chancellor. But Lichnowsky limited his message to the king's support of the proposal for the mediation à quatre; he did not mention the likelihood of Britain remaining neutral. The prince, writing directly to his brother the kaiser, told him that he had found 'Georgie' in a very serious mood, anxious to do everything possible to avoid a world conflagration, and counting on Wilhelm's assistance in keeping the peace. War was nearer than ever but, Georgie said, 'we shall try all we can to keep out of this and shall remain neutral'.[7] Prince Heinrich concluded that the British would remain neutral at the beginning of a conflict, but whether they could remain so permanently—given their relations with the French—he doubted.

The signals reaching Berlin from London were confused and confusing. Where precisely did the British stand on the neutrality issue, whose opinion really counted among them, and whose prognosis was to be believed? Their own man in London, Lichnowsky, was now playing a desperate game in trying to persuade them to drop their all-out support for Austria because Britain might enter a conflict on the side of Russia and France. Lichnowsky

had awakened on Sunday to read Jagow's telegram informing him that
Berlin had accepted the mediation *à quatre*: subject to Germany's obligation
to its allies, Germany was prepared—should Austro-Russian 'strife arise'
(*Streit entstehen*)—to join with the other Great Powers in mediating between
Austria and Russia.[8]

Although this was the news that Lichnowsky hoped to hear, he feared
that Austria's military steps—and Russia's response to them—might precipitate a conflict before the mediation process could be agreed upon. With
Grey off fishing, Lichnowsky was unable to meet with him—in fact, he
complained, it being Sunday, there was 'no one' at the Foreign Office with
whom he could speak. Consequently, the best that he could manage to do
in trying to follow the instructions he had received from Berlin was to write
to Grey to inform him that Germany accepted his proposal, while warning
that a Russian mobilization would certainly be followed by Germany doing
the same.[9] As instructed, he again asked Grey to use his influence at St
Petersburg to localize the conflict and preserve the peace in Europe. When
Benckendorff, the Russian ambassador, saw Lichnowsky that afternoon he
found him very discouraged about the possibility of avoiding war.[10]

During the afternoon the frustrated Lichnowsky received further instructions in a telegram from Bethmann Hollweg. Germany had now received
information (yet to be corroborated) that Russia was about to call up many
of its reservists. Such a step would indicate that it was preparing to mobilize
against Germany as well as Austria. If this information proved to be correct
'we should be forced against our will to adopt measures of counter-action'.
The chancellor repeated Jagow's previous instructions that Lichnowsky was
to request Grey to use his influence at St Petersburg to localize the conflict
and preserve the peace of Europe.[11]

Perhaps Bethmann Hollweg had been persuaded by reports of Prince
Heinrich's initiative with King George that Britain's proposal for mediation
could be interpreted as support for 'localization'. Perhaps mediation could
be used to prevent an Austro-Russian conflict but not the impending one
between Austria and Serbia. The chancellor wrote to the kaiser that, if
Russia undertook preparations for a conflict with Austria, Britain would
then attempt to mediate, with French support. 'As long as Russia undertakes
no hostile action, I think that our attitude must be calm.'[12] He assured the
kaiser that the chief of the general staff, Helmuth von Moltke, who returned
from vacation on Sunday, agreed with this point of view.

On board the *Hohenzollern* Saturday evening, the kaiser had decided to abandon his cruise and return to Germany. He and his entourage believed that once Serbia refused to comply with the Austrian ultimatum it almost certainly meant war and might be 'the first step to war for ourselves as well'.[13] Bethmann Hollweg had protested against the decision to return, fearing it would seem to involve Germany in the crisis and contradict the government's position that the dispute concerned Austria–Hungary and Serbia alone. He assured the kaiser that he was working with the British government to keep the war localized. By Sunday evening the head of the kaiser's military cabinet, with him on board the *Hohenzollern*, recorded that it no longer looked as if a European war were about to break out.[14] In spite of his chancellor's efforts to dissuade him, however, Wilhelm was adamant about returning home: 'My fleet has orders to sail for Kiel and to Kiel it is going to sail.' And he refused Bethmann Hollweg's request to meet with him when he arrived at Kiel on Monday morning.[15]

There was more bad news for Bethmann Hollweg. After receiving his latest instructions from the chancellor, Lichnowsky tried to explain to him that what he was asking for was hopeless. Since the Austrian demands on Serbia had become known, nobody in Britain any longer believed in the possibility of localizing the conflict. No one any longer doubted that a world war would result from Austria's actions. The only hope of avoiding war now was to initiate immediately Grey's proposed mediation *à quatre*. And for this to succeed Austria must be willing to waive its claim to 'further laurels'.[16]

Finally, on Sunday evening, Lichnowsky was able to sit down at the Foreign Office with Nicolson and Sir William Tyrrell, Grey's private secretary. He used his report on this meeting to do everything he could to persuade Berlin to agree to the proposed conference. Nicolson and Tyrrell believed, he said, that this was the only way to avoid a general war. Moreover, they virtually promised that Austria would get what it wanted at a conference: the Serbs would be more likely to give in to the combined pressure of the Powers than to submit to Austrian threats. The absolute prerequisite was a cessation of military activities because once the Serbian frontier was crossed 'all would be lost'. No Russian government could tolerate such a step. Russia would be forced to attack Austria or lose its status among Balkan nations forever.

According to Lichnowsky, Tyrrell, who had met with Grey before he left London on Saturday and who was fully cognizant of his views, emphasized the importance of Serbian territory remaining inviolate until the question of the conference was settled. Otherwise a world war was inevitable. 'Localization', the ambassador once again stressed, was 'wholly impossible' and must now be abandoned as impractical. On the other hand, he promised the chancellor that if Germany and Britain between them were to succeed in preserving peace in Europe, Anglo-German relations would be placed on a secure foundation 'for all time' (*immerwährende Zeiten*).

Lichnowsky attempted to present Berlin with a stark choice: preserve the peace and achieve Bethmann Hollweg's goal of an Anglo-German partnership for the future or involve the German people in a struggle in which 'they have nothing to win and everything to lose'.[17] Nicolson, reporting on the meeting to Grey, noted that the ambassador 'was very excited'.[18]

Little wonder. Germany and Britain appeared to be on the verge of solving the crisis through a process of mediation that Lichnowsky believed could result in a historic partnership between them. On the other hand, if Russia were to mobilize in response to Austria's military steps, Germany would insist on doing the same and Europe would spiral into the abyss of war. Lichnowsky warned Nicolson and Tyrrell that although Germany could tolerate a partial mobilization at Odessa or Kiev, it could not view with indifference a mobilization on its Russian frontier. A partial mobilization would enable Russia to demonstrate its support of the Serbs and perhaps restrain the Austrians from attacking them. Nicolson told him that it would be 'difficult and delicate' for Britain to ask Russia not to mobilize at all when Austria appeared to be contemplating such a step. The British would not be listened to in St Petersburg if they took such a line.

Nicolson, who worked throughout the day Sunday, visited both the Russian and the Austrian embassies in the afternoon. Recognizing the reality that military preparations were now under way, he urged that the critical necessity was for Russia, Austria, and Serbia to suspend military *operations* until Grey's proposed conference could convene. *Preparations* they would all have to agree to live with.

The Russian ambassador in London believed that the British were finally awakening to the dangers of the crisis. Up until now it seemed that they had been completely absorbed by the situation in Ulster. The 'slow English imagination', Benckendorff reported to St Petersburg, had not yet taken in that Britain might be drawn into a European war—but officials at the Foreign Office were now opening their eyes.[19]

At almost precisely the same moment in Berlin they believed that localization was still a possibility—and that the British were working for it. Bethmann Hollweg believed that Austria's disavowal of any intention to acquire Serbian territory ought to be sufficient to keep the peace. He instructed his ambassadors in St Petersburg, Paris, and London to make this point: it now depended on Russia 'whether a European war is to occur'.[20] He urged France and Britain to use their influence to restrain the Russians. At St Petersburg Pourtalès was instructed to insist that the peace of Europe depended on Russia alone. 'Trusting in Russia's love of peace and in our long-established friendly relations, we trust that she will take no step that will seriously endanger the peace of Europe.'[21]

★

There were hopeful signs. The German military attaché reported from St Petersburg in the afternoon that while it appeared certain mobilization had been ordered for the Kiev and Odessa districts, he doubted that the Warsaw and Moscow districts had received such orders.[22] This was the scenario that Lichnowsky had indicated to the British would be acceptable to Germany.

The German ambassador in St Petersburg was optimistic. Meeting with Sazonov in the afternoon, Pourtalès described him as 'much quieter and more conciliatory'. The foreign minister stated emphatically that Russia did not desire war and that he would exhaust every means to avoid it. He was ready to recognize the justice of the Austrian demands relating to the prosecution of the assassins, but insisted that some of the demands must be modified because they violated Serbian sovereignty. He asked for Germany's assistance in persuading Vienna to soften some of the points. He denied that Russia was motivated by Slav 'sympathies' for Serbia: what Russia could not tolerate was the transformation of Serbia into Austria's vassal. Pourtalès was encouraged that Sazonov now abandoned his earlier talk about Europe 'investigating' the findings of Austria's judicial inquiry into the assassination. Finally, the foreign minister had seemed reassured when the ambassador argued that if Austria were seeking a pretext for an attack on Serbia they would already have commenced it.[23]

When Bethmann Hollweg received the latest news of the military steps being taken in Russia he predicted the worst. Any preparatory measures adopted by Russia that appeared to be aimed at Germany would force Germany to adopt counter-measures. This would mean the mobilization of the German army—and mobilization 'would mean war'. The chancellor, familiar with the French military obligations to Russia, concluded that war would have to be waged simultaneously on both fronts.

Although this was the clearest statement yet that a full-scale European war might begin soon, Bethmann Hollweg's prediction was not yet unequivocal. What preparations would Germany consider to be 'aimed at Germany'? This was not clear. Nor did he really believe that Russia would launch such a war under current circumstances. Given Austria's disavowal of any intention to seize Serbian territory, he thought that it ought to be possible for Russia to adopt a 'waiting attitude' in regard to the dispute (*Auseinandersetzung*) between Austria and Serbia. He was prepared to promise that Germany would uphold the integrity of the Serbian kingdom. He believed that this might serve as the basis for agreement.[24]

According to the German chancellor, everything now turned on the issue of Russia's military moves. If these were deemed to be aimed at Germany, mobilization and war would surely follow. But Bethmann Hollweg had not yet received his ambassador's report on that afternoon's meeting between Sazonov and Count Szápáry, the Austrian ambassador, which had preceded the one between Sazonov and Pourtalès. At the end of the day Pourtalès reported that both Sazonov and Szápáry had emerged from their discussion with the same 'pleasant impression' (*befriedigenden Eindruck*). Szápáry's assurance that Austria had no plans for the conquest of Serbia, and Sazonov's willingness to accept many of the points in the Austrian demands, seemed to open the door to a mediated settlement. After the meeting with Szápáry, Sazonov asked Pourtalès to suggest how best to proceed with a mediation.

The German ambassador replied that he was not authorized to make any propositions, but he did offer his 'personal' ideas. If the Austrians were prepared to soften the form of some of their demands—which, according to what Szápáry had told him, was not impossible—perhaps Austria and Russia could discuss this directly. If the two of them could reach agreement, Russia might then advise Serbia to accept the Austrian demands on that basis while notifying Austria of this through the intermediary of a third power. Pourtalès emphasized that he was suggesting this on his own, that he was not speaking on behalf of his government.

Sazonov liked the idea. He promised to telegraph immediately to the Russian ambassador in Vienna along these lines. And so he did. In order to bring the tense situation to a speedy end he asked Vienna to authorize the Austrian ambassador in St Petersburg to engage in a 'private exchange of ideas' with him. Their aim would be to revise some of the articles in the

Austrian note in a formula that would be acceptable to Serbia while giving satisfaction to the principles of Austria's demands.[25] Pourtalès was optimistic: Sazonov gave him the impression (perhaps because of advice he had received from Paris and London) of having lost some of his nerve. Sazonov, who was 'now looking for a way out', urged that something be done to quieten the German press and he promised to do the same in Russia.[26]

Count Szápáry was as impressed as Pourtalès with the change in Sazonov's demeanour between Friday and Sunday. In contrast with his annoyed attitude (*verschnupften Haltung*) then, Sazonov was most cordial now and expressed regret that he had failed to maintain his self-control. Szápáry seized the opportunity of this new attitude to reassure Sazonov that Austria neither aimed to drive into the Balkans as a prelude to a march on Salonika or Constantinople, nor to engage in a preventive war against Russia designed by Germany. Austria aimed only to preserve and defend itself against hostile words and deeds that threatened its integrity. 'No one in Austria-Hungary dreamt of threatening Russian interests or picking a quarrel with Russia.'[27] But Austria was absolutely determined to achieve its objectives and would carry on regardless of the consequences—even at the risk of a conflict among the Great Powers.

Sazonov seemed pleased with these reassurances. He assured the Austrian ambassador that he, the entire cabinet, and the tsar wished to avoid a quarrel with Austria. He had no feelings for the Balkan Slavs, and complained that they were actually a heavy burden on Russia and had given him great trouble. Austria's aims, as Szápáry had portrayed them, seemed to him to be perfectly legitimate, and he only regretted the form in which these had been presented. Going through the Austrian note in detail, he concluded that seven of the ten points could be accepted without much difficulty. Only the fifth and sixth points regarding the cooperation of Austrian and Serbian officials in Serbia and the fourth point concerning the dismissal of Serbian officers and officials at the discretion of Austria seemed to him unacceptable as they stood. Generally, he thought that the difficulty with the note was mainly one of wording, and that it ought to be possible to find a way of overcoming these difficulties. Would Austria accept the mediation of its ally, the king of Italy? or perhaps the king of England?

This dramatic change in attitude impressed Szápáry. The Russian foreign minister had, in two short days, moved from a discourteous rejection of Austria's procedure and a harsh judgement on Austria's dossier to a recognition of the legitimacy of Austria's claims and a proposal that they search for an acceptable mediator. Szápáry warned, however, that in spite of this diplomatic turn, military activity in Russia was proceeding at a pace that was not in Austria's favour. He had been careful not to raise the issue of Russian mobilization with Sazonov, believing that it would be better to allow his German colleague to do so. By Sunday afternoon there was clear evidence in St Petersburg that preparations for mobilization were under way.

Pourtalès raised the issue of mobilization immediately following Szápáry's conversation with Sazonov. The German ambassador warned that resorting to mobilization was a dangerous diplomatic weapon: if the German general staff took offence there would be 'no stopping things'. Sazonov gave his word of honour that the rumours of mobilization were false, that no reserves had been called up, and that military activities amounted to no more than preparatory measures in the military districts of Kiev and Odessa, and perhaps in Kazan and Moscow.[28]

Fearing that his assurances might not be satisfactory, Sazonov arranged for the Russian minister of war, General Sukhomlinov, to meet with the German military attaché, Major von Eggeling, in order to explain Russia's military preparations to him. Sukhomlinov proceeded to give his word of honour that the order for mobilization had not yet been given. He gave his assurances that only preparatory measures had been undertaken thus far—'not a horse and not a reserve had been called to service'. If Austria were to cross the frontier into Serbia, he said, Russia would then mobilize in the direction of Austria: in Kiev, Odessa, Moscow, and Kazan. But under no circumstances would mobilization occur along the German frontier—there would be no mobilization in the military districts of Warsaw, Vilna, or Petersburg. 'It is the urgent desire of Russia to remain at peace with Germany.'

Eggeling replied that although Russia's friendly intentions towards Germany were appreciated, even a mobilization directed at Austria would be regarded as seriously threatening. Sukhomlinov, appearing 'excessively nervous and disquieted', repeatedly expressed Russia's wish to maintain the peace. The military attaché was convinced of the war minister's sincerity and he did not believe that mobilization had begun. Nevertheless, he reported to Berlin that extensive measures were being prepared. The Austrian ambassador repeated the information to Vienna and concluded that the military measures being taken were well suited 'to the dissembler' Tsar Nicholas, since warlike measures—'which he detests'—were avoided, while at the same time eventualities were prepared for.[29]

★

By late Sunday afternoon, the situation seemed precarious but not hopeless. Would the change in Sazonov's attitude combine with Sukhomlinov's reassurances to encourage the Germans and the Austrians sufficiently to agree to some form of mediation on the outstanding issues? Or would the military measures already set in motion create more anxieties leading to counter-measures?

From Vienna, the German ambassador reported that Sazonov's declaration that Russia would go to war with Austria if it were to devour Serbia was being interpreted to mean that Russia would not go beyond diplomatic action.[30] Tschirschky confidently assured the British ambassador that Russia would keep quiet during Austria's 'chastisement of Serbia'.[31] At the same time Pourtalès was reporting from St Petersburg that Sazonov had lost his nerve. Austro-German diplomats on Sunday took Sazonov's improved demeanour as proof that Russia was prepared to back down—in spite of the military preparations that had begun.

The views of the diplomats contradicted the conclusions of military representatives. The kaiser's personal representative at the Russian court, Lieutenant-General von Chelius, the 'military plenipotentiary' (*Miltärbevoll-mächtigte*[32]), reported the impression he had formed on Saturday that although Russia had not yet mobilized, all necessary preparations were being made to do so.[33] The regiments were returning to their garrisons, manoeuvres had been cancelled, and military cadets were commissioned earlier than planned. General headquarters were 'in the throes of great excitement' over Austria's procedure. Later in the day on Sunday he sent a fuller explanation, based on what he witnessed at court and what he heard from army officers. He concluded that the entourage of the tsar was united in its belief that a war between Austria and Serbia must mean war between Russia and Austria. All attempts made by Chelius to counter this belief had proved of no avail: 'Every argument or explanation failed.'[34] At court, they believed that Berlin had known about, and approved of, the Austrian note to Serbia before it was delivered. The belief had taken root in St Petersburg that the firmer bond between Russia and France demonstrated by the visit of Poincaré and Viviani was the real issue—that the Triple Alliance had chosen to 'deliver a blow in the face of the Russian Monarchy' by trampling Serbia underfoot.

According to Chelius, by Sunday the excitement in St Petersburg had been fanned into an enormous blaze. Many of those with whom he spoke had expected war between Austria and Serbia to break out on Saturday night when the Austrian deadline expired. But that had not happened. Austria seemed to be holding back and opening the door to mediation. Had the Austrians occupied Belgrade last night, he complained, they could have presented the world with a fait accompli. The Austrian failure to do so would give new vitality to the Russian opinion that 'Austria barks but does not bite'.

Chelius concluded that from everything that he had seen and heard the tsar was unsympathetic to the policy of friendship with France. He had treated Poincaré 'coldly and haughtily' during the visit. The tsar's personal entourage cared little for the association with France and were more inclined to a monarchical alliance with Germany. On Sunday evening he suggested—through the German ambassador—that the kaiser send a telegram direct to the tsar. This ought 'to appeal to the tsar's monarchical feelings' by emphasizing the blow that had been dealt to the monarchical principle through the murder at Sarajevo, and warning of the danger that would threaten the existence of all European monarchies in the case of a general war.[35]

Twenty-four hours after the expiry of the Austrian deadline, not only had war not broken out, but it now appeared that a new diplomatic initiative might be launched. But this would depend on the kaiser.

★

By Sunday evening Wilhelm had received Pourtalès' report of his Saturday interview with Sazonov. His marginal comments indicated that he was in a fighting mood. He dismissed Sazonov's arguments as 'nonsense' (*Blech*), applauded the ambassador's refusal to submit Austria's position to a European tribunal, and was not surprised that references to the monarchical principle had made little impression on Sazonov—such appeals had been ineffective with Russia since it had begun 'fraternizing with the French socialist republic!' But he disagreed with the conclusion his ambassador had reached that Russia's desire to Europeanize the question indicated that it was not likely to intervene immediately. This was not correct. As for Sazonov's declaration that Russia would go to war with Austria if it attempted to devour Serbia: 'go to it'.[36]

At the Wilhelmstrasse they feared that the return of the kaiser to Berlin would fuel speculation and excitement.[37] After all, the position established by Germany's diplomats had been that the dispute was a purely 'local' affair between Austria and Serbia, that Germany had had nothing to do with the

Austrian ultimatum—had not even been informed of what it contained beforehand—and that Germany, along with Russia and the other Great Powers, should not become involved.

Now the kaiser—who had been literally and figuratively absent from diplomatic decisions while at sea—would be at the centre of decision-making. On his return he was immediately presented with a number of options from which to choose: to align Germany with Grey's proposal to join in a mediation *à quatre* in London, now that the Austro-Serbian dispute had become an Austro-Russian one as well; to support Sazonov's request that Germany should encourage Austria to accept his proposal that Austria and Russia negotiate directly in St Petersburg to modify the most problematic items in the list of Austrian demands on Serbia; to act on the advice of General Chelius that he enter into a dialogue directly with the tsar to mitigate Russia's support of Serbia. His choice could determine the course of events.

But the kaiser was not the only one to return to Berlin that day. General Helmuth von Moltke, the chief of the general staff, finally abandoned his vacation at Karlsbad in order to direct any military preparations himself.

★

Moltke, 66 years old in 1914, was the nephew of the great military hero of the Franco-Prussian war, his namesake, Count Helmuth von Moltke. Moltke 'the younger' had entered the army in 1869 and quickly distinguished himself in the battle of Sedan. After the war, he attended the War Academy and was appointed to the general staff in 1880. He then served as his uncle's personal adjutant until the elder's death in 1891, whereupon the kaiser appointed him as his personal aide-de-camp. The two formed a close, friendly relationship that would last into the First World War. Although Moltke was certainly well-qualified for the position, he had many critics within the high command of the army and it was largely because of his friendship with the kaiser that he was appointed to replace General Alfred von Schlieffen as chief of the general staff in 1906.

Moltke did not fit the stereotypical image of a Prussian general. He was 'philosophical', devoted to the works of Nietzsche, Schopenhauer, and Spencer; a dedicated reader of high literature; a player of the cello and a painter. He was honest, earnest, and hard-working—but he was also anti-Semitic, racist, xenophobic, and a dabbler in the occult.[38] His wife was a follower of the Austrian spiritualist Rudolf Steiner and his 'anthroposophy', which postulated the existence of a spiritual world that could be accessed by

Helmuth von Moltke (1848–1916); chief of the general staff of Germany (1906–14)

human beings through the development of their imagination and intuition. Once, on board the *Hohenzollern*, he lectured the kaiser and his entourage on anthroposophy and theosophy. He was warned to stop dabbling in the occult once he became chief of staff. His philosophical and spiritual interests were shared by Conrad, the chief of the Austrian general staff, which drew the two men closer together.

Moltke returned to Berlin on Sunday the 26th in response to the reports of Russia's military preparations. German strategic planning meant that no time could be lost if Russia was preparing for war. As Moltke and the German general staff saw it, their single greatest advantage was the speed with which Germany was able to mobilize. Detailed planning had been done to facilitate the mobilization: by 1914 the plans provided the logistical support to move over three million men and 600,000 horses in 650 trains a day for thirteen days. The undertaking was massive: Germany was to transport, equip, and supply 6 per cent of its total population in order to fight a war against France and Russia.

The basic lines of German strategy had been laid down years before by Moltke's famous predecessor. Schlieffen, who had anticipated the likelihood that Germany would find itself fighting a two-front war in the future, planned to deliver a knock-out blow against France by invading through Luxembourg, Belgium, and the Netherlands.[39] He believed it possible to achieve victory in the west while standing on the defensive in the east against Russia, utilizing only minimal forces. Moltke accepted Schlieffen's basic premise: 'On the fight against France depends the outcome of the war. The Republic is our most dangerous opponent, but we can hope to achieve a decision here quickly.' France lacked the reserves of manpower to sustain a long struggle, whereas Russia could withdraw its forces into the interior and drag out a war for a long time. Germany must therefore 'end the war on at least one side with a few big strokes as soon as possible'.[40] By 1914 this could only mean France.

The disasters of the Russo-Japanese war had encouraged Schlieffen to believe that only the most minimal forces were necessary to defend against Russia. Moltke was compelled to revise this calculation. Russia's strength had increased significantly over the last few years, along with the strategic resources needed to mobilize it. But defeating France quickly meant that overwhelming force was necessary in the west: by July 1914 the German strategic plan provided for seventy divisions to participate in the invasion of France, leaving only nine to defend Germany against a Russian offensive in the east. The assistance of Austria-Hungary—and even Italy—was now vital to Moltke's calculations. German military strategy meant that Moltke would have to involve himself in German diplomacy. That afternoon he sent to the Wilhelmstrasse a draft of the notification that he proposed they present to Belgium, announcing Germany's intention to violate its neutrality—along with a plea that the diplomats find a way to keep Italy committed to the Triple Alliance.

★

Moltke could count on General Alberto Pollio, chief of the Italian general staff since 1908, to uphold Italy's military commitments to the alliance. Pollio had long been a zealous supporter of the Triple Alliance and Italy's place in it. Believing that the Triple Alliance 'must act as one state', he had offered in 1913 to provide two Italian cavalry regiments to serve on the

Rhine under German command and suggested the possibility that the Italian navy might be able to land troops in Provence.[41] And in March 1914 the Italian king, prime minister, and foreign secretary agreed to make this a formal promise. During the summer he had even discussed with Conrad the possibility of sending Italian forces to assist Austria in a war with Russia. But, on the day of the assassination, 28 June, Pollio had died suddenly and unexpectedly of a heart attack, misdiagnosed as a gastric ailment. Moltke's best hope for Italian military assistance might have died with him. Weeks passed before Pollio's replacement was at last named on 20 July.

In Italy the gap between the military on the one hand, and the politicians and diplomats on the other, was even wider than elsewhere. Successive chiefs of staff in Italy were never given access to the terms of the Triple Alliance. When the minister of war asked for the details of the recently renewed Triple Alliance in 1912, San Giuliano dismissed the request by simply informing him that it contained no military provisions. Strategic plans and diplomatic policies could head off in entirely different directions. When General Luigi Cadorna was appointed to replace Pollio on 20 July, he continued to plan and prepare for a war against France—in spite of the fact that since the assassination San Giuliano had warned repeatedly that Italy might not participate in a war against the Entente. Since the Austrian ultimatum of the 23rd, his reluctance to commit Italy had become more and more pronounced. His reluctance generated increasing concern in Berlin—and increasing frustration with Vienna's unwillingness to do much, if anything, to secure Italian cooperation.

When Moltke raised the issue of Italy's support with Bethmann Hollweg the chancellor immediately told the ambassador in Vienna that the chief of the general staff deemed it an 'urgent necessity' that Italy be held fast to the Triple Alliance. Vienna and Rome should come to an agreement—and Vienna must stop evading it by adopting questionable interpretations of the terms of the alliance.[42]

If the German chancellor in Berlin was frustrated with the unwillingness of the Austrians to do something to bind the Italians to the alliance, the German ambassador in Rome was equally dismayed by the uncooperative attitude of the Austrian ambassador. Flotow, who was doing his best to persuade, cajole, or browbeat the Italians into upholding their commitment to the alliance, complained that the Austrians were doing nothing to assist him. Mérey, the Austrian ambassador, had not come to see him during the past two weeks. The Austrian embassy, Flotow bitterly complained, was a

Count Kajetan von Mérey von Kapos-Mérey (1861–1931); Austro-Hungarian ambassador at Rome (1910–15)

complete failure—during the long period running up to the presentation of their ultimatum they had failed to make any effort to influence public opinion in Italy via the Italian press. Finally, the day after presenting the ultimatum, they had requested a substantial sum of money from Vienna to use in 'influencing' the press—by which they meant bribing journalists and editors. Nevertheless, Flotow asked that Berlin say nothing in Vienna about his complaints, as further discord with Mérey, who was ill, might have disastrous results. He asked for money himself to use in 'influencing' the large Italian newspapers.[43]

No love was lost between the German and Austrian ambassadors in Italy. Mérey suspected Flotow of having surreptitiously let the Italians in on the secret of Austria's plans for dealing with Serbia. He believed that San Giuliano had then passed the information on to Italy's ambassadors in St Petersburg, Belgrade, and Vienna. Mérey seems to have convinced Berchtold that this amounted to disloyalty on the part of Austria's German partner and that Rome should henceforth be kept in the dark as much as possible. Flotow, who exploited the close personal friendship he enjoyed with San Giuliano, believed that Mérey was jeopardizing the Triple Alliance through his obvious contempt for the Italians. It was unlikely, therefore, that Rome would be the place where the cohesion of the Triple Alliance could be cemented.

Flotow met again with San Giuliano on Sunday afternoon in Fiuggi Fonte. The Italian foreign minister repeated his objections to the manner in which Austria had proceeded against Serbia. The Austrians, he said, could use the same arguments and procedures against Italy: they could cite Italy's irredentist ambitions, along with the fact that these ambitions were supported by the press and various organizations. Nor did San Giuliano believe the Austrian promises that they would not claim any Serbian territory—and therefore he proposed that discussions should begin at once on the subject of how Italy might be compensated for Austria's gains. But Mérey's illness combined with his opposition to any accommodation of Italy made this almost impossible to negotiate at Rome.

Vienna was no more promising as a venue as far as San Giuliano was concerned. There, the Italian ambassador was the Sicilian nobleman Giuseppe Avarna—the Count of Gualtieri. By 1914 he had served as Italian ambassador in Vienna for ten years. He had proven himself to be a devoted adherent of the Triple Alliance and regarded cooperation with Austria-Hungary as his life's work. He loved the pomp and ceremony of the Viennese court, and had himself taken to meetings at the Ballhausplatz not in an automobile but in a coach and four.[44] Avarna consistently watered down Italy's demands for compensation in order to make them more palatable to Austrian tastes. San Giuliano had little hope of arranging a deal in Vienna. As the German ambassador in Rome pointed out, the deep-seated distrust between Austria and Italy meant that 'the only available road lies through Berlin'.[45] Flotow claimed not to know what his government thought about the compensation issue, and argued to San Giuliano that it was too soon to begin discussions on it.

San Giuliano was not to be diverted. He told the prime minister that his strategy was to keep everyone in the dark: not knowing which way Italy would jump was the best opportunity to gain an advantage. For the first time a German secretary of state was saying that the moment had arrived for Italy to be given the Trentino.[46] Failing an agreement on compensation, he warned Flotow that Italy would be forced 'to stand in Austria's way'. And, he complained, Germany was giving too much encouragement to Austria. He suggested that Berlin should take care not to reject too abruptly Sir Edward Grey's proposed mediation *à quatre* because this would likely push him onto the side of the Entente.[47]

★

Given their worries that Russian mobilization was about to begin and Moltke's insistence that Italy's contribution was vital to Germany's war plans, the Germans felt they must find a way to resolve the Austro-Italian impasse. From Vienna, Tschirschky assured Bethmann Hollweg that he was continuously discussing with both Berchtold and Macchio the whole range of issues arising from Italy's claims to compensation. And, as earlier instructed, he was striving to get the Austrians to drop their 'futile theoretical discussions' concerning the interpretation of Article VII of the Triple Alliance. He had to admit that he was not getting far. In a meeting on Sunday afternoon General Conrad had supported him, but Berchtold—although not refusing Italian claims to compensation outright—took the position that permitting Italy to remain in occupation of islands in the Aegean, following the war with Turkey, constituted compensation 'in advance'.[48]

Tschirschky told Berchtold that Germany agreed with the Italian position. Every occupation, whether temporary or otherwise, of territory '*dans les régions des Balcans*' (the expression used in Article VII) gave the other party the right to compensation. When Berchtold tried to argue that the formula had been intended to apply only to Turkish territory, Tschirschky insisted that Italy's claim was perfectly justified. If it came to a vote, Germany would side with Italy, and the result would be the defeat of Austria 2 to 1. Berchtold replied that if Italy chose to raise the issue of compensation now, when Austria had declared its intention to do no more than hold Serbian land temporarily as a transitory operation of war, Austria would demand to receive compensation for Italy's occupation of Rhodes, Karpathos, Stampalia, and islands in the Aegean.

A speedy resolution of the dispute between Italy and Austria did not seem likely. Tschirschky, while reporting to Berlin that he was doing his best to follow instructions, may have been misleading his masters. Conrad recorded that Tschirschky had advised Austria to treat Italy's claims 'in a dilatory manner'—i.e. telling them that compensation would be discussed later, at a more suitable time.[49] Or perhaps Conrad was trying to mislead posterity: it would not be the first time (or the last).

Tschirschky assured Jagow that no one was more convinced than he of the necessity of holding Italy firmly to the Triple Alliance. He promised that he was persevering to achieve this objective. This was not a simple task, however: 'the Austrians will always remain Austrians'.[50] Their pride and their recklessness (*Hochmut und Leichtsinn*) were not easy to overcome. He knew them only too well.

Tschirschky was working closely with the Italian ambassador in Vienna. He received from Avarna the impression that San Giuliano was attempting to set the highest possible price on Italy's maintaining a neutral position in an Austro-Serbian conflict. This was not a good reason to abandon the search for a way out of the compensation difficulty, however, because it was in Germany's interest to find a solution. With this in mind, he had approached Macchio at the Ballhausplatz to persuade him to drop the theoretical arguments and to convince Berchtold that some means of compensating Italy had to be found, and found quickly. The Austrian agreed that the arguments over Article VII were leading nowhere, but grumbled that Italy could not ask Austria to 'cut the compensation out of our own flesh'. Neither the emperor nor the military would ever consent to surrendering the Trentino to Italy.

Tschirschky concluded from his latest initiative that the Austrians would certainly not make any significant concessions in exchange for minor territorial gains on the Serbian frontier. Only after a 'great and victorious' war, in which Austria received carte blanche in the Balkans, might the Austrians consider such concessions. The ambassador suggested that Germany ought to eradicate any such illusions of this kind that were entertained in Rome. As a way out of the morass of technical and legal arguments, he proposed to Macchio that Austria should simply tell the Italians that it recognized their right to compensation if the monarchy extended its territory in the Balkans—and thus avoid any reference to the contentious Article VII altogether. Avarna, he told Jagow, approved of this as a way out.

By Sunday evening it remained far from clear which way Italy would jump if the Austro-Serbian dispute turned into an Austro-Russian war. While Berlin and Vienna were pressing Rome for a promise to adhere to the alliance, St Petersburg, London, and Paris were encouraging the Italians to promote a European-mediated settlement. The British ambassador in Rome, Sir Rennell Rodd, had been absent for most of the crisis, scouring the towns of Tuscany for art treasures. A poet who had formed an intimate friendship with Oscar Wilde as a young man, he had become an enthusiastic booster of all things Italian since his appointment in 1908, helping to establish the *Journal of Roman Studies* in 1912. Until late July he seemed to discount the seriousness of the political situation, preferring to pursue his historical and aesthetic interests. After returning to his post he formed the impression that if war broke out Italy would argue that the *casus foederis* of the alliance did not arise because Austria had not consulted Italy before delivering the note and because an attack on Serbia could be construed as a 'constructive provocation' of Russia.[51] By Sunday evening he was reporting that San Giuliano welcomed Grey's proposed mediation *à quatre*.

Meanwhile, the Russian ambassador was instructed to inform San Giuliano that it would be impossible for Russia to refrain from coming to Serbia's assistance if Austria attacked. He suggested that Italy should take up an 'adverse attitude' to the conflict and use its good offices to influence Austria.[52] The French ambassador was making similar arguments. Camille Barrère, who had served in Rome since 1897, had worked throughout his long tenure to detach Italy from the Triple Alliance. He believed that the lack of support Italy's Austrian and German allies had given during the war with Turkey provided a golden opportunity for France. But his plan opened a rift with Poincaré, who regarded the balance between the two alliances as the best guarantee of French security. With the president and premier at sea and barely in touch, Barrère pursued his own agenda in Rome.

Not only was Italy being pushed and pulled in two different directions, but by Sunday evening it was unclear what the 'mediation' process might consist of. While the British were pushing the Italians to support Grey's proposed London conference—the mediation *à quatre*—the Russians were pushing them to use their influence with the Austrians to persuade them to negotiate directly with Sazonov via their ambassador in St Petersburg—the new 'bilateral' proposition. The Austrian ambassador, Mérey, who received a visit in his sick-room from San Giuliano's secretary that afternoon, advised against making any concessions to Italy. He proposed that they stand firm against the cries of the Italian government and newspapers: the more resolved and inexorable the Austrians were, 'the more we will gain in the eyes of Italy'.[53]

★

By Sunday evening more than twenty-four hours had passed since the Austrian legation had departed from Belgrade and Austria had severed diplomatic relations with Serbia. Many had assumed that war would follow immediately, but there had been no invasion of Serbia or even a declaration of war. The Austrians, in spite of their apparent firmness in refusing any alteration of the terms or any extension of the deadline, appeared not to know what step to take next, or when additional steps should be taken. Given the increasing pressures on Vienna to agree to one of the two proposals for mediation or negotiation, and given Italy's inexorable demands for compensation to be promised in advance, Berchtold was now anxious that war should be declared as soon as possible.

On Sunday he asked the chief of the general staff when he wanted the declaration to be made. Conrad's answer was not what Berchtold wanted to hear: the chief of the general staff wanted to put off the declaration until he was ready to commence operations—until about the 12th of August. This was more than two weeks away. In the meantime, the pressures to negotiate with Russia and/or Serbia would continue to mount. Berchtold told him that the diplomatic situation would not hold that long, although he could perhaps manage to defer the declaration of war for a few days. Conrad insisted that he needed to know definitely what attitude Russia would take beforehand—and he would need this information by the 4th or 5th of August at the latest. Berchtold complained that he was asking for the impossible. Conrad explained that if the Russians were going to go against Austria, it would be necessary to proceed against them from the start; if they were not, he could proceed against Serbia directly. And he raised a third possibility: Russia might not go after Austria now but delay an attack until sometime later; if so, Austria would then find itself weak in the north, having already committed its forces against Serbia in the south.[54]

Military considerations were now beginning to influence diplomacy. The Serbs had ordered the mobilization of their forces at the end of the day on Saturday; the Austrians began mobilizing theirs on Sunday; the Russians had taken the first steps towards a mobilization—although it remained unclear exactly what these consisted of, and where they were to be taken; the German fleet was ordered to return to Germany from its annual manoeuvres in Norway; Luxembourg called up its reserves. The intersection of diplomacy and strategy lay in the German response to Russia's action: Bethmann Hollweg warned that a Russian mobilization meant a German mobilization, and that German mobilization meant war. How, then, were Russia's actions to be interpreted? On Sunday, both the Russian foreign minister and minister of war assured the Germans that the steps they were taking did not mean mobilization—not a horse, not a reservist, had been called up into service. There was still a chance for diplomacy to avert a cataclysm.

Day Four

Monday, 27 July

B y the time the diplomats, politicians, and officials arrived at their offices on the morning of Monday, the 27th of July, more than thirty-six hours had elapsed since the Austrian deadline to Serbia had expired. And yet—at least to the naked eye—nothing much had happened as a consequence. True, the Austrian legation had packed up and left Belgrade, Austria had severed diplomatic relations with Serbia and had announced a partial mobilization. But there had been no declaration of war, no shots fired in anger or in error, no wider mobilization of European armies. Most of the action occurred behind the scenes, at the Foreign Office, the Ballhausplatz, the Wilhelmstrasse, the Consulta, the Quai d'Orsay, and at the Chorister's Bridge. Even on Sunday there had been discussions and negotiations, but these had been largely inconclusive and left most of the crucial questions hanging. Perhaps they would be answered today.

Steps were being taken. Not dramatic steps, but tentative, precautionary, ones. In Russia, all lights along the coast of the Black Sea were ordered to be extinguished. The port of Sevastopol was closed to all but Russian warships. All flights were banned over the military districts of St Petersburg, Vilna, Warsaw, Kiev, and Odessa. The French minister of war ordered that over 100,000 troops stationed in Morocco and Algeria should return to metropolitan France. Bienvenu-Martin cabled Poincaré and Viviani, and asked them to sail for home immediately; the *France* changed course from Denmark to Dunkirk. In Britain the cabinet agreed to keep the First and Second Fleets together at Portland; Winston Churchill, first lord of the admiralty, notified his naval commanders that war between the Triple Alliance and the Triple Entente was 'by no means impossible'.[1] The German minister of war ordered that all troops be confined to barracks and instructed that wheat should be purchased 'in great quantities'.[2] On the Danube, Hungarian authorities seized two Serbian vessels at Orsova, but reports of shots being fired farther downstream at Temes-Kubin turned out to be false.

Many of those who had been absent from the scene during the first days of the crisis were now returning to their duties at home or at their post. The Russian ambassadors to Austria-Hungary and France had been instructed to return to Vienna and Paris on Friday; Schebeko had arrived in Vienna on Sunday, Izvol'skii returned to Paris on Monday. 'We can now expect to be spoken to more sharply', the Austrian ambassador in Paris told Berchtold.[3] The British ambassador to Germany, Sir Edward Goschen, arrived in Berlin on Monday morning and immediately arranged to meet with the secretary of state. That evening the French ambassador to Britain, Paul Cambon, returned to London after a brief trip to Paris. San Giuliano returned to Rome from Fiuggi Fonte. The French government announced that the president and the premier had cancelled the rest of their voyage and would arrive in Paris on Wednesday.

Kaiser Wilhelm, against the advice of his chancellor, arrived at Kiel on Monday morning. He then set out for the 200-mile railway journey to Berlin in his private carriage, arriving at 1 p.m., when he was intercepted by Bethmann Hollweg at Wildpark station in Potsdam. There, in the Kaiser-bahnhof, the chancellor pleaded with him not to proceed into Berlin: his sudden appearance there would make the situation seem more ominous. The German government wished to maintain the impression that the dispute concerned only Austria and Serbia and that Germany did not expect to become involved. The kaiser agreed and called for a meeting at the Neues Palais in Potsdam for 3 p.m. There, the chancellor, the chief of the general staff, and several more generals reviewed the situation with him, but no dramatic decisions were taken. General Hans von Plessen, the adjutant general, noted in his diary that they still hoped to localize the war, and that Britain seemed likely to remain neutral. 'I have the impression that it will all blow over.'[4]

Although there was a growing sense of urgency throughout Europe there were few signs of panic. Everyone continued to wonder what would happen next. Would Austria now proceed to declare war on Serbia, invade and occupy Belgrade? Would this precipitate a Russian response in defence of Serbia? If the Russian response consisted of a mobilization, would Germany reply by attacking Russia? Would Germany's war plans mean that a defence of Austria would necessitate an attack on France? Would Britain come to the aid of its Entente partners, or remain on the sidelines?

Would Italy come to the aid of its alliance partners, remain on the sidelines, or perhaps join the enemy?

In spite of these unanswered questions and a growing sense of urgency, there were hopeful signs. Most encouraging was the fact that Austria had yet to declare war on Serbia. Many had expected this to happen immediately following the expiry of the ultimatum on Saturday evening. But when Sunday came and went, then Monday began without any announcement, there was hope that the military steps begun by Austria were mere posturing and amounted to no more than a bluff. Perhaps the Austrians could be satisfied with a resounding diplomatic victory—if one were offered to them.

★

In St Petersburg on Monday morning Sazonov met with the German ambassador, then with the Austrian. Both ambassadors found him surprisingly positive and optimistic. Sazonov seemed relieved that Austria had yet to take any hostile steps against Serbia and encouraged by Austria's declaration of its territorial *désinteressement*. He assured Count Pourtalès of his readiness to go to the limit in accommodating the Austrians if it meant bringing the crisis to a peaceful conclusion. He proposed that they 'build a golden bridge' for them—and the means they adopted to create this were immaterial to him.[5] The only necessity was that those points in the Austrian demands that infringed upon Serbian sovereignty be moderated: could they not find some way of giving the Serbs the lesson they deserved without infringing on their sovereignty? When Pourtalès criticized the Serbs for failing to behave in a civilized manner—and insisted that they would have to give guarantees to Europe for their good behaviour in the future—Sazonov's objections, he reported, were much more feeble than they had been in previous days.

The German ambassador noted a striking change in Sazonov's attitude. He attributed this to Austria's declaration that it did not intend to make any territorial acquisitions and to Germany's energetic refutation of the insinuation that it had prodded Austria into fomenting a conflict. Sazonov, trying to find a way out, was now prepared to recognize the justice of Austria's complaints against Serbia. And the Russian government was trying to quiet opinion—although there was little apparent enthusiasm for war in Russia. When the troops recalled from the camp at Krasnoje Selo marched through the streets of St Petersburg, the people of the city regarded them with indifference, and no one seemed to think of applauding them. Last night there had been another clash between the police and working men, although it was difficult to obtain much information about this because the government was no longer permitting anything to be published on the demonstrations. Generally, the public appeared to be in a dejected mood.[6] So the word to Berlin was that the Russians appeared to be backing away from a confrontation and—perhaps desperately—seeking an accommodation.

Pourtalès did not encourage Sazonov's hope that Austria might moderate the terms of the ultimatum. Instead, he advised him to speak directly with the Austrian ambassador on the issue. This Sazonov did almost immediately. After meeting with him, Count Szápáry confirmed the conclusions of his German colleague: Sazonov's manner on Monday contrasted vividly with the one that he had displayed on Friday, when they had gone over the terms of the Austrian ultimatum. Although he said that it might be unwise for him to admit it to the Austrian ambassador, the Russian foreign minister confessed that he had 'no heart' for the Balkan Slavs, who were a heavy burden for Russia and who had no conception of what Russia had already suffered on their behalf.[7] He accepted that Austria's aim of preserving itself and defending itself against the propaganda which threatened its integrity was perfectly legitimate. The Austrian note to Serbia, however, was not the most desirable way to achieve this, and he proposed to go through it with the ambassador point-by-point.

Szápáry made it clear that he was not authorized to discuss the note or to interpret it, but said that he would be interested to hear what the foreign minister had to say about it. Sazonov surprised the ambassador by declaring that seven of the ten points raised no particular difficulty. However, those referring to the collaboration of Austrian officials in Serbia and the dismissal of Serbian officers and officials named by Austria were—in their present form—unacceptable. Some other means ought to be found for dealing with those who could be proved guilty of complicity in the crime. Serbia could not accept the demands as formulated without risking the overthrow of the Karadjeordjević dynasty—and surely Austria would prefer that regime to an 'anarchist witches cauldron'? The whole affair, he argued, came down to one 'of words' and surely it was possible to find a way to overcome their differences. Would Austria accept the mediation of the king of Italy? or of England?[8]

Szápáry concluded that the Russians had travelled a considerable distance over the last three days. They had moved from a discourteous rejection of Austria's plans for dealing with Serbia to a search for an acceptable mediator.

Although there was an energetic military influence still at work in Russia which must not be overlooked, there seemed no great urgency. Sazonov declared himself to be much comforted by their conversation and promised to report this to the tsar when he was scheduled to see him at a diplomatic reception this coming Wednesday.

Things seemed to be coming together. Russia now appeared to be reluctant to confront Austria and offered to build a 'golden bridge' if the Austrians would agree to some form of mediation. And that mediation would only be asked to find a way to moderate the two or three most contentious demands. The Serbian reply to the Austrian ultimatum, the details of which became known throughout the day on Monday, seemed to confer on the Austrians a great diplomatic victory. Perhaps this crisis, like many others before it, would end in a diplomatic solution. Perhaps the Serbs would be duly chastised, agree to clamp down on propaganda aimed at the Dual Monarchy, ban nationalist organizations devoted to achieving a greater Serbia, and agree to some form of European oversight in finding and punishing all those involved in the crime of Sarajevo.

★

The Serbian minister in London appeared at the Foreign Office first thing Monday morning to give Sir Edward Grey a copy of his government's reply to the Austrian ultimatum. Instead of Grey, who had not yet returned to the office, he met with the permanent under-secretary. Sir Arthur Nicolson, after a quick perusal of the document, concluded that the Serbs had conceded practically all of the Austrian demands. 'It is difficult to see how Austria can honestly proceed to hostile operations when Servia has yielded so much.'[9] Fortunately, military intelligence indicated that there was sufficient time to act on the reply as the basis for a settlement: Austria's mobilization would not be completed until the end of the week at the earliest, and the forces to be concentrated along the Serbian frontier would not be in place until the following week—not until Wednesday, the 5th of August.

When Grey returned from his day of fishing to the Foreign Office later that morning he was astonished to discover just how far the Serbs had gone in agreeing to the Austrian demands. When he met with Lichnowsky he told him that the Serbs had gone farther than he would ever have believed possible.[10] As far as he was concerned, they had practically agreed to everything except the point concerning the participation of Austrian officials in the judicial investigation. And this reservation was hardly surprising, given that the German secretary of state himself had anticipated that the Serbs could hardly be expected to comply with all of the demands made upon them.[11] Grey emphasized another point: that Serbia's submission must be due to pressure exerted upon them from St Petersburg. In other words, this provided convincing proof that the Russians were eager to resolve the crisis diplomatically, even at the cost of Serbia's public humiliation.

So Russia, according to the British foreign secretary, had demonstrated its peaceful intentions. Would Austria now do the same? Grey wanted to know. If the Austrians refused to accept the Serbian reply as the foundation for peaceful negotiations, or if they proceeded to occupy Belgrade—which now lay undefended—it would be 'absolutely clear' that Austria was only seeking an excuse to crush Serbia. If this were the case, he warned, Russia could not regard it with equanimity and was bound to regard it as a direct challenge. 'The result would be the most frightful war that Europe had ever seen.'[12] The Serbian reply was a critical step in Grey's estimation of the nature of the crisis; the Austrian response to it promised to be a turning-point in his diplomacy.

The acting foreign minister in France was equally impressed with the extent of Serbia's compliance. Bienvenu-Martin, practically illiterate when it came to the language of diplomacy and untutored in the subtleties of diplomatic negotiation, had taken a juridical view of the crisis from the start. He had seen nothing wrong in the Austrian determination to punish those responsible for the crime of Sarajevo—or in their insistence that Serbia take the steps necessary to prevent further attacks upon the integrity of the Dual Monarchy. His initial assessment of the Austrian demands on Serbia was only that these appeared to be 'very sharp' (*très accentuée*).[13] After a more thorough perusal of the demands, he told the German ambassador that while the punishment of those implicated in the crime was certainly legitimate, measures that threatened the dignity and sovereignty of Serbia might lead to a revolution there. He hoped that if the Serbs promised to punish those responsible and to offer guarantees that they would suppress anti-Austrian propaganda, then the means for doing so could be examined. If Serbia gave proof of its goodwill, surely Austria would not refuse to engage in discussions?[14]

The Serb reply transformed Bienvenu-Martin. As far as he was concerned, the Serbs had yielded to all of the demands. The Austrian refusal to accept Serbia's submission was 'incomprehensible'.[15] He told the Austrian ambassador that Serbia had accepted Austria's demands on 'almost every point' and that the differences that remained could be overcome by mutual goodwill and with the help of the Powers who wished to maintain the peace. But Austria's declaration that it intended to take the 'severest measures' the next day was—for the second time—making cooperation impossible. He warned that Austria was assuming a grave responsibility in running the risk of precipitating a war 'the limits of which it was impossible to foresee'.[16]

The Austrian ambassador, Count Nikolaus Szécsen von Temerin, claimed not to know what Austria's next move would be. There might be another ultimatum, a declaration of war, or a crossing of the frontier—he had not received precise information from Vienna. Although he was regarded in Vienna as a capable diplomat, with the ability to serve as foreign minister, Szécsen's appointment as ambassador to republican France in 1911 had not been without its challenges. A Magyar magnate, descended from a Croatian family ennobled in the eighteenth century, he typified aristocratic hauteur, playing the role of the grand *seigneur* in Paris. His own military attaché there referred to him as 'our knight of the Golden Fleece with the degenerate nasal voice'.[17] Szécsen warned Vienna that its attitude in response to the Serbian answer had produced the general impression in France that Austria wanted war 'at any price'.[18]

Bienvenu-Martin took some of the credit for persuading the Serbs to respond in such a submissive manner. France had joined together with Russia and Britain to persuade Belgrade to yield to the maximum extent possible—and in this they had succeeded. Were their efforts to be wasted? The Entente had done its part to see that the crisis could be resolved peacefully. Bienvenu-Martin concluded that it was now up to Germany to do the same by putting pressure on Austria to accept the mediation *à quatre* proposed by Grey. If the Germans failed to do so, it would justify the suspicions people had of them and they would have to assume the responsibility for bringing about a general war. He instructed the French ambassador in Berlin to cooperate with his British colleague in persuading the German government to accept the proposed mediation.

When Jules Cambon met with the German foreign minister in Berlin that afternoon Jagow assured him that he was disposed to join the Powers in the proposed mediation and to do all he could to preserve peace. But Germany had alliance obligations to Austria-Hungary, just as France had to Russia— and if Russia were to mobilize, Germany would be forced to do the same. France would then be forced to follow suit and 'a conflict would be almost inevitable'. What if Russia were to mobilize only on the Austrian frontier, Cambon asked: would Germany be bound to mobilize then? 'No', Jagow said—and authorized Cambon to communicate this commitment formally to Bienvenu-Martin. On the other hand, if Russia were to attack Austria, Germany would be obliged to respond by attacking Russia at once. Jagow warned that the proposed mediation could succeed only if events did not transpire as he had outlined.[19]

Cambon had worked diligently for years to improve Franco-German relations. Although he had fought in the Franco-Prussian war as a young captain, when he was appointed as ambassador to Berlin in 1907 he was determined to achieve a rapprochement with Germany. As governor-general of Algeria from 1901 to 1907 he had become convinced that France's future lay overseas—especially in North Africa—and that this could be more easily achieved if tensions between France and Germany were reduced in Europe. In his seven years as ambassador in Berlin he had established a friendly relationship with the kaiser himself—they shared an interest in tapestries and paintings—along with high-ranking officials in the German government.

Cambon was becoming impatient and frustrated with the Germans. Jagow's continuing insistence that Germany could not agree to a conference to deal with the affairs of Austria and Russia was most unfortunate. Merely for the sake of form Germany appeared prepared to forgo the best opportunity of keeping the peace. Jagow, who had often told him how much he regretted the division of Europe into two groups always opposed to one another, now had the opportunity to prove that there was a 'European spirit' by coming together with France, Britain, and Italy to find a way of preventing a conflict. But Jagow had evaded the ambassador's point by arguing that Germany was obliged to maintain its commitments to Austria. Cambon asked him if this bound Jagow 'to follow her everywhere with his eyes blindfolded'.[20]

Cambon wanted to know what Jagow made of the Serbian reply to the Austrian demands. The secretary of state claimed—on Monday afternoon—not yet to have had time to read the document that he had received that morning. Too bad, Cambon said—for he would see that Serbia had yielded entirely, except on a few points of detail. Really, since Germany had been instrumental in obtaining for Austria the satisfaction that it sought, Germany should now advise acceptance of the reply or at least agree to examine the differences that remained in a discussion with Serbia.

Jagow failed to reply clearly to this suggestion. Cambon asked him if Germany wanted war. Jagow protested that this was not so. If this were true, Cambon entreated him 'in the name of humanity' to weigh his conscience and not to assume part of the responsibility for the catastrophe that would ensue.

Against these arguments Jagow appeared to bend a little. He assured Cambon that he was prepared to join with Britain and France in a common effort to avert war. But it was necessary to find an acceptable form for such an intervention. It was his understanding that direct conversations between Vienna and St Petersburg had now begun and were currently in progress. He was hopeful that these would achieve good results. Perhaps a formal mediation *à quatre* would not be necessary.

Cambon was not persuaded. About to leave the meeting, he told Jagow that in the morning—when he read the Serbian reply—he had the impression that the hour of détente had arrived. But he now saw that there was nothing in this. He suggested to Bienvenu-Martin that Grey be asked to renew his proposed conference in a revised form, one that would deprive Germany 'of any pretext for failing to accept it'—and leaving Germany with the responsibility for its failure in British eyes.[21] Cambon had almost abandoned hope that Germany would participate in the mediation effort and his aim now was to utilize Germany's refusal to bolster the coherence of the Entente.

Shortly before his meeting with Cambon, Jagow had seen Edward Goschen, who had returned to his post as ambassador at Berlin the night before. Goschen (originally Göschen) was the youngest of the twelve children of a German banker located in London. He had been raised to be thoroughly English, however, attending Rugby School, then Christ Church, Oxford, before entering the diplomatic service in 1869. He had served abroad continuously for the past forty-four years, including stints in Belgrade and Vienna before his appointment to Berlin in 1908. During his three years in Vienna he had become convinced that Austria was entirely under the thumb of the Germans and would do nothing without their approval. In spite of his German heritage, he was not happy in Berlin, finding the people as uncongenial as the climate. Over the course of his six years there he failed to get close to the kaiser's inner circle and was rarely in a position to report accurately on what they were thinking. He advised that a meaningful détente with Germany was impossible.

Goschen told the French ambassador that in his meeting with Jagow the secretary of state had persisted in the line that Grey's proposed conference would 'practically amount to a court of arbitration' and that this could not be called together except at the request of Austria and Russia.[22] Goschen denied that Grey's proposal had anything to do with arbitration. He simply intended to call together the representatives of the four nations not directly involved in the dispute to discuss the situation and find the means by which to avoid a dangerous situation. Jagow insisted that the proposal was impractical and instead put his faith in the direct discussions that were now under way between St Petersburg and Vienna. He again warned that if Russia were to mobilize against Germany, Germany would have to follow suit.

Goschen wondered what 'mobilizing against Germany' meant. Jagow explained that if Russia mobilized only in the south, he could promise that Germany would not mobilize. Given that the Russian system of mobilization was very complicated, however, he added that it might be difficult to locate exactly the mobilization—and Germany would have to be careful not to be taken by surprise.

★

The military situation was uncertain and confusing. In spite of Germany's best efforts to gather accurate intelligence on Russia's moves, by Monday afternoon the chancellor, Bethmann Hollweg, could tell the kaiser only that based on the most recent reports Russia did not yet seem to be mobilizing. Equally perplexing was the information that Austria, which had begun mobilizing the day before, would not be able to begin war operations against Serbia until the 12th of August. The chief of the German general staff told his wife that the situation remained 'extremely obscure' and that it would be another two weeks before anything definite would be known.[23] Any remaining hope that quick and decisive action on the part of Austria might forestall a determined response by Russia and its Entente partners now seemed to have evaporated. Jagow told the Austrian ambassador that he deeply regretted their delay in undertaking military action.[24]

Bethmann Hollweg admitted to the kaiser that he found the diplomatic situation as unclear as the military situation. He did believe, however, that Britain, France, and Italy all desired peace. The fact that Serbia appeared to have accepted almost all of the points in the Austrian ultimatum further complicated things, because it appeared that Austria-Hungary was close to accomplishing everything it wanted. But for now Bethmann Hollweg had repeated his instructions to all German diplomats that they were to continue to adhere to the line that the Austro-Serbian conflict concerned those two states alone.[25] In the meantime Jagow sought detailed information from Austria in order to refute British assertions that the Serbian reply indicated their willingness to comply with the chief points contained in the Austrian note.[26]

The Serbian reply perplexed the Austrians as well. Berchtold explained to the emperor that the Serbs had been very clever in composing their response. Although he dismissed the contents of their reply as 'totally worthless' (*ganz wertlos*) the form of the note was most courteous—which made it virtually certain that the Powers of the Triple Entente would renew their efforts to find a peaceful solution.[27] In order to prevent an initiative from succeeding he proposed to Franz Joseph that they declare war against Serbia on Tuesday morning. The excuse for this was to be that Serbian troops had fired upon some Austrian ships on the Danube, the Austrians had returned fire, and thus hostilities had already commenced. Berchtold confided to the German ambassador that the declaration of war was to be issued tomorrow—or Wednesday at the very latest—in order to frustrate any diplomatic attempt to intervene in the dispute.[28]

At the Ballhausplatz they decided that they ought to counter Serbia's 'clever' manoeuvre by issuing a rebuttal. By evening they had put some materials together and sent them to the Austrian embassies and legations throughout Europe. Serbia, they argued, had endeavoured to convey the false impression that it was prepared to comply with most of Austria's demands. The Serbian response was insincere and they did not seriously contemplate acting against those who engaged in intrigues against the Dual Monarchy. Serbia's reply was full of evasions and reservations which rendered worthless the concessions that they appeared to make. The refusal to agree to Austrian participation in discovering the perpetrators of the crime of Sarajevo, to deal adequately with propaganda publications and the dissolution of societies hostile to the monarchy amounted to an altogether unsatisfactory response. The fact that the Serbian government had given the orders to mobilize its armed forces three hours prior to handing over its reply to the Austrian minister was further proof of its insincerity.[29]

The Serbian reply to the Austrian ultimatum deepened the divide between the Entente and the Triple Alliance. Grey, Bienvenu-Martin, and Sazonov all believed that the Serbs had gone as far as they possibly could in meeting the demands—and farther than they had imagined possible. If the Austrians insisted on proceeding against the Serbs anyway, it would prove that they were only looking for a pretext.[30] They also believed that it was the pressure they had exerted that had induced the Serbs to be so accommodating. Surely the reply and the fact that it was pressure from the Entente that had brought it about ought to be sufficient to induce the Austrians to negotiate the few small differences that remained?

When Lichnowsky met with Grey in London that morning he found him irritated for the first time during the crisis. It was the German government, Grey complained, that had requested he exert his influence to induce Russia to proceed with moderation. This he had done, and done so successfully. Now it was Germany's turn to exert its influence at Vienna and get the Austrians either to accept the Serb reply as satisfactory or at least as the basis for a conference. The resolution of the crisis now lay in Germany's hands. He would be making a statement to this effect in the House of Commons later in the day.

Lichnowsky now warned the Wilhelmstrasse that if it came to war Germany would no longer be able to count on British sympathy or support. In London, they believed the key to the situation was to be found in Berlin, where they had the power to restrain Austria from proceeding with its foolhardy policy.[31]

Lichnowsky did not hide his frustration or his concern from his Austrian colleague in London. After meeting with Grey, he told Count Mensdorff that the foreign secretary had concluded that if Austria-Hungary was not satisfied with the 'unexampled humiliation' of Serbia that it had achieved, then it would demonstrate beyond a doubt that it was simply seeking a pretext for war and that its real aim was to do away with Serbia altogether and remove Russian influence from the Balkans. If Austria were to occupy Belgrade it would unleash a great European conflagration. Lichnowsky was convinced that if Austria marched into Serbia Britain would go over completely to the other side.[32]

In the House of Commons Grey explained how he had responded since receiving a copy of the Austrian ultimatum on Friday. In meetings with the European ambassadors he had expressed the view that as long as the dispute was one between Austria-Hungary and Serbia alone, Britain had no title to interfere—but that if relations between Austria-Hungary and Russia became threatening, then the question would become one of European peace and would concern Britain. Subsequently, he had proposed that the French, German, and Italian ambassadors in London should meet with him in conference immediately to endeavour to find a solution to the difficulties. He had asked the governments of Austria-Hungary, Russia, and Serbia to suspend active military operations pending the results of such a conference.

Grey explained to the House that what he had done was unusual, that normally one would undertake the preliminary step of determining whether such a proposal would be well received before making it. But the gravity of the situation and the shortness of the time available meant that the risk of proposing something that might be unwelcome or ineffective could not be avoided. He felt, however, that the Serbian reply was such that it should at least provide the basis on which a 'friendly and impartial group of Powers' should be able to arrange a settlement that would be generally acceptable. On the other hand, it ought to be obvious to anyone that if the dispute ceased to be one between Austria-Hungary and Serbia alone and involved another Great Power 'it can but end in the greatest catastrophe that has ever befallen the Continent of Europe at one blow'.[33]

Grey was addressing his colleagues in the cabinet as much as members of parliament and European diplomats. He was well aware that few of his colleagues believed there was any British interest involved in the dispute between Austria-Hungary and Serbia. John Burns, the president of the board of trade, complained that no one could understand why 'four Great Powers should fight over Serbia', and he was determined to have 'nothing to do with such a criminal folly'.[34] A more important member of the cabinet, Herbert Samuel (president of the local government board), told his wife after the cabinet met on Monday evening that he was feeling pessimistic about the situation but that they were doing their best 'to localize the conflict'.[35] More important still, the chancellor of the exchequer, Lloyd George, assured C. P. Scott of the *Manchester Guardian* after the meeting that 'there could be no question of our taking part in any war in the first instance'. Lloyd George assured him that he knew of no minister who would be in favour of it.[36] Complications might arise if the German fleet attacked French towns along the Channel—but even so he hoped that if Germany and Austria went to war with France and Russia, Britain might 'pair' with Italy and agree that the two of them should both keep out of it.

★

The Austrian ambassador, Count Albert Victor Jules Michael Mensdorff-Pouilly-Dietrichstein, was working assiduously to convince Grey that Austria did not want a war. Mensdorff was well connected: his grandmother

Count Albert von Mensdorff-Pouilly-Dietrichstein (1861–1945); Austro-Hungarian
ambassador at London (1904–14)

was a sister of Queen Victoria's mother, giving him an entrée into royal
circles when first appointed to Britain in 1889. His standing in British
society resulted in his serving continuously in London from 1896: as first
secretary, then councillor, and then, at only 42, as ambassador in 1904. The
son of an Austrian foreign minister, his personal wealth was sufficient to
enable him to give brilliant dinners and to entertain lavishly. Proud of his
friendship with his cousins, Edward VII and then George V, they referred to
him at the Ballhausplatz as 'Royal Albert'.[37] He believed that his connections and his knowledge of Britain gave him greater influence than other
diplomats.

Following Grey's address to the House, Mensdorff met with him to try to
persuade him that Austria's policy was purely defensive. He denied that
Austria was seeking either territorial conquest or the destruction of Serbian

independence. On the contrary, Austria's only motive was self-preservation. Grey ought to appreciate that Austria believed the moment had arrived to obtain—by means of the strongest pressure—guarantees 'for the definite suppression' of Serbian aspirations and for the security of peace and order on Austria's south-eastern frontier.[38] Surely, given the British sense of justice, they could not blame the Austrian government if it 'defended by the sword what was theirs'?[39] This fight had been forced upon Austria by Serbia and he counted on Britain's assistance in keeping it localized.

Grey was not persuaded. He could not understand Austria's response to the Serbian reply. They had treated the reply as if it were a 'decided refusal' to comply with Austria's wishes, whereas in fact the ultimatum was 'really the greatest humiliation to which an independent State has ever been subjected'. As far as he was concerned, Serbia had accepted all the points demanded of it. In any case, there was certainly sufficient ground in the reply to believe it could serve as the foundation of a settlement to be proposed by the four disinterested Powers acting together in conference. It was essential that Austria refrain from military operations while the others were conferring.

Mensdorff feared that it was now too late for this. Grey was blunt: if Austria was resolved to have a war with Serbia under any circumstances— on the assumption that Russia would keep quiet—it would be 'taking a very great risk'. If Austria could persuade Russia to keep quiet, that was fine with him, but, if it failed to do so, 'the possibilities and dangers were incalculable'.[40] If Russia were to mobilize and Germany were to act in response, the conference idea, the mediation à quatre, would be dead. As a symptom of Britain's anxiety, Grey told the ambassador that the great British fleet, which was supposed to have dispersed today following the annual manoeuvres, had been given orders to remain together at Portsmouth.

The timing of military steps was becoming perilous. Austria was mobilizing rapidly, but it was now widely understood that it would be at least two weeks before it would be ready to launch an attack against Serbia. On the other hand, no one was certain precisely what steps had been authorized and undertaken in Russia. When the French ambassador visited Warsaw station that evening, he noted that the trains were packed with officers and men: 'This looks like mobilization.'[41] If Germany were to interpret the steps being taken in Russia as a mobilization directed at them, or if Russia were to intervene against Austria-Hungary in an Austro-Serbian war, everyone involved anticipated that Germany would react with an attack of its own—certainly against Russia and probably against France as well.

In London, Grey and Lichnowsky feared that any additional military steps would nullify their efforts to mediate the dispute. Almost from the beginning, Lichnowsky had warned Berlin that its support for Austria to 'solve' the 'Serbian problem' militarily was likely to alienate Britain. He had been sent to London specifically to achieve the Anglo-German détente that Bethmann Hollweg believed essential to German foreign policy. The ambassador believed their relations were now better than they had been for many years, but this crisis threatened to jeopardize his achievement. He warned that 'our entire future relations' with Britain depended on the success of Grey's proposed mediation à quatre. If it were to succeed, with Germany's cooperation, 'I will guarantee that our relations with Great Britain will remain, for an incalculable time to come, of the same intimate and confidential character that has distinguished them for the last year and a half.' On the other hand, if Germany stood behind Austria and subordinated its good relations with Britain to the special interests of its ally, 'it would never again be possible to restore those ties which have of late bound us together'.[42] He predicted that if—in the words of Sir Edward Grey—Austria seized the opportunity to 'crush' Serbia, Britain would place itself unconditionally on the side of France and Russia. If it came to war, Germany would have Britain against it.

Lichnowsky reiterated the widespread view that the Serbian reply had gone so far in complying with the Austrian demands that it should be possible to avoid war. He refuted the directive he received from Bethmann Hollweg during the afternoon that he should 'urgently' continue to advocate in London the 'necessity' of localization.[43] While he admitted it was true that Grey was happy to avoid becoming embroiled in an Austro-Serbian dispute as long as it did not develop into an Austro-Russian conflict, it was now pointless to attempt to separate one dispute from the other. 'How can I argue for localization of the conflict when nobody here doubts that Austria has jeopardized important Russian interests, and that if we do not exert pressure on Vienna, Russia will find herself compelled to intervene, even against her own wishes?'[44]

France and Italy had already indicated their support of Grey's proposal for a conference à quatre in London. The question now was whether Germany would also accede to it. If Germany joined the initiative it was practically certain that the Austrians would have to agree to it, that they could not possibly risk a war with Russia without German backing.

★

By the end of the day, Lichnowsky's arguments appeared to have convinced Bethmann Hollweg. Shortly before midnight the chancellor instructed the ambassador in Vienna that Germany could no longer oppose the conference suggested by Grey '*a limine*' (at the outset). Were they to refuse every proposal for mediation 'we should be held responsible for the conflagration by the whole world'.[45] Serbia's decision to yield to Austria's demands to such a very great degree had complicated the situation. The position of the German government would be made impossible within Germany itself unless it appeared that it had been forced into war. Therefore, Germany could not refuse a mediatory role and must submit Grey's proposal for the consideration of the Austrian government. To Lichnowsky, Bethmann Hollweg wrote that Germany had initiated the proposed mediation at Vienna 'along the lines desired by Sir Edward Grey'.[46]

What this actually meant however, and what it would mean, was unclear. Bethmann Hollweg followed up his terse announcement to Lichnowsky with a longer explanation of his position on the proposed mediation. If, as appeared to be the case, Grey was now asking Germany to persuade Austria to accept the Serbian reply as satisfactory, he could not possibly do so. Whether the Serbs had gone as far as possible in meeting the demands of Austria he could not yet say, although the fact that they had undertaken mobilization before handing in their reply was suspicious. Nor did he believe it to be reasonable to assume—as Grey did—that the Austrians aimed to crush Serbia, as they had disavowed any intention of acquiring Serbian territory and promised not to infringe upon its integrity. It was not only Austria's right but its duty to secure itself against the undermining of its existence through the Greater Serbian propaganda that had resulted in the crime of Sarajevo. This had 'absolutely nothing to do with a policy of prestige or with playing off the Triple Alliance against the Triple Entente'.[47]

If Bethmann Hollweg's support for the Grey proposal was half-hearted, his secretary of state's support for it was even less enthusiastic. Before the communication containing the Grey proposal was sent to Vienna, Jagow met with the Austrian ambassador in Berlin. The secretary of state informed him 'in strictest privacy' that Berchtold would shortly receive from the German government the details of the mediation proposed by Britain. But, he assured Szögyény, the government most decidedly did not identify itself with the proposal. On the contrary, he advised Austria to disregard it. Germany had agreed to forward the proposal only to avoid refusing the British request that they do so.

Jagow explained why. The German government now believed it to be of the greatest importance to keep Britain from siding with Russia and France. Therefore everything that could be done must be done to prevent 'the wire' between Berlin and London from breaking—which was likely to occur if Germany flatly refused to act on Grey's request. Thus, Jagow had sent the mediation proposal to Tschirschky in Vienna, but had not instructed him to present it to Berchtold. In this way it was possible to inform the British government that Germany had complied with Grey's request by sending the note to Vienna. Jagow asked Szögyény to ensure that Berchtold did not misunderstand his position—that although he had acted as an intermediary 'he did not in the slightest degree support the proposed mediation'.[48]

This seemed clear enough. But was it? Szögyény's report on Jagow's explanation would not be received at the Ballhausplatz until the morning of the 28th—at 9 a.m. In the meantime, Bethmann Hollweg had instructed Tschirschky to present the British proposal to the Austrian government for its consideration. The German embassy in Vienna received the directive from the chancellor at 5 a.m. on the 28th. At almost the same moment, Bethmann Hollweg informed the kaiser that he had submitted Grey's suggestion to Berchtold 'in accordance with Your Majesty's orders'. It would, he told the kaiser, then be Austria's business to decide what to do about it.[49] Bethmann Hollweg wanted to know what Berchtold's opinion of the proposal was—as well as his opinion of Sazonov's alternative suggestion that Russia and Austria should negotiate directly with one another in St Petersburg.

★

By the end of the day, there was more confusion than clarity, more questions than answers. Did Germany's forwarding of the Grey proposal to Vienna indicate German support for the initiative—as Bethmann Hollweg's instructions seemed to suggest? Or was this manoeuvre merely a subterfuge—as Jagow seemed to have explained to Szögyény? And where did the kaiser stand on the apparent difference between the two? Before Wilhelm met with his advisers that afternoon Moltke wrote to his wife that the situation was obscure and that nothing definite would be known for another fortnight. At the meeting nothing of any consequence was decided.

General Plessen recorded in his diary that Germany still hoped to localize the war, that Britain was likely to remain neutral, and that the whole thing was likely to blow over.[50] About the only clear and decisive action that came out of the meeting arose from the kaiser's belief that it was 'absolutely necessary' that Austria should come to an understanding with Italy on the compensation issue immediately.[51]

Nor was the confusion limited to Berlin. In St Petersburg the French ambassador told the British ambassador that Sazonov had decided to propose a direct conversation between Russia and Austria concerning modifications to be made to the Austrian demands on Serbia. When this news was received in London it bewildered officials at the Foreign Office. The permanent under-secretary, Sir Arthur Nicolson, complained that this meant that Sazonov had made one suggestion and two proposals—each differing from the other—on three consecutive days:

- on Saturday the 25th he suggested that if Serbia appealed to the Powers, Russia would stand aside and leave the question in the hands of Britain, France, Italy, and Germany;

- on Sunday the 26th he proposed to the Austrian ambassador that Britain and Italy should collaborate with Austria with the aim of putting an end to the present tension;

- today, on Monday the 27th he now proposed to converse directly with Vienna.

'One really does not know where one is with M. Sazonov,' he grumbled, 'and I told Count Benckendorff so this afternoon.'[52]

Nicolson would probably have been even more dismayed had he known that Tsar Nicholas on Monday was suggesting yet another approach. He told his foreign minister that an idea 'had just come to him': could they not suggest to France and Britain, and then to Germany and Italy, that Austria submit the dispute with Serbia to the Hague Tribunal? Perhaps it was not too late. 'My hope for peace is not yet exhausted.'[53]

If the British found the Russian position confusing, the Russians found the British position no less so. Meeting with Sazonov on Monday, the British ambassador, Sir George Buchanan, reiterated that Grey 'could not promise to do more' than he already had.[54] Russia was wrong to believe that anything would be accomplished by Britain telling the Germans that if they supported the Austrians by force of arms they would have Britain to deal with as well as France and Russia. Such a menacing attitude would only stiffen Germany's resolve. Only by approaching the German government as 'a friend' who was anxious to preserve peace could Britain induce it to use its influence at Vienna to avert war. And, for Britain to succeed with this initiative, Russia must do nothing to precipitate a conflict. So Buchanan urged that the *ukase* ordering mobilization be deferred as long as possible. If Russia did mobilize he urged that troops not be allowed to cross the frontier.

Sazonov was perplexed. He did not understand how Britain could believe it could win Germany over to the cause of peace except by publicly proclaiming its solidarity with France and Russia. The British must understand that if Russia continued to delay mobilization this would only enable Austria to complete its preparations, which were now under way.

The diplomats and officials behind Grey were themselves divided on which course to pursue: coordination with Germany or solidarity with the Entente. While Nicolson was annoyed by Sazonov's various—and contradictory—proposals, others warned of the consequences for Britain if they went too far—or not far enough—in standing with Russia. From Paris, one of the leading proponents of the Anglo-French agreement of 1904, Sir Francis Bertie, wanted to encourage France to put pressure on the Russian government 'not to assume the absurd and obsolete attitude of Russia being the protectress of all Slav States, whatever their conduct'.[55] This, he warned, 'will lead to war'. Izvol'skii, who would be returning to Paris sometime soon, was not 'an element of peace'. Unlike most of his colleagues, Bertie did not believe that the kaiser and his government had been accessories before the fact in composing the terms of the Austrian note to Serbia, and he advised Grey to stay away from using the word 'conference' to describe the discussions that he was proposing to hold in London, because this would suggest a repetition of the 1912 conference and lead the Austrians to feel that they were being treated as a minor Balkan state. On Monday, the 27th of July, the British ambassador to France was adamantly opposed to anything that suggested a forceful and determined solidarity on the part of the 'Triple Entente'.

Back in London the assistant under-secretary of state responsible for both the western and eastern departments advised otherwise. Eyre Crowe, the author of a famous memorandum on the state of British relations with France and Germany in 1907,[56] predicted that the real difficulty confronting Britain would arise over the complicated issue of mobilization. Austria was already mobilizing—and this posed a serious menace to Russia because it would take them approximately twice as long to mobilize compared with Austria and Germany. But Britain had been warned that if Russia were to mobilize Germany would do the same—and, as German mobilization would be directed almost entirely against France, 'the latter cannot possibly delay her own mobilization for even the fraction of a day'.[57] Where Bertie proposed that pressure be brought to bear on Russia to drop the 'absurd and obsolete' position of acting as protector of the Slavs, Crowe argued that it was 'neither possible nor just and wise' to do anything to restrain Russia from mobilizing. But the consequences of following his advice would be stark: within twenty-four hours the British government could be forced to decide whether it would stand 'idly aside' if France were drawn into the quarrel.

The question, Crowe recognized, was a momentous one. Although he chose not to elaborate upon it, he pointed to a historical precedent that ought to be borne in mind by the government. In 1805 Prussia had insisted on keeping out of a war between other Powers over questions that were not, apparently, of direct interest to it. The war was duly waged in 1805 without Prussian participation. The consequence of avoiding a commitment was that in the following year Prussia fell victim to the Power that had won the war in 1805 'and no one was ready either to help her or to prevent her political ruin and partition'.[58] This was a parable.

Crowe's warning relied partly on the latest information received from Vienna. Late on Monday afternoon Sir Maurice de Bunsen reported to London that after meeting with all of his ambassadorial colleagues he had concluded that Austria-Hungary had determined from the outset to go to war with Serbia. The Austrians believed that their position as a Great Power was at stake and had drawn up their demands on Serbia 'so as to make war inevitable'.[59] According to Schebeko, the Russian ambassador recently returned from St Petersburg, German efforts to localize the conflict would fail because Russia would be compelled to act if Austria were to attack Serbia. According to Avarna, the Italian ambassador, war was practically inevitable, although he was privately trying to find a formula that might prevent it. De Bunsen predicted that if the war were to be postponed or prevented it would be a great disappointment in Austria, 'which has gone wild with joy' at the prospect of war. When he read this message Crowe concluded that the outlook was bad and that everything would now depend on the line taken by Germany.

★

Entente eyes had indeed been opened during the course of Monday. The Serbian reply to the Austrian ultimatum had come as a revelation: it suggested that the Serbs were prepared to go farther than anyone had expected in meeting the demands made upon them. Their only reservations were those that it seemed no state could agree to and retain its sovereignty. Surely, at the very least, their reply ought to open the door to discussion of the few issues that remained. In fact, the Serbs themselves were beginning to worry that all of the talk of a European mediation implied that they were likely to be forced to go further than they already had.[60] Their suspicions were not unfounded: Sazonov and Grey had both hinted as much to the Austrians and the Germans.

Moreover, to the British and the French, the extent of the concessions that the Serbs were prepared to make indicated that St Petersburg had put pressure upon them to induce their compliance. This seemed to prove that Russia was doing what it could to avoid a confrontation with Austria in the Balkans. Further proof came on Monday. Three days had passed since the regent, Prince Aleksandar, had appealed to the tsar's 'noble Slav heart' to come to Serbia's assistance. The only responses from Russia had consisted of Sazonov's urging that the Serbs ought to be conciliatory, retreat to the south, and appeal to 'Europe' in the event of an Austrian attack. Now the tsar himself wrote to the prince, assuring him of his 'heart-felt good will' towards the people of Serbia. But he promised nothing except to give the situation his serious attention and his assurance that his government was making every effort to resolve the existing difficulties. 'I do not doubt that Your Highness and the Royal Government are eager to facilitate this task' by exploring every opportunity to avert the horrors of war. Together they must make every effort to avoid bloodshed. If they failed in this, the tsar gave his assurance that Russia would not 'remain indifferent' to the fate of Serbia.[61]

An assurance that Russia was not 'indifferent' to the fate of Serbia was certainly not the kind of support the Serbs had hoped for. And it was certainly a considerable distance from the warnings of those—like Francis Bertie in Paris—who feared that Russian feelings of 'Slavic brotherhood' might draw the Entente into a war it did not want.

Even as it now stood, the Serbian reply offered a great and unmistakable triumph for Austro-Hungarian diplomacy. More and more Entente voices were to be heard saying that if Austria was not prepared to accept these concessions at least as the basis for further discussion it could only be because it was determined to have a war—and had probably been so determined from the outset.

By the end of the day on Monday, uncertainty was still widespread. Would the proposals for mediation get off the ground? Germany claimed to be supporting both the Grey proposal for discussions *à quatre* in London, and the Sazonov proposal for bilateral discussions with Austria in St Petersburg. Jagow's 'support' for the Grey proposal at Vienna was demonstrably disingenuous, but it remained to be seen how far Bethmann Hollweg was prepared to go in placating the British by supporting it. His instructions to Lichnowsky in London and Tschirschky in Vienna were confused and contradictory. Would Britain continue to preach restraint at St Petersburg? Would Grey accept Bertie's advice that they exert pressure on France to exert pressure on Russia not to act as the protector of Slavs in the Balkans? Or would he be persuaded by Crowe's arguments that Russia could not afford to remain inert while Austria mobilized and prepared to crush Serbia? Would the return of Poincaré and Viviani to Paris result in a more vigorous French diplomacy? And if so, how would this vigour be asserted: more determined support for its Russian ally, or more coherent efforts to restrain it? On board the *France* Poincaré wondered if Europe would permit Austria to go to war with Serbia: 'That would mean taking Austria's part and giving it open season vis-à-vis Serbia.'[62]

Warnings that further military preparations might take the crisis out of the hands of the diplomats continued to mount. Fears were growing that once the military men began to initiate their strategic plans there would be little time—or space—left for diplomacy. The Austrians, fearing a Russian mobilization on their frontier, were pushing the Germans to reaffirm their commitment to the alliance and to warn Russia that Germany would mobilize if Russia did so. But by Monday the Germans were prepared to go only halfway, warning that a general mobilization in Russia would produce a German mobilization in response—while indicating that a Russian mobilization in the south, aimed at Austria–Hungary alone, would not precipitate a German mobilization. The chief of the German general staff was insisting that the Italian commitment to the Triple Alliance was essential to his strategic planning—which seemed to mean that diplomatic negotiations were required between Austria and Italy before the military went any further. And perhaps the timing was not as fragile as it appeared: although Austria was mobilizing, war on Serbia had not yet been declared and the chief of the Austrian general staff was advising that it would be at least two weeks before the Austrian army could attack Serbia. The time for a diplomatic solution had not yet run out.

There were signs of excitement growing in Russia, however. In St Petersburg a crowd of several thousand gathered in front of the army barracks, sang the national anthem, then marched to the Serbian legation. An official there addressed the crowd from the balcony, expressing Serbia's gratitude to Russia for its support against the Austrian oppressor. The legation was deluged by young men (mainly students) wishing to volunteer to fight on behalf of Serbia. At a concert hall a delegation, led by officers, met with the management to urge that Wagner's *Parsifal* be excluded from the evening's programme and that Tchaikovsky's '1812' be substituted. Management agreed, and the playing of Tchaikovsky was greeted with enthusiastic cheering and followed by the singing of the national anthem. In Moscow diners overheard speaking German in restaurants were ordered to speak Russian. A committee was formed to raise money to equip a Red Cross unit to be sent to Serbia.

In Paris the Caillaux trial resumed, but attention was beginning to shift. The syndicalist *Confédération générale du travail* (CGT), whose official policy it was to declare a general strike in the event of war, organized a mass demonstration of some 30,000 to protest against French participation in a war. The demonstrations quickly spread to the provinces. An editorial, 'On the Brink of the Abyss', in *La Bataille Syndicaliste*, declared that a cataclysm could be unleashed 'that will surpass in horror what men with the fullest imagination could never conceive of'.[63] Fighting broke out that evening on the boulevards of Paris between the anti-war protesters and pro-government supporters. Police on horseback charged a group of syndicalists who had gathered in front of the *Matin* newspaper offices shouting '*A bas la guerre*' ('Down with war'). The street was cleared but more fighting broke out.

There was little excitement in Germany. Holiday trains had been packed as usual with vacationers coming and going from the seaside. But a run on the banks seemed about to begin: in Berlin at 5 a.m. on Monday morning a crowd of a couple of thousand people gathered in front of the municipal savings bank, the *Sparkasse*, determined to withdraw their savings when doors opened for business at 9 a.m. At one bank some 15,000 depositors had presented themselves by 11 a.m. The run on the banks continued in other German cities throughout the day.

The Vienna stock market, fearing a panic would follow the declaration of war on Serbia, did not open for trading on Monday.

Nicholas II, however, appeared unperturbed by the events of the day. He continued with preparations for the royal family to leave that evening on board the imperial yacht for their annual sailing trip to the Finnish Skerries.

Day Five

Tuesday, 28 July

On Tuesday morning in Vienna Count Tschirschky invited Count Berchtold and Count Forgách to join him for breakfast. The German ambassador laid out two problems that he wished to discuss with them. After weeks of pushing and prodding the Austrians to come to some arrangement with Italy in order to keep the Triple Alliance intact, he had accomplished nothing. Now Tschirschky had been given explicit instructions—from the kaiser himself—that it was 'absolutely necessary' for Austria to come to an understanding with Italy on the issue of compensation 'in time'.[1] The German secretary of state warned that without an agreement Italy might become 'directly' anti-Austrian; he urged an immediate conference between Berchtold and the Italian ambassador.[2] Tschirschky's second problem was the Grey proposal for a mediation *à quatre*. Shortly before breakfast Tschirschky had received instructions from the chancellor that he was to ask Berchtold for his opinion of Grey's suggestion. Bethmann Hollweg explained to him that he simply could not refuse every proposal for mediation, otherwise Germany would be seen as the instigator of the war and would be held responsible by the whole world for the conflagration.[3]

Tschirschky believed he solved the first problem over breakfast. Berchtold and Forgách appeared to accept Germany's views on the issue of Italian compensation. Austria would reaffirm its promise not to acquire additional territory in the Balkans as a result of the crisis. If, against their will, the Austrians were forced to occupy any Serbian territory more than temporarily, they would then be prepared to enter into an exchange of views with Italy on the subject of compensation. In return, they expected Italy to maintain the friendly attitude of an ally 'as promised'.[4] Tschirschky seemed confident that this would settle the issue. Berchtold, he wrote privately to Jagow, 'is in very good spirits' and proud of the countless telegrams of congratulation he was receiving from every portion of Germany.[5]

The second problem would be solved before noon: the Grey proposal would be nullified by Austria's declaration of war on Serbia.

★

Tschirschky was unaware that a bombshell was being dropped by the kaiser in Berlin at the same time that he was meeting with the Austrians over breakfast in Vienna. A copy of the Serbian reply to the Austrian demands had been sent from the Foreign Office to the kaiser at the Neues Palais in Potsdam on Monday night.[6] When Wilhelm read it over the next morning he reached the startling conclusion that the Habsburg monarchy had achieved its aims and that the few remaining reservations on the part of Serbia could be settled by negotiation. Their announcement represented a humiliating capitulation—and with it *every cause for war* collapsed (*entfällt*).[7]

If the kaiser were to commit himself to this position the crisis might be over. Ultimately, it was Wilhelm II who was responsible for decisions in Germany—not the chancellor and certainly not the secretary of state or the general staff. They all answered to him. If he decided that there was no longer any need for war, Austria-Hungary would find itself alone. Without the promise of German support the Austrians would never have gone down this road to begin with—and they could not go down it now without Germany's continued approval and support.

As far as the kaiser was concerned, the Austrians had won the diplomatic contest. As he noted on his copy of the text, the Serbian reply was 'a great moral success for Vienna'. In fact, he said, the Austrians had behaved improperly when they received the reply: Giesl ought not to have left Belgrade. If he had been the emperor of the Dual Monarchy, the kaiser would 'never have ordered mobilization' given the extent of the Serbian concessions.[8]

What was now to be done? The Serbian reply was insufficient as far as the kaiser was concerned. It amounted to no more than a piece of paper and was of little value unless its words were translated into deeds. Or, as he put it in his typically colourful language: 'The Serbs are Orientals, and therefore liars, fakers and masters of evasion [*Verschleppen*].' In order to turn their 'beautiful promises' into facts, Belgrade should be taken and held hostage by Austria. This would not only guarantee that the Serbs would carry out their promises, but would satisfy the honour of the Austro-Hungarian army, which had now been mobilized unnecessarily for the third time in two years. The army would be given the opportunity to stand on foreign soil and thus achieve an ostensible success in the eyes of the world. Perhaps even more important, if the Austrian government were simply to abandon its campaign now it might create a dangerous wave of bad feeling against the monarchy. The Austrian army must march into Serbia.

The kaiser suggested to Jagow that they congratulate Austria on having forced Serbia to retreat in the most humiliating manner. With that humiliation every cause for war had vanished. Now the Austrians should receive a guarantee that the promises would be carried out by a military occupation of at least part of Serbia—similar to the way the Germans had kept troops in France in 1871 until billions of francs had been paid to them in indemnity. On this basis—and this basis alone—the kaiser would now be willing 'to mediate' with Austria in order to maintain peace in Europe.

Wilhelm would entertain no other proposals. The Powers had all appealed to him for his assistance in keeping the peace, and he was prepared to act—but only in his own way. He was determined to respect Austria's nationalistic feeling and military honour as much as possible. Thus, it must be given a visible *satisfaction d'honneur* as a prerequisite to his mediation.

The kaiser instructed the secretary of state to draft a proposal along these lines and submit it to him. This would then be communicated to Vienna. He had already instructed his adjutant general, Hans von Plessen, 'who is entirely in accord with my views', to write along these lines to the chief of the general staff.

★

Bethmann Hollweg, Jagow, and all those who had worked under the kaiser in the past were well acquainted with his volatile personality and unwanted interventions. They knew, on Monday, that the Austrians intended to declare war on Tuesday—or Wednesday at the latest. They had, therefore, tried to keep the details of the Serbian reply from the kaiser for as long as possible, anticipating that he might respond in just the way that he had. Wilhelm was following a familiar pattern: extreme language, aggressive declarations, warlike expressions—until the moment of decision arrived. Then he would draw back and find excuses for inaction—which was precisely what he seemed to be doing now.

On Monday at midday Bethmann Hollweg had established Germany's position on the Grey proposal for a mediation *à quatre*. He had told Lichnowsky in London that Germany could not take part in the proposed conference because this would be tantamount to summoning Austria before a 'European court of justice'.[9] But after his meeting with the kaiser at Potsdam that afternoon he changed his tune, instructing Tschirschky in Vienna to submit the Grey proposal for the consideration of the Austrian government.[10] He then assured the kaiser that he had submitted the pro- posal to Count Berchtold 'in accordance with Your Majesty's orders'.[11] Jagow assured the Austrian ambassador in Berlin that evening that Germany did not support the Grey proposal and in fact advised Austria to disregard it. It was only to please the British that Germany passed along the suggestion, he insisted. There was no mention of the kaiser or his views.

Wilhelm's opinion that the Serbian reply removed any cause for war threatened to create a rift between him and his officials. While Bethmann Hollweg continued to assure him that he was proceeding with the *démarche* at Vienna as instructed, Jagow was at the same time telling the French and British ambassadors in Berlin that it was impossible for Germany to accept Grey's proposed conference of ambassadors at London.[12]

At the same time, the chancellor was setting about to procure the support of the federated governments of the German empire. Although it now seems anachronistic, in the structure of the empire created in 1871 Prussia maintained embassies at Darmstadt (Hesse-Darmstadt), Karlsruhe (Baden), Munich (Bavaria), Stuttgart (Württemberg), Dresden (Saxony), Weimar (Thuringia), Oldenburg, and Hamburg (Hanover).[13] Because it was polit- ically important to keep the states marching in step with Prussia, Bethmann Hollweg directed Prussia's representatives to explain the position of the imperial government to them.[14] The crime of Sarajevo had been planned with the connivance of members of the Serbian government and army; it had resulted from years of agitation for the creation of a Greater Serbia. Serbia had failed to live up to the promises of good behaviour made in 1909. Austria could no longer stand by and watch the machinations across the border that constantly threatened its security and integrity. The procedure that the Austrians had followed and the demands they had made on Serbia were fully justified.

The line taken by the chancellor in this directive clearly contradicted the views of the kaiser. Where Wilhelm concluded that the Serbian reply had removed any cause for war, Bethmann Hollweg asserted that the reply demonstrated the 'ruling authorities' in Serbia were unwilling to cease their trouble-making activities. This left Austria with no choice but to enforce its demands by asserting heavy pressure—and, if need be, by resorting to military force—unless it was prepared to sacrifice its standing

as a Great Power. He blamed the Russians for complicating the situation by
their insistence that they had both the right and the duty to take Serbia's
side. Some Russian newspapers were even asserting that Germany would be
responsible for any European conflagration because it had failed to persuade
Austria to yield. If a wider war were to break out Russia's responsibility
would be 'as plain as day'—especially considering that Berchtold had
officially announced that Austria wished neither to acquire any Serbian
territory nor to encroach upon Serbia's independence, but aimed solely to
put an end to the intrigues that endangered Austria's existence.

The position of the German government was that the real objective of
Panslav agitation was to destroy the Habsburg monarchy and thus break up
the Triple Alliance and isolate the German Empire. Thus, 'our most vital
interests summon us to the side of Austria-Hungary'. But, as it was also
Germany's duty to save Europe from a general war, the government was
making every effort to localize the conflict. Bethmann Hollweg insisted,
however, that if Russia interfered Germany would have no choice but to
come to the assistance of its ally with all of the power of the empire. 'We
should take to the sword only under compulsion, but should do so in the
calm conviction that we were in no way guilty of the misery that a war
would necessarily bring to the nations of Europe.'[15]

By Tuesday Bethmann Hollweg had become preoccupied with the issue
of responsibility for war breaking out. He knew that Austria was likely to
declare war today, and that this would probably precipitate the intervention
of Russia, which would lead to a great European war. As expected, at 11
a.m. Austria declared war on Serbia via telegram—the first time in history
that war had been declared in this manner. The chancellor immediately took
up the suggestion of General Chelius, the German military plenipotentiary
to the court at St Petersburg, that Kaiser Wilhelm write directly to Tsar
Nicholas via telegram. This had been suggested to Chelius by 'peacefully
disposed' and 'monarchically inclined' higher officers in the entourage of
the tsar. The kaiser, he suggested, ought to appeal to the monarchical
sensibilities of the tsar and should draw attention to the dangers that would
threaten all monarchies in the event of a general European war.[16]

Bethmann Hollweg urged the kaiser to do so. Why? Because such a
telegram would—if war became inevitable—'throw the clearest light on
Russia's responsibility'. He presented the kaiser with a draft of the message
to be sent. At the same time he assured the kaiser that he was encouraging 'a
frank conference' between the Austrians and the Russians. What was the

purpose of such a conference? To allow the Austrians to explain 'unambiguously' the object and the extent of their procedure against Serbia. That they had already declared war 'need make no difference'.[17] Bethmann Hollweg wrote to Tschirschky in Vienna that Berchtold's declaration of territorial disinterestedness in Serbia should be deemed sufficient to keep Russia from interfering.[18] Clearly, this was not to be the negotiation of terms that Sazonov had proposed.

Following the Austrian declaration of war Germany ruled out Grey's proposal for a conference à quatre in London. Instead, Germany suggested that something might be achieved via the proposed 'bilateral' talks between the Austrians and the Russians in St Petersburg. If nothing else, Bethmann Hollweg explained, such talks might clarify for the Russians why the Austrians had proceeded as they had, and could be used to reaffirm Berchtold's assurances that Austria had no intention of seizing Serbian territory. But this left Bethmann Hollweg with the problem of how to handle the British.

That afternoon the chancellor received a reminder of the puzzle from his minister to Baden at Karlsruhe. His friend, von Eisendecher, who had been attending the annual regatta at Cowes, had decided to return to his post, given the gravity of the international situation. He advised Bethmann Hollweg that the German strategy of attempting to localize the war depended principally upon the attitude of Britain: 'if Petersburg and Paris should receive a determined warning from London, they would hardly plunge themselves into the adventure of a great war'.[19] He suggested that Germany was now paying the price of failing to preserve good relations with Britain. Previous German statesmen, who could have prevented the British ententes with the French and the Russians, had instead squandered British friendship. Now Germany could not even count on the benevolent neutrality of Britain in the event of war.

The complaint was not news to Bethmann Hollweg, whose primary objective in foreign policy when he became chancellor had been to improve relations with Britain. In various initiatives since 1908 he had suggested that in return for ending the Anglo-German naval race Britain ought to come to some political agreement with Germany and the Triple Alliance. The strategy had failed but he had not abandoned hope of reviving it.

The problem was, how was Bethmann Hollweg to get Britain to agree to 'localizing' the Austro-Serbian conflict at the same time as he rejected

Grey's proposal for a meeting of ambassadors *à quatre* in London? For this, he would have to rely on his ambassador in London.

Lichnowsky had warned Berlin against supporting Austria as soon as the crisis began. When Austria declared war on Serbia, he went further. He angrily reported that the Austrian ambassador and the rest of the Austrian embassy in London had never made the least attempt to conceal from him and his staff that their sole aim was to destroy Serbia. The Austrian ultimatum to Serbia had been carefully designed to ensure that it would be rejected—and the Austrians in London had been stunned by the extent to which the Serbs were willing to submit to their demands. Nevertheless, only yesterday the Austrian ambassador had assured him that in Vienna they were absolutely set on war and that Serbia was to be 'beaten into the earth'.[20] It was Austria's intention to hand over portions of Serbia to Bulgaria and, Lichnowsky presumed, to Albania as well.

Nevertheless, the ambassador assured Berlin that he constantly and energetically stood up for the Austrian point of view. He insisted that he had explained to Grey that Berchtold had been forced to take energetic measures purely on the basis of self-preservation, otherwise Austria would have found itself in an impossible situation. He believed that the British seemed to recognize the truth of this.

Lichnowsky's assurances that he was standing up for the Austrian point of view rang hollow. Bethmann Hollweg was not persuaded that the ambassador was working strenuously to uphold the Austro-German line that the affair concerned only Austria and Serbia. Lichnowsky's argument that both Liberals and Unionists in Britain believed that peace could best be preserved by maintaining the balance of power between the two competing alliances annoyed the chancellor. The argument was flawed: if Germany compelled Austria to give in to Serbia it would undermine this balance by weakening the Triple Alliance.

Bethmann Hollweg insisted that the conflict in the Balkans was not a test of strength between the two European groups. Instead, all of Europe shared an interest in putting a 'final end' to the Serbian provocations which had endangered the peace of Europe three times in the last five years. Therefore, Germany would not agree to a conference on the subject but instead would continue its mediation efforts at St Petersburg. 'I have confidence in Your Serene Highness being able to get Sir Edward Grey to see our point of view.'[21]

Would he? Could he? How would Grey interpret Germany's rejection of his proposed conference?

★

By Tuesday those officials working under Grey at the Foreign Office had been able to study carefully the Serbian reply to the Austrian ultimatum. Their impressions seemed likely to undermine any efforts Lichnowsky might make to get Grey to see Germany's point of view. The senior clerk in the eastern department, George Clerk, after carefully comparing the Austrian note and the Serbian reply, concluded that Austria's rejection of the reply showed that it had been read at Vienna 'with a fixed determination to find it unsatisfactory'.[22] Going through the reply point-by-point, he demonstrated that the Serbs were prepared to swallow nearly all of the Austrian demands and that the few reservations they had stipulated were quite reasonable. His superior, Eyre Crowe—assistant under-secretary of state and head of the eastern and western departments—went even further. If Austria demanded absolute compliance with its ultimatum 'it can only mean that she wants a war'.[23] The Austrians knew perfectly well that some of their demands were such that no state could accept because they were 'tantamount to accepting a protectorate'.

If Grey agreed with his officials, it would be very difficult to interpret Germany's rejection of his proposed conference as anything other than a full backing for Austria's determination either to destroy Serbia or to turn it into a protectorate.

The British ambassador in Berlin met with his French and Italian counterparts to discuss what they might do next, now that Germany had rejected the idea of a conference à quatre. As Jagow had assured them that he was still anxious to work with them in order to maintain the general peace, they deduced that it was the proposal of a conference that was unacceptable, not the idea of a mediation. Thus, they wondered if Sir Edward might be able to revise his proposal, omitting the word 'conference'. Or perhaps he might ask Germany to suggest a form of mediation that would be acceptable.[24] At the Foreign Office, Eyre Crowe thought there was much sense in suggesting to the Germans that if they were as anxious to work for peace as they claimed, they ought to be asked what they proposed that the Powers should do.[25]

Grey explained that what he envisioned was not an 'arbitration' but a 'private and informal discussion' that might lead to a suggestion for a settlement.[26] He promised that no suggestion would be put forward by the four Powers that had not previously been deemed acceptable to Austria and Russia. Nevertheless, he was prepared to suspend his proposal as long as there was a chance that 'bilateral' Austro-Russian talks in St Petersburg might succeed.

The Grey proposal was put on ice. There were to be no talks *à quatre* in London.

★

Only Germany's clear and energetic support for the Grey proposal could have convinced the Austrians to accede to it. When the Germans instead indicated—*sotto voce*—that they had no intention of supporting the proposal but presented it at Vienna with the explanation that they were only doing so in order not to offend the British, the Austrians felt free to reject it. On Tuesday morning in Vienna, when Count Berchtold met with the British ambassador, he rejected Grey's argument that the Serbian reply offered sufficient grounds for negotiations to take place and for warlike operations to remain in abeyance. Instead of an 'integral acceptance' of Austria's demands Serbia had prevaricated. The Serbs must not be treated 'as if they were a cultivated nation': any attempt at mediation would only encourage them to go on behaving as they had in the past.[27] De Bunsen concluded from this that the prestige of the Dual Monarchy was engaged: 'nothing could now prevent conflict.'[28]

As a guarantee that the war with Serbia was both just and inevitable Berchtold offered the 'well-known pacific character' of both the Emperor Franz Joseph and himself. He insisted that the issues at stake could only be settled between the two parties concerned.[29] War was declared and a full mobilization of the Austro-Hungarian armies was announced. By late afternoon in Vienna the future seemed clear.

Was it? Conrad, the chief of the general staff, had warned that it would still be some two weeks before he would be in a position to launch an invasion of Serbia. Before undertaking a campaign he insisted it was imperative that he know whether they would be fighting Serbia on its own, or Serbia combined with Russia. The war plans for the two scenarios were entirely different. If they were fighting Serbia alone, the bulk of Austrian forces would be utilized for the invasion to the south, with only a small force remaining on the defensive in the north-east. If they were fighting Serbia and Russia combined, the bulk of Austrian forces would attack Russia, and only a small force would remain on the defensive in the south. It was essential that he know which scenario to prepare for.

Berchtold trusted that the threat of Germany coming to the assistance of Austria would be sufficient to deter Russia. He worried that Germany might abandon Austria at the last moment, leaving it to face Russia alone. His fears were not unjustified.

At the end of the day on Tuesday Bethmann Hollweg let loose his complaints and concerns about Austria's behaviour. In spite of their assurances that they were not considering any territorial acquisitions in Serbia, the Austrian government had left Germany in the dark concerning their intentions 'despite repeated interrogations'.[30] The Serbian reply had created a political problem for Germany—as attested to by the kaiser's reaction to it. The Serbs had gone so far in agreeing to the demands made on them that if the Austrians were to take a completely uncompromising attitude they would have to reckon on a negative public reaction throughout Europe. Given that an Austrian invasion of Serbia could not begin until August the 12th, Germany would be placed in the 'extraordinarily difficult position' of having to respond to mediation efforts and conference proposals coming from the other Powers in the meantime. Germany could not maintain its aloofness in dealing with such proposals without incurring the odium of having been responsible for a world war—even among the German people themselves: 'a successful war on three fronts cannot be commenced and continued on such a basis.' Bethmann Hollweg insisted that it was imperative that the 'odium' for a wider European war must fall on Russia.

How was this to be done? Bethmann Hollweg suggested that Austria ought to repeat at St Petersburg its declaration that it did not intend any territorial acquisitions in Serbia. If it proved necessary to occupy Belgrade or other areas of Serbia, Austria ought to make it clear that this was only a temporary expedient employed to force the Serbian government to carry out the demands made upon it and to secure the necessary guarantees for good behaviour in the future. Taking up the kaiser's analogy, Bethmann Hollweg suggested that the occupation be explained in terms of Germany's occupation of French territory following the treaty of Frankfurt—i.e. for securing payment of a war indemnity. This seemed to make sense: no one now supposed that the German occupation of France had destroyed the sovereignty of the French state. The Austrians could promise to evacuate Serbian territory once their demands had been met. If his advice were followed, Bethmann Hollweg believed that Russia would either have to recognize the justice of such a procedure or have the public opinion of Europe turn against it. At the moment, opinion was turning against Austria-Hungary.

If Austria followed his suggestions, Bethmann Hollweg believed that the diplomatic and military situations would be appreciably altered in favour of the Triple Alliance. He instructed Tschirschky to press these points emphatically on Berchtold, who ought to then make the appropriate move at St Petersburg.

Having staked out a clear path for Austria to follow, Bethmann Hollweg instinctively worried that he might have gone too far. He told Tschirschky that he would have to find a way of presenting the proposal to Berchtold without giving the impression that Germany was attempting to hold Austria back. He explained that if the Austrians accepted his suggestions, they would have succeeded in cutting the cord of the Greater Serbia propaganda without simultaneously bringing about a world war. If, in the end, such a war could not be avoided, following his plan would at least improve the conditions under which Germany and Austria would wage it.

Bethmann feared the loss of his Austrian ally more than he feared the consequences of a European war. If Austria were to abandon the alliance because it believed that it could not count on Germany's support of its vital interests, Germany would find itself isolated and encircled by potential enemies. Bismarck's nightmare after Germany's successful wars against Denmark, Austria, and France—the *cauchemar des coalitions*—might become real. France and Russia had now been allies for a generation; Britain had associated itself with their alliance through its ententes with them; Italy seemed prepared to abandon the Triple Alliance; Romania seemed unwilling to live up to its promises.

Berchtold was beginning to worry that he might not be able to rely on Germany. On Tuesday evening, twelve hours after declaring war on Serbia, he directed Szögyény in Berlin 'to go immediately' either to Bethmann Hollweg or Jagow in order to outline Austria's perspective on the military situation. Austria believed it was clear that Russia was making extensive military preparations and that it would mobilize its forces in the Kiev, Odessa, Moscow, and Kazan military districts the moment that Austrian troops crossed the Serbian frontier. Under these circumstances it was imperative that Austria know whether it could march against Serbia with strong forces, or whether it must reserve the bulk of them for use against Russia. At the moment, Russia was gaining time in making its preparations,

making it 'absolutely imperative' that Austria—and Germany—take immediate and comprehensive counter-measures.[31]

Jagow's assurances to Entente diplomats that Germany would not take
military steps as long as Russia mobilized only against Austria resonated in
Vienna. Berchtold requested that Berlin warn St Petersburg that mobilizing
in the military districts bordering on Austria-Hungary would have to be
countered by military counter-measures not only by the Dual Monarchy
but by its ally 'the German empire' as well.

In fact, Berchtold proposed, as a first step, that Germany ought to take this
initiative on its own. 'Plain language' (deutliche Sprache) would be the most
effective way to warn Russia of the consequences of adopting a threatening
attitude. As a second step, he wanted Germany to press Romania into action.
King Karl ought to warn Russia—by a solemn démarche in St Petersburg, or
by a private telegram to the tsar, or simply through publication—that
Romania had joined the Triple Alliance. In order for this to be effective,
it must be done no later than Saturday, August the 1st.

While Berchtold was trying to push Bethmann Hollweg into threatening
Russia with military action, Bethmann Hollweg was trying to push Berch-
told into negotiating with Russia in St Petersburg. While Austria wanted
Romania to commit itself publicly to the Triple Alliance, Germany wanted
Austria to offer sufficient inducements to Italy to keep it within the fold of
the alliance. The German ambassador in Rome assured San Giuliano that
Germany regarded it as a necessity that Austria come to an agreement with
Italy and that it was pressing this point at Vienna.[32]

The Austrian ambassador in Rome continued to resist. Ill and irascible,
Mérey complained of Italy's 'not inoffensive' (nicht unbedenklichen) attitude
on the issue of compensation and he refused to thank Italy for its expressions
of friendship. The Italians had not yet done anything to deserve Austrian
gratitude.[33] Privately, he warned Berchtold against an optimistic interpretation of the assurances given to him by Avarna in Vienna. In fact, Mérey
grumbled that the reception of Italy's assurances had been overdone. If it
were left to him, he would deny the right of Italy to any compensation
whatsoever and would not even enter into discussions on the issue. If
Austria were to act otherwise, it would be allowing Italy to play the role
of a man who says to a friend drowning in the Danube 'I won't help you
out, but if you get out by your own efforts, you will have to pay me an
indemnity.'[34]

Even on the 28th of July, and even after Austria-Hungary had declared
war on Serbia, the Triple Alliance remained divided on how to deal with its
Italian and Romanian problems. Nor could they agree on how to handle the
Russian threat. For the moment, the only thing they could agree on was
that Grey's proposed conference *à quatre* in London was unacceptable.
Tschirschky, acting upon direct orders from the kaiser, explained to Berchtold that Germany interpreted Article VII of the Triple Alliance in the same
way as the Italians: i.e., that it gave Italy the right to receive compensation
for any change in Austria's favour in the Balkans. He appealed, solemnly and
emphatically, to the foreign minister to clarify the situation with Italy:
Germany's military plans would be jeopardized 'if Italy refused to recognize
the *casus foederis*'.[35]

★

Berchtold was proving to be no pawn of the Germans. He remained
intransigent. In spite of the kaiser's admonitions to come to an understanding
with Italy 'for God's sake', he would not go farther than to declare that, while
it was not Austria's intention to make territorial acquisitions, he would be
prepared to enter into negotiations over compensation if it became necessary
for Austria to occupy Serbian territory more than temporarily. And he
persevered in his expectation that Italy would not hinder its ally in attaining
its goals and would maintain the friendly attitude which it had promised.

The only bright spot on the horizon for the Triple Alliance emanated from
Constantinople. Even before the crisis began, prior to the assassination in
Sarajevo, the Austrian strategic plan had been to draw Turkey into an align-
ment against Serbia. The Austrians believed it ought to be possible to line up
Bulgaria, Turkey, and Greece against the Serbs, effectively encircling them
and, if war were to come, reducing their power by distributing their people
and territory to the surrounding states.[36] The alliance with the Italians—against
whom the Turks had fought a war in 1911–12—was an impediment to this
design. But, when the assassination of the archduke opened the possibility of an
Austro-Serbian confrontation, the Austrian ambassador in Constantinople
argued that the moment of opportunity had arrived.

The Marquess Pallavicini surmised that if it appeared to the Turks that
Austria was about to secure for itself a commanding position in the Balkans
by acting against Serbia, they might be inclined to seek the support of Austria
and align themselves with the Triple Alliance. On 14 July Berchtold—more
than a week before presenting the ultimatum to Serbia—had asked Jagow

whether he agreed that the time had arrived to persuade Turkey to join the alliance.[37]

Jagow had not been encouraging. On account of the poor state of its army, he said, Turkey ought to be considered a 'passive factor' for years to come. If Germany were to propose that they join the Triple Alliance, the Turks would undoubtedly make demands on them—which would likely include a demand for protection against Russia in Armenia—a guarantee that the Triple Alliance was not in a position to offer. Under the circumstances, Turkey could be expected to do little more than side with the strongest and most successful group. If Austria were to act energetically and successfully against Serbia and establish a commanding position in the Balkans, Turkey would likely seek their support. Until then, for Germany to act at Constantinople as Berchtold proposed seemed to him both pointless and dubious.

The German ambassador in Constantinople strongly supported Jagow's position. Having Turkey join the Triple Alliance would only add to its burdens without offering the slightest advantage. 'Turkey is today unquestionably worthless as an ally.'[38] For now, the Triple Alliance should try to maintain friendly relations with Turkey in case it succeeded in becoming a power factor some years hence. In the meantime, the Turks should be advised to avoid political adventures and to maintain friendly relations with their neighbours. Even a neutral Turkey would give the Triple Alliance the advantage of detaining several Russian corps along the Armenian frontier.

This clear and consistent view changed when, on the 24th of July—the day after the presentation of the Austrian ultimatum to Serbia—the kaiser intervened personally. He believed that 'for reasons of expediency' Germany should take advantage of Turkey's inclination to align itself with the Triple Alliance. Consequently, Jagow instructed the ambassador in Constantinople to work on this assumption and to think of the connection with Turkey as an alliance 'ad hoc' for the moment, as Germany was not in a position to undertake any far-reaching obligations.[39] Although the ambassador remained dubious about the value of Turkey as a military ally he carried out his instructions.[40]

Late in the evening of Monday, the 27th of July, the Grand Vizier, Said Halim Pasha, sent for the German ambassador and asked him to present a proposal to the kaiser for a secret offensive and defensive alliance against Russia. The *casus belli* would occur if Russia were to attack either Germany or Turkey, but also if it were to attack Austria-Hungary; in fact, it would occur even if Germany or a member of the Triple Alliance were to attack Russia. Turkey would request protection against Russia—no one else— along with a promise that the kaiser would leave the German military mission in Turkey. Turkey would give the supreme command of the entire Turkish army and the field command of one-quarter of the army to the German military mission upon the outbreak of war. Negotiations were to be conducted in absolute secrecy.

Little negotiation was necessary. The kaiser instantly agreed to the proposed terms. A few details were added. Germany and Turkey were to bind themselves to 'strict neutrality' in the conflict between Austria and Serbia; Germany guaranteed Turkish territory against Russia; if war between Germany and Russia did not break out the agreement would become inoperative. The ambassador was instructed to finalize the agreement on these terms—but he was not to say anything to anyone about the discussions—not even to his colleague, the Austrian ambassador.

★

On Tuesday the 28th, the day that war was finally declared by Austria-Hungary on Serbia, the Triple Alliance was far from cohesive. Publicly, Germany stood behind its ally and rejected the initiative of Sir Edward Grey to join Britain in a mediated settlement of the crisis. But beyond that there were numerous diplomatic, political, and military issues that divided the three (or four) members of the alliance. Austria was pressing Germany to warn Russia that military preparations aimed at Austria would be regarded as a threat against Germany—but the Germans had so far refused the request. Austria pressed Germany to insist that Romania 'go public' with its secret participation in the Triple Alliance—but the Germans believed this to be impolitic and unwise at the moment. Germany was pressing Austria to find a way to assure Italy's continuing adherence to the alliance—but the Austrians adamantly continued to refuse to offer anything of substance. Germany was negotiating an alliance with Turkey but chose to keep this secret from Austria. Finally, the kaiser had, on Tuesday morning, read the text of the Serbian reply to the Austrian ultimatum and concluded that it removed any cause for war. Under these circumstances, how likely was it that the alliance would act cohesively and remain intact in the days to come?

All eyes now turned to St Petersburg; everything seemed to depend on how Russia would react to the Austrian declaration of war on Serbia. Would Austria's denial that it aimed to acquire Serbian territory be sufficient to deter the Russians from continuing with their military preparations? Would Russia continue to negotiate as long as Austria did not cross the frontier into Serbian territory? Could Russia depend on the support of its French ally and its British friend? If it could not depend on them would it be prepared to intervene on its own on behalf of Serbia?

The day before, on Monday the 27th, Sazonov had argued that Serbia's reply at the very least offered the possibility of a diplomatic solution to the crisis. He had proposed that he undertake to mediate between Austria and Serbia through direct discussions with the Austrian ambassador in St Petersburg. Germany had utilized this suggestion as an excuse to reject the Grey proposal for a conference à quatre in London, and Grey had then withdrawn his proposal in favour of the 'bilateral' discussion between Russia and Austria.

But Berchtold, when he met with the recently returned Russian ambassador in Vienna on Tuesday, flatly rejected Sazonov's suggestion. It was too late for negotiations: Austria had already declared war on Serbia in response to its provocations and was determined to establish a peaceful arrangement that would last. The only way to achieve this was by military action. Public opinion in Austria-Hungary demanded this as well; it was a course of action congruent with the dignity of the monarchy.[41]

Sazonov was pleading for the British to act: they ought to recognize that Germany had encouraged Austria's intransigence. The key to the situation 'undoubtedly lies in Berlin', where they ought to be exerting pressure.[42] The British should insist on mediation and demand that Austria suspend military measures. Unless this was done immediately, Austria would crush Serbia completely and 'acquire a dominant position in the Balkans'.[43]

The British were perplexed by his plea. At the Foreign Office, the permanent under-secretary of state wrote personally to the ambassador at St Petersburg to explain the quandary they faced in London. Sazonov, he grumbled, had been making fresh proposals almost daily, throwing the diplomatic initiative into disarray. Nicolson could only hope that Austria would now abstain from actually entering Serbian territory. Such an invasion could not possibly be regarded with indifference by Russia, and in that case 'all hope of a peaceful solution will vanish'. He dismissed all the talk about 'localization' as meaning simply that the Powers were supposed to stand by 'while Austria quietly strangles Servia'. This was preposterous and iniquitous. Especially after the Serbian reply, the Austrians must realize that if they continued to insist on giving them 'a lesson' it would probably lead to a general European conflagration, with disastrous consequences. The

Germans, he complained, had not been playing straight with them. When asked to assist at Vienna, they had done no more than pass along Grey's proposal, and then brushed aside the *à quatre* idea as impractical.[44]

Nicolson explained Britain's dilemma. The Russians were taking the current crisis as a test of the Anglo-Russian Entente—and 'all hope of a friendly and permanent understanding' would disappear if the British were to disappoint them. But the British government could not take any clear line unless it felt that it had public opinion behind it. And, although the British press was gradually coming around to the realization that it would be difficult—if not impossible—for Britain to remain outside a general European conflict, for the time being they could do no more than make it clear to Germany and Austria that they could not rely on the certainty that Britain would remain neutral. The decision to keep the fleet together seemed to have given weight to this point. Although the British government was unable to give Sazonov the definite undertaking he sought, 'there is no doubt whatsoever that were we drawn into this conflagration we should be on the side of our friends'.

In spite of such ruminations, nothing clear or concrete emanated from London on Tuesday: far from it. There were two small indications that the British were unlikely to intervene quickly or forcefully on the side of the Russians. The ambassador in Paris, Sir Francis Bertie, had from the beginning of the crisis warned against going too far in support of Russia's 'Slavic' pretensions in the Balkans. Now the Austrian ambassador in Paris reported Bertie as telling him that if Russia intervened it would lead to the intervention of Germany and France as well. Britain, however, 'would be an idle spectator and interfere only if France were threatened by utter ruin'.[45] The report was eagerly relayed from Vienna to Berlin by Tschirschky.[46]

At the same time, the kaiser's younger brother, Prince Heinrich—Grand Admiral of the German fleet—reported on the meeting that he had had with their cousin, King George, in London on Sunday. 'Georgie' had assured him that both he and his government would do everything possible to localize the conflict between Austria and Serbia. The king's own words, according to the prince, were that 'we shall try all we can to keep out of this and shall remain neutral'.[47] Heinrich believed him to be serious, although he himself doubted that Britain could remain neutral permanently, given her relationship with France. On the other hand, he had witnessed no trace of excitement among the people of London during the weekend.

★

Such interest as there was among the British people as of Tuesday the 28th focused on the issue of neutrality. There were few signs of enthusiasm for a war in support of Serbia. Perhaps the single most famous anti-war spokesman in the decade before the war, Norman Angell (whose book, *The Great Illusion* [1909], had become a best-seller), got together with some of his friends to form 'The Neutrality League'. On Tuesday they issued a manifesto arguing that if Britain intervened on the side of Russia and assured its victory in a continental war it would have the effect of making Russia the dominant military power in Europe, and possibly the dictator there and in Asia. Germany, on the other hand—a highly civilized, cultured nation 'racially allied to ourselves and with moral ideals largely resembling our own'—was wedged in between hostile states. The last war fought by Britain on the European continent was for the purpose of checking the growth of Russia; now Britain might be asked to go to war to promote Russian expansion. Half a million copies of the pamphlet 'Shall We Fight for a Russian Europe?' were printed.[48]

At the same time, the focus of the French began to change. On Tuesday, the trial of Madame Caillaux finally ended. The two thousand people who had squeezed into the Palais de Justice (built to hold 500) cheered wildly when she was acquitted of murder. Thus far few had paid much attention to what had been going on in the Balkans.

French socialists now began to join the syndicalists in their opposition to participation in a war. On Sunday, the editor of the socialist newspaper *L'Humanité* had written to his German colleague, Karl Kautsky, that although there were some bad signs, there was no need to move up the date of the annual meeting of the International Socialist Bureau.[49] But by Tuesday, fifty of the 104 Socialist deputies in the French chamber had met to discuss the crisis. When they emerged from their meeting they issued a declaration that intervening in a war on behalf of Russia would extend and aggravate the evils of war without any benefit to Serbia. A committee was appointed to call on Bienvenu-Martin and ask him to call parliament together immediately.

The most persuasive and influential of French socialists, Jean Jaurès, issued a manifesto in the name of the permanent administrative committee of the *Section française de l'Internationale ouvrière* (SFIO) urging the French and German governments to restrain their allies. When he learned of the Austrian declaration of war on Serbia he called it a 'relapse into barbarism' and wondered if man was not 'eternally destined for suffering'. In spite of everything, he called on people to rally behind the forces for good, for progress—the only barriers against the flood of barbarism.[50]

On behalf of the syndicalists, *La Bataille* warned that war would be 'a horrifying carnage, a grandiose slaughter in which blood would run in streams. The almost total extermination of people and of things, a renewal of ancient barbarity without precedent.'[51]

Another group within the French socialist movement took a different view, declaring that Europe could not permit a small nation to be crushed by a colossus. If their socialist brethren in Germany and Austria were unable to prevent the imperialist crimes of their leaders, then the duty of all French citizens was clear: to take up arms for the defence of their country and for the rights of all people and for civilization.

Perhaps the socialist movement in Germany would have some effect in restraining their government? *Die Sozialdemokratische Partei Deutschlands* (SPD: Social Democratic Party of Germany) had called on its supporters to demonstrate against war, and on Tuesday evening thirty-two separate demonstrations were held in greater Berlin. Over 100,000 attended. At each meeting a party leader delivered a short speech blaming Austria for the trouble. Later in the evening parades began marching from the outlying working-class districts into the centre of Berlin. By 10 p.m. thousands were marching up and down Unter den Linden, singing the '*Arbeitermarseillaise*', shouting 'Down with war' and 'Long live social democracy'.[52] Lining up along the sidewalks were the bourgeoisie, singing patriotic songs; the police moved in and cleared the street before a confrontation occurred.

The anti-war protests in Germany were not confined to Berlin: hundreds of thousands in other German cities joined in. Karl Kautsky, Rosa Luxemburg, and Hugo Haase, the most important German socialist leaders, left Germany for Brussels and a meeting of the executive committee of the International Socialist Bureau. But on the same day the SPD newspaper, *Vorwärts*, while criticizing Austria-Hungary, stated that socialists would rally to Germany's defence in the event of an attack from Russia.

Franz Joseph attempted to rally his subjects by issuing a manifesto following the declaration of war on Serbia. He explained that he had attempted to do his best to maintain the peace and spare his people from the sacrifices and burdens of war but 'Providence, in its wisdom, has decreed otherwise'. The intrigues of a malevolent opponent had compelled him, for the honour of the monarchy, for the protection of its dignity, for its position as a Power, and for the security of its possessions, 'to grasp the sword after long years of peace'.

The emperor's hope that Serbia would appreciate the patience and love of peace that his government had demonstrated had not been fulfilled. 'The flame of its hatred for myself and my House has blazed always higher' as Serbia attempted to tear away by force 'inseparable portions of Austria-Hungary'. A criminal propaganda, extending across the frontier, aimed to lead astray the youth of the monarchy, 'inciting it to mischievous deeds of madness and high treason'. A series of murderous attacks had been organized and carried out in a carefully prepared conspiracy that could be traced back to Serbia. Now, in this solemn hour, 'I am fully conscious of the whole significance of my resolve and my responsibility before the Almighty. I have examined and weighed everything, and, with a serene conscience, I set out on the path to which my duty points.'

★

The news that Austria-Hungary had declared war on Serbia reached Sazonov in St Petersburg late that afternoon. He immediately arranged to meet with the tsar at the Peterhof. After their meeting the foreign minister instructed the Russian chief of the general staff to draft two *ukases*—one for partial mobilization of the four military districts of Odessa, Kiev, Moscow, and Kazan, another for general mobilization. The tsar had remained steadfast in his determination to do nothing that might antagonize Germany and would go no further than authorize a partial mobilization aimed at Austria-Hungary. This was in spite of the warnings from his military advisers who knew that such a mobilization was impossible. The head of the mobilization division and the quartermaster general both argued that partial mobilization would result in chaos, make it impossible to prosecute a successful war against Austria-Hungary, and render Russia vulnerable in a war with Germany.

A partial mobilization served the requirements of Russian diplomacy, however. Sazonov attempted to placate the Germans by assuring them that the decision to mobilize in only the four districts indicated that Russia had no intention of attacking them. Keeping the door open for negotiations, he decided not to recall the Russian ambassador from Vienna—in spite of Austria's declaration of war on Serbia.[53]

That night Belgrade was bombarded by Austro-Hungarian artillery: two shells exploded in a school, one at the Grand Hotel, others at cafés and banks. Offices, hotels, and banks had been closed. The city had been left defenceless.

Day Six

Wednesday, 29 July

Late on Tuesday evening, Bethmann Hollweg and Kaiser Wilhelm had decided to seize the initiative. Every one of the Great Powers had been increasing the pressure on them to act. Berchtold was pleading for them to live up to their commitments and warn Russia that mobilizing against Austria would be taken as a threat against them as well. Sazonov was pleading for Germany to pressure Austria to negotiate a settlement at St Petersburg. Italy was insisting that Germany recognize the validity of its claims for compensation in the Balkans in return for upholding the alliance. Britain was persevering in its attempts to persuade Germany to restrain Austria from precipitating a general European war by invading Serbia. France was stressing the urgency of initiating some form of mediation: in the face of German recalcitrance, Jules Cambon bluntly asked Jagow if Germany wanted a war.[1]

Bethmann Hollweg had persuaded the kaiser the day before to act on General Chelius' suggestion that he contact the tsar directly via telegram.[2] Late Tuesday evening a telegram was drafted (in English) for the kaiser and despatched to St Petersburg after midnight. As suggested by Chelius, the telegram emphasized that a crime against monarchy had been perpetrated by the assassins at Sarajevo. The kaiser connected the crime directly to the 'unscrupulous agitation' that had been going on for years in Serbia: 'The spirit that led Serbians to murder their own king and his wife still dominates the country.' He trusted that the tsar would agree with him that they shared a common interest in punishing all of those 'morally responsible' for the dastardly murder. 'In this politics play no part at all.' On the other hand, the kaiser expressed his understanding of the difficulties faced by the tsar, given the drift of Russian public opinion. In view of this, and of the 'hearty and tender friendship which binds us both', he was exerting his utmost influence to induce Austria to deal directly with Russia in order to arrive at an understanding. 'I confidently hope you will help me in my efforts to smooth over the difficulties that may still arise.'[3]

At almost the same moment that the kaiser was wiring the tsar, the tsar was wiring the kaiser. At 1 a.m. on Wednesday the 29th, Nicholas appealed to Wilhelm for his assistance: 'An ignoble war has been declared on a weak country.' The indignation that this had caused in Russia—an indignation that Nicholas fully shared—was enormous. He anticipated that he would soon be overwhelmed by the pressure being brought to bear upon him, and that he would be forced to take 'extreme measures' that would lead to war. To avoid this terrible calamity, Nicholas begged Wilhelm, in the name of their old friendship, 'to do what you can to stop your allies from going too far'.[4]

To these messages, which crossed one another in the middle of the night, was added a third. Arriving in Berlin at 3.42 a.m. was one from General Chelius in St Petersburg, reporting on his meeting with Prince Grigorii Troubetskoy on Tuesday. Chelius was anxious to convey directly to the kaiser the views of such an important figure in the entourage of the tsar. The prince told him that the Serbian reply testified to their intention of complying wholly and completely with the demands made by Austria. But the Serbian government could not accept the contested points without running the risk of a revolution. If Austria failed to recognize this, it would assume the responsibility for turning the affair into a European conflict. When Chelius complained that the responsibility would lie not with Austria, but with Russia, Troubetskoy insisted that although the Russians 'did not love' the Serbs, they were their Slavic brothers 'and we cannot leave our brethren in the lurch'.[5] Russia would not permit Austria to annihilate Serbia. Chelius denied this was the intent: Austria had wished only to be left alone and had proclaimed that it would not seize a single tract of Serbian territory. Troubetskoy refused to accept this: 'war is war'—and if the Austrians crushed the Serbs, what would come afterward could not be foreseen.

The prince was attempting to add weight to Sazonov's efforts to induce the Germans to intervene at Vienna in support of a compromise. Oceans of blood would be shed if they failed to negotiate, and Troubetskoy hoped that the kaiser would give his Austrian ally the good advice 'not to over-draw the bow', to recognize the good intentions of Serbia from the promises already given, and to submit the remaining points at issue either to a decision of the Great Powers or to the Hague Court of Arbitration. He warned of the inadequacies of those in charge at Vienna: the emperor was old, the heir to the throne inexperienced, the foreign minister weak. The return of the kaiser to Berlin had made the Russian court feel easier, for they trusted that he did not want war—just as the tsar did not. The prince hoped that the two monarchs would be able to come to an understanding via their telegraphic exchanges.

Chelius emphasized that the opinions expressed to him came from one of the most influential men at Russian headquarters, and probably represented 'the opinion of the entire *entourage*'.

The kaiser read the telegrams from the tsar and Chelius early on Wednesday morning. They did not please him. He dismissed the tsar's message as an admission of weakness: Nicholas was attempting to shift the responsibility for the situation onto Wilhelm's shoulders. The telegram was offensive: it contained a concealed threat and a demand that he should tie the hands of his Austrian ally. The tsar gave no indication of any sense of monarchical solidarity: in fact he betrayed a Panslavic conception of the situation. The kaiser saw no need for the Russians to act now, before the results of Austria's action were known; there would be time for negotiation afterwards. There was certainly no reason why Russia needed to mobilize at this moment. Instead of demanding that Germany check its ally, the tsar ought to deal directly with the emperor.

The kaiser took a similar view of the report from Chelius. Troubetskoy's hope that the kaiser would restrain the Austrians he interpreted as simply another attempt to throw the responsibility onto him. 'I refuse it.' On Troubetskoy's point that the Russians could not leave their Slavic brethren in the lurch, the kaiser exclaimed: 'Murderers of kings and princes!' He had done as Troubetskoy had suggested in sending a personal telegram to the tsar, but whether an understanding would follow from this, the kaiser had his doubts. He instructed Jagow to draft a reply to the tsar to be sent later in the day.

The view from Berlin on Wednesday morning was cloudy. On the one hand, with the Austrian declaration of war against Serbia, the crisis seemed close to a resolution. Austria had publicly disavowed any intention of taking Serbian territory, and therefore its action could—or should—be regarded only as a reasonable and understandable step to remove the most persistent threat to the cohesiveness of the Habsburg monarchy. The kaiser believed that a European war could be avoided as long as Russia was prepared to accept Austria's assurances and permit it to give the Serbs the lesson they needed in order to keep them in check in the future.

But when Berlin looked to St Petersburg, Paris, Rome, London—and even within Berlin itself—the view became much bleaker.

★

On Wednesday the German general staff summarized their view of the situation for the chancellor.[6] The generals left no doubt where they stood: for the past five years the Austrians had 'with a patience approaching weakness' put up with continual provocations from a people who engaged in regicide at home and in the murder of princes abroad. In spite of the threat to its national stability it was only after the crime of Sarajevo that Austria resorted to extreme measures 'in order to burn with a glowing iron a cancer that has constantly threatened to poison the body of Europe'. It would seem reasonable that all Europe should be grateful to the Austrians for properly chastising such a mischief-maker and restoring order to the Balkans. But Russia was choosing to align itself with a 'criminal nation' (*verbrecherischen Landes*) and thereby create a thunder-cloud that threatened to break over Europe at any moment. The Austrians, who had given their assurances that they would neither make any territorial acquisitions at Serbia's expense nor infringe upon its sovereignty, were only taking such steps as were necessary to compel the Serbs to live up to their promises.

The general staff argued that the quarrel between Austria and Serbia ought to have been regarded as a purely private one—and would have been had Russia not intruded. Austria had mobilized only a portion of its armed forces against Serbia: eight army corps, just enough to conduct a punitive expedition. But Russia had responded by making preparations to mobilize twelve army corps in the districts of Kiev, Odessa, and Moscow, and was preparing to undertake similar measures in the north, along the German border and the Baltic. And then the Russians had announced that they would mobilize if Austria advanced into Serbia because they could not permit the destruction of Serbia.

What would be the consequences of Russia's steps? If the Austrians advanced into Serbia they would face not only the Serbian army but the vastly superior strength of Russia. Thus, they could not contemplate fighting Serbia without securing themselves against an attack by Russia. This would force them to mobilize the other half of their army—at which point a collision between Austria and Russia would become inevitable. And that would be the *casus foederis* for Germany, who, if it were not to be false to its word and permit Russia to annihilate its ally, must mobilize. If Germany were to mobilize, this would compel Russia to mobilize in the remaining military districts. The Russians would then claim that they were being attacked by Germany, thus obliging France to support them—'and the mutual butchery of the civilized nations of Europe would begin'.

According to the general staff, Russia had cunningly contrived the entire situation. By giving repeated assurances that it was not mobilizing but only preparing for it, Russia was now ready to move its armies forward within days of issuing the mobilization order. This had placed Austria in a desperate position, Germany in an invidious one. By forcing Austria and Germany to mobilize against them, the Russians would be able to proclaim to the world that they did not want war, that Germany had brought it about. Unless a miracle were to prevent it, war was about to 'annihilate for decades the civilization of almost all Europe'.

Germany must live up to its responsibilities. If it failed to come to the assistance of its ally at such a decisive moment, it would violate the deeply rooted feelings of fidelity 'which are among the most beautiful traits of the German character'. The French had now begun to undertake preparatory military measures, demonstrating that they and the Russians were moving hand-in-hand. When the collision between Austria and Russia became inevitable, Germany would have to mobilize and prepare to take up the fight on two fronts. This placed Germany in a difficult position: the further that Russia and France got with their preparations the quicker they would be able to mobilize. The situation was becoming more unfavourable to Germany with each passing day. Allowing this to continue would 'lead to disastrous consequences for us'.

The warnings of the general staff were intensified by the exhortations of the Austrians. Late Tuesday night Berchtold had instructed Szögyény to prod the Germans into action and on Wednesday morning the ambassador took the unusual step of presenting a formal note at the Wilhelmstrasse. Russia's military preparations were proceeding to the point that General Conrad considered it absolutely essential that he know whether Austria-Hungary could utilize its full strength in the war with Serbia or whether most of its forces would have to be used against Russia. Germany should warn Russia that it would take extensive and immediate counter-measures if Russia mobilized in the military districts bordering on Austria-Hungary. 'Plain speech', Berchtold suggested, was the best way to make the Russians recognize the consequences of their threatening behaviour. The German government should also join the Austrian in persuading King Karl to warn

Tsar Nicholas of Romania's adhesion to the Triple Alliance. The Austrian government trusted that it could rely upon its German ally to support its suggestions.

The situation that seemed so clear to Berchtold and the German general staff was murky to the German chancellor. Bethmann Hollweg took seriously the reports of Russian and French military preparations—and by midday he issued warnings to both governments of dire consequences should they proceed. If France continued with its preparations, he threatened to proclaim '*Kriegsgefahr*' (the risk of war) and begin to undertake steps to prepare Germany for mobilization.[7] He cautioned Sazonov that if Russia continued moving towards mobilization, Germany would be forced to do the same. A European war would then be difficult to prevent.[8]

In spite of what appeared to be his clear and decisive warnings to France and Russia, Bethmann Hollweg was perplexed. He was anxious and angry—not only with the French and Russians but with the Austrians. The chancellor was dismayed that, after weeks of diplomatic activity, the Austrians had failed to secure the adhesion of the Italians to the Triple Alliance. Moltke had advised him that the participation of Italy was essential to German war plans. Vienna had been warned, over and over again, that it should drop its 'juridical' interpretation of the compensation clauses of the alliance and instead act upon the realization that it was vital to keep Italy as a partner in the alliance. But nothing had happened.

Bethmann Hollweg now directed Jagow to send another telegram to Vienna, stating pointedly that the manner in which it was handling the Italian issue was 'absolutely unsatisfactory'.[9] The responsibility would rest on Vienna's shoulders if the Triple Alliance broke apart on the eve of a European conflagration. He complained that Austria's policy was contradictory: at Rome they were promising to come to an arrangement with Italy if it chose to remain in permanent occupation of Serbian territory; at St Petersburg they were proclaiming that they had no interest in acquiring Serbian territory. What the Austrians were saying in Rome was certainly known in St Petersburg. As Austria's ally, Germany could not support such a 'two-faced policy' (*doppeltem Boden*).

Bethmann Hollweg told Jagow that he refused to be placed in a position where he might be accused of double-dealing. He could not continue to mediate at St Petersburg as long as this remained the case: otherwise, Germany would find itself 'completely entangled in Vienna's tow-rope'. He instructed Jagow to draft an appropriate telegram to send to Berchtold.

By midday on Wednesday the 29th, even with Austria-Hungary having declared war on Serbia, relations within the Triple Alliance were still complicated and confusing.

★

Even more tangled were relations within the Triple Entente. The Russians, supported by the French, continued to press the British to align themselves squarely with them. On Tuesday morning the British cabinet met for the purpose of considering the crisis in Europe—the first time they devoted themselves exclusively to the topic. The question was, what would Britain do in the event of war in the west between Germany and France? The nineteen men sitting around the table in Downing Street were unable to reach agreement. They could not even agree to support France in the event of a German invasion: public opinion would not allow it.

Grey found himself opposed by almost everyone in the cabinet at every turn—the only ones prepared to support him were the prime minister, Asquith, and the first lord of the admiralty, Churchill. Grey tried to argue that at the very least Britain was obligated to uphold the neutrality of Belgium, and he used a report prepared by the Law Officers in 1870 of British obligations under the treaty of 1839 to support his stand. The vast majority of the cabinet disagreed: whether Britain should intervene to uphold Belgian neutrality was a matter of policy, not law.

After carefully reviewing the situation from all points of view the cabinet 'decided not to decide'.[10] Most in the cabinet believed this to be prudent: 'if both sides do not know what we shall do, both will be less willing to run risks.'[11] Grey was instructed to inform both the French and the German ambassadors that Britain was unable to make any promises. As the prime minister reported to the king: 'After much discussion it was agreed that Sir E. Grey should be authorised to inform the German and French Ambassadors that at this stage we were unable to pledge ourselves in advance, either under all conditions to stand aside, or in any conditions to join in.'[12] At the same time it also seemed prudent to prepare for the worst: Churchill was to send a 'warning' telegram to the fleet authorizing preparations for an immediate mobilization; the First Squadron was moved to concentrate at Scapa Flow; the Committee of Imperial Defence was directed to implement the 'precautionary stage' of the British War Book.

Immediately following the cabinet meeting, Grey undertook to act as instructed. He met first with Lichnowsky, then with Cambon.

Grey began by making it clear to the German ambassador that he was displeased that Berchtold had flatly declined the Russian suggestion that Austria negotiate in St Petersburg in an effort to solve the Austro-Serbian dispute. A direct discussion of that kind appeared to Grey to be the most feasible way of proceeding—particularly as Germany had declined his suggestion of a conference of ambassadors in London. As Germany had accepted the idea of a mediation *à quatre* in principle, perhaps it could come up with a revised proposal?

Lichnowsky could only reaffirm the German position. The dispute, he maintained, was between Austria and Serbia alone, and Austria could not be subjected to the humiliation of being called before a European tribunal. Austria aimed only to establish peace and order on its frontiers. He insisted that Serbia was no concern of Russia's, particularly once Austria disavowed any intention of acquiring Serbian territory.[13]

Grey replied that no humiliation of Austria was intended. He hoped that a way could be found to give the Austrians full satisfaction, but Russia could not be expected to remain inactive while the Austrians attained their aims by war. Austria could turn Serbia into its vassal without annexing it. Russia could not stand by and allow this to happen: its position among orthodox Christians and its standing in the Balkans was at stake.[14] Russia could not possibly accept such a humiliation.

Lichnowsky warned Berlin that in London they were firmly convinced that unless Austria was willing to enter into a negotiation on the Serbian question 'a world war is inevitable'. He presented the case as starkly as he could: Germany had to find a way to get Austria to the negotiating table or it would find itself embroiled in a world war.

Grey did not go so far. He told Lichnowsky, 'in a quite private and friendly way', that he regarded the situation as very grave. Although Britain had no wish to interfere, if Germany became involved—and then France— the situation would involve all of Europe. He did not wish the ambassador to mistake the friendly tone of their conversation to mean that Britain would stand aside. When Lichnowsky asked if this meant that Britain would—under certain circumstances—intervene, Grey refused to go that far. He avoided making threats or applying pressure. As long as Germany did not become involved, or even if France was not involved, there would be no question of Britain intervening. But, if it reached the point where he believed British interests required intervention, a decision would have to be made very quickly.

Before his meeting with Lichnowsky, Grey had received an updated report on Russia's position from his ambassador in St Petersburg. Sir George Buchanan had met with Sazonov on Tuesday evening and asked whether Russia might be satisfied with Austria's assurances that it would respect Serbia's independence and integrity. Sazonov flatly rejected any such promises: if the Austrians crossed the Serbian frontier Russia would mobilize. The whole nation would be behind the Russian government in the event of war. When Buchanan asked if the tsar could not appeal directly to the emperor to limit Austria's actions in a way that would be acceptable to Russia, Sazonov replied that the only way to avert war now was for Britain to make it clear that it would join France and Russia.

Although circumstances were now changing quickly, with war declared between Austria and Serbia, shots being exchanged between them, and military preparations beginning in Russia, the arguments being presented to Grey in London had not altered. The Germans and the Austrians continued to insist that the affair was a local one in which the other Powers ought to remain aloof. The Russians and the French continued to insist that the only way to prevent a general European war was for Britain to warn the Triple Alliance that it would join its entente partners if war were to break out.

Even if Grey himself was inclined to succumb to the Russo-French pressure to join them, he was constrained by the cabinet from doing so. Although he warned Lichnowsky against mistaking his friendly and conciliatory words as indicating that Britain would not intervene, neither did he promise anything to Russia or France. He would only commit himself to continue making every effort to maintain peace. When he met with the French ambassador later that afternoon, he warned him not to assume that Britain would take the same view of this crisis as it had in Morocco in 1905—when it had stood by France in its dispute with Germany. Public opinion in Britain, he told Paul Cambon, took a quite different view of this dispute. In Morocco, it had appeared that Germany was attempting to crush France. Now, 'the dispute between Austria and Serbia was not one in which we felt called to take a hand'.[15] He went further: even if the question became one between Austria and Russia, Britain would still not feel called upon to take a hand in it. In a conflict between 'Teuton or Slav' for supremacy in the Balkans Britain had no interest. Britain's policy had always been to avoid being drawn into war over a Balkan question.

Grey confessed to Cambon that he remained undecided what policy to follow should Germany and France become involved in the quarrel. Britain was free from engagements 'and we should have to decide what British interests required us to do'.[16] Just as he warned Lichnowsky not to take his friendly tone to indicate that Britain would stand aside, he cautioned Cambon not to assume that the precaution of keeping the British fleet together indicated what Britain would do 'in a contingency that I still hoped might not arise'. If the question became one of European hegemony, Britain would then decide what was necessary. Cambon did not seem surprised.

★

The British cabinet had not involved itself directly in the European crisis until Wednesday the 29th—and neither had the French. With the president and the premier at sea or in Scandinavia since Austria presented Serbia with its ultimatum on the 23rd, there was little direction or central control in French diplomacy. Communications between Bienvenu-Martin in Paris and Poincaré and Viviani on board the *France* were slow and unreliable. The French ambassadors in St Petersburg, London, and Berlin were left much to their own devices and pursued their own diplomacy. Things changed in France on the 29th.

That morning the French presidential party landed at Dunkirk. Heavy fog had delayed their arrival: a crowd of 2,000 had formed to greet them at the Gare du Nord at ten that morning. When they finally arrived at 1.30 p.m. the crowd numbered over 10,000. When the president's carriage emerged from the station the crowd began to sing the *Marseillaise*; more people lined the streets along the route to the Elysée Palace, shouting '*Vive la France!*' '*Vive la République!*' '*Vive Poincaré!*' '*Vive l'Armée!*' When they passed the Place de la Concorde they were greeted by members of the League of Patriots marching around the statue of Strasbourg.

Shortly after their arrival at the palace Poincaré convened a meeting of the cabinet for 5.30 p.m. He had determined to seize control of foreign affairs from Viviani, who, besides his ignorance, had—according to Poincaré—proved himself to be hesitant and faint-hearted. But then Poincaré had suggested that Viviani combine the post of foreign minister with that of premier largely because he was pliable and ignorant of foreign affairs—enabling Poincaré to exert much greater influence on diplomacy than presidents had in the past. The Quai d'Orsay had no confidence in Viviani, an excitable anti-clerical socialist who did not understand even the fundamental diplomatic conventions. Under Poincaré's chairmanship, the cabinet—until now ignored as the crisis had unfolded—would meet every morning. On the evening of the 29th they met and discussed the crisis for two hours.

With the moment of decision rapidly approaching, and Austria-Hungary having refused to negotiate directly at St Petersburg, Sazonov desperately attempted to revive Grey's proposal. He was now willing to accept any arrangements for mediation that were approved by Britain and France: he no longer cared what form these took. If efforts to maintain peace failed, he trusted the British public to understand that Russia was not to blame. There was still time; he promised that Russia would not precipitate war by crossing the frontier immediately. It would take a week or more before Russia could complete its mobilization.[17]

According to this timetable, by the evening of Wednesday, 29 July it appeared that the diplomats might still have until 5–6 August before fighting would begin and the soldiers took over.

Anyone who thought that the Austrian declaration of war on Serbia would signal the end of diplomacy was proved wrong. On Wednesday morning Count Szápáry met with Sazonov in St Petersburg in order to reject his proposal that they negotiate directly. Sazonov, although visibly disappointed, discussed the situation in a calm and friendly manner. He requested a copy of the dossier of the Austrian case against Serbia—which the ambassador believed to mean that Sazonov was searching to find something that would enable him to withdraw his support of Serbia. Szápáry concluded that Sazonov wanted to avoid a conflict with Austria and was 'clinging to straws in the hope of escaping from the present situation'.[18]

Not long after their morning meeting rumours began to circulate in St Petersburg that the tsar was about to issue a *ukase* to mobilize in the four military districts. Szápáry approached Sazonov again. He denied that Austria was refusing to negotiate with Russia: although he was not authorized to discuss the text of the note presented to Serbia, he could propose 'a far broader basis' for discussions with Russia. He assured Sazonov that Austria had no intention of damaging Russian interests, did not intend to acquire any Serbian territory, and would not question Serbia's right to sovereignty.

Sazonov insisted that it was the terms of the note that were the issue, because if Serbia were to accept them as they stood, it would be reduced to a vassal of Austria. This would upset the balance of power in the Balkans and damage Russian interests. He promised the ambassador that if they negotiated on the basis of Sir Edward Grey's proposal, Austria's legitimate demands would be recognized and fully satisfied.

Sazonov confirmed that the mobilization *ukase* was to be issued later in the day but denied that he had anything to do with it. The decision was entirely the responsibility of the tsar and his military advisers. The announcement need not mean the end of diplomacy, however. He assured the ambassador that Russian troops were not about to sweep down upon Austria. They were only to be kept in readiness in case Russia's Balkan interests were threatened. Mobilization was merely a precautionary measure.

Their conversation was interrupted by a telephone call. The Austrians had begun to bombard Belgrade. The news instantly transformed Sazonov: he now saw how right the tsar had been to order mobilization. 'You only want to gain time by negotiations and in the meantime you are advancing and bombarding an unprotected city.' What else would Austria wish to conquer once it was in possession of Belgrade? 'What is the good of continuing our conversation?' he asked.[19]

Sazonov informed the German ambassador that Austria's mobilization of eight army corps had compelled Russia to mobilize in the military districts along the Austrian frontier. He assured Pourtalès that this did not mean war: the Russian army could remain under arms for weeks without crossing the frontier. They could still find a way to avoid war. The ambassador warned him that Russia's decision to mobilize would undoubtedly lead the general staffs of Germany and Austria to press for counter-measures as they would not be prepared to sacrifice the advantage of getting a head-start over Russia in their own mobilization. He begged the foreign minister to consider this danger.[20]

At almost the same moment, General Chelius was reporting to the kaiser that the mood among the tsar's entourage had changed entirely. Yesterday they had all hoped for peace—but since Austria's declaration of war they now considered a general war almost inevitable. Austria's refusal to consider the very compliant reply of the Serbs as sufficient grounds for negotiation had convinced them that Austria had been acting in bad faith and that it was determined to have a war. The Russians, he reported, did not want war and regretted that no one had succeeded in restraining Austria.[21]

Early that evening Sazonov sent for the German ambassador to tell him that Austria had categorically refused to engage in direct negotiations with him. He confessed that he was becoming desperate, that he was continuing to look for some way out of the impasse, that he was 'grasping at every straw' (*klammere sich dabei an jeden Strohhalm*).[22] Perhaps they could revive Grey's proposal for a conference *à quatre* in London? Pourtalès warned that the impending Russian mobilization would make it more difficult to find a peaceful solution. Sazonov replied that Austria had forced Russia to take this step.

But what step, or steps, had been taken? That afternoon the German military attaché met with the chief of the Russian general staff. General Nikolai Yanushkevich, who had just come from a meeting with the tsar and the minister of war, assured Major von Eggeling that nothing had changed. Yanushkevich gave his word of honour that up until 3 p.m. no mobilization had commenced anywhere, that not a single man or horse had been called up. Although he could give no guarantees for the future, he assured the attaché that the tsar was opposed to a mobilization on the German frontier.

Eggeling dismissed these assurances as disingenuous. He had received too many credible reports from various parts of the empire detailing the calling up of reservists and the requisitioning of horses. When he confronted the chief of staff with this information, Yanushkevich gave him his word as an officer that the reports were mistaken, and simply cases of false alarms here and there. He admitted that troops had been moved to protect the frontier, but dismissed these movements as precautionary; he reiterated Russia's desire for peace. It was difficult to have confidence in Yanushkevich, who had been appointed chief of staff only five months earlier and had not yet familiarized himself with Russia's mobilization plans. Eggeling did not believe him. The reports he was receiving were too numerous to disregard. The Russians, he concluded, were trying to mislead them as to the extent of the measures that they were undertaking.

Bethmann Hollweg issued precise instructions to Pourtalès that afternoon. The ambassador was to tell Sazonov that if Russia continued to mobilize, Germany would be forced to do the same. At that point 'a European war could scarcely be prevented'.[23] The reports coming from Russia were putting the chancellor in an invidious position. On Tuesday evening the kaiser had repeated that he no longer believed war to be necessary.[24] But at the same time Moltke submitted a secret situation report to Bethmann Hollweg, arguing that Germany was out of options and must act within the next seventy-two hours: even a partial Russian mobilization must be countered by Germany.[25] And the minister of war pressed the point, demanding that Germany ought to declare an 'imminent danger of war' (the *drohende Kriegsgefahr*). Bethmann Hollweg opposed this, arguing that Russia must appear to be the aggressor, for the sake of public opinion in Germany and in Britain. By late Wednesday afternoon the German government had still not made a decision.

★

At 4 p.m. the German general staff received intelligence that Belgium was calling up reservists, raising the numbers of the Belgian army from 50,000 to 100,000, equipping its fortifications, and reinforcing defences along the frontier. Forty minutes later a meeting at the Neue Palais in Potsdam considered Germany's next step. The kaiser discussed the situation with his chancellor, his minister of war, his chief of the general staff, and his adjutant general. The military representatives presented a united front against the civilian chancellor. Moltke argued that the military situation would never be more favourable and wanted war now; Bethmann Hollweg resisted, wanting to avoid anything 'that might start similar measures in France or Britain and set the ball rolling'.[26] 'There is no doubt that the Chief of the General Staff is in favour of war whereas the Chancellor is holding back.'[27] The kaiser again reversed his position, siding with his military advisers against the civilian chancellor.

Bethmann Hollweg did not give up easily. He arranged for Moltke and Falkenhayn (the minister for war) to meet with him at the Reichskanzlerpalais in Berlin later that night. Over the past two days the chancellor had begun meeting with leaders of the Social Democratic Party. He was convinced that the socialists would support the government in a war if it were 'defensive'. That night he succeeded in bringing Moltke around to see his point, that Russia must be made to appear responsible for a war. The British would not side with the Russians if they 'unleashed the general fury of war by way of an attack on Austria'.[28] Falkenhayn reluctantly agreed. After their meeting, shortly before midnight, the chancellor asked the British ambassador to see him.

In the meantime, Bethmann Hollweg had received Pourtalès' report of his meeting with Sazonov, at which he warned him that even a partial mobilization by Russia could precipitate a war. The ambassador explained to the foreign minister that this was not a threat (*Drohung*) but only a 'friendly opinion' (*freundschaftliche Meinung*). Sazonov, greatly excited, promised to convey the warning to the tsar. He assured him a partial mobilization did not mean that Russia intended to go to war, only that it would enter into a state of 'armed neutrality'.[29]

Ten minutes after receiving this report in Berlin Bethmann Hollweg wired St Petersburg that he feared that Sazonov's hopes for peace would not be realized: it was difficult to say to what extent the rolling stone could now be stopped. Russia's mobilization on Austria's frontiers would almost certainly be met with corresponding measures on the part of Austria. Nevertheless, he was still attempting to avoid the impending catastrophe by persuading Vienna to declare formally to Russia that it did not intend to acquire any Serbian territory, that it envisioned no more than a temporary military occupation in order to force a guarantee of good behaviour from Serbia in the future. 'If Austria-Hungary makes such a declaration, Russia would obtain all she desires.'[30]

Did the German chancellor genuinely believe that such a declaration on the part of Austria should—and would—satisfy Russia's concerns? His dealings with Austria on the same day offer some clues.

Bethmann Hollweg transmitted to his ambassador in Vienna Lichnowsky's complaints from London concerning Austria's hidden agenda for Serbia. He told Tschirschky that the comments of Austrian diplomats appeared to reflect 'new wishes and aspirations' that dismayed him. He regarded the procedure of the Austrians in saying different things to different governments 'with increasing astonishment' (wachsendem Befremden). He complained that at St Petersburg the Austrians announced their territorial disinterestedness; at Rome they put off the Italians with meaningless phrases on the compensation issue; at London they proposed to give away parts of Serbia to Bulgaria and Albania; at Berlin they left the Germans 'entirely at sea' regarding their true intentions.

Bethmann Hollweg drew the conclusion that Vienna was formulating plans that it deemed advisable to keep secret from Berlin in order to assure itself of German support.[31]

Nevertheless, in spite of Bethmann Hollweg's own irritation with the Austrians, he instructed Tschirschky to keep his frustration with them to himself for now. For the moment, the ambassador should simply advise Berchtold that Austria ought to avoid arousing suspicions regarding the future integrity of Serbia. He should also make it clear that the instructions received by Mérey in Rome regarding compensation could scarcely be expected to satisfy the Italians.

Bethmann Hollweg concluded that Austrian diplomacy was duplicitous, unreliable, jeopardizing the harmony of the Triple Alliance and threatening to coalesce the opposition of the Entente. By midnight, he was prepared to

accept the Grey proposal for a mediation *à quatre*, given the compliance of
Serbia as indicated in its formal response to Austria's demands—if Austria
was permitted to occupy 'a portion of Serbian territory as a hostage'.[32] The
kaiser's favourable response on Tuesday to the Serbian reply might still be
acted upon: the need for war had disappeared; Serbia was already humiliated; a temporary military occupation by Austria would publicize the
humiliation and provide a hostage for arrangements to be made for the
future.

The German chancellor seemed prepared to accept Sazonov's explanation of Russia's military steps. Shortly after midnight he wired Vienna that
Russia's mobilization in the four military districts was in response to Austria's
mobilization of eight corps, which must be regarded as partly directed
against Russia. The Russian mobilization did not mean war: relations with
Austria were not being broken off and Russia still wanted to avoid war if at
all possible. In light of these facts, he instructed Tschirschky to present
Germany's urgent request that in order to prevent a catastrophe 'or at least
to put Russia in the wrong' Vienna should initiate and continue the discussions with Russia.[33] Suddenly, both negotiation/mediation options—the
Grey *à quatre* and the Sazonov 'bilateral'—seemed to be back on the table.

Bethmann Hollweg's position clearly reflected the kaiser's idea that an
Austrian occupation of Belgrade was essential for the sake of Austria's
honour and to guarantee that the Serbs—those 'liars, tricksters, and masters
of evasion'—would translate their words into deeds.

On Wednesday evening, following his meeting with his chancellor and
military advisers, the kaiser reiterated this argument when he replied to the
tsar's telegram of the day before. He denied that Austria's war against Serbia
was 'ignoble': the Austrians knew from experience that Serbian promises
were wholly unreliable. They required guarantees that Serbia would fulfil
its promises. Russian intervention was unnecessary: the Austrians had disavowed any intention of territorial conquest at Serbia's expense. He believed
that a direct understanding between Russia and Austria was possible and his
government was continuing to promote it. If Russia undertook military
measures that appeared to threaten Austria, however, this could jeopardize
his ability to act as mediator and precipitate a calamity.[34]

By Wednesday evening the German government seemed to be speaking
with one voice. The secretary of state met with the French ambassador and
explained that Germany regarded the Serbian reply as having established
the foundations necessary for negotiations to begin. Consequently, he was

encouraging the Austrians to engage in direct conversations with the
Russians in St Petersburg. But 'with oriental peoples one could never obtain
sufficient guarantees' and thus Austria had to be guaranteed that the promises made would be carried out.[35] This the Serbs had refused. Nevertheless,
Germany was continuing to encourage direct negotiations on this point
while agreeing that the proposed à quatre conference of ambassadors in
London was still a possibility.

Cambon suggested to Jagow that when Austria finally entered into Serbia
and thus satisfied its military prestige, perhaps the moment would have
arrived for the four disinterested Powers to discuss the situation and to come
forward with suggestions for preventing graver complications. Jagow agreed
that this was worth considering, as it sounded quite different from Grey's
proposal.[36]

At the same time newspapers in Paris began to report the beginnings of
French military preparations. Bethmann Hollweg instructed the German
ambassador to warn the French that Germany might be forced to undertake
similar measures and to proclaim a state of Kriegsgefahr ('risk of war').[37]
When Schoen met with Viviani late that afternoon, the French foreign
minister admitted that France had begun to take precautionary measures,
but insisted that these were only small and discreet steps. Mobilization was
not imminent. Nor would he object if Germany were to do the same
thing—although such measures might alarm public opinion.[38]

Germany had now to face the reality that the Franco-Russian alliance was
not showing any sign of cracking, and that a war between Austria and Russia
over Serbia would mean German participation. But German war plans
meant standing on the defensive in the east while knocking out France
quickly in the west. Moltke had reiterated this strategic reality in the
meetings that day. By late evening Bethmann Hollweg had decided that if
Russia did not back down from its planned mobilization, a general European war was bound to result.

★

With war now clearly emerging on the horizon, Bethmann Hollweg
decided that the moment had come to launch a bold new initiative. After
his meetings with the kaiser, Moltke, and Falkenhayn, he sent for the British
ambassador. He told Sir Edward Goschen that he feared a Russian attack on
Austria would precipitate a general European war. Suddenly, out of the
blue, with no prior hints or preparations he proposed that Britain agree to

remain neutral in the event of war, in exchange for a German promise not to seize any French territory in Europe when it ended. He explained that he understood the main principle governing Britain's foreign policy to be that it would not allow France to be crushed. Such was not Germany's aim—and this offer proved it.

The proposal was perhaps not as astonishing as it seemed. Bethmann Hollweg had been trying to use the offer of abandoning the naval race with Britain in exchange for a neutrality agreement ever since he had become chancellor. His offer to leave France intact was the latest variation on that theme. He implied that a worse fate would be in store for France if Britain were to intervene on its behalf. What led him to believe that such an offer might be acceptable?

On 20 July Albert Ballin, the pro-British head of the Hamburg Steamship line, had undertaken a mission to London at the behest of the German secretary of state. Jagow had asked him to sound out his British friends on what course Britain would follow in the event of a European war. His mission was authorized by Bethmann Hollweg and the kaiser himself. Lichnowsky had not been informed.

On the evening of 23 July, at the same moment that the Austrian ultimatum was being presented in Belgrade, Ballin sat down to dinner at the home of Richard, Viscount Haldane of Cloan, the lord chancellor, who had undertaken the famous mission to Berlin in 1912 in an attempt to bring about an end to the Anglo-German naval race. Also at dinner that night were Sir Edward Grey and John Morley—Viscount Morley of Blackburn, who served in the cabinet as lord president of the council. According to Ballin, the three cabinet ministers assured him that Britain would not intervene in a war between Germany and France unless Germany 'swallowed' France and altered the balance of power in Europe by annexing French territory.[39] The next day Ballin met with Winston Churchill, first lord of the admiralty, and suggested a deal: that Britain remain neutral if Germany promised beforehand that it would not annex any French territory and limit its gains to only a few French colonies.

Ballin returned to Germany on 27 July. The following day he assured the *Hamburg Correspondent* that Britain would not intervene in a European war, that 'the highest authorities in London are positively determined to take no steps based on participation in the war'. The next day Bethmann Hollweg proposed a formula almost identical to the one that Ballin had suggested to his friends in the British cabinet while in London.

Perhaps a statement made by the British ambassador in Paris that Britain would interfere in a continental war only if France were threatened with ruin also influenced the German chancellor. The comments, made to the Austrian ambassador in Paris, had been relayed immediately from Vienna to Berlin. Sir Francis Bertie's comments seemed to verify Ballin's summary of the British attitude. Perhaps a guarantee that Germany would respect the territorial integrity of France might be enough to keep Britain on the sidelines?

Goschen asked Bethmann Hollweg whether his proposal applied to French colonies as well. The chancellor replied that he was unable to give a similar undertaking concerning them. What about Holland? The chancellor said that as long as Germany's adversaries respected Dutch integrity he was prepared to give an assurance that Germany would do likewise. And Belgium? What operation Germany might be forced to undertake would depend on what actions France might undertake. In any case, when the war ended, Belgian integrity would be respected. That is, as long as it had not sided against Germany.

Bethmann Hollweg concluded his conversation with the British ambassador by saying that ever since becoming chancellor he had aimed to achieve an understanding with Britain. He hoped that the assurances that he was now proposing to give would form the basis of such an understanding. What he had in mind was a general neutrality agreement between Britain and Germany, although it would be premature to discuss the details of such an arrangement at the moment.[40]

What would they make of this in London? This was the first time that even a whisper of the future of French colonies, or the neutrality of Holland and Belgium, had been raised during the crisis. Until today all the talk had been of Serbia and what conditions could be imposed, how, in order to prevent further acts of terror aimed against Austria.

The telegram summarizing the conversation between Bethmann Hollweg and Goschen would not arrive at the Foreign Office until 9 a.m. Thursday, so the British reaction would not be known until later that day. When Bethmann Hollweg asked Goschen how he thought Sir Edward Grey would respond to his proposal, the ambassador was guarded: he thought Grey would wish to retain 'full liberty of action' and he thought it unlikely that the foreign secretary would care to bind himself in any way at this stage.

Goschen did not raise a red flag immediately concerning the issue of Belgian neutrality. Perhaps he would have done so had he realized that— simultaneous with the Bethmann Hollweg initiative—the German secretary of state was warning the Belgians that the French were preparing to attack Germany through Belgian territory. He explained that it was natural for Germany to worry that even with the best of intentions the Belgians would not be able to resist the French without assistance. For the sake of its self-preservation, therefore, Germany had no choice but to anticipate such an eventuality: Germany might be forced to enter Belgian territory.

In order to avoid a misunderstanding, Jagow outlined the principles upon which Germany proposed to proceed:

1. Germany contemplated no hostile action against Belgium and would bind itself to guarantee its sovereignty and independence at the end of hostilities—should Belgium adopt an attitude of benevolent neutrality during the conflict. Moreover, Germany would look upon with favour any claims Belgium might have for territorial compensation at the expense of France.

2. Germany would evacuate Belgian territory at the conclusion of peace.

3. If Belgium were to adopt a friendly attitude, Germany would be willing to buy for cash all the necessities required for its troops and to reimburse Belgium for any damages caused by them.

If Belgium were to oppose Germany as an enemy and place obstacles in its way—by using its Meuse fortifications for resistance, by destroying railroads, roads, or tunnels—then Germany would be compelled to regard it as an enemy. In that case Germany could make no promises and would leave the future of their relations 'to the decision of arms'. The German minister at Brussels was to insist on an 'unequivocal' reply to this within the next twenty-four hours.[41]

★

Grey, who was beginning to despair, might have abandoned any hope had he known of the German initiative at Brussels. Even so, he told the Austrian ambassador that it was a bad day 'for the peace of Europe'. The rejection of his proposed mediation *à quatre* meant that the Powers were not to be permitted 'to help in getting satisfaction for Austria'—which they might succeed in doing, were they given the opportunity. When Mensdorff repeated Austria's disavowal of any territorial aggrandizement, Grey dismissed the promise, repeating that it was possible to turn Serbia into a vassal state without taking away any of its territory.[42]

Giving up on Austria, Grey turned again to Germany. He told Lichnowsky that he was disappointed that Germany seemed to regard his suggestions of a conference, consultation, or conversations à quatre in London as too formal a method. He urged the German government to suggest any method by which the influence of the four Powers could be used to prevent war between Austria and Russia. France and Italy had both agreed to his proposal, and the three of them were ready to initiate mediation 'by any method that Germany could suggest' if it would only 'press the button' in the interests of peace.[43]

And a report from Rome gave Grey a glimmer of hope. The Serbian chargé d'affaires there had apparently told the Italian foreign minister that Serbia was now inclined to swallow even articles 5 and 6 of the Austrian ultimatum if the terms by which Austrian agents were to participate in the investigations could be agreed upon. Thus, Serbia would have accepted all of the demands. San Giuliano believed it possible to reach an agreement on this basis, and Grey encouraged the Italians to present the proposal at Berlin and Vienna.[44]

Grey's permanent under-secretary at the Foreign Office was much less optimistic. Sir Arthur Nicolson asked himself what would be the use of continuing to exchange views regarding mediation at this juncture. The only possibility of avoiding war now was to ask Austria to take no military action pending conversations—and the Austrians had made it quite clear that they would peremptorily reject such a request and that it would not be supported by Germany. 'I am of opinion that the resources of diplomacy are, for the present, exhausted.'[45]

Nicolson was despondent. He argued that two undoubted facts faced them: Austria would invade and endeavour to crush Serbia; Russia would then act to support Serbia. Appeals to either Austria or to Russia to alter their course would be futile and only lead to misunderstandings.

Whether Grey would share this gloomy view was not yet clear. Lichnowsky, he noted, had assured him today that Germany had in fact accepted the principle of mediation between Austria and Russia. He summoned the ambassador to meet with him again that evening. Although apprehensive, Grey had not given up hope. He outlined a new scenario: Austria might, after occupying Belgrade, stop there and announce its conditions. If mediation were not possible, perhaps this 'halt in Belgrade' might avert the impending catastrophe.

Grey also wanted to warn Germany. Although Britain wished to maintain their friendship and was prepared to stand aside as long as a conflict was limited to Austria and Russia, the situation would be altered if France were to become involved. Britain would be forced to make its mind up very quickly as it would not be practicable to stand aside for any length of time. 'If war breaks out, it will be the greatest catastrophe the world has ever seen.' Grey assured the ambassador that this was not a threat, but an explanation of his personal opinion.

He warned Lichnowsky that public opinion in Britain was shifting. While it had generally favoured Austria to begin with, it was now turning completely to the other side because of Austria's stubbornness. On the other hand, if the Austrians would accept his proposed mediation he could promise to secure for them 'every possible satisfaction'. There could no longer be any question of a humiliating retreat for them because the Serbs would be punished and compelled—with the agreement of Russia—to subordinate themselves to the Austrians. Austria could thus secure for itself the guarantees it sought for the future without a war that would jeopardize the peace of Europe.[46]

The news from Vienna was discouraging. The British ambassador reported that he and his French and Italian colleagues agreed that there was now no step which could be taken to stop the war against Serbia, to which the government was fully committed.[47] The Russian ambassador left a meeting with Berchtold 'white as chalk'.[48]

Everything seemed to confirm the validity of their fears. At the end of the day Berchtold instructed Szögyény to make it clear tomorrow to them in Berlin that Austria would not permit anything to stop its warlike operations in Serbia. The way to prevent a general European war was for Germany and Austria to warn St Petersburg—and perhaps Paris—that a continuation of the Russian mobilization would result in Austro-German counter-measures.[49]

Bethmann Hollweg's frustration with the Austrians was watered down considerably when his views were transmitted to them by Tschirschky on Wednesday. After presenting the suggestion that Austria confirm that it did not intend any territorial aggrandizement and that any military occupation of Serbian territory would only be temporary, the ambassador explained that this declaration was intended solely for the purpose of saddling Russia alone 'with the odium of having caused a world war'.[50] Otherwise, the blame might be laid at Austria's door.

Tschirschky assured Berchtold that Bethmann Hollweg wished to make it clear that he was not attempting to bring any pressure to bear on him. Nor did he wish to restrain Austria from acting against Serbia. He wanted only to improve the conditions under which they should fight a world war. Particularly with regard to public opinion in Britain it would be of great value to make it clear that if the war against Serbia was widened to include other Great Powers it would be Russia's fault, not Austria's.

★

At 7 p.m. in St Petersburg the German ambassador visited the Russian foreign minister for the third time that day. He brought with him Bethmann Hollweg's message warning that if Russia continued with its military preparations Germany would be compelled to mobilize, in which case it would take the offensive. Sazonov replied that this removed any doubts he might have had concerning the real cause of Austria's intransigence. Pourtalès jumped up from his seat and protested against 'this insulting assertion' (*cette assertion blessante*).[51]

Shortly afterwards the tsar rang Sazonov on the telephone to tell him that he had just received another telegram from the kaiser, this one containing a plea that he should not permit Russian military measures to jeopardize German efforts to promote a direct understanding between Russia and Austria. Sazonov summarized what the German ambassador had told him, which seemed to contradict the conciliatory message from the kaiser. They agreed that the tsar should wire Berlin immediately to ask for an explanation of the apparent discrepancy. At 8.20 p.m. the wire asking for clarification was sent. Trusting in his cousin's 'wisdom and friendship', Tsar Nicholas suggested that the 'Austro-Serbian problem' be handed over to the Hague conference.[52]

While the Russians were attempting to sort out just where the Germans stood Sazonov met with the minister for war and the chief of the general staff to discuss the military situation. News had been received from Vienna that the Austrians were preparing to announce a general mobilization the next day.[53] In St Petersburg they concluded that, as a war with Germany was now likely, they ought to prepare for it. As they could not undertake a partial mobilization without making it more difficult to undertake a general mobilization afterwards, they ought to begin a general mobilization immediately.

They reported their conclusions to the tsar by telephone. He authorized the general mobilization.

The tsar was not happy. He recorded in his diary that night: 'During the day we played tennis; the weather was magnificent. But the day was singularly unpeaceful. I was constantly being called to the telephone, now it was Sazonov, now Sukhomlinov or Yanushkevich.' And then there was the telegram from Wilhelm to deal with as well.[54]

The message announcing a general mobilization was drafted and ready to be sent out by 9 p.m. Then, just minutes before sending out the instructions to begin general mobilization, a personal messenger from the tsar arrived, instructing his officials to postpone it. The general mobilization was to be cancelled and the partial one reinstituted. The tsar wanted to hear how the kaiser would respond to his latest telegram before proceeding. 'Everything possible must be done to save the peace. I will not become responsible for a monstrous slaughter.'[55] Instead of a general mobilization, the order for a partial one went out at midnight.

Just after 10 p.m. the French military attaché, General Pierre de Laguiche, was informed by Russian military authorities that a general mobilization was about to be ordered. He was asked to inform Paris, but not to tell Paléologue of the decision until after midnight—because of the ambassador's reputation for indiscretion. But Paléologue learned of it anyway. At 11 p.m. the deputy director of the chancellery at the Russian Foreign Office, Nicholas-Alexandrovich Basily, arrived at the French embassy to tell him that Russia had decided to announce the mobilization of thirteen army corps against Austria-Hungary—and, secretly, to commence a general mobilization as well. Paléologue, who believed that French ciphers had been cracked by the Austrians, attempted to send a telegram to Paris from the Russian foreign ministry to inform them of the Russian decision. But this was intercepted by General Laguiche, who had since been told that the tsar had rescinded his instructions. Accordingly, Laguiche deleted the sentence saying that Russia was secretly beginning a general mobilization.[56]

Sazonov had already sent telegrams to Paris and London thanking the French for their promise of support and asking the British to join with their Entente partners in upholding the European balance of power. When Viviani received Sazonov's message late that night he was terrified that war was about to begin. He dashed to the residence of Messimy, the minister of war, and the two of them decided to go to the Elysée Palace, where—at 2 a.m.—they roused Poincaré, who was asleep in bed. The three of them drafted a message pleading with Russia not to take any step that could provide Germany with a pretext for mobilizing its forces.[57]

When they received the tsar's telegram in Berlin they decided that Pourtalès ought to approach Sazonov once again in order to clarify the German position. Sometime after midnight the ambassador managed to rouse Sazonov from his bed to continue their discussion. Would Russia not be satisfied with an Austrian assurance not to violate Serbia's integrity? Sazonov said it would not. When Pourtalès pressed him, he drew up a formula of conditions that would have to be met in order for Russia to cease its military preparations. They would have to wait until the next day to see whether Austria-Hungary might be willing to meet these conditions.

★

Pacifists, internationalists, and anti-militarists at last began to feel a sense of urgency as the signs of war became more evident. In Germany it was announced that both the *Landwehr* and *Landsturm* reserves were to be called up—including men up to 50 years old. The *Landsturm* had not been called up since the war with Napoleonic France in 1806. Bavarian soldiers who had been given leave to assist in bringing in the harvest were now ordered to return to their units. The call up of reservists in Austria-Hungary had almost brought the harvest to a standstill. The trains in France that night were filled with soldiers returning to their regiments: the 1st, 2nd, 6th, 7th, 20th, and 21st army corps were brought up to their full strength of 240,000 men. All airplane factories were placed under military protection. The wireless station at the Eiffel Tower was surrounded by a military guard.

The ships of Germany's Baltic Sea fleet returned to their base at Kiel in the morning. Cadets at the Russian naval school were, in the presence of the tsar himself, promoted to the rank of officers. The British First Fleet, running with lights extinguished, sailed past Dover during the night, heading to their war stations in the North Sea.

Could the movement against war stop this?

In Brussels, the Bureau of the International organized a mass demonstration against war that evening. At the Cirque Royale thousands of protesters gathered, singing the '*Internationale*' and applauding the delegates.

At the same time, the International Socialist Union was meeting there and condemned any and all moves in the direction of war as a capitalist conspiracy. Workers ought to refuse to fight. Crowds marched through the city shouting '*A bas la guerre*' and singing the '*Internationale*':[58]

Arise, ye workers from your slumber,
Arise, ye prisoners of want.
For reason in revolt now thunders,
And at last ends the age of cant!
Away with all your superstitions,
Servile masses, arise, arise!
We'll change henceforth the old tradition,
And spurn the dust to win the prize!
    So comrades, come rally,
    And the last fight let us face.
    The Internationale
    Unites the human race.
    So comrades, come rally,
    And the last fight let us face.
    The Internationale
    Unites the human race.

No more deluded by reaction,
On tyrants only we'll make war!
The soldiers too will take strike action,
They'll break ranks and fight no more!
And if those cannibals keep trying,
To sacrifice us to their pride,
They soon shall hear the bullets flying,
We'll shoot the generals on our own side.
    So comrades, come rally,
    And the last fight let us face.
    The Internationale
    Unites the human race.
    So comrades, come rally,
    And the last fight let us face.
    The Internationale
    Unites the human race.

No saviour from on high delivers,
No faith have we in prince or peer.
Our own right hand the chains must shiver,
Chains of hatred, greed and fear.
E'er the thieves will out with their booty,
And to all give a happier lot,
Each at his forge must do their duty,
And we'll strike the iron while it's hot.
    So comrades, come rally,
    And the last fight let us face.

The Internationale
Unites the human race.
So comrades, come rally,
And the last fight let us face.
The Internationale
Unites the human race.

Hugo Haase, chairman of the German Social Democratic Party, threw his arms around Jean Jaurès, leader of the French Socialist Party, signifying their unity against war.[59] And the Bureau agreed to move up the date for the next Congress to the 9th of August with 'war and the proletariat' to be placed at the top of the agenda. In Paris Gustave Hervé, a leading French syndicalist, wrote an anti-war article under the headline 'Neither Insurrection! Nor General Strike! DOWN WITH WAR.'[60]

In London eleven radicals within the Liberal Party's 'Foreign Affairs Group' met and agreed on a resolution to submit to Sir Edward Grey: that 'Great Britain in no conceivable circumstances should depart from a position of strict neutrality'.[61]

In Vienna Victor Adler, leader of the Social Democratic Workers' Party of Austria, reported that the war against Serbia was popular in Austria-Hungary and that the socialist movement could do little to stop it.

The sentiments of international socialism were about to be put to the test. The Austrian shelling of Belgrade began at 11 p.m. that night and continued for hours.

Day Seven

Thursday, 30 July

The shelling of Belgrade that began on the evening of the 29th ceased at 3 a.m. The respite was brief: the shelling resumed at 6 a.m. No casualties were reported from Serbia, but two people were found dead in Germany. Eugen Bieber, the head of the M. & J. Bieber bank of Potsdam, was discovered alongside his wife in a Berlin hotel room that morning. Having already lost a fortune because of the war crisis, they had poisoned themselves. The appearance of a German reconnaissance balloon above the site of the 1870 Franco-Prussian battle of Gravelotte caused a panic in towns and cities near the German frontier: the banks in Nancy were besieged by thousands of depositors, desperately trying to withdraw their money. In Paris, business almost came to a standstill because of the absence of cash: cafés posted notices that they were unable to cash bank notes—even for as little as 50 francs. A large grocery store was overrun when it opened in the morning by customers determined to purchase pasta, rice, and whatever preserved food they could lay their hands on. A crowd of hundreds gathered at the Banque de France, trying to exchange bank notes for gold. The London stock exchange was the only one in Europe open for business on Thursday morning.

Before the day dawned, Chancellor Bethmann Hollweg had already despatched a series of telegrams to Germany's ambassadors in London, St Petersburg, and Vienna. He assured Sir Edward Grey that Germany was continuing to mediate in Vienna and was advising acceptance of his proposal for a mediation *à quatre* to resolve the crisis. He assured Sazonov that Germany was willing to mediate, but would continue to do so only if Russia suspended its 'unfriendly actions' against Austria. The telegram he sent to Tschirschky in Vienna was marked urgent—and it was threatening.[1]

Bethmann Hollweg sent Tschirschky a copy of Lichnowsky's telegram recounting yesterday's conversation with Grey. The chancellor had concluded from Grey's warning that, if Austria were to refuse mediation, Germany and Austria would soon find themselves at war with Russia, France, and Britain. And it looked as if neither their Italian nor their Romanian allies would come to their assistance.[2] In this scenario, the burden of the fighting would fall mainly upon Germany, thanks to Britain aligning itself with Russia and France.

Bethmann Hollweg argued that Austria's political prestige and its military honour could be amply satisfied by an occupation of Belgrade. Austria now had the opportunity to enhance its status in the Balkans while strengthening itself against Russia through the humiliation of Serbia. He therefore suggested 'urgently and emphatically' that Austria accept mediation under the conditions proposed.[3] The consequences of a refusal, he warned, would be heavy to bear.

The chancellor was shocked to be told by Germany's ambassador in St Petersburg that Austria had declined to discuss the situation with Russia. He immediately drafted a second telegram to Tschirschky: there seemed to be some misunderstanding and he wanted it cleared up. An Austrian refusal to exchange ideas with Russia would provoke their armed intervention, which would be a mistake. It was in Austria's interest to prevent it. While Germany was prepared to fulfil the obligations of its alliance with Austria, it would decline 'to be drawn wantonly into a world conflagration by Vienna'.[4] And, as if that were not enough, Vienna appeared to be still disregarding Germany's advice in regard to the question of compensation for Italy. Tschirschky was instructed to speak at once to Berchtold and impress upon him the great seriousness of the situation.

Bethmann Hollweg's insistence that Austria negotiate directly with Russia and his support for the conference à quatre meant that a diplomatic solution to the crisis was now within sight. Confusing and contradictory reports concerning Russia's military preparations continued to complicate matters. At 1.45 a.m. Thursday the tsar's latest message was received at the kaiser's Neue Palais in Potsdam. Attempting to reassure Wilhelm that nothing new or radical was taking place in Russia, Nicholas explained that the military measures now being undertaken had been decided upon five days ago—and only as a defence against Austria's preparations. 'I hope from all my heart that these measures won't in any way interfere with your part as mediator which I greatly value.'[5] Russia, he said, needed the kaiser to exert pressure on Austria to come to an understanding.

Wilhelm instantly erupted. He was shocked to discover first thing on Thursday morning that the 'military measures which have now come into force were decided five days ago'. He construed this to mean that these measures had begun then, giving Russia a head-start of a week on Germany. He dismissed the tsar's logic: Austria had undertaken only a partial mobilization—against Serbia, and only in the south. How could the tsar claim to be acting defensively when Austria was neither threatening nor preparing to attack Russia?

The kaiser would no longer put any pressure on Austria: 'I cannot agree to any more mediation.' The tsar, while requesting mediation, 'has at the same time secretly mobilized behind my back.' The Russians were merely manoeuvring, attempting to hold the Germans back while they gained the advantage. 'My work is at an end!'[6]

Things quickly got worse. At 6 a.m. that morning Bethmann Hollweg despatched a messenger to Potsdam with a copy of yesterday's telegram from St Petersburg announcing that Russia's partial mobilization had begun. The Russian ambassador in Berlin confirmed that the military districts of Kiev, Kazan, Odessa, and Moscow were mobilizing—although he insisted that this did not mean war or even the breaking off of diplomatic relations with Austria.

By 7 a.m. the kaiser had read and commented on this additional information. 'According to this', he complained, the tsar 'has simply been tricking us with his appeal for my assistance'. He believed that the deception was deliberate: the tsar was asking for the kaiser's help at the same time that he was mobilizing his forces. Russia's mobilization had not begun yesterday, on the 29th, but on the 24th. Thus, the measures were already in full swing when the tsar had begged him by telegram to mediate: 'he simply lied to me'. The tsar's diplomacy was no more than a childish manoeuvre to lure Germany into the mire. Instead of awaiting the results of the kaiser's mediation, the tsar had mobilized behind his back. Now 'I must mobilize too!'[7]

Was all hope of peace now lost? Along with the reports from his chancellor on Thursday morning the kaiser received and commented (in English) upon a newspaper clipping from the British *Morning Post* entitled 'Efforts towards Peace'. After reading it Wilhelm concluded that the only way left to avoid war was for the British to tell their French and Russian allies 'to remain quiet, i.e. neutral'. If they were to do so, Germany could also remain quiet. But if Britain 'continues to remain silent or to give lukewarm assurances of neutrality' this would encourage its allies to attack 'Austro-Germany'. Catastrophe could be prevented only if the British intimated to their allies that they could not count on their help: 'That would put a stop to all war.'

The messages received in Berlin from London were mixed. On the one hand, Prince Heinrich had conveyed his belief that King George intended Britain to remain neutral. On the other hand Sir Edward Grey—in a private conversation with Prince Lichnowsky—had indicated that if Germany made war on France, Britain would immediately attack Germany with its fleet. 'Consequently Sir E. Grey says the direct contrary to what his Sovereign communicated to me through my brother and places his King in the position of a double-tongued liar.'[8]

Wilhelm went even further: 'The whole war is plainly arranged between England, France and Russia for the annihilation of Germany, lastly through the conversations with Poincaré in Paris and Petersburg, and the Austro-Serbian strife is only an excuse to fall upon us! God help us in this fight for our existence, brought about by falseness, lies and poisonous envy!'

The kaiser was not alone in his pessimism. By mid-morning his chancellor drafted a telegram to the German minister in Stockholm telling him that he had reason to assume 'that England will very soon take part in the war on the side of the Dual Alliance'.[9] His gloomy impression was corroborated by the Italian foreign minister. On Thursday morning the German ambassador in Rome reported that San Giuliano was insistent that 'at the outbreak of a general European war England will take part in the war on the side of Russia and France'.[10]

In fact, no decision had been reached in London. The cabinet had yet to discuss the issue of how it would proceed if the war widened beyond one between Austria-Hungary and Serbia. Before that decision was made Grey had to decide how to respond to Bethmann Hollweg's proposal of the day before that Britain should agree to remain neutral if Germany promised to respect the territorial integrity of France in Europe.

The assistant under-secretary of state and head of the western and eastern departments at the Foreign Office drew a clear and straightforward conclusion from the proposal. Eyre Crowe said only one comment was necessary on these 'astounding proposals': they reflected discredit on the statesman who made them. He thought it was interesting, however, that Germany practically admitted its intention to violate Belgian neutrality. 'It is clear that Germany is practically determined to go to war, and that the one restraining influence so far has been the fear of England joining in the defence of France and Belgium.'[11] Grey, who received the telegram and Crowe's comments on it on Thursday morning, would spend most of the working day contemplating and composing his response to Bethmann Hollweg.

★

In Vienna, Berchtold was grappling with Bethmann Hollweg's other initiative. The chancellor's telegram to his ambassador instructing him to insist that Austria agree to engage in direct negotiations with the Russians was brought to Tschirschky while he was having breakfast with Berchtold. The Austrian foreign minister sat 'pale and silent' while the ambassador read aloud—twice—the chancellor's message.

Tschirschky emphasized the point made by Bethmann Hollweg, that Austria's claims against Serbia, with guarantees of its good behaviour in the future as part of the mediation proposal, meant that Austria's aims 'would be attained without unleashing a world war'. Under these circumstances to refuse mediation completely 'was out of the question'. The occupation of Serbian territory by Austrian troops would satisfy its military honour. That such a military occupation would proceed with the express consent of Russia would unquestionably mean a strengthening of Austria's position in the Balkans. Refusing mediation now would have 'incalculable consequences'.[12]

Berchtold had to excuse himself from the meeting with Tschirschky in order to dress for an audience with the emperor. Franz Joseph was returning to Vienna from Ischl. When he made the journey in an open carriage from the railway station to Schönbrunn Palace at midday he was cheered by thousands who lined the route.

After his meeting with the emperor that afternoon, Berchtold undertook to explain that his apparent rejection of mediation talks was all an unfortunate misunderstanding. He instructed Szápáry, the ambassador in St Petersburg, to explain to Sazonov that his position must have been misunderstood. Berchtold was, in fact, prepared to explain the points made in the Austrian note to Serbia. Moreover, he would very much like to discuss 'amicably and confidentially' all of those questions that directly affected Austro-Russian relations.[13] Szápáry was to ask Sazonov—as if the question came from the ambassador—what subjects the foreign minister wished to include in such a discussion, and to indicate his willingness to engage in such a discussion.

While Szápáry was pursuing this initiative in St Petersburg, Berchtold met with the Russian ambassador in Vienna and explained the 'misunderstanding' to him. He suggested that Sazonov had misinterpreted his conversation with Schebeko on Tuesday the 28th to mean that the Austrian foreign minister was flatly refusing Sazonov's proposal that they exchange views. He now informed the ambassador that he had instructed Szápáry to engage in such an exchange in St Petersburg and reminded Schebeko that the two of them had, in fact, already discussed the questions at issue for three-quarters of an hour on Tuesday. On the other hand, while a friendly discussion of all the issues was desirable, there could be no question of Austria yielding on any of the points contained in the note to Serbia.[14]

Until his meeting with Berchtold Thursday afternoon, Schebeko had become progressively more pessimistic. In fact, after hearing rumours that the Russian mobilization might lead to a declaration of war on them by Austria, he had begun that morning to make preparations for himself and the embassy staff to leave Vienna and return to St Petersburg. But Berchtold's sudden and unexpected willingness to engage in further discussions encouraged him. He explained that the Russian government could not help but view the situation anxiously because they did not know what Austria's intentions were. Did they intend to deprive Serbia of its sovereignty? Overthrow the regime? Crush the kingdom altogether? Although Russia could not remain indifferent to Serbia's fate, it had brought all possible pressure to bear on Belgrade to accept the demands made by Austria.

To these arguments Berchtold gave his usual response: Austria was neither pursuing a policy of conquest in Serbia, nor attempting to deprive it of its sovereignty. All that Austria was seeking was to establish a state of things that would provide guarantees against Serbian agitation aimed at the monarchy. And he complained that Russia's mobilization in the four military districts of Odessa, Kiev, Moscow, and Kazan was a move of a hostile character against Austria—in spite of the fact that Austria had mobilized only against Serbia, as demonstrated by the fact that the 1st, 10th, and 11th army corps had not been mobilized. Now the Russian move would force Austria to respond by extending its mobilization to Galicia.

In spite of Berchtold's warning of further military steps, Schebeko told the British and French ambassadors that their meeting had been friendly. In fact, he was encouraged by Austria's willingness to engage in discussions at St Petersburg. Although Russia must be assured that Serbia would not be crushed, it understood that Austria was compelled to exact from Serbia

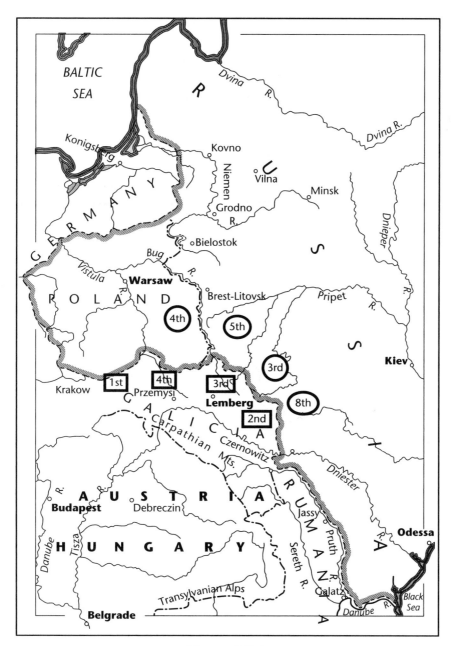

Map 5. Galicia

measures that would secure its Slav provinces against hostile propaganda emanating from Serbia.[15]

Austria and Serbia had now been at war since Tuesday. On Wednesday, Russia had decided to mobilize its forces in four military districts. Today, Austria was preparing to respond by announcing a general mobilization. But, in spite of these developments, a negotiated settlement now appeared to be within reach. Austria had agreed—at the prompting of Germany—to renew discussions in St Petersburg.

Shortly before noon Russia's partial mobilization was announced in St Petersburg. The Austrian ambassador had already assured Berchtold that when the announcement was made it would only be a bluff. Sazonov, he said, dreaded war 'as much as his Imperial Master', but he was apparently attempting 'to deprive us of the fruits of our Serbian campaign without going to Serbia's aid if possible'.[16] Count Szápáry believed that the tsar had been won over to mobilization only by the argument that it would enable Russia to secure its interests without going to war.

News of Russia's partial mobilization—and that it was aimed at them— was kept secret from the people of Austria-Hungary. The government chose to keep it out of the newspapers, which had been carefully censored since the assassination of the archduke.

★

Was Russia really bluffing? Was there any possibility, with the ongoing bombardment of Belgrade and the Austrian preparations for an invasion, that a general war could still be avoided? Was Russia's partial mobilization a diplomatic move or a military manoeuvre that meant the march to war had begun?

Peaceful signs emanating from Berlin were encouraging. Bethmann Hollweg had instructed Tschirschky in Vienna to push the Austrians to agree to discussions with the Russians in St Petersburg. He had informed Lichnowsky in London that he was urging Vienna to accept Grey's renewed proposal for the mediation *à quatre*. He had directed Pourtalès in St Petersburg to reassure Sazonov that Germany was continuing to mediate.

Bethmann Hollweg arranged to meet with the minister of war (Falkenhayn) and the secretary of state for the navy (Tirpitz) at 1 p.m. to discuss their response to Russia's announcement of the partial mobilization. When the chief of the general staff got wind of the meeting he showed up, uninvited. Moltke's officials were insisting that Germany must seize the initiative, that Russia was gaining a critical advantage by mobilizing first. Sometime during the day news was received from Warsaw that 'Russia is already fully in a state of preparation for war'.[17] The German consul there reported that Russian troops were assembling against Germany along the Niemen. Nevertheless, the chancellor was able to convince the chief of the general staff to support his diplomatic initiatives.

When Moltke met with the recently arrived representative of the Austrian general staff, General Fleischmann, he reiterated that Germany would not mobilize in response to Russia's partial mobilization. Germany would mobilize only if war broke out between Austria-Hungary and Russia. Why? Because a German mobilization would mean war. And he urged Austria not to declare war, but to wait for Russia to do so in order 'to avoid producing any appearance of an aggressive move on our part in the eyes of Europe'.[18] Moltke assured him that if Russia were to declare war Britain would refuse to cooperate with the Entente.

But now another danger loomed. If Russia simply mobilized and then waited—as Sazonov was saying was its intention—Austria might commit itself fully to the war against Serbia in the south. This would mean that the Austrians would be unable to fulfil their role of taking the offensive against Russia in Poland while Germany vanquished France in the west. Germany's strategic plan was to maintain only a minimal defensive force in the east— but if Russia did not have to defend itself against an Austrian attack it would be free to launch a massive offensive against Germany. The general staff calculated that they would need six weeks to defeat France in the west, during which time they could afford only to keep the Eighth Army in the east to defend against Russia.

Moltke began to panic. Early in the afternoon he asked the Austrians to tell him what they intended to do. A few hours later he pleaded with them to mobilize fully against Russia, and to announce this in a public proclamation. Austria should immediately promise compensation to Italy to keep it on the side of the Triple Alliance—and Austria should leave no troops on the frontier with Italy. The only way to preserve Austria-Hungary was to endure (*durchhalten*) a European war. 'Germany is with you unconditionally.'[19] Moltke then decided to contact Conrad directly, pressing him to mobilize immediately against Russia and promising that Germany would then do the same.

Meanwhile, the chancellor was meeting with the Prussian cabinet and warning them that even though all governments involved wanted peace

they were beginning to lose control of the situation and that the 'stone had
started to roll'. But he was not giving up. Peace could still be preserved.
Vienna might agree with his *démarche* and consent to negotiate with Russia.
But if it came to war the mood in Germany was good and they need not fear
the opposition of the Social Democrats. 'A general strike . . . or sabotage
were out of the question.'[20]

After the meeting that evening Bethmann Hollweg met with Moltke and
Falkenhayn. But by now Moltke had reversed his position from earlier in
the day, insisting that Germany must begin to mobilize no later than midday
on Friday. He was in favour of war: 'His changes of mood are hardly
explicable, or not at all.'[21] Bethmann Hollweg resisted: he and his officials
at the Foreign Office—Jagow and Zimmermann—'apparently still hope for a
miracle'. But Moltke and Falkenhayn apparently convinced him that the
mobilization announcement had to be made no later than midday tomorrow.

Around midnight Moltke called in his personal adjutant, Major-General
Hans von Haeften, and instructed him to draft a declaration to be made
by the kaiser to the German people announcing mobilization. He now
believed that Germany must mobilize immediately—even if Russia did
not—or Germany would find itself entering the war in the worst possible
circumstances. 'This war will turn into a world war in which England will
also intervene. Few can have an idea of the extent, the duration and the end
of this war. Nobody today can have a notion of how it will all end.'[22]
Haeften concluded that his boss was now suffering from serious psycho-
logical turmoil.

The Austrian ambassador in Berlin was dismayed. Whereas the Germans
had appeared calm about the possibility of a European war, now they
seemed to have been seized 'by an attack of nerves'.[23] It seemed to Szögyény that the reason for the change in mood was their worry about Italy:
that, if the Triple Alliance was not to act as a solid block, it would seriously
impair their chances of success in a European war. He urged Berchtold to be
as 'generous as possible' in meeting Italy's wishes and to begin negotiations
on compensation immediately. Although there was no reason to doubt
Germany's loyalty to Austria-Hungary, they 'absolutely' needed Italy on
their side in the event of a general war.

★

Sir Edward Grey certainly believed that peace now had a chance. On
Wednesday he had suggested that if the Austrians were to 'halt in Belgrade'

this would enable a mediation to take place that could prevent the conflict from escalating. Nothing—not even Bethmann Hollweg's 'astonishing' proposal for British neutrality—had crushed his hopes. Prince Lichnowsky, who had preached moderation and mediation from the beginning of the crisis, immediately upon receiving his latest instructions from Bethmann Hollweg sent a letter to Grey notifying him of Germany's support for his mediation proposal.

But would the kaiser, given his reactions that morning to the news from Russia and Britain, be willing to endorse these moves by his chancellor? He had already lashed out in anger at Russia's decision to mobilize in the four military districts, declaring that his mediation efforts were now 'at an end'. And he was furious with the British for their duplicity in offering neutrality on the one hand while preparing to attack Germany on the other. Shortly before noon on Thursday, Bethmann Hollweg attempted to steer Wilhelm back onto the path of mediation. He sent, via automobile from the Wilhelmstrasse to Potsdam, a copy of yesterday's telegram from Lichnowsky in London, along with a brief report on his own moves to insist that the Austrians negotiate with the Russians. He told the kaiser that he had submitted Grey's proposals for mediation to Berchtold 'for his serious consideration'. Personally, he believed that if Britain were prepared to act vigorously to secure the results Austria sought, the Austrians could be satisfied.

Bethmann Hollweg's efforts exploded in his face. When the kaiser received the copy of Lichnowsky's account of his interview with Grey of the day before, he again erupted. He angrily denounced Grey's diplomacy as 'the worst and most scandalous piece of English pharisaism that I ever saw! I will never enter into a naval convention with such scoundrels.' Instead of mediation, 'a serious word to Petersburg and Paris, to the effect that England would not help them would quiet the situation at once'. Grey was no more than a 'common cheat!!' (*Der gemeine Täuscher*). His suggestion that Britain might be forced to intervene were the war to widen to include Germany and France meant that Germany was supposed 'to leave Austria in the lurch as if we were common as dirt'. The idea was 'thoroughly English'. Grey's assurances that he did not intend to threaten Germany really meant that 'they will attack us'. The British foreign secretary, he bitterly complained, had demonstrated his bad faith for years now.[24]

By Thursday afternoon the kaiser concluded that Britain was at last showing its true colours. 'That common crew of shopkeepers has tried to

trick us with dinners and speeches.' Grey had proved his own king to be a
liar and he had spoken to Lichnowsky in the way that he had because he had
a guilty conscience for having deceived them. What Grey was aiming at was
to combine a threat and a bluff in an attempt to separate Germany from
Austria and to stop Germany from mobilizing its forces against Russia.
Instead of quieting things by issuing a sharp warning to Paris and St
Petersburg, Grey had chosen to threaten Germany. 'Common cur!' Britain
alone, the kaiser warned, would now bear the responsibility for peace or
war. That ought to be made clear to the world.[25]

Bethmann Hollweg's mediation initiative seemed doomed by the kaiser's
reaction. Had the copy of Lichnowsky's telegram not been doctored before
it was sent to him his reaction might have been even more extreme.
Removed from the telegram were the words that Germany 'had already
accepted in principle' Grey's proposal for a mediation *à quatre*. The chancellor had anticipated some difficulty with the kaiser, but the extent of his
anger went beyond what he might have expected. Dismissing Grey and Tsar
Nicholas as duplicitous liars might mean the end of any attempt to negotiate
a settlement without a general European war.

Bethmann Hollweg begged the kaiser not to abandon his role as mediator
between Austria and Russia. He drafted a reply to the tsar's latest telegram
for Wilhelm's consideration. If the kaiser agreed, this would make it clear
that there was no discrepancy between his efforts to mediate a settlement
and the strong language that had been used by Count Pourtalès, which was
meant only to draw attention to the dangers of serious consequences arising
from a Russian mobilization. If Russia now mobilized against Austria—who
had mobilized only against Serbia—then the kaiser's role of mediator
(undertaken at the tsar's request) 'will be endangered, if not made impossible'. Bethmann Hollweg pleaded with the kaiser to recognize that, as this
telegram would be a particularly important document 'historically', he
ought not to express in it the fact that his role as mediator had now ended.[26]

The kaiser accepted the chancellor's advice. That afternoon he replied to
the tsar in a telegram that Wilhelm drafted himself—in English. It closely
followed Bethmann Hollweg's suggestions. The essential point was that if
Russia mobilized against Austria, the kaiser's role as mediator would be
'endangered if not ruined'. His final words, however, were starker and more
dramatic: 'The whole weight of the decision lies solely on you[r] shoulders
now, who have to bear the responsibility for peace or war.'[27]

Everything now seemed to hinge on the Russian mobilization. At Bethmann Hollweg's insistence, Berchtold had agreed to resume the bilateral discussions with Sazonov in St Petersburg. But, given the kaiser's outrage at what he regarded as the misleading efforts of the Russians to gain a military advantage over Germany, the proposed discussions might fail before they began.

Although Wilhelm was equally furious with the British, he nevertheless authorized another diplomatic effort through his brother. Prince Heinrich, now in Berlin and meeting with the kaiser in person, drafted a telegram that he proposed to send to King George. He would begin by assuring the king that the kaiser was trying his utmost to fulfil the tsar's appeal to him to work to maintain peace. He proposed to warn the king that Russia's military measures—now confirmed to have begun five days ago—combined with French preparations, might force Germany to respond in kind. If Russia and France continued with their military steps it might 'mean a European war'. If George really wanted to prevent this terrible disaster, he ought to use his influence to keep France and Russia out of the conflict between Austria-Hungary and Serbia. This was perhaps the only chance of maintaining the peace of Europe. Wilhelm, he assured him, was most sincerely endeavouring to maintain peace, but the military preparations of Germany's two neighbours might force him to follow their example for the safety of his own country, 'which otherwise would remain defenceless'.[28]

The kaiser approved the draft and it was despatched that afternoon.

★

If Wilhelm and Heinrich genuinely believed that their cousin, King George, was in a position to direct, or even influence, British diplomacy in the crisis, they were badly mistaken. Sir Edward Grey continued to direct policy. And by Thursday afternoon—at the time that Wilhelm and Heinrich were in the process of sending the telegram to King George—he had prepared his reply to Bethmann Hollweg's proposal of the day before that Britain should promise to remain neutral in a European war.

Grey was blunt: the proposal 'that we should bind ourselves to neutrality on such terms cannot for a moment be entertained'. Bethmann Hollweg was asking that Britain should stand by while French colonies were taken and France was beaten in exchange for Germany's promise that it would refrain from taking French territory in Europe. Such a proposal was unacceptable, 'for France could be so crushed as to lose her position as a Great Power, and become subordinate to German policy'. Besides, for Britain to make such a bargain with Germany at the expense of France 'would be a disgrace from which the good name of this country would never recover'.[29]

Nor would Grey bargain away Britain's obligation to uphold Belgian neutrality.

Grey refused to consider the possible advantages of a general neutrality agreement with Germany in the future in return for tying Britain's hands now. 'We must preserve our full freedom to act as circumstances may seem to us to require.' Instead, he asserted that the only way to maintain good relations between Britain and Germany was for them to work together now in preserving the peace of Europe. If they succeeded in this, their relations would *ipso facto* be improved and strengthened.

If the current crisis passed and the peace of Europe was preserved, Grey promised to endeavour to promote some arrangement by which Germany could be assured 'that no hostile or aggressive policy would be pursued against her or her allies by France, Russia, and ourselves, jointly or separately'. This was what he had desired and worked for during the last Balkan crisis—and Anglo-German relations had improved as a result. 'The idea has hitherto been too Utopian to form the subject of definite proposals, but if this present crisis, so much more acute than any that Europe has had for generations, be safely passed, I am hopeful that the reaction and relief that will follow may make some more definite *rapprochement* between the powers possible than was possible before.'[30]

By late Thursday afternoon Grey and Bethmann Hollweg had traded promises of a new, friendlier relationship in the future—if they could find a way of avoiding a cataclysm. Each proposed a different formula for attaining it: Bethmann Hollweg wanted a promise of British neutrality in the event of a continent-wide war; Grey wanted Germany to promote a mediated settlement that would limit a conflict to the one already under way between Austria and Serbia.

Although he rejected Bethmann Hollweg's proposal, Grey rejected Eyre Crowe's conclusion that it proved Germany was determined to go to war. He still believed that he had German support for his 'halt in Belgrade' proposal: on Thursday afternoon, Lichnowsky assured him that Germany would endeavour to influence Austria not to advance beyond Belgrade and the frontier region. The Powers could then endeavour to arrange for Serbia to give satisfaction sufficient to pacify Austria.

Grey believed Russia to be the key to any such arrangement. He feared that the proposed arrangement might not meet the formula that Sazonov had drawn up at his meeting with the German ambassador at 2 a.m. that morning: 'If Austria, recognizing that her conflict with Servia has assumed the character of a question of European interest, declares her willingness to eliminate from her ultimatum points which violate [the] principle of Serbian sovereignty, Russia engages to stop all military preparations.'[31] Grey instructed Buchanan in St Petersburg to urge Sazonov to modify his terms: the Powers would examine how Serbia could 'fully satisfy' Austria without impairing its 'sovereign rights or independence'. If Russia accepted this formula, and if Austria agreed to cease its advance further into Serbian territory while a settlement was worked out, he hoped that Russia would suspend further military preparations—provided the other Powers did the same. 'It is a slender chance of preserving peace, but the only one I can suggest.'[32]

Grey tried to enlist French support to persuade the Russians. In London, Paul Cambon seemed disposed to recommend the arrangement to Paris, but he raised the possibility that German military preparations were a prelude to aggression against France. He predicted that Germany might demand that France should cease its military preparations or that it promise to remain neutral in a war between Germany and Russia. France could not agree to either of these demands, and Cambon asked Grey what Britain would do in such circumstances. He reminded Grey of the promise the foreign secretary had given him in 1912, that the two of them would discuss what Britain and France would do together if the peace of Europe was seriously threatened. Grey promised to raise the issue at the cabinet meeting scheduled for tomorrow morning and to meet with him afterwards.[33]

In Paris that morning the French had already attempted to restrain the Russians. On Wednesday evening Izvol'skii had explained to Viviani that Russia had decided to expedite her military preparations because of Austria's mobilization of eight army corps and its continuing refusal to settle its differences peacefully with Serbia. Russia was counting on the support of its French ally and hoped that the British would join the two of them. At 7 a.m. Thursday Viviani responded: France was resolved 'to fulfil all the obligations of its alliance'.[34] France would not neglect any opportunity to solve the crisis peacefully, however, and he urged Russia to do nothing that might offer Germany a pretext for either the total or even the partial mobilization of its forces.

Shortly afterwards Poincaré convened a meeting of the French cabinet. The mood was sombre. They agreed that—for the sake of public opinion— they must take care that 'the Germans put themselves in the wrong'.[35] They agreed to avoid the appearance of mobilizing French forces, but consented to at least some of the requests being made by the army. Covering troops— the *couverture*—could take up their positions along the German frontier from Luxembourg to the Vosges mountains, but were not to approach closer than 10 kilometres. No train transport was to be used, no reservists were to be called up, no horses or vehicles were to be requisitioned. The chief of the general staff was not pleased with the decision.

★

General Joseph Joffre, a veteran of the Franco-Prussian war, had been appointed chief of staff three years earlier. The son of a barrel-maker in the Pyrenees, Joffre had risen from his humble beginnings to graduate from the prestigious École Polytechnique. From 1911 on he had worked assiduously to reform French military planning to conform with the doctrine of the offensive. He dismissed the idea of the counter-offensive, enshrined in the army's Plan XVI, as outdated. He convinced his Russian counterpart to make specific plans for taking the offensive in the east against Germany by the sixteenth day of mobilization. At a minimum the Russian offensive should tie down five to six German army corps. He also planned on the assistance of the British Expeditionary Force, assuming that Germany might attack through Belgium. By 1912 he had gone as far as proposing a plan by which France would violate Belgian neutrality in the event of war with Germany. The Quai d'Orsay had argued against this, however, insisting that the French army could move into Belgium only once Germany had violated its neutrality, and Poincaré had refused to agree to Joffre's proposal. Nevertheless, in his new plan—XVII—Joffre still envisioned taking the offensive by attacking Germany through Lorraine.[36]

The cabinet's decision to create a 10-kilometre buffer zone and to take only hesitant steps in the direction of mobilization frustrated Joffre. These measures would make it difficult to execute the offensive thrust of Plan XVII. Nevertheless, the orders went out at 4.55 p.m.

Poincaré was not hopeful that the Austrians would accept Sazonov's promise to halt the Russian mobilization in exchange for their promise to respect Serbian sovereignty and to submit those articles of their note that Serbia had not accepted to an international discussion. As Poincaré saw it,

Joseph Joffre (1852–1931); commander-in-chief of army of France (1911–16)

the preservation of peace was now in the hands of the British. If they would only declare that in the event of a conflict between Germany and France they would come to the aid of France 'there would be no war' because Germany would modify its attitude at once.[37] When the British ambassador tried to explain how difficult it would be for the British government to take such a position, Poincaré insisted that it would be in the interests of peace. France was pacific and did not wish to go to war, but had to make preparations to mobilize so as not to be taken unawares. He had received reports that German troops were already concentrated around Thionville and Metz and were ready for war. If a continental war were to erupt, Britain would inevitably become involved in order to protect its vital interests—

whereas a declaration of intent to support France now would almost certainly deter Germany from embarking on the path to war.

In Berlin, Jules Cambon was growing increasingly pessimistic about the prospect of a mediated settlement. When he met with Jagow in the afternoon, he asked him how he planned to reply to Grey's renewed proposal for a conference à quatre. The secretary of state replied that in order 'to gain time' he had asked Austria to tell him directly on what terms they were prepared to open discussions.[38] Cambon dismissed this as a mere ploy to eliminate Britain, France, and Italy from the negotiations and instead to entrust Tschirschky—whose pan-German sentiments were well known—with the responsibility of persuading Vienna to adopt a conciliatory attitude. Moreover, Jagow now seemed to be backing down from his earlier pledge that Germany would mobilize only if Russia mobilized along the German frontier. Even though he recognized that Russia was not yet doing this, Jagow warned that Germany might have to take military measures because the heads of the army were insisting on it. Besides, he said, the words he had used when promising that Germany would not mobilize in response to a partial Russian mobilization did not constitute a firm engagement on his part. Cambon concluded that 'the chances of peace have again decreased'.[39]

From London, Lichnowsky was continuing to do what he could to convince Berlin of the merits of Grey's mediation proposal. Perhaps it could be made more attractive if they were to convene somewhere other than London? He suggested that Bethmann Hollweg consider Berlin as the location. Besides, the Austrian ambassador in London, Count Mensdorff, was 'too timid and lacked influence at Vienna'.[40]

By evening there was confusion everywhere. Bethmann Hollweg had pushed the Austrians to reverse their stand against the direct 'bilateral' discussions with the Russians in St Petersburg; Berchtold had reluctantly restarted them; Lichnowsky had assured Grey that Germany would promote his latest proposal for an ambassadorial conference—while advising his government to consider holding it in Berlin rather than London; Sazonov had laid down the formula he required the Austrians to meet—that the sovereignty and independence of Serbia must be upheld—if Russia was to reverse its mobilization order; Grey had continued to refuse to commit Britain to either stand aside and remain neutral in a European war, or to reassure its Entente partners that it would stand with them.

Moreover, no one was quite certain who was undertaking exactly what military measures. In the middle of the day in Berlin, news that Germany's mobilization had begun was reported by the *Lokal Anzeiger*—but then this was immediately denied by the government. In St Petersburg, Sazonov was convinced that Germany had begun naval preparations for an attack on Russia in the Baltic. The chief of the German general staff encouraged the chief of the Austrian general staff to produce his plans for full mobilization of the Austro-Hungarian armies by the end of the day.

Could Bethmann Hollweg convince Wilhelm to continue 'mediating' the dispute, or would the kaiser's fury at what he regarded as Russian duplicity convince him to mobilize against Russia? Would the Austrians accept the proposed 'halt in Belgrade' and agree to a conference to impose terms on Serbia? Would the Russians be influenced by French warnings not to give the Germans any pretext for mobilizing? Would the British come down clearly on the side of either remaining neutral in a European war or committing themselves to join in on the side of Russia and France?

In St Petersburg Sazonov, the war minister, and the chief of the general staff all worried that the tsar's change of heart on the general mobilization would put Russia in peril. Sukhomlinov and Yanushkevich tried to persuade Nicholas over the telephone that partial mobilization was a mistake. The tsar refused to budge. He did agree to allow Sazonov to present the case to him in person later that afternoon—but he claimed to be too busy to meet with Krivoshein, who hoped that Sazonov would succeed in changing the tsar's mind because otherwise 'we should be marching towards a certain catastrophe'.[41]

When Sazonov met with the tsar at Peterhof at 3 p.m. he argued that general mobilization was essential because war was almost inevitable. The Germans, he said, were resolved to bring it about—otherwise they would not have rejected the various proposals for a peaceful solution; they could easily have made the Austrians see reason. Irritated and distraught, the tsar eventually gave way to Sazonov's arguments. An hour later the foreign minister telephoned the chief of staff that the tsar had authorized a general mobilization. At 5 p.m. the official decree was sent out.

★

Bethmann Hollweg convened a meeting of the Prussian state council on Thursday afternoon at which he attempted to clarify where things stood. The situation, he told his ministers, was changing from hour to hour and the outcome of the crisis remained uncertain. He explained that the kaiser had been attempting to mediate between Russia and Austria, thus far without success. It was of the greatest importance to put Russia in the position of being the guilty party—and the way to accomplish this was to have Austria issue a declaration that would render the Russian position absurd. Unfortunately, this was complicated by the fact that the Serbs had consented to almost all of the Austrian demands except in unimportant points. At the same time, the kaiser and the tsar were corresponding directly with one another, but thus far this had failed to reach any conclusion. Britain and Germany had taken 'all possible steps to avoid a European war'.[42] He did not inform them of the bargain he had proposed to Grey for British neutrality in a war between Germany and France.

On the issue of mobilization, Bethmann Hollweg explained that the kaiser had decided they should wait for Vienna's decision concerning the British and German proposals before taking any step. A declaration of 'threatening danger of war' (*drohenden Kriegsgefahr*) was tantamount to mobilization—and mobilization would mean war.

The chancellor dismissed any hope that they could count on the British, who would probably take the side of the Franco-Russian alliance. The attitude of the Italians was unclear, but they regarded the war as threatening their interests in the Balkans. He had tried—unsuccessfully, thus far—to persuade Austria to come to an understanding with them, but Austria was uncompromising. Romania could not be counted on for support, nor could Bulgaria. The outlook was bleak.

Bethmann Hollweg maintained that while each of the governments involved, including that of Russia, were peaceable themselves, they were losing control of the situation. The stone had started rolling and would be difficult to stop. He would not give up hope, however, and he promised to continue his efforts to maintain peace. He would wait to see what Vienna would make of his recent *démarche*. The public mood in Germany was good, and they had nothing to fear from the Social Democrats; there would be no talk of a general strike or of sabotage.

When the minister of war, General von Falkenhayn, and the minister of the navy, Admiral von Tirpitz, objected to the delay in declaring the *Kriegsgefahr*, Bethmann Hollweg invited them to submit their objections directly to the kaiser.

Wilhelm had already lashed out at Tsar Nicholas and Sir Edward Grey when, on Thursday evening, he received the report of Pourtalès' 2 a.m. interview with Sazonov. He believed that he now understood what the tsar was up to: he had asked the kaiser to mediate in order to quiet 'his uneasy conscience' even though he knew that he was not strong enough to stand up against his ministers and stop the Russian mobilization. 'Frivolity and weakness' would plunge the world into a frightful war which was aimed at Germany's destruction: Britain, Russia, and France had agreed among themselves to use the Austro-Serbian conflict as an excuse to wage a 'war of extermination' (*Vernichtungskrieg*) against Germany. This explained Grey's cynical manoeuvre of warning Germany that Britain would move against it in the event of a Franco-German war—which would force Germany either to betray shamefully its allies to Russia (and thus break up the Triple Alliance) or to be attacked by the Triple Entente for maintaining its fidelity to its allies.[43]

According to the kaiser the dilemma now confronting Germany had been cleverly devised by Edward VII, then systematically developed and brought to a conclusion by George V. The stupidity and ineptitude of Austria had been used as a trap. The encirclement of Germany was now complete. The net had been thrown over Germany's head, with Britain scornfully (*hohnlächelnd*) reaping a brilliant success in opposing German world-policy, twisting the noose of Germany's political and economic destruction while the Germans squirmed isolated in the net. He had to admire the greatness of this achievement, even if it was about to destroy his empire. 'Edward VII after his death is stronger than I, who am still alive! And to think that there are those who believed that Britain could be won over or pacified by this or that puny measure!!!'[44]

According to the kaiser, the British had pursued this policy unremittingly and relentlessly. And Germany had walked into the trap—even agreeing to limit its shipbuilding programme in the hope of pacifying them. All of the kaiser's warnings and pleas had been for nothing. Germany now faced the dilemma that maintaining its fidelity 'to the venerable old Emperor of Austria' placed it in the position of giving Britain the pretext it sought to annihilate Germany under the hypocritical cloak of justice—of appearing to help France and preserve the 'balance of power' in Europe. Germany must now rip off this mask of Christian peacefulness and expose their hypocrisy. Germany's consuls and agents in Turkey and India should fire up 'the whole Mohammedan world' to rebel against the hateful, lying, conscienceless nation of shopkeepers. 'If we are to be bled to death, England shall at least lose India.'[45]

Bethmann Hollweg, who was long accustomed to such outbursts, would not see these comments until the next day. In the meantime, the diplomatic initiative to prevent a general European war not only continued but appeared to be succeeding.

★

Most diplomats now seemed to be agreed that an Austrian occupation of Belgrade and frontier territories would be acceptable and need not precipitate a general war. To avoid a European war, however, would require a formula to be devised that would assure Russia that Serbia's sovereignty and independence would be maintained while assuring Austria that measures would be imposed sufficient to eradicate the movement for a Greater Serbia. Grey's suggestion—supported by Germany—was that this was an appropriate subject for discussion at a conference if Austria were to 'halt in Belgrade' and Russia agreed to suspend further military operations.

Grey attempted to persuade the Austrians by warning them of the consequences if they refused his proposal. He told the Austrian ambassador late Thursday evening that 'we are all steering for a general war'. He found it incomprehensible that Vienna had broken off the discussions between Sazonov and Szápáry in St Petersburg, which had been a 'ray of hope to the whole of Europe'. Russia was now mobilizing; Germany and France might follow suit as soon as tomorrow. On the other hand, he was continuing to work with Berlin, endeavouring to find a peaceful solution. If he were to achieve anything at St Petersburg, he must have something to offer: if he approached the Russians 'with empty hands' and demanded that they stand aside while Austria finished its reckoning with Serbia, his efforts were doomed to fail.[46]

Grey warned that if the Austrians believed that the Russians could be persuaded to stand quietly to one side while they crushed Serbia they were mistaken. Thus far Austria had offered nothing to the other Powers that they might make use of in St Petersburg. The Austrian ambassador attempted to press him on what he had in mind; Grey refused to offer any details on the grounds that Austria might regard this as interference. Mensdorff concluded that the British sincerely desired peace and that they were prepared to assist in giving Austria satisfaction and guarantees for the future against Serbia in order to avoid a European war.

While he attempted to cajole Austria into agreement, Grey asked Viviani for French support in persuading Russia. Time was now of the essence. German military and naval authorities were warning that they could stand by no longer while Russia began to mobilize. French strategists argued that

Germany was already taking steps and that they could not afford to be left behind. Although the politicians and diplomats were busily denying rumours of mobilization and secret preparations, the generals and admirals everywhere were insisting that if they waited any longer they ran the risk of defeat. Everyone involved continued to believe that mobilization meant war.

By late Thursday evening something close to a consensus on how to proceed seemed to be emerging. Germany had pressed the Austrians to renew discussions at St Petersburg—and this Berchtold had agreed to do. That evening the Wilhelmstrasse received the news that he had instructed Szápáry to provide Sazonov with the explanations of the note to Serbia that he had asked for. He promised to consider any suggestions made by Russia and to discuss all questions concerning Austro-Russian relations. He promised to hold a similar discussion in Vienna: he would reassure the Russian ambassador that any occupation of Serbian territory would be purely temporary, and only in order to assure the fulfilment of Austria's demands. After this had been achieved, Austria would evacuate. The kaiser was pleased: 'my proposition is accepted as I telegraphed it to the Tsar . . . .'.[47]

At a family dinner at Potsdam that night, the kaiser's brother Heinrich and four of his six sons argued that if Russia mobilized on the German frontier, Germany ought to mobilize in response. The kaiser was hesitant: with Serbia having agreed to almost every Austrian demand, and with London and St Petersburg apparently willing to allow an Austrian occupation of Belgrade, there seemed little point in launching a European war. 'The Kaiser absolutely wants peace. . . . He even wants to influence Austria and to stop her continuing further.'[48] The chief of the naval cabinet believed that the kaiser was on the verge of a nervous breakdown.

Shortly before midnight a telegram from King George arrived at Potsdam. Responding to the telegram from Prince Heinrich, the king assured him that the British government was doing its utmost to suggest to Russia and France that they suspend further military preparations. This seemed possible 'if Austria will consent to be satisfied with [the] occupation of Belgrade and neighbouring Servian territory as a hostage for [the] satisfactory settlement of her demands'. He urged the kaiser to use his great influence at Vienna to induce Austria to accept this proposal and prove that Germany and Britain were working together to prevent a catastrophe.

The kaiser ordered his brother to drive into Berlin immediately to inform Bethmann Hollweg of the news. Heinrich delivered the message to the chancellor at 1.15 a.m. and had returned to Potsdam by 2.20. Wilhelm planned to answer the king on Friday morning. The kaiser noted, happily, that the suggestions made by the king were the same as those he had proposed to Vienna that evening.

Surely a peaceful resolution was at hand?

Day Eight

Friday, 31 July

By Friday people throughout Europe began to panic at the prospect of war among the Great Powers. Smaller states began preparing for the worst. The government of the Netherlands ordered the mobilization of all of its land forces. The Bundesrat in Switzerland summoned all three divisions of the Swiss army—the *Elite*, the *Landwehr*, and the *Landsturm*—to ready themselves for mobilization. In Belgium troops currently absent from their garrisons were being sent back to their quarters via special trains commandeered for the purpose, and orders had gone out in preparation for calling to the colours the last three annual drafts of reserves. The government issued a decree prohibiting the export of grain, cattle, horses, fodder, and automobiles.

The internationalist, pacifist, and socialist movements at last realized that time was quickly running out. An emergency meeting of the *Bureau international de la paix* was convened in Brussels on Friday. Approximately fifty representatives attended, representing every state in Europe except Austria. They agreed to send telegrams to the governments concerned, pleading that they restrain themselves.[1] Socialists in the House of Commons in Britain passed a resolution denouncing a war into which every European Power would be dragged because of secret alliances that had never been sanctioned by, or communicated to, the people. They supported yesterday's resolution of the International Socialist Bureau calling upon all workers to unite to prevent their governments from embarking on war.

In Britain the movement against war began to focus on the issue of British intervention. They were against it. The council of the International Arbitration League met on Friday and agreed to advocate British neutrality. It had 20,000 copies of the flysheet 'Britain's First Duty. No War!' printed and handed out in London. The journal *War and Peace* issued its own flyer, 'Stand Clear, England!', arguing against fighting a war on behalf of Russia and the balance of power.[2] Leading liberals and socialists formed a Neutrality Committee. Norman Angell launched the Neutrality League, which distributed half-a-million leaflets in two days, put up 10,000 posters, and had 362 sandwich-men walking the streets of London. Socialists in the House of Commons protested against any step being taken by the government in support of Russia, 'as being not only offensive to the political traditions of the country but disastrous to Europe'.[3]

★

By the end of the day on Thursday, 30 July, one week had passed since Austria-Hungary had presented its ultimatum to Serbia. Although Austria had declared war, begun the bombardment of Belgrade, and announced the mobilization of its army in the south, negotiations to reach a diplomatic solution continued. A wide array of peaceful outcomes still seemed possible, ranging from a settlement negotiated directly between Austria and Russia in St Petersburg, to a conference of the four 'disinterested' Great Powers in either London or Berlin to mediate between Austria and Russia.

Activity was now frantic. Officials everywhere were overworked and nerves were fraying. Work at the British embassy in Berlin was so overwhelming that 'one or two of the Staff showed signs of collapsing'.[4] No one knew what to expect next. Almost anything seemed possible. Would the alliances hold or fall apart? If it came to war, which way would the uncommitted jump? Were the Austrians about to march into Belgrade? Would they halt once they occupied the city? Would negotiations continue in spite of the fighting? Would Austria's repeated promises to respect Serbian sovereignty be sufficient to persuade the Russians to stop their mobilization? How long would Germany and Austria be willing to delay general mobilization in light of Russia's preparations?

By now Chancellor Bethmann Hollweg had become exasperated with the Austrians. Their intransigent refusal to negotiate with the Russians was placing the alliance in an untenable position. If Vienna declined to make any concessions it would be impossible to blame Russia for the outbreak of a general European war. In fact, the kaiser had personally intervened at Vienna at the request of the tsar because, if he had refused, it would create 'the irrefutable suspicion' (*unwiderleglichen Verdacht*) that Germany wanted war. On the other hand the partial mobilization of Russia against Austria had complicated things, and Bethmann Hollweg had insisted that Russian and French preparations for war must cease if negotiations were to continue. If

Sir Edward Grey succeeded in restraining Russia and France while Vienna declined to negotiate it would be disastrous: it would appear to everyone that the Austrians absolutely wanted a war. Germany would be drawn in, but Russia would be free of responsibility. 'That would place us in an untenable situation in the eyes of our own people.' Bethmann Hollweg advised Austria to accept Grey's proposal.[5]

From London, Lichnowsky confirmed that the proposed formula could succeed. Germany should persuade Berchtold to announce that, out of regard for the peace of Europe and the wishes of his allies, he was satisfied with what Austria had accomplished and that he was prepared to suspend further military operations. Then, through German mediation, Berchtold could discuss with Sazonov the conditions to be imposed upon Serbia—during which time Russia would cease to undertake further military preparations.[6]

All this seemed encouraging until Bethmann Hollweg suddenly changed his mind shortly before midnight Thursday. At 11.20 p.m. he directed Tschirschky not to act upon his previous instructions. The chancellor had now been persuaded by the general staff that the military preparations of Russia and France would force Germany to make an immediate decision regarding its own mobilization; to wait any longer could be disastrous.[7] The Wilhelmstrasse was now convinced that, if Germany and Austria-Hungary found themselves at war with Russia and France, Britain would attack them immediately.

On Friday morning Germany set about to bolster the Austro-German position in the Balkans. Bethmann Hollweg had a message drafted to be sent from the kaiser to King Constantine of Greece.[8] At 6 a.m. Friday morning he had this draft sent to the kaiser by special messenger. The chancellor argued that if the conflict remained limited to one between Austria and Serbia, the interference of Turkey and Bulgaria would not be permitted. But if it came to a general European war they—and all Balkan nations—would have to choose sides.

The chancellor wanted the kaiser to suggest to the king 'that the very memory of your father, who fell at the hand of a murderer, will keep you and Greece from taking the part of the Serbian assassins against my person and the Triple Alliance'. And this would be in the self-interest of Greece: 'No nation has regarded Greece's remarkable rise under your leadership with more envious eyes than has Russia.' There would never be a better opportunity than the present for Greece, 'under the mighty shield of the

Triple Alliance', to deny Russia the hegemony it was seeking to impose on the Balkans.[9] If Greece were to align itself with Serbia it would expose itself to attack from Italy, Bulgaria, and Turkey.

At 6.45 a.m. the kaiser refused to send the message proposed by his chancellor. He pointed out that Britain's latest proposal—to negotiate a settlement while the Austrian army occupied Belgrade—was very similar to his own position. He wanted to wait to hear from King George and Tsar Nicholas before taking any action.

An hour later, however, the kaiser did agree to try to persuade King Karl of Romania to stick with his allies in the crisis. Germany and Romania ought to support their 'venerable friend and ally', the Emperor Franz Joseph, in his demand for atonement from Serbia. Russia, attempting to establish hegemony in the Balkans, was using Serbia to undermine the Austrian monarchy. The Panslavist design was to destroy the monarchy, dissolve the Triple Alliance, and isolate and enfeeble Germany in order to achieve 'the domination of Russia over all of south-eastern Europe'.[10] King Karl had 'created a civilized nation' in eastern Europe, and erected 'a dam against the Slavic flood'. He trusted that as a king and as a Hohenzollern, Karl would stand faithfully by him and fulfil unconditionally the obligations of their alliance.

There was, however, little evidence that Romania was inclined to support Austria against Russia, or that King Karl could overcome public antipathy to the Austrians for their treatment of Romanians in Transylvania.

There was even less evidence that Italy would uphold the alliance in a general European war. None of Germany's efforts to persuade the Austrians to offer sufficient inducement to the Italians to commit them to support the alliance had succeeded. For more than a month in Berlin, Vienna, and Rome, German diplomats had proposed a variety of incentives to be offered to the Italians but nothing had been offered. Instead, the Austrians would discuss 'compensation' only if their occupation of Serbian territories proved to be more than a temporary military necessity.

Overnight Thursday/Friday the Austrian ambassador in Rome recounted a meeting in which the Italian foreign minister explained what attitude Italy proposed to take in the event of a general European war. The Triple Alliance, San Giuliano insisted, was supposed to be of a purely defensive character. But Austria's 'violent proceedings' against Serbia were provoking a European conflagration.[11] As Austria had refused to come to an understanding with him regarding compensation, Italy was under no obligation to take part in a war. He would, however, continue to ask himself whether it was in Italy's interests to remain neutral or provide armed assistance to Austria. San Giuliano told the German ambassador that he was not saying that Italy would not participate in a war: 'I am only saying that she is not obliged to take part.'[12]

The Austrian ambassador in Rome had ceased to conceal his irritation with his government. He reminded Berchtold that he had repeatedly argued against offering Italy any prospect of compensation, but, in spite of this advice, the foreign minister had gone 'more than halfway' in encouraging Italy to hope for compensation. Italy's blackmail tactics appeared to be succeeding and Mérey wanted no part in them. He would make any offer of compensation contingent upon Italy fulfilling exactly its duty as an ally.[13]

The clash between San Giuliano and Mérey in Rome explained why the Italian foreign minister wanted discussions concerning compensation to be conducted in Vienna. However, this raised another difficulty. In Vienna, the Duke d'Avarna was proving to be as pro-Austrian as Mérey was anti-Italian. On Friday the Italian ambassador visited the German ambassador to suggest that Berlin ought to give some blunt hints to Rome. Although Avarna did not wish to suggest that Italy was about to act disloyally to the alliance, he felt that the time had come for 'plain speech by Berlin to Rome'. Tschirschky suggested they keep this strictly confidential, as any leak would compromise Avarna, 'who has always shown himself to be unswervingly loyal to the Triple Alliance'. Tschirschky had again pointed out to Berchtold that it was Austria's 'duty' to bind Italy unconditionally to the alliance by making 'the greatest concessions'.[14]

★

The kaiser continued to hope that the initiatives he had undertaken at St Petersburg, London, and Vienna might avert war. Everywhere he looked, the signs were discouraging: Romania appeared disinclined to honour its commitment to the Triple Alliance; Austria and Italy seemed unable to come to an agreement; neither Bulgaria nor Greece appeared inclined to join Germany and Austria against Serbia; Britain had responded negatively to Bethmann Hollweg's proposal that it should remain neutral; Belgium did not appear willing to abandon its neutrality in the face of German threats. The only hopeful sign on the horizon came from Constantinople, where it seemed that the Turks might be prepared to join Germany in a war against Russia. On the other hand most German strategic assessments suggested that the Turks would contribute little of value. If Austria could humiliate, reduce, and occupy Serbia without a general European war, surely this would be victory enough for the Triple Alliance?

The German secretary of state put together a brief memorandum outlining the state of affairs as they had evolved by Friday. Germany, he said, was to sound Austria, Britain, and Russia to determine whether it was possible for the four disinterested Powers to secure 'complete satisfaction' for Austria, provided that this did not infringe on Serbia's sovereignty and territorial integrity. Austria, he pointed out, had already declared that it would respect Serbia's sovereignty and its integrity—so perhaps the four Powers might inform Russia that they would guarantee that Austria's demands would not go too far. All Powers would then agree to suspend military preparations and operations.[15] From London, Lichnowsky urged Bethmann Hollweg to propose to the tsar that he halt the Russian mobilization provided that Austria agree to suspend its military operations against Serbia. But would the Austrians agree?

In Vienna at 9 a.m. Berchtold convened a meeting of the common ministerial council. The Austrian and Hungarian prime ministers were present, along with the minister of finance, the minister of war, and several others. Berchtold explained that the Grey proposal for a conference à quatre was back on the agenda and that the German chancellor was insisting that this must be carefully considered: if Austria-Hungary declined every sort of mediation, Germany and Austria would find themselves opposed by a coalition of the whole of Europe as neither Italy nor Romania would stand by the alliance. Bethmann Hollweg was arguing that Austria's political prestige and military honour could be satisfied by the occupation of Belgrade and other points, while the humiliation of Serbia would weaken Russia's position in the Balkans.[16]

Berchtold reported that he had consulted the emperor on this and that they had agreed it was now impossible to stop hostilities against Serbia. Austria could, however, do its best to appear to be meeting Britain's wishes and avoid giving offence to the German chancellor. The Foreign Office was currently drafting a response according to the following principles:

1. Warlike operations against Serbia must continue.

2. Austria could not negotiate the British proposal unless the Russian mobilization ceased.

3. Austria demanded the 'integral' acceptance of its demands, on which it was not prepared to negotiate.

Berchtold warned that in a conference such as that proposed by Grey it was inevitable that the other Powers involved would attempt to reduce the demands made by Austria-Hungary. In this instance France, Britain, and Italy were likely take Russia's part; Austria could not even count on the support of the German ambassador in London. If everything that Austria had undertaken were to result in no more than a gain in 'prestige', all of their work to this point would have been in vain. A mere occupation of Belgrade would be of no use—even if Russia were prepared to allow it. This was all a fraud (*Flitterwerk*). Russia would pose as the saviour of Serbia—which would remain intact—and in two or three years they could expect the Serbs to attack again in circumstances far less favourable to Austria. Thus, he proposed to respond courteously to the British offer while insisting on Austria's conditions and avoiding a discussion of the merits of the case.

Everyone supported Berchtold. Tisza agreed that it would be dangerous to discuss the merits of the case and that military operations against Serbia must continue. He suggested they reply to the British by saying they were prepared to agree to the proposal in principle, but that the war with Serbia must continue and the Russian mobilization must be stopped. Prime Minister Stürgkh went even farther: the idea of a conference was so odious that he wished to avoid even the appearance of agreeing to it.

The cabinet sided with Tisza and agreed to proceed as he proposed. Austria would inform the Powers that it was prepared to meet in conference *à quatre* only if Russia agreed to halt its mobilization while Austria continued with the war against Serbia.

There was also the issue of the Italian problem to resolve. Berchtold explained that Italy was holding Austria responsible for provoking the conflict, arguing that it was contrary to the defensive terms of the Triple Alliance. The real aim of the Italians was compensation, on which the Germans were unfortunately siding with them.

Krobatin, the minister of war, pointed out that both the kaiser and the chief of the German general staff were adamant that they needed the active assistance of Italy in the coming war. Both of them were urging that Austria meet Italy's demands for compensation. Berchtold explained that the perception in Rome seemed to be that the coming war was against Italian interests because, if successful, it would strengthen Austria's position in the Balkans—in which case Italy would intervene only if its claims to compensation were recognized. He had responded to the Italians with vague phrases and assurances that Austria did not intend to seize any territory.

The council divided on the issue. Some felt that the Italian interpretation of the alliance was easily refuted, while others believed that this legalistic argument was beside the point. Biliński pointed out that the great struggle which was now imminent meant a fight for the survival of the monarchy, and that if Italy's assistance was of such great importance, Austria should make the necessary sacrifices 'in order to purchase this assistance'. But the ministers sided with Berchtold and agreed that he should promise Italy compensation only if Austria's occupation of Serbian territory proved to be more than temporary.

The Austrians refused to be diverted from the course they had embarked upon. At 12.30 p.m. they announced a general mobilization: all men aged 19–42 were now called to the colours. The first day of mobilization was set for Tuesday, the 4th of August.

★

Immediately following the council meeting the emperor wired the kaiser to inform him that he had decided to respond to the Russian mobilization by mobilizing all of his forces. Austria could not permit a Russian intervention to rescue Serbia, which would have 'serious consequences' for the monarchy. 'I am fully aware of the meaning and the implications of my decision'—which he had arrived at with confidence in 'the justice of God' and the certainty of the kaiser's unflinching fidelity.[17]

The kaiser was already angry when he received news of the Austrian decision. He had learned that morning that the Russians had decided to mobilize all of their forces. Placards had gone up at street-corners throughout St Petersburg overnight Thursday–Friday ordering reservists to report to the nearest police station by 6 a.m. Saturday. The kaiser believed this left Germany with little choice but to take preventive measures in response. 'The responsibility for the disaster which is now threatening the whole of the civilized world', he wired to the tsar, 'will not be laid at my door.'[18]

Still, Wilhelm did not abandon hope altogether. He told Nicholas that he still had the power to avert disaster. As neither the honour nor the power of Russia was being threatened, the tsar could afford to await the result of the kaiser's mediation. 'My friendship for you and your Empire, transmitted to me by my grandfather on his deathbed, has always been sacred to me.' Peace could still be saved if only the tsar would agree to stop the military measures that threatened Germany and Austria.

Shortly before sending his telegram to the tsar the kaiser met with Bethmann Hollweg and Moltke. At 2 p.m. the the *drohenden Kriegszustand* ('imminent peril of war') was announced. At 3.30 p.m. Bethmann Hollweg instructed Pourtalès in St Petersburg to explain that Germany had been compelled to take this step because of Russia's mobilization. Germany would mobilize unless Russia agreed to suspend 'every war measure' aimed at Austria-Hungary and Germany within twelve hours. Once the ambassador had presented this demand to Sazonov, he was to wire back to Berlin the precise timing of his communication. The twelve-hour clock would begin ticking from the moment that the demand was presented in St Petersburg.

Still, Bethmann Hollweg held out some hope. Perhaps the Russians had chosen to mobilize because of yesterday's false report that Germany had begun to mobilize. When they were reassured that Germany had not done so, perhaps they would reverse their decision. For the time being, the *Kriegszustand* meant only that military authorities could supersede civilian, that the news would be strictly censored, that railways, bridges, and other strategically important sites would come under special protection, and that restrictions would be placed on the use of telegraphs and telephones.

The kaiser and his wife entered Berlin an hour after the announcement, driving through the Brandenburg Gate in an open automobile, proceeding down Unter den Linden on their way to the palace. They were surrounded by cheering crowds all the way. At 4 p.m. an officer accompanied by a contingent of soldiers marched from the palace across the bridge to the Zeughaus, the Prussian military museum on Unter den Linden, where, with the soldiers forming a square and with drummers beating their drums, a proclamation declaring a state of siege (*Belagerungszustand*) was read to a cheering crowd. Within a few hours most Germans would learn that they were now governed by martial law.

Tens of thousands began to gather in the pleasure gardens in front of the imperial palace. At 6.30 p.m. the kaiser, accompanied by his wife and Prince Adalbert, addressed them from the balcony. He declared that those who envied Germany had forced him to take measures to defend the Reich. He had been forced to take up the sword but had not ceased his efforts to maintain the peace. If he did not succeed 'we shall with God's help wield the sword in such a way that we can sheathe it with honour'.[19] He and the family then left the palace by automobile while the crowd sang '*Heil dir im*

Siegerkranz' ('Hail to Thee in Victor's Crown'—the unofficial anthem of
the empire since 1871, sung to the melody of 'God Save the Queen'):

> Hail to thee in victor's crown,
> Ruler of the fatherland!
> Hail, Emperor, to you.
> Feel in the splendour of the throne
> Fully the highest joy:
> To be the favourite of the people!
> Hail, Emperor, to you.
>
> Neither steed nor weapons
> Secure the steep height
> Where princes stand:
> Love of the fatherland,
> Love of the free man
> Founds the sovereign's throne
> Like a rock in the sea.
>
> Holy flame, glow,
> Glow and expire not
> For the fatherland!
> We all will stand then
> Courageous for one man,
> Fight and bleed with joy
> For throne and empire!
>
> Trade and sciences
> May rise upwards their head
> With courage and power!
> Warriors' and heroes' deeds
> May find their laurels of fame
> Faithfully preserved
> On your throne!
>
> Be, Emperor Wilhelm, here
> A long time your people's glory,
> The pride of mankind!
> Feel in the splendour of the throne
> Fully the highest joy:
> To be the favourite of the people!
> Hail, Emperor, to you.

The kaiser's chancellor was pessimistic that peace could now be preserved.
Declaring the *Kriegszustand* meant that Germany would be mobilized within
forty-eight hours, which 'inevitably means war'. He chaired a meeting of the

imperial council that issued orders to prohibit the export of provisions, livestock, fodder, automobiles, oil, and coal. He instructed the ambassador in Vienna to make it clear that Germany expected immediate and active Austrian participation in the war against Russia.[20] At 11.45 p.m. he addressed a crowd of several thousand who had gathered outside his office. Thanking them for their support, he declared that 'all Germans were prepared to fight, regardless of his or her views or beliefs'.[21]

But precisely when did 'inevitable' become inevitable? An hour and a half after Bethmann Hollweg made his gloomy prediction to Tschirschky he wired Lichnowsky in London to inform him of Germany's decision. Perhaps, he told him, Russia's decision to mobilize had been taken because of the false rumours of Germany's imminent mobilization that were circulated by the *Lokal Anzeiger* in Berlin yesterday. It was not too late: they were giving Russia the opportunity to suspend all military preparations aimed at Germany and Austria. Only if Russia refused would Germany begin to mobilize.[22]

Bethmann Hollweg met with the British ambassador shortly before the proclamation of the *Kriegszustand*. He told him that he had received information that Russia had burned a cordon of houses along the German frontier, sealed its public offices in the frontier districts, and carried off its chests of money into the interior. If this information proved correct it could only mean that Russia now looked upon war as a certainty. And the Russians had taken these steps in spite of Germany's attempt to mediate. If the Russians were taking military measures aimed at Germany as well as Austria, he could not leave his country defenceless. He wanted Goschen to inform Grey that Germany might have to take some very serious steps in a short time—perhaps today.[23]

When this news reached London on Friday afternoon, officials at the Foreign Office dismissed Bethmann Hollweg's arguments. Eyre Crowe interpreted them as an effort to throw the blame for military preparations onto Russia—but in fact Germany, while stopping short of issuing an actual mobilization order, had begun mobilizing on all three German frontiers some time ago. Arthur Nicolson argued that Russia was simply taking very reasonable and sensible precautions, which should not be interpreted as provocative. Germany, 'who has been steadily preparing now wishes to throw the blame on Russia—a very thin pretext'.[24]

How would Grey respond? When he met with the cabinet in the morning they considered the French request for a promise of British

intervention before Germany attacked. The cabinet divided into three
factions: those who opposed intervention, those who were undecided,
and those who wished to intervene. Only two ministers, Grey and Churchill, favoured intervention. Most agreed that public opinion in Britain would
not support them going to war for the sake of France. But opinion might
shift if Germany were to violate Belgian neutrality. Grey was instructed to
request—from both Germany and France—an assurance that they would
respect the neutrality of Belgium. They were not prepared to give France
the promise of support that it had asked for. One cabinet minister concluded
it was now clear 'that this Cabinet will not join in the war'.[25]

Grey continued to hope that if Austria and Russia resumed negotiations
war might still be averted. However, he did not see how Russia could be
persuaded to suspend its military preparations unless Austria 'put some limit
to her advance into Serbia'.[26] This was precisely what the cabinet in Vienna
had decided it would not do when it met that morning.

After the cabinet meeting, Grey met with the French ambassador, who
pressed him as hard as he could for a decision on coming to the assistance of
France. Cambon asked him whether it was the position of the British
government to wait for a German invasion of French territory before it
would intervene. Because, if so, this would come too late: Germany was
already preparing to invade. If Britain remained indifferent it would be
repeating the mistake of 1870, when it had failed to foresee the danger that
would be created by the formation of a powerful Germany in the centre of
Europe. The danger was even graver today: if Germany were to be victorious once again, Britain would find itself isolated and in a state of depend-
ency. The French were counting on the assistance of the British, and if this
was not forthcoming it would bolster the arguments of those in France who
preferred to do a deal with Germany. Cambon asked that Grey go back to
the cabinet and insist on a pledge being given to France 'without delay'.[27]

Grey refused. He would promise only that if the situation were to change
the cabinet would immediately be called together again. Even in mid-
afternoon he attempted once again to resuscitate his proposal for a conference à quatre. He wired to Berlin to ask whether Germany might be willing
to sound out Vienna, while he sounded out St Petersburg, on the possibility
of agreeing to a revised formula that could lead to a conference. Perhaps the
four disinterested Powers could offer to Austria to undertake to see that it
would obtain 'full satisfaction of her demands on Servia'—provided that
these did not impair Serbian sovereignty or the integrity of Serbian territory.

After all, Austria had already given assurances that it would respect both sovereignty and territorial integrity. Russia could then be informed by the four Powers that they would undertake to prevent Austrian demands from going to the length of impairing Serbian sovereignty and integrity. All Powers would then suspend further military operations or preparations.[28]

Goschen approached Jagow with this proposal in Berlin that evening, urging him to accept it and to make one more attempt to prevent the 'terrible catastrophe of a European war'. The secretary of state indicated that while he was sympathetic to Grey's suggestion he could not consider it until Russia had responded to Germany's ultimatum to cease mobilization. If Russia failed to comply, Germany would mobilize at once. Up until Thursday night Germany had been urging Austria to continue diplomatic discussions with Russia—and indications from Vienna had been positive—'but Russia's mobilization had spoilt everything'.[29] If Russia responded positively to Germany's demand to stop mobilizing he would take Grey's proposal to the chancellor and the kaiser for their consideration.

The kaiser was unlikely to have been receptive to the British proposal, had it been presented to him. At midday he sought to explain the situation to the heads of the German navy. On Thursday Britain had, in effect, given Germany an ultimatum: either betray its Austrian ally and refuse to participate in the war against Russia or immediately face an attack from the British navy. Thus, he told them, Grey was making a liar of his own king, who had, on Wednesday, forwarded to him through his brother Prince Heinrich 'a plain declaration of neutrality'.

The kaiser was now convinced that the entire crisis had been caused by Britain, and Britain alone. And the crisis could now be ended by the British on their own, by putting pressure on the 'Russians and Gauls'. King George ought to order his allies to cease their mobilization at once, to remain neutral, and to await Austria's proposals—which the kaiser would transmit to Russia and France as soon as he received them. Thus, the full responsibility for the most frightful conflagration in the history of the world would rest on the king's shoulders. He, the kaiser, could do nothing more—it was up to the king to prove that the British loved peace.[30]

Fortunately, Wilhelm assured the admiralty staff, King George had made proposals similar to those he had himself made at Vienna—with the result that discussions between Vienna and St Petersburg had now resumed. Reports from Russia indicated that there was no enthusiasm for war there. In fact, on Thursday night there had again been violent confrontations between revolutionaries and the police. The court and the army appeared to be coming to their senses, having received a scare about the possible consequences of their premature mobilization. There was still reason to hope that Russia might back down.

By mid-afternoon Germany had announced the *drohenden Kriegszustand*. Austria had announced general mobilization. Nevertheless, the Russian ambassador at Vienna was undeterred. Schebeko assured Sazonov that in spite of the mobilization he would continue to 'exchange views' with Berchtold.[31] And Count Forgách, one of the 'hawks' at the Ballhausplatz, assured the British ambassador in Vienna that neither the Austrian nor the Russian mobilization ought necessarily to be regarded as hostile acts. Although de Bunsen failed to get any suggestion of what a compromise might consist of, 'he spoke in a conciliatory tone and evidently did not regard the situation as desperate'.[32]

Surprisingly, the chief of the Austrian general staff appeared to agree with these optimistic voices. At 4.15 p.m. he telephoned to the office of the general staff in Berlin in order to explain the Austrian position: the emperor had authorized full mobilization only in response to Russia's actions and only for the purpose of taking precautions against a Russian attack. Austria had no intention of declaring war against Russia. In other words, he agreed with Sazonov: Russia could mobilize along the Austrian frontier and Austria could match this on the other side. And there the two forces could wait, without going to war.

This prospect terrified Moltke. He replied to Conrad immediately: Germany would probably mobilize its forces on Sunday and then commence hostilities against Russia and France. Would Austria abandon Germany (*im tich lassen*)?[33] Moltke's suggestion dismayed Conrad. At 9.30 p.m. he called Berlin to confirm that Austria's decision to mobilize forces in Galicia proved it was prepared to go to war; its reluctance to declare war and begin hostilities was only in response to Germany's requests that they should avoid appearing to be the aggressor and wait for Russia to begin hostilities. It was news to him that Germany now intended to launch a war against Russia and France. Would Moltke please confirm that this was Germany's intention?

Minutes later Conrad decided that he ought to put the question more clearly to Moltke. In his next call he asked for a 'definite statement' whether Austria should now anticipate 'a major war against Russia immediately and unconditionally'.[34] Was he now to rule out the possibility of fighting a war against Serbia without having to come to grips with Russia at the same time?

Moltke replied to the first call by informing Conrad that Germany had presented ultimatums to both Russia and France. Answers were required by 4 p.m. Saturday, and if these were unsatisfactory Germany would begin mobilization immediately. At 2.20 a.m. he replied to Conrad's second call, elaborating on the timetable and concluding that 'I regard acceptance of German demand by Russia as impossible'.[35] Conrad directed the Austrian military attaché in Berlin to assure Moltke that Austria would do everything in its power to assist Germany. But he could not help but complain that Germany had failed to give him this information earlier. In fact, in spite of the evidence, Conrad until this moment had appeared to believe that somehow he would be left to fight Serbia without having to deal with Russia simultaneously.

In St Petersburg Sazonov informed Szápáry that he would not be satisfied with an Austrian declaration that it would respect the sovereignty of Serbia and would not attempt to reduce its size. Instead of being satisfied with a promise that Austria would not injure Russian interests in the Balkans or elsewhere, Russia had chosen to mobilize. Under the circumstances, Szápáry believed it best to abstain from engaging in the renewed discussions that Berchtold had directed—at least not without further instructions to that effect. This telegram was not received at the Foreign Office in Vienna until 9 a.m. on Saturday, 1 August.[36]

In spite of this, Szápáry painted a surprisingly optimistic picture of how things stood in St Petersburg. He reported that while the Russian cabinet had met again, nothing definite seemed to have been decided on. But the signs were encouraging. Whereas for days a howling mob had surrounded the Austrian embassy—probably hooligans in the pay of the ministry of internal affairs, Szápáry thought—today all was quiet and calm now reigned. Within industrial and financial circles, the bourgeoisie were beginning to react as they began to anticipate the fearful economic consequences of a war. Within the Russian cabinet, both Sazonov and the most influential minister, Krivoshein, were said to be arguing in favour of peace. Only the military men and the prime minister, Goremykin, were believed to be in favour of war.[37]

Szápáry realized that his decision not to act on the instructions directing him to resume discussions with Sazonov might appear to contradict the messages being conveyed by the kaiser and his ambassador. Thus, he decided to approach Sazonov again. At the very least another initiative would enable

Austria to appear as the victim of a Russian attack by giving further proof of its goodwill 'and thus put Russia in the wrong'.[38]

On Friday afternoon Pourtalès gave up trying to persuade Sazonov. Instead of continuing discussions with him he submitted a memorandum to the Russian foreign ministry and sought an audience with the tsar himself. The memorandum credited Germany for having convinced Austria to issue the assurance to Russia that it had no intention either of injuring Russia's legitimate interests or of infringing Serbia's territorial integrity. In the opinion of the German government, Austria's declaration to this effect 'should be sufficient for Russia'. It was, after all, a very great concession for a Great Power in a state of war to tie its hands in advance in such a manner. Russia, by insisting that Austria go beyond this declaration, was demanding something that was incompatible 'with her dignity and her prestige as a Great Power'. Nor should Russia lose sight of the fact that Austria's standing as a Great Power was a matter of interest to Germany. Russia ought to recognize the extreme gravity of the situation that it would cause if it continued to insist on its demands.[39] The tsar agreed to meet with the ambassador that evening.

★

In London, Lichnowsky was deeply pessimistic that any concession could be gotten out of the Austrians without 'very energetic pressure' being exerted on them from Berlin. And if Berchtold failed to do more than continue to repeat his familiar declarations and explanations, the Russian government would be forced—against its will—by public opinion to intervene against the destruction of Serbian cities and towns. Grey indicated to him that everything depended on whether Austria was willing to make sufficient concessions as to put Russia in the wrong. If the Austrians made such concessions Grey would put pressure on St Petersburg and Paris. The foreign secretary, while reaffirming that Britain was not bound by any agreements, could justify not taking the French side in a conflict only if some tangible concession by Austria placed Russia in the wrong—public sentiment in Britain would demand this. Lichnowsky thought that Grey still seemed to have in mind his earlier suggestion that military operations in Serbia be suspended while the conference à quatre proceeded.[40]

But the Austrians had already decided against any suspension of their military operations against Serbia and instead had announced the general mobilization. What, then, would the British do? Grey had already refused

Bethmann Hollweg's proposal for obtaining British neutrality, but he had also refused to make any promises of support to the French.

The cabinet had directed Grey on Thursday to ask both Germany and France whether they would respect Belgian neutrality in the event of a conflict. When Goschen presented the question to Jagow, the secretary of state refused to commit Germany to any position before he had the opportunity to consult with the kaiser and the chancellor. Nevertheless, he told the ambassador that he doubted whether they could answer at all: any reply might disclose their strategic plans. Moreover, he confided that the Belgians had already committed acts 'which he could only qualify as hostile'. They had, for example, embargoed a consignment of grain destined for Germany. Before replying to the British enquiry Germany would need to know how France had responded to the same question.[41]

The question had not yet been put to France—and would not be until Friday evening. But in the meantime Grey refused to accept Poincaré's argument that peace now lay in his hands, that if he were to announce that Britain would come to the aid of France in the event of war with Germany, there would be no war. This was 'quite untrue', he told his ambassador in Paris: 'Germany does not expect our neutrality.' On the other hand, no one in London believed that British treaties or obligations were yet involved, and the feeling was quite different than it had been during the Moroccan crisis of 1905, which was a dispute that directly involved France. 'In this case France is being drawn into a dispute which is not hers.'[42] Although he promised the French ambassador that the government would reconsider its decision if the situation changed, it was unwilling to give a definite pledge to intervene in a war at this time.

Instead of giving in to the pressure of French and Russian pleas for a promise of assistance, Grey renewed his efforts to find a diplomatic solution. He thought that Sazonov's stated position—that Russia would cease military preparations only if Austria declared its willingness to eliminate from its ultimatum to Serbia all those points that endangered the principle of Serbian sovereignty—might be modified. Grey suggested that Russia cease its military preparations in exchange for an undertaking from the other Powers that they would seek a way to give complete satisfaction to Austria without endangering the sovereignty or territorial integrity of Serbia. On Friday afternoon in Paris Sir Francis Bertie handed a note to Viviani to this effect. Grey asked that France join his initiative by urging its acceptance in St Petersburg.

Viviani agreed. The French would tell Sazonov that Grey's formula furnished a useful basis for a discussion among the Powers who sought an honourable solution to the Austro-Serbian conflict and to avert the danger of war. The formula proposed 'is calculated equally to give satisfaction to Russia and to Austria and to provide for Serbia an acceptable means of escaping from the present difficulty'.[43] The French ambassador was instructed to urge Sazonov to adhere to the proposal 'without delay'. In the meantime France would continue to show military restraint in spite of German movements along the frontier: the government was determined not to appear the aggressor 'under any circumstances', for the sake of both French and British opinion.[44]

In fact, Sazonov had already agreed to modify his position at the urging of the British alone. His revised formula now stated:[45]

> If Austria consents to stop her troops from marching into Serbian territory, and if, recognizing that the Austro-Serbian conflict has assumed the character of a question of European interest, she agrees that the great Powers may examine how Serbia might satisfy the Austro-Hungarian Government without infringing upon her sovereign independence as a state, Russia undertakes to maintain her waiting attitude.

This was vaguer than the Grey formula: 'stopping the march' of Austrian troops lacked the specificity of the occupation of Belgrade—and given that it was not yet occupied, that no Austrian troops had yet crossed the frontier, it was not readily apparent what the formula meant. Nor was it clear that the promise to 'maintain her waiting attitude' was equivalent to ceasing military operations or preparations.

Would the new formula go far enough?

★

Early Friday evening Count Pourtalès had the private audience with Tsar Nicholas that he had sought at the beginning of the day. Above all, he wanted to point out to the tsar the impact that the decision to mobilize all Russian forces had made on Germany—especially when this had followed repeated assurances that only the mobilization of forces in the military districts along the Austrian frontier was being contemplated. By evening, the German ambassador warned that Russian measures might already have produced 'irreparable consequences'. It was entirely possible that the decision to mobilize when the kaiser was attempting to mediate the dispute might be regarded by him as offensive—and by the German people as provocative. 'I begged him . . . to check or to revoke these measures.'[46]

The tsar replied that, for technical reasons, it was not now possible to stop the mobilization. For the sake of European peace it was essential, he argued, that Germany influence, or put pressure on, Austria. Pressure, Pourtalès replied, would not be considered: Germany's position in Europe made the friendship of Austria indispensable. But Germany had always shown its willingness to exercise a friendly influence encouraging mediation and was continuing to do so.

Pourtalès came away with the impression that the tsar was not yet conscious of the gravity of the situation. The ambassador had not yet received the telegram instructing him to present the twelve-hour ultimatum to Russia to cease its mobilization or face the consequences. That evening in Berlin the newspapers announced the ultimatum to Russia in extra broadsheets; mobilization might follow the next day, depending on the response of Russia. Large crowds began to gather immediately and soon they were parading through the streets and singing patriotic songs.

The French learned of Germany's decisions before the Russians did. Jagow informed Jules Cambon of the decision to declare the *Kriegsgefahrzustand* late in the afternoon—and that they would be demanding that Russia should demobilize on both the German and the Austrian frontiers or face a German mobilization in reply.[47] Immediately following their meeting, Bethmann Hollweg sent urgent instructions to the German ambassador in Paris: Schoen was to ask the French government if it intended to remain neutral in the event of a Russo-German war. Germany required an answer within eighteen hours. Schoen was to telegraph Berlin immediately once he had made this enquiry, informing them of the hour at which it had been made. The utmost haste was necessary. There were now two deadlines: the one on France was added to the twelve-hour ultimatum given to Russia.

Secretly, Bethmann Hollweg clarified how Germany would respond in the unlikely case that France agreed to remain neutral. Ambassador Schoen was to inform the French that the fortresses of Verdun and Toul must be handed over to Germany as a pledge of their neutrality. They would be handed back to France at the conclusion of the war with Russia. The deadline by which France must agree to this demand was set for 4 p.m. the next day—Saturday, the 1st of August.[48] Schoen met with Viviani at 7 p.m. The deadline for the French reply was thereby set for 1 p.m. the next day.

Viviani said that he was not yet prepared to give up hope that war could be avoided, but promised to have an answer by the deadline.[49]

At almost the same moment as the meeting between Schoen and Viviani in Paris, the British minister, Sir Francis Villiers, was meeting with the Belgian foreign minister in Brussels. Grey wanted to inform the Belgians that he had asked France and Germany whether they were prepared to respect its neutrality in the event of war. Villiers was to tell Julien Davignon, the Belgian foreign minister, that he assumed Belgium would 'to the utmost of her power maintain neutrality'.[50]

When they met that evening Davignon assured Villiers that Belgium was determined to do so. He was convinced that the other Powers, 'in view of the excellent relations of friendship and confidence which had always existed between us', would respect Belgium's neutrality.[51] Nevertheless, Belgium had decided to mobilize its forces in order to ensure that it would be able to defend itself 'energetically' if its territory were violated. Mobilization was to begin on Saturday. According to official Belgian estimates, this would enable it to bring its strength up to 230,000 men.

By Friday evening virtually everyone involved had come to expect the worst. With Austria refusing to stop its military operations against Serbia, with Russia refusing to desist in mobilizing against Austria and Germany, with Germany threatening to mobilize unless Russia desisted, with Belgium mobilizing the next day, with Germany demanding a declaration of French neutrality by Saturday afternoon, it now seemed that there was little hope left for diplomacy.

★

At the Foreign Office in London, Sir Arthur Nicolson urged that Britain ought to mobilize the army immediately. 'It is useless to shut our eyes to the fact that possibly within the next twenty-four hours Germany will be moving across the French frontier.'[52] If Britain were not mobilized, its aid to France would come too late. Mobilization ought to be regarded as a precautionary, not a provocative, measure—and it was now essential.

Sir Edward Grey concurred that there was much force in Nicolson's argument and promised that it would be considered early on Saturday.

At the same time Sir Eyre Crowe hastily put together a memorandum for Sir Edward that incorporated his thoughts on the gravity of the situation that Britain now faced. 'If you think them worthless please put them aside.

Nothing is further from my mind than to trouble you needlessly or add to your grave perplexities at this moment.'[53]

Crowe argued against those who maintained that Britain was unprepared to engage in a big war. If this were true it would mean the abdication of Britain as an independent state: it could be brought to its knees and made to obey any Power or group of Powers willing to go to war—'of whom there are several'. The general principle on which Britain's whole foreign policy had been based in the past—the balance of power—would become 'an empty futility'. A balance of power could not be maintained by a state incapable of fighting. Those who pointed to the panic in the financial markets as evidence that Britain ought to remain aloof were also wrong. There was always a commercial panic at the beginning of any war: commercial opinion was generally timid. The panic currently under way in London was largely influenced by the deliberate acts of German financial houses, working closely with the German government and the German embassy in London.

Germany had, since the beginning of the crisis, made an unremitting effort to induce Britain to declare its neutrality. But Britain had persistently declined to do so. Why had Britain just yesterday rejected Germany's request as 'dishonourable' if it was now going to remain neutral and stand aside while Germany fell upon France? At least the bargain that Germany had proposed would have offered some value for France and Belgium.

Crowe agreed that there was no written bond binding Britain to France. This was strictly correct: there was no contractual obligation. 'But the *Entente* has been made, strengthened, put to the test and celebrated in a manner justifying the belief that a moral bond was being forged.' The whole policy of the Entente would be rendered meaningless if Britain was not prepared to stand by its friends in a just quarrel. If they were to repudiate this expectation their good name would be exposed to grave criticism. The question was not whether Britain was capable of taking part in a war, but whether it ought to enter this war. And this was a question first of right or wrong, and, secondly, of political expediency. 'If the question were argued on this basis, I feel confident that our duty and our interest will be seen to lie in standing by France in her hour of need. France has not sought the quarrel. It has been forced upon her.'

Crowe was not hopeful that the cabinet would see things his way. Later that evening he took a copy of a telegram from St Petersburg reporting on Russia's general mobilization to the chief of the general staff. He told

General Sir Henry Wilson that after having had forty-five minutes with Grey he felt hopeless. The foreign secretary talked about the ruin of commerce, etc., and 'in spite of all Crowe's arguments appeared determined to act the coward'.[54] Crowe was in despair.

In St Petersburg, at 11 p.m., the German ambassador presented the twelve-hour ultimatum to Sazonov. If Russia did not abandon its mobilization by noon Saturday, Germany would mobilize in response. And, as Bethmann Hollweg had already declared, 'mobilization means war'.

★

The socialist anti-war movement was confounded by the developments of the day. In Germany the Social Democratic Party now realized that they might soon have to decide whether to vote for or against the granting of war credits in the Reichstag. They decided to seek common ground with their counterparts in France and an emissary was despatched that evening to Paris. He expected to meet with Jean Jaurès in order to discuss a common strategy on Saturday.

Jaurès had led a delegation of socialists to meet with Viviani on Thursday evening, seeking an explanation of French policy. The premier had explained that the government was still seeking a peaceful resolution to the crisis but that it was necessary to begin fortifying the frontier. He assured Jaurès that the government would not round up those socialists and syndicalists who constituted most of those on the notorious *Carnet-B*, the secret 'enemy list' of those deemed dangerous to the French state.

The next day Jaurès published an editorial in *L'Humanité*. Under the headline '*Sang-froid nécessaire*' he pleaded for everyone to remain calm and to display 'nerves of steel'. He attacked Russian foreign policy and vowed that the socialist party would struggle against war 'until the very end'.[55] That evening he and some colleagues from the newspaper went out for a late dinner. As the Montmartre restaurant was crowded and the night was warm they were seated next to open windows, with a screen separating them from the street for privacy.

Waiting on the sidewalk was a fanatic determined to murder Jaurès for his anti-militarist, anti-war proclamations. He pushed the screen aside and put a bullet through the base of Jaurès' skull and into his brain. He died within minutes. The international socialist movement lost its most popular and persuasive advocate.

PART THREE

Days of Decision

Saturday to Tuesday,
1–4 August

Saturday, 1 August

The choice between war and peace now hung in the balance. All those involved saw themselves as standing on the edge of the precipice. Austria-Hungary and Russia were proceeding with full mobilization of their armed forces: Austria-Hungary was now preparing to mobilize along the Russian frontier in Galicia; Russia was now preparing to mobilize along the German frontier in Poland. On Friday evening in Paris the German ambassador had presented the French government with a question: would France remain neutral in the event of a Russo-German war? They were given eighteen hours to respond—until 1 p.m. Saturday. Five hours later in St Petersburg the German ambassador presented the Russian government with another demand: Russia had twelve hours—until noon Saturday—to suspend all war measures against Germany and Austria-Hungary, or Germany would mobilize its forces.

Would mobilization mean war? Sazonov put the question to the German ambassador. 'No', he replied. But they would find themselves 'extraordinarily close to war'.[1]

But they were also extraordinarily close to peace. Russia and Austria had resumed negotiations in St Petersburg at the behest of Britain, Germany, and France. Austria had declared publicly and repeatedly that it did not intend to seize any Serbian territory and that it would respect the sovereignty and independence of the Serbian monarchy. Russia had declared that it would not object to severe measures against Serbia as long its sovereignty and independence were respected. Surely, when the two of them were agreed on the fundamental principles involved, a settlement was within reach?

The Austrian ambassador at St Petersburg assured Sazonov that Berchtold was prepared to negotiate with Russia 'on a broad basis' and was willing to discuss the text of Austria's note to Serbia. Sazonov assured the ambassador that Russia's mobilization was insignificant, as the tsar had given his word to the kaiser that the army 'would not budge' as long as the discussions with Austria continued. The Russian army was well-disciplined and it could be withdrawn from the frontier upon the utterance of 'a single word' from the tsar. Count Szápáry concluded that if Berchtold wished to proceed with negotiations there was a basis available for them in St Petersburg.[2]

Count Pourtalès, the German ambassador, tried another manoeuvre. The head of the tsar's imperial court, Count V. B. Frederycksz, known to be a leading advocate of an understanding with Germany and a critic of the alliance with France, regarded a Prussian-led Germany as a bastion of conservatism and the monarchical principle. On Saturday morning Pourtalès turned to him in desperation. The situation, he explained, was now extremely serious and he was seeking every means to avert the catastrophe of war, which was enormously dangerous to all monarchies. Germany would be forced to mobilize if Russia failed to suspend its military preparations by noon—and 'you know what that means'. They were only the breadth of a finger away from war. The ambassador understood how difficult it was to stop a machine once it was set in motion, but the tsar could do so. He entreated Frederycksz to do whatever he could 'to prevent a catastrophe'.[3]

Similar language was used in London that morning. Sir Edward Grey's private secretary, Sir William Tyrrell, called the German ambassador on the telephone to tell him that Grey hoped to provide him with some facts following the cabinet meeting to be held that morning. These 'facts' might be helpful in 'avoiding the great catastrophe'. Grey himself followed this up with a second call to ask Lichnowsky whether Germany might give its assurance that it would not attack France if France were to remain neutral in a Russo-German war. Lichnowsky gave him this assurance. Grey, he reported, would use this at the cabinet meeting.[4]

The cabinet met at 11 a.m. for two and a half hours. The discussion was devoted exclusively to the European crisis. They were badly divided. Winston Churchill was the most bellicose, demanding immediate mobilization. At the other extreme were John Morley and John Simon, who

Herbert Henry Asquith (1852–1928); prime minister of Great Britain (1908–16)

insisted that the government should declare that Britain would not enter the war under any circumstances. According to the prime minister, Asquith, this was 'the view for the moment of the bulk of the party'. Grey threatened to resign if the cabinet adopted an uncompromising policy of non-intervention. If Grey went, Asquith told his mistress, he would too. He felt sure there would be a cabinet split and he anticipated the resignations of Morley and Simon—but believed that peace still had a chance.[5]

One cabinet minister, Herbert Samuel, proposed a solution to their dilemma: they should put the onus on Germany. Intervention should depend on whether Germany launched a naval attack on the northern coast of France or violated the independence of Belgium. His suggestion raised more questions: did Britain have the duty, or merely the right, to intervene if Belgian neutrality were violated? If German troops merely 'passed through' Belgium in order to attack France, would this constitute a violation of neutrality? The meeting was inconclusive.

Shortly before noon Saturday Belgium mobilized. The government announced its determination to uphold neutrality 'to the utmost of her power'. The minister of foreign affairs insisted that relations with the neighbouring Powers were excellent and that 'there was no reason to suspect their intentions'.[6] The Belgians turned neither to Britain nor France for support. Besides leading the campaign against Belgian atrocities in the Congo, the British were regarded as unreliable and as having joined an alliance which cared 'only about victory, and not Belgium'.[7] The French minister in Brussels repeatedly warned that the Belgians would do little in a conflict until they could anticipate who would be victorious. He quoted the Belgian chief of staff as declaring that Belgium would defend itself against all aggressors, 'last-comers as well as first-comers': if the French came in after the Germans, Belgium would defend against them equally. 'Our interest is to make common cause with nobody.'[8]

Moltke had, six days previously, drafted an ultimatum to be presented to Belgium when war broke out. Officials at the Foreign Office amended this slightly and Bethmann Hollweg had approved it on Wednesday. It was sent to the German minister in Brussels on 29 July inside a sealed envelope, which he was instructed to open only when he received instructions to do so by telegram from Berlin. Few were aware of its terms: Moltke, his adjutant, Bethmann Hollweg, and Wilhelm von Stumm of the Wilhelmstrasse.

★

While the British cabinet was arguing about intervention that morning, the German chancellor was chairing a session of the federal council (Bundesrat) in Berlin. According to the German constitution, the approval of the Bundesrat was required to mobilize the armies of the empire or to declare war—unless the territory of the Reich itself was under attack.

Bethmann Hollweg began with a gloomy assessment. He warned the fifty-eight delegates representing the states of Germany that, unless God performed a miracle at the eleventh hour, a crisis 'greater than any ever seen' was about to destroy the peace of Europe. He then proceeded to outline the events that had occurred since the assassination of 28 June, while explaining the policy that the German government had followed:

– Austria-Hungary had chosen to act against the 'Greater Serbia movement', which was not only its right, but its duty.

- It was in Germany's interests that Austria-Hungary should remain powerful and not succumb in its struggle with the southern Slavs, over whom Russia had chosen to act as protector.
- Support for Austria had been the guiding principle of German policy for thirty years.
- Although Germany had expressed no opinion of the steps taken by Austria, it had promised to stand faithfully by its ally.
- Although Serbia had appeared to agree to many of Austria's demands, it had placed important conditions on acceptance, and its promises were worthless.
- Germany had, from the beginning, attempted to localize the conflict between Austria and Serbia.
- Russia had initiated secret military preparations, directed first against Austria-Hungary.
- At Russia's request the kaiser had undertaken to mediate between it and Austria-Hungary.
- Russia had then mobilized openly against Austria-Hungary, in spite of Austrian promises to respect the territorial integrity and sovereign independence of Serbia.
- While Austro-Russian negotiations had begun again in St Petersburg yesterday (instigated by Germany) Russia had undertaken the full mobilization of its forces on land and at sea.

Bethmann Hollweg argued that Germany was left with no choice: Russia's mobilization must be regarded as a hostile act. Germany must respond or sacrifice its security and its honour. If Germany were to accept Russia's promise not to begin hostilities it would squander the advantage it enjoyed of a more rapid mobilization of its forces. The government had therefore presented an ultimatum to Russia to suspend its mobilization while asking France what it would do in the case of a Russo-German war. Bethmann Hollweg feared that Russia would not comply and that France would join its ally. If this proved to be the case, the kaiser would declare that a state of war existed.

The chancellor hoped that the delegates would agree it was impossible for Germany to bear Russia's provocation, 'if we are not to abdicate as one of the Great Powers of Europe'. Germany did not wish the war, which had been forced upon it—a war which would require the German people to make the greatest sacrifices that they had ever made.

There was no argument. The delegates of the states unanimously approved of the government's actions. The chancellor closed the meeting: 'If the iron dice are now to be rolled, may God help us.'[9]

The kaiser was ready. Riding in the Tiergarten that morning with an Austrian diplomat, he had stressed that Austria must direct all the military means at its disposal against Russia, whose preparations along the Austro-Russian frontier were 'colossal'.[10] He authorized the general mobilization of German forces. He approved the formal German note to be handed to Russia later that day, once it had failed to respond positively to the German demand that it demobilize: 'His Majesty the Emperor, my August Sovereign, accepts the challenge in the name of the Empire, and considers himself as being in a state of war with Russia.'[11]

Germany's diplomats were frantically engaged in trying to cement the alliance to fight the war that they could now see clearly in sight. Italy and Romania were vital. It was of the 'greatest importance' that Romania should put its whole army into the field against Russia. It would not do so, however, unless it could be guaranteed of its security along its frontier with Bulgaria. What was needed was a 'binding declaration' from Bulgaria that in the event of war it would act 'according to our wishes'.[12] Berchtold was to undertake this move at Sofia.

By midday Saturday the Austrians and the Germans were convinced that they at last had a deal regarding compensation that would keep Italy within the Triple Alliance. The Austrian ambassador in Vienna had agreed to it with Berchtold, in the presence of the German ambassador. Berchtold instructed Mérey in Rome to call upon San Giuliano immediately to inform him that Austria now accepted the Italian interpretation of Article VII of the Triple Alliance 'presuming that Italy would fully perform its duties as an ally in the present conflict'.[13] Five minutes later Jagow instructed the German ambassador at Rome to communicate the deal at once to San Giuliano in Rome, as he understood that 'the attitude of the government there would be altered by it'.[14]

Would it? Really? The Austrian military attaché at Rome had reported that 'the tide of public sentiment' had turned in favour of Austria and Germany several days ago.[15] Conrad wrote to the new Italian chief of the general staff asking what forces Italy would make available, and when, to support both Austria-Hungary and Germany. At the same time the Austrian ambassador was warning that the Italians could not be trusted, that they were still pursuing a policy of blackmail, trying to get guarantees of compensation beforehand—whether the war remained localized or became general. Flotow warned Berlin from Rome that Mérey was continuing to impede any agreement with Italy.

The situation with Turkey was much clearer. The Grand Vizier had approached the Germans with a proposal for a secret offensive and defensive alliance earlier in the week, on Tuesday the 28th. But the Germans had hesitated: it could complicate their diplomatic initiatives in the Balkans. Now, however, they no longer had the luxury of delay: any opportunity to make things more difficult for Russia was an advantage. If the head of the German military mission in Turkey, General Liman von Sanders, confirmed to the German ambassador in Constantinople that Turkey would, in the event of war with Russia, 'stand with us actively and effectively', the ambassador was authorized to sign the proposed alliance.[16]

Simultaneously, the Austrians were moving to make a deal with Montenegro. Given the affinity between the Montenegrins and the Serbs, the best the Austrians could hope for was that the king might be persuaded—or bribed—to remain neutral. In exchange for neutrality Austria-Hungary promised to respect its independence and the inviolability of its territory, its extension into Albania and the Sanjak of Novibazar, and 'financial support'.[17]

An hour after despatching the telegram to St Petersburg containing the German declaration of war, another telegram arrived in Berlin from the tsar. Nicholas said he understood that, under the circumstances, the kaiser was obliged to mobilize, but he asked Wilhelm to give him that same guarantee that he had given Wilhelm: 'that these measures DO NOT mean war' and that they would continue to negotiate 'for the benefit of our countries and universal peace dear to our hearts'. With God's help, their friendship must succeed in avoiding bloodshed.[18]

In Berlin that morning crowds had begun to gather around the newspaper offices, anxiously awaiting news. By afternoon they numbered in the tens of thousands—perhaps over one hundred thousand near the palace. At 3 p.m. the kaiser, the kaiserin, and other members of the royal family left the Neues Palais in Potsdam and drove down the great Middle Way of the Unter den Linden in open cars on their way to the Stadtschloss in Berlin. The kaiser, wearing the dress uniform of Cuirassiers of the Guard, maintained a salute to the cheering crowds along the way.

★

In London Sir Edward Grey continued to believe that peace might be saved if only a little time could be gained before shooting started. After the cabinet meeting ended at 1.30 that afternoon Grey wired the ambassador in Berlin: Russia and Austria had both now agreed on the terms by which a mediation could commence. The British government would carefully abstain from any act that might precipitate matters. 'Things ought not to be hopeless while Russia and Austria are ready to converse.'[19]

Grey was as good as his word. He met with both the French and German ambassadors in the afternoon and held out little hope to either of them: to Cambon, no promise of British assistance; to Lichnowsky, no promise of British neutrality. Instead, he proposed that, following the mobilization of French and German forces on their frontier, they should remain there, both agreeing not to cross as long as the other refrained from doing so.

Grey contacted Lichnowsky to tell him that he wished to see him in order to make another proposal regarding British neutrality, 'even in the event that we should have war with France as well as Russia'.[20] When this news reached Berlin the kaiser was elated, the civilians pleased, and Tirpitz satisfied. The kaiser proposed that they turn the bulk of their armies against Russia; the civilians were convinced that their diplomacy had succeeded in securing British neutrality in a continental war. Tirpitz declared: 'The risk theory works!'[21]

When Lichnowsky met with Grey in person following the cabinet meeting, the offer did not turn out to be what he had hoped for. The foreign secretary began by reading out a statement which, he said, had been unanimously agreed upon by the cabinet. The cabinet greatly regretted the reply of the German government regarding Belgian neutrality: if it could give the same positive reply that the French government had given it would 'relieve anxiety and tension' in Britain. On the other hand, if one combatant violated Belgium's neutrality while the other respected it, 'it would be extremely difficult to restrain public feeling in this country'.[22] Lichnowsky asked him if he could promise that Britain would remain neutral if Germany respected Belgian neutrality. Grey was not prepared to give such a promise.

Grey asked if it might be possible for Germany and France to remain facing one another under arms, without attacking, in the event of a Russian war. Lichnowsky, evidently unaware of Germany's deployment plan, replied that this might be possible—if Germany could be certain of Britain's neutrality. He reported to Berlin that Britain wanted to keep out of the war

Alfred von Tirpitz (1849–1930); state secretary, imperial navy office of Germany (1897–1916)

if it could possibly do so, but that Jagow's reply concerning Belgian neutrality 'has caused an unfavourable impression'.

If Lichnowsky was disappointed, Cambon was dismayed. Grey informed him that the current situation 'differed entirely' from those they had faced over Morocco. In the earlier crises Germany had made demands on France that the French could not accept and over which Britain was obligated to support them. British public opinion would have supported the government. This time, however, Germany appeared willing to agree not to attack France if France remained neutral in a war between Russia and Germany.

If France was unable to take advantage of this offer 'it was because she was bound by an alliance to which we were not parties, and of which we did not know the terms'. Although he would not rule out assisting France under any circumstances, France must make its own decision 'without reckoning on an assistance that we were not now in a position to give'.[23]

Cambon was shocked. He said that he could not transmit to Paris what Grey had told him. He proposed instead to tell his government that the British cabinet had yet to make a decision. He complained that France had left its Atlantic coast undefended because of the naval convention with Britain in 1912 and that the British were honour-bound to assist them. His complaint fell on deaf ears. He staggered from Grey's office into an adjoining room, close to hysteria, 'his face white'.[24] The elderly, distinguished, white-haired diplomat could see the achievements of sixteen years of effort disappearing before his eyes.

Immediately after the meeting the shaken ambassador met with two influential Unionists. He made no effort to hide his bitterness. 'Honour! Does England know what honour is?' Although he had to admit that there was no written obligation to assist France, if they remained neutral they would deliver control of the French coast to Germany: 'If you stay out and we survive, we shall not move a finger to save you from being crushed by the Germans later.'[25]

Hiding his bitterness and his disappointment, Cambon provided Paris with only a vague summary of his discussion with Grey. He reported that the foreign secretary intended to seek the cabinet's approval for stating to the House of Commons on Monday that the British government would not permit a violation of Belgian neutrality. He would, moreover, propose to his colleagues an announcement that Britain would oppose the passage of the Straits of Dover by the German fleet or any 'demonstration' of Germany's fleet on the French coasts.[26] He held out at least a glimmer of hope that Britain might join France if Germany attacked.

★

Would Cambon's treatment of the situation matter in Paris? That morning General Joffre, chief of the general staff, had threatened to resign if the government refused to order mobilization. Attending the meeting of the cabinet that afternoon, he warned that France had already fallen two days behind Germany in preparing for war. The cabinet was not unanimous. One-third to one-quarter of them expressed reservations about mobilizing immediately. But, in the end, they agreed to distribute mobilization notices that afternoon at 4 p.m.—hours before Cambon's report on the British position was received in Paris. They agreed, however, to maintain the 10-kilometre buffer zone: 'No patrol, no reconnaissance, no post, no element whatsoever, must go east of the said line. Whoever crosses it will be liable to court martial and it is only in the event of a full-scale attack that it will be possible to transgress this order.'[27]

Shortly after the cabinet meeting notices began to appear throughout French cities: '*MOBILISATION GENERALE. Le premier jour de la mobilisation est le dimanche 2 août.*' Still, Poincaré hastened to assure everyone that 'mobilization is not war'. In a two-page explanation of policy that was distributed to journalists the president insisted that it was still the ardent desire of the government to settle the crisis peacefully. They were only taking precautions while continuing their diplomatic efforts. The government was relying on 'the composure of this noble nation not to allow itself to indulge in unjustified emotion'. And they knew that they could rely on the patriotism of all Frenchmen and were confident that they were ready to do their duty. 'In this hour there are no parties. There is a France *éternelle*, peaceful and resolute France. There is the *patrie* of right and justice, completely united in calm vigilance and dignity.' When the proclamation was presented to the waiting journalists there were cries of '*Vive la France*'.[28]

By 5 p.m. the streets of Paris were almost deserted: people were at home, preparing for the mobilization. The only traffic consisted of vehicles carrying reservists headed for railway stations. Except for post offices, all public services were suspended or transformed for military purposes. Buses disappeared from the streets as they were all commandeered to assist in transporting troops to the frontier. Later in the evening, detachments of reservists began marching down the boulevards to their assembly-points, waving their *képis* in the air to the cheers of those gathered in cafés. Searchlights, including one atop the Eiffel Tower, began scanning the skies in search of airplanes and zeppelins.

In the village of Vatilieu in the *département* of Isère in south-eastern France two police cars arrived in the square with the mobilization order. The *tocsin* was sounded. 'Nobody spoke for a long while. Some were out of breath, others dumb with shock. Many still carried their pitchforks in their hands. . . . Wives, children, husbands—all were overcome by anguish and emotion. The wives clung to the arms of their husbands. The children, seeing their mothers weeping, started to cry too. All around us was alarm and consternation.'[29] Throughout France war was now regarded as a virtual certainty.

The French government continued to insist this was not so. The political director at the Quai d'Orsay assured the Austrian ambassador that 'it was a long way from mobilization to a declaration of war'.[30] The French consti- tution stipulated that the consent of the chamber was required for such a declaration—and it had not even convened yet. When Viviani met with the German ambassador at 5.30 p.m. he assured him that mobilization did not indicate any aggressive intentions on the part of France. He offered the continuation of the 10-kilometre buffer zone along the frontier as proof of this. Viviani continued to cling to the latest Grey proposal that everyone should cease further military measures while negotiating a solution to the crisis. If Germany agreed to this France would too. The French premier was encouraged by Austro-Russian conversations in St Petersburg; he 'would not abandon his hope for peace'.[31]

Viviani was not alone. When the Russian ambassador in Vienna met with Berchtold that afternoon the foreign minister seemed anxious to clear up the 'misunderstanding' between them. Schebeko concluded from their conversation that Austria might welcome an opportunity to escape from the current situation 'without damaging its *amour propre*' or its prestige in the Balkans and within Austria-Hungary.[32]

★

Would the Germans agree? By 4 p.m. Russia had not responded to the ultimatum that expired at noon. Falkenhayn, the minister of war, went to Bethmann Hollweg to persuade him that they should go together to see the kaiser and ask him to promulgate the order for mobilization. Bethmann Hollweg, after some argument, agreed. They called up Moltke and Tirpitz and asked them to come along. At 5 p.m., in the Sternensaal ('Hall of Stars') at the Berlin Stadtschloss, the mobilization order sat on a table made from the timbers of Nelson's *Victory*. As the kaiser signed it, Falkenhayn declared, 'God bless Your Majesty and your arms, God protect the beloved Father- land.' Both had tears in their eyes as they shook hands.[33]

Then another diplomatic bombshell hit. Lichnowsky's telegram of that morning, holding out the prospect of British neutrality, arrived at the palace shortly after the kaiser signed the mobilization order. If what the ambassador said was true, it suddenly seemed possible that Britain would remain neutral, and guarantee France's neutrality, if Germany were to refrain from attacking

France.[34] This might mean that the war could be limited to the eastern front and that Russia would face the German and Austro-Hungarian armies on its own. The kaiser, Bethmann Hollweg, and Jagow greeted this news 'with great joy'.[35] Wilhelm wanted to deploy the whole army in the east. Moltke, who had already left, returned in haste to the palace. He was distraught: a war against Russia alone was impossible!

The kaiser was adamant. He ordered a bottle of champagne while Jagow assisted him and Bethmann Hollweg in drafting telegrams to King George and Lichnowsky indicating that Germany was prepared to accept Britain's offer to guarantee French neutrality. But news of the British proposal had arrived after Germany had already proclaimed mobilization and troops were on their way to Luxembourg, and, for technical reasons, the mobilization order could not now be countermanded. 'I am sorry', the kaiser wrote, 'your telegram came so late.' But, if French neutrality were to be guaranteed by the British fleet and army, Germany would refrain from attacking France. The kaiser hoped that France would not become nervous: 'The troops on my frontier are in the act of being stopped by telegraph and telephone from crossing into France.'[36] Lichnowsky was authorized to promise that German forces would not cross the French frontier before Monday, 3 August at 7 p.m. if Britain's agreement could be obtained before that time.[37] Jagow told the ambassador in Paris that they hoped to reach agreement with Britain on a guarantee of French neutrality: 'Please keep the French quiet for the time being'; no hostile action against France was contemplated, despite mobilization.[38]

When the kaiser's telegram to the king was received in London Sir Edward Grey was enjoying an after-dinner game of billiards at his club. He was summoned to Buckingham Palace to explain what was going on, and to draft a reply to the kaiser. 'I think there must be some misunderstanding' was what he had the king telegraph to the kaiser in response.[39] A suggestion 'had passed' between Grey and the German ambassador that afternoon when they were discussing how fighting between the German and French armies might be avoided while there was still a chance of some agreement between Austria and Russia. Grey would see Lichnowsky early on Sunday morning 'to ascertain whether there is a misunderstanding on his part'.[40]

By late Saturday evening the confusion was widespread. In St Petersburg Count Pourtalès had, as instructed, presented the German declaration of war to Sazonov at 7 p.m. local time. But shortly after Lichnowsky's encouraging messages were received from London, Bethmann Hollweg drafted another telegram for the kaiser to send to the tsar. At 10.30 p.m. the kaiser wired to explain that he had been forced to mobilize his army because Russia had failed to respond to the demand that it demobilize its forces. 'Immediate, affirmative and unmistakable answer from your Government is the only way to avoid endless misery.' The kaiser could not promise the tsar that Germany would not to go to war and that it would continue to negotiate in spite of mobilization until Russia responded to Germany's demand. 'I must request you to immediately order your troops on no account, to commit the slightest act of trespassing over our frontiers.'[41]

Was Germany at war with Russia or not? Even the 'declaration' of war was rather opaque: at 7 p.m. Pourtalès had told Sazonov that the kaiser 'considers himself as being in a state of war with Russia'. Rather strange, then, to insist several hours later that Russian troops ought to be ordered not to cross the German frontier.

The Germans continued to be encouraged throughout the evening that Grey's 'proposal' to guarantee French neutrality would change everything. The kaiser instructed that the Italians should be informed immediately of the British proposal, as they would remain timid supporters of the Triple Alliance as long as they feared that Britain might intervene.[42]

The kaiser's hopes were soon dashed. Not only did King George suggest that there must have been 'some misunderstanding' in how Lichnowsky had interpreted Grey's words, but now the Italians seemed ready to declare their position clearly and publicly. The German ambassador warned Berlin that San Giuliano was still inclined to refuse to participate in a European war, although he would bring the matter before the cabinet meeting scheduled for later Saturday night. Flotow confirmed the impression that Britain's attitude was the determining factor for the Italians, as San Giuliano had repeatedly insisted that Italian coasts and harbours could not be subjected to the guns of the British navy; Italian troops in Libya could be cut off from supplies. Sometime around midnight the Italian cabinet agreed to declare neutrality and San Giuliano was to draft a declaration to that effect the next day.

By the end of the day the federal council in Germany had met, the British cabinet had met, the Russian cabinet had met, and the Italian cabinet had met. At midnight at the Elysée Palace Poincaré convened a meeting of the French cabinet, which was to last until 4 a.m. Half an hour before the meeting the Russian ambassador came to Poincaré with the news that Germany had declared war on Russia. Izvol'skii wanted to know how France would respond. With Grey's suggestion for a military standstill in front of him, the French president was not very encouraging. He told the ambassador that both France and Russia had an interest that mobilization should be taken as far as possible before war was declared. It would be much better if the declaration of war came 'not from France but from Germany'.[43] This was advisable for both military and political reasons: 'a defensive war would raise the whole country'.[44] Poincaré, who recognized that the alliance with Russia was not popular, wished, if at all possible, to avoid the appearance that it was France's commitments to its ally that drew it into the war.

Izvol'skii waited at the palace until 4 a.m. in order to hear the results of the meeting. The cabinet confirmed that it would uphold the commitment of France to the alliance with Russia. France should complete its mobilization before military operations began, and this would take ten days. This 'is a matter of the greatest secrecy'.[45]

The British ambassador was also waiting while the French cabinet deliberated. And, while he waited, he wondered what Grey's conversation with Lichnowsky really meant. 'Do you desire me to state to French Government that after mobilisation of French and German troops on Franco-German frontier we propose to remain neutral so long as German troops remain on the defensive and do not cross French frontier, and French abstain from crossing German frontier?' Bertie could not imagine that it would be consistent with French obligations to the Russians to remain quiescent in the event of them being at war with Austria and being attacked by Germany. 'If French undertook to remain so, the Germans would first attack Russians and, if they defeated them, they would then turn round on the French.'[46]

News of the German declaration of war on Russia spread quickly throughout St Petersburg immediately following the meeting between Pourtalès and Sazonov. Vast crowds began to gather on the Nevsky Prospekt; women threw their jewels into collection bins to support the families of the reservists who had been called up. By 11.30 that night around 50,000 people surrounded the British embassy calling out, 'God save the King', 'Rule Britannia', and '*Bozhe Tsara Khranie*' ('God save the Tsar'). The crowd then moved along to continue their demonstration in front of the French embassy.

Shortly after midnight the German minister of war convinced the chief of the general staff to go with him to see the secretary of state in order to convince him 'to prevent the foolish and premature declaration of war on Russia'. Jagow told him that it was now too late.[47] The kaiser, he told the British ambassador, was 'fearfully depressed'.[48]

Sunday, 2 August

By Sunday morning everyone involved in the crisis was utterly exhausted. All were awake into the small hours of Sunday; some had been up all night. In Berlin Horace Rumbold was still sending telegrams at 1.30 a.m., having sent the attachés to bed because they were dead beat. 'The crisis is telling on our nerves,' he wrote to his wife.[49] 'We are all worn out and that is the truth. I don't think we could stick it for another 48 hours.'[50]

Confusion was still widespread. On Saturday Germany and France had joined Austria-Hungary and Russia in announcing their general mobilization; by 7 p.m. Germany appeared to be at war with Russia. Still, the only shots fired in anger consisted of the bombs that the Austrians continued to shower on Belgrade. Sir Edward Grey continued to hope that the German and French armies might agree on a standstill behind their frontiers while Russia and Austria proceeded to negotiate a settlement over Serbia. No one was certain what the British would do. Especially not the British.

Shortly after dawn, German troops crossed the frontier into the Grand Duchy of Luxembourg. Trains loaded with soldiers crossed the bridge at Wasserbillig and headed to the city of Luxembourg, the capital of the Grand Duchy. By 8.30 a.m. German troops occupied the railway station in the city centre. Marie-Adélaïde, the grand duchess, protested directly to the kaiser, demanding an explanation and asking him to respect the country's rights. The chancellor responded to her protest: Germany's military measures should not be regarded as hostile, but only as steps to protect the railways under German management against an attack by the French; he promised full compensation for any damages suffered. Luxembourg's prime minister demanded to know 'whether the entire country is to be occupied' or only a portion of it.[51]

The neutrality of Luxembourg had been guaranteed by the Powers in the Treaty of London of 1867. The prime minister protested the violation to Berlin, Paris, London, and Brussels. Jagow replied by repeating Bethmann

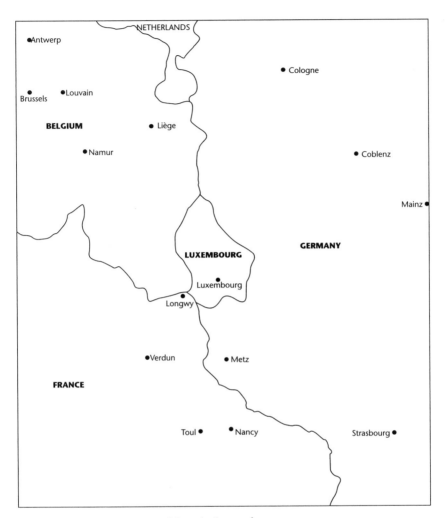

Map 6. Luxembourg

Hollweg's reassurance that no hostile action was intended and promising compensation. He regretted that there had been no time to make arrangements with the government of Luxembourg, but the danger of a French attack was imminent: Germany had received 'reliable information' that French armed forces were advancing on Luxembourg.[52] It was necessary to act in order to protect the German army and to secure the railways. At the same time the German ambassador in Paris informed the French government that Germany's actions did not constitute an act of hostility but must be regarded as 'purely preventive measures' taken to protect the railways which were, by treaty, under German administration.[53]

Paul Cambon received the news in London from Viviani at 7.42 a.m. He immediately requested a meeting with Sir Edward Grey. The foreign secretary tried to put him off until after the cabinet meeting, which was scheduled for 11 that morning. But Cambon persisted and Grey relented. The French ambassador brought with him a copy of the 1867 treaty—but Grey took the position that the treaty was a 'collective instrument', meaning that if Germany chose to violate it, Britain was released from any obligation to uphold it.[54] Disgusted, Cambon declared that the word 'honour' might have 'to be struck out of the British vocabulary'.[55]

There was no sign that anyone who mattered in Britain regarded the violation of Luxembourg's neutrality as a cause worth fighting for. It was barely spoken of when the cabinet met that morning.

The cabinet was to meet at 10 Downing Street at 11 a.m. Before it convened Lloyd George held a small meeting of his own at the chancellor's residence next door. He, 'Loulou' Harcourt (colonial secretary), the Earl of Beauchamp (commissioner of works), John Simon (attorney-general), Walter Runciman (president of the board of trade), and 'Jack' Pease (president of the board of education) discussed what position they ought to take when the full cabinet met. They were untroubled by the German invasion of Luxembourg and agreed that, as a group, they would oppose Britain's entry into the war in Europe. They might reconsider under certain circumstances, however, 'such as the invasion wholesale of Belgium'.[56]

Richard, Viscount Haldane, former minister of war, a 'Liberal imperialist', friendly with Sir Edward Grey and now lord chancellor, found himself caught in the middle. Before the cabinet meeting he wrote to his sister that both extremes of opinion were wrong: 'that on the one hand we can wholly disinterest ourselves and on the other that we ought to rush in'. The correct course, he believed, was for Britain to prepare to intervene if it were called upon at a decisive moment. Unfortunately, he found it difficult to formulate this policy in any clear terms.[57] Precisely what were the conditions in which Britain should intervene?

The cabinet found it almost impossible to answer this question. The government appeared to be on the verge of collapse. Opinions ranged from opposition to intervention under any circumstances to immediate mobilization of the army in anticipation of despatching the British Expeditionary Force to France in the coming week. Grey revealed his frustration with the behaviour of Germany and Austria-Hungary: they had chosen to play with the most vital interests of civilization and had declined the numerous attempts he had made to find a way out of the crisis. While appearing to negotiate they had continued their march 'steadily to war'.[58] But the views of the foreign secretary proved unacceptable to the majority of the cabinet. Asquith believed they were on the brink of a split.

After almost three hours of heated debate the cabinet agreed to authorize Grey to give the French a qualified assurance. The British government would not permit the Germans to make the English Channel the base for hostile operations against the French. Even this caused John Burns, president of the board of trade—and the first working-man ever appointed to the cabinet—to resign on the spot. He feared that such a statement might be regarded by Germany as an act of hostility and lead it to declare war on Britain. The prime minister managed to talk Burns out of resigning for the moment at least, until they gathered again that evening.

All the 'Beagles'—Asquith's term for the lesser members of the cabinet—backed by Lloyd George, Morley, and Harcourt, remained adamantly opposed to any kind of intervention. If the cabinet agreed with them, Grey would quit—and Asquith would likely go with him. Several ministers remained in the middle, believing that intervention might be called for in certain circumstances. What those circumstances might be remained unclear.

One of the waverers in the middle, Herbert Samuel (president of the local government board), attempted to explain under what conditions he believed intervention would be justified. Britain must protect the northern coast of France: it could not afford to see it bombarded by the German fleet and occupied by German armies. Britain must also insist on the independence of Belgium, 'which we were bound by treaty to protect and which again we could not afford to see subordinated to Germany'. On the other hand, he did not believe that they could justify entering the war for the sake of their goodwill for the French or in order to maintain the strength of France and Russia against that of Germany and Austria.[59]

Complicating things for Asquith was his estimate that three-quarters of Liberal members in the House of Commons were 'for absolute non-interference at any price'. For his part, the prime minister emerged from the meeting clear in his own mind as to what was right and what was wrong. He listed his guiding principles in a letter to his mistress after the meeting that afternoon:

1. We have no obligation of any kind either to France or Russia to give them military or naval help.

2. The despatch of the Expeditionary Force to help France at this moment is out of the question and wd. serve no object.

3. We mustn't forget the ties created by our long-standing and intimate friendship with France.

4. It is against British interests that France should be wiped out as a Great Power.

5. We cannot allow Germany to use the Channel as a hostile base.

6. We have obligations to Belgium to prevent her being utilized and absorbed by Germany.[60]

As the cabinet were meeting in the afternoon a great anti-war demonstration was beginning only a few hundred yards away in Trafalgar Square. Trade unions organized a series of processions, with thousands of workers marching to meet at Nelson's Column from St George's Circus, the East India Docks, Kentish Town, and Westminster Cathedral. Speeches began around 4 p.m.—by which time 10,000–15,000 had gathered to hear Keir Hardie and other labour leaders, socialists, and peace activists. With rain pouring down, at 5 p.m. a resolution in favour of international peace and for solidarity among the workers of the world 'to use their industrial and political power in order that the nations shall not be involved in the war' was put to the crowd and deemed to have carried.[61]

If the British cabinet was divided, so however were the British people. When the crowd began singing 'The Red Flag' and the '*Internationale*' they were matched by anti-socialists and pro-war demonstrators singing 'God Save the King' and 'Rule Britannia'. When a red flag was hoisted, a Union Jack went up in reply. Part of the crowd broke away and marched a few hundred feet to Admiralty Arch where they listened to patriotic speeches. Several thousand marched up the Mall to Buckingham Palace, singing the national anthem and the *Marseillaise*. The king and the queen appeared on the balcony to acknowledge the cheering crowd. Later that evening demonstrators gathered in front of the French embassy to show their support.

In Paris that afternoon the general staff began to receive reports of German incursions across the French frontier. General Joffre pleaded with the cabinet to remove the restriction on French forces to maintain the 10-kilometre buffer between themselves and the frontier; at 2 p.m. they agreed. Even so, the chief of the general staff instructed his officers that it

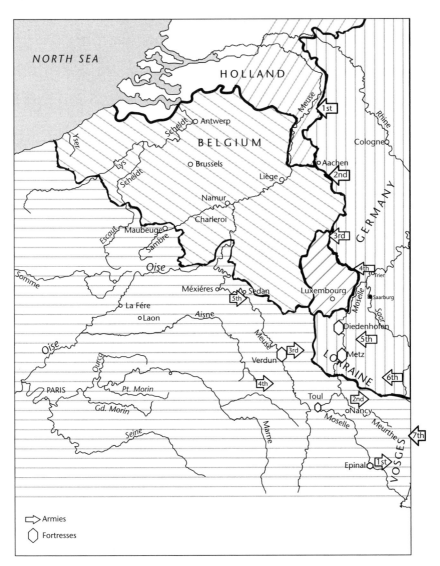

Map 7. Armies and fortifications

was 'indispensable' that the Germans be made responsible for any hostilities. 'Consequently, and until further notice, covering troops will restrict themselves to expelling across the frontier any assault troops without giving chase any further and without encroaching on opposing territory.'[62]

The anti-war sentiment, which was still strong among labour groups and socialist organizations in Britain, was rapidly dissipating in France. The day after the assassination of Jaurès one socialist newspaper declared, 'National Defence above all! They have murdered Jaurès! We will not murder France!'[63] On Sunday morning the Socialist Party announced its intention to defend France in the event of war. The newspaper of the syndicalist CGT declared 'That the name of the old emperor Franz Joseph be cursed'; it denounced the kaiser 'and the pangermanists' as responsible for the war.[64] One influential socialist was persuaded to write to Ramsay MacDonald— the leader of the Independent Labour Party in Britain—and plead with him to support British intervention in support of France.

In Germany three large trade unions did a deal with the government. In exchange for promising not to go on strike, the government promised not to ban them.

In Russia, organized opposition to war practically disappeared. In St Petersburg on Sunday at 3 p.m. five or six thousand people assembled in the massive St George's Gallery in the Winter Palace. Court officials attended in full dress; military officers in field dress. An altar was erected in the centre of the room, featuring the miraculous icon of the Virgin Mary, borrowed from the Cathedral of Our Lady of Kazan on the Nevsky Prospekt. Tsar Nicholas and his cortège proceeded in silence to the altar, where mass was performed. The tsar prayed 'with a holy fervour which gave his pale face a movingly mystical expression'.[65] When prayers were finished the court chaplain read aloud a manifesto to the people from the tsar.

BY the Grace of God, We, Nicholas II, Emperor and Autocrat of all Russia, Tsar of Poland, Grand Duke of Finland, etc., etc., etc., proclaim to all Our loyal subjects:

Following her historical traditions, Russia, united in faith and blood with the Slav nations, has never regarded their fate with indifference. The unanimous fraternal sentiments of the Russian people for the Slavs have been aroused to special intensity in the past few days, when Austria-Hungary presented to Serbia demands which she foresaw would be unacceptable to a Sovereign State.

Having disregarded the conciliatory and peaceable reply of the Serbian Government, and having declined Russia's well-intentioned mediation, Austria hastened to launch an armed attack in a bombardment of unprotected Belgrade.

Compelled, by the force of circumstances thus created, to adopt the necessary measures of precaution, We commanded that the army and the navy be put on a war footing, but, at the same time, holding the blood and the treasure of Our subjects dear, We made every effort to obtain a peaceable issue of the negotiations that had been started.

In the midst of friendly communications, Austria's Ally, Germany, contrary to our trust in century-old relations of neighbourliness, and paying no heed to Our assurances that the measures We had adopted implied no hostile aims whatever, insisted upon their immediate abandonment, and, meeting with a rejection of this demand, suddenly declared war on Russia.

We have now to intercede not only for a related country, unjustly attacked, but also to safeguard the honour, dignity, and integrity of Russia, and her position among the Great Powers. We firmly believe that all Our loyal subjects will rally self-sacrificingly and with one accord to the defense of the Russian soil.

At this hour of threatening danger, let domestic strife be forgotten. Let the union between the Tsar and His people be stronger than ever, and let Russia, rising like one man, repel the insolent assault of the enemy.

With a profound faith in the justice of Our cause, and trusting humbly in Almighty Providence, We invoke prayerfully the Divine blessing for Holy Russia and our valiant troops.[66]

The tsar then approached the altar and raised his right hand to the gospel held out to him. Slowly and deliberately he solemnly declared 'that I will never make peace so long as one of the enemy is on the soil of the fatherland'. Nicholas had copied the words used by Alexander I in 1812. Following the declaration the tsar appeared on the balcony of the palace. The huge crowd that had gathered there knelt and sang the Russian national anthem.

Before the ceremony at the palace the tsar had authorized a telegram to be sent in reply to one he had received from King George the day before. The king had pleaded with the tsar to do anything he could to avoid the 'terrible calamity which . . . threatens the whole world'. He hoped that there was still an opportunity for negotiation and peace and expressed his willingness to contribute in any way that he could to reopening the discussions between the Powers involved.[67] The tsar now replied to say that he had been given no choice, that he had been presented with a declaration of war from Germany in spite of the categorical assurances that he had given the kaiser that Russian troops would not move as long as negotiations continued. Now that war had been forced upon him, 'I trust your country will not fail to support France and Russia in fighting to maintain the balance of power in Europe. God bless and protect you.'[68]

★

Shortly before dinner that evening the British cabinet met once again to decide whether they were prepared to enter the war. The prime minister had received a promise from the leader of the Unionist opposition, Andrew Bonar Law, that his party would support Britain's entry into the war. Now, if the anti-war sentiment in cabinet led to the resignation of Sir Edward Grey—and most likely of Asquith, Churchill, and several others along with him—there loomed the likelihood of a coalition government being formed that would lead Britain into war anyway.

Nothing was decided. Burns and Simon continued to warn the others that they would resign if Britain entered the war under almost any circumstances. The others were generally agreed that intervention might be warranted if Germany sent her fleet into the Channel or invaded Belgium. They continued to hope that the stand they had taken in the morning might deter Germany. If so, Herbert Samuel argued, Britain would have accomplished a brilliant stroke of policy: protecting France's north coast and her 150 miles of frontier with Belgium 'without firing a shot'. If they failed to accomplish this then the failure would be Germany's responsibility 'and my conscience will be easy in embarking on the war'.[69]

After the meeting the attorney-general submitted his resignation to Asquith. Simon believed that the statement that Grey had been authorized to make to Cambon that afternoon, regarding the protection of France's north coast against the German fleet, was tantamount to a declaration that Britain was prepared to take part 'in this quarrel with France and against Germany'. As he believed that Britain should not take part, 'I must resign my post'.[70]

While the British cabinet were meeting in London they were unaware that the German minister at Brussels was presenting an ultimatum to the Belgian government. At 6.30 p.m. Walter von Below-Saleske requested an immediate appointment with the foreign minister. Half an hour later he arrived at the office of Viscomte Julien Davignon, pale and trembling. 'What is the matter, are you not well?' Davignon asked. Below replied that he had come up the stairs too quickly, that it was nothing to worry about. He handed the foreign minister a sealed envelope.

The note contained in the envelope claimed that the German government had received reliable information that French forces were preparing to march through Belgian territory in order to attack Germany. Germany feared that Belgium would be unable to resist a French invasion. For the sake of Germany's self-defence it was essential that it anticipate such an attack, which might necessitate German forces entering Belgian territory. Thus, Germany declared:[71]

1. Germany has in view no act of hostility against Belgium. In the event of Belgium being prepared in the coming war to maintain an attitude of friendly neutrality towards Germany, the German Government bind themselves, at the conclusion of peace, to guarantee the possessions and independence of the Belgian Kingdom in full.

2. Germany undertakes, under the above-mentioned condition, to evacuate Belgian territory on the conclusion of peace.

3. If Belgium adopts a friendly attitude, Germany is prepared, in co-operation with the Belgian authorities, to purchase all necessities for her troops against a cash payment, and to pay an indemnity for any damages caused by German troops.

4. Should Belgium oppose the German troops, and in particular should she throw difficulties in the way of their march by a resistance of the fortresses on the Meuse, or by destroying railways, roads, tunnels, or other similar works, Germany will, to her regret, be compelled to consider Belgium as an enemy.

In this event, Germany can undertake no obligations towards Belgium, but the eventual adjustment of the relations between the two States must be left to the decision of arms.

Belgium was given until 7 a.m. the next morning—twelve hours—to respond. Davignon was incredulous. 'No, surely? . . . No, it is not possible!'[72] He said he would immediately inform the king and the cabinet and that they would reply within twelve hours. Davignon 'could not conceal his pained surprise at the unexpected communication'.[73] Within the hour the prime minister took the German note to the king. They agreed that Belgium could not agree to the demands. The king called his council of ministers to the palace at 9 p.m. They discussed the situation until midnight. The council agreed unanimously with the position taken by the king and the prime minister. They recessed for an hour, resuming their meeting at 1 a.m. to draft a reply.

The French minister in Brussels was convinced that the Belgian government was preparing to yield to Germany. Rumours abounded that there is 'some sort of connivance between the two countries'.[74]

Monday, 3 August

At 7 a.m. Monday morning the official reply of the Belgian government was handed to the German minister in Brussels. The German note had made 'a deep and painful impression' on the government. France had given them a formal declaration that it would not violate Belgian neutrality, and, if it were to do so, 'the Belgian army would offer the most vigorous resistance to the invader'. Belgium had always been faithful to its international obligations and had left nothing undone 'to maintain and enforce respect' for its neutrality. The attack on Belgian independence which Germany was now threatening 'constitutes a flagrant violation of international law'. No strategic interest could justify this. 'The Belgian Government, if they were to accept the proposals submitted to them, would sacrifice the honour of the nation and betray at the same time their duties towards Europe.' The government refused to believe that Belgium's independence could be preserved only at the price of its neutrality being violated and are 'firmly determined to repel, by all the means in their power, every encroachment upon their rights'.[75]

Would they? Really? The French minister continued to doubt it. He confided to his Russian colleague his fears that Belgium's defence would amount to no more than a 'sham'.[76] When he had assured the foreign minister that if Belgium were to appeal to the Powers who had guaranteed neutrality, France would respond at once, he had declined to make such an appeal. The French military attaché offered the support of five army corps, but this too was declined. Instead, King Albert appealed only to King George for Britain's 'diplomatic intervention' to safeguard the integrity of Belgium.[77]

Before the British cabinet reconvened at 11 a.m. the prime minister had received notice that two more ministers intended to join John Burns in resigning. When the cabinet met, Burns, John Morley, and John Simon were joined by Beauchamp. There were now four ministers prepared to resign over the issue of British intervention. Lloyd George appealed to them to stay, or at least to delay their departure until further events unfolded. The four agreed to say nothing publicly for now and to take their usual seats in the House when it met that afternoon. 'The rest of us stood firm as we are sure our policy is right, much as we hate the war.' The cabinet discussion lasted for three hours, at the end of which they agreed on the line to be taken by Sir Edward Grey when he addressed the House of Commons at 3 p.m. 'The Cabinet was very moving. Most of us could hardly speak at all for emotion.'[78]

Grey began his address to the House by explaining that the present crisis differed from that of Morocco in 1912. That had been a dispute which involved France primarily, to whom Britain had promised diplomatic support, and had done so publicly. The situation they faced now had originated as a dispute between Austria and Serbia—one in which France had become engaged because it was obligated by honour to do so as a result of its alliance with Russia. But this obligation did not apply to Britain. 'We are not parties to the Franco-Russian Alliance. We do not even know the terms of that Alliance.'[79]

Britain did, however, have a long-standing friendship with France. They had cleared away their differences of the past. How far that friendship entails obligation 'let every man look into his own heart, and his own feelings'. Because of that friendship the French had concentrated their fleet in the Mediterranean because they were secure in the knowledge that they need not fear for the safety of their northern and western coasts. Those coasts were now absolutely undefended. 'My own feeling is that if a foreign fleet engaged in a war which France had not sought, and in which she had not been the aggressor, came down the English Channel and bombarded and battered the undefended coasts of France, we could not stand aside and see this going on practically within sight of our eyes, with our arms folded, looking on dispassionately, doing nothing!'[80] He believed that this would be the feeling in the country.

Looking at the matter without sentiment and from the point of view of British interests, he had grave concerns. What if, in order to defend its northern and western coasts, the French withdrew their fleet from the Mediterranean? Britain no longer had a fleet there capable on its own of dealing with a combination of other fleets, nor would it be in a position to send more ships there. Therefore, the government felt strongly that France was entitled to know 'and to know at once!' whether in the event of an attack on her coasts it could depend on British support.[81] Thus, he had given the government's assurance of support to the French ambassador yesterday.

There was now the more serious consideration, 'becoming more serious every hour', of the question of Belgian neutrality.[82] After a brief review of the treaty of 1839 and the history of Britain's commitment to it, Grey explained that he had asked both the French and German governments whether they were prepared to respect Belgian neutrality. France had given its assurance that it would do so, unless neutrality were violated by another Power; Germany had declined to answer on the grounds that to do so would be to disclose its plan-of-campaign. In reply to another query, Belgium had given its assurance that it was determined to defend its neutrality if it were violated by another Power. Now there were reports that Germany had presented Belgium with an ultimatum. Where did this leave British diplomacy?

Appealing to Liberal tradition, he invoked the great name of William Gladstone—no friend of militarism, imperialism, or interventionism. The greatest Liberal prime minister of the nineteenth century had denounced those who were prepared to stand aside while the independence of Belgium was extinguished. Those who were prepared to witness 'the perpetration of the direst crime that ever stained the pages of history' would themselves 'become participators in the sin'.

> We have great and vital interests in the independence—and integrity is the least part—of Belgium. If Belgium is compelled to submit to allow her neutrality to be violated, of course the situation is clear. Even if by agreement she admitted the violation of her neutrality, it is clear she could only do so under duress. The smaller States in that region of Europe ask but one thing. Their one desire is that they should be left alone and independent. The one thing they fear is, I think, not so much that their integrity but that their independence should be interfered with. If in this war which is before Europe the neutrality of one of those countries is violated, if the troops of one of the combatants violate its neutrality and no action be taken to resent it [*sic*], at the end of the war, whatever the integrity may be the independence will be gone....
>
> No, Sir, if it be the case that there has been anything in the nature of an ultimatum to Belgium, asking her to compromise or violate her neutrality, whatever may have been offered to her in return, her independence is gone if that holds. If her independence goes, the independence of Holland will follow. I ask the House from the point of view of British interests, to consider what may be at stake. If France is beaten in a struggle of life and death, beaten to her knees, loses her position as a great Power, becomes subordinate to the will and power of one greater than herself—consequences which I do not anticipate, because I am sure that France has the power to defend herself with all the energy and ability and patriotism which she has shown so often—still, if that were to happen, and if Belgium fell under the same dominating influence, and then Holland, and then Denmark, then would not Mr. Gladstone's words come true, that just opposite to us there would be a common interest against the unmeasured aggrandisement of any Power?
>
> It may be said, I suppose, that we might stand aside, husband our strength, and that whatever happened in the course of this war at the end of it intervene with effect to put things right, and to adjust them to our own point of view. If, in a crisis like this, we run away from those obligations of honour and interest as regards the Belgian Treaty, I doubt whether, whatever material force we might have at the end, it would be of very much value in face of the respect

that we should have lost. And do not believe, whether a great Power stands outside this war or not, it is going to be in a position at the end of it to exert its superior strength. For us, with a powerful Fleet, which we believe able to protect our commerce, to protect our shores, and to protect our interests, if we are engaged in war, we shall suffer but little more than we shall suffer even if we stand aside.

We are going to suffer, I am afraid, terribly in this war whether we are in it or whether we stand aside. Foreign trade is going to stop, not because the trade routes are closed, but because there is no trade at the other end. Continental nations engaged in war—all their populations, all their energies, all their wealth, engaged in a desperate struggle—they cannot carry on the trade with us that they are carrying on in times of peace, whether we are parties to the war or whether we are not. I do not believe for a moment, that at the end of this war, even if we stood aside and remained aside, we should be in a position, a material position, to use our force decisively to undo what had happened in the course of the war, to prevent the whole of the West of Europe opposite to us—if that had been the result of the war—falling under the domination of a single Power, and I am quite sure that our moral position would be such as to have lost us all respect. I can only say that I have put the question of Belgium somewhat hypothetically, because I am not yet sure of all the facts, but, if the facts turn out to be as they have reached us at present, it is quite clear that there is an obligation on this country to do its utmost to prevent the consequences to which those facts will lead if they are undisputed. . . .

The most awful responsibility is resting upon the Government in deciding what to advise the House of Commons to do. We have disclosed our mind to the House of Commons. We have disclosed the issue, the information which we have, and made clear to the House, I trust, that we are prepared to face that situation, and that should it develop, as probably it may develop, we will face it. We worked for peace up to the last moment, and beyond the last moment. How hard, how persistently, and how earnestly we strove for peace last week, the House will see from the Papers that will be before it.

But that is over, as far as the peace of Europe is concerned. We are now face to face with a situation and all the consequences which it may yet have to unfold. We believe we shall have the support of the House at large in proceeding to whatever the consequences may be and whatever measures may be forced upon us by the development of facts or action taken by others. I believe the country, so quickly has the situation been forced upon it, has not had time to realise the issue. It perhaps is still thinking of the quarrel between Austria and Servia, and not the complications of this matter which have grown out of the quarrel between Austria and Servia. Russia and Germany we know are at war. We do not yet know officially that Austria, the ally whom Germany is to support, is yet at war with Russia. We know that a good deal has been happening on the French frontier. We do not know that the German Ambassador has left Paris.

The situation has developed so rapidly that technically, as regards the condition of the war, it is most difficult to describe what has actually happened. I wanted to bring out the underlying issues which would affect our own conduct, and our own policy, and to put them clearly. I have put the vital facts before the House, and if, as seems not improbable, we are forced, and rapidly forced, to take our stand upon those issues, then I believe, when the country realises what is at stake, what the real issues are, the magnitude of the impending dangers in the West of Europe, which I have endeavoured to describe to the House, we shall be supported throughout, not only by the House of Commons, but by the determination, the resolution, the courage, and the endurance of the whole country.[83]

If Grey hoped to carry his party with him, he could not have been encouraged. His hour-long speech was not impassioned and failed to move his audience. Instead, he was cautious, tactful, and hesitant, leaving— Asquith complained—'ragged ends'. Recognizing how Liberals felt about Russia, he had carefully avoided any reference to it. Most of the speakers who followed from the Liberal and Labour benches spoke against intervention. One, Josiah Wedgwood, declared: 'Starvation is coming to this country, and the people are not the docile serfs they were a hundred years ago. They are not going to put up with starvation in this country. When it comes, you will see something far more important than a European War— you will see a revolution.'[84] That Grey got the support of the Unionists was neither surprising nor encouraging.

When he returned to the Foreign Office, however, Grey was greeted with applause from the staff. Still, when Nicolson went to his office to offer his congratulations, he found him depressed. Grey raised clenched fists above his head then crashed them down on the table: 'I hate war, I hate war.'[85]

Lichnowsky, who was not present in the House but received a brief summary of the speech, concluded that Britain 'has no immediate intention of participating in the struggle' or of abandoning its neutrality. Moreover, Grey's statement concerning the protection of French coasts was meaningless as Germany had already given assurances that it did not intend to attack from the Channel. He found Grey's views on Belgian neutrality unclear, but believed he would oppose any reduction of Belgian territory or sovereignty. 'We can regard the speech as satisfactory.' He considered it a great victory that Britain was not immediately entering the fight on the side of

Russia and France; he was convinced that the British government would continue to strive to be neutral.

While Grey was speaking in the House the king and queen were driving along the Mall to Buckingham Palace in an open carriage, cheered by large crowds. In Berlin the Russian ambassador was being attacked by a mob wielding sticks, while the chancellor was sending instructions to the German ambassador in Paris to inform the French government that Germany considered itself to now be 'in a state of war' with France:[86]

> The German administrative and military authorities have established a certain number of flagrantly hostile acts committed on German territory by French military aviators. Several of these have openly violated the neutrality of Belgium by flying over the territory of that country; one has attempted to destroy buildings near Wesel; others have been seen in the district of the Eifel, one has thrown bombs on the railway near Karlsruhe and Nuremberg.

The declaration of war was handed by Baron Schoen to Viviani in Paris at 6 p.m. The ambassador then requested that he be given his passports in order that he might return to Germany.

Poincaré welcomed the declaration. It came as a relief, given that war was by this time inevitable. 'It is a hundred times better that we were not led to declare war ourselves, even on account of repeated violations of our frontier.... If we had been forced to declare war ourselves, the Russian alliance would have become a subject of controversy in France, national [élan?] would have been broken, and Italy may have been forced by the provisions of the Triple Alliance to take sides against us.'[87]

When the British cabinet met again briefly in the evening they had before them the text of the German ultimatum to Belgium and the Belgian reply to it. They agreed to insist that the German government withdraw the ultimatum. After the meeting Grey told the French ambassador that if Germany refused 'it will be war'.[88]

Tuesday, 4 August

At 6 a.m. in Brussels the Belgian government was informed that German troops would be entering Belgian territory. Later that morning the German minister assured them that Germany remained ready to offer them 'the hand of a brother' and to negotiate a modus vivendi.[89] But the basis for any agreement must include the opening of the fortress of Liege to the passage of German troops and a Belgian promise not to destroy railways and bridges.

At the same time the British government was protesting against Germany's intention to violate Belgian neutrality and requesting 'an assurance that the demand made upon Belgium will not be proceeded with, and that her neutrality will be respected by Germany'.[90] The British ambassador in Berlin asked for an immediate reply.

In Berlin they had already anticipated British objections and attempted to reassure them. Lichnowsky was instructed to 'dispel any mistrust' by repeating, positively and formally, that Germany would not, under any pretence, annex Belgian territory. He was to impress upon Sir Edward Grey the reasons for Germany's decision: they had 'absolutely unimpeachable' information that France was planning to attack through Belgium. Germany thus had no choice but to violate Belgian neutrality because it was a matter 'of life or death' that it prevent such a French advance.[91]

Jagow's assurance was received in London at almost the same moment that the Foreign Office received news that German troops had begun their advance into Belgium. Jagow's urgent telegram to Lichnowsky had crossed one from Lichnowsky to the Foreign Office in Berlin. At 1.37 p.m. Jagow was informed that Lichnowsky had been mistaken in his assessment of Grey's speech to the House of Commons the day before because he had relied on a short summary of the speech. He now warned that Germany could not count much longer on Britain to remain neutral. The violation of Belgian neutrality was the key, and unless Germany was able to evacuate Belgian territory very quickly, it should prepare for early intervention on Britain's part. Outside of the left wing of the Liberal Party the government could count on the overwhelming support of parliament. The news of the invasion of Belgium by Germany had brought about 'a complete reversal of public opinion'.[92]

Lichnowsky might have gone even farther. He did not know that two of the four cabinet ministers who had threatened to resign changed their minds. Following a plea from Asquith and after hearing the news about Belgium, Simon and Beauchamp had 'returned to the fold & attended the Cabinet this morning'.[93] The news that Germany had entered Belgium and announced that they would 'push their way through by force of arms' had simplified matters for the cabinet—'so we sent the Germans an ultimatum to expire at midnight'.

At 10.30 a.m. Grey instructed the British minister in Brussels that Britain expected the Belgians to resist any German pressure to induce them to depart from their neutrality 'by any means in their power'. The British government would support them in their resistance and was prepared to join France and Russia in immediately offering to the Belgian government 'an alliance' for the purpose of resisting the use of force by Germany against them, along with a guarantee to maintain Belgian independence and integrity in future years.[94]

Grey may have felt he had gone too far. An hour and forty-five minutes later, at 12.15 p.m., a second telegram was sent altering 'an alliance' to 'common cause'. In between the two messages Lichnowsky had brought Jagow's telegram, with its reassurances, to the Foreign Office.

At 2 p.m. Grey instructed Goschen to repeat the request he had made last week and again this morning that the German government assure him that it would respect Belgian neutrality. A satisfactory reply was required by midnight, Central European time. If this were not received in time the ambassador was to request his passports and to tell the German government that 'His Majesty's Government feel bound to take all steps in their power to uphold the neutrality of Belgium and the observance of a Treaty to which Germany is as much a party as ourselves'.[95]

Before Goschen could present these demands, Bethmann Hollweg addressed the Reichstag that afternoon in Berlin:[96]

A terrible fate is breaking over Europe. For forty-four years, since the time we fought for and won the German Empire and our position in the world, we have lived in peace and protected the peace of Europe. During this time of peace we have become strong and powerful, arousing the envy of others. We have patiently faced the fact that, under the pretence that Germany was warlike, enmity was aroused against us in the East and the West, and chains were fashioned for us. The wind then sown has brought forth the whirlwind which has now broken loose. We wished to continue our work of peace, and, like a silent vow, the feeling that animated everyone from the Emperor down to the youngest soldier was this: only in defence of a just cause would our sword fly from its scabbard.

The day has now come when we must draw it, against our wish, and in spite of our sincere endeavours. Russia has set fire to the building. We are at war with Russia and France—a war that has been forced upon us. . . .

From the first moment of the Austro-Servian conflict we declared that the question must be limited to one between Austria-Hungary and Servia, and we worked with this end in view. All governments, especially that of Great

Britain, took the same attitude. Russia alone asserted that she had to be heard in the settlement of this matter.

Thus the danger of a European crisis raised its threatening head.

As soon as the first definite information regarding the military preparations in Russia reached us, we declared at St. Petersburg—in a friendly but emphatic manner—that military measures against Austria would find us on the side of our ally, that military preparations against ourselves would oblige us to take countermeasures, and that mobilization would come very near to actual war.

Russia assured us in the most solemn manner of her desire for peace, and declared that she was making no military preparations against us.

In the meantime, Great Britain, warmly supported by us, tried to mediate between Vienna and St. Petersburg.

On July 28th the Kaiser telegraphed to the tsar to ask him to take into consideration the fact that it was Austria-Hungary's duty and right to defend herself against the pan-Serb agitation which threatened to undermine her existence. The kaiser drew the tsar's attention to the solidarity of interest among all monarchs in face of the murder at Sarajevo. He asked for the latter's personal assistance in smoothing over the difficulties between Vienna and St. Petersburg. About the same time, and before receipt of this telegram, the tsar asked the kaiser to come to his aid and to induce Vienna to moderate her demands. The kaiser accepted the role of mediator.

But scarcely had active steps on these lines begun when Russia mobilized all her forces directed against Austria, while Austria-Hungary had mobilized only those of her corps which were directed against Servia. To the north she had mobilized only two of her corps, far from the Russian frontier. The kaiser immediately informed the tsar that this mobilization of Russian forces against Austria rendered the role of mediator, which he had accepted at the tsar's request, difficult, if not impossible.

In spite of this we continued our task of mediation at Vienna and carried it to the greatest extent compatible with our position as an ally.

Meanwhile Russia, of her own accord, renewed her assurances that she was making no military preparations against us.

We come now to July 31st. The decision was to be taken at Vienna. Through our representations we had already obtained the resumption of direct conversations between Vienna and St. Petersburg, after they had been interrupted for some time. But before the final decision was taken at Vienna, the news arrived that Russia had mobilized her entire forces and that her mobilization was therefore directed against us also. The Russian Government, who knew from our repeated statements what mobilization on our frontiers meant, did not notify us of this mobilization, nor did they even offer any explanation. It was not until the afternoon of July 31st that the kaiser received a telegram from the tsar in which he guaranteed that his army would not assume a provocative attitude towards us. But mobilization on our frontiers had been in full swing since the night of July 30th–31st.

While we were mediating at Vienna in compliance with Russia's request, Russian forces were appearing all along our extended and almost entirely open frontier, and France, though indeed not actually mobilizing, was admittedly making military preparations. What was our position? For the sake of the peace of Europe we had, up till then, deliberately refrained from calling up a single reservist. Were we now to wait further in patience until the nations on either side of us chose the moment for their attack? It would have been a crime to expose Germany to such peril. Therefore, on July 31st we called upon Russia to demobilize as the only measure which could still preserve the peace of Europe. The Imperial ambassador at St. Petersburg was also instructed to inform the Russian Government that in case our demand met with a refusal, we should have to consider that a state of war (*Kriegszustand*) existed.

The Imperial ambassador has executed these instructions. We have not yet learned what Russia answered to our demand for demobilization. Telegraphic reports on this question have not reached us even though the wires still transmitted much less important information.

Therefore, the time limit having long since expired, the kaiser was obliged to mobilize our forces on the 1st August at 5 p.m.

At the same time we had to make certain what attitude France would assume. To our direct question, whether she would remain neutral in the event of a Russo-German War, France replied that she would do what her interests demanded. That was an evasion, if not a refusal.

In spite of this, the kaiser ordered that the French frontier was to be unconditionally respected. This order, with one single exception, was strictly obeyed. France, who mobilized at the same time as we did, assured us that she would respect a zone of 10 kilometres on the frontier. What really happened? Aviators dropped bombs, and cavalry patrols and French infantry detachments appeared on the territory of the Empire! Though war had not been declared, France thus broke the peace and actually attacked us. . . .

Gentlemen, we are now in a state of necessity (*Notwehr*), and necessity (*Not*) knows no law. Our troops have occupied Luxemburg and perhaps have already entered Belgian territory.

Gentlemen, that is a breach of international law. It is true that the French government declared at Brussels that France would respect Belgian neutrality as long as her adversary respected it. We knew, however, that France stood ready for an invasion. France could wait, we could not. A French attack on our flank on the lower Rhine might have been disastrous. Thus we were forced to ignore the rightful protests of the governments of Luxemburg and Belgium. The wrong—I speak openly—the wrong we thereby commit we will try to make good as soon as our military aims have been attained.

He who is menaced as we are and is fighting for his highest possession can only consider how he is to hack his way through (*durchhauen*).

Gentlemen, we stand shoulder-to-shoulder with Austria-Hungary.

As for Great Britain's attitude, the statements made by Sir Edward Grey in the House of Commons yesterday show the standpoint assumed by the British Government. We have informed the British Government that, as long as Great Britain remains neutral, our fleet will not attack the northern coast of France, and that we will not violate the territorial integrity and independence of Belgium. These assurances I now repeat before the world, and I may add that, as long as Great Britain remains neutral, we would also be willing, upon reciprocity being assured, to take no warlike measures against French commercial shipping.

Gentlemen, so much for the facts. I repeat the words of the kaiser: 'With a clear conscience we enter the lists.' We are fighting for the fruits of our works of peace, for the inheritance of a great past and for our future. The fifty years are not yet past during which Count Moltke said we should have to remain armed to defend the inheritance that we won in 1870. Now the great hour of trial has struck for our people. But with clear confidence we go forward to meet it. Our army is in the field, our navy is ready for battle, and behind them stands the entire German nation united to the last man.

Gentlemen, you know your duty and all that it means. The proposed laws need no further explanations. I ask you to pass them quickly.

Immediately following the speech excerpts were forwarded to London in an effort to reassure the British that Germany was not preparing to launch a naval attack against the French coasts.

Before this arrived, and before Goschen had presented the British ultimatum in Berlin, Grey had already concluded that the German invasion of Belgium had made war inevitable. When he met with the US ambassador at 3 p.m. there was 'a touch of finality in his voice'. It would not end with Belgium, he predicted: next would come Holland, and after Holland, Denmark. Germany had already made overtures to Sweden to come into the war on the side of the Triple Alliance. If Britain sat by while Belgian neutrality was violated it would be 'forever contemptible'. Grey told the ambassador that there were 'two Germanies' and that the 'war party' had gotten the upper hand. 'The efforts of a lifetime' had now come to nothing: 'I feel like a man who has wasted his life.'[97]

At the same moment that Sir Edward Grey was despairing in London, Raymond Poincaré was arousing the French people in Paris. Unlike Bethmann Hollweg in Germany, the French constitution barred the French president from addressing the Chamber of Deputies directly, so it was left to the minister of justice, Bienvenu-Martin, to read to them the words of the president:[98]

Gentlemen:

France has just been the object of a violent and premeditated attack, which is an insolent defiance of the law of nations. Before any declaration of war had been sent to us, even before the German Ambassador had asked for his passports, our territory has been violated. The German Empire has waited till yesterday evening to give at this late stage the true name to a state of things which it had already created.

For more than forty years the French, in sincere love of peace, have buried at the bottom of their heart the desire for legitimate reparation.

They have given to the world the example of a great nation which, definitely raised from defeat by the exercise of will, patience, and labour, has only used its renewed and rejuvenated strength in the interest of progress and for the good of humanity.

Since the ultimatum of Austria opened a crisis which threatened the whole of Europe, France has persisted in following and in recommending on all sides a policy of prudence, wisdom, and moderation.

To her there can be imputed no act, no movement, no word, which has not been peaceful and conciliatory.

At the hour when the struggle is beginning, she has the right, in justice to herself, of solemnly declaring that she has made, up to the last moment, supreme efforts to avert the war now about to break out, the crushing responsibility for which the German Empire will have to bear before history. Our fine and courageous army, which France today accompanies with her maternal thought has risen eager to defend the honour of the flag and the soil of the country.

The President of the Republic interpreting the unanimous feeling of the country, expresses to our troops by land and sea the admiration and confidence of every Frenchman.

Closely united in a common feeling, the nation will persevere with the cool self-restraint of which, since the beginning of the crisis, she has given daily proof. Now, as always, she will know how to harmonize the most noble daring and most ardent enthusiasm with that self-control which is the sign of enduring energy and is the best guarantee of victory.

In the war which is beginning, France will have Right on her side, the eternal power of which cannot with impunity be disregarded by nations any more than by individuals.

She will be heroically defended by all her sons; nothing will break their sacred union before the enemy; today they are joined together as brothers in a common indignation against the aggressor, and in a common patriotic faith.

She is faithfully helped by Russia, her ally; she is supported by the loyal friendship of Great Britain.

And already from every part of the civilized world sympathy and good wishes are coming to her. For today once again she stands before the universe for Liberty, Justice, and Reason.

'Haut les coeurs et vive la France!'

At almost the same moment Asquith was informing the House of Commons that Britain had given Germany an ultimatum regarding the violation of Belgian neutrality. Now the waiting began. Germany had until midnight to respond—11 p.m., London time.

Shortly after 9 p.m. a small group convened in the cabinet room at 10 Downing Street. Besides Asquith and Grey, several cabinet ministers— Lloyd George, Churchill, and McKenna—were there. An unciphered (*en clair*) telegram, in English, from Berlin to the German embassy in London had been intercepted: 'English Ambassador just demanded his passports shortly after seven o'clock declaring war.'[99] But two hours remained before the British deadline expired. What were they to do?

Foreign Office officials had been preparing messages to be sent following the expiry of the deadline. At 9.45 a messenger burst in to announce that Germany had declared war on Britain. The draft announcement was now revised to read: 'The German empire having declared war upon Great Britain...'. An official was sent to take this announcement to Lichnowsky, along with his passports. But when he returned to the Foreign Office shortly after 10.15, a telegram was received from Goschen telling them that Bethmann Hollweg had informed him via telephone that Germany would not be replying to the British ultimatum—and therefore a state of war would arise at midnight. It turned out that the intercepted German message had only been intended to warn German shipping that war with Britain was imminent. The British Admiralty was responsible for the mistake. The Foreign Office now realized that it had made the horrible mistake of handing Lichnowsky an incorrect declaration of war. Sir Arthur Nicolson despatched his son Harold—a junior in the office—to retrieve the faulty note and substitute the correct one:[100]

Grasping the correct declaration in a nervous hand, he walked across the Horse Guards Parade and rang the bell at the side-door of the Embassy which gives on the Duke of York's steps. It was by then some five minutes after eleven. After much ringing a footman appeared. He stated that Prince Lichnowsky had gone to bed. The bearer of the missive insisted on seeing His

Excellency and advised the footman to summon the butler. The latter appeared and stated that His Highness had given instructions that he was in no circumstances to be disturbed. The Foreign Office clerk stated that he was the bearer of a communication of the utmost importance from Sir Edward Grey. The butler, at that, opened the door and left young Nicolson in the basement. He was absent for five minutes. On his return he asked Sir Edward Grey's emissary to follow him and walked majestically toward the lift. They rose silently together to the third floor and then proceeded along a pile-carpeted passage. The butler knocked at a door. There was a screen behind the door and behind the screen a brass bedstead on which the Ambassador was reclining in pyjamas. The Foreign Office clerk stated that there had been a slight error in the document previously delivered and that he had come to substitute for it another, and more correct, version. Prince Lichnowsky indicated the writing table in the window. 'You will find it there' he said. The envelope had been but half-opened, and the passports protruded. It did not appear that the Ambassador had read the communication or opened the letter . . .

Nicolson required a signed receipt from the ambassador, and while Lichnowsky was signing it 'the sound of shouting came up from the Mall below, and the strains of the *Marseillaise*. The crowds were streaming back from Buckingham Palace.' At the palace at 10.45 the king had convened a meeting of the Privy Council for the purpose of authorizing the declaration of war. They waited for 11 p.m. to come, and when Big Ben struck they were at war. Meanwhile people had begun gathering outside the palace. When news began to spread throughout the crowd that war had been declared the excitement mounted; and when the king, the queen, and their eldest son appeared on the balcony 'the cheering was terrific.'[101]

By the end of the day five of the six Great Powers of Europe were at war, along with Serbia and Belgium. Diplomacy had failed. The tragedy had begun.

PART FOUR

The Aftermath

Making Sense of the Madness

And surely it was madness? For what purpose were over 9 million men killed, almost 30 million injured, maimed, or disfigured? To what end were millions of women made widows, condemned to a life of poverty, millions of children left fatherless, millions of young women rendered childless? Did those men who made the choice between war and peace envision that the frontiers of Europe would be redrawn, new states created, old ones destroyed as a result of their choices? Did no one anticipate the collapse of empires, the triumphant expansion of others, and the unleashing of anti-colonial, anti-European movements in the world beyond Europe? Who among them foresaw that their decision to go to war would unleash the revolutionary forces of communism and fascism? Was there no foreboding that war would unleash the seething resentments and hatreds that bubbled beneath the surface of European society, that xenophobia and anti-Semitism might be transformed into acceptable political doctrines?

The enormity of the consequences that the war produced, the extent of the personal suffering that it involved, would lead Europeans to think of it in apocalyptic terms. The war was Armageddon, it was a cataclysm, it was destroying, would destroy, had destroyed civilization. If this were so, there must be deep, profound causes for it. Those who had sown the wind would reap the whirlwind. But sown with what?

The first explanations offered came from those responsible for the sowing. And those explanations were simple and straightforward. Every one of the monarchs and statesmen who addressed their people claimed to have acted in self-defence. They had done everything in their power to preserve the peace. But their enemies had given them no choice: the fatherland, the motherland, *la patrie*, the empire was in danger. The war was a fight for existence. The enemy was encircling, threatening, seeking to overwhelm

them. They could not abandon their friends and allies who needed and
trusted them—and without whom they could not survive into the future.
The honour and dignity of the country and its people were at stake: to back
down in the face of threats would reduce them all to servitude or slavery.

The explanations and excuses, justifications and recriminations that began
to flow in the first days of August would soon turn into a flood. People
everywhere were called upon to make sacrifices, to forget their differences, to
unite in the common cause. Fear of losing the war ought to be sufficient to
rally them. With the anticipation that the war would be over quickly,
probably by Christmas, there seemed little point in debating whether the
struggle had a meaning deeper than the right to defend the nation against its
enemies.

Attention focused first on diplomacy. All parties involved professed that
the diplomatic record would demonstrate the lengths to which they had
gone to preserve the peace, that in the end they had been given no choice.
The German government got the ball rolling. Even before Britain declared
war on them the Germans issued a 'White Book' on the outbreak of the
'German-Russian-French War': *How Russia and her Ruler betrayed Germany's
confidence and thereby made the European War.*[1] This contained excerpts from
diplomatic correspondence to demonstrate that Germany had behaved
honourably throughout the crisis, that the kaiser and his government had
done their best to mediate the dispute but that Russian military preparations
left them no choice but to act.[2] The British government responded quickly,
publishing a 'Blue Book' consisting of 159 diplomatic documents on
5 August. The Russians came out with an 'Orange Book' in September,
followed by the Belgians with their 'Grey Book' in October. The French
produced a 'Yellow Book' at the end of November: 'How Germany forced
the War'. The Austrians lagged far behind; their 'Red Book' was not
published until the summer of 1915.

The coloured books were aimed first and foremost at their own subjects
and citizens. Although general strikes to stop the war failed to materialize,
although conscripts and reserves everywhere obeyed orders to report for
duty, and although volunteers heeded the call to arms, there were those
who opposed the war from the start. Dissident socialists, pacifists, and
conscientious objectors questioned the validity and the necessity of the
war. Before these few voices could turn into a chorus, the governments
involved attempted to defend their policies by putting 'the documents'
before their people. Of course in doing so they chose to cheat. Not only

were the documents carefully and skilfully selected, they were excised, revised, and merged in order to produce the desired impression.[3] Documents that might contradict the government line were omitted altogether.

Had the war been the short-lived affair that almost everyone—especially the strategists—expected, the war of words over who was responsible for initiating the carnage might have been equally brief. But the failure of the offensive in August and September bogged down into trench warfare on the western front and a virtual stalemate on the eastern. As it became clear that the war would be fought at vast expense and with untold human misery it became harder to believe that the answers to questions concerning responsibility and guilt could be found in a selection of diplomatic documents. Did it really matter who said what to whom, when? Must there not be deeper, more profound causes of such bloodletting?

Academics and intellectuals, writers and journalists rallied to the cause and began to offer their own explanations for the war. Ninety-four of Germany's most famous professors protested as 'representatives of German science and art' against the 'lies and calumnies' with which Germany's enemies were 'endeavoring to stain the honor of Germany in her hard struggle for existence—in a struggle which has been forced upon her'. The kaiser had demonstrated throughout the twenty-six years of his reign that he was an upholder of peace. It was only when a 'numerical superiority which had been lying in wait on the frontiers assailed us' that Germany rose as one to defend itself. The militarism denounced by Germany's enemies had in fact saved German civilization by protecting it against the 'bands of robbers' that had plagued it for centuries. People should have faith in Germany and believe that 'we shall carry on this war to the end as a civilized nation, to whom the legacy of a Goethe, a Beethoven, and a Kant is just as sacred as its own hearths and homes'.[4]

In a further appeal from 'the German universities' they argued that a systematic campaign of lies and slander had been conducted against the German people and the German empire for years before the outbreak of the war. As the 'appointed trustees of culture and education' in the fatherland, they believed it was their duty to protest against these attacks and to draw the attention of the world to the inheritance of German culture, to the industry and uprightness, the sense of order and discipline of the German people, the profound love of the sciences and the arts in Germany. The charges of barbarism levelled against 'the country's best sons' in the German army were slanderous and unfounded: they were simply caught up in the bitterness of defensive warfare. Germany was fighting for its very existence and for its entire civilization. The responsibility for the horrors of war rested on the shoulders of those who let loose this ruthless war: 'They alone are the guilty authors of everything which happens here. Upon their heads the verdict of history will fall for the lasting injury which culture suffers.'[5]

And thus the war of words between men of culture, intelligence, and the arts began. British scholars pointed out that influential German writers such as Nietzsche, Treitschke, Bülow, and Bernhardi had advocated national aggrandizement through war. They regretted that 'under the baleful influence of a military system and its lawless dreams of conquest, she whom we once honored now stands revealed as the common enemy of Europe and of all peoples which respect the law of nations'.[6] French intellectuals joined in. The philosopher Henri Bergson declared that Germany had launched the war to impose its domination, its 'culture' on others. But it was bound to fail because, in its worship of brute force, it had lost its idealism—and once its material strength was shattered it would have no ideals capable of reviving it. French soldiers, by contrast, were inspired by ideals that could not be worn down, by their belief in justice and liberty: 'To a force nourished only by its own brutality we oppose one that seeks outside of itself, above itself, a principle of life and renewal.' The one would destroy the other.[7]

Within months of the outbreak of war almost every intellectual in Europe had joined battle in the war of words. And governments were happy to utilize them. Propaganda before the war had been a rather amateurish affair. While everyone knew that certain newspapers were used by governments as mouthpieces for their policies, and while diplomats attempted to influence public opinion by bribing journalists, there were no government departments, no systems in place to mould opinion, deflect criticism, mobilize sentiment. This all changed rapidly as governments saw the need to justify the sacrifices they were calling upon their people to make. It was not enough to insist that they had acted in self-defence: some greater cause had to be found to sustain support. That cause became the ideals that the state, the nation, the empire, represented. And those ideals became attached to explanations of the war's causes.

All parties involved blamed the other side for the war. In the beginning, this consisted of utilizing a carefully cleansed version of the diplomatic record to demonstrate that everything possible had been done to avoid a war which had been forced on them. But now the stakes were raised: what accounted for the other side's warlike determination? Structures, systems, movements, philosophies were uncovered, revealed to be at the root of things. 'Prussian militarism', Panslavism, imperialism, autocracy, pan-Germanism, the perfidy of Albion—the list was long. Attention shifted from the moves made during the July crisis to analysis of the sins of competing systems. Governments, now getting into the propaganda game as they never had before, encouraged writers to rally to the cause, subsidized publications, and organized lectures, speeches, and talks.

Some attempted to rise above the fray. Or to sidestep it. Not all pacifists and socialists abandoned their ideals. They too disputed the war's meaning, the nature of its causes. And a long list of Europe's ills began to emerge—a list that could be used to guide to make a better, more peaceful world when the war ended. Only days before the assassination at Sarajevo an English socialist, H. N. Brailsford, published *The War of Steel and Gold: A Study of the Armed Peace*. There, he argued that the competition in armaments was not only an economic disaster, but was making war between the most powerful states highly likely. A month later, this seemed prophetic. The book immediately became a best-seller, and 'armaments' emerged as a cause of war. But Brailsford offered more: it was the capitalist system that encouraged and enabled armaments manufacturers to profit; it was the absence of true democracy that resulted in war. The best promise of a peaceful future lay in a democratic, socialist system of government.

Others soon joined Brailsford with many variations on his theme. Secret diplomacy was the culprit: if diplomats and politicians had been forced to carry out their work in the full light of day, the promises they had made in the dark would never have been permitted and the peoples of Europe would not have awakened to discover that they were committed to going to war without their knowledge or consent. Secret diplomacy was first cousin to the system of alliances. The alliances that had divided Europe into two armed camps were only made possible by the secretiveness in which they had been conceived. Armed and divided in this way meant that it would only take one spark to set the whole of Europe alight.

And what was it that had caused Europe to be armed and divided in this way? Empire. It was the desire to control the world beyond Europe's frontiers that created the competition within it. Africa had been partitioned, most of south Asia seized by Britain, Russia, or France. Germany had been left on the outside looking in. But the old Ottoman empire was falling apart; China seemed certain to disintegrate. If Germany was to take its place in the sun in the twentieth century, it had to be prepared to compete overseas. But why? Who benefited? It was the capitalists, the traders, the financiers, the investors who saw the opportunity for greater profits than they could have at home. And the taxpayers picked up the tab: they paid for the armies and the navies. And the newspapers, at the beck and call of the special interests, whipped up jingoist support and xenophobic fears in order to convince ordinary people to pay for the expensive tools of imperialism.

Thus, there emerged on the European Left an analysis of the war's causes and a remedy for the future. The combination of capitalism and imperialism had created militarism and navalism. The absence of truly democratic governments and the orchestration of opinion by the capitalist press had sustained secret diplomacy and the alliance system. From this point of view the only purpose in studying the diplomatic history of the pre-war years was to demonstrate how far governments had gone in making their dirty deals behind the backs of the public.

How was war to be prevented in the future? The 'Union of Democratic Control' was formed in Britain to change 'the system of official intercourse between nations'. This would produce 'permanent peace' when the war ended, instead of ushering in a period of renewed armaments. If they were to achieve this it was essential that they 'create a public opinion which will insist upon such terms of peace and such changes and modifications of diplomatic procedure ... as will ensure a lasting settlement and herald the dawn of a new era for civilised mankind'. Included in the UDC's general council were H. N. Brailsford (*The War of Steel and Gold*), Norman Angell (*The Great Illusion*), J. A. Hobson (*Imperialism: A Study*), and E. D. Morel (*Truth and the War*), along with Bertrand Russell, the future prime minister J. Ramsay MacDonald, and Sir Daniel Stevenson—who would bankroll the Stevenson Chair of International History at the University of London.

Understanding the true nature of the war's causes became essential to devising a remedy capable of sustaining a peaceful future. Even while the war was being fought on the battlefields, another war had broken out at home between the upholders of the old regime and the proponents of the new. Gradually, the movement would coalesce around the idea of creating a 'League of Nations' at the end of the war—an organization that would conduct diplomacy in the light of day, that would replace the system of alliances with the promise of collective security, that would redraw frontiers on the principle of the right of national self-determination, that would oversee a process by which all states would disarm, that would replace imperialist rivalry with a trusteeship system in which European states acted on behalf of African and Asian peoples until they were capable of governing themselves, that would require states to submit their disputes to a process of legal arbitration.

The pamphlets and books, the newspaper and journal articles, purporting to understand what had caused the war and how it was to be prevented in the future became a veritable tidal wave flooding Europe for the duration of the war. The schemes for a new system of international relations multiplied almost daily. But the essence of their proposals was similar: the old system perpetuated a struggle among nations that inevitably led to war. And the past was to be studied to prove this point. The sins of empire, the sorrows of those who suffered under the rule of other nationalities, the conspiracies operating between armaments manufacturers, shipbuilders, and governments, the secret deals perpetrated by the old aristocrats who conducted diplomacy were now to be laid bare for all to see. A brave new world could emerge from the ashes of the old if people were told the truth about their histories.

Thus did the fascination of the July crisis fade from view over the course of the war. Attention was refocused on the systemic ills of pre-war Europe. Critics condemned the old diplomacy as symptomatic of the diseases that plagued the past: authoritarianism, militarism, imperialism, secretiveness. Propagandists—both paid and amateur—condemned the other side not for their diplomacy of July but for their systematic pursuit of empire, or for their opposition to the rights of nationalities, or for allowing their policies to be shaped by self-interested elites. Critics and propagandists alike agreed that whatever errors had been made in July were merely symptoms of underlying causes.

The July crisis might, therefore, have been consigned to the rubbish-bin of history. The diplomacy of that fateful month might have been reduced to a topic of interest only to specialists and antiquarians. That it did not was the result of two developments in 1918 and 1919 that would change forever the course of diplomatic history.

A revolution occurred in Germany in November 1918 when the war appeared to be lost. Sailors began to mutiny and soldiers began putting down their arms. A republic was declared and the kaiser abdicated, fleeing to the Netherlands. A social-democratic government took the place of the monarchy and signed the armistice of 11 November. One member of the new government was Karl Kautsky, who was installed at the German Foreign Office as under-secretary of state. Kautsky had begun to make a reputation for himself as a Marxist spokesman in the late 1880s, and by 1914 was widely regarded as one of the leading theorists of the movement. When war was declared in August he defended the decision as a necessary defensive war against the tsarist autocracy—a point of view first taken by Karl Marx himself.

The new government confiscated all of the documents they found at the Foreign Office with the intention of handing them over to a commission to study them. Kautsky led the investigation. His intention was to prove that he, other socialists, and the German people as a whole had been wilfully misled by the kaiser's government. The German people themselves were not militaristic or imperialistic: they had been duped by the military and the finance capitalists who backed the opportunity to fight an expansionist war.

Kautsky and the new government regarded it as imperative to make the case. If they failed to do so, and if the burden of responsibility for the war came to rest on Germany, they could expect humiliating and crushing terms of peace. If successful, they could simultaneously discredit the old regime and defend the new one at Paris. Kautsky undertook most of the work himself, assisted by his wife. What they discovered was a mixed blessing: the documents seemed to support the view that the old regime in Germany could be held responsible for the war. But would the responsibility end there? What if the peacemakers, meeting in Paris as the documents were being reviewed and assembled, simply concluded that 'Germany'—and not the old regime—was responsible and should bear the burden of its costs? Officials at the Wilhelmstrasse did everything they could to stop, or at least delay and revise, the documents that Kautsky proposed to publish. Among other motives, officials feared that the allies might launch legal proceedings against those 'criminally responsible' for the war.

The new government decided to delay publication of the documents. An 'Office of Peace Negotiations' was created and charged with the task of proving that France, Russia, and Britain shared as much, or more, responsibility for the outbreak of the war—that they had systematically prepared for a war against Germany. The official position at Paris was to be that Germany had acted in self-defence against 'tsarism'—'the most dreadful system of enslavement ever devised . . . before the present peace treaty'. In the midst of the peace negotiations the German government launched a much broader review of pre-war policy: experts were to be assigned the task of going back further than the July crisis, to include the years that preceded it in order to provide 'context' to the documents concerning the crisis itself—perhaps as far back as 1870. And calls were made for the victorious allies to open their files as well. Eventually, this would become *Die Grosse Politik der Europäischen Kabinette, 1871–1914*—a monumental series of forty volumes. Published between 1922 and 1927, it would set the precedent for similar government publications from Britain, France, Italy, and the United States. The unprecedented detail available in published form would change forever the study of diplomatic history.[8]

Once again, the intention was to shift the focus from the diplomacy of the July crisis to the 'roots' of the European problem, which were to be discovered years, perhaps decades, before the crisis itself. But in the first instance this strategy failed. Kautsky published four volumes of documents that he collected in December 1919 and suddenly Europeans were again immersed in details and arguments about precisely who said what, when, and how their words and decisions produced the cataclysm of war. Head-lines appeared concerning the 'Potsdam War Council'; the kaiser's volatile notations on the documents were now available for all to see—and the legend of the 'peace kaiser' who had done everything he could to prevent war was almost instantly discredited. Kautsky himself 'connected the dots' between the documents he had assembled by offering a commentary on their meaning in *The Guilt of William Hohenzollern*—the title of which speaks for itself.[9]

The revelations of the Kautsky collection might have been of only passing interest, or consigned to debates among specialists, had it not been for the so-called 'war guilt clause'—Article 231 of the Treaty of Versailles. The victorious powers had established a commission on the 'Responsibility of the Authors of the War and on Enforcement of Penalties' when the peace conference began in Paris in January 1919. By the end of March it reported that the primary responsibility for the war rested with Germany and Austria-Hungary.[10] The report was then used to justify Article 231: 'The Allied and Associated Governments affirm and Germany accepts the responsibility of Germany and her Allies for causing all the loss and damage to which the Allied and Associated Governments and their nationals have been subjected as a consequence of the war imposed upon them by the aggression of Germany and her allies.'[11]

The apparent linkage between 'war guilt' and the reparations imposed on Germany at Paris gave a whole new life to the subject of the war's origins. The discussion was transformed. When the commission had deliberated on responsibility it had not much more to go on than the scattered, doctored, and invented documents contained in the coloured books produced for the purposes of propaganda during the war itself. Germans especially came to believe that if they could disprove their 'guilt' they could undercut what they believed to be the unjust terms imposed upon them by the *Diktat* of Versailles. This is why the new German government found the Kautsky initiative so perplexing: while discrediting the diplomacy of the old regime, it also discredited the efforts of the new regime to ameliorate the peace terms. The new German republic ended up with the worst of all scenarios: it was saddled with responsibility for the peace terms—terms which Germans would blame for every problem they faced after the war—while outside Germany the new government was lumped together in sharing responsibility for causing the war. Thus the determined efforts of successive Weimar governments to share guilt for the war with the victorious allies.

Almost simultaneously, the new republican government in Austria published hundreds of diplomatic documents covering July–August 1914 in three volumes. And a trickle of accounts from participants in the July crisis—autobiographies, memoirs, recollections, and reminiscences—began to appear. By 1920 historians, journalists, and anyone interested in the subject had substantial new sources to study. Over the next few years the trickle of accounts coming from participants would turn into a flood. The range and scale of these publications was unprecedented. Never before in European history had so much attention been focused on a historical event.

Within the German Foreign Office a special department was created, the *Kriegsschuldreferat* (War Guilt Section), which then spun off a subsection, the 'Working Committee of German Associations for Combating Lies Concerning War Responsibility', whose mission it was to spread the truth to the German people. And a special centre was created to propagate ongoing study into the war's origins (the *Zentralstelle zur Erforschung der Kriegsschuldfrage*); the centre then undertook to publish a monthly journal, *Die Kriegsschuldfrage*. The issue of responsibility was topical, political, and emotional. Far from disappearing, the arguments, controversies, and debates on the topic got hotter as time went on.

A whole new round of historical argument began when a young American historian, Sidney B. Fay, utilized the new documents (and some of the memoirs) to publish a trilogy of articles in the *American Historical Review*.[12] Fay, compared with most of those historians and other academics who had entered the debate, was relatively unencumbered by pre-war bias, wartime activity, or national prejudice. He was representative of the new professionalism, receiving his doctorate from Harvard in 1900, supplemented by further studies at the Sorbonne and the University of Berlin before the war. He taught at Dartmouth until 1914, publishing several textbooks on European history, and was then appointed to Smith College.[13] His articles on the subject would make his career: they became the basis for a monumental two-volume study of the subject in 1928, which would lead to his appointment at Harvard the following year.

As might be expected, Fay was more dispassionate than most of those coming to the subject in the immediate post-war years. Rather than expunging guilt or assigning blame he suggested that it was the 'monstrous influence' of the militarists in Vienna, Berlin, and St Petersburg that was the fundamental factor at play. But, in spite of his distance as an American and as a professional, he still played the blame game: Berchtold, for example, was 'more than any one else responsible for the World War'.[14] And most historians have continued to play this game ever since. This is not so much partisanship but omniscience: they know who the guilty are; they know what the mistakes were; they know how the war could have been avoided.

Fuelled by the unprecedented amount of documentary information that was becoming available, detailed diplomatic histories began to appear. Germany's Erich Brandenburg published *Von Bismarck zum weltkriege: die deutsche politik in den jahrzehnten vor dem kriege* in 1924;[15] France's Pierre Renouvin published *Les origines immédiates de la guerre (28 juin–4 août 1914)* in 1925;[16] the US historian Harry Elmer Barnes published his *Genesis of the World War* in 1926, and Britain's R. W. Seton-Watson published *Sarajevo: A Study in the Origins of the Great War*, in 1927. Their treatments were far more detailed, more carefully documented, and more sophisticated than the propagandistic works that had preceded them. But, perhaps because of these very characteristics, they failed to seize hold of the public imagination.

Although these works varied considerably, their aims were similar: the wish to discover who, or what, was responsible for the war. What they discovered turned out to fit as neatly into nationalist proclivities as the propaganda works that had preceded them. Brandenburg claimed no one could show that Germany 'wished for war or strove to bring it about': 'our policy was . . . too anxious and too peace-loving rather than too militant'.[17] Renouvin concluded that Germany and Austria-Hungary, after 'careful deliberation' and 'coolly considering the consequences', had 'deliberately provoked' the confrontation that led to war.[18] Seton-Watson said that it was not too much to assert that Vienna and Berlin undertook deliberate action 'thought out to the smallest details' that created a diplomatic situation 'from which nothing short of a miracle could have saved Europe'; the main responsibility for the outbreak of war 'must therefore rest upon their shoulders'.[19]

But by the end of the 1920s the sizzle had gone out of the debate. The German campaign to revise the treaty of Versailles by disproving German war guilt had failed. By 1926 'the spirit of Locarno' was in the air: Germany was admitted to the League of Nations, and a new era of international cooperation had begun. The disputes over responsibility faded into the background. What was the point of them? There was hardly a monarch, a statesman, a practising politician left who had been in a position of prominence in 1914. Men like Asquith and Lloyd George were now on the sidelines, relegated to hurling abuse at one another and publishing their memoirs (from which many made small fortunes).

There was another reason why the sizzle was lost. From the mid-1920s on, historians—although still inclined to apportion blame to one side more than the other—began to stress the 'underlying' causes of war more than the immediate. Seton-Watson argued that the ultimate causes of the war 'are infinitely complex', and that every nation 'must bear some of the share of the blame'.[20] This emerging attitude reached its apogee two years later when Sidney Fay built upon his earlier articles to publish his massive two-volume study: *The Origins of the World War*. Here, students of the subject would discover that there were five 'Underlying Causes of the War':

(a) The System of Secret Alliances
(b) Militarism
(c) Nationalism
(d) Economic Imperialism
(e) The Newspaper Press

Within a few years, almost every high-school student in North America was committing these causes to memory. And, in line with this approach, coming to believe that no one, and no one thing, was responsible. Fay was certain of one thing: that the 'verdict' of Versailles that Germany and its allies were responsible for the war was, in light of the evidence now available, 'historically unsound'. To a greater or lesser degree 'all the European countries' were responsible. The dictum of Versailles was 'exacted by victors from vanquished, under the influence of the blindness, ignorance, hatred, and the propagandistic misconceptions to which war had given rise'.[21] He called upon historians to explain this to the public in order that the peace treaty could be revised accordingly.

Fay's approach to the subject resonated with Americans in particular. His position fitted neatly into some deeply rooted traditions, from George Washington's warnings about the dangers of 'entangling alliances' to beliefs in American exceptionalism and the dangers of authoritarian governments with their large standing armies. Another American took a similar view: Bernadotte Schmitt had visited Germany before the war while studying for his bachelor's degree at Oxford (having already received one from the University of Tennessee). He had been profoundly disturbed at the militarism that he saw as pervading German society and culture. After graduating from the University of Wisconsin, he received a Rhodes Scholarship to study at Oxford in 1914. In 1930 he produced another massive, door-stopping study of war origins, equalling that of Fay: over 1,000 pages in two volumes. Schmitt's *The Coming of the War: 1914* emphasized the responsibility of Germany and the fault of its militaristic traditions. But he also spread the guilt around: everyone shared some degree of responsibility. The crisis had turned into war because it was viewed as a test of strength between the two rival alliances 'and it was the tragedy of Europe that among its many gifted statesmen there was no one of the caliber of a Canning or a Cavour to cut through the web of alliances ... '.[22]

But, according to Schmitt, the diplomats were not solely to blame. Behind them stood public opinion, urging a resolute stand and opposing concessions that might have averted war. In every country involved there was an instinctive feeling that any nation which failed to play its part 'would be outdistanced in the eternal competition of peoples'. Modern European history as a whole was to blame: in the face of the intense nationalism 'born of the French Revolution and intensified by the events of the nineteenth century, pacific instincts, socialistic programmes, religious scruples and humanitarian ideals were of no avail'.[23] Schmitt's book made him famous. He won the Pulitzer Prize for it, along with the American Historical Association's prize for the best book on European international history. Both he and Fay would become presidents of the Association.

The debate over war origins ushered in the golden age of diplomatic history. Never before—or since—was there such widespread interest among the general public in what historians of diplomacy had to say. Not only did these massive studies sell in unprecedented numbers for serious works of historical scholarship, but they made their authors famous. And interest in the topic, along with those writing on it, was not confined to historians of diplomacy. Harry Elmer Barnes was no diplomatic historian, yet his revisionist *Genesis of the World War* was a best-seller and made him a public figure. And, at almost the same moment that his book appeared, a Cambridge classicist—with no real knowledge of or training in diplomatic history—produced an immensely popular book on the subject.

Goldsworthy Lowes Dickinson had opposed Britain's participation in the war and had been a founding member of the Union of Democratic Control.[24] A close friend of John Maynard Keynes, he joined those who attacked the *Diktat* of Versailles as a 'Carthaginian peace'. And he believed that discrediting the 'war guilt' thesis was essential to revising the treaty and putting international relations on a new foundation: 'it is the future of mankind that is at stake'.[25] Historians, he complained, were hypnotized. They concentrated on the superficial and failed to consider the 'fundamental conditions which make war inevitable'. The existence of a number of independent and armed states was the problem, not the particular policies pursued by any one of them. In this anarchical situation every state seeks to gain an advantage over others, leading to the competition in armaments. The hope that this would produce a balance of power among them had been shattered. War always resulted; a peaceful balance had never been maintained. Until men agreed to lay down their arms and to substitute a method of resolving their disputes peacefully, war would never cease.

Dickinson's 500-page book amounts to a prolonged plea for the League of Nations to substitute for the anarchy of international relations. All states must join the League; all must agree to lay down their arms; all must agree to submit their disputes to conciliation or arbitration. The time had come to end the arguments about 'who was the good or the bad boy'. People needed to take stock of the real situation: 'The time is short, and the danger imminent.'[26]

By 1930 the debate over war origins had ended. Massive studies of the July crisis, of the decade (or so) before the war, and of the system of international relations all seemed to have rendered the debate sterile. A consensus had now emerged: in the anarchic system that had prevailed prior to 1914, responsibility for the war could not be assigned to any one state or person. Cries of 'Hang the kaiser' ceased to be heard. The Hohenzollerns, along with their Prussian militarism, had disappeared; the Habsburgs, along with their ramshackle multinational empire had disappeared;

the Romanov autocracy had disappeared. Raymond Poincaré had retired from politics, as had Sir Edward Grey. What point was there in pursuing sterile debates about guilt, when the tens of thousands of documents now available, pored over and studied from every possible point of view by historians and others, demonstrated that responsibility was shared, that everyone involved had pursued self-interest, made mistakes?

When Hitler came to power and began his campaign to tear up the treaty of Versailles, there was no one left to speak up for it. By the mid-1930s almost everyone was convinced that the peace was illegitimate, that the whole edifice had been erected on the false foundation of German war guilt. It had been a victors' peace: German colonies seized, territory taken, the nation divided, disarmament imposed, reparations exacted; Austria-Hungary dismantled; Turkey reduced to Asia Minor. All this proved what the revisionists had said from the beginning—that the victors had had these aims in mind all along, that their imperialist gains and the humiliation of their enemies illustrated their culpability in the war's origins. Questions concerning how the war began now seemed to be of interest only to antiquarians—who might as well have been studying the origins of the Peloponnesian or Punic wars, so far as the European public was now concerned.

And just such a person emerged in the unlikely form of an Italian journalist. Luigi Albertini had begun to undertake (more as a hobby than anything else) his own investigation of war origins in the early 1920s. In 1914 he had been an ardent interventionist, advocating that Italy intervene in the war in 1914. And he occupied an influential position in doing so: he was editor of one of Italy's most important newspapers, the *Corriere della Sera* of Milan. After the war he had become one of Mussolini's early supporters. In developing his fascination with the war's origins he joined numerous other journalists and historians of the day. But where he differed from them was the dogged determination with which he continued to pursue the subject for the next twenty years. He published almost nothing on the subject while he was alive. When he died during the Second World War in 1941, he was still at work on his magnum opus, preparing his conclusions.

Albertini's was one of the most ambitious research projects undertaken in the twentieth century. He examined almost every published document on the subject—which, by the time that he wrote, numbered in the tens of thousands. His research far exceeded the already richly detailed, two-volume works of Fay and Schmitt, as he was able to incorporate substantial French and Russian documents made available after 1930. And he went farther still, interrogating participants either personally or through correspondence. His work is unique in the annals of diplomatic history. He defied what had become the conventional approach to the subject: he offered no analysis of the 'underlying causes'. There is no exploration of the role played by nationalism, imperialism, or militarism. Instead, he produced a truly massive narrative history: three volumes consisting of over 2,000 pages and exceeding a million words. *Le origini della guerra del 1914* was published under the supervision of his faithful collaborator, Luciano Magrini, in 1942 and 1943.

As magnificent an undertaking as it is, it is doubtful that more than a handful of enthusiasts have ever read it—even after it was translated into English as *The Origins of the War of 1914* in 1952. Its massive size and copious documentation present a formidable challenge to even the most dedicated enthusiast. And its fractured narrative makes it very difficult to follow: chapters follow the diplomacy pursued by one state, usually in conjunction with a particular event or decision. Successive chapters in the second volume, for example, are:

  XI.   German Policy after the Austrian Declaration of War on Serbia; The Threat of English Intervention
  XII. The Russian General Mobilization
  XIII. France and Russian Mobilization; Last English Efforts to Save Peace

This approach means that readers must constantly go back and forth in time, as successive chapters go over the same ground from different perspectives. This also entails a good deal of repetition from one chapter to the next. And, finally, even these smaller narratives break down as Albertini investigates the conflicts and contradictions that arise in the different accounts of events given by participants. As fascinating as these excursions may be, they often read more like extended asides or lawyer's briefs than as intrinsically important parts of the story itself.

Partly for those reasons, partly because it was not really clear what Albertini's purpose was, his three volumes made little impact. He stimulated no new debate. The fundamental dimensions of the subject remained intact: that the 'real' causes of the war were the 'underlying' ones first delineated by Sidney Fay; that all of the participants shared some of the responsibility for the outbreak of war in August 1914. Albertini's work became a standard work assigned to PhD students. It is doubtful that the circle of readership extended much wider.

But the experience of Hitler, the Holocaust, and the Second World War turned everything upside down. In the midst of a consensus that individuals could not be held personally responsible for such earth-shattering events as a world war, that causes of great historical events were profound and systemic, along came the guiltiest man in history. After the Second World War another, completely different, consensus emerged. It was Hitler, sustained by Nazi fanaticism, who launched the world into that war. The only meaningful historical question to be answered was why his opponents had failed to stop him earlier: was it weakness of character, ideological sympathy, or simple stupidity that led the leaders of Britain and France to turn a blind eye to Hitler's aggressive, racist ambitions?

Ironically, it was a German historian who linked Hitler and the Second World War with Wilhelm II and the First World War—and re-ignited a debate that had lain dormant for three decades. Fritz Fischer saw a line of continuity stretching back from Hitler—not only to Wilhelm II but to Bismarck and the founding principles of the German empire. In 1961, at the height of the Cold War, he published *Griff nach der Weltmacht: die Kriegszielpolitik des Kaiserlichen Deutschland, 1914–18*. By 1961 it had become a historical convenience to treat Hitler and Nazism as aberrations, as departures from the normal course of German history. A conference of French and German historians in 1952 had concluded that no government or nation had wanted war in 1914.[27] As far as 'history' was concerned, they could be accounted for as part of the war origins narrative: blaming Germany for causing the First World War had enabled the victorious allies to impose their *Diktat* at Versailles. Their unjustified punishment of Germany, based on the erroneous charge of war guilt, had undercut the foundations of the fledgling Weimar republic and enabled a small group of fanatics to capture the state and lead Germany down the road to war. Fischer's book created an immediate sensation in Germany because he challenged this convenient consensus.

Fischer argued that Germany had not acted in self-defence in 1914, but had chosen to make a 'Grab for World Power' (*Griff nach der Weltmacht*).[28] Germany's war aims were defined almost immediately when the war broke out. The 'September Programme' demonstrated that it would not have been satisfied with the incorporation of all German peoples within the Reich, that it would eradicate the independence of smaller states and abolish the liberties of their people. It was an aggressive, expansionist Germany that encouraged Austria-Hungary to push the crisis to the point of war, convinced that it could win (partly because Britain would stay out), disrupt the Triple Entente, destroy the balance of power, and dominate south-eastern Europe and the Middle East.

Fischer himself had little background or training in the subject. In his fifties by the time that he began publishing on the subject, he had specialized in early modern history. But after becoming intrigued by the debates on war origins, he had managed to gain access to archives in the German Democratic Republic of East Germany. In almost 900 pages of densely written text, he quoted extensively from the new documents that he and his students had unearthed at Potsdam. Still, his work would not likely have caused a stir outside of academic circles had he not proposed the thesis that there was a line of continuity that ran from the First to the Second World War.

The German public became aware of Fischer's work shortly after the sensational trial of Adolf Eichmann had begun in Jerusalem. Was it true that there was no difference between Germans of the First World War and the Nazis responsible for the Holocaust? If so, this would seem to play directly into the hands of the communist regime in East Germany. Was it possible that the line coming from Moscow was right? Was it the capitalist-generated imperialism of Germany that had led it to launch two world wars—aimed principally at Russia/USSR? The gentlemanly, reserved Hamburg professor was turned into a pariah by his enemies.

Fischer turned the clock back. The debate on responsibility was renewed, but with a couple of new twists. First, critics assailed the idea that the aims elucidated by Germany once war broke out were necessarily the reasons why it had gone to war. Other states, they argued, had equally ambitious and expansive wish-lists. New research was undertaken to examine the war aims of Britain, France, and Russia. Second, Fischer's emphasis on the peculiarities of German history stimulated new research on the 'structural' components of Germany's foreign policy: had Prussian militarism fused with finance capital and big business to create a system that was predisposed to a war of expansion? The idea that there were generic, underlying causes of the war for which no one was responsible faded from view: now the systemic factors of imperialism and militarism could be attributed to the self-interest of the governing elite of the aristocracy, financiers, and industrialists. And a meticulous examination of the historical records would demonstrate how this elite functioned and how it managed to use the state for its own purposes.

Fischer attempted to undercut the criticism of his 'continuity' thesis by undertaking a study of German diplomacy before the war. Eight years after *Griff nach der Weltmacht* he published *Krieg der Illusionen* ('War of Illusions').[29] And here the First World War was made inevitable. Germany had been making careful preparations to launch a war of expansion for years: its leaders, including the supposedly peace-loving Bethmann Hollweg, were only waiting for the best possible moment to mount the attack. War became inevitable from the time of the 'war council' in December 1912 when it was decided that more time was necessary to prepare for it—but that it must be launched while Germany still had the military advantage over Russia. From that point forward it was only a matter of time.

The controversy over the 'Fischer thesis' revived interest in a subject that had been dying a lingering death for thirty years. The consensus that responsibility was shared by all who participated, and that the real causes of the war were to be found in the failures of the pre-war international system with its balance of power, alliances, armaments race, and secret diplomacy, was shattered in the 1960s. A whole new generation of historians turned to the subject again, and the volume of literature devoted to the Fischer debate has now exceeded the volume of Fischer's own writings on the subject.[30]

The arguments between admirers and critics became highly charged and increasingly strident. Unlike the debate of the 1920s this one was not overtly political: there was no 'war guilt clause' to be attacked or defended, no linkage to a peace treaty that might—or might not—be revised. But with a war raging in Vietnam and with a Cold War that threatened to turn hot, the issues at the centre of the debate were essentially political. Did elites control foreign policy? Was there a military–industrial complex that profited from the competition in armaments? Was capitalism inherently expansionist and warlike? Did states choose war over peace in order to avoid domestic difficulties, avert demands for political reform?

The long-term result of the Fischer controversy was to stimulate the creation of a vast new literature on the subject. This was fuelled, in part, by unprecedented access to the documentary record. In the 1920s the argument over war guilt had pushed governments into publishing multi-volume collections of their diplomatic correspondence. As useful and authoritative as these were, they were in every instance overseen by 'safe' historians who were not likely to publish anything that might damage the national interest or discredit the nation's reputation. No one outside the inner circle was given untrammelled access to the documents themselves. The access granted to Fischer by the communist government of East Germany set a precedent. Historians began to demand access to their own national archives. In September 1965 a letter to the editor of *The Times* of London declared that

> We, historians of many countries, have attended the discussions of the International Congress of Vienna on German war aims in the First World War. We feel strongly that British war aims, as well as the war aims of other belligerents, should be discussed with the same frankness, and therefore appeal to the British Government that they should open the British archives for the First World War without delay or restrictions.

Signatories of the letter included Fritz Fischer, Bernadotte Schmitt, and A. J. P. Taylor. Access was not long in coming. Doctoral dissertations and scholarly articles soon began to flow from those who immersed themselves in the newly accessible documents. In the 1970s, in the English language alone, over 100 new books were published on various aspects bearing upon the origins of the First World War. And then, over the course of the next twenty years, historians began the work of synthesizing these new works. Dividing the topic along national lines, Volker Berghahn (for Germany), Zara Steiner (for Britain), Dominic Lieven (for Russia), Richard Bosworth (for Italy), and Samuel Williamson (for Austria-Hungary) examined afresh the copious literature that had been produced.

As a result of all this activity we know vastly more today about decision-making, court circles, political parties, bureaucracies, strategic thought, military organizations, public opinion, and trade and finance. Perhaps surprisingly, we do not know a good deal more about the crisis of July. Students of the subject have inclined to examine structures and to investigate the assumptions of those working within those structures. All of this activity has been carried out in the shadow created by a dark cloud of predeterminism, of profound forces having produced a situation in which war was inevitable, in which what individual human beings said and did between the 28th of June and the 4th of August matters little.

This is wrong. War was not inevitable. It was the choices that men made during those fateful days that plunged the world into a war. They did not walk in their sleep. They knew what they were doing. They were not stupid. They were not ignorant. The choices they made were rational, carefully calculated, premised on the assumptions and attitudes, ideas and experience that they had accumulated over the years. Real people, actual flesh-and-blood human beings, were responsible for the tragedy of 1914— not unseen, barely understood forces beyond their control.

★

During the war there had been pressing reasons for all governments to prove to their people that their enemies were responsible for the cataclysm. As the war dragged on year after year, as the casualties moved from hundreds of thousands to millions, the need to justify the decision to go to war increased. The War of the Coloured Books is understandable, as was the war of words—the propaganda campaign—that followed. Those in power insisted that they had done their best to keep the peace, that their enemies had forced war upon them, that the war had been planned long in advance. At the same time critics on what came to be called 'the home front' joined the battle, arguing that it was the wickedness, the venality, the stupidity of their leaders that was to blame. The 'system' had to be reformed. Governments had to be more representative of their people, had to be made more responsible to them. States must agree to arbitrate disputes, stop negotiating in secret, agree to disarm. Arguments about the future of Europe hinged upon assessments of the past: determining the causes of the war, assigning responsibility for it, would enable a brave new world to rise from the ashes of the old.

Normally, arguments about responsibility for its outbreak would fade into the background once the war was over. Historians and antiquarians might pursue the subject, but did it really matter? What did matter was who won. A treaty would be negotiated and the world would move on. But not so in the aftermath of this war. The treaty of Versailles produced an unprecedented war after the war: the fight over 'war guilt'. Once again, the debate was momentous and real: the terms of the peace and the future of the new international system hung in the balance. If Germany and its allies could not be held responsible, could the harshness of the peace terms be justified? If it was not the inherent wickedness of the authoritarian governments with their militarist ethos in Germany and Austria-Hungary that was to blame for the war, was the new world being erected on a false foundation?

By 1930 the debate was over. The revisionists had won. Responsibility for the war was shared by all. A few specialists might continue to argue over the exact portion of the blame to be assigned to individual states and statesmen—but their argument ceased to be a matter of public interest. When Hitler began toppling each of the component parts of the Versailles system, no one could be found to defend them. They were illegitimate, unsupportable because they had been erected on the false premise of German war guilt.

The consensus concerning war origins played an important part in the turmoil of the 1930s. The crises in the Rhineland, over German rearmament, the *Anschluss* with Austria, the fate of the Sudeten Germans, the future of Danzig and the Polish corridor raised fundamental issues concerning nationality and sovereignty. How could Germany be denied the right to place its troops on its own soil? Why should Germany remain disarmed when others had refused to do so themselves? By what right did the victors in 1919 deny Germans the right to come together as citizens in a single state? Was the principle of national self-determination meaningless? Was the entire treatment of Germany based on hypocrisy? Was it not the refusal of Austria-Hungary to permit its Serbs to join their brethren in the Serbian kingdom that lit the fuse that would ignite the world conflagration? Were international relations once again to be conducted not on the basis of principles and ideals such as sovereignty and nationality, but on force and threats of force?

The errors made by the statesmen in 1914 were not to be repeated: the conference between the great and the powerful that was never held in July convened instead at Munich in 1938. No stone must be left unturned if it could preserve the peace and prevent a repeat performance of the cataclysm of 1914. Chamberlain would not be Sir Edward Grey: no fishing for him in the midst of a crisis. Men do learn from their mistakes: they learn how to make new ones.[31]

Hitler believed that he too had learned. The choice made by the kaiser and his circle to challenge British commerce and colonialism meant that they squandered the opportunity of an alliance. Failing this, Germany ought to have turned to Russia for support. Instead, it found itself in 1914 'forsaken by all except the Habsburg hereditary evil' and thus 'stumbled into the World War'.[32] The Nazi–Soviet Pact was the result of Hitler's interpretation of Germany's mistakes between 1900 and 1914.

Hitler and Chamberlain were not alone in acting upon interpretations of war origins. The French accepted the premise that it was the military preparations for offensive war that ultimately brought it about. No one would be able to accuse them of such a plan this time: they would proclaim their commitment to a defensive war by constructing the Maginot Line—the most ambitious and expensive fortification programme undertaken in modern times. The Russians believed that a sentimental attachment to a small Slav state, combined with a naïve faith in Anglo-French assistance, had led them down the road to disaster in 1914. Stalin would not repeat the mistake of Nicholas II.

★

The experience of the Second World War and the revelations of the Holocaust afterwards turned the world upside down. War became respectable once again: it was essential to confront evil men, to counter wicked ideas, to stand up to aggression. The 'lessons' of the First World War had to be forgotten, new ones remembered. Alliances made a come-back: blamed for precipitating the First World War, the absence of an Anglo-French-Russian coalition was now seen as opening the door to Hitler's aggression. Armaments were essential: the legend of the 'armed camps' in Europe before 1914 gave way to the belief that military weakness deprived Germany's opponents of the strength to resist—until they were left with no choice but to go to war unprepared for the struggle. A 'league' of nations would give too much weight to the small; nations must be 'united' instead—led by a small group of great powers who would be responsible for calling the shots.

People prefer simple explanations. Statesmen find them convenient. Tapping into simple-minded conclusions enabled Western leaders to sell NATO, arm to the teeth, confront the enemy on every front. This was an astonishing reversal of what people believed they had learned from the experience of 1914. But did it affect our understanding of that experience?

One central truth seemed to remain. Hitler would not have triumphed in Germany, Nazism would not have flourished, had it not been for the error made at Versailles in punishing Germany for its guilt. Making Germany pay the price for a war that was no one's fault, that had been caused by 'the system', had put Europe back on the road to ruin. The consensus that had triumphed between the wars endured. Luigi Albertini's massively detailed study did nothing to alter anyone's perspective. There was no doubt who was guilty for the second of the world wars: Hitler and Nazism. The Nazis were criminals who must be punished, but they were an aberration, and the mistake of 1919 would not be repeated. The German people would not be made to suffer; Germany would be 'de-nazified', democratized, and restored to its rightful place among the comity of nations.

This is why Fritz Fischer caused such a storm. By linking Hitler to Bismarck, the 'third Reich' to Wilhelmine Germany, he suggested that the phenomenon of Nazism was no aberration. The will to dominate, establish hegemony in Europe, make a 'grab' for world power was deeply rooted in Germany's history. When the 'Fischerites' examined the structural realities of German society and politics they discovered the underlying forces that produced the will to expand and rule. They turned upside down the famous dictum of the great nineteenth-century historian, Leopold von Ranke, who had proclaimed the 'primacy of foreign affairs' (*Primat der Aussenpolitik*) in explaining Germany's history. Now it was domestic affairs (*Innenpolitik*) that mattered most. In essence, German foreign policy before 1914 had been determined by the deal done between the Prussian *Junker* aristocracy and the industrialists, the shipbuilders, and the financiers of western Germany. The pact between these forces guaranteed that Germany would remain militarist and undemocratic—but to remain so it would have to repress social democracy and whip up fear and resentment of foreigners—Slavs especially.

The *Innenpolitik* approach reverberated beyond the frontiers of Germany. Opponents of the war in Vietnam took it to heart. Was it not the case that the government of the United States was doing the bidding of a coterie of special interests? Was it not the 'military–industrial complex' that Eisenhower had warned of that was responsible for pushing Americans into fighting an unwinnable land war in Asia? Was it not the 'national security state' in the US that was using the spectre of international communism to whip up support for militarism at home and repressing dissent? Did all of this not resemble the strategy of Wilhelmine and Hitlerian Germany?

The real lesson that seemed to be emerging from studying the wars of the twentieth century was that they began because the states involved were rotten at the core. They were essentially undemocratic, unrepresentative, and unconstitutional. We were, in essence, back where we started. Militarism, the arms race, secret diplomacy were all the products of special interests who had captured the apparatus of the state and twisted it to benefit themselves and their friends.

★

Unfortunately, as historians turned their sights back on the structures, the systems, and the special interests that were once again charged with responsibility for war in 1914, the situation turned out to be vastly more complicated than expected. Years of research into domestic crises, interest groups, and decision-making failed to yield any clear answers, failed to find the villain responsible.

One hundred years on, those who continue the futile search for a guilty man offer us little more than an entertaining parlour game: pin the tail on the kaiser or Moltke; on the tsar or Sazonov; on Berchtold or Conrad; on Grey or Poincaré. Many have played this game, but no one has managed to win it. And, if they had, what would we have learned from it? That great wars are caused by wicked or incompetent individuals—and that we must in the future insist on being led by those who are neither wicked nor incompetent? A sterile and not particularly helpful guideline.

Is the alternative to ignore the role of individuals in history? No: this narrative of events from the assassination to the decisions of August demonstrates the importance of individuals and the role of human agency. Our comprehension of the choices that lay before those involved in the crisis enables us to grasp the values, the hopes, and the fears of those whose decisions led to the cataclysm. It was the choices they made that mattered. Blind 'historical forces' did not devise ultimatums or mobilize millions: men of flesh and blood did.

Assumptions about honour and prestige, the past and the future, were paramount in the decisions that they made. The statesmen responsible for guiding the policies of the Great Powers believed, ultimately, that they could not appear to be weak in the eyes of the others. The perception of weakness would erode the prestige of their state; without prestige they would no longer command respect; without respect their wishes could be ignored. Their study of the past had taught them that the great could decline: they too might go the way of Spain and Portugal, the Netherlands and Sweden—their greatness could gradually erode; they could be pushed to the periphery, their voices barely heard. Worse still, their enemies might descend upon those perceived to be weak and carve them up, annexing and partitioning until they no longer existed. What had become of Poland? The only safeguard against decline, decay, and disappearance was exertion of will. For Austria-Hungary to admit that it lacked the strength or determination to put an end to Serbian propaganda, agitation, and plots on behalf of a Greater Serbia would be an admission that it was no longer a Great Power, capable of confronting those forces that threatened to pull it apart. For Russia to admit that it could do nothing to stop Serbia from becoming the vassal of Austria would confirm the lessons of the Russo-Japanese war: that it was an empire in decay, incapable of exerting itself in the Slavic sphere where the tsars had long proclaimed their special duty, their historic mission, to protect their brethren in the Orthodox Church.

If the past taught the statesmen of 1914 what to fear, the future tantalized them with what they might hope for. The twentieth century promised great rewards for those strong enough, courageous enough, to seize opportunities when they beckoned. The future belonged to the large and the strong—to empires, to world powers. The age of small states was passing into history. Those who lacked the people and the resources would gradually be absorbed by those who had them. The British empire and the United States offered two versions of imperial greatness: one a diverse, world-wide empire of heterogeneous character; the other a continental empire consisting of 'one nation indivisible, with liberty and justice for all'. Russia certainly had the people and the resources to compete with them—if it could only modernize and industrialize before being pulled apart by social revolutionaries or ethnic differences.

Where did this leave the other Great Powers of Europe? Could Germany and France, Austria-Hungary and Italy possibly compete on this scale? With the aid of allies, they believed they could. France, no longer clashing with Britain around the world, could create a modern empire in Africa and Asia of 'Frenchmen' welded together by the universalist principles of the enlightened republic. Building a cohesive empire would take time—during which the alliance with Russia would offer protection against Germany within Europe. Germany could see two versions of an imperial future—sometimes complementary, sometimes competing. A great high-seas fleet could sustain a *Weltpolitik* (world policy) that had already helped to secure footholds in Africa and Asia; a *Mitteleuropa* could create a continental empire stretching from Berlin to Baghdad, capable of competing with the British and the Russian. Essential to both these visions was the continuing existence, and support, of a strong, dependable Austria-Hungary.

Compared with the already vast empires of Britain and Russia, compared with the power and the possibilities already beckoning to Germany and France, the imperial dreams of Austria-Hungary and Italy may appear whimsical. This is a retrospective judgement. The future that beckoned to their statesmen was alluringly real. The Habsburg monarchy had the opportunity to create a multinational empire, one that offered its diverse nationalities and religions a strength and a unity that they could not hope to achieve as tiny, independent entities. Developing and modernizing Bosnia and Herzegovina could show the way to the future—as long as Austria could continue to rely on the protection of Germany against Russia. Maintaining its position in the annexed provinces had become a litmus-test. And Italy? The war with Turkey, the seizure of its territories in north Africa and their transformation into provinces that echoed the greatness of Rome—'Libya' and 'Cyrenaica'—on the 'fourth shore' offered hope for the future. As did expansion along the Adriatic, with a foothold in Albania. For a time, it seemed that this dream might be realized through the alliance with Germany and Austria-Hungary; but it could be wrecked by a war with Britain and France. Italy, the 'least' of the Great Powers, had a choice to make between the two alliances—a choice no other power believed open to them.

There were, however, many choices made between 28 June and 4 August. The choices were made by men of experience and intelligence, and they made their choices consciously, rationally, on the basis of *raison d'état*, on the foundations of the fears they faced in the present and on their hopes for a better future. Few were eager for war—or at least for the great European war that they got in August. Most of the men who mattered in Austria-Hungary were prepared for war with Serbia, but believed it unlikely, under the circumstances of the regicide and given the support of Germany, that the Russians would go to war to defend their Slavic brethren. Most Germans who mattered concurred in this estimate. They were mistaken. Their mistakes consisted of an amalgam of wishful thinking and wilful blindness: Russia was not yet prepared for war and would back down; Britain cared nothing for the fate of Serbia; France might not back Russia without the guarantee of British support. The support of Italy could be purchased; somehow the Romanians could be persuaded to adhere to the alliance. Every one of these estimates proved to be mistaken, but they barrelled ahead anyway, confident that—in spite of everything—they still enjoyed a military advantage; fearful that this advantage would slip away if they waited too long.

Austria-Hungary, with Germany's support, seized the initiative. Russia, France, and Britain—the so-called Triple Entente—reacted to it. Their statesmen and diplomats proved to be as mistaken and as misguided as those of the Triple Alliance. It was not the 'topos of inevitable war' that explains their errors, but the 'topos of avoidable war'.[33] Europe had been through many crises as bad as this one—and some that seemed worse.

Serbia, they believed, would be disciplined, chastised in some manner or other—and indeed Serbia deserved to be punished. The role of the small is not to make trouble for the great. Surely, they believed, it would not take an unprecedented intellectual effort on the part of Europe's statesmen to devise a formula that would satisfy Austrian honour and limit the likelihood of Serbia upsetting the balance of power in the future. They all trusted that Germany would restrain Austria from going too far; even some Germans thought this ought to be their role on the crisis.

War was neither premeditated nor accidental. Premeditation is not to be proven by the existence of war plans or by the warlike pronouncements of military men. Strategists are expected to plan for the next war: the politicians and diplomats decide when that war is most likely to occur. It is then the professional duty of men in uniform to plan accordingly. When they take the next step and advise that a war at any given moment is preferable to waiting, that what might be winnable now might be losable in the future, or—as is actually more often the case—that more needs to be done, that more men, more guns, more ships, that newer, faster, more powerful equipment is essential if victory is to be secured, they are doing what is expected of them. That warriors are prone to be warlike can hardly be a surprise. It certainly does not surprise the civilians who listen to their advice, give it the credence they believe it deserves, then make their decisions accordingly.

Given the size and complexity of the modern armies that would fight a war in 1914, it was essential to have plans in place. Part of these plans, everywhere, involved preparations that had to precede mobilization. Railway carriages had to be commandeered, tracks cleared, railway companies informed of changes to their schedules; horses, foodstuffs, essential materials had to be gathered, secured, and available; personnel had to be put in place to receive reservists when they were called up. In Germany this was the *Kriegsgefahrzustand*,[34] in Austria-Hungary the *Alarmierung*, in Russia the 'period preparatory to war', in Britain the 'precautionary stage', and so on. The extent of these arrangements varied and the publicity given to them was deliberately constrained—making it difficult for observers to determine just how far and how fast things were moving. But in the last week of July, everyone was aware that steps were being taken. None of the Great Powers could carry out a mobilization in secret. The war plans themselves did not make war inevitable. And, when the fighting started in August, no one's plan worked as promised: not Germany's Schlieffen Plan, not Austria's Plan R, not Joffre's Plan XVII. Chaos, not design, was the order of the day.

Some news of the steps being taken prior to mobilization leaked into the newspapers. More detailed information was available through military intelligence. The Russians were the acknowledged leaders here, and they succeeded in intercepting many of the communications between Vienna and St Petersburg. Both they and the French were aware, before 24 July, that the Austrians were about to demand that steps be taken in Serbia to punish those involved in the assassination and to restrict the agitation for a greater Serbia. This was hardly surprising, and Sazonov, in particular, attempted to prevent them from going too far by warning that Russia would not countenance the end of Serbian independence and sovereignty. His warnings fell on deaf ears and he was genuinely shocked when he saw the extent of the demands made upon Serbia in the ultimatum of 23 July. Ignoring his admonitions appeared to prove that the Austrians were determined to reduce Serbia to vassalage and that they must be counting on the backing of Germany.

Thus, from the 24th of July, Sazonov believed that Russia must either prepare for war or abandon Serbia. Still, Russia's preparations did not preclude peace: they brought war closer, ratcheted up the tension, but they did not make conflict inevitable. The record of what those involved actually said and did confutes the thesis of a premeditated war. This narrative shows the lengths to which Austria, encouraged by Germany, was prepared to go in trying to keep Russia on the sidelines in its confrontation with Serbia.

On almost every day of the July crisis a solution seemed to be at hand. Anything short of crushing Serbia's independence appeared to be acceptable to Russia, France, and Britain. No one knows what would have happened had different decisions been taken: had Sir Edward Grey announced that Britain would support Russia at the outset of the crisis; had Poincaré warned Russia that France might not fight a European war for the sake of Balkan interests; had Sazonov calculated that upholding Serbian sovereignty was too risky for Russia; had Berchtold advised the emperor that a diplomatic humiliation of Serbia would be victory enough for Austria-Hungary; had Bethmann Hollweg insisted that the Austrians negotiate a settlement by meeting in conference with the other Great Powers. Those historians who claim to know how things would have turned out had one decision gone the other way are not to be trusted. They are not omniscient. We cannot know, will never know, how things might have been. What we can know, and what we do know, is how the participants behaved—and how, from each of their perspectives, their behaviour was grounded in rational self-interest, on their experiences in the past and their expectations of the future.

History offers no simple lessons, no short guidebook on how to behave. When the fighting of the First World War proved to be more horrific than anything anyone had imagined, people everywhere began searching for solutions, devising slogans like 'the war to end war'. Everyone's solution varied according to their nationality, ideology, age, and experience. Believing that alliances were the ultimate cause, some promoted the new device of collective security, to be engineered by the fledgling League of Nations. Believing that unfulfilled national dreams would inevitably lead to discontent, agitation, and assassinations, the principle of 'national self-determination' was enshrined in the League's principles. Believing that Europe 'of the armed camps' made war inevitable, the victorious powers promised to disarm 'to the lowest point consistent with national safety'. Believing that the competition for empire was at the root of the trouble, the territories of the German and Ottoman empires were handed over to 'mandated' powers who were to act as 'trustees' until those Africans and Arabs in their charge were capable of forming their own, independent states. Believing that the German people would inevitably dominate Europe if permitted to unite without restriction, the Rhineland was demilitarized, the new republic was disarmed, Sudeten Germans assigned to Czechoslovakia, Austrian Germans debarred from becoming part of Germany. The lessons 'learned' in studying the outbreak of the First World War laid the groundwork for the Second.

There is not, and there never will be, a neat explanation that ties up all of the loose ends, that satisfactorily answers everyone's questions concerning the outbreak of the First World War. Missing from the documentation on which this narrative is based are the 'unspoken assumptions' identified by James Joll many years ago. What went on in the schools, how young men and women were turned into patriotic subjects and citizens through the education that they received, how ideas of honour and valour, manhood and courage, were formed, how the belief that fighting 'for king and country', for 'holy mother Russia', for *Das Vaterland*, for *La Patrie* lay at the bottom of the choices men made in July 1914 is undeniable. They were present, however, long before July 1914; they are present still. They did not result in perpetual war. Instead, Europe had enjoyed something close to perpetual peace for almost half a century.

The existence of alliances, mass conscript armies, huge navies, unprecedented armaments, imperial rivalries, nationalist discontents were all factors in the outbreak of war. But they, like the underlying assumptions formed by Europeans in the age before the war, had been present for decades. While such factors may explain why wars break out, they do not explain why this one broke out at this time, in this way, with the opposing sides arrayed as they were. We can never know what the alternative was, whether, if war was avoided in August, it would have broken out in September, or 1915, or ever. Would the Triple Alliance have disintegrated? Would the Anglo-Russian entente have broken down because of growing friction in the Middle East and Central Asia? Would the Habsburg empire have endured, in spite of the fissiparous tendencies that bedevilled it in 1914? Would the agitation, the plots, the conspiracies against Austria-Hungary have continued within Serbia? Would the tsarist autocracy, with its pretensions to act on behalf of Slavdom and Orthodoxy, have gradually transformed into a democratic, representative system embodying different values? Would social democracy have eventually triumphed in Germany, supplanting the authoritarian rule enshrined in the constitution of 1871? These are only a few of the possible scenarios that might have occurred, had war been avoided in July 1914. How such changes might have affected issues of war and peace are unfathomable. Would a Great, a European, or a World War have erupted anyway? We shall never know.

What we do know is how those in positions of authority made the choices that produced unprecedented suffering and upheaval. The tragic era that followed can be explained only by their hubris, combined with chance and circumstance.

Notes

ABBREVIATIONS USED IN THE NOTES

BD, XI   *British Documents on the Origins of the War*, ed. G. P. Gooch and
             Harold Temperley, vol. XI (London, 1926)

BGB   *Diplomatic Correspondence Respecting the War (July 24–August 29)*, in
             *Collected Diplomatic Documents Relating to the Outbreak of the European
             War* ('The Belgian Grey Book') (London, 1915)

DAVK, III   *Diplomatische Aktenstücke zur Vorgeschichte des Krieges 1914*, teil III
             (Berlin, 1922), no. 97.

DDF, X   *Documents diplomatiques français (1871–1914)*, 3ᵐᵉ série, 1911–14,
             Tome X (Paris, 1929)

DDI, XII   *I documenti diplomatici italiani*, 4th series, vol. XII, ed. A. Torre
             (Rome, 1954) DDK, I *Die deutschen Dokumente zum Kriegsausbruch*,
             ed. M. Montgelas and W. Schücking, Band I (Berlin, 1919)

DSP   *Dokumenti o spolnoj politici Kraljevine Srbije*, ed. Vladimir Dedijer and
             Života Anić, VII/2

Int. Bez.   *Die Internationalen Beziehungen im Zeitalter des Imperialismus*, ed. Otto
             Hoetzsch (Berlin, 1931)

O-UA, VIII   *Österreich-Ungarns Aussenpolitik von der Bosnischen Krise 1908 bis zum
             Kriegsausbruch 1914*, ed. L. Bittner et al., Band VIII (Vienna, 1930)

SBB   'The Serbian Blue Book', in *Collected Diplomatic Documents Relating
             to the Outbreak of the European War* (London, 1915)

PROLOGUE: THE LONG EUROPEAN PEACE

1. On Angell, see: J. D. B. Miller, *Norman Angell and the Futility of War* (London, 1986); Martin Ceadel, *Living the Great Illusion: Sir Norman Angell, 1872–1967* (Oxford, 2009); Cornelia Navari, 'The Great Illusion Revisited: The International Theory of Norman Angell', *Review of International Studies* 15 (1989), 341–58; and L. Brescia, 'Norman Angell and the Pacifist Muddle', *Bulletin of the Institute of Historical Research* xlv (1972), 104–21.

2. *The Great Illusion*, 3rd edn (London, 1911), 269.

3. Paul Laity, *The British Peace Movement, 1870–1914* (Oxford, 2001), 186–94.

4. See Azar Gat, *The Development of Military Thought: The Nineteenth Century* (Oxford, 1992), 17–18.

5. *The War of the Future in its Technical, Economic and Political Relations* (London, 1899), 6.

6. On Suttner, see Caroline Playne, *Bertha von Suttner and the Struggle to Avert the World War* (London, 1936).

7. Quoted in Sandi E. Cooper, *Patriotic Pacifism: Waging War on War in Europe, 1815–1914* (New York, 1991), 60 n. 1.

8. Quoted in Cooper, *Patriotic Pacifism*, 81 n. 203.

9. Cooper, *Patriotic Pacifism*, 87 n. 259.

10. On these issues generally, see James Joll and Gordon Martel, *The Origins of the First World War*, 3rd edn (London, 2007), ch. 8: 'The mood of 1914', pp. 254–98.

11. Karl Marx, 'The war', *New York Daily Tribune*, 15 November 1853, in Eleanor Marx (ed.), *The Eastern Question* (London, 1897), 151.

12. Michael Hurst (ed.), *Key Treaties for the Great Powers, 1814–1914*, vol. 2: *1871–1914* (London, 1974), 590.

13. Hurst, *Key Treaties*, 611.

14. An English translation of the text of all of the treaties may be found in Alfred Pribram, *The Secret Treaties of Austria-Hungary, 1879–1914* (Cambridge, Mass., 1920), tr. A. G. Coolidge.

15. Hurst, *Key Treaties*, 663.

16. The Franco-Russian alliance is sometimes referred to as the 'Dual Alliance', but as this term is also sometimes used to describe the Austro-German alliance, I have chosen to use 'Franco-Russian' in order to avoid any confusion.

17. Hurst, *Key Treaties*, 668–9.

18. Nicholas II to Wilhelm II, 29 October 1904, in Johannes Lepsius, Albrecht Mendelssohn-Bartholdy, and Friedrich Thimme (eds), *Die Große Politik der Europäischen Kabinette, 1871–1914. Sammlung der diplomatischen Akten des Auswärtigen Amtes* (henceforth *DGP*), Band 19, Teil 2, nr 6119.

19. Quoted in Zara Steiner and Keith Neilson, *Britain and the Origins of the First World War*, 2nd edn (London, 2003), 158.

20. Nicolson to Goschen, 5 May 1914. Quoted in Steiner and Neilson, *Britain and the Origins*, 229.

21. Quoted in J. C. G. Röhl, *The Kaiser and his Court: Wilhelm II and the Government of Germany* (Cambridge, 1987), 168.

22. Helmuth von Moltke, chief of the general staff; Alfred von Tirpitz, chief of the naval staff; August von Heeringen, Tirpitz's predecessor; and Georg von Müller, chief of the naval cabinet.

23. See J. C. G. Röhl, 'Admiral von Müller and the Approach of War, 1911–1914', *The Historical Journal* 12/4 (1969), 651–73.

24. The conversation of that day has been interpreted by Fritz Fischer, and his students and followers—Imanuel Geiss, J. C. G. Röhl, Volker Berghahn, and others—as making war inevitable from that time forward, as Germany was now bent on unleashing it when the most favourable moment arrived. 'German foreign policy from then onwards until July 1914 readily becomes plausible as the execution of the programme laid down on that occasion.' 'With the decision of 8 December 1912, the German Empire had entered a course which was to lead straight to war.' Imanuel Geiss, *German Foreign Policy, 1871–1914* (London, 1976), 144, 145. Röhl has reconsidered this and now argues that it 'was not so much the point at which Germany's leaders decided to begin a European war in the summer of 1914, but rather the meeting at which a decision to begin an immediate war which had been taken four weeks earlier was reversed again in favour of a postponement'. My thanks to John for providing me with his unpublished paper on the subject, 'War Premeditated? The "War Council" of 8 December 1912 Revisited'.

25. Quoted in Konrad Jarausch, *The Enigmatic Chancellor* (New Haven, 1972), 134.

26. Jarausch, *The Enigmatic Chancellor*, 134.

27. The decision of the kaiser required the approval of the upper, federal house—the Bundesrat—but it had become a rubber-stamp under Bismarck and his successors.

28. Quoted in Röhl, *Kaiser and his Court*, 11.

29. On his love of parade and his sensitivity to public perceptions of his greatness, see Thomas A. Kohut, *Wilhelm II and the Germans* (New York, 1991).

30. Quoted in Wilhelm Deist, 'The Kaiser and his Military Entourage', in John C. G. Röhl and Nicolaus Sombart (eds), *Kaiser Wilhelm II: New Interpretations* (Cambridge, 1982), 180.

31. See Paul Kennedy, 'The Kaiser and German *Weltpolitik*: Reflections on Wilhelm II's Place in the Making of German Foreign Policy', in Röhl and Sombart, *Kaiser Wilhelm II*, 157.

32. Röhl, *Kaiser and his Court*, 13.

33. The foremost proponent of the 'personal monarchy' thesis is John C. G. Röhl. The most detailed exposition of the thesis is to be found in his immensely detailed three-volume biography, now available in English: *Young Wilhelm: The Kaiser's Early Life, 1859–1888* (Cambridge, 1998), tr. Jeremy Gaines and Rebecca Wallach; *Wilhelm II: The Kaiser's Personal Monarchy, 1888–1900* (Cambridge, 2004), tr. Sheila de Bellaigue; *Wilhelm II: Into the Abyss of War and Exile, 1900–1941* (Cambridge, 2014), tr. Sheila de Bellaigue and Roy Bridge. For a contrasting interpretation see Christopher Clark, *Kaiser Wilhelm II* (London, 2000).

34. Richard J. Evans, *Rethinking German History: Nineteenth-Century Germany and the Origins of the Third Reich* (London, 1987), 63.

35. Quoted in Röhl, *Kaiser and his Court*, 159.

36. Lamar Cecil, 'William II and his Russian "Colleagues"', in Carole Fink, Isabel V. Hull, and MacGregor Knox (eds), *German Nationalism and the European Response, 1890–1945* (Norman, Okla., 1985), 97.

37. Quoted in Lamar Cecil, *The German Diplomatic Service, 1871–1914* (Princeton, 1976), 212.

38. Graydon A. Tunstall, Jr, 'Austria-Hungary', in Richard F. Hamilton and Holger H. Herwig (eds), *The Origins of World War I* (Cambridge, 2003), 130.

39. Quoted in Steven Beller, *Francis Joseph* (London, 1996), 186.

40. Quoted in F. R. Bridge, *From Sadowa to Sarajevo: The Foreign Policy of Austria-Hungary, 1866–1914* (London, 1972), 336.

41. Quoted in Dominic Lieven, *Nicholas II: Emperor of All the Russias* (London, 1993), 195.

42. Lieven, *Nicholas II*, 60.

43. Quoted in G. P. Gooch, *Before the War* (London, 1938), ii. 312.

44. Cecil, *German Nationalism*, 126.

45. Quoted in John Keiger, *Raymond Poincaré* (Cambridge, 1997), 22.

46. Keiger, *Raymond Poincaré*, 44.

47. Ironically, the French constitution had failed to provide for the position that evolved as the *président du conseil*—and thus the man who would function as premier/prime minister was required to take on a ministry in order to sit in the council that he had formed.

48. Quoted in Keiger, *Raymond Poincaré*, 130.

49. See Leslie Derfler, *President and Parliament: A Short History of the French Presidency* (Boca Raton, Fla., 1983).

50. Quoted in Steiner and Neilson, *Britain and the Origins*, 40.

THE KILLING

1. *Zeleni Venac*—'Green Wreath'; *Zlatna Ribica*—'Little Goldfish'; *Žirovni Venac*—'Oak Garland'.

2. Albert Mousset, *Un drame historique: l'attentat de Sarajevo. Documents inédits et text intégral des sténogrammes du procès* (Paris, 1930), 130.

3. Quoted in R. W. Seton-Watson, *Sarajevo: A Study in the Origins of the Great War* (London, 1926), 70.

4. A quotation found in the notes of several Bosnian youths arrested after the assassination of the archduke. Vladimir Dedijer, *The Road to Sarajevo* (London, 1967), 178.

5. Quoted in István Diószegi, *Hungarians in the Ballhausplatz: Studies on the Austro-Hungarian Common Foreign Policy* (Budapest, 1983); tr. Kornél Balás, rev. Mary Borsos, 118–19.

6. Dedijer, *Road to Sarajevo*, 374.

7. Quoted in Dedijer, *Road to Sarajevo*, 185.

8. Quoted in Bernadotte Schmitt, *The Coming of the War, 1914* (New York, 1930), i. 244.

9. Quoted in Luigi Albertini, *Le origini della guerra del 1914* (1942–43); tr. Isabella M. Massey as *The Origins of the War of 1914* (Oxford, 1952), ii. 113.

10. Quoted in Seton-Watson, *Sarajevo*, 79.

11. Seton-Watson, *Sarajevo*, 84.

12. Quoted in Gordon Brook-Shepherd, *Victims at Sarajevo: The Romance and Tragedy of Franz Ferdinand and Sophie* (London, 1984), 136.

13. Mousset, *Un drame historique*, 485.

14. Quoted in Schmitt, *Coming of the War*, i. 256.

15. *Coming of the War*, i. 256.

16. *Coming of the War*, i. 257.

17. Quoted in Albertini, *Origins of the War*, ii. 42–3.

THE REACTION

1. Dedijer, *Road to Sarajevo*, 324–7.

2. Schmitt, *Coming of the War*, ii. 258–62.

3. Ritter von Storck to Berchtold, 29 June, *O-UA*, VIII, nr 9943.

4. Descos to Viviani, 1 July 1914, *DDF*, X, no. 469.

5. Quoted in Mark Cornwall, 'Serbia', in Keith Wilson (ed.), *Decisions for War* (London, 1995), 60.

6. From *Pester Lloyd*; cited in Seton-Watson, *Sarajevo*, 126.

7. Graf Franz Conrad von Hötzendorf, *Aus meiner Dienstzeit, 1906–1918*, 5 vols (Vienna, 1921–25), iv. 31.

8. Baron von Margutti, *The Emperor Francis Joseph and his Times* (New York, 1921), 307.

9. Lawrence Sondhaus, *Franz Conrad von Hötzendorf: Architect of the Apocalypse* (Boston, 2000), 84.

10. Sondhaus, *Franz Conrad von Hötzendorf*, 110–11. Sondhaus's extensive use of this correspondence makes his work an indispensable source for anyone interested in the outbreak of the First World War.

11. Sondhaus, *Franz Conrad von Hötzendorf*, 119.

12. Sondhaus, *Franz Conrad von Hötzendorf*, 135.

13. Sondhaus, *Franz Conrad von Hötzendorf*, 140.

14. Tschirschky to Bethmann Hollweg, 30 June, *DDK*, I, nr 7. This is available in English translation as *Outbreak of the World War: Documents Collected by Karl Kautsky and edited by M. Montgelas and W. Schücking* (New York, 1924), tr. Carnegie Endowment for International Peace. The numbering of the documents is identical in the two versions. The translations are not entirely reliable, and some German terms and phrases are open to different renderings.

15. Storck to Berchtold, 30 June, *O-UA*, VIII, nr 9950.

16. Tschirschky to Bethmann Hollweg, 30 June, *DDK*, I, nr 7.

17. Tschirschky remained as ambassador in Vienna until his death in 1916—so he was one of the few leading diplomatists who did not attempt to explain afterwards his role in the outbreak of war in a memoir or autobiography.

18. Rumbold to Grey, 30 June, *BD* XI, no. 22.

19. Bollati to San Giuliano, 30 June, *DDI*, XII, 25; quoted in R. J. B. Bosworth, *Italy, the Least of the Great Powers: Italian Foreign Policy before the First World War* (Cambridge, 1979), 380.

20. Lamar Cecil, *Wilhelm II*, vol. 2: *Emperor and Exile, 1900–1941* (Chapel Hill, 1996), 198.

21. Pashitch [Pašić] to All the Royal Serbian Legations abroad. Belgrade, 1 July, *SBB*, no. 8.

22. Tschirschky to Foreign Office, telegram, 2 July, *DDK*, I, nr 8.

23. Tisza to Franz Joseph, 1 July, *O-UA*, VIII, nr 9978.

24. Bridge, *Sadowa to Sarajevo*, 361.

25. Memorandum by Baron von Matscheko, undated, secret, *O-UA*, VIII, nr. 9918; a good English translation of the memorandum is available in Bridge, *Sadowa to Sarajevo*.

26. H. B. A. Petersson, 'Das osterreichisch-ungarische Memorandum an Deutschland vom 5. Juli 1914', *Scandia* 30 (1964), 138–90.

27. Franz Joseph to Wilhelm II, 2 July, *O-UA*, VIII, nr 9984. Presented in Berlin on 5 July.

28. Franz Joseph to Wilhelm II, 2 July, *O-UA*, VIII, nr 9984.

29. Tisza to Franz Joseph, 1 July, *O-UA*, VIII, nr 9978.

30. *O-UA*, VII, nr. 9482.

31. Quoted in Gabor Vermes, *István Tisza: The Liberal Vision and Conservative Statecraft of a Magyar Nationalist* (New York, 1985), 230.

32. Berchtold to Conrad, *O-UA*, VIII, nr. 9976.

33. Conrad to Berchtold, *O-UA*, VIII, nr. 9995.

34. Daily report [*Tagesbericht*] by Berchtold on meeting with Tschirschky, 3 July, *O-UA*, VIII, nr 1006.

35. Tschirschky to Bethmann Hollweg, 2 July, *DDK*, I, nr 11.

36. Tschirschky to Bethmann Hollweg. 2 July, *DDK*, I, nr 11.

37. Tschirschky to Bethmann Hollweg. 2 July, *DDK*, I, nr 11. Kaiser's marginal note.

38. de Bunsen to Grey, 2 July, *BD*, XI, no. 28.

39. de Bunsen to Nicolson, 3 July, *BD*, XI, no. 29.

40. Vesnitch to Pashitch, telegram, 2 July, *SBB*, no. 10.

41. de Bunsen to Grey, 5 July, *BD*, XI, no. 40.

42. Dumaine to Viviani, 2 July, *DDF*, X, no. 470.

43. Keith Eubank, *Paul Cambon: Master Diplomatist* (Norman, Okla., 1960), 168.

44. Ernst Lichtenau (Saxon minister in Berlin) to Vitzthum, 2 July 1914, in Annika Mombauer, *The Origins of the First World War: Diplomatic and Military Documents* (Manchester, 2013), 176.

45. An English translation of Hoyos' account of their conversation (from *O-UA*, VIII, nr 9966) can be found in Imanuel Geiss, *July 1914: The Outbreak of the First World War: Selected Documents* (New York, 1967), 64–5.

46. Quoted in Robert A. Kann (ed. Stanley B. Winters), *Dynasty, Politics and Culture: Selected Essays* (Boulder, Colo., 1991), 136.

47. William Godsey Jr, *Aristocratic Redoubt: The Austro-Hungarian Foreign Office on the Eve of the First World War* (West Lafayette, 1999), 160, 167, 191.

48. Szögyény to Berchtold, 5 July, *O-UA*, VIII, nr 10058.

49. The kaiser, as commander of the armed forces, maintained his own military cabinet that operated quite apart from the 'cabinet' chaired by the chancellor.

50. Hans Plessen (aide-de-camp to the kaiser), diary, 5 July, in Mombauer, *Diplomatic and Military Documents*, 195.

51. Quoted in Annika Mombauer, *Helmuth von Moltke and the Origins of the First World War* (Cambridge, 2001), 191.

52. On Bethmann Hollweg generally, see Jarausch, *Enigmatic Chancellor*; on his relationship with the kaiser, see Cecil, *Wilhelm II*, vol. 2; with the pan-Germans, Roger Chickering, *We Men Who Feel Most German: A Cultural Study of the Pan-German League, 1886–1914* (Boston, 1984).

53. Quoted in Jarausch, *Enigmatic Chancellor*, 68.

54. Jarausch, *Enigmatic Chancellor*, 147.

55. Szögyény to Berchtold, telegram, 6 July, *O-UA*, VIII, nr 10076.

56. Kaiser's marginalia on Bethmann Hollweg to Wilhelm II, 3 October 1912, quoted in John Röhl (ed.), *1914: Delusion or Design? The Testimony of Two German Diplomats* (London, 1973), 42–3.

57. Quoted in Harry F. Young, *Prince Lichnowsky and the Great War* (Athens, Ga., 1977), 11.

58. Young, *Prince Lichnowsky*, 40–1.

59. Lichnowsky to Bethmann Hollweg, 6 July, *DDK*, I, nr 20.

60. Grey to Rumbold, 6 July, *BD*, XI, no. 32.

61. Young, *Lichnowsky*, 103.

62. Wayne C. Thompson, *In the Eye of the Storm: Kurt Riezler and the Crises of Modern Germany* (Iowa City, 1980), 74.

63. Tschirschky to Foreign Office, telegram, 7 July, *DDK*, I, nr 18.

64. Berchtold to Franz Joseph, 7 July, *O-UA*, VIII, nr 10116.

65. His remarks may be found in Hötzendorff, *Aus meiner Dienstzeit*, iv. 43–56.

66. Berchtold to Tisza, 8 July, *O-UA*, VIII, nr 10145.

67. Tschirschky to Foreign Office, telegram, 8 July, *DDK*, I, nr 19.

68. Quoted in Gary W. Shanafelt, *The Secret Enemy: Austria-Hungary and the German Alliance, 1914–1918* (Boulder, Colo., 1985), 27.

69. Tunstall, 'Austria-Hungary', in Hamilton and Herwig (eds), *Origins of World War I*, 132.

70. Fritz Fellner, 'Austria-Hungary', in Wilson, *Decisions for War*, 12–14. 'Flucht nach Vorne' translates more directly as a 'flight to the front'—but this does

not convey the sense of confronting danger in order to head it off. I am grateful to Stuart Robson for suggesting an English idiom.

71. Berchtold to Tisza, 8 July, *O-UA*, VIII, nr 10145.

72. The lengths to which Berchtold went undercuts the (preposterous) argument of Hugo Hantsch that he had sent Hoyos to Berlin in the hope that the Germans would not give any promises of support for vigorous action against Serbia: *Leopold Graf Berchtold: Grandseigneur und Staatsmann*, 2 vols (Graz, 1963). But the biography is nevertheless useful for its usage of primary Berchtold materials.

73. Tisza to Franz Joseph, 8 July, *O-UA*, VIII, nr 10146.

74. Riezler diary, 8 July, in Karl Dietrich Erdmann (ed.), *Kurt Riezler: Tagebücher, Aufsätze, Dokumente* (Göttingen, 1972), 184; the diary was reprinted in 2009 with a new introduction by Holger Afflerbach.

75. Tisza to Berchtold, 9 July, quoted in József Galántai, *Hungary in the First World War* (Budapest, 1989), 37.

76. Berchtold, diary for 9 July; quoted in Hantsch, *Berchtold*, ii. 570.

77. Bollati to San Giuliano, 9 July, *DDI*, XII, no. 123; quoted in Richard Bosworth, *Least of the Great Powers* (Cambridge, 1979), 382.

78. Grey to Rumbold, 9 July, *BD*, XI, no. 41.

79. Lichnowsky to Bethmann Hollweg, 9 July, *DDK*, I, nr 30.

80. Lichnowsky to Bethmann Hollweg, 9 July, *DDK*, I, nr 30.

81. Grey to Buchanan, 8 July, *BD*, XI, no. 39.

82. Tschirschky to Foreign Office, telegram, 10 July, *DDK*, I, nr 29.

83. A *sanjuk* was an administrative district within the Ottoman Empire.

84. Tschirschky to Foreign Office, telegram, 10 July, *DDK*, I, nr 29.

85. Szögyény to Berchtold, 12 July, *O-UA*, VIII, nr 10215.

86. Conrad to Berchtold, *c.*12 July 1914, *O-UA*, VIII, nr 10226.

87. d'Apchier le Maugin to Viviani, 11 July, *DDF*, X, no. 498.

88. de Bunsen to Grey, 11 July, *BD*, XI, no. 46. He was not sufficiently alarmed to send this communication via telegram; it was not received in London until 15 July.

89. Flotow to Foreign Office, telegram, 12 July, *DDK*, I, nr 38.

90. Quoted in Richard F. Hamilton and Holger H. Herwig, 'Italy', in Hamilton and Herwig, *Origins of World War I*, 358.

91. Quoted in Bosworth, *Least of the Great Powers*, 84.

92. Bosworth, *Least of the Great Powers*, 53.

93. Berchtold to Mérey, telegram, 12 July, *O-UA*, VIII, nr 10221.

94. Friedrich Ritter von Wiesner to Berchtold, 13 July, *O-UA*, VIII, nr 10252.

95. Burián to Tisza, and Burián, diary, 12 July, in Galántai, *Hungary in the First World War*, 40.

96. de Bunsen to Grey, 13 July, *BD*, XI, no. 55.

97. A. J. Anthony Morris, *Radicalism Against War, 1906–1914: The Advocacy of Peace and Retrenchment* (London, 1972), 384.

98. Pourtalès to Bethmann Hollweg, 13 July, *DDK*, I, nr 53.
99. Quoted in Harold Nicolson, *Sir Arthur Nicolson, Bart., First Lord Carnock: A Study in the Old Diplomacy* (London, 1930), 405.
100. Tschirschky to Foreign Office, telegram, 13 July, *DDK*, I, nr 40.
101. Berchtold to Franz Joseph, 14 July, *O-UA*, VIII, nr 10272.
102. Tschirschky to Bethmann Hollweg, 14 July, *DDK*, I, nr 49.
103. Tschirschky to Bethmann Hollweg, 14 July, *DDK*, I, nr 50.
104. Riezler, diary, 14 July, in Erdmann, *Kurt Riezler*, 185.
105. Cornwall, 'Serbia', in Wilson, *Decisions for War*, 68.
106. Berchtold to Szögyény, telegram, 15 July, *O-UA*, VIII, nr 10276.
107. Jagow to Tschirschky, 15 July, *DDK*, I, nr 46.
108. Lichnowsky to Foreign Office, telegram, 14 July, *DDK*, I, nr 43.
109. Jagow to Lichnowsky, telegram, 15 July, *DDK*, I, nr 48.
110. Jagow to Ballin, 15 July, *DDK*, I, nr 56.
111. Bethmann Hollweg to Roedern, 16 July, *DDK*, I, nr 58.
112. Lichnowsky to Bethmann Hollweg, 16 July, *DDK*, I, nr 62.
113. Flotow to Bethmann Hollweg, 16 July, *DDK*, I, nr 64.
114. Flotow to Bethmann Hollweg, 16 July, *DDK*, I, nr 73.
115. Mérey to Berchtold, telegram, 18 July, *O-UA*, VIII, nr 10364.
116. Schebeko to Sazonov, 16 July, *Int. Bez.*, Bd. IV, nr 247. The tsar's note was made on the 19th.
117. de Bunsen to Nicolson, Private, 17 July, *BD*, XI, no. 56.
118. A summary of the conversation was sent by telegram the previous day—without Lützow being referred to by name; de Bunsen to Grey, telegram, 16 July, *BD*, XI, no. 50.
119. Bošković to Pašić, 16 July, *DSP*, no. 449; quoted in Cornwall, 'Serbia', in Wilson, *Decisions for War*, 69 n. 86.
120. 18 July, *DSP*, no. 462; quoted in Cornwall, 'Serbia', in Wilson, *Decisions for War*, 70 n. 91.
121. Tunstall, 'Austria-Hungary', in Hamilton and Herwig (eds), *Origins of World War I*, 140; Lawrence Sondhaus, *The Naval Policy of Austria-Hungary, 1867–1918: Navalism, Industrial Development, and the Politics of Dualism* (West Lafayette, Ind., 1994), 245.
122. Jagow to Tschirschky, telegram, 18 July, *DDK*, I, nr 70.
123. Jagow to Lichnowsky, private letter, 18 July, *DDK*, I, nr 72.
124. Jagow to Lichnowsky, private letter, 18 July, *DDK*, I, nr 72.
125. Quoted in Volker Berghahn and Wilhelm Deist, 'Kaiserliche Marine und Kriegsausbruch 1914', *Militärgeschichtliche Mitteilungen* (1970), 55.
126. Stolberg to Jagow, private letter, 18 July, *DDK*, I, nr 87.
127. Jagow to Tschirschky, telegram, 19 July, *DDK*, I, nr 77.
128. Quoted in Cecil, *Wilhelm II*, ii. 202.
129. Flotow to Foreign Office, telegram, 19 July, *DDK*, I, nr 78.
130. de Bunsen to Grey, 19 July, *BD*, XI, no. 156.

131. Lichnowsky to Foreign Office, telegram, 20 July, *DDK*, I, nr 92.
132. Grey to Buchanan, telegram, 20 July, *BD*, XI, no. 67.
133. Grey to Rumbold, 20 July, *BD*, XI, no. 68.
134. Jagow to Tschirschky, 20 July 20, *DDK*, I, nr 83.
135. Report by Berchtold on meeting with Tschirschky, 20 July, *O-UA*, VIII, nr 10398.
136. Tschirschky to Bethmann Hollweg, 20 July, *DDK*, I, nr 94.
137. Szögyény to Berchtold, telegram, 21 July, *O-UA*, VIII, 10445.
138. Szögyény to Berchtold, private letter, 21 July, *O-UA*, VIII, 10448.
139. Jagow to Bethmann Hollweg, 21 July, *DDK*, I, nr 106.
140. Maurice Paléologue, *An Ambassador's Memoirs*, 4th edn (New York, 1925), i. 17.
141. Szápáry to Berchtold, telegram, 21 July, *O-UA*, VIII, 10461.
142. This is clear from Poincaré's diary; see Gerd Krumeich, *Armaments and Politics in France on the Eve of the First World War: The Introduction of Three-Year Conscription 1913–1914*, tr. Stephen Conn (Leamington Spa,1984), 218.
143. Spalajković to Pašić, 22 July, *DSP*, quoted in Cornwall, 'Serbia', in Wilson, *Decisions for War*, 72 n. 107.
144. Quoted in Krumeich, *Armaments and Politics*, 219. Stefan Schmidt has argued that Poincaré was pushing Russia to take a hard line against Austria, and that he promised French military support for such a line. The evidence for this is not convincing; *Frankreichs Außenpolitik in der Julikrise 1914* (Munich, 2007), esp. 354–6.
145. Pourtalès to Bethmann Hollweg, 21 July, *DDK*, I, nr. 120.
146. Report on visit of the French Ambassador to the Foreign Office, 22 July, *O-UA*, VIII, nr 10491.
147. See M. B. Hayne, *The French Foreign Office and the Origins of the First World War 1898–1914* (Oxford, 1993), 73–4.
148. Grey to Bertie, 21 July, *BD*, XI, no. 72.
149. Grey to Buchanan, 22 July, *BD*, XI, no. 79.
150. Jules Cambon to Bienvenu–Martin, telegram, 21 July, *DDF*, X, no. 539.
151. Barrère to Bienvenu–Martin, telegram, 21 July, *DDF*, X, no. 546.
152. Rodd to Grey, telegram, 22 July, *BD*, XI, no. 78.
153. Berchtold to Giesl, 20 July, *O-UA*, VIII, nr 10395.
154. Jagow to Tschirschky, telegram, 22 July, *DDK*, I, nr 112.
155. Berchtold to Giesl, telegram, 23 July, *O-UA*, VIII, 10518.
156. Quoted in Chickering, *We Men Who Feel Most German*, 287.
157. Bethmann Hollweg to Wilhelm II, telegram, 20 July, *DDK*, I, nr 84.
158. Wilhelm II to Crown Prince, telegram, 21 July, *DDK*, I, nr 105.
159. Bethmann Hollweg to Foreign Office, telegram, 21 July, *DDK*, I, nr 101.
160. Behnke to Foreign Office, 22 July, *DDK*, I, nr 111.
161. Bethmann Hollweg to Wedel, telegram, 23 July, *DDK*, I, nr 125.
162. Jagow to Wilhelm II, telegram, 23 July, *DDK*, I, nr 121 (filed at Foreign Office at 1.30 p.m.—received by Imperial office at 8.30 p.m.).

163. Riezler, diary, 23 July, in Erdmann, *Kurt Riezler*, 189–90.
164. Quoted in Holger Afflerbach, *Kaiser Wilhelm II* (Munich, 2005), 127.
165. From Paléologue's unpublished diary; quoted in Krumeich, *Armaments and Politics*, 291.
166. Giesl to Berchtold, telegram, 23 July, *O-UA*, VIII, nr 10526.
167. Cornwall, 'Serbia', in Wilson, *Decisions for War*, 73.

DAY ONE: FRIDAY 24 JULY

1. Reprinted in Gordon Martel, *The Origins of the First World War*, 3rd edn, rev. (Harlow 2008), 116–17.
2. Szápáry to Berchtold, telegram, 3.35 p.m., 24 July, *O-UA*, VIII, nr. 10616.
3. Szápáry to Berchtold, telegram, 8.25 p.m., 24 July, *O-UA*, VIII, nr. 10617.
4. Szápáry to Berchtold, telegram, 8.00 p.m., 24 July, *O-UA*, VIII, nr. 10619.
5. Buchanan to Grey, telegram, 5.40 p.m., 24 July, *BD*, XI, no. 101.
6. Paléologue to Bienvenu-Martin, telegram, 9.12 p.m., 24 July, *DDF*, XI, no. 21.
7. Hayne, *French Foreign Office*, 117–18.
8. Buchanan to Grey, telegram, 5.40 p.m., 24 July, *BD*, XI, no. 101.
9. Buchanan to Grey, telegram, 5.40 p.m., 24 July, *BD*, XI, no. 101.
10. The source for this summary is the unpublished memoir of the minister of finance, Peter Bark; summarized in D. C. B. Lieven, *Russia and the Origins of the First World War* (London, 1983), 141–4.
11. Quoted in David MacLaren McDonald, *United Government and Foreign Policy in Russia 1900–1914* (Cambridge, Mass., 1992), 302.
12. Quoted in D. W. Spring, 'Russia and the Coming of War', in R. J. W. Evans and Hartmut Pogge von Strandmann (eds), *The Coming of the First World War* (Oxford, 1988), 60.
13. The council had stipulated 'Black Sea fleet' but the tsar, in his own hand, inserted 'Baltic' and changed 'fleet' to 'fleets'.
14. An English translation of the council's decisions may be found in R. C. Binkley, 'New Light on Russia's War Guilt', *Current History* XXIII (January 1926), 533.
15. Pourtalès to Foreign Office, telegram, 1.08 a.m., 25 July, *DDK*, I, nr 160; Szápáry to Berchtold, telegram, 2.30 a.m., 25 July, *O-UA*, VIII, nr. 10620.
16. Pourtalès to Foreign Office, telegram, 1.08 a.m., 25 July, *DDK*, I, nr 160.
17. Quoted in Albertini, *Origins*, ii. 301.
18. Riezler, diary, 27 July, in Erdmann, *Kurt Riezler*, 191–2.
19. Bienvenu-Martin to Viviani [and to Belgrade, London, St Petersburg, Berlin, Vienna, Rome], telegram, 9.30 p.m., 24 July, *DDF*, XI, no. 22.
20. Quoted in Katherine Lerman, 'The Kaiser's Elite? Wilhelm II and the Berlin Administration, 1890–1914', in Annika Mombauer and Wilhelm Deist (eds),

The Kaiser: New Research on Wilhelm II's Role in Imperial Germany (Cambridge, 2003), 75.

21. Jules Cambon to Bienvenu-Martin, 24 July, *DDF*, XI, no. 29.
22. Paléologue to Bienvenu-Martin, telegram, 9.12 p.m., 24 July, *DDF*, XI, no. 21.
23. Paul Cambon to Bienvenu-Martin, telegram, 5.53 p.m., 24 July, *DDF*, XI, no. 23.
24. Grey to de Bunsen, telegram, 1.30 p.m., 24 July, *BD*, XI, no. 91.
25. Grey to Bertie, 24 July, *BD*, XI, no. 98.
26. *H. H. Asquith: Letters to Venetia Stanley*, ed. Michael and Eleanor Brock (Oxford, 1982), 123.
27. Grey to Rumbold, telegram, 7.45 p.m., 24 July, *BD*, XI, no. 99.
28. Lichnowsky to Foreign Office, telegram, 9.12 p.m., *DDK*, I, nr 157.
29. Grey to Crackanthorpe, telegram, 9.30 p.m., 24 July, *BD*, XI, no. 102.
30. Crown Prince Aleksandar to Tsar Nicholas II, telegram, 24 July, *SBB*, no. 37; Strandtmann to Sazonov, telegram, 24 July, *Int. Bez.*, V, nr 37.
31. Spalajković's report came in three separate telegrams, arriving at 4, 10, and 11 a.m. on the 25th; see Cornwall, 'Serbia', in Wilson, *Decisions for War*, 79–81.
32. Mérey to Berchtold, telegram, 4.30 p.m., 24 July, *O-UA*, VIII, nr 10611.
33. Szécsen to Berchtold, telegram, 4.55 p.m., 24 July, *O-UA*, VIII, nr 10606.
34. Mensdorff to Berchtold, telegram, 8.48 p.m., 24 July, *O-UA*, VIII, 10601.
35. Szécsen to Berchtold, telegram, 8.45 p.m., 24 July, *O-UA*, VIII, nr. 10607.
36. Szécsen to Berchtold, telegram, 7.40 p.m., 24 July, *O-UA*, VIII, nr 10608.
37. Tschirschky to Bethmann Hollweg, 24 July, *DDK*, I, nr 138.
38. Jagow to Tschirschky, telegram, 2.05 p.m., 24 July, *DDK*, I, nr 142.
39. Flotow to Foreign Office, telegram, 7.30 a.m., 24 July, *DDK*, I, nr 136.
40. Jagow to Flotow, telegram, 6.45 p.m., 24 July, *DDK*, I, nr 145.
41. Jagow to Tschirschky, telegram, 9.15 p.m., 24 July, *DDK*, I, nr 150.
42. San Giuliano to Bollati and Avarna, 24 July, *DDI*, XI, no. 488. Quoted in Bosworth, *Least of the Great Powers*, 388.
43. Flotow to Foreign Office, telegram, 8.10 p.m., 24 July, *DDK*, I, nr 156.
44. Jagow to Wangenheim, telegram, 6.40 p.m., 24 July, *DDK*, I, nr 144.
45. Kudashev to Sazonov, 24 July, *Int. Bez.*, V, nr 32.
46. Lichnowsky to Foreign Office, telegram, 6.16 p.m., 24 July, *DDK*, I, nr 152.

DAY TWO: SATURDAY, 25 JULY

1. Szögyény to Berchtold, telegram, 8.45 p.m., 25 July, *O-UA*, VIII, nr. 10659.
2. Grey to Buchanan, telegram, 25 July, *BD*, XI, no. 112.
3. Bienvenu-Martin to Viviani, telegram, 5.00 p.m., 25 July, *DDF*, XI, no. 47.
4. Szécsen to Berchtold, telegram, 5.20 p.m., 25 July, *O-UA*, VIII, nr 10679.
5. Paléologue to Bienvenu-Martin, telegram, 6.22 p.m., 25 July, *DDF*, XI, no. 50.

6. Pourtalès to Foreign Office, telegram, 12.30 a.m., 26 July, *DDK*, I, nr. 194.

7. Spalajković to Paču, telegram, 4.10 a.m., 26 July, *DSP*, 584; quoted in Christopher Clark, *The Sleepwalkers: How Europe Went to War in 1914* (New York, 2012), 468.

8. Quoted in Schmitt, *Coming of the War*, i. 508.

9. Journal of the Russian General Staff Committee, *Int. Bez.*, V, nr 79.

10. Daily journal of the Russian council of ministers, 24 July, *Int. Bez.*, V, nr 19.

11. Sazonov to Kudashev, Bronevsky, Sevastopulo, Benckendorff, Krupenski, and Pokievski, *Int. Bez.*, V, nr 23.

12. Macchio to Berchtold, telegram, 1.45 p.m., 25 July, *O-UA*, VIII, nr 10703. Berchtold to Szápáry, telegram, 9.00 p.m., 25 July, *O-UA*, VIII, nr 10683.

13. Pourtalès to Bethmann Hollweg, 25 July, *DDK*, I, nr 204. This was a more detailed report of his conversation with Sazonov of the previous day; it was received in Berlin in the afternoon of the 26th.

14. Pourtalès to Foreign Office, telegram, 1.08 a.m., 25 July, *DDK*, I, nr 160.

15. Buchanan to Grey, telegram, 8 p.m., 25 July, *BD*, XI, no. 125.

16. Pourtalès to Bethmann Hollweg, 25 July, *DDK*, I, nr 204.

17. Sazonov to Strandtmann, telegram, 24 July, *Int. Bez.*,V, nr 22.

18. Grey to Bertie, 24 July 1914, *BD*, XI, no. 98.

19. Grey to Bertie, telegram, 12.10 a.m., 25 July, *BD*, XI, no. 105.

20. Bronevsky to Jagow, 25 July, *DDK*, I, nr 172.

21. Buchanan to Grey, telegram, 8 p.m., *BD*, XI, no. 125.

22. Sazonov to Benckendorff, 25 July, *Int. Bez.*, V, nr 48.

23. Buchanan to Grey, telegram, 8 p.m., *BD*, XI, no. 125.

24. Grey to Buchanan, telegram, 2.15 p.m., 25 July, *BD*, XI, no. 112.

25. On Benckendorff see Marina Soroka, *Britain, Russia and the Road to the First World War: The Fateful Embassy of Count Aleksandr Benckendorff (1903–16)* (Farnham, 2011).

26. Grey to Buchanan, 25 July, *BD*, XI, no. 132.

27. Grey to Buchanan, 25 July, *BD*, XI, no. 132.

28. Buchanan to Grey, telegram, 5.40 p.m., 24 July, *BD*, XI, no. 101.

29. Bertie to Grey, telegram, 8.30 p.m., 25 July, *BD*, XI, no. 129.

30. Bertie to Grey, private, 25 July, *BD*, XI, no. 134.

31. Grey to Rumbold, telegram, 3 p.m., *BD*, XI, no. 116.

32. Lichnowsky to Jagow, telegram, 2 p.m., 25 July, *DDK*, I, nr. 179.

33. Lichnowsky to Foreign Office, telegram, 11.10 a.m., 25 July, *DDK*, I, nr 165.

34. Tschirschky reported to Berlin Kudashev's request that the deadline be extended, and Macchio's negative response; to Foreign Office, telegram, 2.10 p.m., 25 July, *DDK*, I, nr 178.

35. Szögyény to Berchtold, telegram, 2.15 p.m., 25 July, *O-UA*, VIII, nr 10656.

36. Szögyény to Berchtold, telegram, 8.45 p.m., 25 July, *O-UA*, VIII, nr 10658.

37. Schoen to Foreign Office, telegram, 1.30 p.m., 25 July, *DDK*, I, nr. 169.

38. Szécsen to Berchtold, telegram, 5.20 p.m., 25 July, *O-UA*, VIII, nr. 10679.

39. Lichnowsky to Foreign Office, telegram, 2.02 p.m., 25 July, *DDK*, I, nr 180.
40. Lichnowsky to Foreign Office, telegram, 2.02 p.m., 25 July, *DDK*, I, nr 180.
41. Jagow to Lichnowsky, telegram, 11.05 p.m., 25 July, *DDK*, I, nr 192.
42. Rumbold to Grey, telegram, 3.16 p.m., 25 July, *BD*, XI, no. 122.
43. Theodore Wolff, *Eve of 1914*, tr. E. W. Dickes (New York, 1936), 450–1.
44. Boppe to Bienvenu-Martin, telegram, 3 p.m., 25 July, *DDF*, XI, no. 63.
45. Giesl to Berchtold, telegram, 8 p.m., 25 July, *O-UA*, VIII, nr 10647.
46. 15/28—'old style' and 'new style' dates. The old style calendar was still in use in Serbia and Russia.
47. French text in *O-UA*, VIII, nr 10648.
48. Grey to Bertie, telegram, 4.30 p.m., *BD*, XI, no. 120.
49. Lichnowsky to Foreign Office, telegram, 6.09 p.m., 25 July, *DDK*, I, nr. 186. The telegram was received in Berlin at 9.25 p.m.; Jagow forwarded to Tschirschky by telegram the text of Grey's letter at 1.05 a.m. on the 26th.
50. Dumaine to Bienvenu-Martin, 5 p.m., 25 July, *DDF*, XI, no. 45.
51. Telephone report, 7.45 p.m., *O-UA*, VIII, nr 10646.
52. Tisza to Franz Joseph, 25 July, *O-UA*, VIII, nr 10708.
53. de Bunsen to Grey, telegram, 11.20 p.m., 25 July, *BD*, XI, no. 135.
54. Quoted in Jeffrey Verhey, *The Spirit of 1914: Militarism, Myth and Mobilization in Germany* (Cambridge, 2000), 30.
55. Quoted in Michael S. Neiberg, *Dance of the Furies: Europe and the Outbreak of World War I* (Cambridge, Mass., 2011), 74.
56. Quoted in Verhey, *Spirit of 1914*, 18.
57. Quoted in James Joll, *The Second International* (London, 1974), 160.
58. Quoted in Martin Gilbert, *Sir Horace Rumbold: Portrait of a Diplomat, 1869–1941* (London, 1973), 111.
59. Quoted in Krumeich, *Armaments and Politics*, 220.
60. Berchtold to Foreign Office, private, telegram, 2 p.m. *O-UA*, VIII, nr 10704.
61. Bethmann Hollweg to Kaiser Wilhelm, telegram, 10.45 p.m., 25 July, *DDK*, I, nr 191.
62. Paléologue to Bienvenu-Martin, telegram, 12.45 a.m., 25 July, *DDF*, XI, no. 34.
63. Baron Schilling, *How the War Began in 1914. Being the Diary of the Russian Foreign Office from the 3rd to the 20th of July* [16 July–2 August], *1914* (London, 1925), 31–2; Albertini, *Origins of the War*, iii. 267.
64. Jules Cambon to Bienvenu-Martin, 25 July, *DDF*, XI, no. 60.
65. Davignon to Belgian ministers at Rome, The Hague, and Luxembourg, 25 July, *BGB*, no. 3.

DAY THREE: SUNDAY, 26 JULY

1. Quoted in Galántai, *Hungary in the First World War*, 57.
2. A *ukase* was an imperial edict issued by the tsar.
3. Quoted in Nicolson, *Arthur Nicolson*, 406.

4. Nicolson to Grey, telegram, undated [26 July], *BD*, XI, no. 139.

5. Nicolson to Grey, 26 July, *BD*, XI, no. 144.

6. Lichnowsky to Bethmann Hollweg, telegram, 11.49 a.m., 26 July, *DDK*, I, nr 201.

7. Prince Heinrich to Kaiser Wilhelm, 28 July, *DDK*, I, nr. 374.

8. Jagow to Lichnowsky, telegram, 11.05 p.m., 25 July, *DDK*, I, nr 192.

9. Lichnowsky to Grey, 26 July, *BD*, XI, no. 145.

10. Benckendorff to Sazonov, 26 July, *Int. Bez.*, V, nr 91.

11. Bethmann Hollweg to Lichnowsky, telegram, 'urgent', 1.35 p.m., 26 July, *DDK*, I, nr 199.

12. Bethmann Hollweg to Wilhelm, telegram, 1 p.m., 26 July, *DDK*, I, nr. 197.

13. Lyncker (chief of the military cabinet) to wife, 25 July, quoted in Albertini, *Origins of the War*, ii. 428.

14. Albertini, *Origins of the War*, ii. 437.

15. Quoted in Cecil, *Wilhelm II*, 203.

16. Lichnowsky to Foreign Office, telegram, 4.25 p.m., 26 July, *DDK*, I, nr 218.

17. Lichnowsky to Foreign Office, telegram, 8.25 p.m., 26 July, *DDK*, I, nr 236.

18. Nicolson to Grey, 26 July, *BD*, XI, no. 146.

19. Benckendorff to Sazonov, telegram, 26 July, *Int. Bez.*, V, nr 91.

20. Bethmann Hollweg to Schoen, telegram, 1.35 p.m., 26 July, *DDK*, I, nr 200.

21. Bethmann Hollweg to Pourtalès, telegram, 1.35 p.m., 26 July, *DDK*, I, nr 198.

22. Pourtalès to Foreign Office, telegram, 3.25 p.m., 26 July, *DDK*, I, nr 216.

23. Pourtalès to Foreign Office, telegram, 3.15 p.m. (received at Foreign Office 7.01 p.m.), 26 July, *DDK*, I, nr 217.

24. Bethmann Hollweg to Pourtalès, telegram, urgent, 7.15 p.m., 26 July, *DDK*, I, nr 219.

25. Sazonov to Schebeko, telegram, 26 July, *Int. Bez.*, V, nr 86.

26. Pourtalès to Foreign Office, telegram, 10.10 p.m., 26 July, *DDK*, I, nr 238.

27. Szápáry to Berchtold, telegram, 2.15 p.m. [26 July], *O-UA*, VIII, nr 10835. This telegram has clearly been misdated by the editors of *O-UA*, who assigned it to the 27th—but the internal evidence, Szápáry's other communications of those two days, and the reports of Pourtalès and Sazonov make it clear that the conversation it reported occurred on the afternoon of the 26th.

28. Pourtalès summarized his conversation to Szápáry, who then reported it to Berchtold, telegram, private, 4.30 a.m., 27 July, *O-UA*, VIII, nr 61. Pourtalès did not refer to Sazonov's promise in his own report to Berlin on his conversation with Sazonov; see Pourtalès to Foreign Office, telegram, 3.15 p.m., 26 July, *DDK*, I, nr 217.

29. Szápáry to Berchtold, telegram, private, 4.30 a.m., 27 July, *O-UA*, VIII, nr 10758. The reports of the military attaché to Berlin are not to be found in *DDK* because of the administrative/political structure of the *Kaiserreich*. In Bismarck's time attachés reported to the chancellor, through the German

minister in the country of their posting. But in 1890 the kaiser instituted a new regime by which attachés were responsible to him directly—and upon receiving their messages and reports, he would determine who else might receive them. Thus, it was entirely possible for even the chancellor—let alone the secretary of state—not to know what a military or naval attaché was telling the kaiser. See Cecil, *German Diplomatic Service*, 124–38.

30. Tschirschky to Foreign Office, telegram, 6.10 p.m., 26 July, *DDK*, I, nr. 222.
31. de Bunsen to Grey, telegram, 7 p.m., 26 July, *BD*, XI, no. 150.
32. The military plenipotentiary was a position entirely separate from that of the military attaché. As the kaiser's personal envoy to the court, the military plenipotentiary reported directly to him, and was not required to show the ambassador what he was reporting.
33. Pourtalès to Foreign Office, telegram, 25 July—sent at 12.30 a.m. 26 July; received at Foreign Office 3.28 a.m., received at Kaiser's Court Office, 4 a.m., 27 July; *DDK*, I, nr. 194.
34. General Chelius to Kaiser Wilhelm, 26 July, *DDK*, I, nr. 291.
35. Pourtalès to Foreign Office, telegram, 8.50 p.m., 26 July, *DDK*, I, nr. 229.
36. Pourtalès to Foreign Office, telegram, 1.08 a.m., 26 July—received at Foreign Office at 3.45 a.m.; sent to kaiser at 1.15 p.m.; received at kaiser's Court Office at 5.30 p.m.; kaiser's reply received at Foreign Office, 27 July.
37. Rumbold to Grey, telegram, 2.20 p.m., 26 July, *BD*, XI, no. 147.
38. On Moltke, see especially Mombauer, *Helmuth von Moltke*, but also Isabel V. Hull, *The Entourage of Kaiser Wilhelm II, 1888–1918* (Cambridge, 1982).
39. There has been some controversy over the existence of the Schlieffen Plan, owing to the work of Terence Zuber, who has argued that the plan was a 'myth' invented after Germany's defeat in 1918. See his *Inventing the Schlieffen Plan: German War Planning, 1871–1914* (Oxford, 2002) and *German War Planning, 1891–1914: Sources and Interpretations* (Woodbridge, 2004). The argument has not convinced many experts in the field: see the excellent summary of the debate by Annika Mombauer, 'Of War Plans and War Guilt: The Debate Surrounding the Schlieffen Plan', *Journal of Strategic Studies* 28 (2005), 857–85.
40. Quoted in Mombauer, *Helmuth von Moltke*, 91.
41. Quoted in Bosworth, *Least of the Great Powers*, 216–17.
42. Bethmann Hollweg to Tschirschky, telegram, 3 p.m., 26 July, *DDK*, I, nr 202.
43. Flotow to Foreign Office, telegram, 12.10 p.m., 25 July, *DDK*, I, nr 167.
44. Richard Bosworth, *Italy and the Approach of the First World War* (London, 1983), 38.
45. Flotow to Foreign Office, telegram, 3.40 p.m., 26 July, *DDK*, I, nr 211.
46. San Giuliano to Salandra, telegram, 8 p.m., 26 July, *DDI*, XII, 560 (Mombauer, *Diplomatic and Military Documents*, 367).
47. Flotow to Foreign Office, telegram, 4.50 p.m., 26 July, *DDK*, I, nr. 225.

48. Tschirschky to Foreign Office, telegram, 4.50 p.m., 26 July, *DDK*, I, nr. 212.
49. Conrad, *Aus meiner Dienstzeit*, iv. 131.
50. Tschirschky to Jagow, private letter, confidential, 26 July, *DDK*, I, nr. 326. This letter, written in Tschirschky's own hand, while useful in explaining his activities, had no immediate effect on Jagow because it was not sent for two days. Tschirschky added several paragraphs on 28 July before posting it.
51. Rodd to Grey, telegram, 3.45 p.m., 26 July, *BD*, XI, no. 148.
52. Sazonov to Krupensky, telegram, 26 July, *Int. Bez.*, V, nr. 84.
53. Mérey to Berchtold, telegram, confidential, 2 a.m., 27 July, *O-UA*, VIII, nr. 10750.
54. Conrad, *Aus meiner Dienstzeit*, iv. 131.

DAY FOUR: MONDAY, 27 JULY

1. Winston Churchill, *The World Crisis* (London, 1923), i. 206.
2. Quoted in Holger Herwig, 'Germany', in Hamilton and Herwig, *Origins of World War I*, 179.
3. Szécsen to Berchtold, telegram, 8.05 p.m., 27 July, *O-UA*, VIII, nr 10822.
4. Quoted in Albertini, *Origins of the War*, ii. 438.
5. Pourtalès to Foreign Office, telegram, 8.40 p.m., 27 July, *DDK*, I, nr. 282. The editors of *DDK* mistakenly identified this telegram as being despatched on the 28th.
6. Pourtalès to Bethmann Hollweg, 27 July, *DDK*, I, nr 339.
7. Szápáry to Berchtold, telegram, private, 2.15 p.m., 27 July, *O-UA*, VIII, nr 10853.
8. Szápáry to Berchtold, telegram, private, 2.15 p.m., 27 July, *O-UA*, VIII, nr 10853.
9. Nicolson to Grey, 27 July, *BD*, XI, no. 171.
10. Lichnowsky to Foreign Office, telegram, 1.31 p.m., 27 July, *DDK*, I, nr 258.
11. Grey to Goschen, telegram, 8 p.m., 27 July, *BD*, XI, no. 176.
12. Lichnowsky to Foreign Office, telegram, 1.31 p.m., 27 July, *DDK*, I, nr 258.
13. Bienvenu-Martin to Viviani [on board *La France*], telegram, 11.30 a.m., 24 July, *DDF*, XI, no. 4.
14. Bienvenu-Martin to Poincaré and ambassadors, telegram, 6.40 p.m., 24 July, *DDF*, XI, no. 20.
15. Bienvenu-Martin to Jules Cambon, telegram, 12 p.m., 27 July, *DDF*, XI, no. 121.
16. Bienvenu-Martin to ambassadors, telegram, 8.20 p.m., 27 July, *DDF*, XI, no. 147.
17. Quoted in Godsey, *Aristocratic Redoubt*, 192.
18. Szécsen to Berchtold, telegram, 8.05 p.m., 27 July, *O-UA*, VIII, nr 10822.

19. Cambon to Bienvenu-Martin, telegram, 12.55 p.m., 27 July, *DDF*, XI, no. 134.

20. Cambon to Bienvenu-Martin, 27 July, *DDF*, XI, no. 167. This longer explanation of his meeting with Jagow, which was sent in a despatch supplementary to the telegram, was received in Paris on the 28th.

21. Cambon to Bienvenu-Martin, 27 July, *DDF*, XI, no. 167.

22. Goschen to Grey, telegram, 6.17 p.m., 27 July, *BD*, XI, no. 185.

23. Quoted in Albertini, *Origins of the War*, ii. 437.

24. Szögyény to Berchtold, telegram, strictly private, 5.50 p.m., 27 July, *O-UA*, VIII, nr 10792.

25. Bethmann Hollweg to Kaiser Wilhelm, telegram, 11.20 a.m., 27 July, *DDK*, I, nr 245. The telegram was received at the kaiser's court office at 1.20 p.m.

26. Szögyény to Berchtold, telegram, private, 5.50 p.m., 27 July, *O-UA*, VIII, nr 10790.

27. Berchtold to Emperor Franz Joseph, 27 July, *O-UA*, VIII, nr 10855.

28. Tschirschky to Foreign Office, telegram, 3.20 p.m., 27 July, *DDK*, I, nr 257.

29. Circular decree, telegram, 6 p.m., 27 July, *O-UA*, VIII, nr 10781.

30. Sazonov to ambassadors in Paris, London, Berlin, Vienna, Rome, and Constantinople, 27 July, *Int. Bez.*, V, nr 119.

31. Lichnowsky to Foreign Office, telegram, 1.31 p.m., 27 July, *DDK*, I, nr 258.

32. Mensdorff to Berchtold, telegram, 2.12 p.m., 27 July, *O-UA*, VIII, nr 10812.

33. Hansard, House of Commons debate, 27 July, vol. 65, col. 938.

34. Note in Burns papers, 27 July, quoted in Morris, *Radicalism against War*, 387.

35. Quoted in Bernard Wasserstein, *Herbert Samuel, A Political Life* (Oxford, 1992), 160.

36. Diary entry for 27 July, in Trevor Wilson (ed.), *The Political Diaries of C. P. Scott, 1911–1928* (London, 1970), 91–2.

37. Godsey, *Aristocratic Redoubt*, 24, 35, 191.

38. Grey to de Bunsen, 27 July, *BD*, XI, no. 188.

39. Mensdorff to Berchtold, telegram, 8.05 p.m., 27 July, *O-UA*, VIII, nr 10813.

40. Mensdorff to Berchtold, telegram, 8.05 p.m., 27 July, *O-UA*, VIII, nr 10813.

41. Paléologue, *Ambassador's Memoirs*, 35.

42. Lichnowsky to Foreign Office, telegram, 5.08 p.m., 27 July, *DDK*, I, nr 265.

43. Bethmann Hollweg to Lichnowsky, telegram, 1.30 p.m., *DDK*, I, nr 248.

44. Lichnowsky to Foreign Office, telegram, 6.17 p.m., 27 July, *DDK*, I, nr 266.

45. Bethmann Hollweg to Tschirschky, telegram, 11.50 p.m., 27 July, *DDK*, I, nr 277.

46. Bethmann Hollweg to Lichnowsky, telegram, 11.50 p.m., 27 July, *DDK*, I, nr 278.

47. Bethmann Hollweg to Lichnowsky, telegram, 2 a.m., 28 July, *DDK*, II, nr 279.

48. Szögyény to Berchtold, telegram, 9.15 p.m., 27 July, *O-UA*, VIII, nr 10793.

49. Bethmann Hollweg to Kaiser Wilhelm, 5 a.m. [sent by messenger], 28 July, *DDK*, I, nr 283.
50. Quoted in Albertini, *Origins of the War*, ii. 438.
51. Jagow to Tschirschky, telegram, 9 p.m., 27 July, *DDK*, I, nr 267.
52. Buchanan to Grey, telegram, 2.13 p.m. [received 3.45 p.m.], 27 July, *BD*, XI, no. 179.
53. Nicholas II to Sazonov, private, 27 July; quoted in Schmitt, *Coming of the War*, ii. 30.
54. Buchanan to Grey, telegram, 10 a.m., 27 July, *BD*, XI, no. 170.
55. Bertie to Grey, private, 27 July, *BD*, XI, no. 192.
56. See Steiner and Neilson, *Britain and the Origins*, 46–7.
57. Minute by Crowe on Buchanan to Grey, telegram, received at 1.15 p.m., 27 July, *BD*, XI, no. 170.
58. Minute by Crowe on Buchanan to Grey, telegram, received at 1.15 p.m., 27 July, *BD*, XI, no. 170.
59. de Bunsen to Grey, telegram, 1 p.m., 27 July, *BD*, XI, no. 175.
60. Strandtmann to Sazonov, telegram, 27 July, *Int. Bez.*, V, nr 149.
61. Nicholas II to Aleksandar, 27 July, *Int. Bez.*, V, nr 120.
62. Poincaré, diary, 27 July; quoted in Clark, *Sleepwalkers*, 502.
63. Quoted in Paul B. Miller, *From Revolutionaries to Citizens: Antimilitarism in France, 1870–1914* (Durham, NC, 2001), 207.

DAY FIVE: TUESDAY, 28 JULY

1. Jagow to Tschirschky, telegram, 9.00 p.m., 27 July, *DDK*, I, nr 267.
2. Jagow to Tschirschky, telegram, 9.30 p.m., 27 July, *DDK*, I, nr 269.
3. Bethmann Hollweg to Tschirschky, telegram, 11.50 p.m., 27 July [received in Vienna 5.30 a.m., 28 July], *DDK*, I, nr 277.
4. Tschirschky to Foreign Office, telegram, 9.10 p.m., 27 July, *DDK*, II, nr 328.
5. Tschirschky to Jagow, private letter, 26 July 1914 [the first part of this letter was composed on the 26th, but the second half was written on the 28th], *DDK*, II, nr 326.
6. Jagow to Kaiser Wilhelm, 9.30 p.m., 27 July, *DDK*, I, nr 270. The editor (or translator) of the English version of these documents has erroneously rendered this as 'a.m.'. But the German version clearly lists it as '*nachm.*' (*nachmittag*: afternoon), and it is clear that the German Foreign Office itself did not receive a copy of the Serbian reply until later in the day of the 27th. The special messenger assigned to take the document to the kaiser did not leave Berlin until 11.30 p.m.
7. The emphasis was the kaiser's. Kaiser Wilhelm to Jagow, 10 a.m., 28 July, *DDK*, II, nr 293.
8. Marginal notation by kaiser on the reply of the Serbian government to the Austro-Hungarian ultimatum, *DDK*, I, nr 271.

9. Bethmann Hollweg to Lichnowsky, telegram, 1.30 p.m., 27 July, *DDK*, I, nr 248.

10. Bethmann Hollweg to Tschirschky, telegram, 11.50 p.m., 27 July, *DDK*, I, nr 277.

11. Bethmann Hollweg to Kaiser Wilhelm, 27 July [sent by messenger at 5 a.m., 28 July], *DDK*, II, nr 283.

12. Jules Cambon to Bienvenu-Martin, telegram, 4.25 p.m., 28 July, *DDF*, XI, no. 203; Goschen to Grey, telegram, 2.30 p.m., 28 July, *BD*, XI, no. 215.

13. Although Prussia was clearly in a position to dominate the empire created by the constitution of 1871, considerable powers had been left to the individual states within the empire (education, justice, policing, civil rights) and the federal council, the Bundesrat, could create problems for the government if it chose to do so. Bavaria maintained its own embassies, while Württemberg joined Bavaria in maintaining its own ministry of war.

14. Bethmann Hollweg to Prussian ministers accredited to the Federated German Governments, 28 July, *DDK*, II, nr 307. The explanation appears to have been drafted by Jagow for Bethmann Hollweg's signature.

15. Bethmann Hollweg to Prussian ministers accredited to the Federated German Governments, 28 July, *DDK*, II, nr 307.

16. Pourtalès to Foreign Office, telegram, 8.50 p.m., 26 July, *DDK*, I, nr 229.

17. Bethmann Hollweg to Kaiser Wilhelm, 28 July, *DDK*, II, nr 308. Annotation by kaiser at 10.15 p.m.: 'Agreed'.

18. Bethmann Hollweg to Tschirschky, telegram, 4.10 p.m., 28 July, *DDK*, II, nr 309.

19. Eisendecher to Bethmann Hollweg, 27 July, *DDK*, II, nr 303.

20. Lichnowsky to Foreign Office, telegram, 12.58 p.m., 28 July, *DDK*, II, nr 301.

21. Bethmann Hollweg to Lichnowsky, telegram, 8.40 p.m., 28 July, *DDK*, II, nr. 314.

22. 'Communication by the Servian Minister', 27 July, *BD*, XI, no. 171; minute by Clerk, 28 July.

23. Minute by Crowe, 28 July, *BD*, XI, no. 171.

24. Goschen to Grey, telegram, 2.30 p.m., 28 July, *BD*, XI, no. 215.

25. Goschen to Grey, telegram, 2.30 p.m., 28 July, *BD*, XI, no. 215. Minute by Crowe, 28 July.

26. Grey to Goschen, telegram, 4 p.m., 28 July, *BD*, XI, no. 218.

27. Berchtold to Mensdorff, telegram, 28 July [sent at noon, 29 July], *O-UA*, VIII, nr 10892.

28. de Bunsen to Grey, telegram, 1.10 p.m., 28 July, *BD*, XI, no. 227.

29. de Bunsen to Grey, telegram, 4.10 p.m., 28 July, *BD*, XI, no. 230.

30. Bethmann Hollweg to Tschirschky, telegram, urgent, 10.15 p.m., 28 July, *DDK*, II, nr 323.

31. Berchtold to Szögyény, telegram, strictly private, 11 p.m., 28 July, *O-UA*, VIII, nr 10863.
32. Jagow to Flotow, telegram, 9.30 a.m., 28 July, *DDK*, II, nr 287.
33. Mérey to Berchtold, telegram, 1.30 a.m., 28 July, *O-UA*, VIII, nr 10911. Mérey sent his secretary, Count Ambrózy, to convey his views to the Consulta.
34. Mérey to Berchtold, telegram, 1.30 a.m., private, 28 July, *O-UA*, VIII, nr 10912.
35. Berchtold to Mérey and Szögyény, telegrams, 1 p.m., 28 July, *O-UA*, VIII, nr 10909.
36. Memorandum by Baron von Matscheko, undated, secret, *O-UA*, VIII, nr 9918; Emperor Franz Joseph to Kaiser Wilhelm, 2 July, *O-UA*, VIII, nr 9984.
37. Jagow to Tschirschky and Wangenheim, *DDK*, I, nr 45.
38. Wangenheim to Foreign Office, telegram, 18 July, *DDK*, I, nr 71.
39. Jagow to Wangenheim, telegram, 24 July, *DDK*, I, nr 144.
40. Wangenheim to Foreign Office, telegram, 1.45 p.m., 27 July, *DDK*, I, nr 256.
41. Berchtold to Szápáry, telegram, 11.40 p.m., 28 July, *O-UA*, VIII, nr 10915.
42. Sazonov to Benckendorff, telegram, 28 July, *Int. Bez.*, V, nr 164.
43. Sazonov to Benckendorff, telegram, 28 July, *Int. Bez.*, V, nr 167.
44. Nicolson to Buchanan, private, 28 July, *BD*, XI, no. 239.
45. Berchtold to Szögyény, Mensdorff, and Mérey, telegram, 11 p.m., 28 July, *O-UA*, VIII, nr 10867.
46. Tschirschky to Foreign Office, telegram, 10.45 p.m., *DDK*, II, nr 329.
47. Heinrich to Kaiser Wilhelm, 28 July, *DDK*, II, nr 374.
48. Quoted in Morris, *Radicalism against War*, 412.
49. The Bureau had been established in 1890 in order to coordinate the activities of national socialist parties and trade unions.
50. Quoted in Harvey Goldberg, *The Life of Jean Jaurès* (Madison, Wis., 1962), 464−5 n. 11.
51. Quoted in Miller, *Revolutionaries to Citizens*, 207.
52. Verhey, *Spirit of 1914*, 54.
53. Sazonov to Bronevski, telegram, 28 July, *Int. Bez.*, V, nr 168.

DAY SIX: WEDNESDAY, 29 JULY

1. Cambon to Bienvenu-Martin, telegram, 4.25 p.m., 28 July, *DDF*, XI, no. 203.
2. Pourtalès to Foreign Office, telegram, 26 July, *DDK*, I, nr 229.
3. Kaiser Wilhelm to Tsar Nicholas, telegram, 1.45 a.m., 29 July [dated 28 July], *DDK*, II, nr 335.
4. Tsar Nicholas to Kaiser Wilhelm, telegram, 29 July [received at Neue Palais at 1.10 a.m.], *DDK*, II, nr 332.

5. Chelius to Foreign Office ['for His Majesty'], telegram [received at Foreign Office 3.42 a.m.], 29 July, *DDK*, II, nr 337.

6. Great General Staff to Chancellor, 29 July, *DDK*, II, nr 349.

7. Bethmann Hollweg to Schoen, telegram, urgent, 12.50 p.m., 29 July, *DDK*, II, nr 341.

8. Bethmann Hollweg to Pourtalès, telegram, 12.50 p.m., 29 July, *DDK*, II, nr 342.

9. Bethmann Hollweg to Jagow, 29 July, *DDK*, II, nr 340.

10. Burns, diary, 29 July, quoted in Keith M. Wilson, *The Policy of the Entente: Essays on the Determinants of British Foreign Policy, 1904–1919* (Cambridge, 1985), 136.

11. Samuel, quoted in Wasserstein, *Herbert Samuel*, 160.

12. Asquith to George V, 30 July, MS Asquith 7, Bodleian Library, Oxford. I am grateful to Keith Nielson for this reference.

13. Lichnowsky to Foreign Office, telegram, 2.08 p.m., 29 July, *DDK*, II, nr 357.

14. Grey to Goschen, 29 July, *BD*, XI, no. 286. Grey chose to record this conversation not in a telegram, but in a despatch—and war broke out before it was sent to Berlin.

15. Grey to Bertie, 29 July, *BD*, XI, no. 283.

16. Cambon to Viviani, telegram, very confidential, 7.20 p.m., *DDF*, XI, no. 281.

17. Buchanan to Grey, telegram, 8.40 p.m., 29 July, *BD*, XI, no. 276.

18. Szápáry to Berchtold, telegram, 10 a.m., 29 July, *O-UA*, VIII, nr 10999.

19. Szápáry to Berchtold, telegram, secret, 11 p.m., 29 July, *O-UA*, VIII, nr 11003.

20. Pourtalès to Sazonov, telegram, 1.58 p.m., 29 July, *DDK*, II, nr 343.

21. Chelius to Foreign Office [for His Majesty], 2.30 p.m., 29 July, *DDK*, II, nr 344.

22. Pourtalès to Foreign Office, telegram, 6.10 p.m., 29 July, *DDK*, II, nr. 365.

23. Bethmann Hollweg to Pourtalès, telegram, 12.50 p.m., *DDK*, II, nr 342.

24. John C. G. Röhl, 'The Curious Case of the Kaiser's Disappearing War Guilt: Wilhelm II in July 1914', in Holger Afflerbach and David Stevenson (eds), *An Improbable War? The Outbreak of World War I and European Political Culture before 1914* (New York, 2007), 84.

25. Arden Bucholz, *Moltke, Schlieffen, and Prussian War Planning* (New York, 1991), 311.

26. Wenninger [Bavarian military representative in Berlin] to Kress [Bavarian minister of war], 29 July; in Imanuel Geiss, *Julikrise und Kriegsausbruch 1914: eine Dokumentensammlung* (Hanover, 1963), Bd. II, p. 298.

27. Leuckart [Saxon military representative in Berlin] to Carlowitz [Saxon minister of war], 29 July; in Geiss, *Julikrise*, Bd. II, p. 299.

28. Falkenhayn diary for 29 July; quoted in Mombauer, *Diplomatic and Military Documents*, 426.

29. Pourtalès to Foreign Office, telegram, 8 p.m., 29 July, *DDK*, II, nr 378.
30. Bethmann Hollweg to Pourtalès, telegram, urgent, 11.05 p.m., *DDK*, II, nr 139.
31. Bethmann Hollweg to Tschirschky, telegram, 8 p.m., 29 July, *DDK*, II, nr 361.
32. Bethmann Hollweg to Tschirschky, telegram, 12.30 a.m., 30 July, *DDK*, II, nr. 384.
33. Bethmann Hollweg to Tschirschky, telegram, 12.30 a.m., 30 July, *DDK*, II, nr 385.
34. Kaiser Wilhelm to Tsar Nicholas, telegram, 29 July, *DDK*, II, nr 359. The original draft was produced in German by Jagow; it was then translated into English and sent to the kaiser, who then revised it and signed it at 6.30 p.m.
35. Jules Cambon to Bienvenu-Martin, telegram, 2.15 a.m., 29 July, *DDF*, XI, no. 238.
36. Goschen to Grey, telegram, 11.20 p.m., 29 July, *BD*, XI, no. 281.
37. Bethmann Hollweg to Schoen, telegram, urgent, 12.50 p.m., *DDK*, II, nr 341.
38. Schoen to Foreign Office, telegram, 6.50 p.m., *DDK*, II, nr 367.
39. Lamar Cecil, *Albert Ballin: Business and Politics in Imperial Germany, 1888–1918* (Princeton, 1967), 207.
40. Goschen to Grey, telegram, secret and urgent, 1.20 a.m., 30 July, *BD*, XI, no. 293; note by Bethmann Hollweg, 29 July, *DDK*, II, nr 373.
41. Jagow to Below, sent by imperial messenger, p.m., 29 July, *DDK*, II, nr 376. Jagow's instructions were based on a draft begun on 26 July by the chief of the general staff, then revised by the under-secretary of state and the chancellor.
42. Grey to de Bunsen, 29 July, *BD*, XI, no. 282.
43. Grey to Goschen, telegram, 4.45 p.m., 29 July, *BD*, XI, no. 263.
44. Lichnowsky to Foreign Office, 2.08 p.m., 29 July, *DDK*, II, nr 357.
45. Minute by Nicolson, 29 July, on Rodd to Grey, 29 July, *BD*, XI, no. 252.
46. Lichnowsky to Foreign Office, telegram, 6.39 p.m., 29 July, *DDK*, II, nr 368.
47. de Bunsen to Grey, telegram, 4.30 p.m., 29 July, *BD*, XI, no. 265.
48. Tschirschky to Foreign Office, telegram, 2 p.m., *DDK*, II, nr 356.
49. Berchtold to Szögyény, telegram, 1 a.m., 30 July [dated 29 July], *O-UA*, VIII, nr 10937.
50. Daily report on a visit of the German ambassador, 29 July, *O-UA*, VIII, nr 10939.
51. Daily memorandum of ministry of foreign affairs, 29 July, *Int. Bez.*, V, nr 224.
52. Tsar Nicholas to Kaiser Wilhelm, telegram, 8.20 p.m., 29 July, *DDK*, II, nr 366.
53. Schebeko to Sazonov, 29 July, *Int. Bez.*, V, nr 242.
54. Quoted in Albertini, *Origins of the War*, ii. 569.
55. Quoted in Albertini, *Origins of the War*, ii. 558.

56. The details of precisely what happened that evening were discovered in the diary kept by the Marquise de Laguiche, the attaché's wife. See Keiger, *Poincaré*, 173–5.
57. Viviani to ambassadors in St Petersburg and London, 7 a.m., 30 July, *DDF*, XI, no. 305.
58. The lyrics—to be sung to the tune of *La Marseillaise*—were written by Eugène Pottier, a veteran of the Paris Commune, in June 1871. New music was composed by Pierre De Geyter in 1888. Over the years it was translated into all of the European languages
59. Cited in Goldberg, *Life of Jean Jaurès*, 465.
60. Miller, *Revolutionaries to Citizens*, 210.
61. Arthur Ponsonby to Grey, 29 July, quoted by Cameron Hazlehurst, *Politicians at War, July 1914 to May 1915: A Prologue to the Triumph of Lloyd George* (London, 1971), 36.

DAY SEVEN: THURSDAY, 30 JULY

1. Drafts of all three telegrams were sent to the telegraph office at 2.50 a.m., Central European time; it is not clear when those sent to London and St Petersburg arrived, but that to Vienna was received by Tschirschky at noon.
2. Presumably, Bethmann Hollweg was assuming that Japan would join the Entente through its alliance with Britain.
3. Bethmann Hollweg to Tschirschky, telegram, urgent, 2.55 a.m., 30 July, *DDK*, II, nr 395.
4. Bethmann Hollweg to Tschirschky, telegram, 3 a.m. [received in Vienna at 10 a.m.], 30 July, *DDK*, II, nr 396.
5. Tsar Nicholas to Kaiser Wilhelm, telegram, 1.20 a.m., 30 July, *DDK*, II, nr 390.
6. Kaiser's marginal notations on the tsar's telegram, *DDK*, II, nr 390. It is not clear precisely when the kaiser made his comments; the telegram was received at the Neue Palais at 1.45 a.m. on the 30th, and by that afternoon the annotated telegram was received at the Foreign Office in Berlin.
7. Marginal notation by kaiser, 7 a.m., on Bethmann Hollweg to Kaiser Wilhelm, 6 a.m., 30 July, *DDK*, II, nr 399.
8. Marginal annotations, 30 July, *DDK*, II, nr 402.
9. Bethmann Hollweg to Hadik, telegram, absolutely confidential, 11 a.m., 30 July, *DDK*, II, nr 406, 11 a.m.
10. Flotow to Foreign Office, telegram, 11 a.m., 30 July, *DDK*, II, nr 414.
11. Minute by Crowe, 30 July, on Goschen to Grey, telegram, secret and urgent, 29 July (sent at 1.20 a.m., received at Foreign Office, 9 a.m., 30 July), *BD*, XI, no. 293.
12. Tschirschky to Foreign Office, telegram, 30 July (sent 1.35 a.m., 31 July), *DDK*, II, nr 465.

13. Berchtold to Szápáry, telegram, 1.20 p.m., 30 July, *O-UA*, VIII, nr 11092.
14. Berchtold to Szápáry, telegram, 30 July (sent 1.40 a.m., 31 July), *O-UA*, VIII, nr 11093.
15. de Bunsen to Grey, telegram, 3.50 p.m., 30 July, *BD*, XI, no. 307.
16. Szápáry to Berchtold, telegram, 1 a.m. [received in Vienna, 3.15 p.m.], 30 July, *O-UA*, VIII, nr 11094.
17. Brück to Bethmann, 29 July [received on 30th], quoted in Sean McMeekin, *July 1914: Countdown to War* (New York, 2013), 265.
18. Quoted in Albertini, *Origins of the War*, ii. 672. Fleischmann had been seconded to the military intelligence section of the German general staff.
19. Lieutenant-Colonel Bienerth (Austrian military attaché in Berlin) to Conrad, *Aus meiner Dienstzeit*, iv. 152.
20. Protocol of the meeting of the Prussian Ministry of State, 30 July; Geiss, *Julikrise*, Bd. II, p. 374.
21. Falkenhayn, diary, 30 July; quoted in Mombauer, *Helmuth von Moltke*, 205.
22. Quoted in Mombauer, *Helmuth von Moltke*, 206.
23. Szögyény to Berchtold, telegram, 5.30 p.m., 30 July, *O-UA*, VIII, nr 11030.
24. Marginal notations on Lichnowsky to Foreign Office, telegram, 6.39 p.m., 29 July [kaiser's annotations, 1 p.m., 30 July], *DDK*, II, nr 368.
25. Marginal notations on Lichnowsky to Foreign Office, telegram, 6.39 p.m., 29 July [kaiser's annotations, 1 p.m., 30 July], *DDK*, II, nr 368.
26. Bethmann Hollweg to Kaiser Wilhelm, 11.15 a.m., 30 July, *DDK*, II, nr 408.
27. Kaiser Wilhelm to Tsar Nicholas, telegram, 3.30 p.m., 30 July, *DDK*, II, nr 420.
28. Prince Heinrich to King George, 2.15 p.m., 30 July, *DDK*, II, nr 417.
29. Grey to Goschen, telegram, 3.30 p.m., 30 July, *BD*, XI, no. 303.
30. Grey to Goschen, telegram, 3.30 p.m., 30 July, *BD*, XI, no. 303.
31. Sazonov to ambassadors at Berlin, Vienna, Paris, London, and Rome, 30 July, *Int. Bez.*, V, nr 277.
32. Grey to Buchanan, telegram, 7.35 p.m., 30 July, *BD*, XI, no. 309.
33. Paul Cambon to Viviani, telegram, very confidential, 8.19 p.m., 30 July, *DDF*, XI, no. 363; Grey to Bertie, 30 July, *BD*, XI, no. 319.
34. Viviani to ambassadors at St Petersburg and London, telegram, confidential, 7 a.m., 30 July, *DDF*, XI, no. 305.
35. Note by Abel Ferry, under-secretary of state for foreign affairs, 30 July, *DDF*, XI, no. 305, note 2.
36. See S. R. Williamson, 'Joffre Reshapes French Strategy', in Paul M. Kennedy (ed.), *The War Plans of the Great Powers, 1880–1914* (London, 1979), 133–54.
37. Bertie to Grey, telegram, 8.15 p.m., 30 July, *BD*, XI, no. 318.
38. Jules Cambon to Viviani, telegram, urgent, 1.30 a.m., 31 July, *DDF*, XI, no. 380.
39. Jules Cambon to Viviani, telegram, urgent, 1.30 a.m., 31 July, *DDF*, XI, no. 380.

40. Lichnowsky to Foreign Office, telegram, 11.43 a.m., 30 July, *DDK*, II, nr 418.
41. Daily memorandum of ministry of foreign affairs, 30 July, *Int. Bez.*, V, nr 284; an English translation of the memorandum is given by Mombauer in *Diplomatic and Military Documents*, 440.
42. Minutes of the meeting of the Prussian ministers of state, 30 July, *DDK*, II, nr 456.
43. Minutes on Pourtalès to Foreign Office, telegram, urgent, 4.30 a.m. [received at Foreign Office at 7.10 a.m.], 30 July, *DDK*, II, nr 401. The kaiser noted his minutes as having been made at 7 p.m.; the copy with his comments was returned to the Foreign Office on Friday, 1 August.
44. Minutes on Pourtalès to Foreign Office, telegram, urgent, 4.30 a.m. [received at Foreign Office at 7.10 a.m.], 30 July, *DDK*, II, nr 401.
45. Minutes on Pourtalès to Foreign Office, telegram, urgent, 4.30 a.m. [received at Foreign Office at 7.10 a.m.], 30 July, *DDK*, II, nr 401.
46. Mensdorff to Berchtold, telegram, 10 p.m., 30 July, *O-UA*, VIII, nr 11064.
47. Marginal notation on Tschirschky to Foreign Office, telegram, 2.30 p.m. [received 5.25 p.m.], 30 July, *DDK*, II, nr 433.
48. Diary of General Krafft von Dellmensingen, quoted in Mombauer, *Helmuth von Moltke*, 199. He was disappointed that the kaiser was taking this line.

DAY EIGHT: FRIDAY, 31 JULY

1. Cooper, *Patriotic Pacifism*, 187.
2. Laity, *British Peace Movement*, 220.
3. Quoted in Paul Ward, *Red Flag and Union Jack: Englishness, Patriotism and the British Left, 1881–1924* (Woodbridge, 1998), 120.
4. Quoted in Gilbert, *Horace Rumbold*, 114.
5. Bethmann Hollweg to Tschirschky, telegram, urgent, 3 a.m., 31 July [drafted in the chancellor's hand, and submitted to the telegraph office in Berlin at 9 p.m., 30 July], *DDK*, II, nr 441.
6. Lichnowsky to Foreign Office, telegram, 7.49 p.m., 30 July [received at Foreign Office, 10.25 p.m.], *DDK*, II, nr 447.
7. Bethmann Hollweg to Tschirschky, telegram, urgent, 11.20 p.m., *DDK*, II, nr 450; and see details in the draft of telegram (not sent) from Bethmann Hollweg to Tschirschky, 30 July, *DDK*, II, nr 451.
8. It was drafted by Frederic von Rosenberg, head of the *Orient Referat* (the department responsible for the Balkans and the Middle East) at the *Auswärtiges Amt*.
9. Bethmann Hollweg to Kaiser Wilhelm, 30 July, *DDK*, II, nr 466.
10. Kaiser Wilhelm to King Karl, 31 July, *DDK*, II, nr 472.
11. Mérey to Berchtold, telegram, secret, 2.30 a.m., 31 July, *O-UA*, VIII, nr 11090.

12. Flotow to Foreign Office, telegram, 11.45 a.m., 30 July, *DDK*, II, nr 419.
13. Mérey to Berchtold, telegram, strictly secret, 1.30 a.m., 1 August, *O-UA*, VIII, nr 11172.
14. Tschirschky to Foreign Office, telegram, 4.30 p.m., 31 July, *DDK*, III, nr 510.
15. Jagow memorandum, 31 July, *DDK*, III, nr 496.
16. Cabinet council for mutual affairs, 31 July, *O-UA*, VIII, nr 11203.
17. Emperor Franz Joseph to Kaiser Wilhelm, telegram, 1.06 p.m. [received in Berlin, 2.45 p.m.], 31 July, *DDK*, III, nr 482.
18. Kaiser Wilhelm to Tsar Nicholas, 2.40 p.m., 31 July, *DDK*, III, nr 480.
19. *The Times*, 2 August 1914 (report from Berlin on 1 August), 4.
20. Bethmann Hollweg to Tschirschky, telegram, 1.45 p.m., 31 July, *DDK*, II, nr 479.
21. Quoted in Verhey, *Spirit of 1914*, 61.
22. Bethmann Hollweg to Lichnowsky, telegram, 3.10 p.m., 31 July, *DDK*, III, nr 488.
23. Goschen to Grey, telegram, 11.55 a.m., 31 July, *BD*, XI, no. 337.
24. Minutes on Goschen to Grey, telegram, 11.55 a.m., 31 July, *BD*, XI, no. 337.
25. Pease, diary, 31 July, Quoted in Wilson, *Policy of the Entente*, 136.
26. Grey to Buchanan, telegram, 11.40 a.m., 31 July, *BD*, XI, no. 335.
27. Cambon to Viviani, 31 July, *DDF*, XI, no. 459.
28. Grey to Goschen, telegram, 2.45 p.m., 31 July, *BD*, XI, no. 340.
29. Goschen to Grey, telegram, 31 July, [2 a.m., 1 August], *BD*, XI, no. 385.
30. KaiserWilhelm to Imperial Naval Office and Admiralty Staff (copy to chief of the general staff and minister of war), absolutely secret, noon, 31 July, *DDK*, II, nr 474.
31. Schebeko to Sazonov, telegram, 31 July, *Int. Bez.*, V, nr 361.
32. de Bunsen to Grey, telegram, 4.16 p.m., 31 July, *BD*, XI, no. 360.
33. Quoted in Albertini, *Origins of the War*, iii. 147.
34. Albertini, *Origins of the War*, iii. 48.
35. Albertini, *Origins of the War*, iii. 48.
36. Szápáry to Berchtold, telegram, 2.05 p.m., 31 July *O-UA*, VIII, nr 11177.
37. Szápáry to Berchtold, telegram, 2.55 p.m., 31 July, *O-UA*, VIII, nr 11174.
38. Szápáry to Berchtold, telegram, secret, 11.17 p.m., *O-UA*, VIII, nr 11179.
39. Pourtalès to Foreign Office, telegram, 9.35 p.m., 31 July, *DDK*, III, nr 527.
40. Lichnowsky to Foreign Office, telegram, 12.15 p.m., 31 July, *DDK*, III, nr 489.
41. Goschen to Grey, telegram, 2 a.m., 31 July, *BD*, XI, no. 383.
42. Grey to Bertie, telegram, 7.30 p.m., 31 July, *BD*, XI, no. 352.
43. Viviani to Paléologue, telegram, 5 p.m., 31 July, *DDF*, XI, no. 405.
44. Viviani to Paul Cambon, telegram, 12.30 p.m., 31 July, *DDF*, XI, no. 390.

45. Paléologue to Viviani, telegram, 7.30 p.m., 31 July [received in Paris at 4 a.m., 1 August], *DDF*, XI, no. 453; Sazonov to Russian ambassadors in Berlin, Vienna, Paris, London, and Rome, 31 July, *Int. Bez.*, V, nr 343.
46. Pourtalès to Foreign Office, telegram, 7.10 p.m., 31 July [received in Berlin at 5.45 a.m.], *DDK*, III, nr 535.
47. Cambon to Viviani, telegram, 3.50 p.m., 31 July [received in Paris at 4.25 p.m.], *DDF*, XI, no. 116.
48. Bethmann Hollweg to Schoen, telegram, urgent, 3.30 p.m., 31 July, *DDK*, III, nr 491.
49. Viviani to Paléologue, telegram, very urgent, 9 p.m., 31 July, *DDF*, XI, no. 438; Schoen to Foreign Office, telegram, 8.17 p.m., 31 July, *DDK*, III, nr 528.
50. Grey to Villiers, telegram, 6.15 p.m., 31 July, *BD*, XI, no. 351.
51. Davignon to Belgian ministers at Berlin, London, and Paris, 31 July, *BGB*, no. 11.
52. Nicolson to Grey, 31 July, *BD*, XI, no. 368.
53. Crowe to Grey, private, 31 July, *BD*, XI, no. 369.
54. Quoted in Keith Jeffery, *Field Marshal Sir Henry Wilson: An Irish Soldier* (Oxford, 2006), 128.
55. Goldberg, *The Life of Jean Jaurès*, 470–1.

SATURDAY TO TUESDAY, 1–4 AUGUST

1. Sazonov to Izvol'skii and Benckendorff, telegram, *Int. Bez.*, V, nr 385.
2. Szápáry to Berchtold, telegram, secret, 10.45 a.m., 1 August, *DAVK*, III. Unfortunately, the much more comprehensive Austrian documents in *O-UA* end on 31 July 1914.
3. Pourtalès to Frederycksz, 7.30 a.m., 1 August, *DDK*, III, nr 539.
4. Lichnowsky to Foreign Office, telegram, 11.14 a.m. [received at Foreign Office, 4.23 p.m.], 1 August, *DDK*, III, nr 562.
5. Asquith to Stanley, 1 August, *Letters to Venetia Stanley*, 139–40.
6. Villiers to Grey, telegram, 10.24 a.m., 1 August, *BD*, XI, no. 395.
7. Michael Brock, 'Britain Enters the War', in R. J. W. Evans and Hartmut Pogge von Strandmann (eds), *The Coming of the First World War* (Oxford, 1988), 152.
8. Klobukowski to Viviani, 1 August, *DDF*, XI, no. 551.
9. Protocol of the 27th meeting of the Bundesrat, *DDK*, III, nr 553.
10. Szögyény to Berchtold, telegram, 2.50 p.m., 1 August, *DAVK*, III, nr 84.
11. Jagow to Pourtalès, telegram, urgent, 12.52 p.m., 1 August, *DDK*, III, nr 542.
12. Jagow to Tschirschky, telegram, 1.10 p.m., 1 August, *DDK*, III, nr 544.
13. Berchtold to Mérey, telegram, 12.05 p.m., 1 August, *DAVK*, III, nr 86.
14. Jagow to Flotow, telegram, urgent, 12.10 p.m., 1 August, *DDK*, III, nr 541.

15. Austro-Hungarian embassy note to Foreign Office, Berlin, 1 August, *DDK*, III, nr 557. The note was marked 'received' that afternoon at the Wilhelmstrasse.

16. Bethmann Hollweg to Wangenheim, telegram, 1 August, *DDK*, III, nr 547.

17. Tschirschky to Foreign Office, telegram, 2.05 p.m., 1 August, *DDK*, III, nr 567.

18. Tsar Nicholas to Kaiser Wilhelm, telegram, 2.06 p.m., 1 August; received at palace 2.05 p.m. [Central European time], *DDK*, III, nr 546.

19. Grey to Goschen, telegram, 3.10 p.m., 1 August, *BD*, XI, no. 411.

20. Lichnowsky to Foreign Office, telegram, 2.10 p.m., 1 August, *DDK*, III, nr 570; the telegram reporting the morning telephone conversations (nr 562) was received in Berlin at 4.23 p.m.; the next telegram (570) was received at 6.04 p.m.

21. Diary of Admiral Müller, quoted in Young, *Lichnowsky*, 116.

22. Lichnowsky to Foreign Office, telegram, 5.47 p.m. [received at Foreign Office in Berlin, 10.02 p.m.], 1 August, *DDK*, III, nr 596.

23. Grey to Bertie, telegram, 8.20 p.m., 1 August, *BD*, XI, no. 426.

24. Eubank, *Paul Cambon*, 175.

25. Quoted in Eubank, *Paul Cambon*, 175.

26. Paul Cambon to Viviani, telegram, 6.24 p.m., 1 August, *DDF*, XI, no. 532.

27. Quoted in Keiger, *Raymond Poincaré*, 181.

28. Keiger, *Raymond Poincaré*, 181–2; Viviani to Paul Cambon, telegram, very urgent, 6.50 p.m., 1 August, *DDF*, XI, no. 523.

29. This is the recollection of the village schoolmaster, the *instituteur*, quoted in P. J. Flood, *France 1914–18: Public Opinion and the War Effort* (London, 1990), 7.

30. Szécsen to Berchtold, telegram, 10.50 p.m., 1 August, *DAVK*, III, nr 93.

31. Schoen to Foreign Office, telegram, 7.05 p.m., 1 August, *DDK*, III, nr 598.

32. Schebeko to Sazonov, 1 August, *Int. Bez.*, V, nr 418.

33. Falkenhayn, diary for 1 August, quoted in Albertini, *Origins of the War*, iii. 169.

34. Lichnowsky's telegram of 11.14 a.m. was received at the Foreign Office at 4.23 p.m. (*DDK*, III, nr 562).

35. Tirpitz, diary, 1 August, quoted in Albertini, *Origins of the War*, iii. 172.

36. Kaiser Wilhelm to King George, telegram, urgent, 7.02 p.m., 1 August, *DDK*, III, nr 575.

37. Bethmann Hollweg to Lichnowsky, telegram, 7.15 p.m., 1 August, *DDK*, III, nr 578.

38. Jagow to Schoen, telegram, urgent, 8.45 p.m., 1 August, *DDK*, III, nr 587.

39. King George to Kaiser Wilhelm, telegram [between 8.30 and 9.30 p.m.], 1 August, *DDK*, III, nr 612.

40. See Stephen J. Valone, '"There must be some misunderstanding": Sir Edward Grey's Diplomacy of 1 August 1914', *Journal of British Studies* 27 (1988), 405–24.

41. Kaiser Wilhelm to Tsar Nicholas, telegram, 10.30 p.m., 1 August, *DDK*, III, nr 600; *Int. Bez.*, V, nr 416.

42. Marginal notation by kaiser on Lichnowsky to Foreign Office, telegram, 2.10 p.m. [received at Foreign Office at 6.04 p.m.], *DDK*, III, nr 570.

43. Izvol'skii to Sazonov, telegram, 1 August, *Int. Bez.*, V, nr 409.

44. Poincaré, diary, 2 August, quoted in Keiger, *Raymond Poincaré*, 182.

45. Izvol'skii to Sazonov, telegram, 2 August, *Int. Bez.*, V, nr 412.

46. Bertie to Grey, telegram, 1.15 a.m., 1 August, *BD*, XI, no. 453.

47. Falkenhayn, diary, 1 August; quoted in Albertini, *Origins of the War*, iii. 192.

48. Goschen to Nicolson, private [1 August], *BD*, XI, no. 510.

49. 1 August, quoted in Gilbert, *Horace Rumbold*, 117.

50. 2 August, Gilbert, *Horace Rumbold*, 118.

51. Buch to Foreign Office, telegram, 12.54 p.m., 2 August, *DDK*, III, nr 647.

52. Jagow to Buch, telegram, 2.10 p.m., 2 August, *DDK*, III, nr 648.

53. Note given by Schoen to Foreign Office, 2 August, *DDF*, XI, no. 587.

54. Paul Cambon to Viviani, telegram, secret, 11.20 a.m., 2 August, *DDF*, XI, no. 579.

55. Quoted in Eubank, *Paul Cambon*, 179.

56. Pease, diary, quoted in Wilson, *Policy of the Entente*, 140.

57. Quoted in Wilson, 'Britain', in Wilson, *Decisions for War*, 195.

58. Quoted in Wasserstein, *Herbert Samuel*, 162.

59. Wasserstein, *Herbert Samuel*, 162.

60. Asquith to Stanley, *Letters to Venetia Stanley*, 146.

61. *The Times*, 3 August 1914, p. 8.

62. Quoted in Keiger, *Raymond Poincaré*, 183.

63. Quoted in Miller, *Revolutionaries to Citizens*, 210.

64. Miller, *Revolutionaries to Citizens*, 209.

65. Paléologue, *Memoirs of an Ambassador*, 50.

66. Quoted in Frank Golder, *Documents of Russian History, 1914–1917* (New York, 1927), 29–30.

67. Grey to Buchanan [enclosing message from king], telegram, 3.30 a.m. [received at 5 p.m.], *BD*, XI, no. 384.

68. Tsar Nicholas to King George, telegram, 3.10 p.m., 2 August, *Int. Bez.*, V, nr 451.

69. Quoted in Wasserstein, *Herbert Samuel*, 163.

70. Quoted in Wilson, *Policy of the Entente*, 137.

71. Note presented by Below Saleske to Davignon, *BGB*, no. 20.

72. Quoted in Albertini, *Origins of the War*, iii. 456.

73. Below to Foreign Office, telegram, urgent, 9.48 p.m., 2 August, *DDK*, III, nr 695.

74. Klobukowski to Viviani, telegram, 12.05 p.m., 2 August, *DDF*, XI, no. 586.
75. Quoted in Jean Stengers, 'Belgium' in Wilson, *Decisions for War*, 161.
76. Kudachev to Sazonov, 3 August, *Int. Bez.*, V, nr 498.
77. Albert I to George V, 3 August, *BGB*, no. 25.
78. Quoted in Wasserstein, *Herbert Samuel*, 163–4.
79. Hansard, debates, 3 August, col. 1815.
80. Hansard, debates, 3 August, col. 1816.
81. Hansard, debates, 3 August, col. 1817.
82. Hansard, debates, 3 August, col. 1819.
83. Hansard, debates, 3 August, cols 1823–7.
84. Hansard, debates, 3 August, col. 1838.
85. Nicolson, *Sir Arthur Nicolson*, 422.
86. Bethmann Hollweg to Schoen, telegram, urgent, 1.05 p.m., 3 August *DDK*, III, nr 734. The reports proved to be false.
87. Poincaré, diary, 3 August, quoted in Krumeich, *Armaments and Politics*, 229.
88. Paul Cambon to Viviani, telegram, 12.17 a.m., 4 August, *DDF*, XI, no. 712.
89. Jagow to Below, telegram, urgent, 9.20 a.m., 4 August, *DDK*, III, nr 805.
90. Grey to Goschen, telegram, 9.30 a.m., 4 August, *BD*, XI, no. 573.
91. Jagow to Lichnowsky, telegram, 10.02 a.m., *DDK*, III, nr 810.
92. Lichnowsky to Foreign Office, telegram, 10.02 a.m., *DDK*, III, nr 820.
93. Asquith to Stanley, *Letters to Venetia Stanley*, 4 August, p. 150.
94. Grey to Villiers, telegram 10.45 a.m., *BD*, XI, no. 580.
95. Grey to Goschen, telegram, 2 p.m., 4 August, *BD*, XI, no. 594.
96. *Collected Diplomatic Documents Relating to the Outbreak of the European War* (London, 1915), 436–9.
97. Quoted in B. J. Hendrick, *Life and Letters of W. H. Page* (London, 1923), 313–14.
98. http://www.firstworldwar.com/source/poincare_aug1914.htm
99. Jagow to Lichnowsky, telegram, urgent, 9.05 p.m., 4 August, *DDK*, III, nr 848.
100. Nicolson, *Arthur Nicolson*, 425–6.
101. George V, diary, 4 August, quoted in Kenneth Rose, *King George V* (London, 1983), 168.

MAKING SENSE OF THE MADNESS

1. This was the subtitle given in the English translation.
2. There were precedents for this. 'Coloured books' containing official documents had been issued throughout the nineteenth century. Most recently, the Austro-Hungarian government had produced a Red Book containing almost one thousand diplomatic despatches and telegrams covering the Balkan crisis from August 1912 to November 1913.

3. There was considerable variation in this: the worst was the German, closely followed by the French; the British contain only minimal cuts.

4. 'To the Civilized World', *New York Times Current History of the European War*, vol. 1 (12 December 1914), 43–70, 184–5. The professors were responding in particular to charges of barbarous behaviour on the part of German forces in Belgium.

5. 'Appeal of the German Universities', *New York Times Current History of the European War*, vol. 1 (12 December 1914), 187.

6. 'Reply to the German Professors', *New York Times Current History of the European War*, vol. 1 (12 December 1914), 188.

7. 'The Vital Energies of France', *New York Times Current History of the European War*, vol. 1 (12 December 1914), 153–4.

8. Holger H. Herwig, 'Clio Deceived: Patrotic Self-Censorship in Germany after the Great War', *International Security* 12/2 (1987), 5–44. See also Eric J. C. Hahn, 'The German Foreign Ministry and the Question of German War Guilt in 1918–19', in Carole Fink, Isabel Hull, and MacGregor Knox (eds), *German Nationalism and the European Response, 1890–1945* (Norman, Okla., 1985), 43–70.

9. In the preface Kautsky tells the troubled story of bringing the documentary collection to publication (London, 1920), 1–14.

10. The full report can be found in *The American Journal of International Law* 14/1 & 2 (1920), 95–154.

11. See Sally Marks, 'Smoke and Mirrors: In Smoke-Filled Rooms and the Galerie des Glaces', in Manfred F. Boemeke, Gerald D. Feldman, and Elisabeth Glaser (eds), *The Treaty of Versaille: A Reassessment after 75 Years* (Cambridge, 1998), 337–70.

12. Sidney B. Fay, 'New Light on the Origins of the World War', *American Historical Review* 25/4 (1920), 616–39; 26/1 (1920), 37–53; 26/2 (1921), 225–54.

13. On Fay and some of the others involved in the debate during the 1920s see Gordon Martel, 'Explaining World War One: Debating the Causes', in Nicholas Atkin and Michael Biddis (eds), *Themes in Modern European History 1890–1945* (New York, 2009), 117–45.

14. Fay, 'New Light', *American Historical Review*, 25/4 (1920), 619.

15. Translated by Annie Adams and published as *From Bismarck to the World War* in 1927.

16. Translated by Theodore Hume and published as *Immediate Origins of the War* in 1928.

17. *Bismarck to the World War*, 518.

18. *Immediate Origins*, 355.

19. Seton-Watson, *Sarajevo: A Study in the Origins of the Great War* (London, 1926), 289.

20. Seton-Watson, *Sarajevo*, 289.

21. Sidney B. Fay, *The Origins of the World War*, 2 vols (New York, 1928, 1930), ii. 549.
22. Bernadotte Schmitt, *The Coming of the War: 1914*, 2 vols (New York, 1930), 481.
23. Schmitt, *The Coming of the War: 1914*, 482.
24. See p. 406.
25. G. L. Dickinson, *The International Anarchy, 1904–1914* (London, 1926), 2.
26. Dickinson, *The International Anarchy*, 481.
27. John Langdon, *July 1914: The Long Debate, 1918–1990* (Oxford, 1991), 4.
28. When the book was translated into English and published in 1967 the title was altered: *Griff nach der Weltmacht* was dropped and only the subtitle, *Germany's Aims in the First World War*, was used. 'Griff' does not translate directly into English: it might be better translated as 'Grasping' and is sometimes translated as 'Bid'.
29. *Krieg der Illusionen: die deutsche Politik von 1911 bis 1914* (Düsseldorf, 1969); the English translation was published six years later (New York, 1975).
30. On the debate, see the collections by: John A. Moses, *The Politics of Illusion: The Fischer Controversy in German Historiography* (New York, 1975); Hans W. Koch (ed.), *The Origins of the First World War: Great Power Rivalry and German War Aims*, 2nd edn (London, 1984); and the detailed studies by Annika Mombauer, *The Origins of the First World War: Controversies and Consensus* (London, 2002) and Mark Hewitson, *Germany and the Causes of the First World War* (Oxford, 2004).
31. To paraphrase A. J. P. Taylor: 'Mistaken Lessons from the Past', *The Listener* (6 June 1963).
32. Adolf Hitler, *Mein Kampf*, tr. Ralph Manheim (Boston, 1971), 613.
33. See Holger Afflerbach, 'The Topos of Improbable War in Europe before 1914', in Holger Afflerbach and David Stevenson (eds), *An Improbable War? The Outbreak of World War I and European Political Culture before 1914* (New York and Oxford, 2007), 161–82; and Wolfgang Mommsen, 'The Topos of Inevitable War in Germany in the Decade before 1914', in Volker Berghahn and Martin Kitchen (eds), *Germany in the Age of Total War*, tr. Jane Williams (London, 1981), 23–45.
34. The actual term used in Germany in July 1914 was inconsistent; there were several variations on the same theme.

List of Works Cited

Because the literature concerning the July crisis is so vast, there is insufficient space to list all of the works consulted in the writing of this book. Readers interested in pursuing the subject further may wish to consult my *Origins of the First World War* (revised 3rd edition, 2008) which presents an essay-style guide to further reading, or James Joll and Gordon Martel, *Origins of the First World War* (3rd edition, 2007) which arranges readings according to various subject categories.

I. PUBLISHED DOCUMENTS

Bittner, Ludwig, Pribram, Alfred Francis, Srbik, Heinrich, and Uebersberger, Hans (eds), *Österreich-Ungarns Aussenpolitik von der Bosnischen Krise 1908 bis zum Kriegsausbruch 1914: diplomatische aktenstücke des österreichisch-ungarischen ministeriums des äussern ausgewählt*, 8 vols (Vienna, 1930).

Collected Diplomatic Documents Relating to the Outbreak of the European War (London, 1915).

Correspondance diplomatique du Gouvernement serbe, 16/29 juin–3/16 août 1914 (Paris, 1914); translated as 'The Serbian Blue Book' in *Collected Diplomatic Documents Relating to the Outbreak of the European War* (London, 1915).

Geiss, Imanuel, *July 1914: The Outbreak of the First World War: Selected Documents* (New York, 1967).

Geiss, Imanuel, *Julikrise und Kriegsausbruch 1914: eine Dokumentensammlung*, 2 vols (Hanover, 1963).

Golder, Frank, *Documents of Russian History, 1914–1917* (New York, 1927).

Gooch, G. P., and Temperley, Harold (eds), *British Documents on the Origins of the War*, 11 vols (London, 1926–38).

Hendrick, B. J., *Life and Letters of W. H. Page* (London, 1923).

Hoetzsch, Otto (ed.), *Die Internationalen Beziehungen im Zeitalter des Imperialismus*, Bd. 1–5, *Das Jahr 1914 bis zum Kriegsausbruch* (Berlin, 1931–34).

Hurst, Michael (ed.), *Key Treaties for the Great Powers, 1814–1914*, vol. 2: *1871–1914* (London, 1974).

Lepsius, Johannes, Mendelssohn-Bartholdy, Albrecht, and Thimme, Friedrich (eds), *Die Große Politik der Europäischen Kabinette, 1871–1914. Sammlung der diplomatischen Akten des Auswärtigen Amtes*, 40 vols (Berlin, 1928).

Ministère des Affaires Étrangères, Commission de publication des documents relatifs aux origines de la guerre de 1914, *Documents diplomatiques français (1871–1914)*, 3me série, 1911–14, 11 vols (Paris, 1929).

Montgelas, Maximilian, and Schücking, Walter (eds), *Die deutschen Dokumente zum Kriegsausbruch, vollständige Sammlung der von Karl Kautsky zusammengestellten amtlichen Aktenstücke mit einigen Ergänzungen*, 4 vols (Berlin, 1919).

Mousset, Albert, *Un drame historique: l'attentat de Sarajevo. Documents inédits et text intégral des sténogrammes du procès* (Paris, 1930).

Pribram, Alfred, *The Secret Treaties of Austria-Hungary, 1879–1914*, tr. A. G. Coolidge (Cambridge, Mass., 1920).

Republik Österreich, *Diplomatische Aktenstücke zur Vorgeschichte des Krieges 1914*, 3 vols (Vienna, 1922).

Schilling, Baron, *How the War Began in 1914. Being the Diary of the Russian Foreign Office from the 3rd to the 20th of July* [16 July–2 August]*, 1914* (London, 1925).

II. PUBLISHED PRIMARY MATERIALS: DIARIES, LETTERS, MEMOIRS

Brock, Michael, and Brock, Eleanor (eds), *H. H. Asquith: Letters to Venetia Stanley* (Oxford, 1982).

Churchill, Winston, *The World Crisis* (London, 1923).

Conrad von Hötzendorf, Franz, Graf, *Aus meiner Dienstzeit, 1906–1918*, 5 vols (Vienna, 1921–25).

Erdmann, Karl Dietrich (ed.), *Kurt Riezler: Tagebücher, Aufsätze, Dokumente* (Göttingen, 1972).

Paléologue, Maurice, *An Ambassador's Memoirs*, 4th edn (New York, 1925).

Röhl, John C. G. (ed.), *1914: Delusion or Design? The Testimony of Two German Diplomats* (London, 1973).

Wilson, Trevor (ed.), *The Political Diaries of C. P. Scott, 1911–1928* (London, 1970).

III. SECONDARY SOURCES: BOOKS

Afflerbach, Holger, *Kaiser Wilhelm II* (Munich, 2005).

Afflerbach, Holger, and Stevenson, David (eds), *An Improbable War? The Outbreak of World War I and European Political Culture before 1914* (New York, 2007).

Albertini, Luigi, *Le origini della guerra del 1914*, 3 vols (Milan, 1942–43); tr. Isabella M. Massey as *The Origins of the War of 1914* (Oxford, 1952).

Beller, Steven, *Francis Joseph* (London, 1996).

Bosworth, R. J. B., *Italy, the Least of the Great Powers: Italian Foreign Policy before the First World War* (Cambridge, 1979).

Bosworth, R. J. B., *Italy and the Approach of the First World War* (London, 1983).

Brehm, Bruno, *They Call it Patriotism* (Boston, 1932).

Bridge, F. R., *From Sadowa to Sarajevo: The Foreign Policy of Austria-Hungary, 1866–1914* (London, 1972).

Brook-Shepherd, Gordon, *Victims at Sarajevo: The Romance and Tragedy of Franz Ferdinand and Sophie* (London, 1984).

Bucholz, Arden, *Moltke, Schlieffen, and Prussian War Planning* (New York, 1991).

Ceadel, Martin, *Living the Great Illusion: Sir Norman Angell, 1872–1967* (Oxford, 2009).

Cecil, Lamar, *Albert Ballin: Business and Politics in Imperial Germany, 1888–1918* (Princeton, 1967).

Cecil, Lamar, *The German Diplomatic Service, 1871–1914* (Princeton, 1976).

Cecil, Lamar, *Wilhelm II*, vol. 2: *Emperor and Exile, 1900–1941* (Chapel Hill, 1996).

Chickering, Roger, *We Men Who Feel Most German: A Cultural Study of the Pan-German League, 1886–1914* (Boston, 1984).

Clark, Christopher, *Kaiser Wilhelm II* (London, 2000).

Clark, Christopher, *The Sleepwalkers: How Europe Went to War in 1914* (New York, 2012).

Cooper, Sandi E., *Patriotic Pacifism: Waging War on War in Europe, 1815–1914* (New York, 1991).

Dedijer, Vladimir, *The Road to Sarajevo* (London, 1967).

Derfler, Leslie, *President and Parliament: A Short History of the French Presidency* (Boca Raton, Fla., 1983).

Diószegi, István, *Hungarians in the Ballhausplatz: Studies on the Austro-Hungarian Common Foreign Policy*, tr. Kornél Balás (Budapest, 1983).

Eubank, Keith, *Paul Cambon: Master Diplomatist* (Norman, Okla., 1960).

Evans, Richard J., *Rethinking German History: Nineteenth-Century Germany and the Origins of the Third Reich* (London, 1987).

Flood, P. J., *France 1914–18: Public Opinion and the War Effort* (London, 1990).

Galántai, József, *Hungary in the First World War* (Budapest, 1989).

Gat, Azar, *The Development of Military Thought: The Nineteenth Century* (Oxford, 1992).

Geiss, Imanuel, *German Foreign Policy, 1871–1914* (London, 1976).

Gilbert, Martin, *Sir Horace Rumbold: Portrait of a Diplomat, 1869–1941* (London, 1973).

Godsey Jr, William, *Aristocratic Redoubt: The Austro-Hungarian Foreign Office on the Eve of the First World War* (West Lafayette, Ind., 1999).

Goldberg, Harvey, *The Life of Jean Jaurès* (Madison, Wis., 1962).

Gooch, G. P., *Before the War*, 2 vols (London, 1938).

Hamilton, Richard F., and Herwig, Holger H. (eds), *The Origins of World War I* (Cambridge, 2003).

Hantsch, Hugo, *Leopold Graf Berchtold: Grandseigneur und Staatsmann* (Graz, 1963).

Hayne, M. B., *The French Foreign Office and the Origins of the First World War 1898–1914* (Oxford, 1993).

Hazlehurst, Cameron, *Politicians at War, July 1914 to May 1915: A Prologue to the Triumph of Lloyd George* (London, 1971).

Hull, Isabel V., *The Entourage of Kaiser Wilhelm II 1888–1918* (Cambridge, 1982).

Jarausch, Konrad, *The Enigmatic Chancellor* (New Haven, 1972).

Jeffery, Keith, *Field Marshal Sir Henry Wilson: An Irish Soldier* (Oxford, 2006).

Joll, James, *The Second International* (London, 1974).

Joll, James, and Martel, Gordon, *The Origins of the First World War*, 3rd edn (London, 2007).

Kann, Robert A., *Dynasty, Politics and Culture: Selected Essays*, ed. Stanley B. Winters (Boulder, Colo., 1991).

Keiger, John, *Raymond Poincaré* (Cambridge, 1997).

Kennedy, Paul M. (ed.), *The War Plans of the Great Powers, 1880–1914* (London, 1979).

Kohut, Thomas A., *Wilhelm II and the Germans* (New York, 1991).

Krumeich, Gerd, *Armaments and Politics in France on the Eve of the First World War: The Introduction of Three-Year Conscription 1913–1914*, tr. Stephen Conn (Leamington Spa, 1984).

Laity, Paul, *The British Peace Movement, 1870–1914* (Oxford, 2001).

Lieven, Dominic C. B., *Russia and the Origins of the First World War* (London, 1983).

Lieven, Dominic C. B., *Nicholas II: Emperor of All the Russias* (London, 1993).

McDonald, David MacLaren, *United Government and Foreign Policy in Russia 1900–1914* (Cambridge, Mass., 1992).

Margutti, Baron von, *The Emperor Francis Joseph and his Times* (New York, 1921).

Martel, Gordon, *The Origins of the First World War*, 3rd edn, rev. (Harlow, 2008).

Miller, J. D. B., *Norman Angell and the Futility of War* (London, 1986).

Miller, Paul B., *From Revolutionaries to Citizens: Antimilitarism in France, 1870–1914* (Durham, NC, 2001).

Mombauer, Annika, *Helmuth von Moltke and the Origins of the First World War* (Cambridge, 2001).

Morris, A. J. Anthony, *Radicalism Against War, 1906–1914: The Advocacy of Peace and Retrenchment* (London, 1972).

Neiberg, Michael S., *Dance of the Furies: Europe and the Outbreak of World War I* (Cambridge, Mass., 2011).

Nicolson, Harold, *Sir Arthur Nicolson, Bart., First Lord Carnock: A Study in the Old Diplomacy* (London, 1930).

Playne, Caroline, *Bertha von Suttner and the Struggle to Avert the World War* (London, 1936).

Röhl, John C. G., *The Kaiser and his Court: Wilhelm II and the Government of Germany* (Cambridge, 1987).

Röhl, John C. G., *Young Wilhelm: The Kaiser's Early Life, 1859–1888*, tr. Jeremy Gaines and Rebecca Wallach (Cambridge, 1998).

Röhl, John C. G., *Wilhelm II: The Kaiser's Personal Monarchy, 1888–1900*, tr. Sheila de Bellaigue (Cambridge, 2004).

Rose, Kenneth, *King George V* (London, 1983).

Schmidt, Stefan, *Frankreichs Außenpolitik in der Julikrise 1914* (Munich 2007).

Schmitt, Bernadotte, *The Coming of the War, 1914* (New York, 1930).

Seton-Watson, R. W., *Sarajevo: A Study in the Origins of the Great War* (London, 1926).

Shanafelt, Gary W., *The Secret Enemy: Austria-Hungary and the German Alliance, 1914–1918* (Boulder, Colo., 1985).

Sondhaus, Lawrence, *Franz Conrad von Hötzendorf: Architect of the Apocalypse* (Boston, 2000).

Soroka, Marina, *Britain, Russia and the Road to the First World War: The Fateful Embassy of Count Aleksandr Benckendorff (1903–16)* (Farnham, 2011).

Spender, J. A., and Asquith, Cyril, *Life of Herbert Henry Asquith, Lord Oxford and Asquith* (London, 1932).

Steiner, Zara, and Neilson, Keith, *Britain and the Origins of the First World War*, 2nd edn (London, 2003).

Thompson, Wayne C., *In the Eye of the Storm: Kurt Riezler and the Crises of Modern Germany* (Iowa City, Iowa, 1980).

Verhey, Jeffrey, *The Spirit of 1914: Militarism, Myth and Mobilization in Germany* (Cambridge, 2000).

Vermes, Gabor, *István Tisza: The Liberal Vision and Conservative Statecraft of a Magyar Nationalist* (New York, 1985).

Ward, Paul, *Red Flag and Union Jack: Englishness, Patriotism and the British Left, 1881–1924* (Woodbridge, 1998).

Wasserstein, Bernard, *Herbert Samuel, A Political Life* (Oxford, 1992).

Wilson, Keith, *The Policy of the Entente: Essays on the Determinants of British Foreign Policy, 1904–1919* (Cambridge, 1985).

Wilson, Keith (ed.), *Decisions for War* (London, 1995).

Wolff, Theodore, *Eve of 1914* (New York, 1936).

Young, Harry F., *Prince Lichnowsky and the Great War* (Athens, Ga., 1977).

IV. SECONDARY SOURCES: ARTICLES AND ESSAYS IN BOOKS

Berghahn, Volker, and Deist, Wilhelm, 'Kaiserliche Marine und Kriegsausbruch 1914', *Militärgeschichtliche Mitteilungen* 1 (1970), 37–58.

Brescia, L., 'Norman Angell and the Pacifist Muddle', *Bulletin of the Institute of Historical Research* xlv (1972), 104–21.

Brock, Michael, 'Britain Enters the War', in R. J. W. Evans and Hartmut Pogge von Strandmann (eds), *The Coming of the First World War* (Oxford, 1988), 145–78.

Cecil, Lamar, 'William II and his Russian "Colleagues"', in Carole Fink, Isabel V. Hull, and MacGregor Knox (eds), *German Nationalism and the European Response, 1890–1945* (Norman, Okla., 1985), 95–134.

Cornwall, Mark, 'Serbia', in Keith Wilson (ed.), *Decisions for War* (London, 1995), 55–96.

Deist, Wilhelm, 'The Kaiser and his Military Entourage', in John C. G. Röhl and Nicolaus Sombart (eds), *Kaiser Wilhelm II: New Interpretations* (Cambridge, 1982), 169–92.

Fellner, Fritz, 'Austria-Hungary', in Keith Wilson (ed.), *Decisions for War* (London, 1995), 9–26.

Herwig, Holger, 'Germany', in Richard F. Hamilton and Holger H. Herwig (eds), *The Origins of World War I* (Cambridge, 2003), 150–87.

Kennedy, Paul, 'The Kaiser and German *Weltpolitik*: Reflections on Wilhelm II's Place in the Making of German Foreign Policy', in John C. G. Röhl and Nicolaus Sombart (eds), *Kaiser Wilhelm II: New Interpretations* (Cambridge, 1982), 143–68.

Lerman, Katherine, 'The Kaiser's Elite? Wilhelm II and the Berlin Administration, 1890–1914', in Annika Mombauer and Wilhelm Deist (eds), *The Kaiser: New Research on Wilhelm II's Role in Imperial Germany* (Cambridge, 2003), 63–90.

Navari, Cornelia, 'The Great Illusion Revisited: The International Theory of Norman Angell', *Review of International Studies* 15 (1989), 341–58.

Petersson, H. B. A., 'Das osterreichisch-ungarische Memorandum an Deutschland vom 5. Juli 1914', *Scandia* 30 (1964), 138–90.

Röhl, John C. G., 'Admiral von Müller and the Approach of War, 1911–1914', *The Historical Journal* 12/4 (1969), 651–73.

Röhl, John C. G., 'The Curious Case of the Kaiser's Disappearing War Guilt: Wilhelm II in July 1914', in Holger Afflerbach and David Stevenson (eds), *An Improbable War? The Outbreak of World War I and European Political Culture before 1914* (New York, 2007), 75–94.

Spring, D. W., 'Russia and the Coming of War', in R. J. W. Evans and Hartmut Pogge von Strandmann (eds), *The Coming of the First World War* (Oxford, 1988), 57–86.

Stengers, Jean, 'Belgium', in Keith Wilson (ed.), *Decisions for War* (London, 1995), 151–74.

Tunstall Jr., Graydon A., 'Austria-Hungary', in Richard F. Hamilton and Holger H. Herwig (eds), *The Origins of World War I* (Cambridge, 2003), 112–49.

Valone, Stephen J., '"There must be some misunderstanding": Sir Edward Grey's Diplomacy of August 1, 1914', *Journal of British Studies* 27 (1988), 405–24.

Williamson, S. R., 'Joffre Reshapes French Strategy', in Paul M. Kennedy (ed.), *The War Plans of the Great Powers, 1880–1914* (London, 1979), 133–54.

Picture Acknowledgements

145   Library of Congress

154   Wikimedia

169   Wikimedia

171   Library of Congress

174   Library of Congress

178   Library of Congress

179   Library of Congress

197   Library of Congress

200   Library of Congress

216   From Viscount Grey of Fallodon, Twenty-Five Years (Frederick A. Stokes Co., New York, 1925)

217   Library of Congress

229   Library of Congress

232   Austrian National Library

252   Viscount Grey of Fallodon, Twenty-Five Years (Frederick A. Stokes Co., New York, 1925)

327   Library of Congress

361   Library of Congress

367   Library of Congress

Index